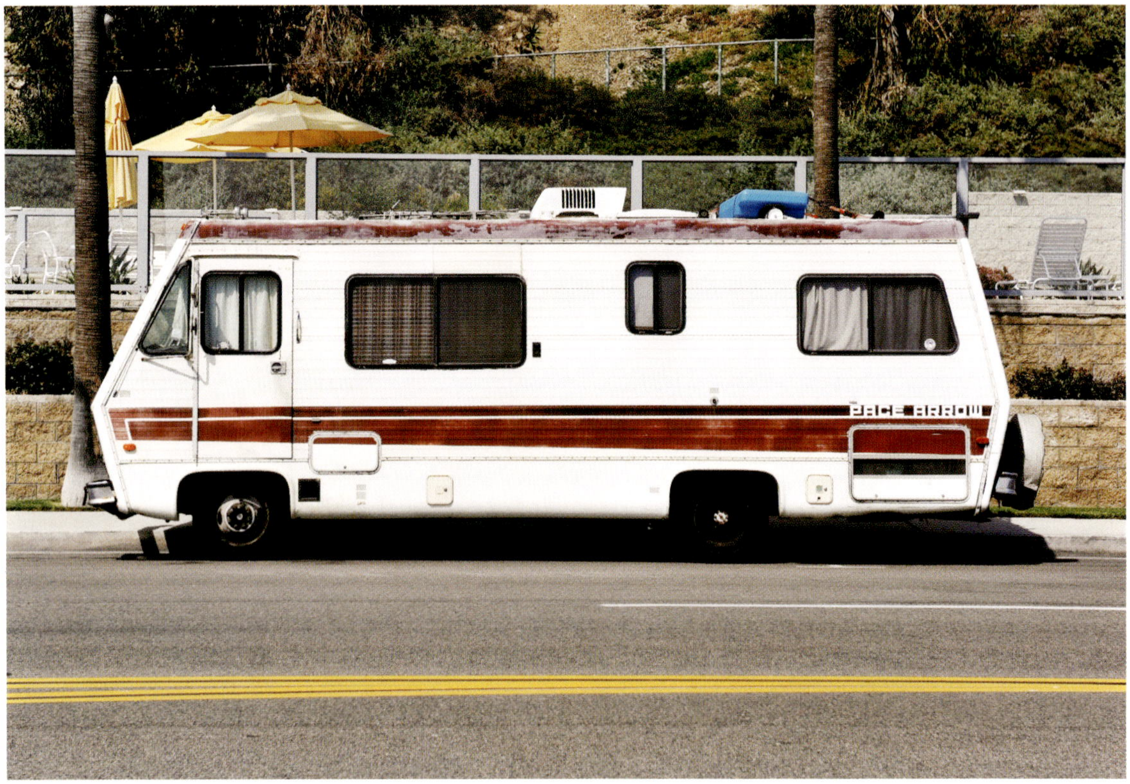

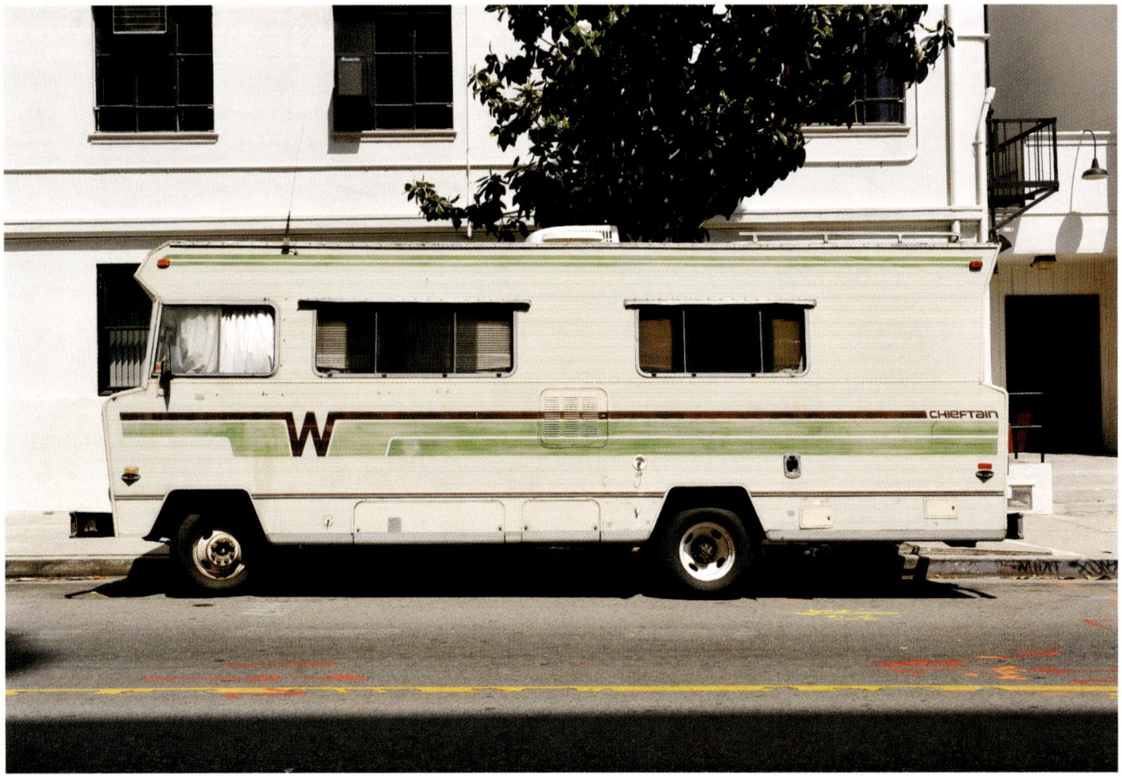

Damon Way
"Motorhome–Orange County"

Damon Way
"Motorhome–San Diego"

RETNA
"Is It a Crime?" 2011
Acrylic on canvas

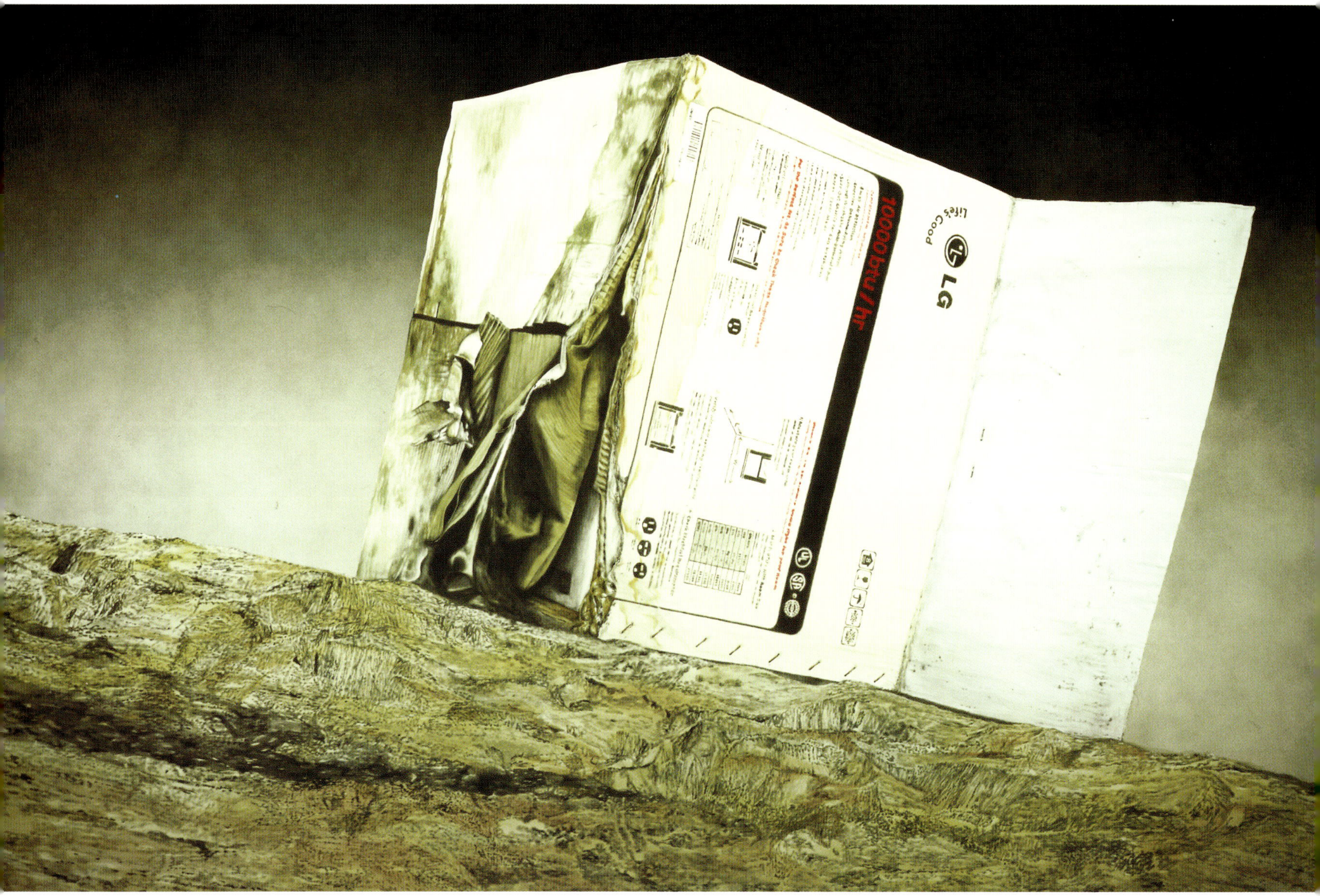

Ed Ruscha
"Psycho Spaghetti Western #6" 2010
Acrylic on canvas
70 x 108 inches

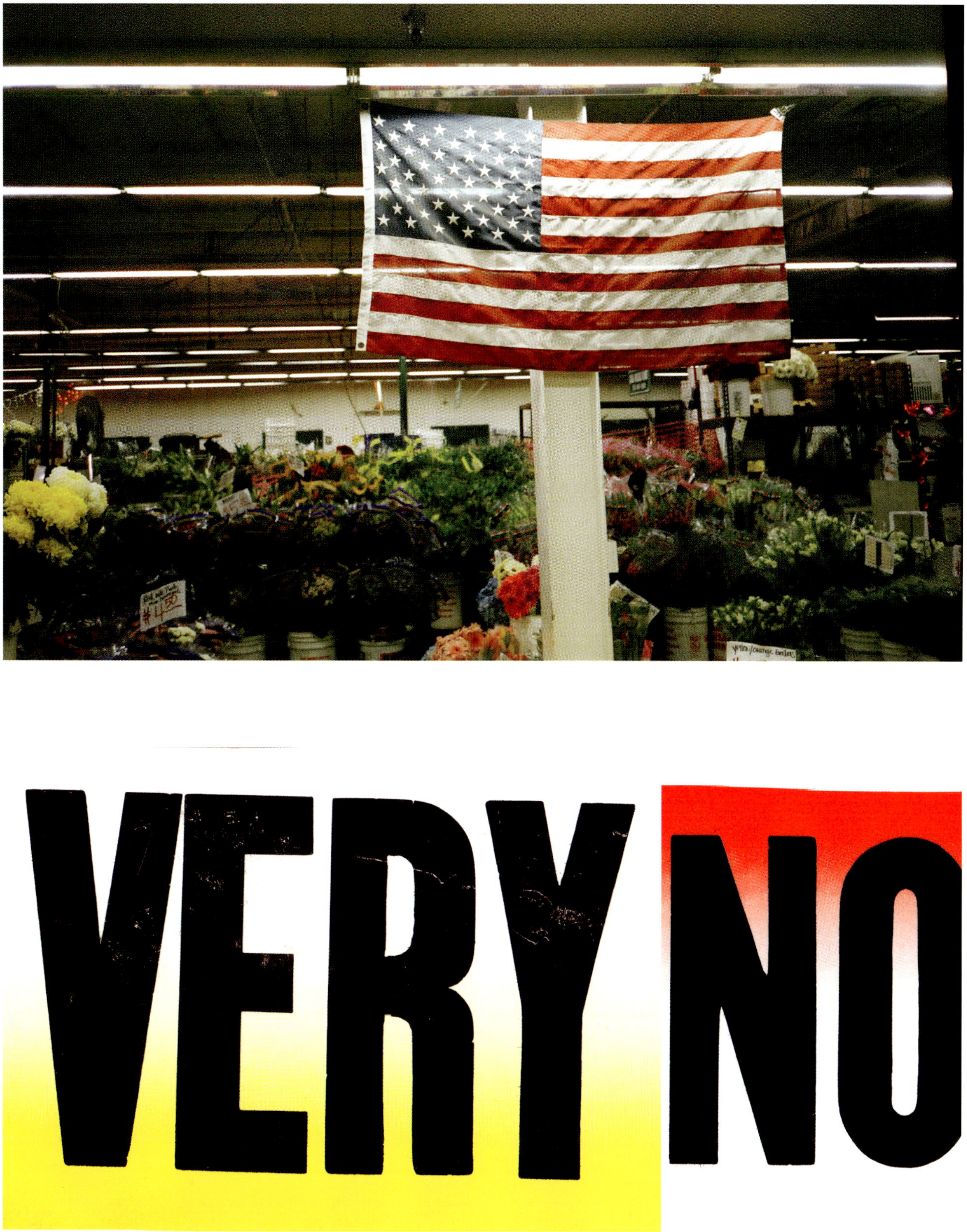

Cali Thornhill deWitt
"Flower Shopping" 2012
Photograph and letterpress
8 x 10 inches

Following spread:
Cleon Peterson
"The Balance of Terror" 2011
Acrylic on panels
84 x 168 inches

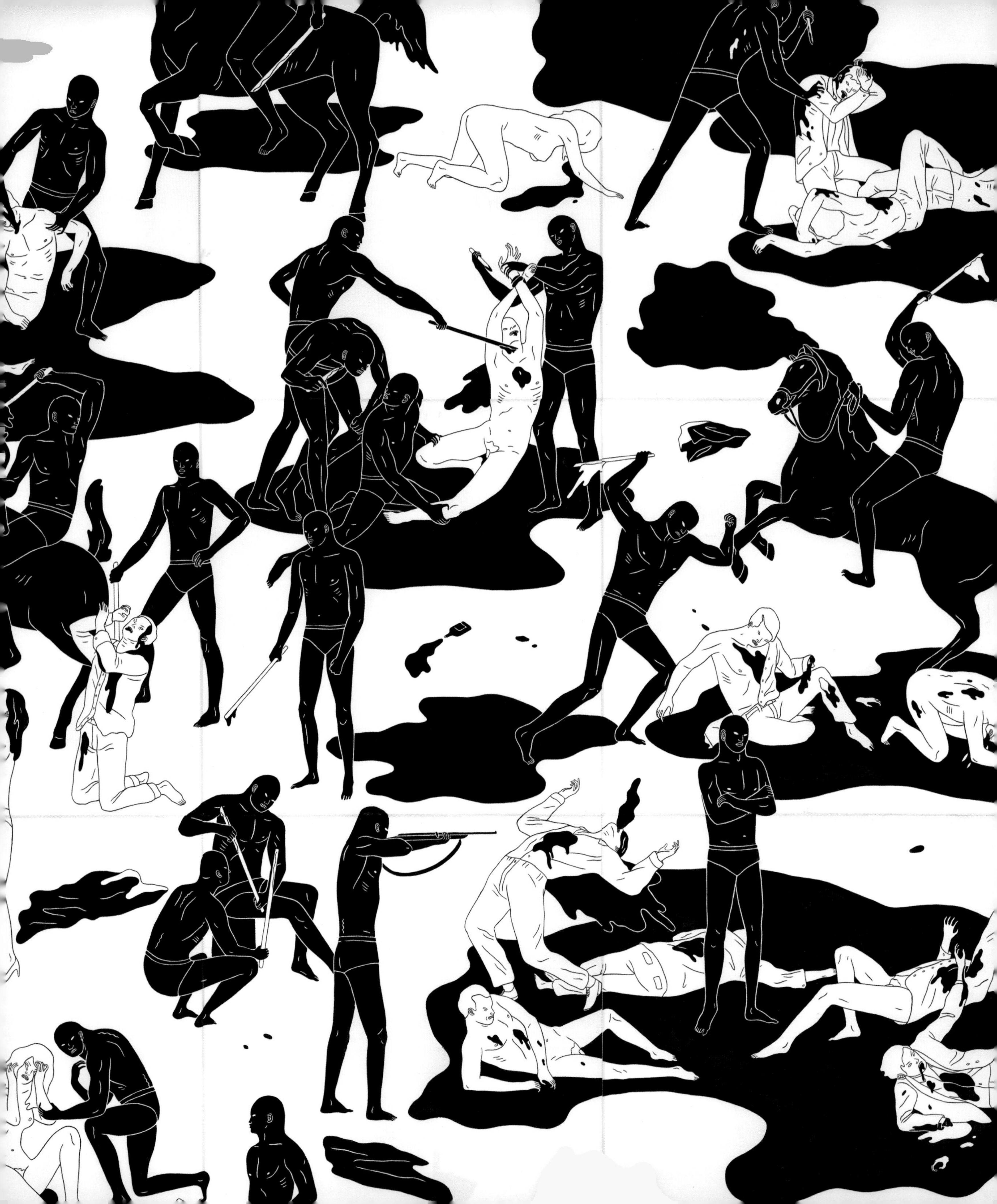

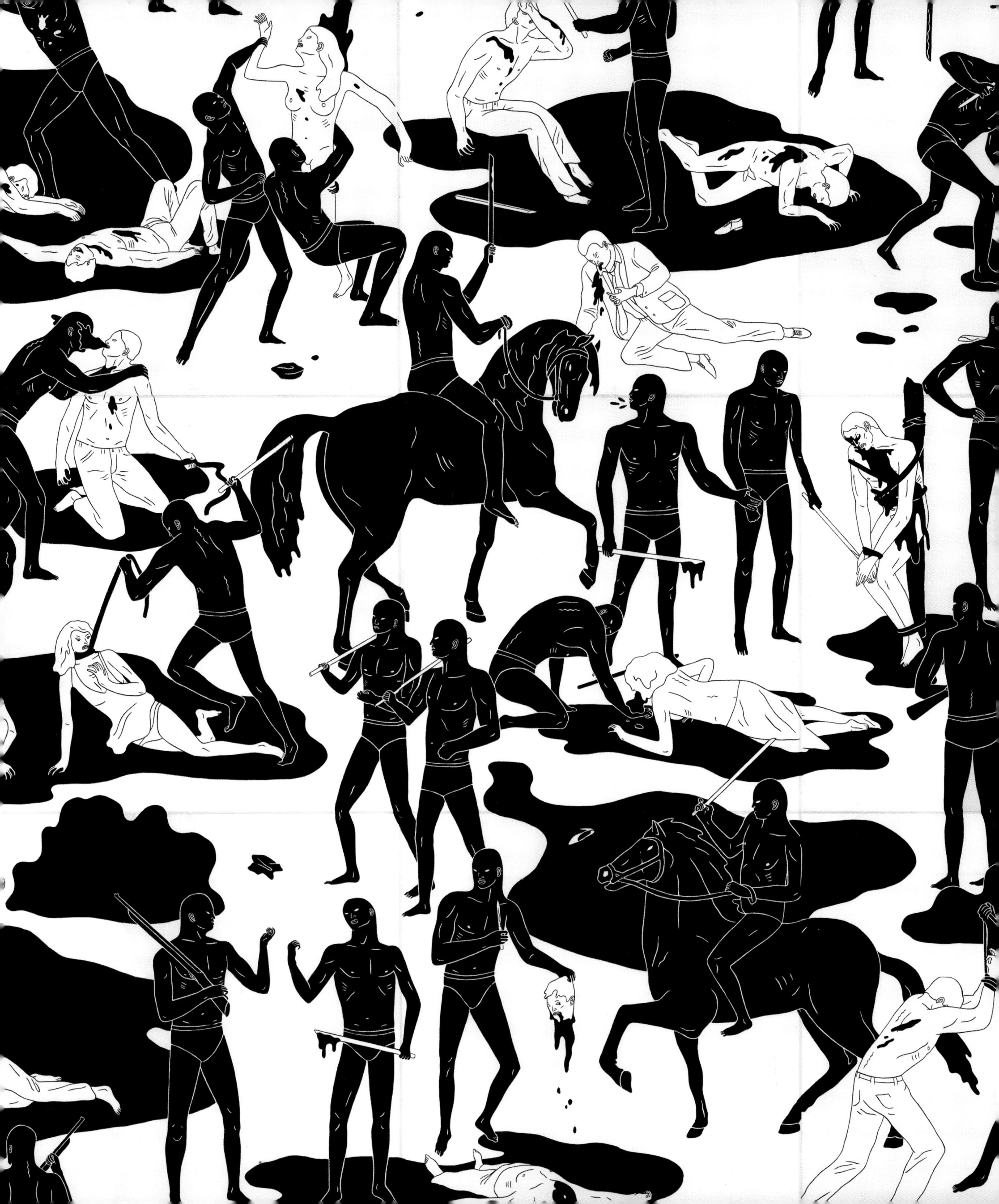

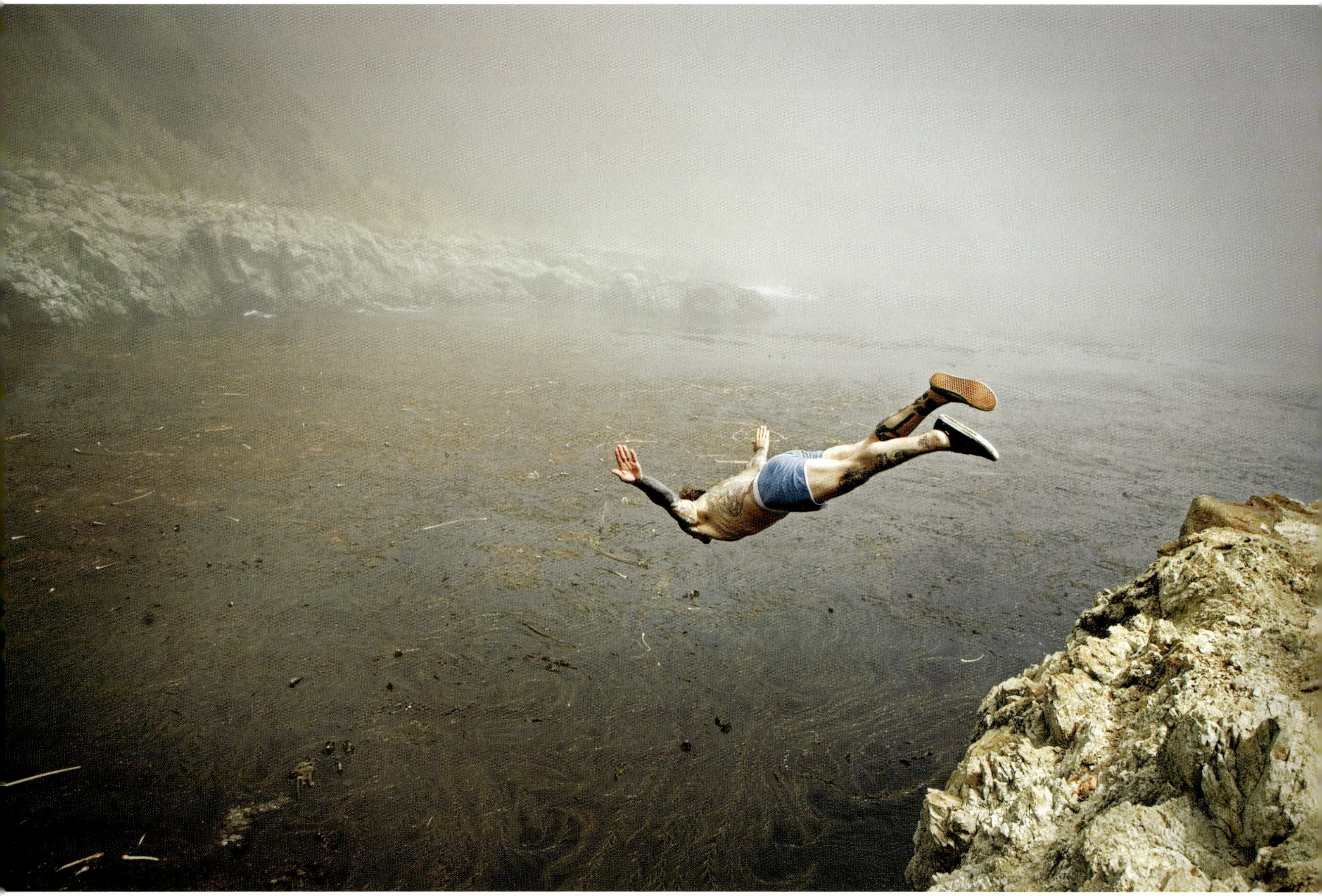

DAY19
"Chris Dive" 2008

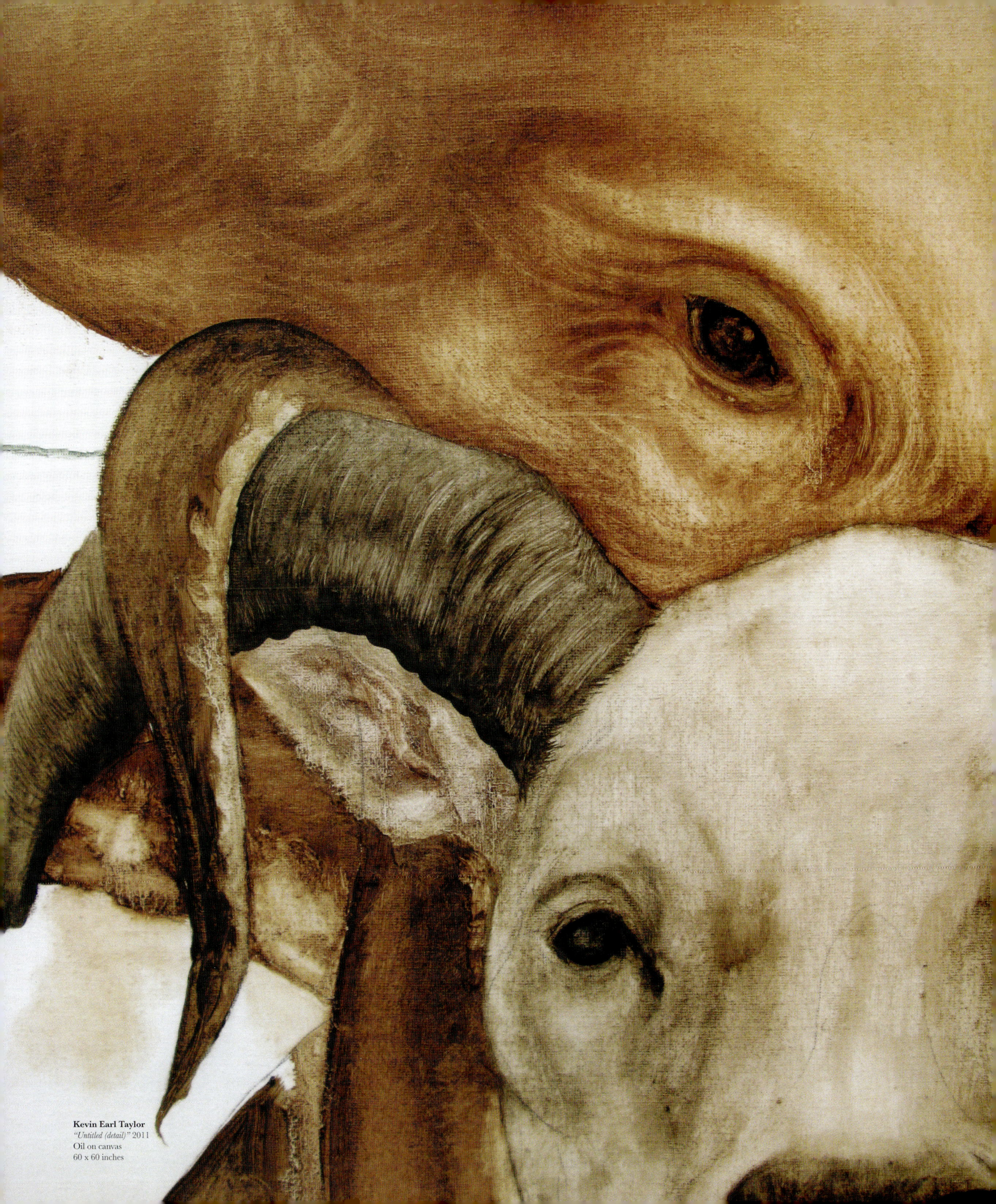

Kevin Earl Taylor
"Untitled (detail)" 2011
Oil on canvas
60 x 60 inches

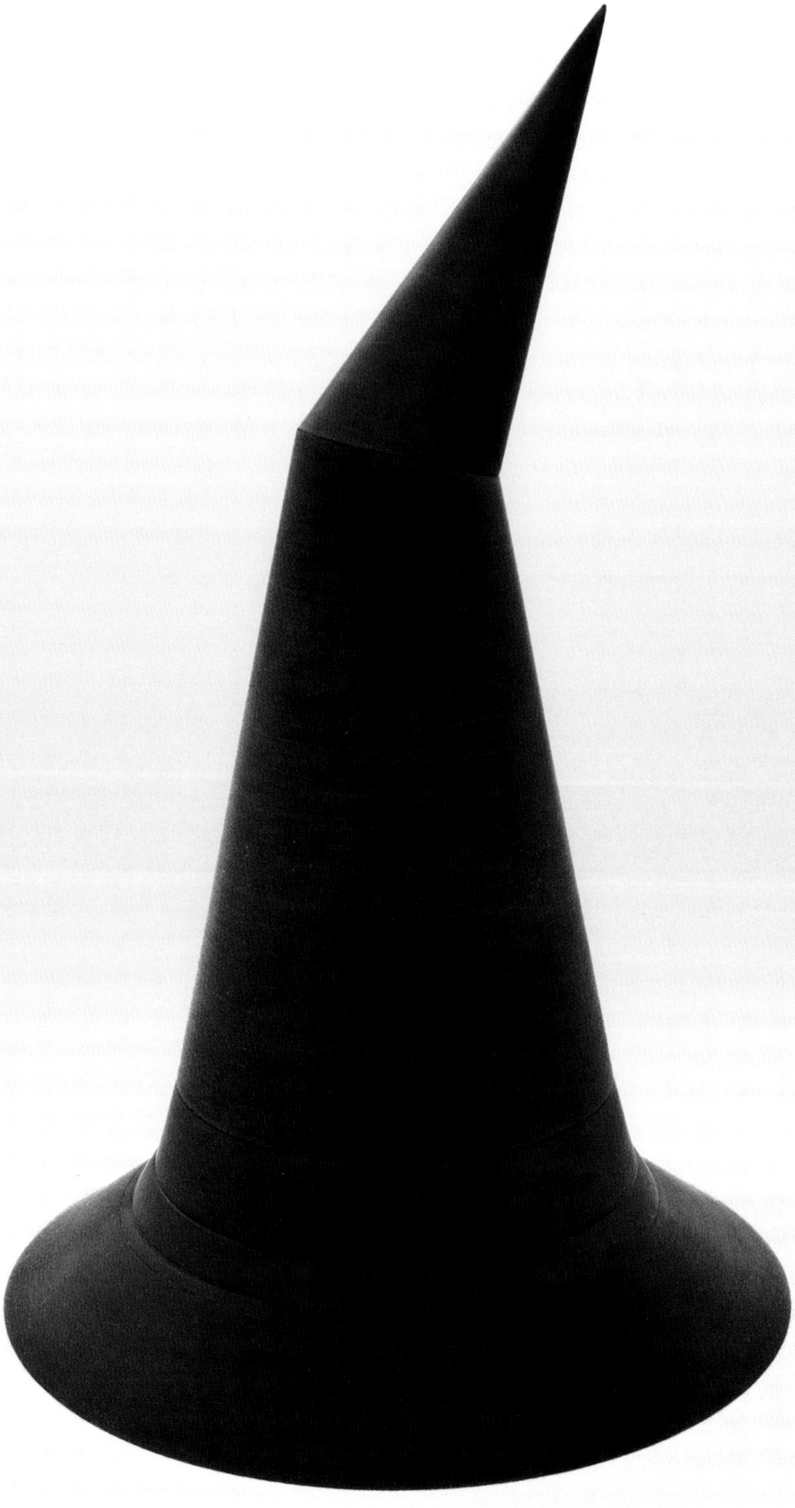

Robert Therrien
"No title (New witch hat)" 2011
Plastic (acetal)
$12^{1}/_{4}$ x 8 x 8 inches

MILK and HONEY

CONTEMPORARY ART *in* CALIFORNIA

BY JUSTIN VAN HOY

AMMO

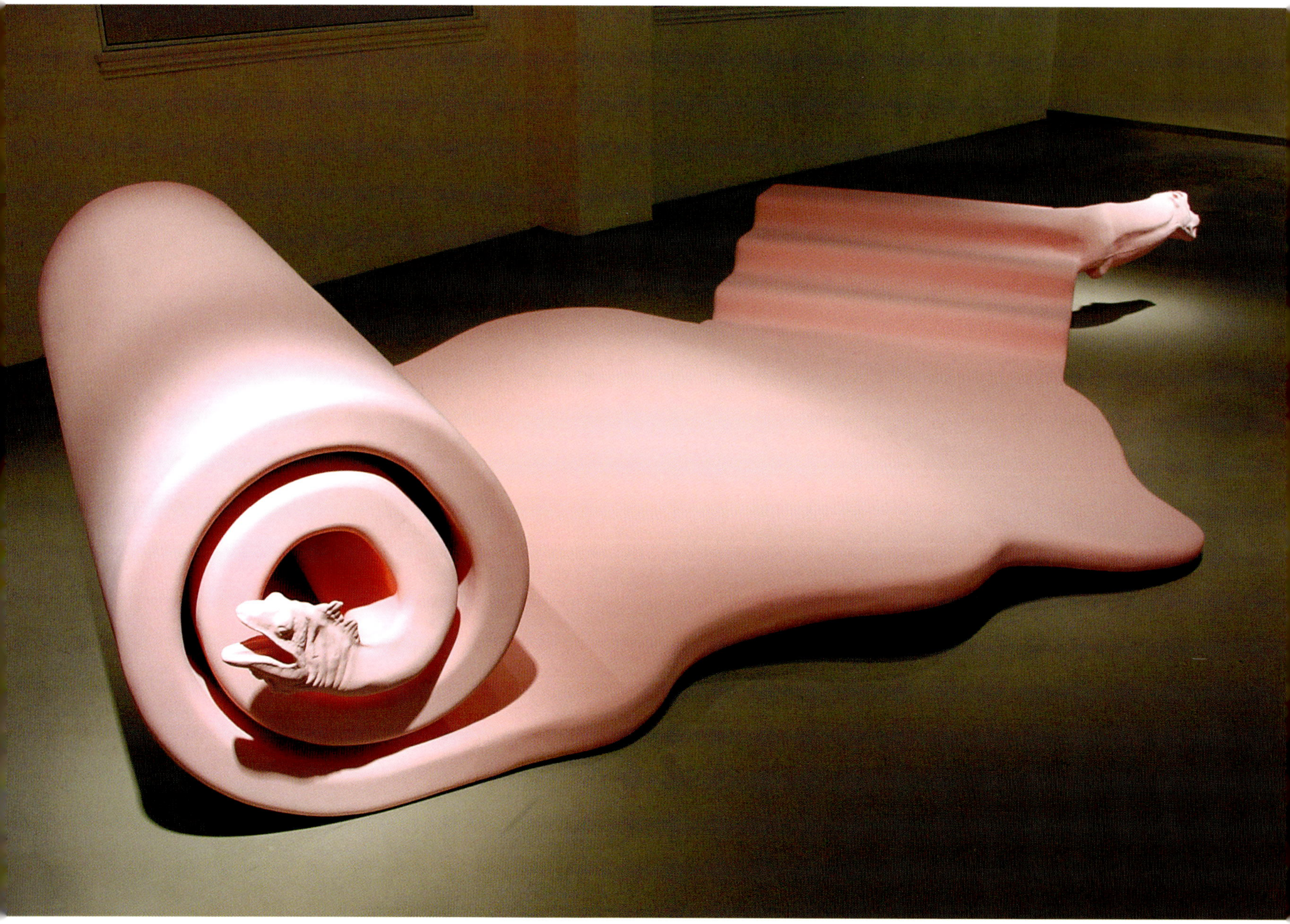

Jon Rajkovich
"Jolly Roll" 2007
Painted plywood and cast resin
164 x 112 x 29 inches

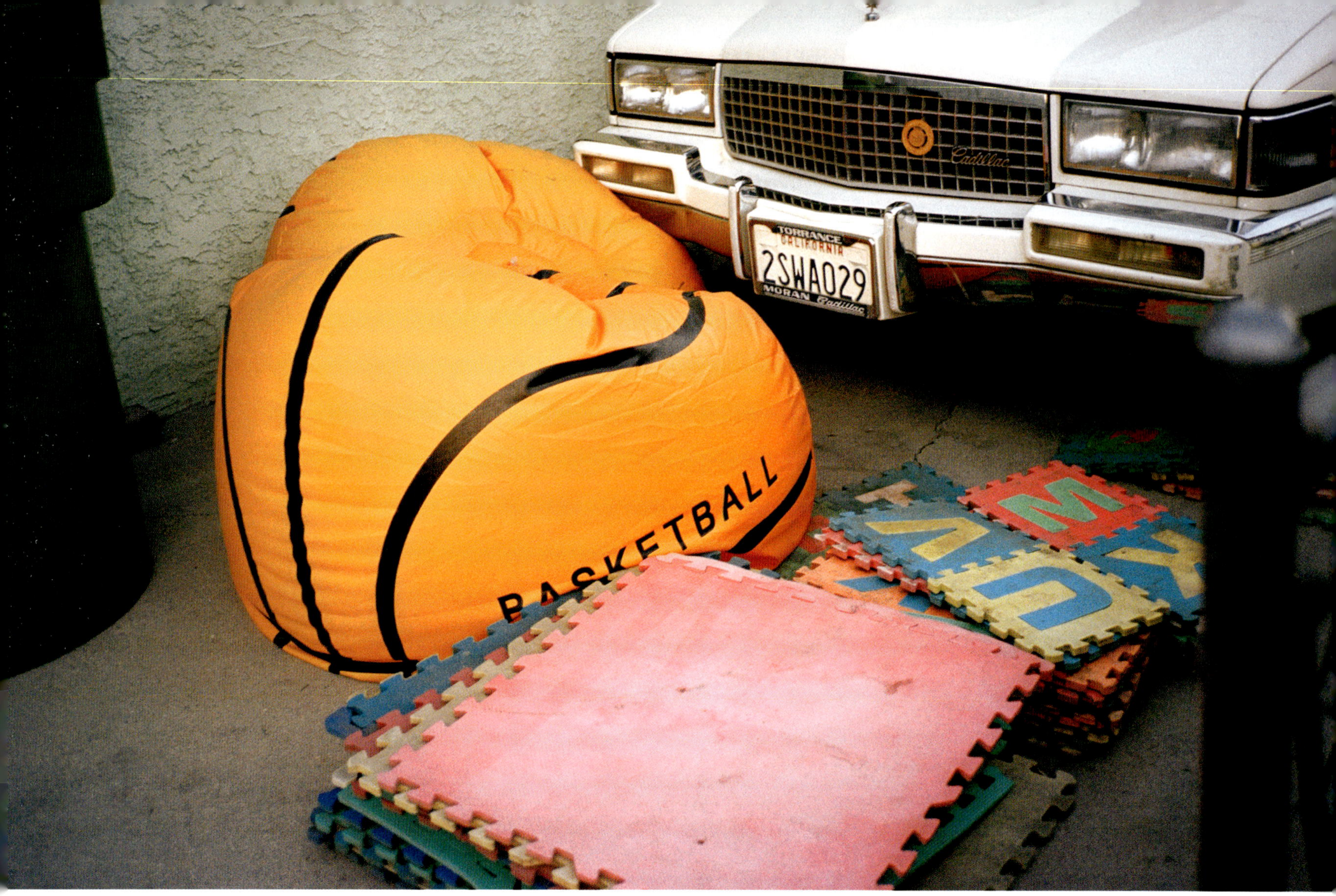

JUSTIN VAN HOY

Los Angeles, California

thedutchpress.com and thislosangeles.com

Milk and Honey: Contemporary Art in California is a book containing contemporary art from (for the most part) late 2011 and early 2012. The origin of the term contemporary art is a result of categorizing artwork created after World War II. From this spawned several other categories to tether artists and their work to—Modern and Postmodern art, High and Low art, Conceptual art, etc.—but they all belong to the greater description of contemporary art.

World War II ended in 1945, sixty-seven years ago, and a lot has changed since then. The seemingly ancient limited lines of communication—post office mail, telephones, and, God forbid, actually speaking face to face with another person—are losing out to the variety of Internet sites and social media wormholes. Conceptual notions are born and killed off in the blink of an eye because everything is visibly available instantly. This accelerated aging in the art world is the Internet's fault, plain and simple.

All of this is creating a very strange time for the art world. New bodies of work, collaborations, and schools of artists are presented and discarded at such a rapid pace that many valuable artists and avenues of visual work are lost due to lack of a proper stage. There is an absence of patience and cadence surrounding themes and viewpoints, and, as a result, we—the audience and participants—are a society

Joey Gallagher
"Inflatable basketball & Cadillac Los Angeles" 2011

that has come to rely on a constant stream of contemporary visual imagery in our everyday world.

Having rambled on about all that, the idea of contemporary art now seems comical. At one time, everything is contemporary and then, not. So, in many ways, the images in this book will be considered old before this book is ever sent to be printed. Still, hope springs eternal that this defined collection of artists and images will act as a visual footprint of 2011 and 2012.

Milk and Honey: Contemporary Art in California is simply a collection of 54 artists currently living and working in California. They are painters, curators, photographers, illustrators, sculptors, designers, and directors. All of these creative personalities spend a large portion, if not all, of their time creating work in the same finite swatch of desert, mountains, and beaches during a time of economic uncertainty for all professions, especially the arts. These artists and their work have been curated and edited to show concurrent themes and images from a wide breadth of talent. Some of the most established artists in the art world: Ed Ruscha, Chris Burden, and Robert Therrien, as well as rising blue chip prospects such as Barry McGee, Joel Morrison, and Piero Golia, and emerging and unknown artists such as Kevin Earl Taylor, Steven Harrington, and others are shown alongside one another in this book. They belong to many collective groups and schools of the arts, but ultimately they are simply all artists creating the most contemporary imagery they can.

Milk and Honey is more than just a label or catch phrase. For many, it has become the idea and, in some instances, the destination that welcomes creativity. Obviously California is not the only place to achieve one's creative goals, but because it is under so many microscopes—political, glamorous, artistic, and educational—it remains so commonly associated with the phrase. The artists showcased in this book have decided, for a variety of reasons, to move to, or remain in, California and create their own story and live their life. The resources are vast and opportunities here are endless.

Most people are normally hit or miss when it comes to California. Whether born here or having emigrated from other states or countries, my fellow California residents and I have committed to stay and figure out what does and doesn't work for us in this place.

Whether you want to admit it or not, California is kind of a big deal. It is the United States' most populous state (approx. 38 million people), and the third most extensive (approx. 163,695.57 sq. miles). It is home to some of the nation's most populated cities (Los Angeles, San Francisco, San Diego) and home to one of the most important art cities in North America: Los Angeles. Throughout its history, California has been viewed as a land of opportunity given its abundance of whatever the commodity of choice happens to be: land, climate, food, or opportunity. It presents a varied landscape of beaches, desert, forests, and mountains, as well as a temperate climate and the attraction of new opportunities in careers. The 54 artists in this book have created work that helps to define the ever-changing creative landscape of California. They have found this place to be an inspirational home to live and work as they create the next wave of timeless contemporary imagery.

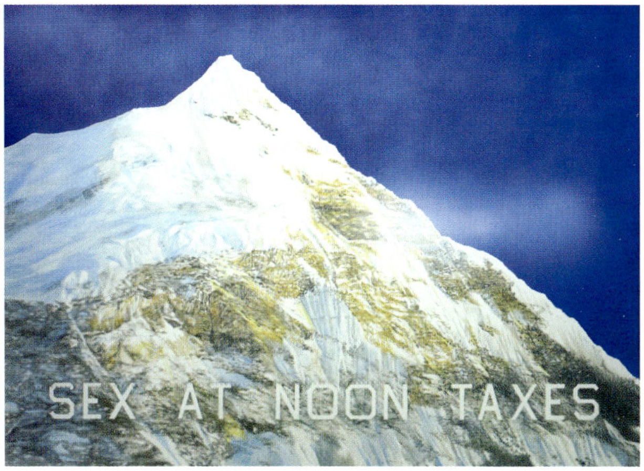

Ed Ruscha
"Sex at Noon Taxes" 2011
Acrylic on canvas
42 x 60 inches

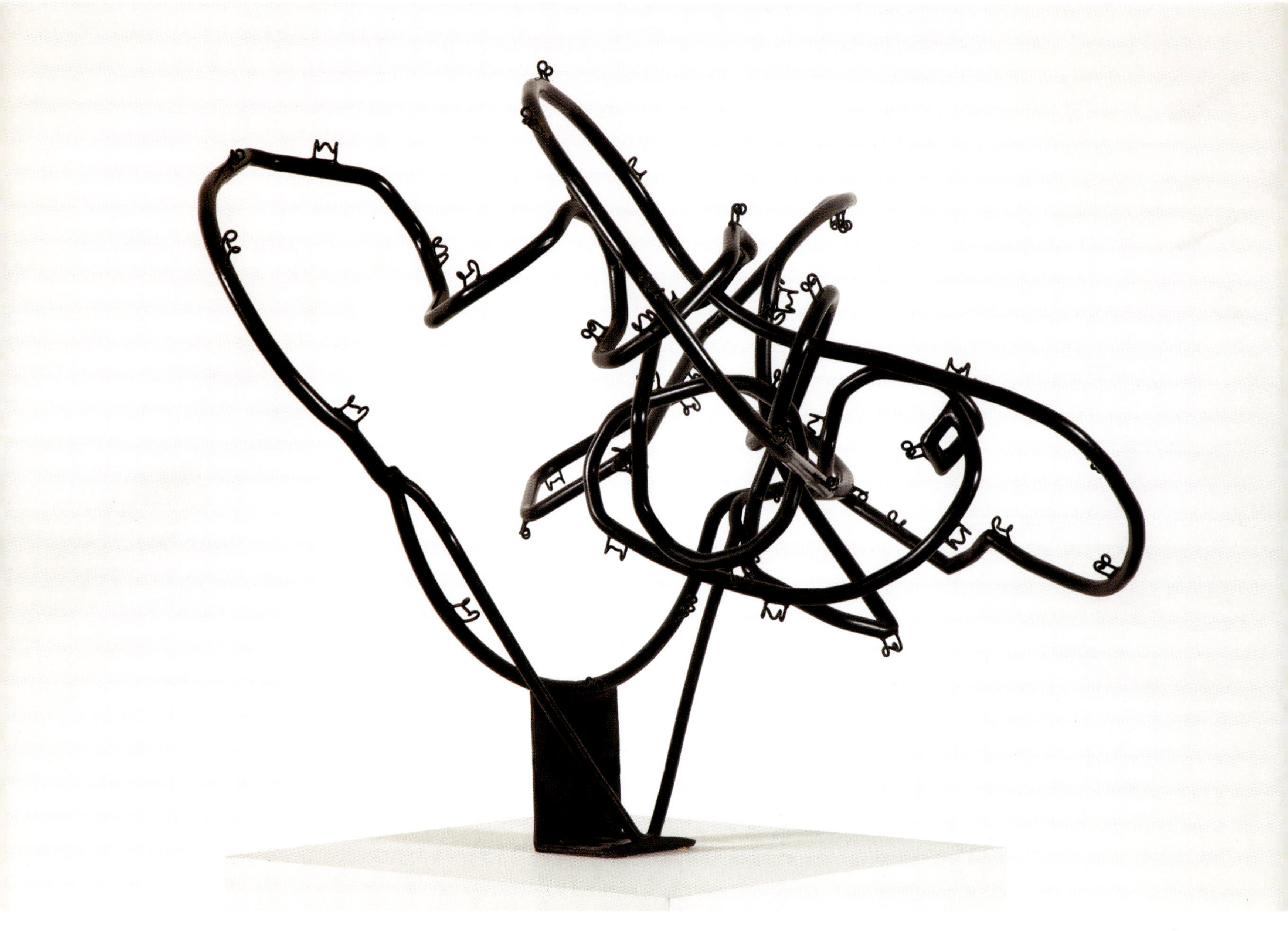

Joel Morrison
"Basketball Rim Drawing" 2012
Bronze with black patina
33 x 41 ½ x 32 ¼ inches

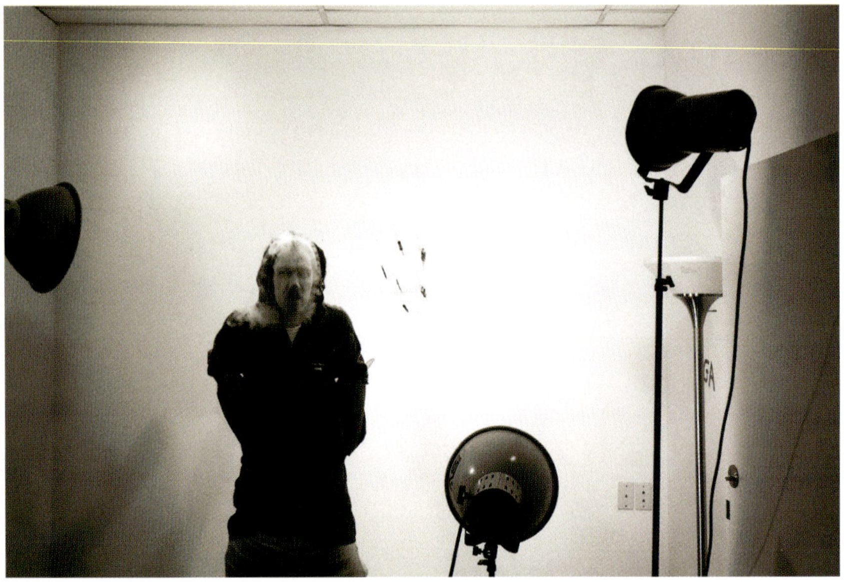

CALI THORNHILL dEWITT

Los Angeles, California
witchhat.biz

Photo by Cali Thornhill deWitt and Jenna deWitt, 2012

My parents initially brought me to California; I was three years old. I have moved away a few times (Vancouver, New York City, Seattle) but never for very long. I always return home, and home is Los Angeles, or as Jesse Spears says, "Los Angeles, the greatest country in the World." I have created my own reality here. People complain about how spread out everything is, but they just haven't figured out how to navigate the space. There is a life here for everyone, regardless of money/class/interest, this is a place where possibility is endless. You just have to look for it, and you'll find what you need.

Advantages: Cheap rent, cheap food, paradise weather, life-affirming light. Disadvantages: I guess Hollywood/ entertainment industry culture, though I feel like that never touches my world. You actually have to welcome that bullshit into your life to have it be present. Same thing goes for all the posers. (Lot's of posers but what do I care? I don't even know their names.)

I am constantly exploring new parts of this city, my neighborhood, my block. It is more a land of discovery to me than ever, and discovery is what I am after. My life feels endless here, and that usually, hopefully gives me a feeling of possibility. California, specifically Los Angeles, gives me everything I need to do what I need to do.

I think of my process mostly as collecting and scavenging. I shoot photos every day. I take notes on what I see, hear, and read. I have a horrible habit of reading the online comments section of human rights and political news stories. But that is somehow crucial. A mental collection of strangers' hatred and bigotry.

At some point I hear something, a phrase or a single word, something simple, and that ties everything together for me.

I take all the images I have made and seen and collected that week/month/season, and I start to put it together, try to make a thing that represents the word or idea that stopped me in my tracks.

And then I put it all aside and start all over again!

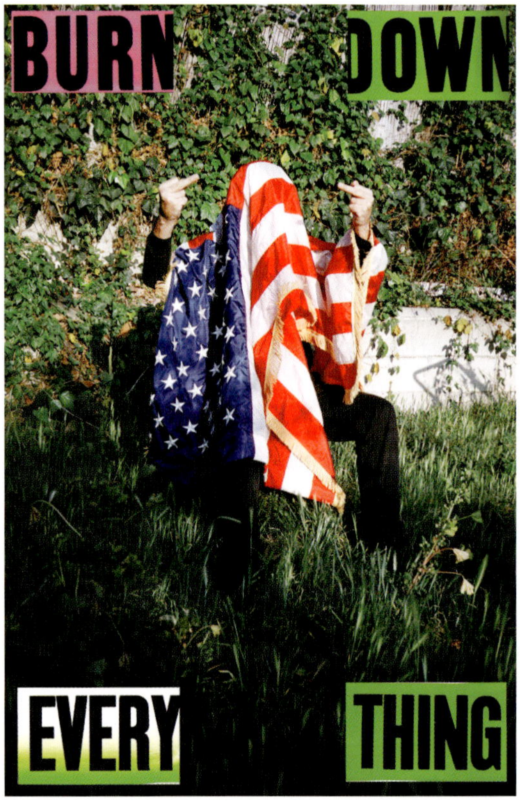

"Stolen Flag" 2012
Photograph and letterpress
8 x 10 inches

"Underneath the 110" 2012
Photograph, letterpress, and ink
8 x 10 inches

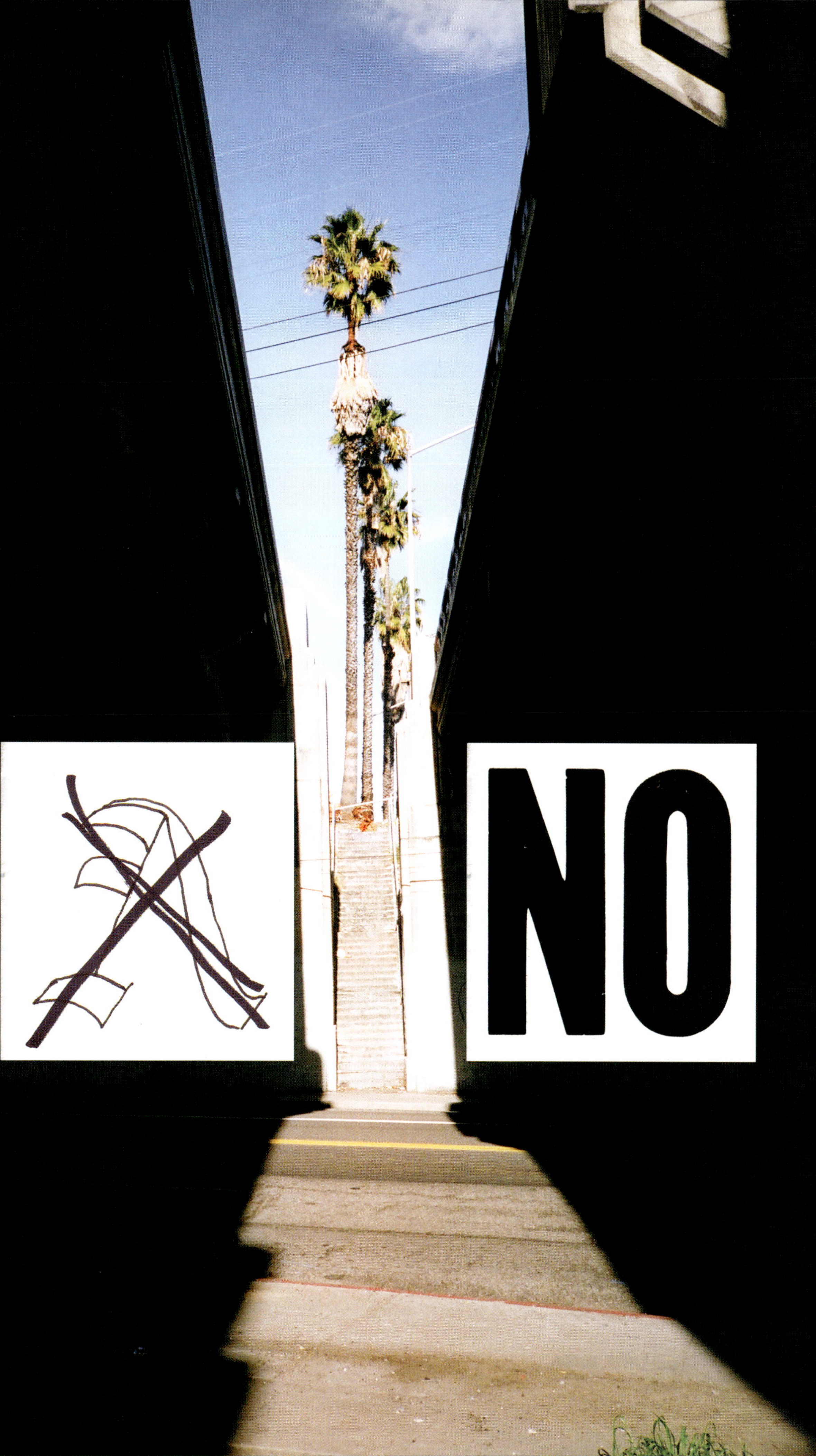
NO

BARE
Elegance
4624 W. Imperial HWY, Hawthorne/LAX Area
(310) 649-1100
Always Hiring Girls 18+. No Experience Needed.
PERIAL HWY AND INGLEWOOD BLVD.

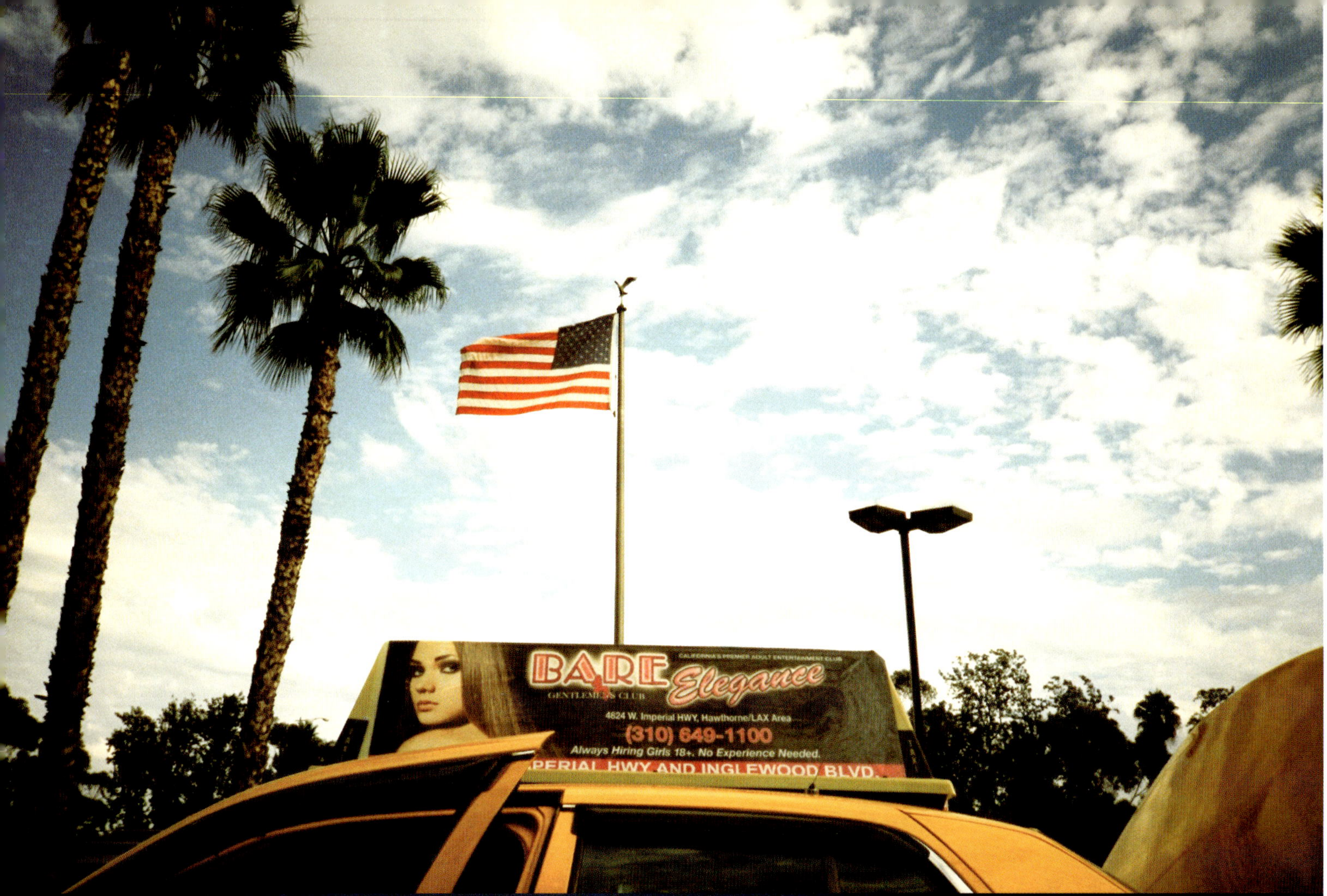

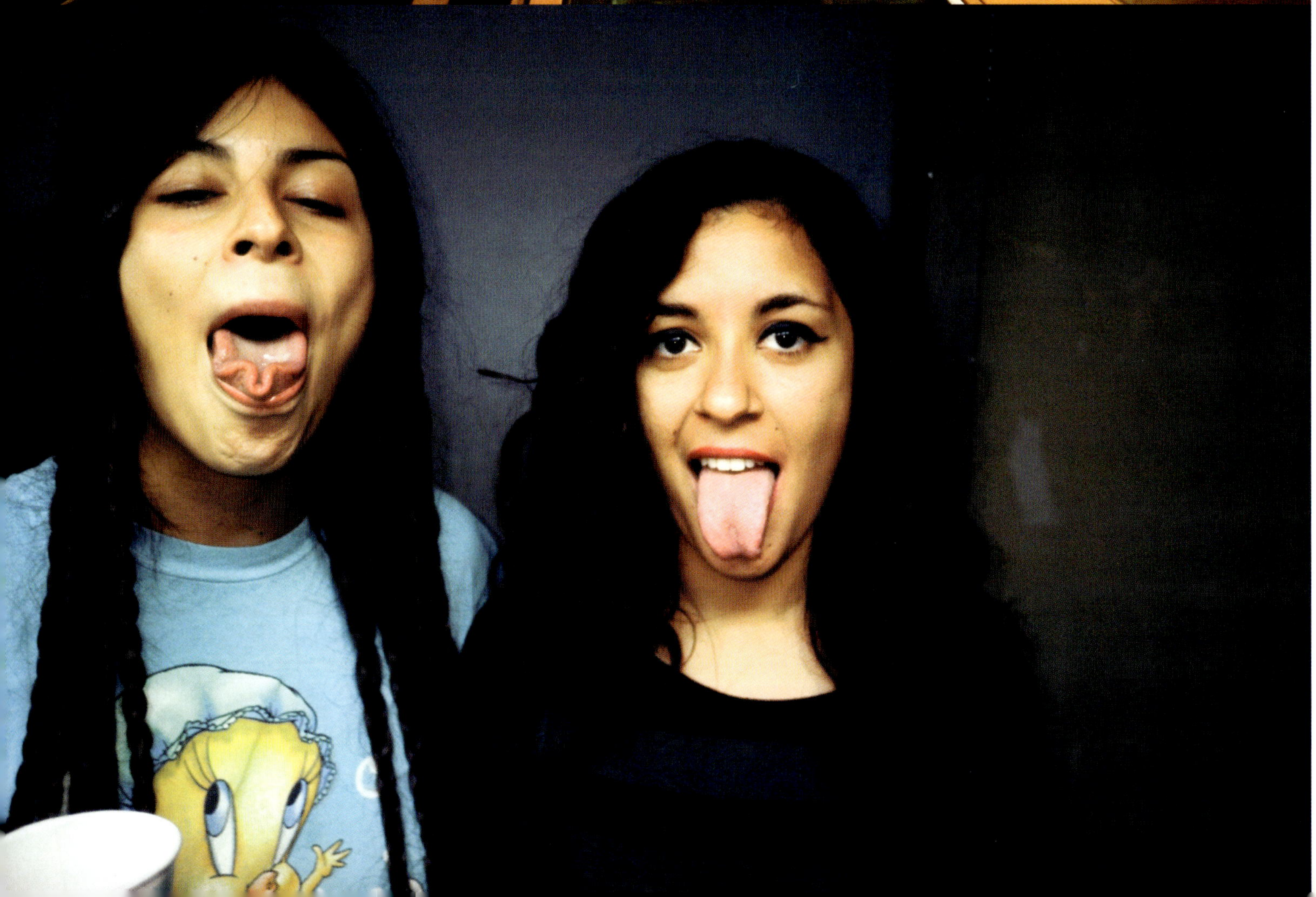

"Real Hair" 2012
Photograph
8 x 10 inches

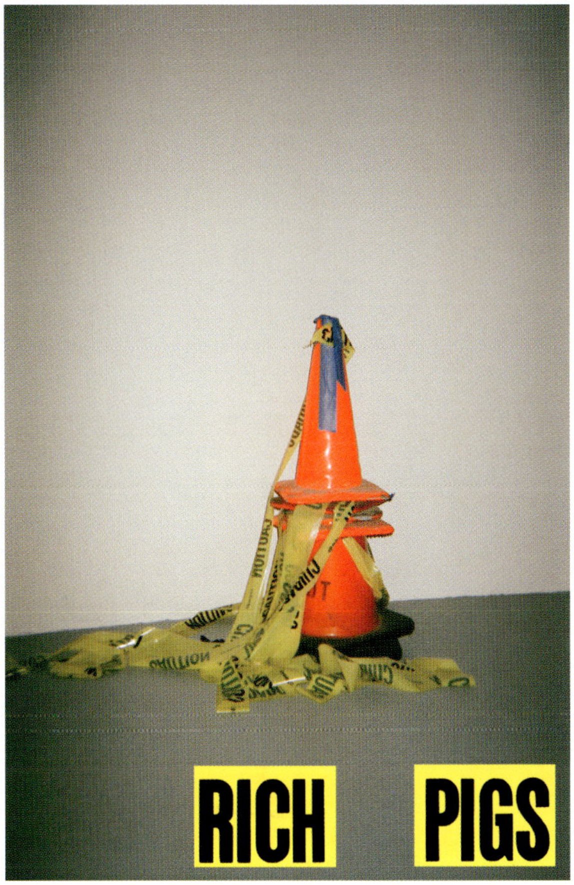

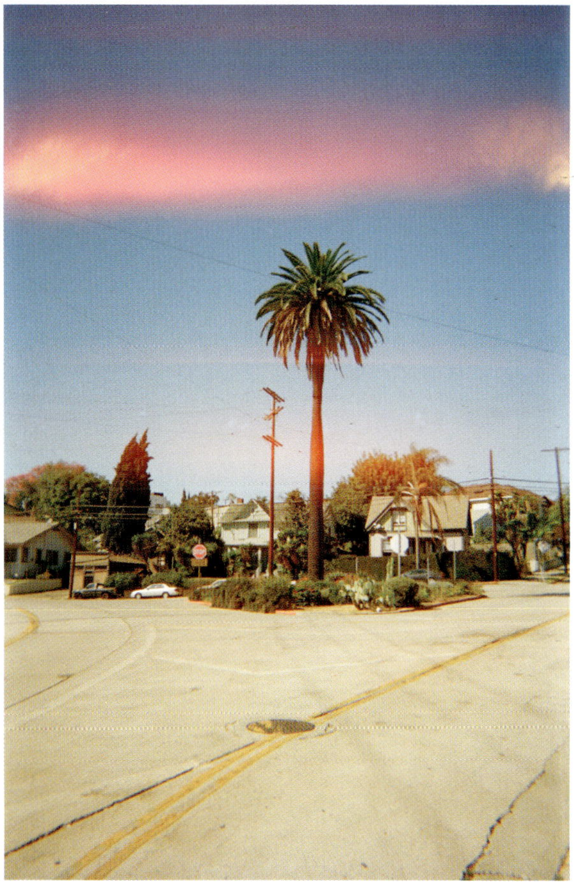

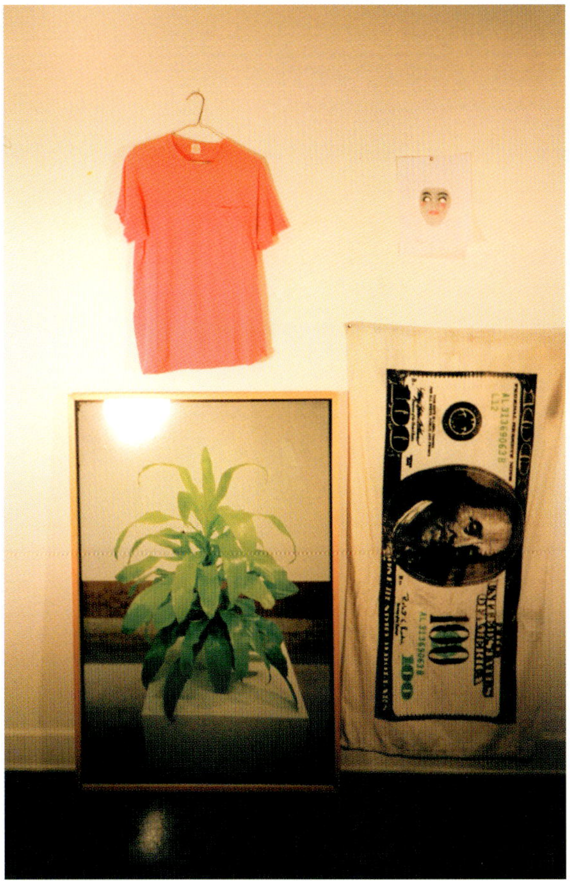

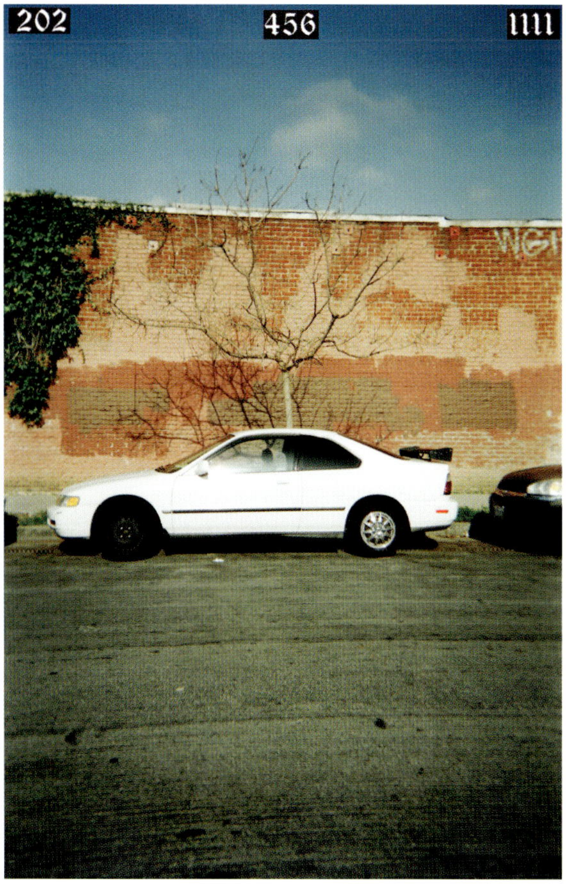

Clockwise from top left: *"Museum"* 2012 Photograph and letterpress 8 x 10 inches; *"My Island"* 2012 Photograph 8 x 10 inches; *"Mandarin Plaza"* 2012 Photograph 8 x 10 inches; *"Call Me"* 2012 Photograph and silkscreen 8 x 10 inches

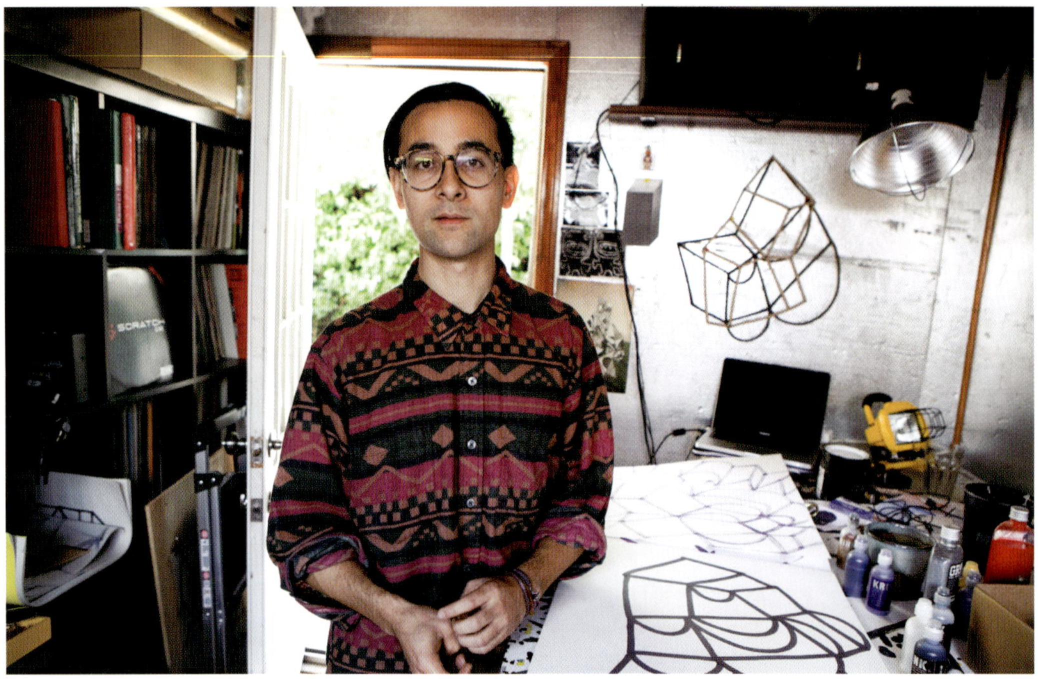

Photo by Aaron Farley, 2012

ERIN GARCIA

Los Angeles, California
erindgarcia.com

I first came out to Los Angeles in 2000 to visit a couple friends that I grew up with in North Carolina. The visit felt very natural, and I was immediately enamored with the atmosphere they had created. Through the years I've built up an amazing community of friends that support all of my creative ideas.

It seems the advantages parallel the disadvantages here. I'm not one to dislike good weather, but a more dramatic change in seasons is a good placeholder for time. Seclusion is easier when you have to drive everywhere, but that reduces random social interaction, which can also spark ideas. I guess I'm really just weighing LA vs. more metropolitan cities, so beyond that I like to be able to escape from LA in any direction and end up in the desert, mountains, or ocean. For now I've chosen California, but you never know what another location might do for you.

Growing up in the South, I always had a vision of what I believed California was like. After being here for 12 years, I'm not sure my original assumption has changed that much; it's only been enhanced by sunshine, bold colors, and surf contests. I think of California as a never-ending expanse, sharing its longest border with a limitless ocean and dotted with natural wonders and celebrity. The foundation of Los Angeles is visual stimulation edited for commerce, supported by endless communities of every culture that barely can be held back by imposing landscape or even the nation's border. The city's promoted aesthetic has everything constantly changing to keep up with the desire to remain brand new and photo-shoot fresh.

This isn't a critique, just an outsider's perspective, and I actually think this makes me enjoy California more and lets these influences seep into my work.

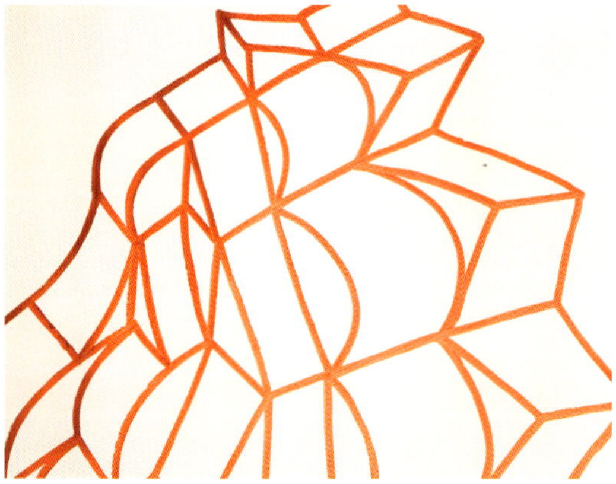

"Stacks #31 (Gold)" 2012
Permanent ink on archival paper
48 x 36 inches

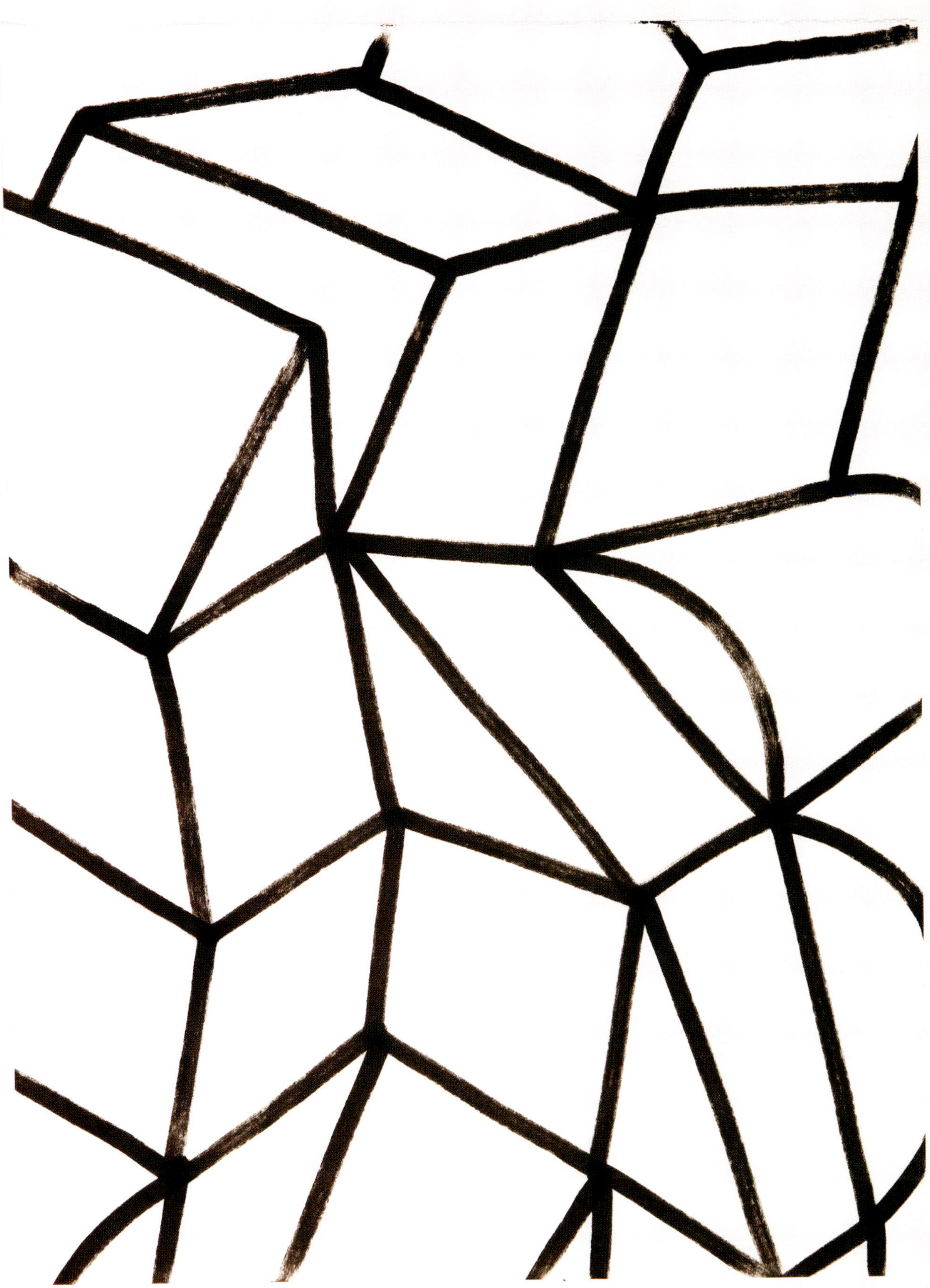

"Stacks #60 (Black)" 2012
Permanent ink on newsprint
18 x 24 inches

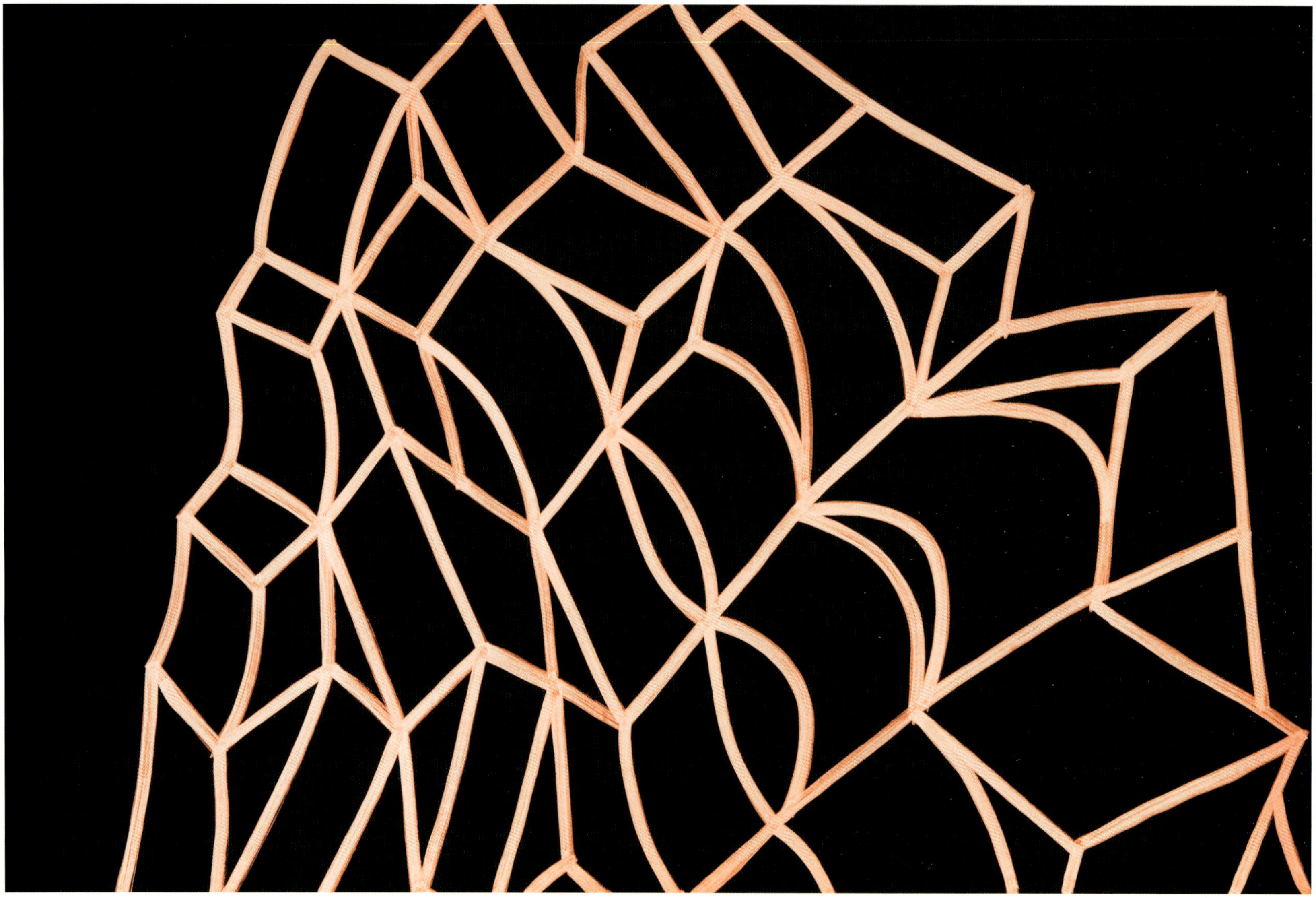

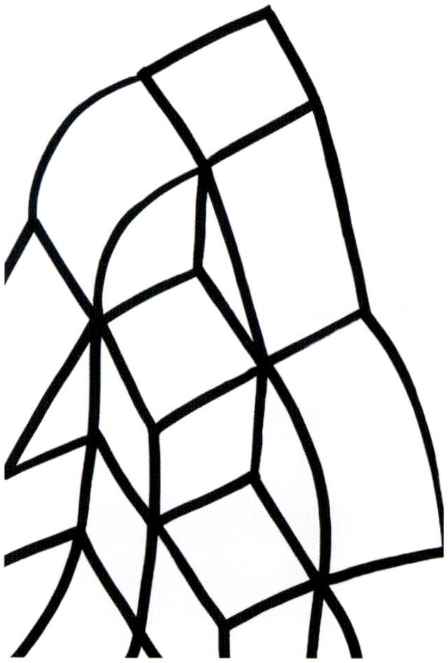

"Stacks #69 (Silver)" 2012
Permanent metallic ink on paper
18 x 24 inches

"Structure #22 (Black)" 2012
Permanent ink on paper
48 x 36 inches

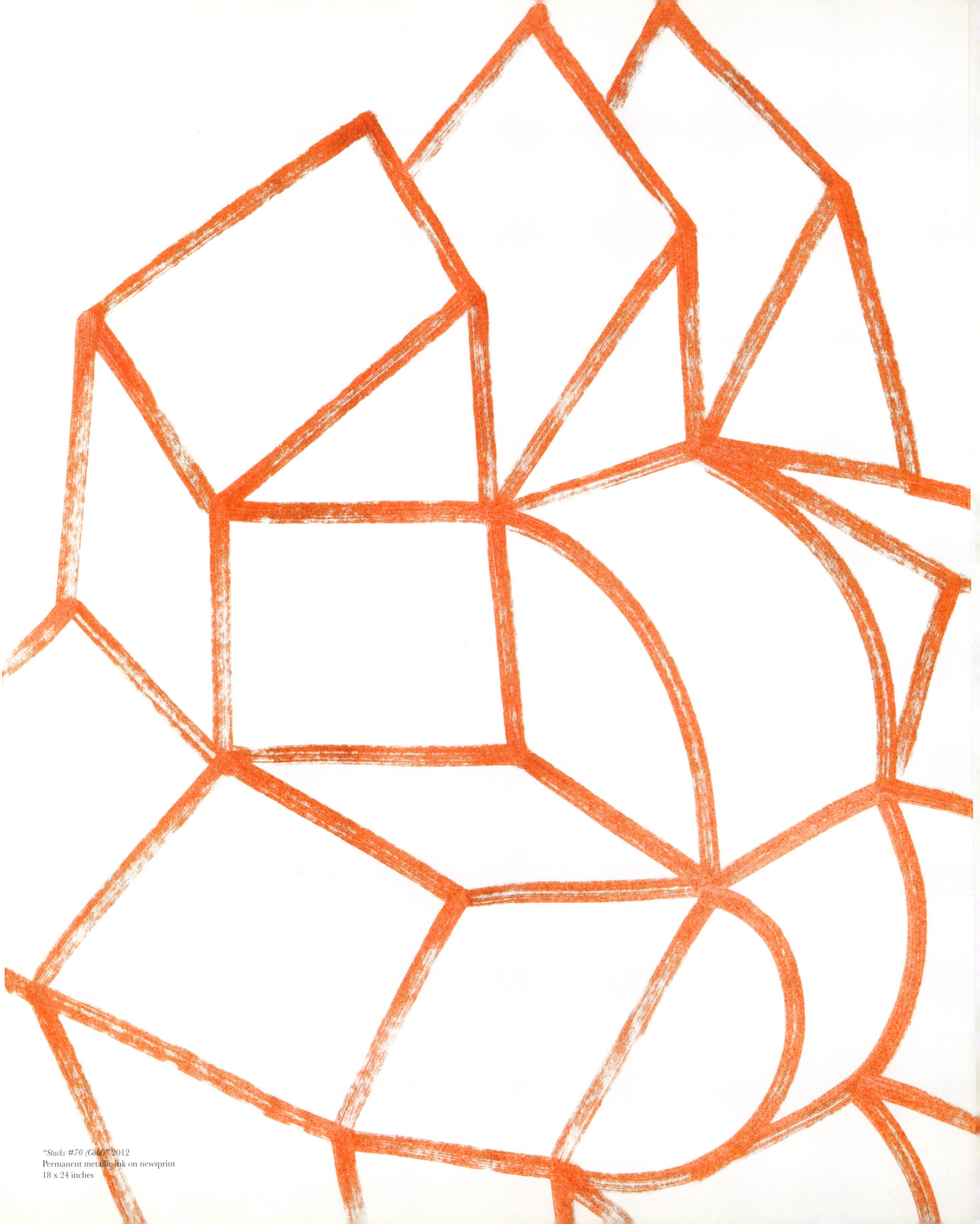

"*Stacks #70 (Gold)*" 2012
Permanent metallic ink on newsprint
18 x 24 inches

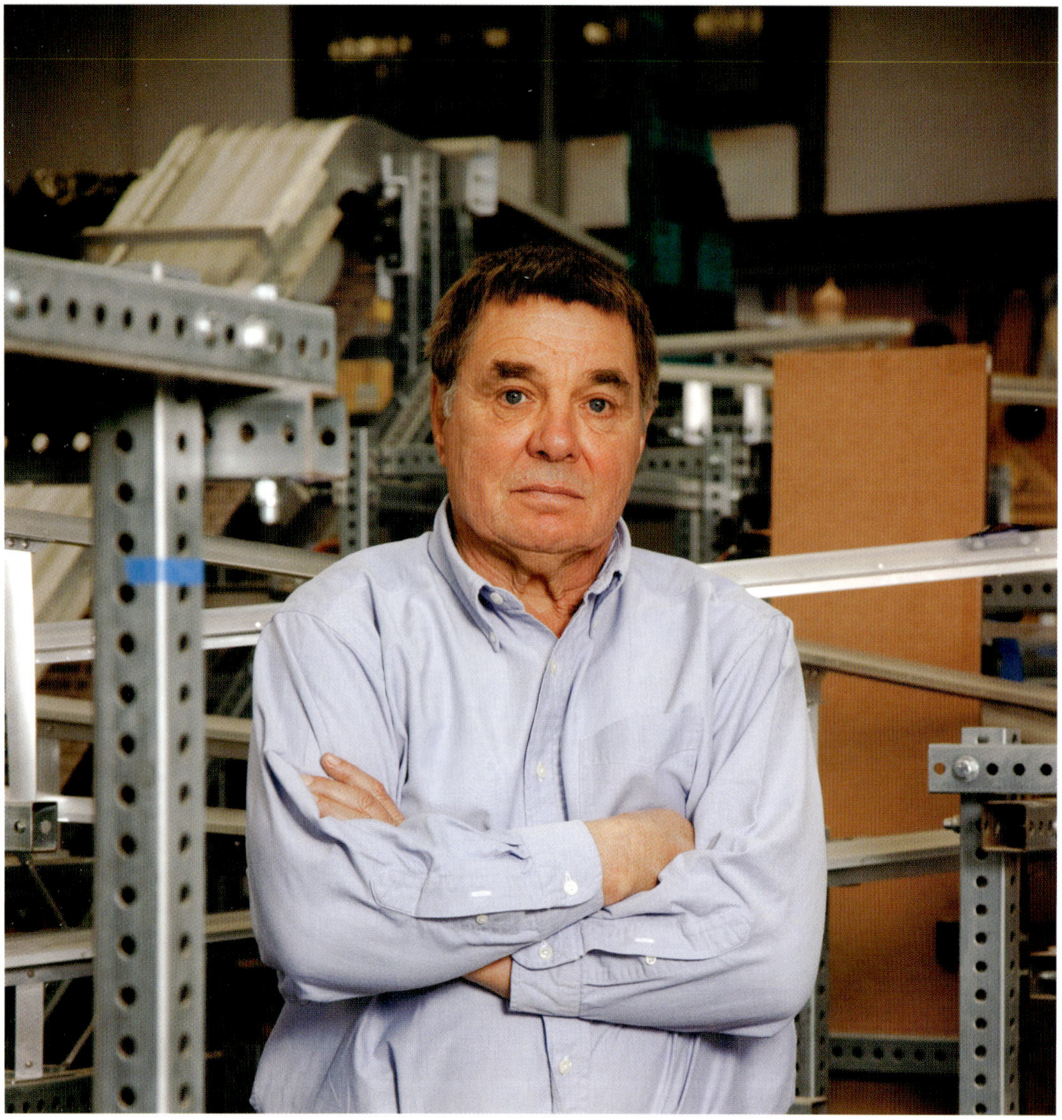

CHRIS BURDEN

Los Angeles, California
Gagosian Gallery

Photo by Joshua White

I first came to California in my junior year of high school, in 1962. I was awarded a National Science Foundation grant to study oceanography at the Scripps Institute in La Jolla. I was so enamored with California, I later applied and was accepted to Pomona College. I have stayed here because I can't imagine making art anyplace else.

There are incredible resources available in Southern California—from inexpensive materials to high-tech companies and their expertise. In addition, one can work outside year-round and store materials outdoors. The biggest disadvantage to Southern California now is the overwhelming traffic.

Conversely, the overwhelming traffic is also an influence. It forces me to stay in my studio and create.

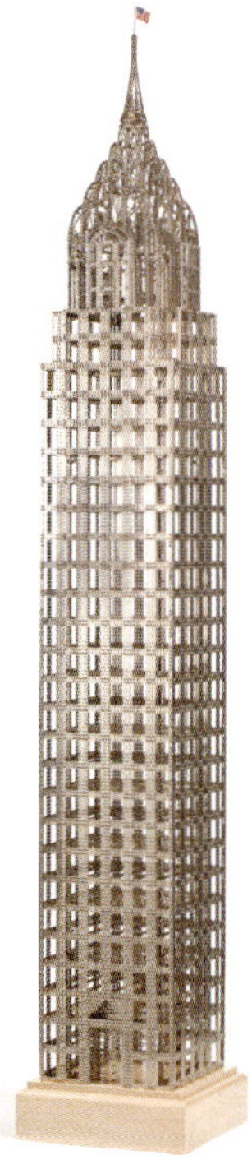

"Chrysler Building" 2011
Nickel-plated metal Eitech toy construction parts, metal flag, wood base
With base: 127 x 20 ½ x 20 ½ inches
Photo by Bryan Forrest

(Detail)
"Chrysler Building" 2012
Nickel-plated metal Eitech toy construction parts, metal flag, wood base
With base: 127 x 20 ½ x 20 ½ inches
Photo by Bryan Forrest

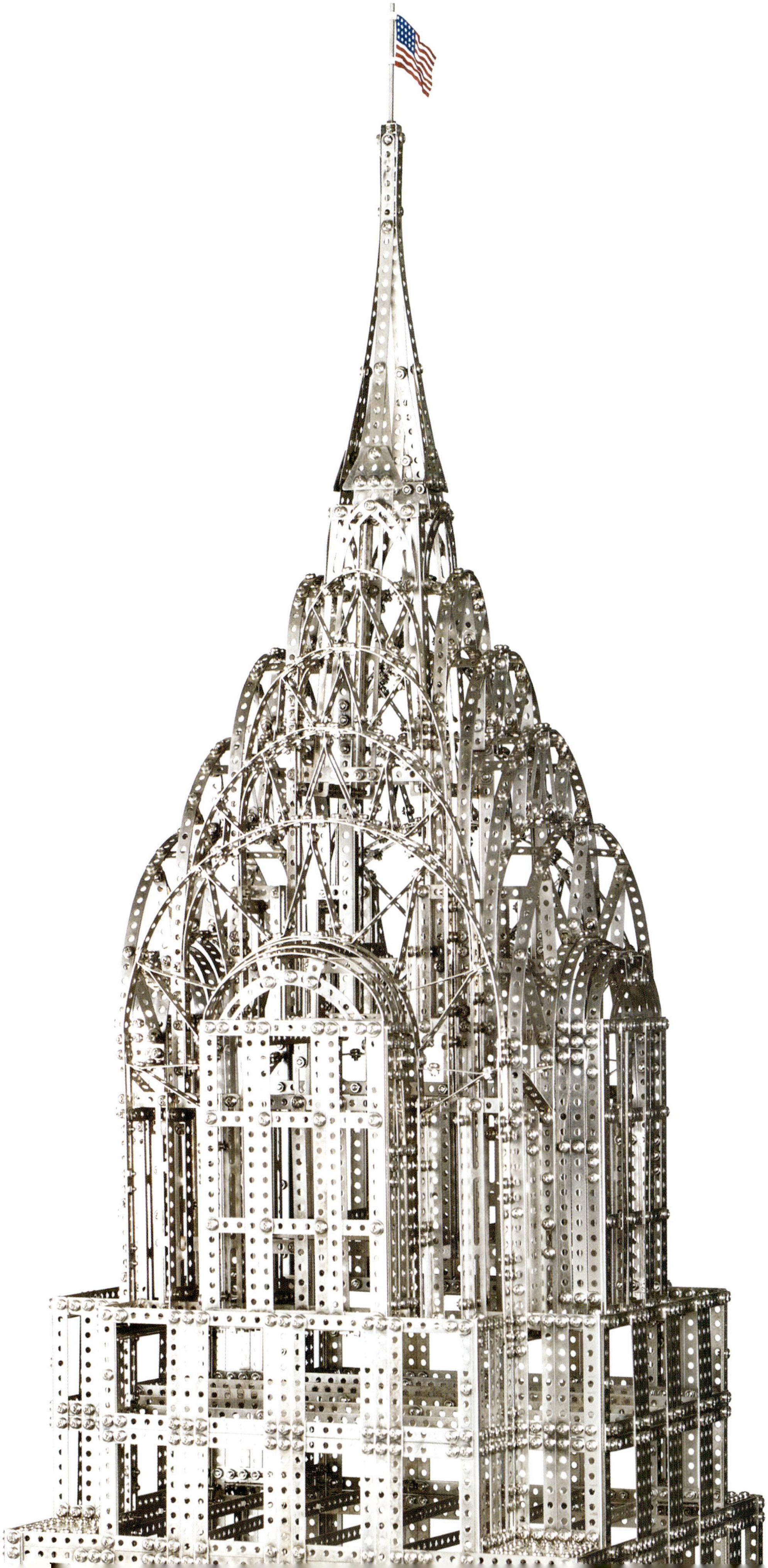

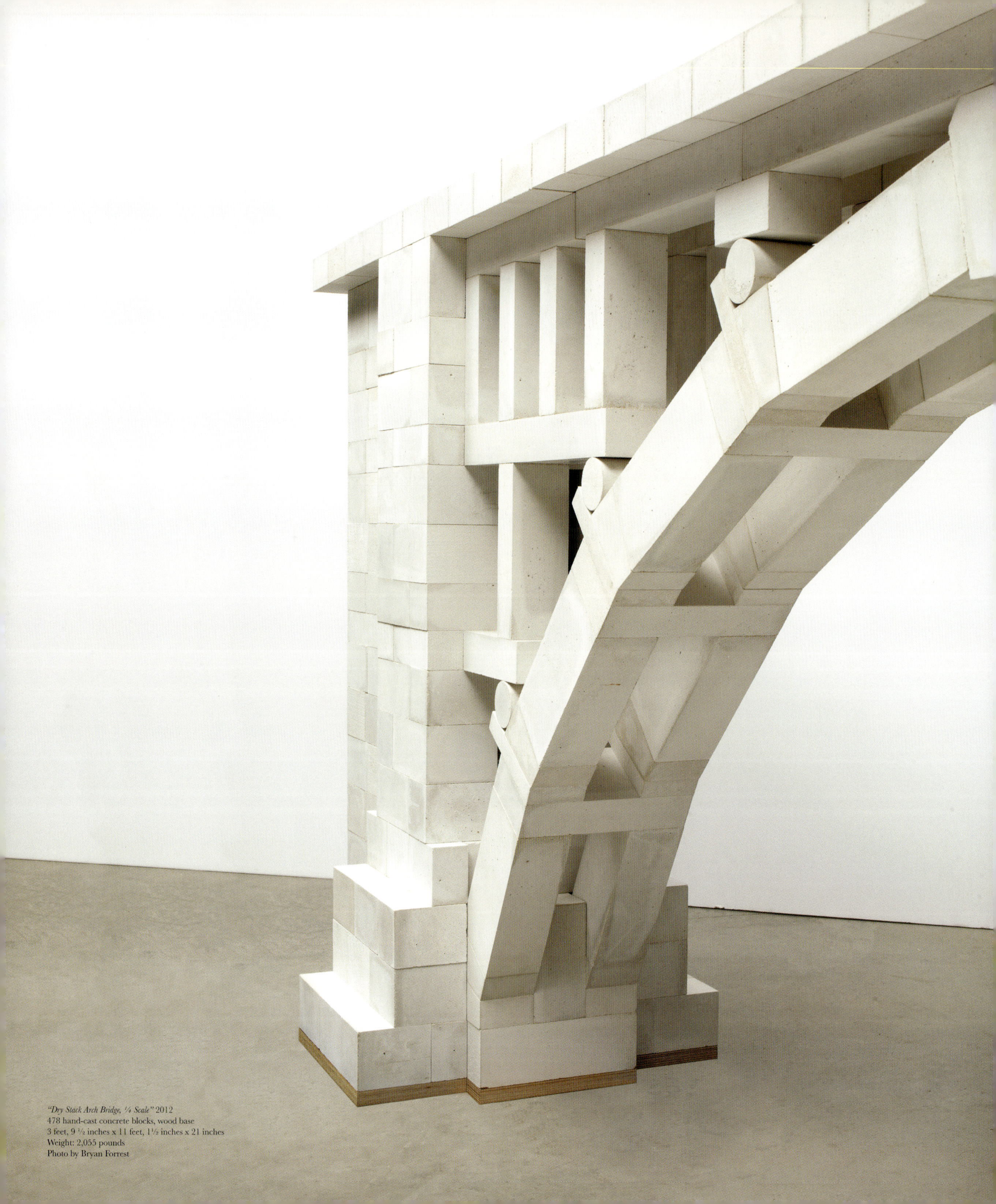

"Dry Stack Arch Bridge, ¼ Scale" 2012
478 hand-cast concrete blocks, wood base
3 feet, 9 ½ inches x 11 feet, 1½ inches x 21 inches
Weight: 2,055 pounds
Photo by Bryan Forrest

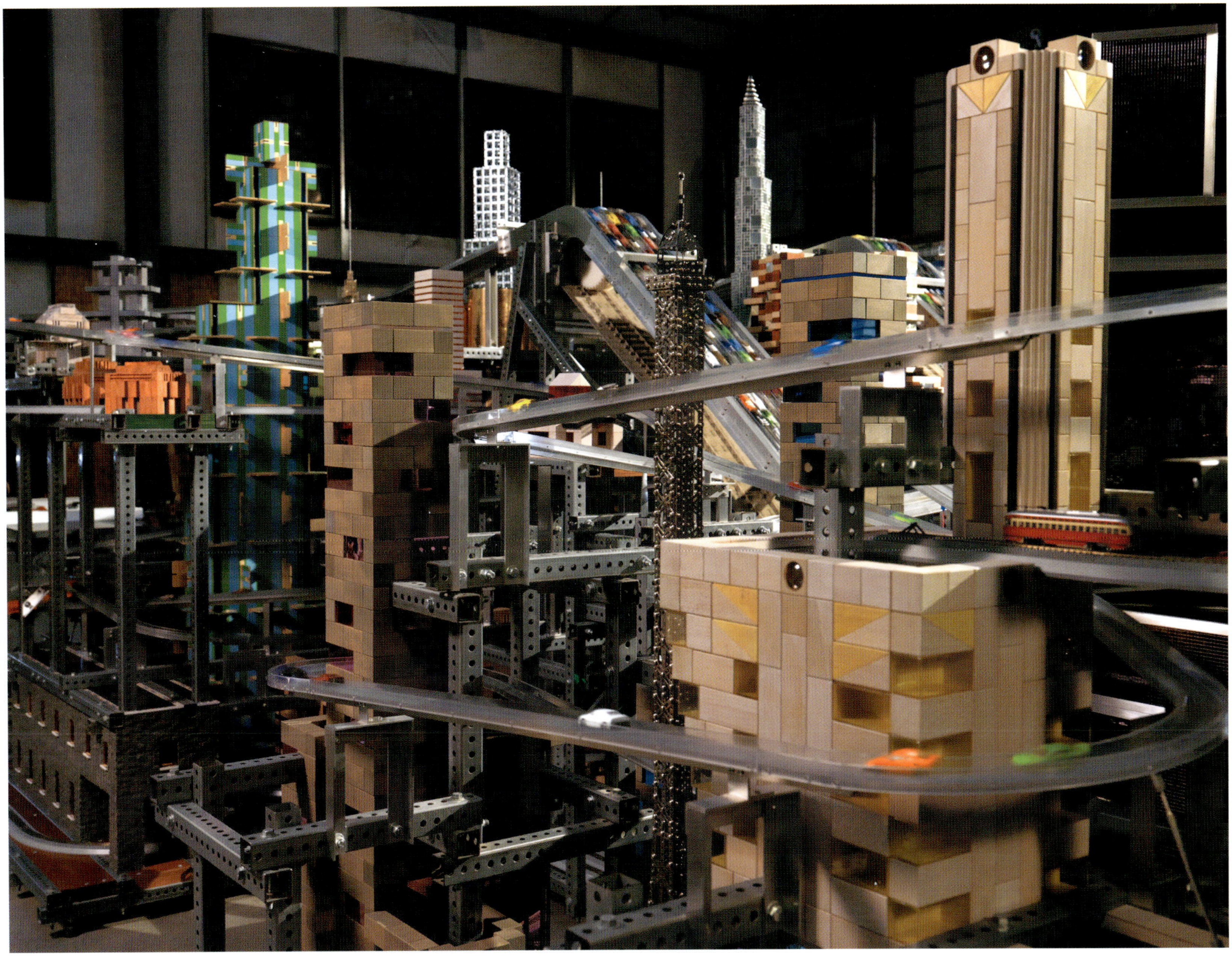

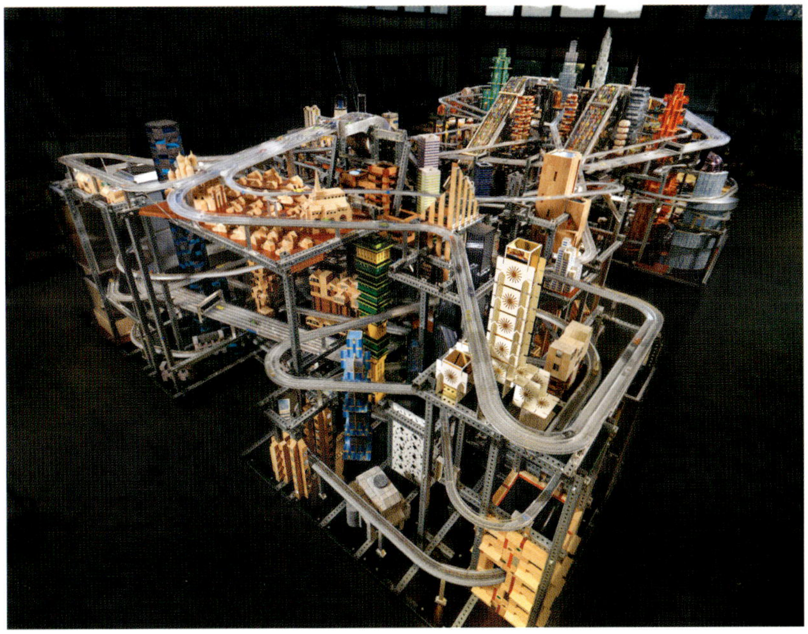

"Metropolis II" 2010
Three ½ hp DC motors with electronic control and sensors, 1100 custom manufactured die-cast cars, HO-scale train sets with controllers and tracks, neodymium magnets, steel, aluminum, shielded copper wire, copper sheet, brass, various plastics, assorted woods and manufactured wood products, Legos, Lincoln Logs, Dado Cubes, glass, ceramic and natural stone tiles, acrylic and oil-base paints, rubber, sundry adhesives
9 feet, 9 inches (H) x 28 feet, 3 inches (W) x 19 feet, 2 inches (D)
Photo by Erich Koyama

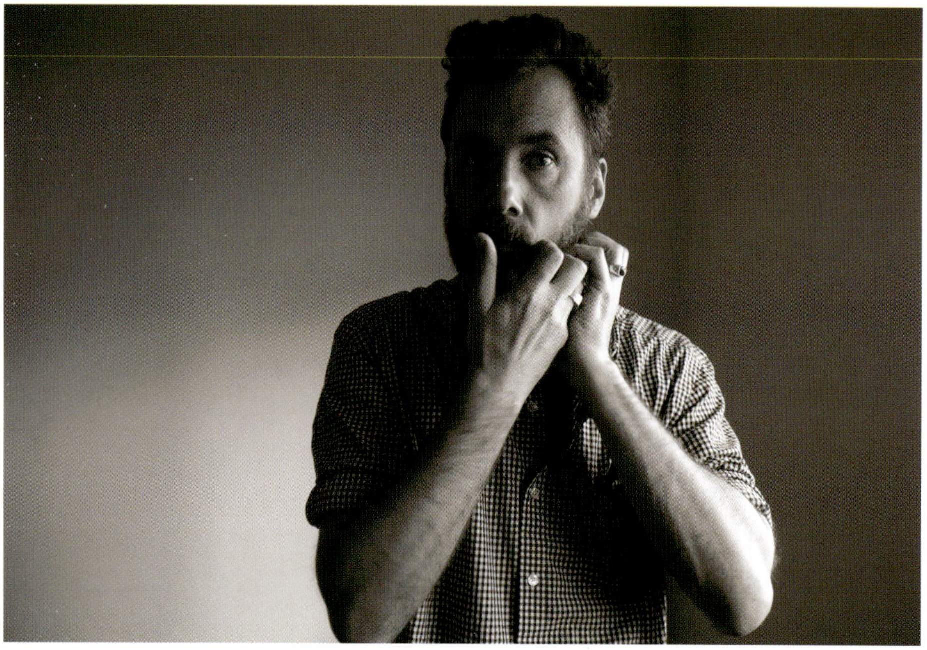

Self portrait, 2012

DAN MONICK

Los Angeles, California
dmonick.com
thegardenpartynyc.com

I initially came to California for the weather and stayed for the space.

There are advantages:
The space
The weather
You have to dig to find what you want
Its bad rap keeps it from being overrun
The ability to isolate and focus
The ability to find such a multitude of inspiration
I love driving
Disadvantages: See advantages

As far as the process, with taking photographs, the technical process will remain the same no matter where I go. The isolating bubble of driving everywhere in Los Angeles creates a more observational state for me. Contrary to what one would think, I strangely see more because of this.

I've always thought about the stories pay phones could tell if they could talk. Silent sentinels that hear so much but never give away the secrets. Fading monuments to the way we used to communicate and exist without being constantly in touch. Once out of the house, one couldn't communicate with someone who was not there until they found a pay phone. Major events of my life have revolved around pay phones, and now I know I have not touched one in over eight years. If those pay phones could talk.

Ed Ruscha's "Every Building On The Sunset Strip" and Hollywood Boulevard 1973-2004 are two major documents in completist recording of somewhat banal subjects. As Ruscha calls these works unemotional and democratic, I feel the momentary focus on these everyday aspects illicit a very emotional response once I take the time to pause and think about how these often-passed-over objects have had a part in my life. From the massive changes of the real estate of Hollywood Boulevard to the fading facades of the phones up and down Sunset Boulevard, a straight forward reminder of change.

This project is directly inspired by and acknowledges Ed Ruscha's work.

These photos are a test run for the full Boulevard. Shot in sequence on the northeast and southwest sides of Sunset Boulevard between Quintero St. and Alvarado St. on December 18th, 2011, and are all shot on 35mm color negative film.

"Every Pay Phone On Sunset Blvd (test)" 2011
35mm color negative film

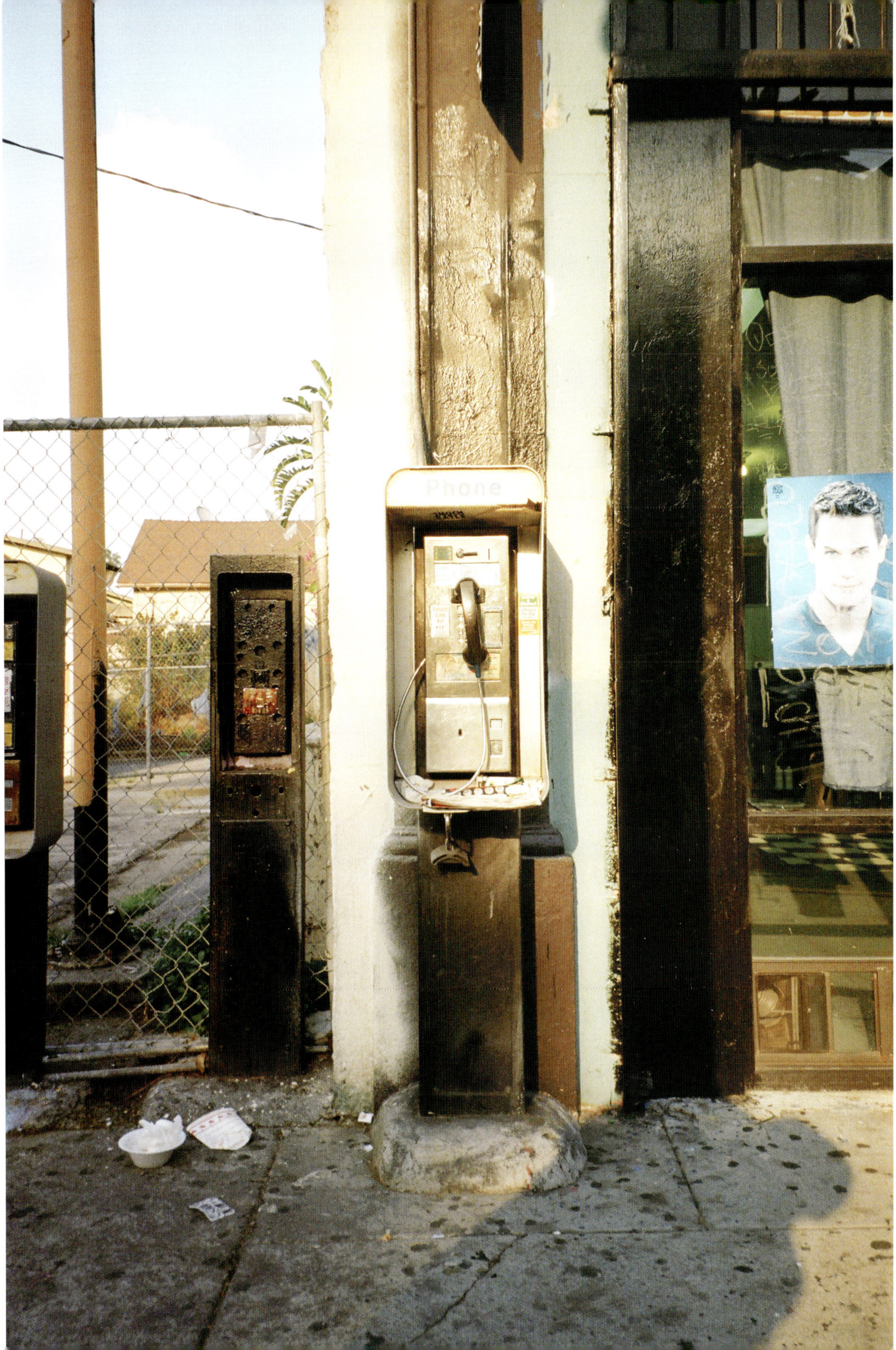
Phone

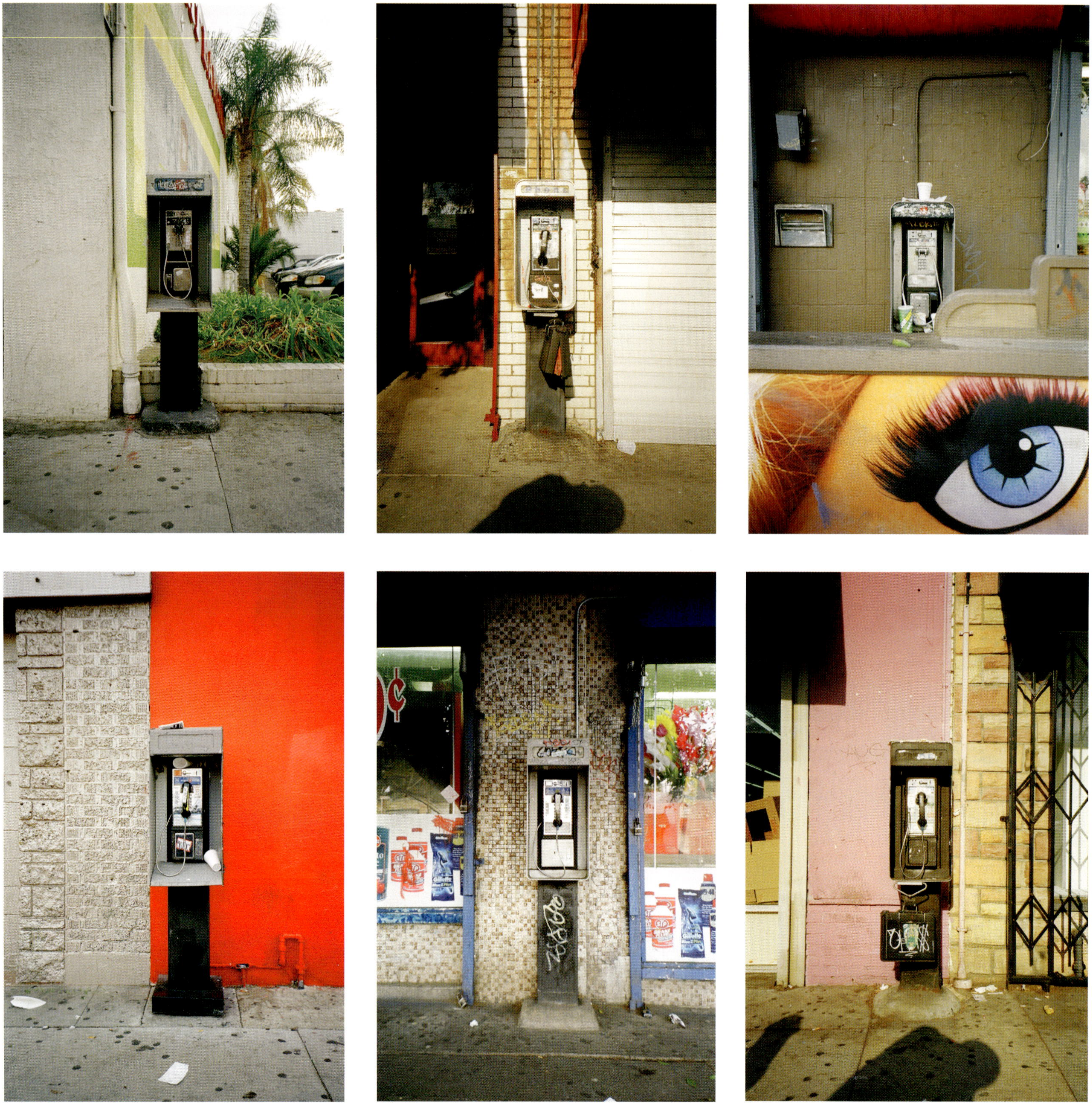

"Every Pay Phone On Sunset Blvd (test)" 2012
35mm color negative film

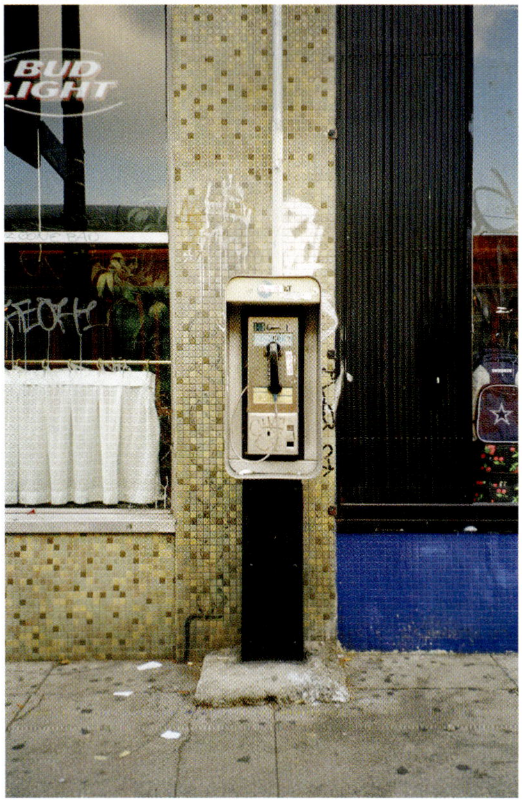
BUD
LIGHT

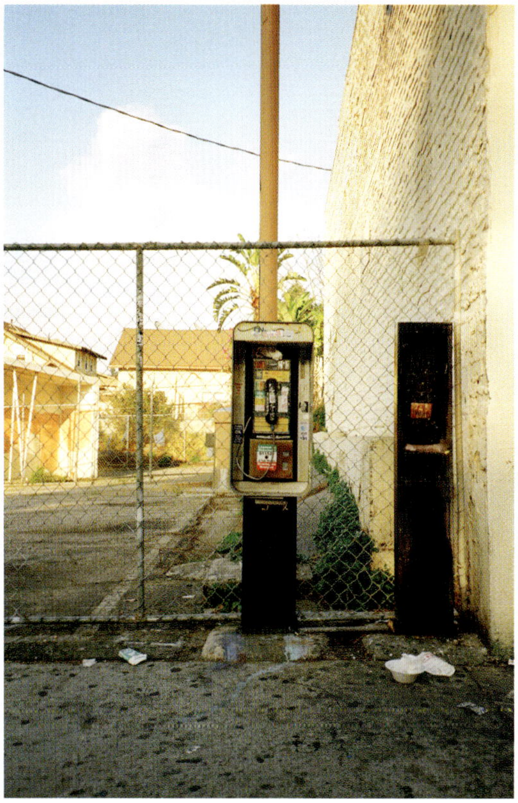

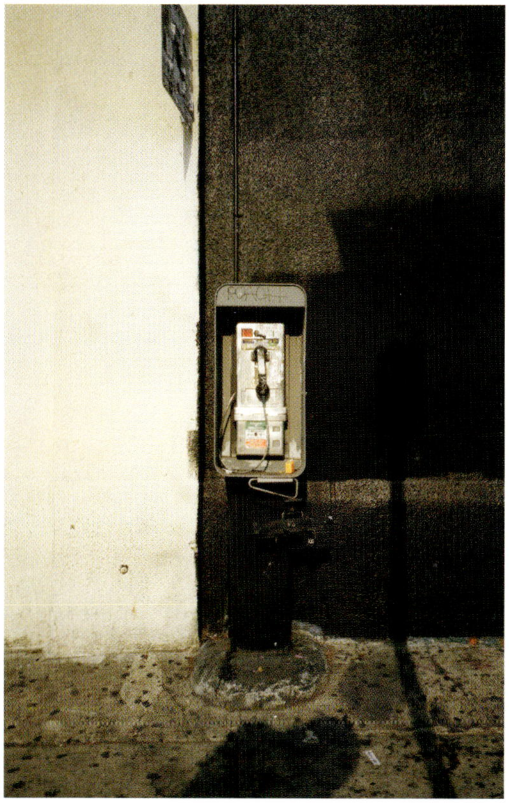

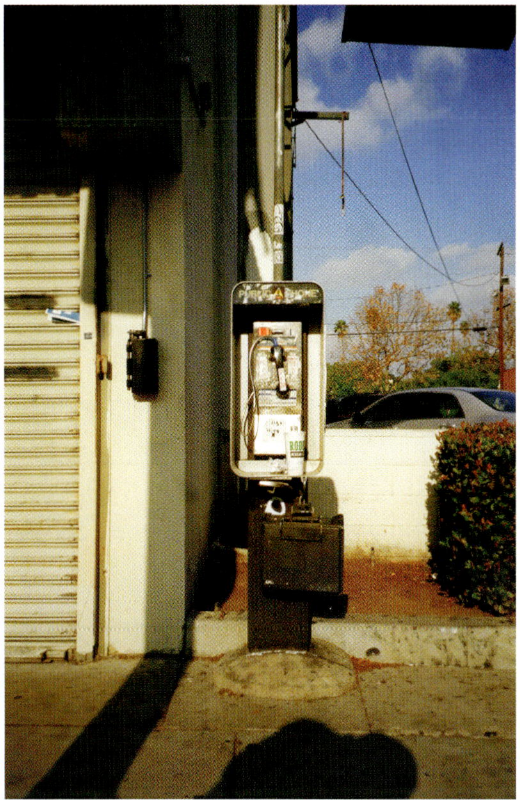

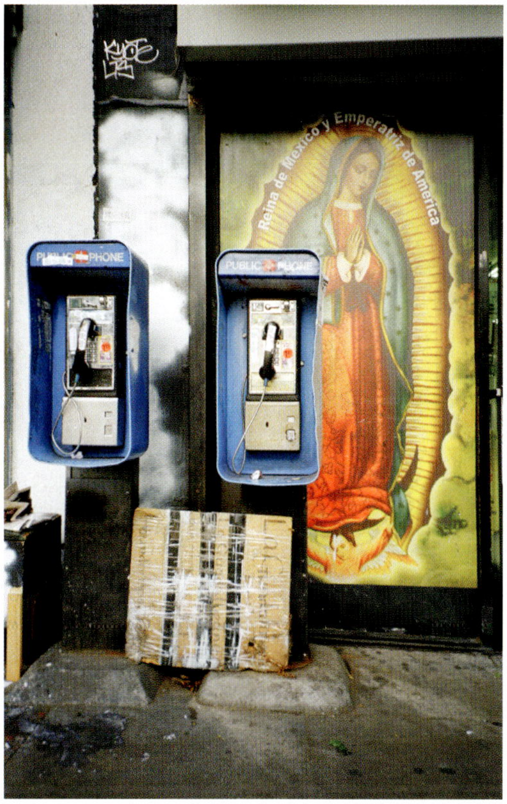
PUBLIC PHONE
PUBLIC PHONE
Reina de Mexico y Emperatriz de America

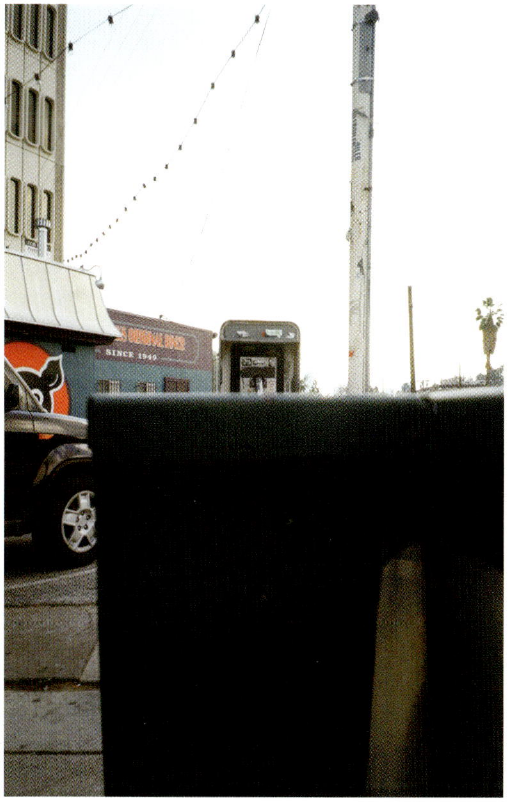
SINCE 1949

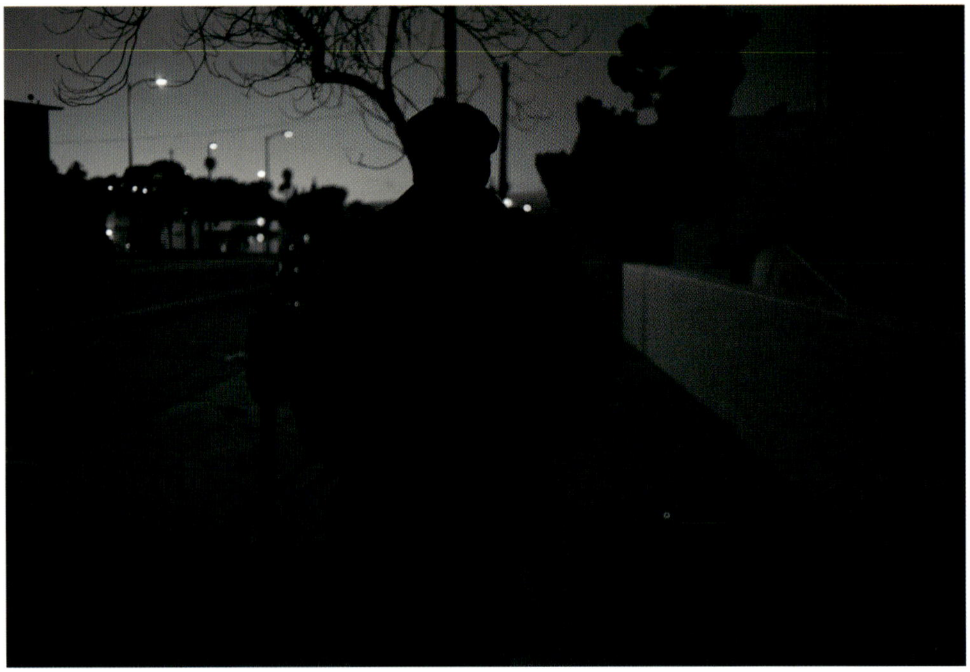

Photo by Andrew Tonkery, 2012

HASSAN RAHIM

Los Angeles, California
hassanrahim.com
shabazzprojects.com

I was born in California, and have been here since. If I had done more traveling, or went to school abroad somewhere, this could be a different outcome. But California is, and has been home, my whole life.

Coming from Orange County (where almost nothing cool existed growing up), the lack of creative surroundings influenced me at an early age. I found solace on the Internet, scouring strange blogs and Google image searching for hours. I started collecting a serious folder of inspiration pictures, which eventually spawned my image blog, hrstudioplus (hrstudioplus.com). So in a way, California influenced me to be on the computer more as a teenager, enough to discover more than I ever could have in Santa Ana.

Our beautiful weather is a double-edged sword. Sometimes it inspires, sometimes it distracts. I'm more creative in a gloomy or rainy climate, which happens far less often than somewhere like New York (or most of Europe). One advantage is the rapid economic growth; there is so much new opportunity arising constantly. Also, the amount of space you can have here is an enormous advantage. It's a true Western expansion town.

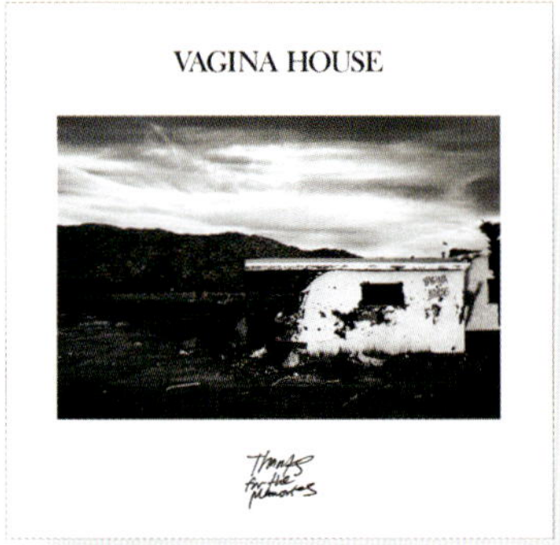

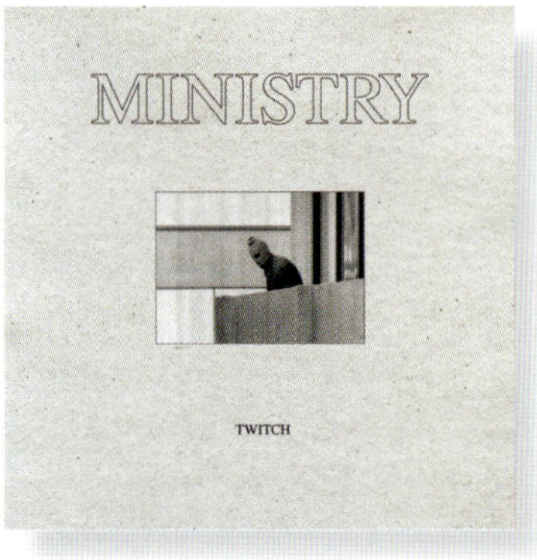

"Vagina House LP" 2012
Digital print on archival paper
12 x 12 inches

"Ministry" 2012
Digital print on archival paper
12 x 12 inches

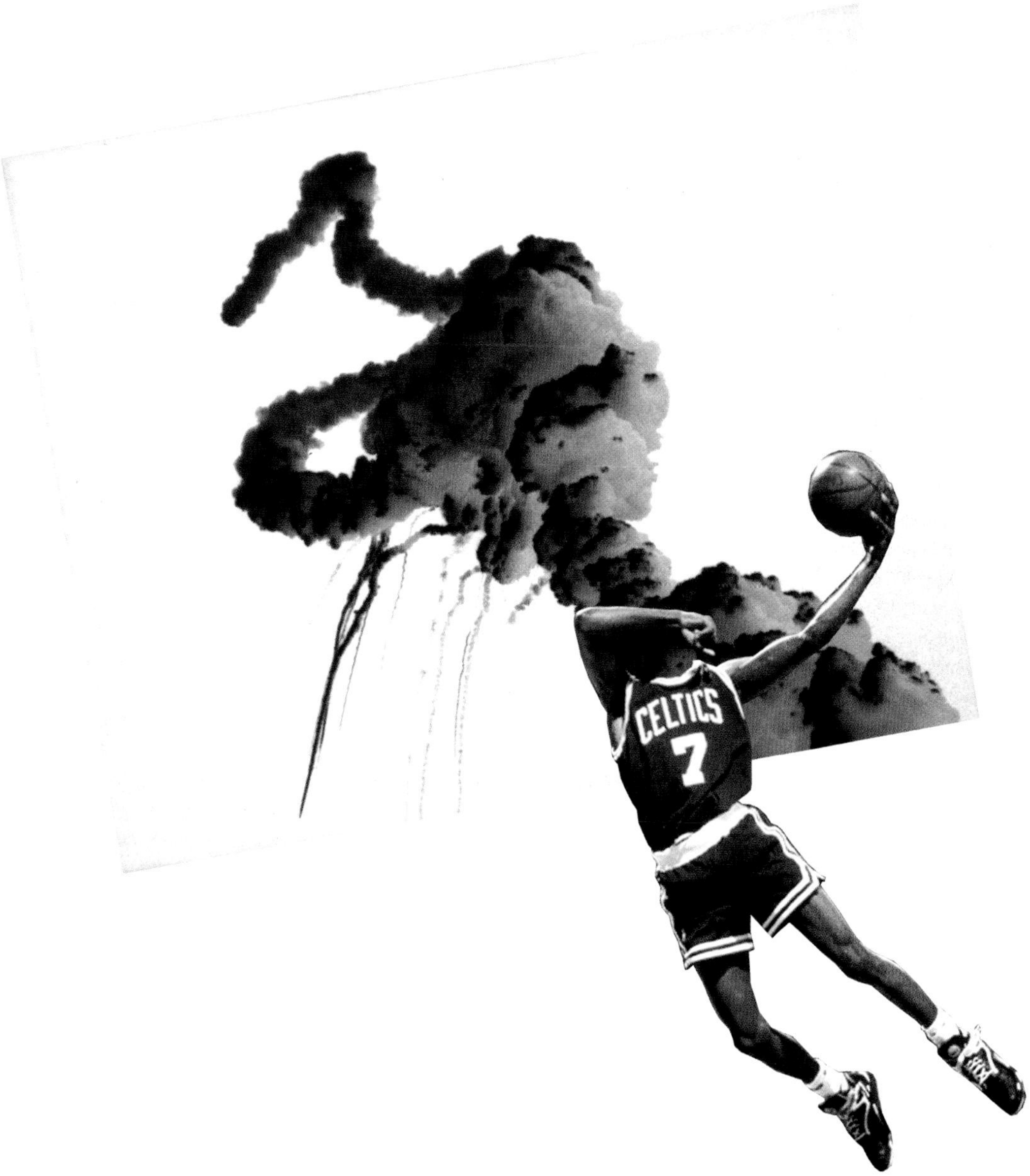

"Dee Brown" 2012
Digital collage

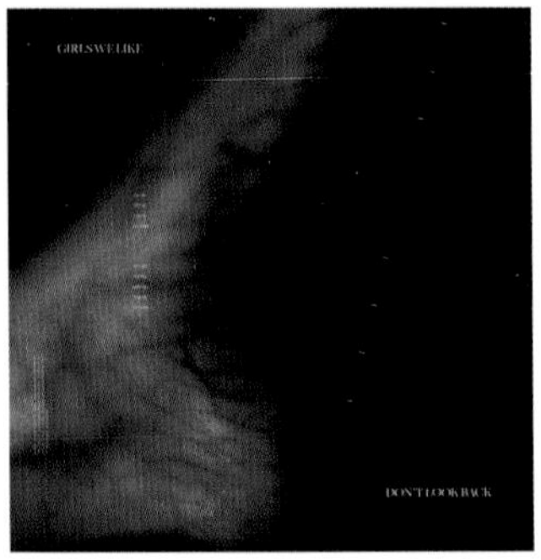

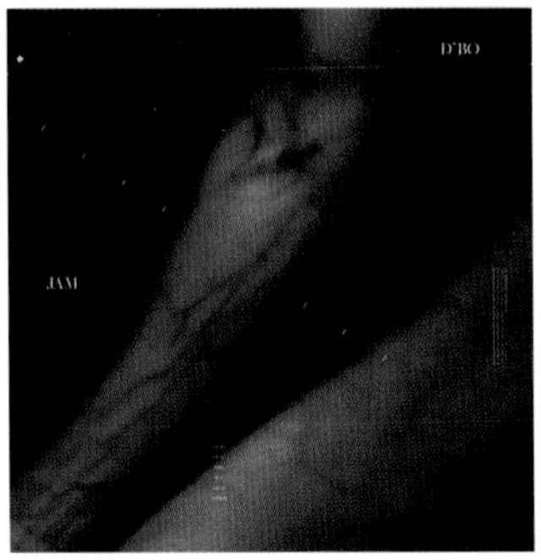

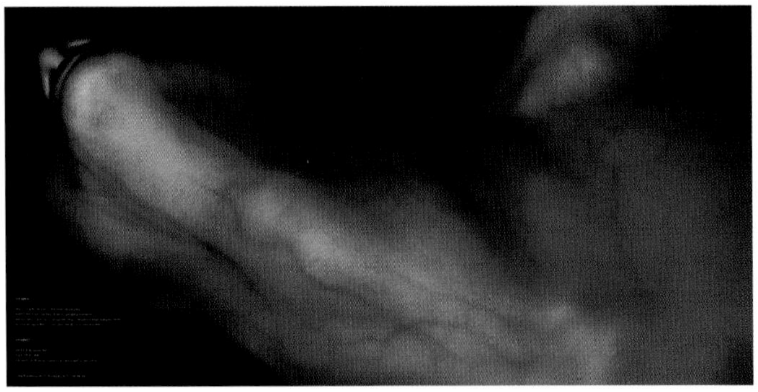

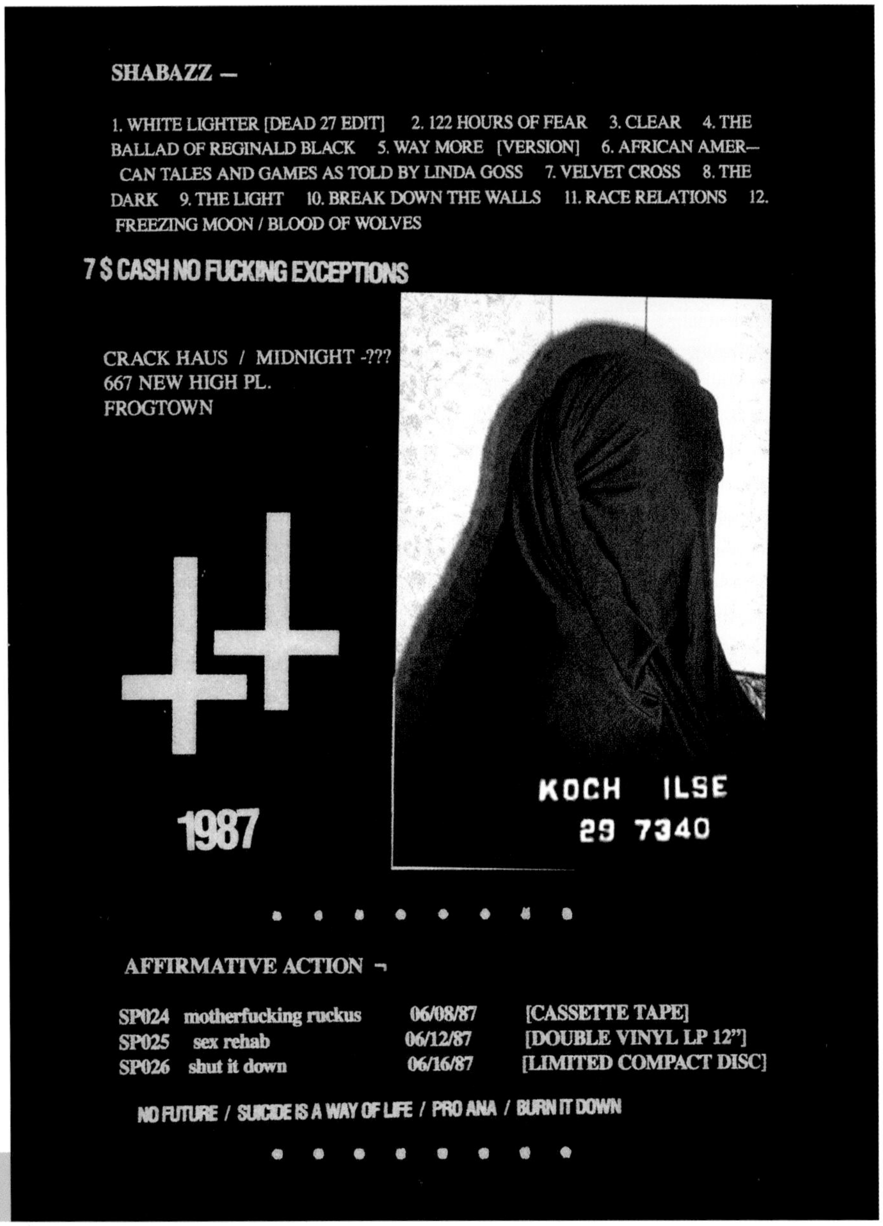
SHABAZZ —
1. WHITE LIGHTER [DEAD 27 EDIT] 2. 122 HOURS OF FEAR 3. CLEAR 4. THE BALLAD OF REGINALD BLACK 5. WAY MORE [VERSION] 6. AFRICAN AMER— CAN TALES AND GAMES AS TOLD BY LINDA GOSS 7. VELVET CROSS 8. THE DARK 9. THE LIGHT 10. BREAK DOWN THE WALLS 11. RACE RELATIONS 12. FREEZING MOON / BLOOD OF WOLVES
7 $ CASH NO FUCKING EXCEPTIONS
CRACK HAUS / MIDNIGHT -???
667 NEW HIGH PL.
FROGTOWN
KOCH ILSE
29 7340
1987
AFFIRMATIVE ACTION ¬
SP024 motherfucking ruckus 06/08/87 [CASSETTE TAPE]
SP025 sex rehab 06/12/87 [DOUBLE VINYL LP 12"]
SP026 shut it down 06/16/87 [LIMITED COMPACT DISC]
NO FUTURE / SUICIDE IS A WAY OF LIFE / PRO ANA / BURN IT DOWN

SANTA ANA
PSYCH
WARD
BLACK MAGIC
WHITE LIES
BLOODSHOT EYES
SUMMER 1987

"Girls We Like" 2012
Album artwork

"(No Future)" 2012
Shabazz Projects
Show flyer

"Santa Ana Psycho Ward" 2012
Album artwork

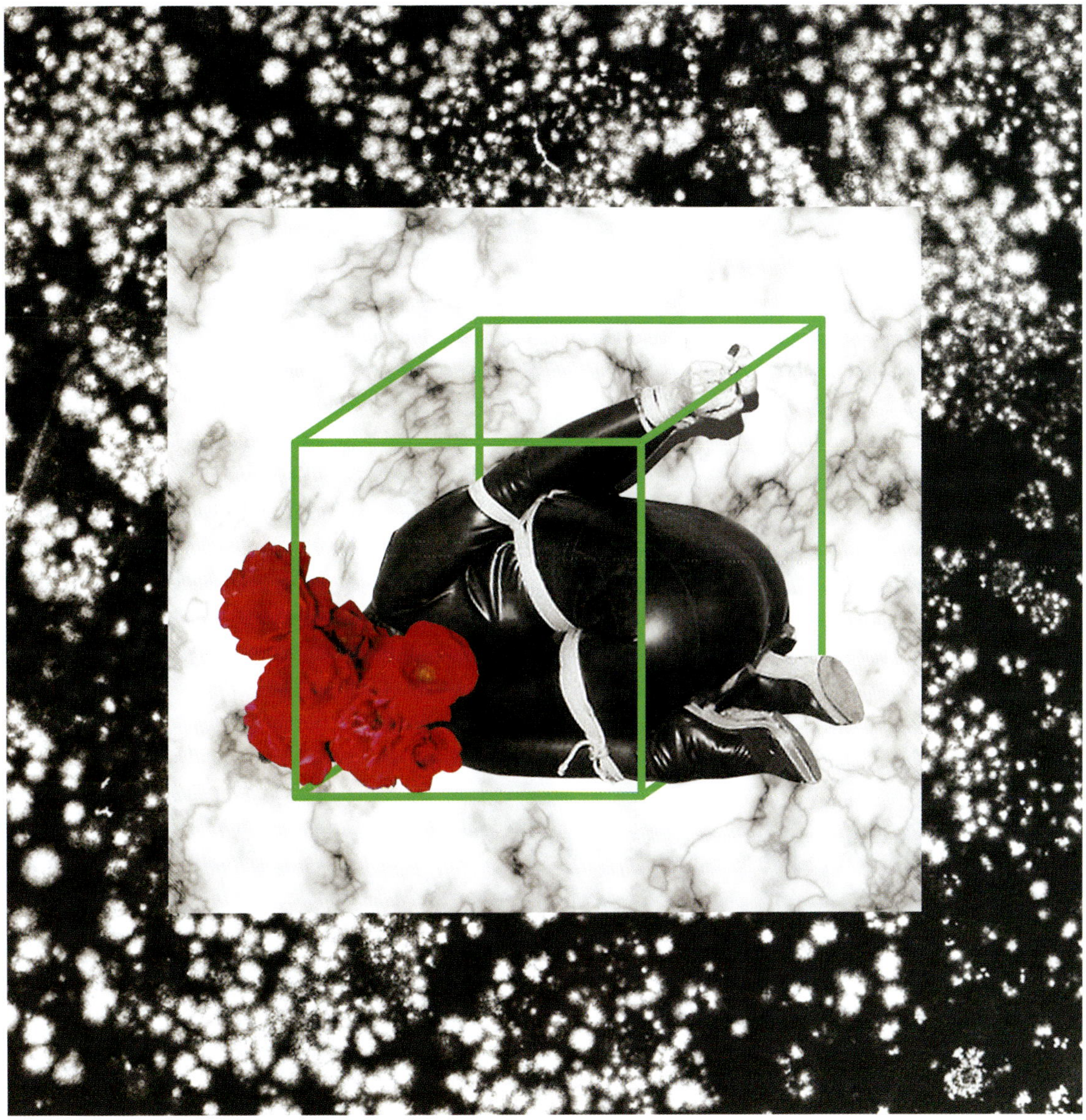

"G.Vamp + Pipes" 2012
Digital collage

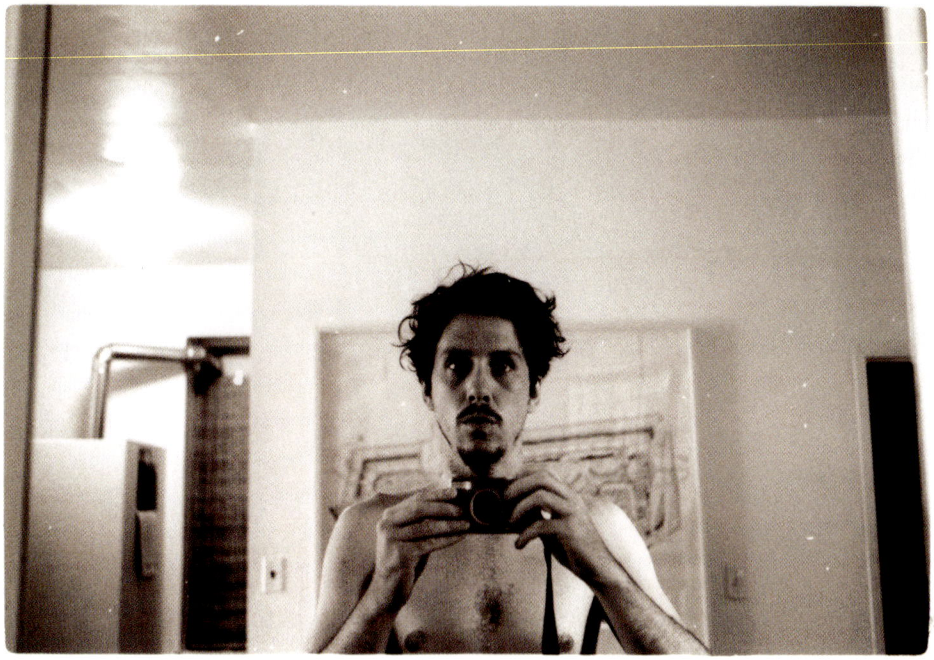

Self Portrait, 2010

JOEY GALLAGHER

Los Angeles, California
joeygallagher.com

I was born in Jersey City but lived in NYC for most of my life. I started visiting SF in the early 2000s when it was either too cold or too hot in NY to skate. I first came to LA for work, mostly video jobs, in the mid 2000s. Not long ago I had the opportunity to direct a music video for Animal Collective and decided to shoot it in LA.

I stayed with my good friend Charlie Smith for 20 days, and he helped me out a lot. I had such a good time and was dreading going back to NY. I looked at a place through mutual friends and wound up moving out here a few months later. That was two years ago.

The weather and access to outdoor spaces and the variety of the whole state convinced me to stay. There's always something new to check out.

There are so many amazing places I've been lucky enough to travel to and visit. Some more than others. But, California is a pretty diverse place. If you don't mind the driving, you can pretty much do anything you want in a day, from mountains to beaches to cities. The biggest disadvantage I would I say is you are a bit cut off from other people because everyone is in their cars. If people walked more, it would be nicer, but I guess that's just the NY'er in me.

The inspiration I find out here comes from a different place than in NY. Here, there's so much more light and open space. In NY I was more inspired from just walking around and observing people. You can do that here, too, but it's just a little more spread out. I've also been more inspired by reading in California, where I was mostly inspired by listening to music in NY. But I guess both forms are just ways of learning about the place you're living.

"Alex Olson—Pool Surf Los Angeles" 2011
35mm film
Dimensions vary

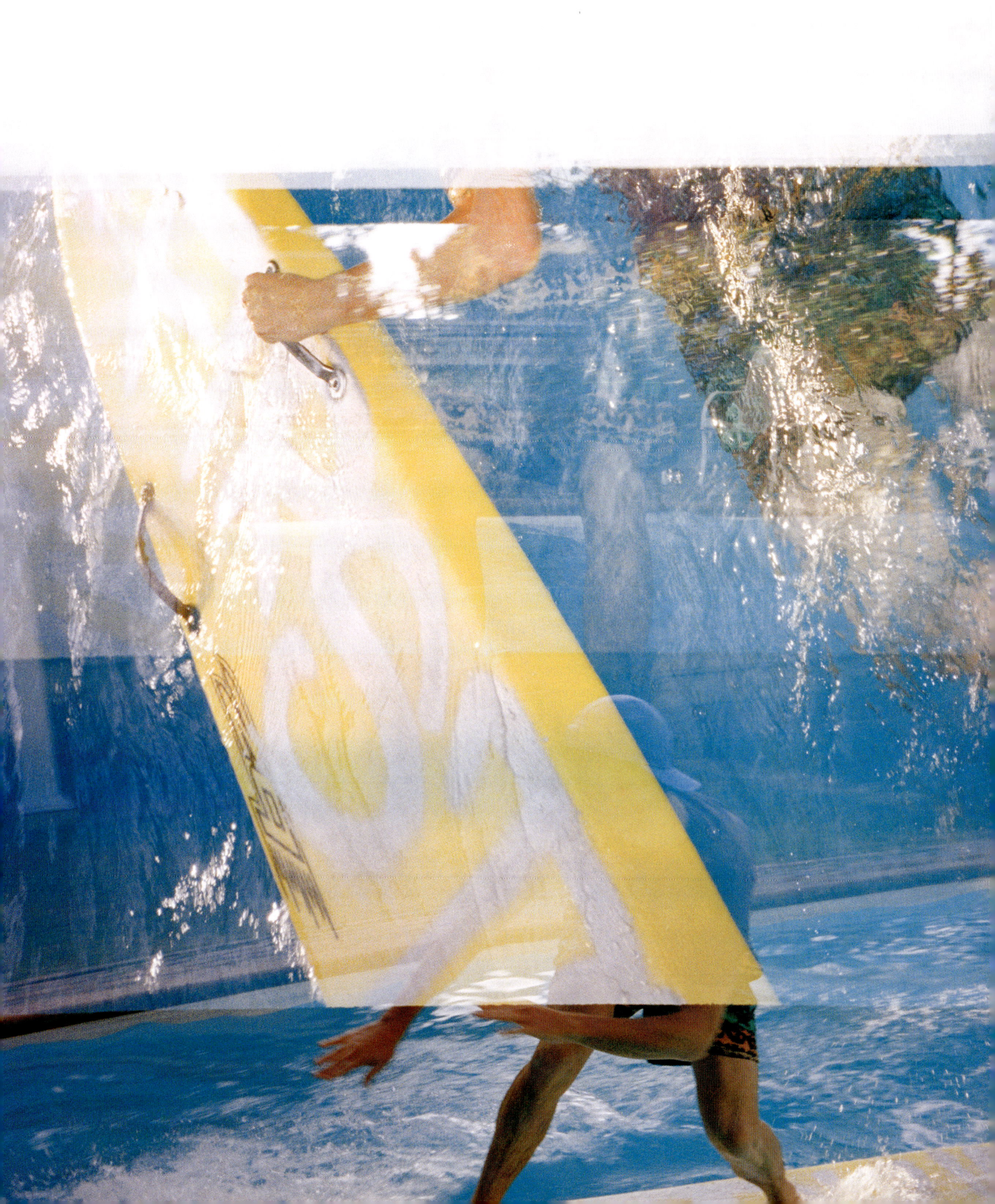

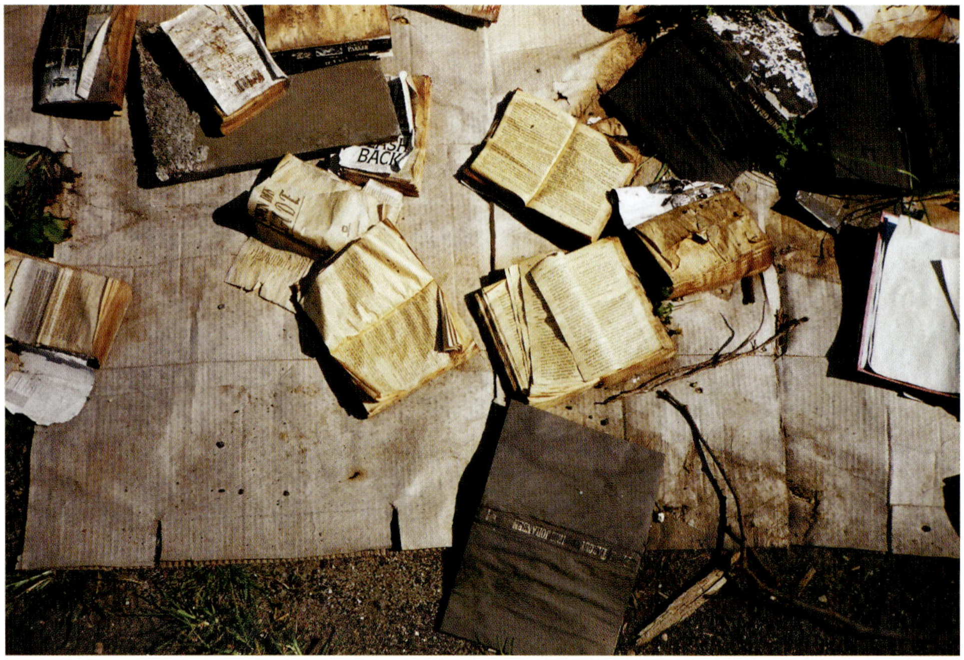

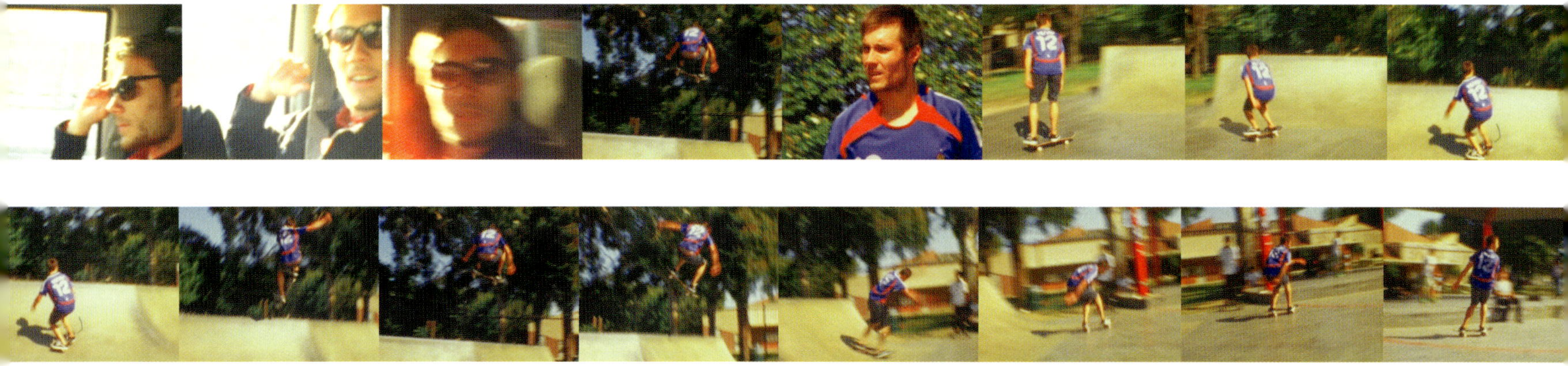

"Homeless Camp—Books: Rockaway Beach, NY" 2011
35mm film

"Alex Olson—Stoner Park Sequence: West Los Angeles" 2012
Super 8 film stills

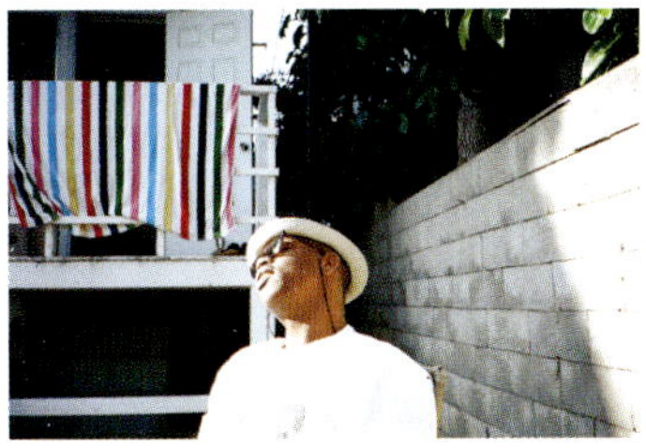

"*Kunle Martins—West Hollywood, CA*" 2011
Digital photograph

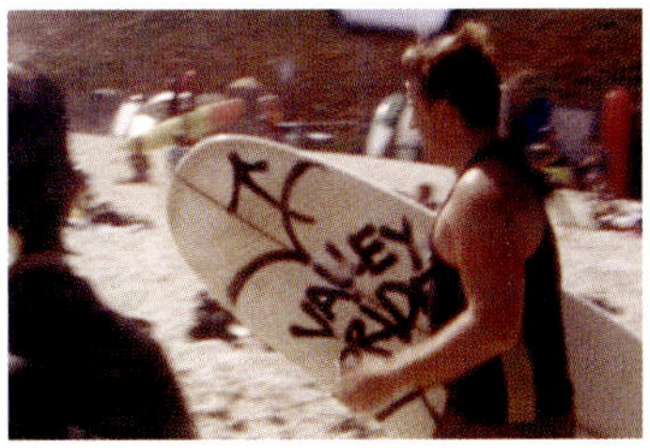

"*Trace Marshall—Malibu, CA*" 2011
Super 8 film still

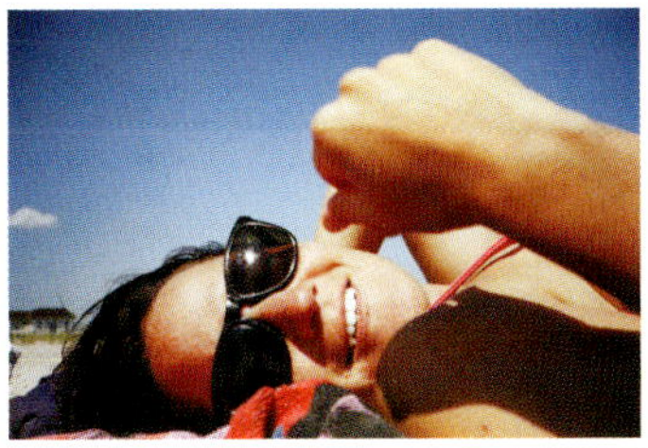

"*Gillian Garcia (Untitled #1)—Rockaway Beach, NY*" 2011
Digital photograph

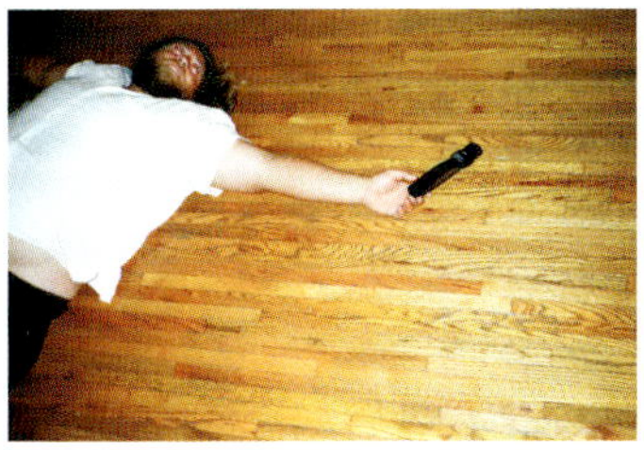

"*Sam Shainberg Remote—Glassel Park, CA*" 2011
Digital photograph

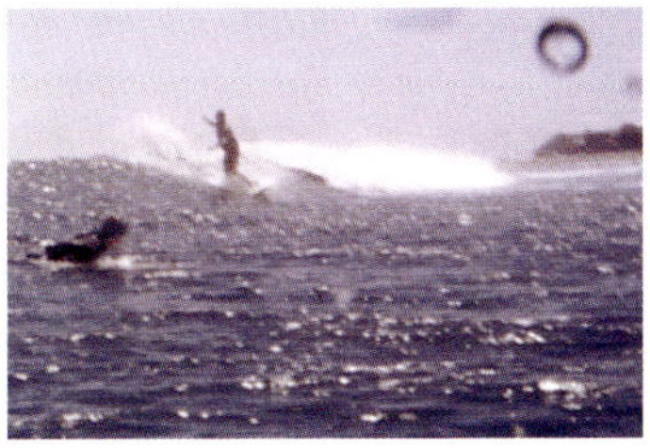

"*Trace Marshall (Untitled #1)—Malibu, CA*" 2011
Super 8 film still

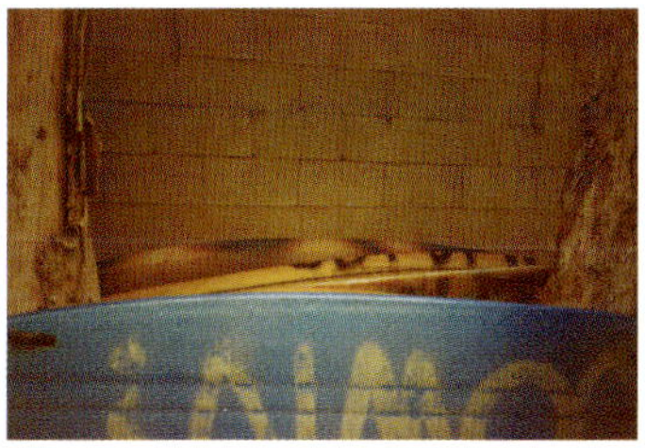

"*Charlie Smith's Driveway—Hancock Park, Los Angeles*" 2011

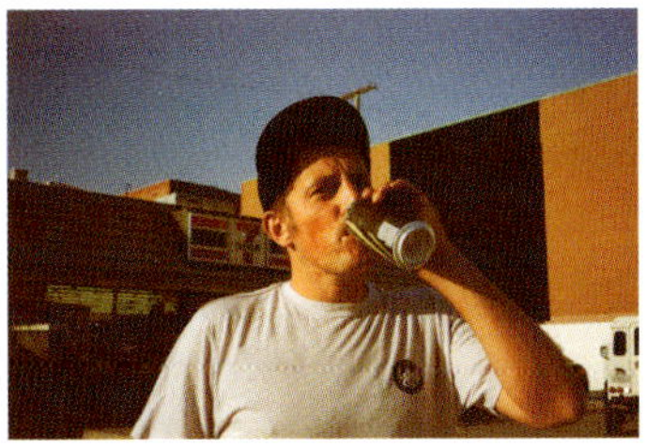

"*Charlie Smith 7Eleven—Los Angeles, CA*" 2011
Digital photograph

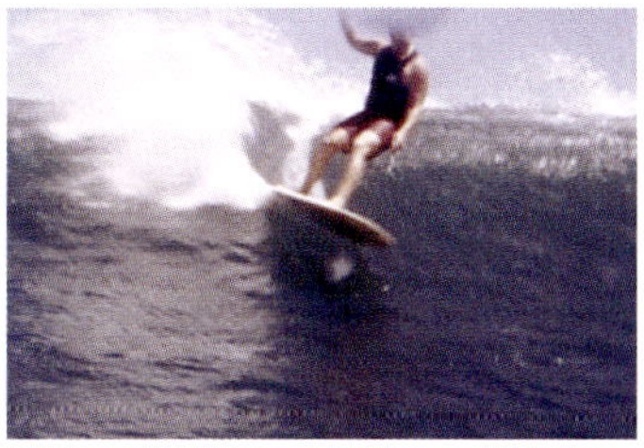

"*Trace Marshall (Untitled #2)—Malibu, CA*" 2011
Super 8 film still

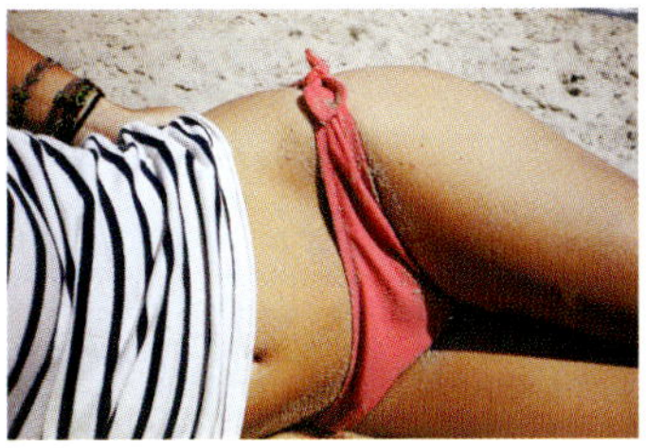

"*Gillian Garcia (Untitled #2)—Rockaway Beach, NY*" 2011
Digital photograph

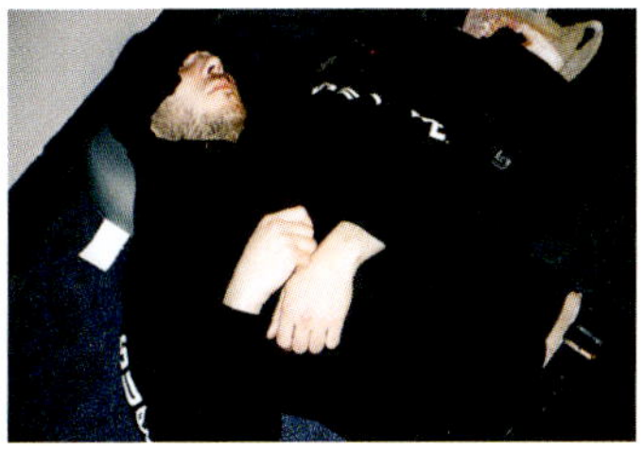

"*Jeff Potocar—Sleeping/Airport—Newark, NJ*" 2011
Digital photograph

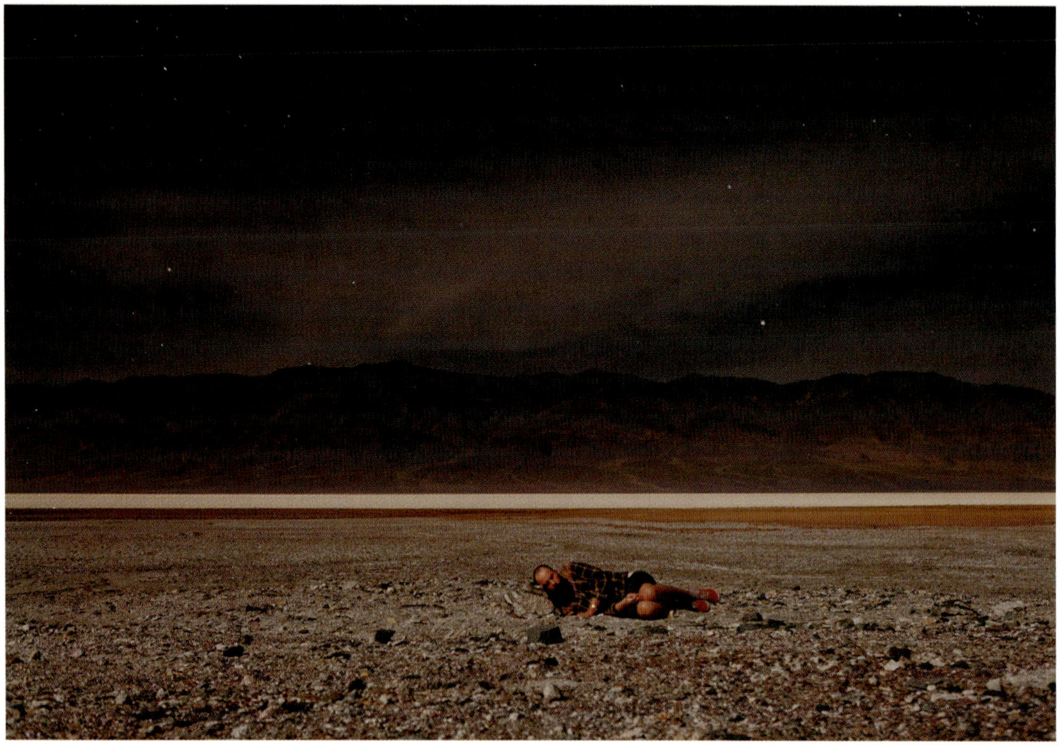

Self portrait, 2012

JARED EBERHARDT

Los Angeles, California
jaredeberhardt.com
Partizan Pictures

I originally moved to California because of how good it felt when I'd visit. I'd get off the plane and walk out to the curb, and it just always smelled like home. That, and I wanted to be able to surf or skate every day. I get a charge out of being here, every day, I love that I have a lemon tree in my front yard, and there is almost always the most beautiful light as the sun goes up and down. There's something special about the light here. I like that there are so many people here doing so many incredible things, big and small, all the time; it's nice to be surrounded by all of it. It feels like anything is possible.

The biggest advantage of being here is there are so many people all doing the same thing with a similar mind-set; it's easy to find whatever you need to get going. There's such easy access to technical knowledge, equipment, and production crews. The question of how to do something is easily answered, leaving you free to focus on what you are doing. You can talk shop with just about anyone, and it's easy to find a community. Which also can be a disadvantage. It's a bit crowded here; you have to work extra hard to keep from getting swallowed up by it all.

My process is scientific. I need to have a lot of parts to organize and consider to feel like I can be creative. I think that's what brought me to filmmaking. It usually starts with some irrational thought or tiny moment that continually replays itself (almost like a gif animation) that just pops into my head, and I just have to do something with it. Then I spend my time and energy trying to justify and support its existence by building a narrative around it. I usually have something that I'm deeply interested in, like a person I want to work with, or a feeling I want to convey, or a type of camera, or even just a technique I want to use that helps drive things. I do a lot of research and a lot of sketching, and that's my favorite part, when a new idea or new bit of information comes up, then the entire thing can change as fast as I can sketch it. It's freedom. Things get more complicated to change when you are actually shooting. By the time I'm actually shooting it feels like I'm just executing the plan. There's still a bit of creative discovery, but mostly I'm trying to reconcile the reality of what the shot looks and feels like with the fantasy of how I imagined it.

All Images:
"Untitled" 2012
Assorted film stills
Dimensions vary

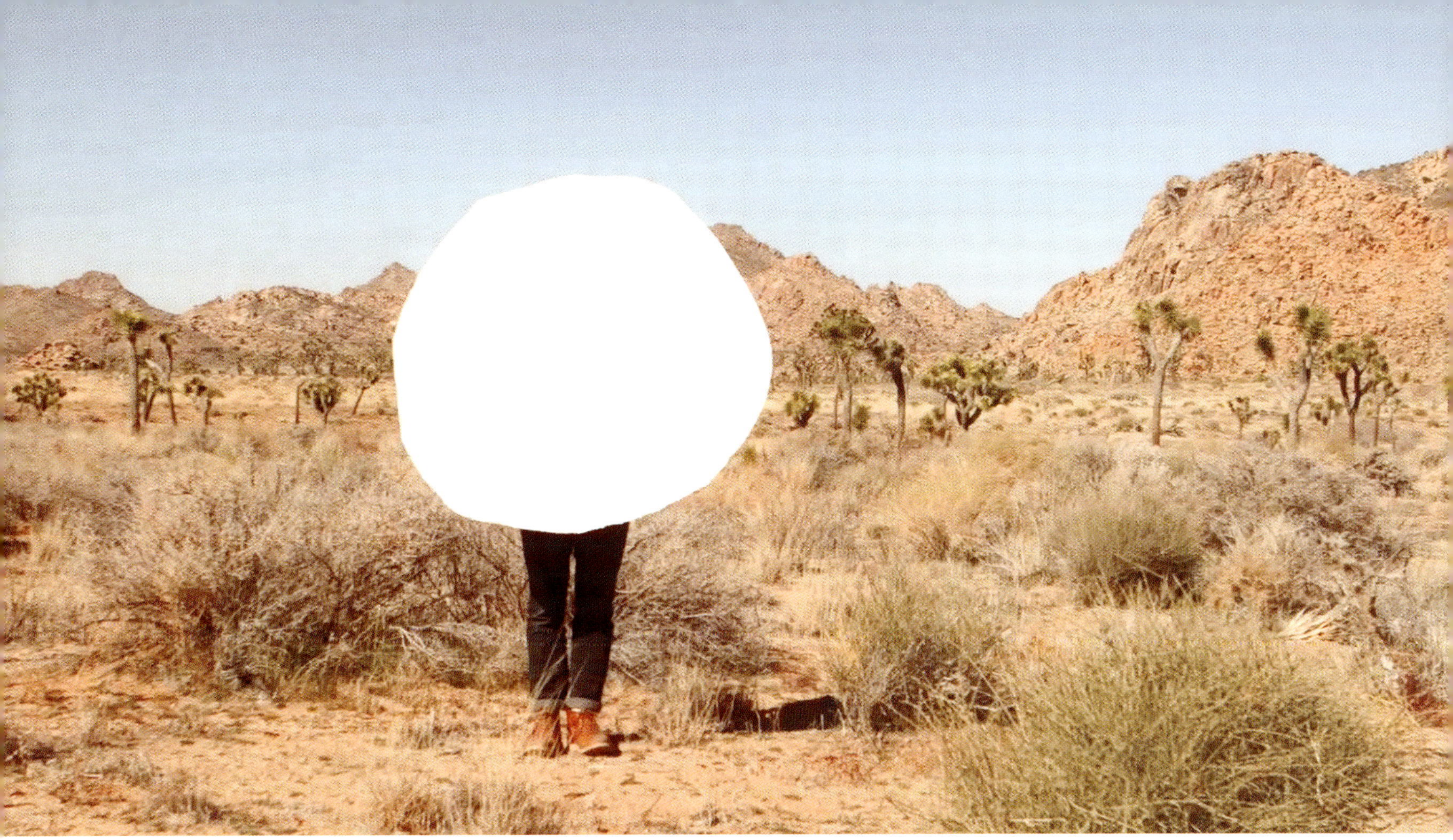

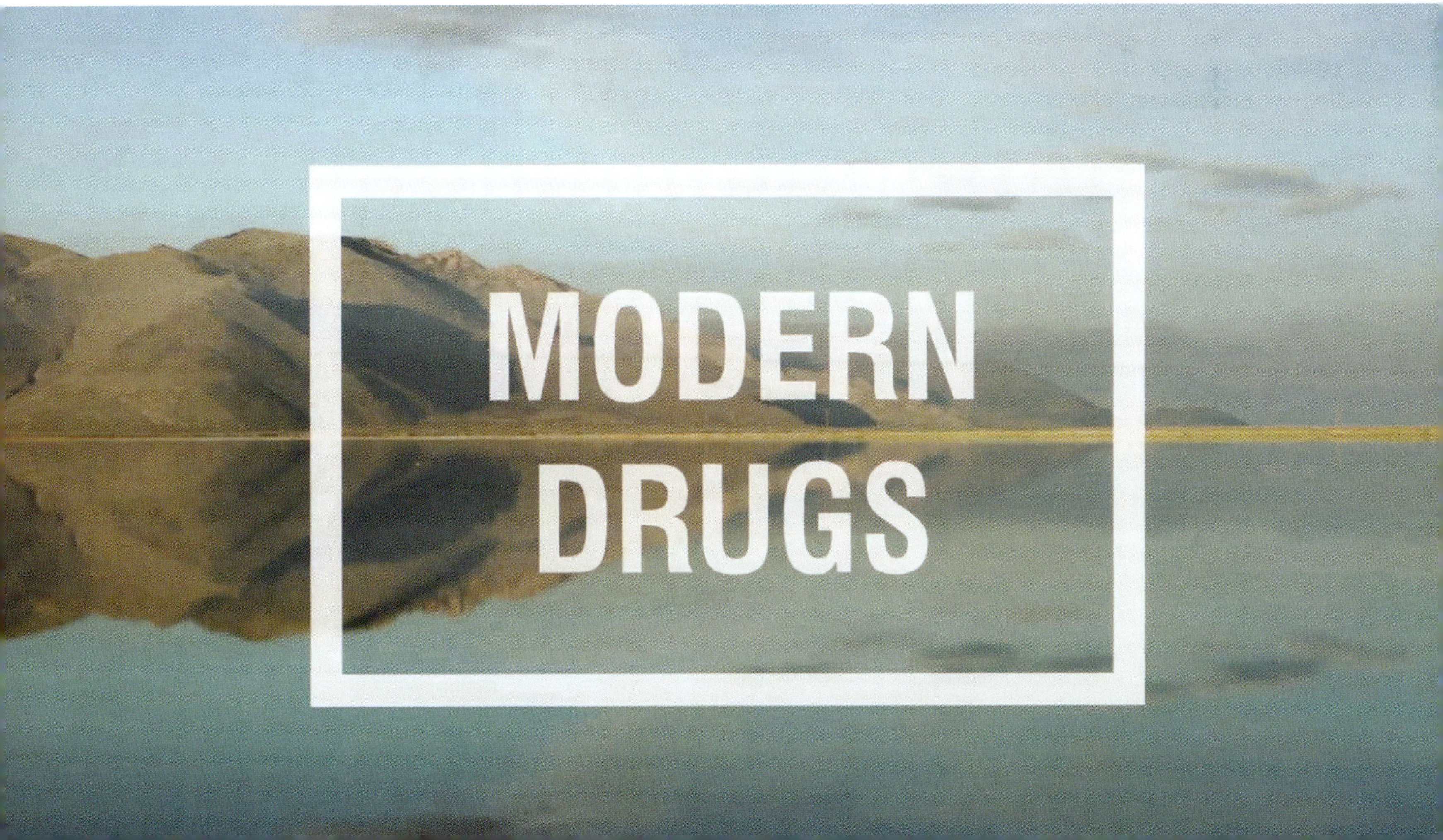

MODERN DRUGS

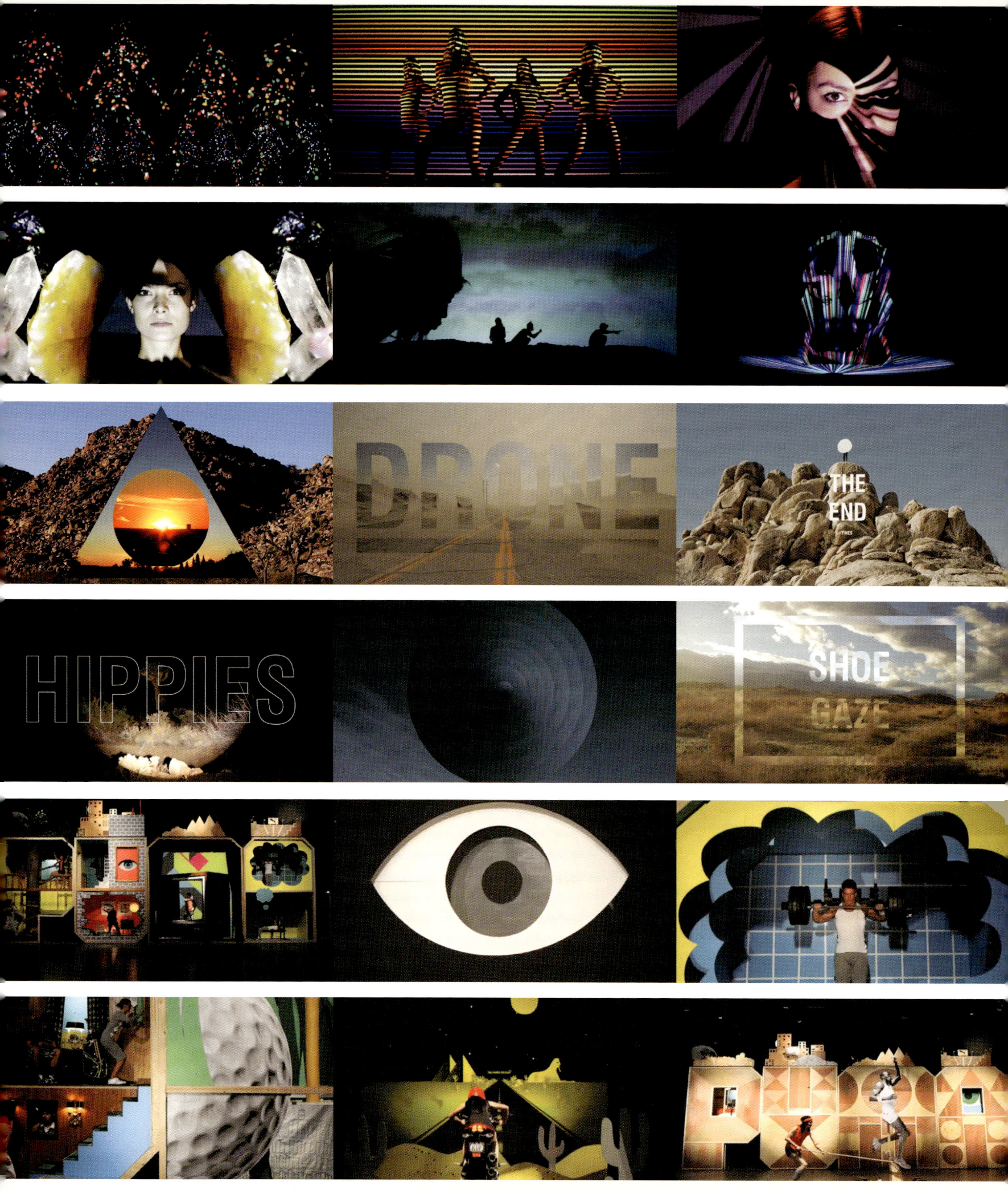
DRONE
THE END
HIPPIES
SHOE
GAZE

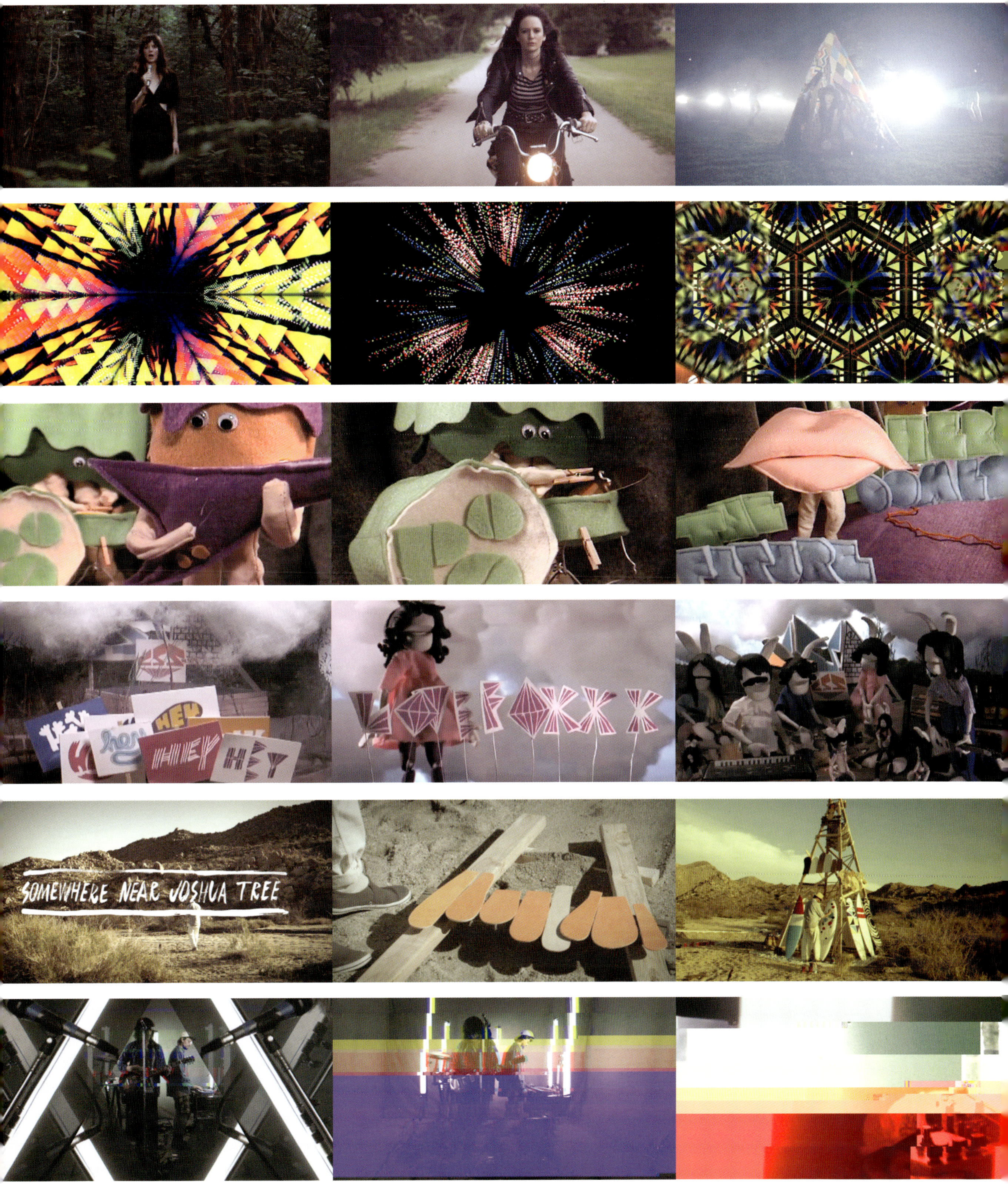
HEY
HEY
SOMEWHERE NEAR JOSHUA TREE

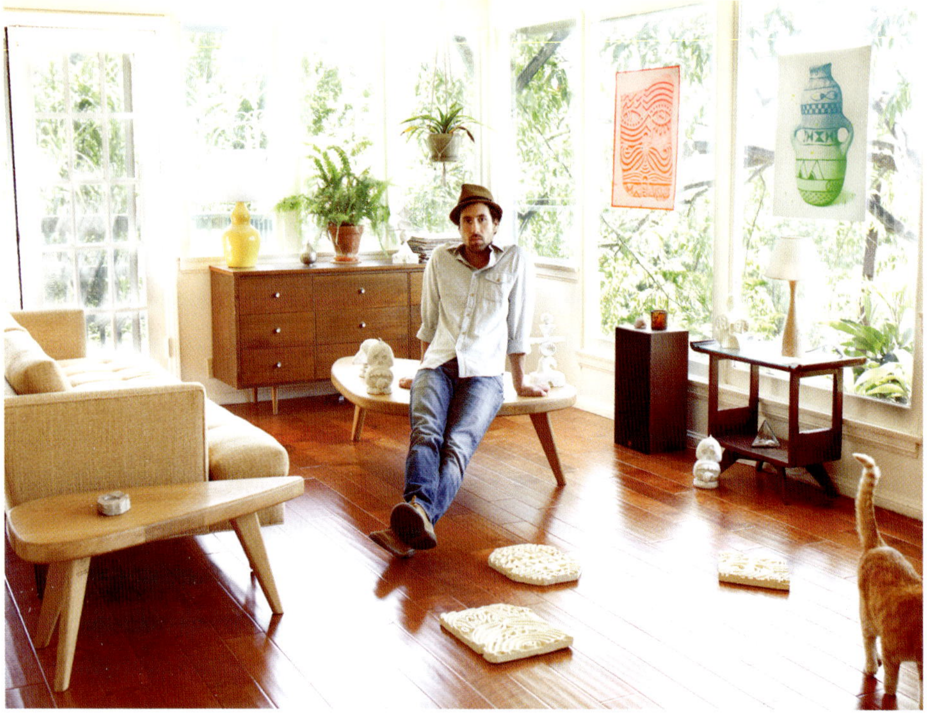

STEVEN HARRINGTON

Los Angeles, California
stevenharrington.com
nationalforest.com

Photo by Brigitte Sire
"Portrait in South Pasadena studio, with Tucker"
California, 2012

To be quite frank, I really had no choice in the matter of coming to California. I was born in California. Since I can remember, I've always loved this part of the planet. My family, friends, sun, sea, and desert and mountains are here. Why move?

Like any large city, Los Angeles has its pros and its cons. Aside from the unpractical urban planning and public transportation system, it has a really unique landscape and thriving mix of cultures.

The sun is shining most of the year, and the ocean and mountains are only twenty-five minutes away in either direction. That's all I need.

Aside from co-owning and operating National Forest Design, I still find time to work on both commissioned and self-inspired art projects. Influenced by images, fashion and graphics discovered in Time Life Encyclopedias from 1972-1997, thrift stores, and Bill Withers, my art might be termed contextual objectivism. Whatever feel or meaning the observer takes away from the piece belongs to the observer. Nothing is shoved down his or her throat. Discovery is the key. Some of my most recent projects include a three-board, custom-shaped signature series for Element Skateboards, contributions to the French clothing line Sixpack France, a signature billboard campaign for Target, a collaboration with Nike SB, contributions to Arkitip Magazine, a special 3-D piece with Kidrobot, and a series of silkscreen prints based on the idea of "connectivity."

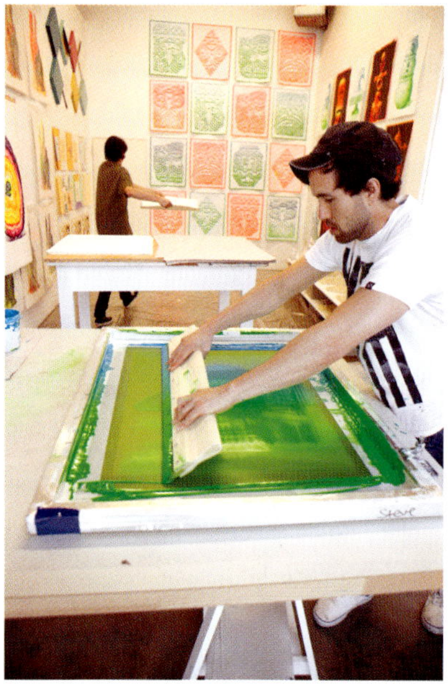

Atwater Village studio, screen printing for Beams Japan art show in 2012
Photo by Brigitte Sire

":)" 2012
White screen print ink on fluorescent enamel sprayed paper
41 x 50 inches

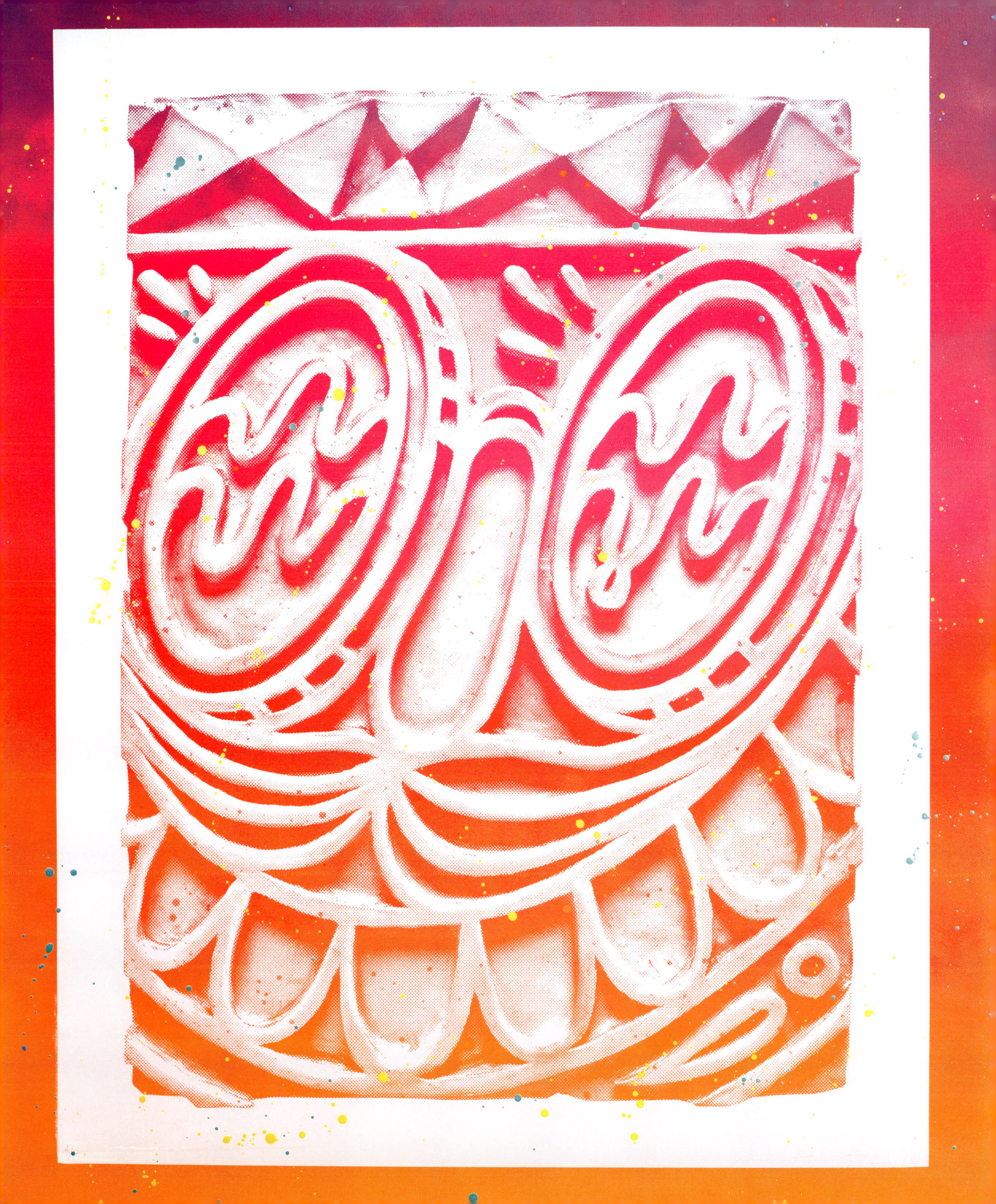

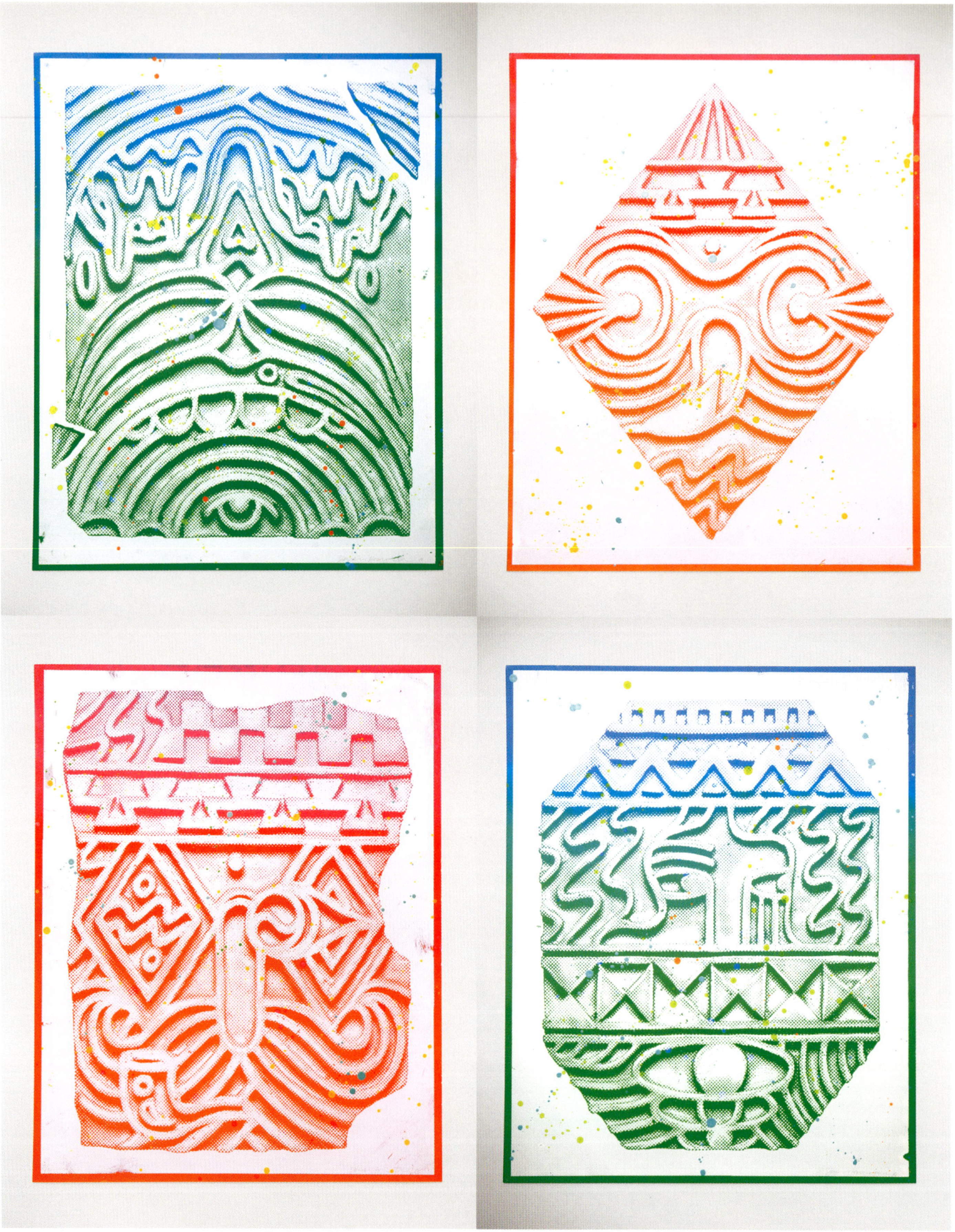

"Stone Tablet Series" 2011-2012
White screen print ink on fluorescent enamel sprayed paper
22 x 30 inches

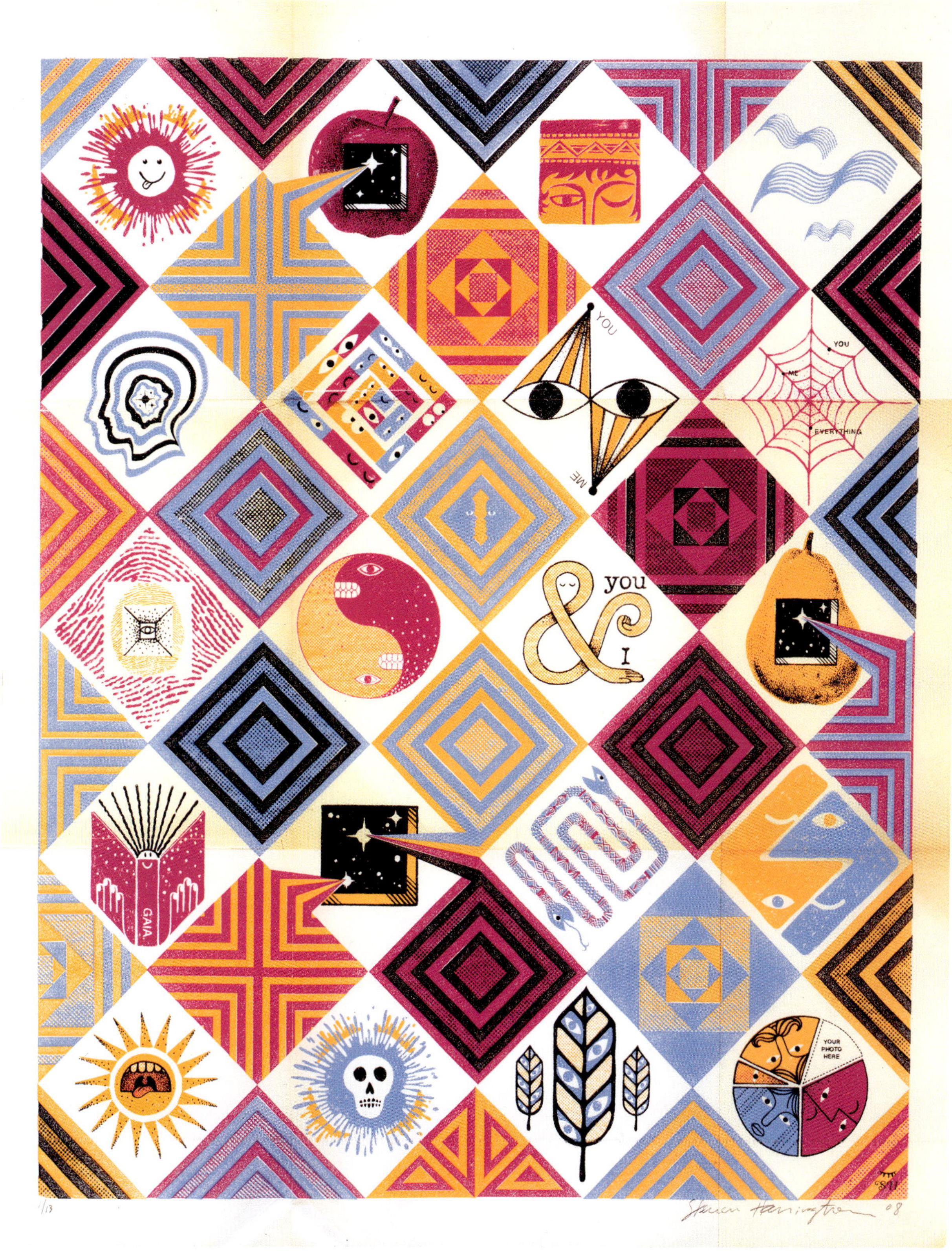

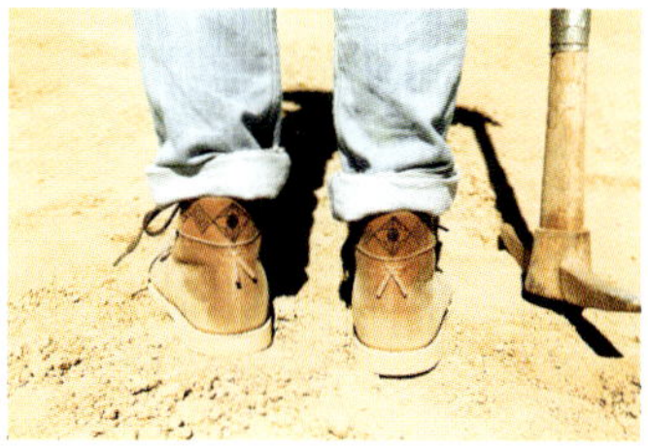

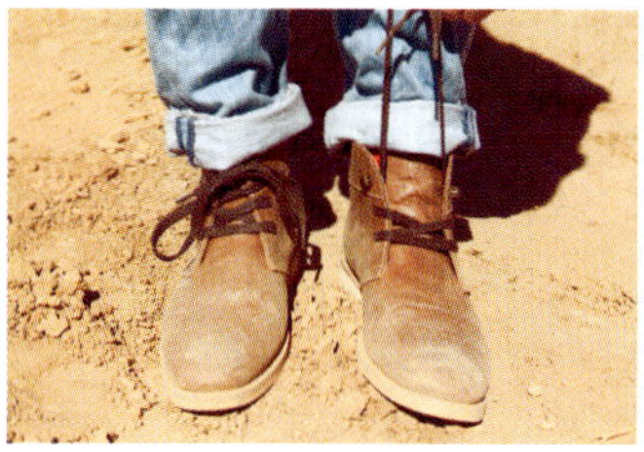

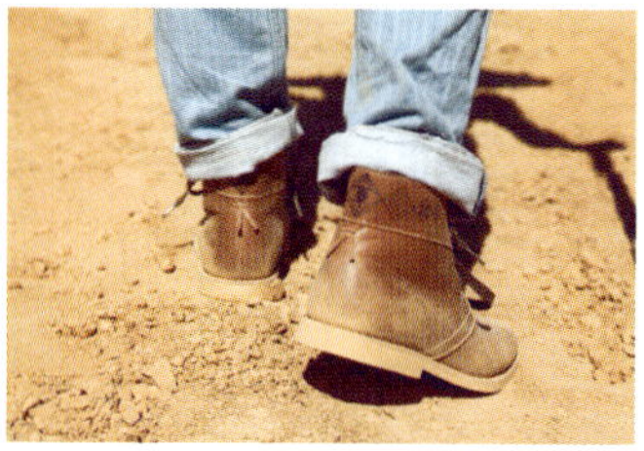

"Balance" 2009
Four color screen print on aged paper stock
24 x 30 inches

"Steven Harrington x Generic Surplus collaborative desert boot" 2012
Tobacco brown beeswax leather with EVA outsole. Artwork embossed in dark earth on insole and heel.

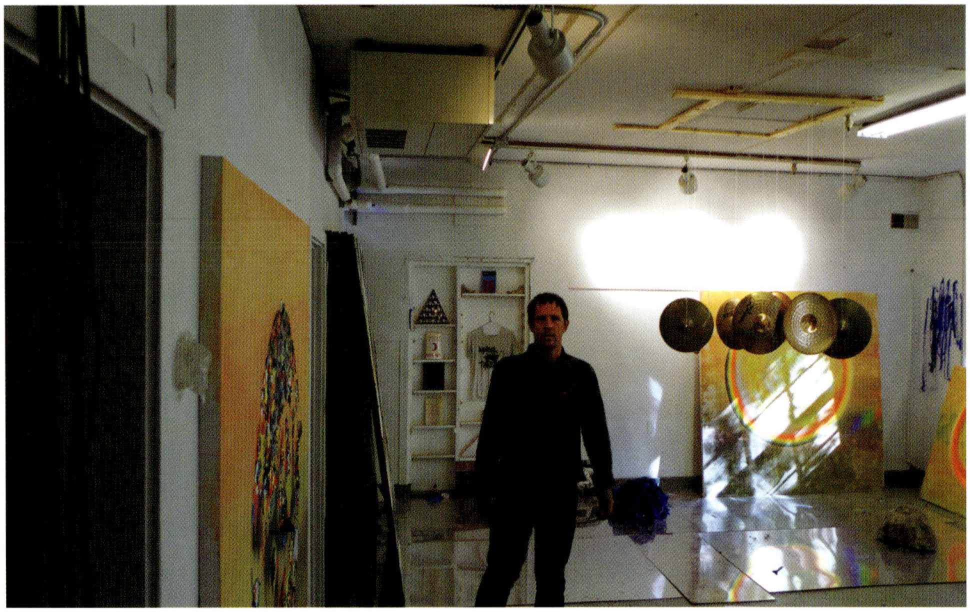

Self Portrait, 2012

CHRIS DUNCAN

Oakland, California

landandseelandandsea.blogspot.com
eliridgwaygallery.com
halseymckay.com

During the winter of 1995, a car brought me from Delaware to Northern California. I was looking to get as far away from what was familiar at home, literally. A dear friend and I flipped a coin on where to land, and California won. Heads I believe. Oakland, California, and all it has to offer keeps me here. My family, proximity to nature, and a strong arts and music community are all factors.

As an artist, California, the San Francisco Bay Area in particular, is all I have ever known. I hear about New York and what it could offer, same with Los Angeles. There are positives and negatives wherever you are. The grass is always greener perhaps. Oakland makes sense to me.

It is hard to pinpoint what about California influences my work and process. I have lived here my whole adult life; my daughter was born here. I have traveled all over California. I take notice of the light, the landscape, people, color, sounds, ideas, concepts. I take it all in.

I employ the use of color, repetition, and reflections, along with a wide variety of materials (tape, crayons, and string) to ponder ideas such as perception and transcendence, in both conceptual and physical forms. Often in flux between the overwhelming and the minimal, my work is a balancing act. Beyond constructing paintings, drawings, publishing, and installations, I have also ventured into experimental sound making and people gathering. Named, THE SUN, under the same premise of my more traditional forms of art-making, I create sonic happenings that, by design, dismantle the idea of audience and performer, and offer a space for anyone willing to contribute and participate.

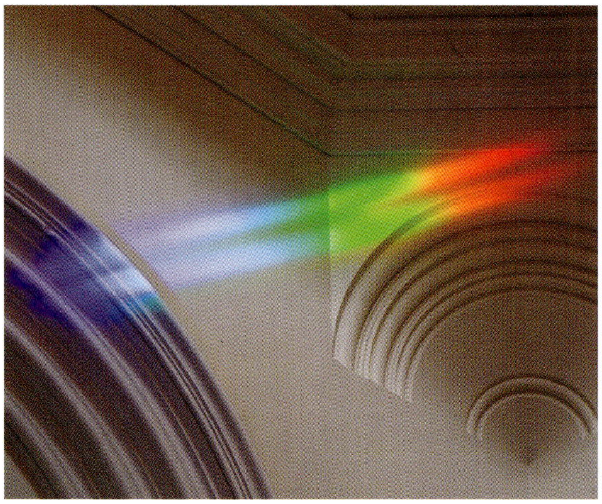

"*PRISM SCHISM*" 2012
Sunlight, film, and architecture
Dimensions vary

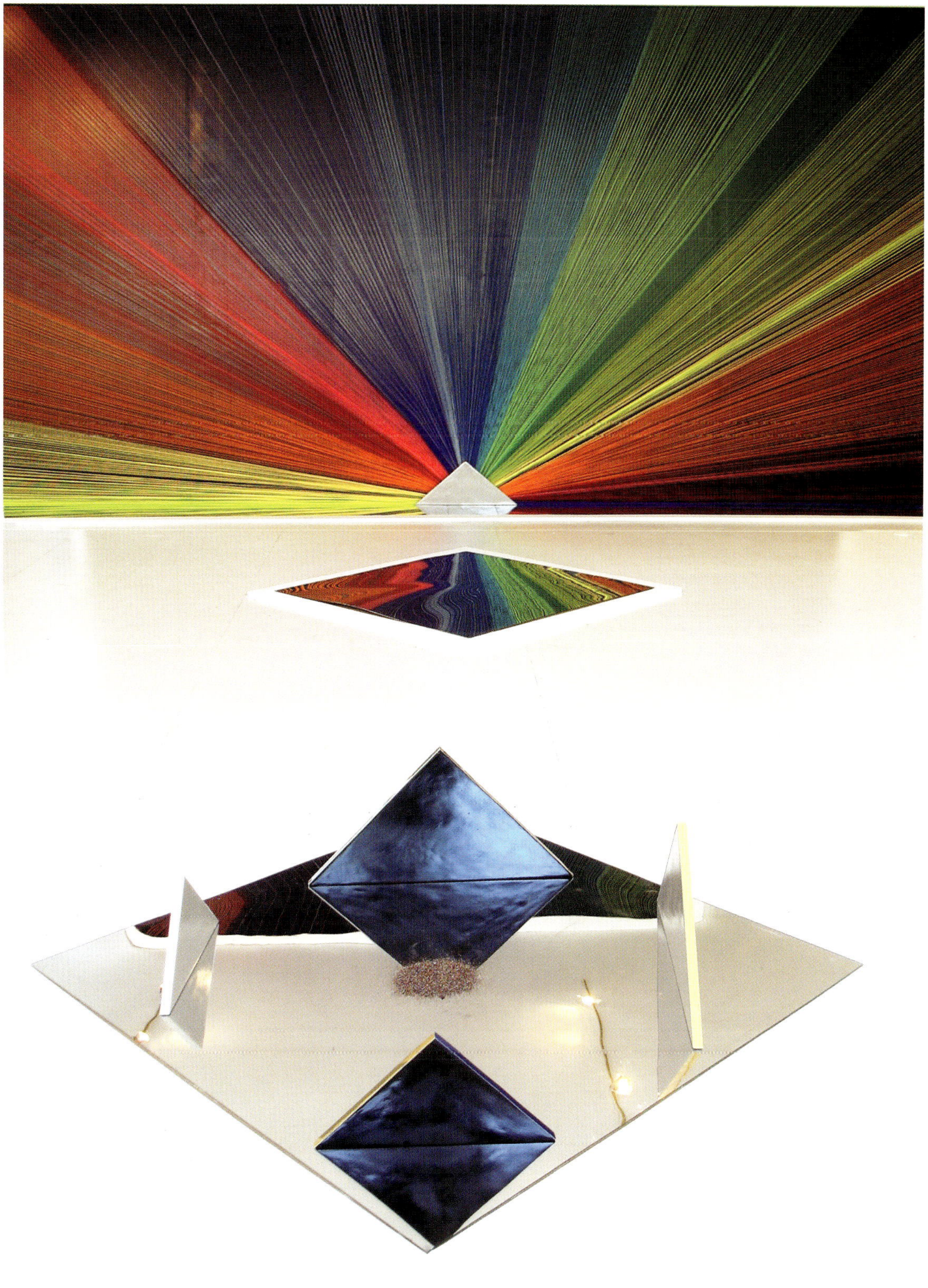

"PRISM SCHISM installation" 2011
Mirrors, string, nails, and wood
Dimensions vary

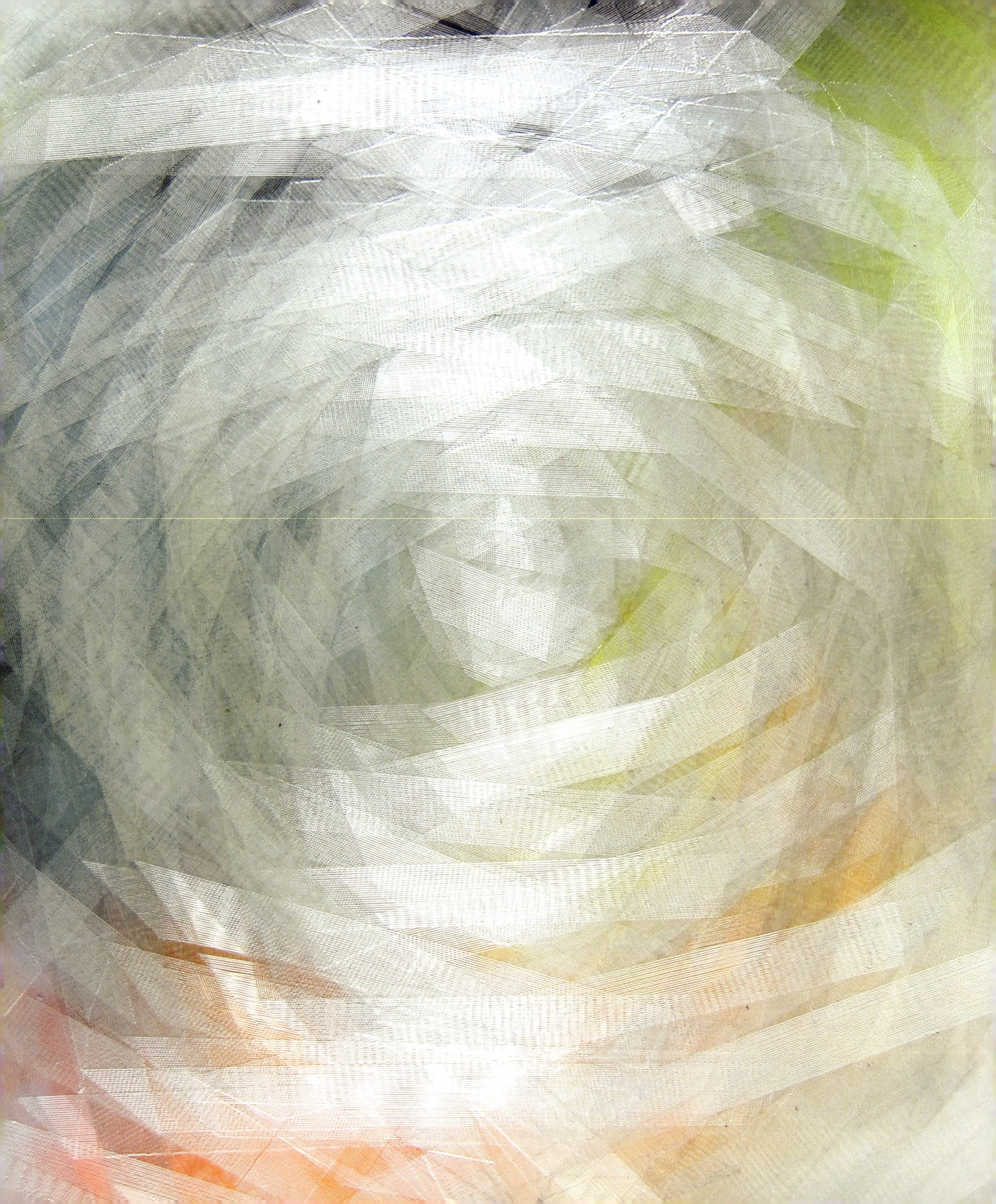

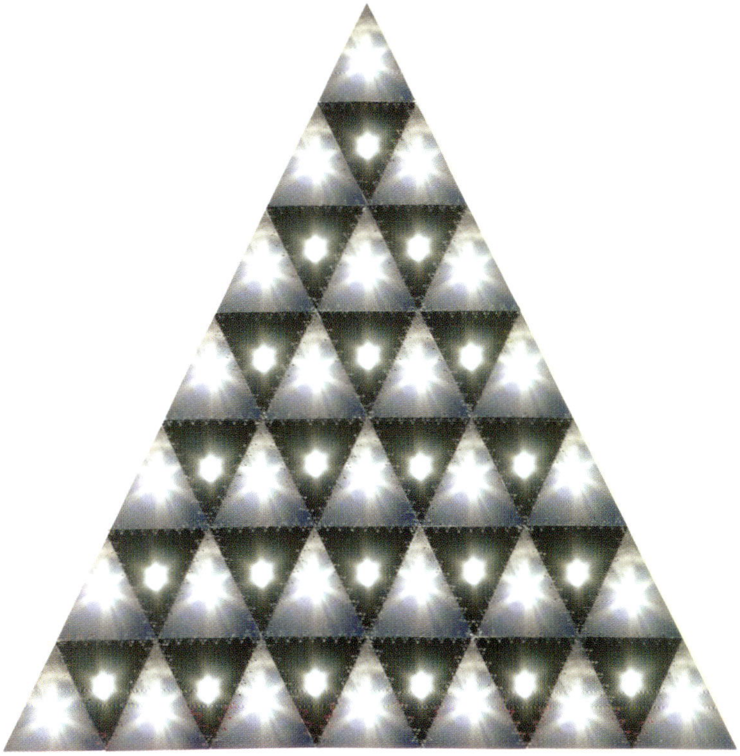

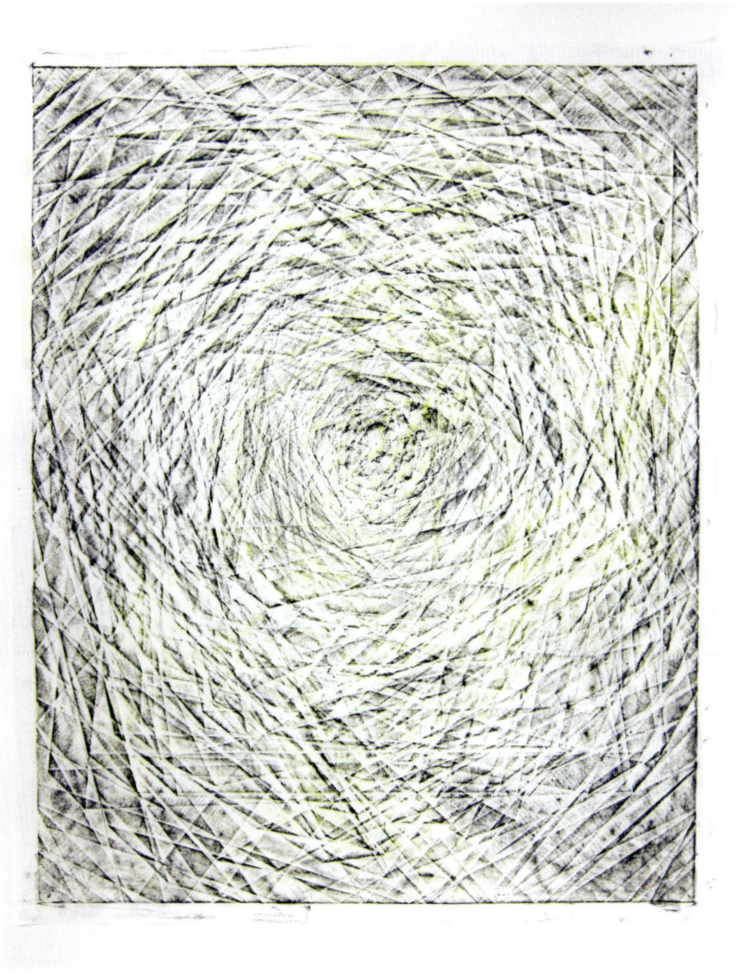

Previous page:
"WORLD WIDE WEB" 2012
Strapping tape, spray paint, on paper
40 x 30 inches

Top:
"Light" 2011
Sewn photographs
18 x 15 x 15 inches

Bottom:
"WORLD WIDE WEB (rubbing #1)" 2012
Crayon rubbing on paper
40 x 30 inches

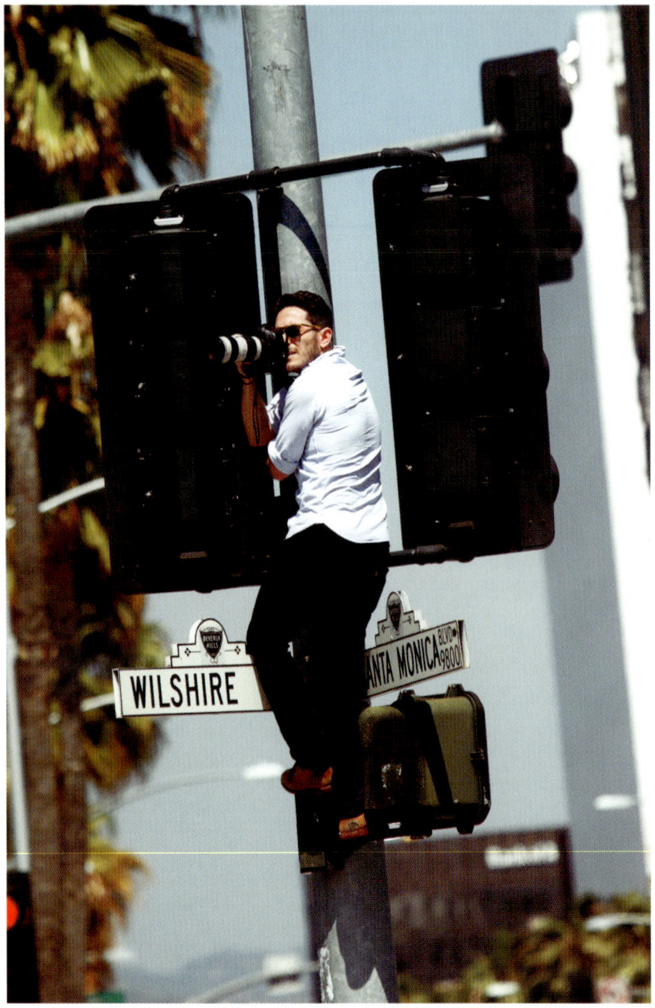

RJ SHAUGHNESSY

Los Angeles, California
rjshaughnessy.com
giantartists.com

Portrait, 2012

I first came to California on vacation with my family in 1992. We flew into Los Angeles and were going to rent a car and drive down to Disneyland the next day. As luck would have it, the day we landed was the first day of the LA Riots. My family and I were stranded in Los Angeles for almost two weeks while the city burned and the rebuilding began. I never got to go to Disneyland, but I did end up volunteering with my family to help clear a burned-out swap meet at the corner of Santa Monica and Western. I've been in love ever since.

The advantages to living in California: Everyone comes to LA to make art. No one works. It is beautiful every day. And it never rains. Disadvantages are the same.

The longer you live somewhere the harder it is to separate yourself from that place. The stereotypes of sunshine and happiness that have become synonymous with Los Angeles have also become a part of who I am and the work I make. I like sunshine, I like happiness, I like the ocean, I like being creative, and I like trying to fold those elements of California into my work.

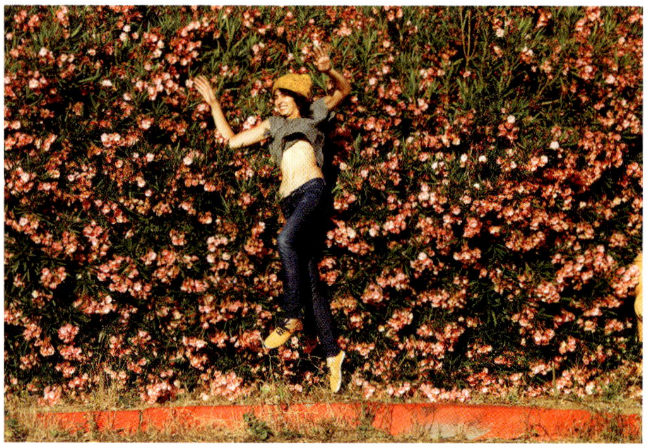

"*Stay Cool #65*" 2012
Digital photograph

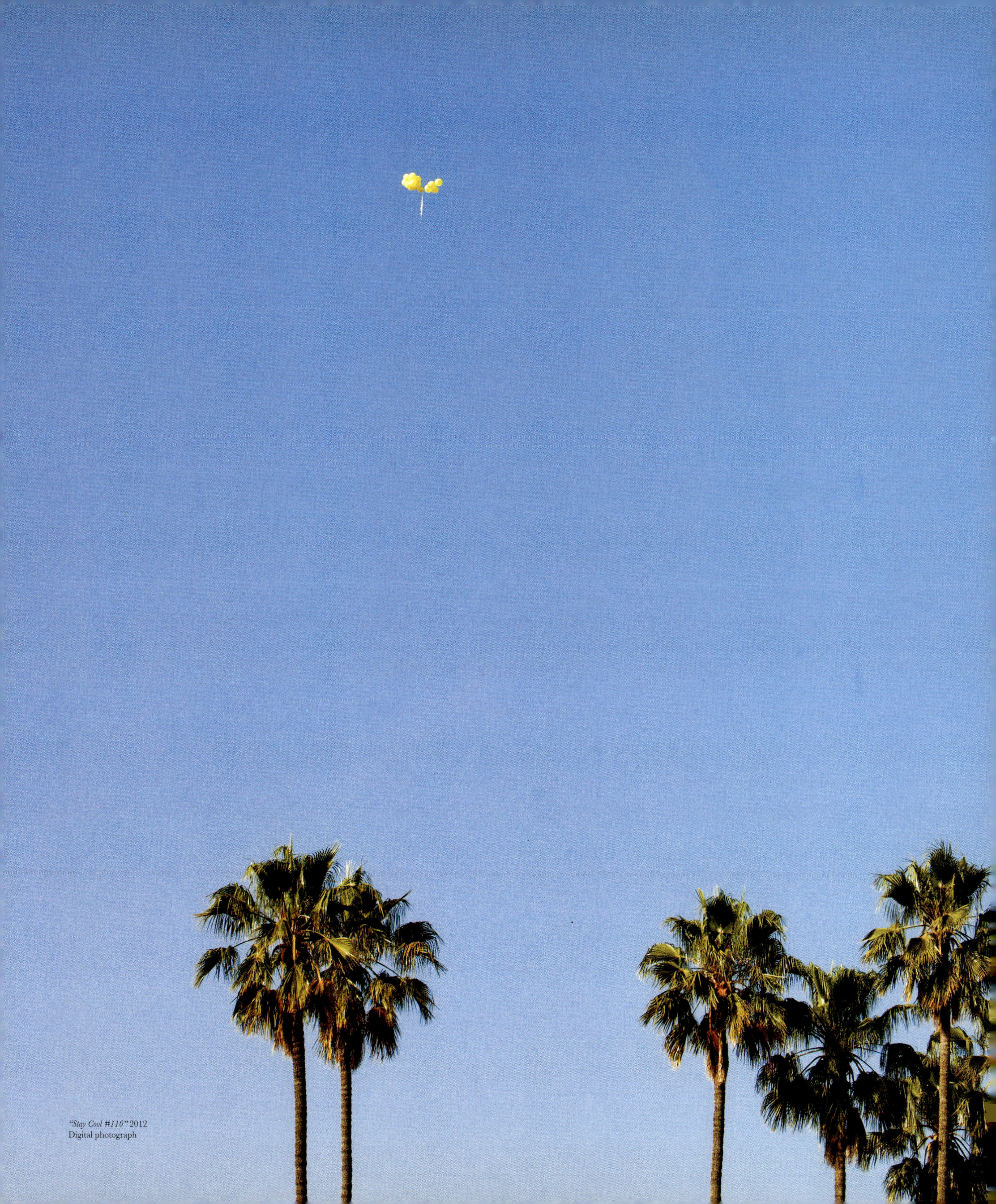

"Stay Cool #110" 2012
Digital photograph

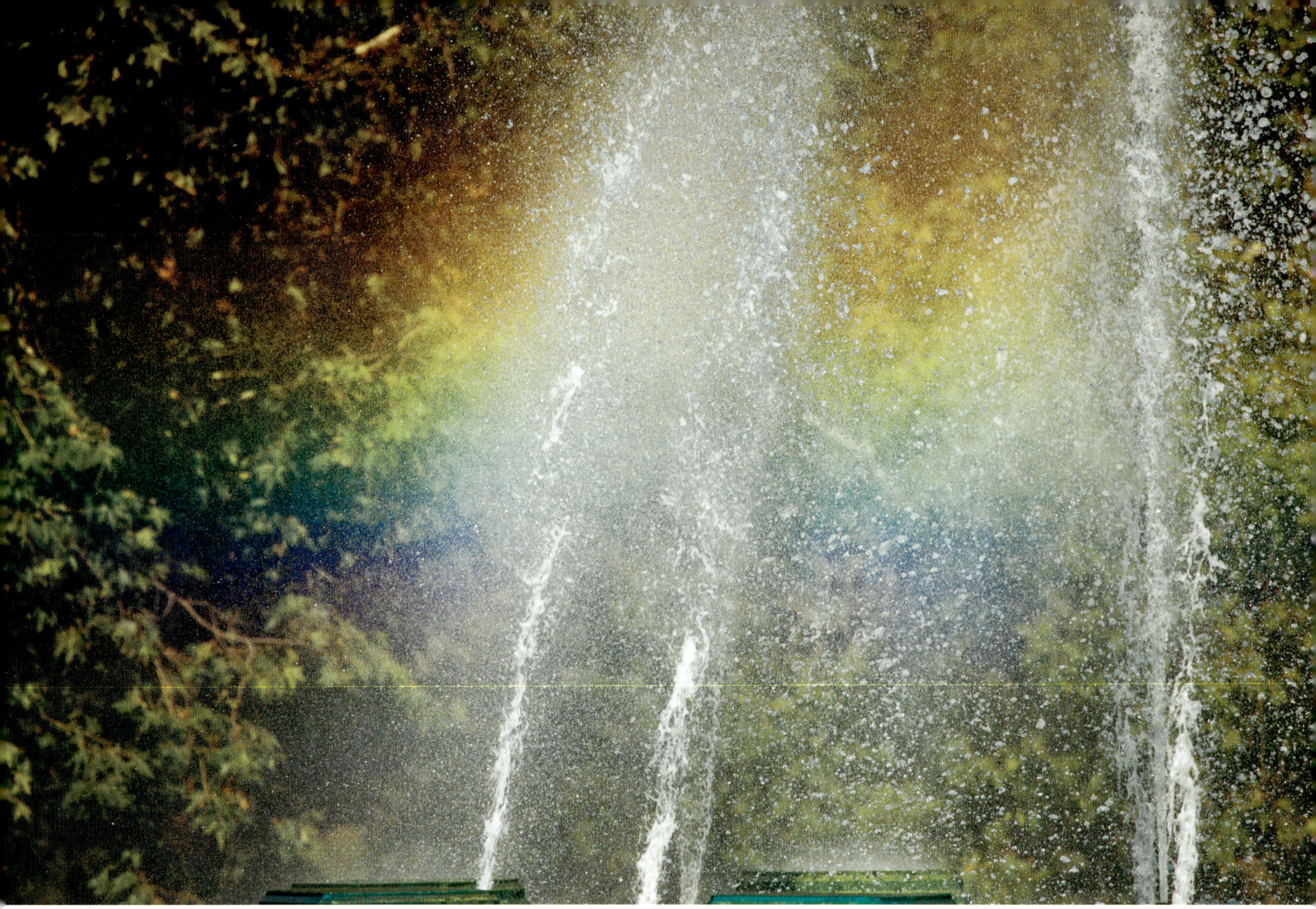

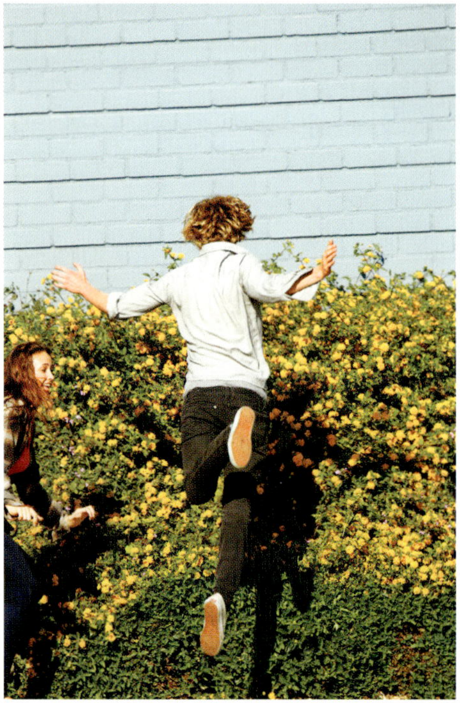

"Stay Cool #55" 2012
Digital photograph

"Stay Cool #113" 2012
Digital photograph

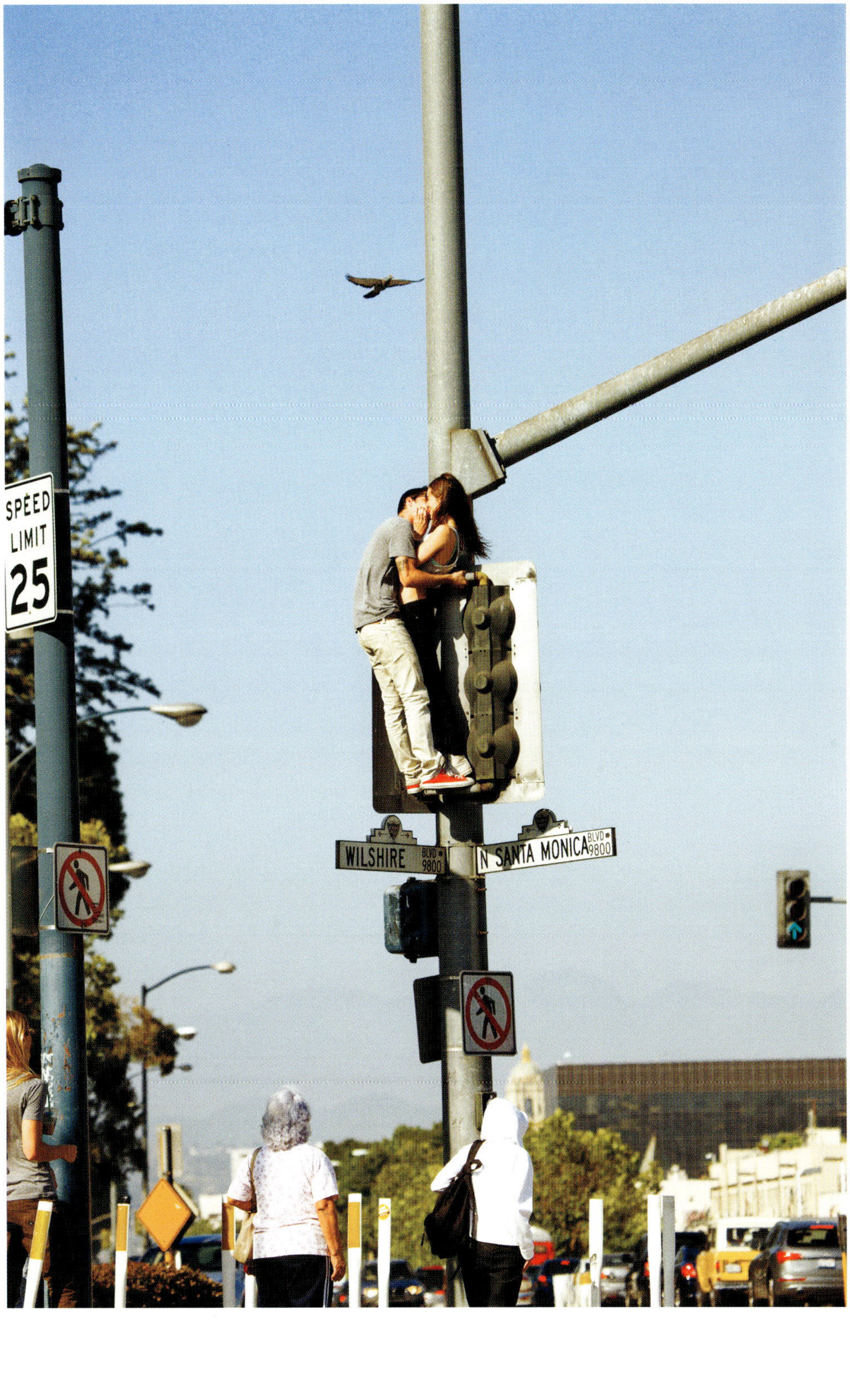
SPEED
LIMIT
25
WILSHIRE
BLVD
9800
N SANTA MONICA
BLVD
9800

"Stay Cool #143" 2012
Digital photograph

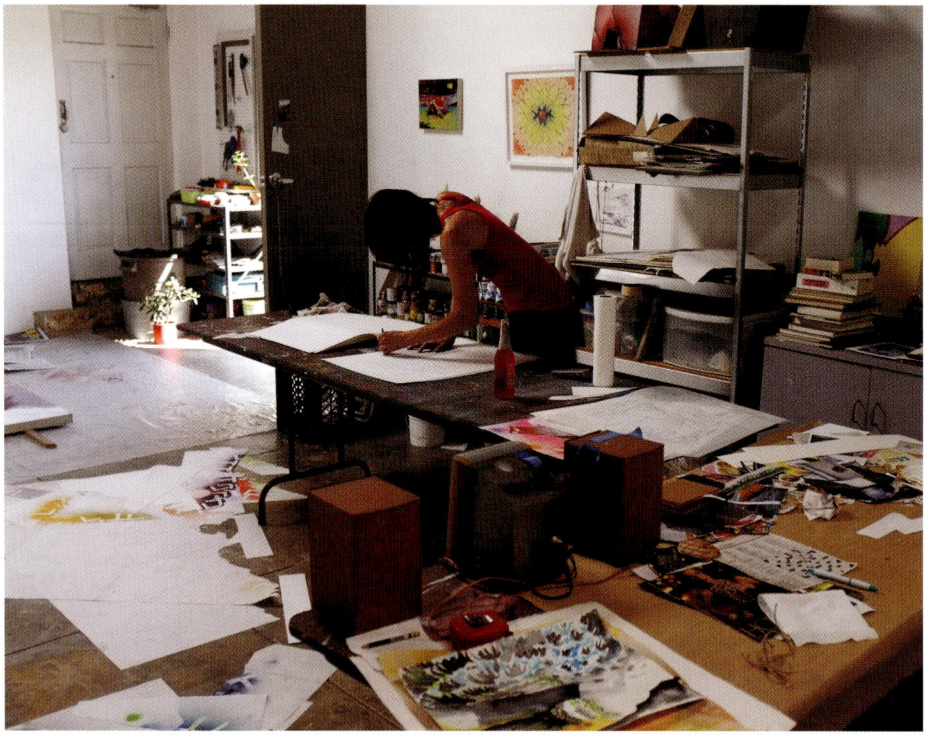

Photo by Steve Kim, 2011

PEARL C HSIUNG

Los Angeles, California
pearlchsiung.com

My parents and I emigrated from Taiwan to Los Angeles when I was four months old. Family, friends, good weather, dreamy daylight, a dynamic cultural environment, affordable living, and studio spaces have all kept me here.

Besides having strong roots and childhood memories here, I have had some of the most meaningful and transformative experiences of my life on California sites such as Yosemite, Big Sur, San Francisco, Mammoth Lakes, Twentynine Palms, Borrego Springs, and probably some Indian Reservations I couldn't direct you to.

To me, the most compelling essence about California is that it has been, and continues to be, a locus for the projections of human desires, big ideas, and aspirations. Throughout its history, California has been a space where people have brought their dreams, speculations, delusions, and greed, often manipulating and distorting the concept of California to enable their/our desires and plans for the future.

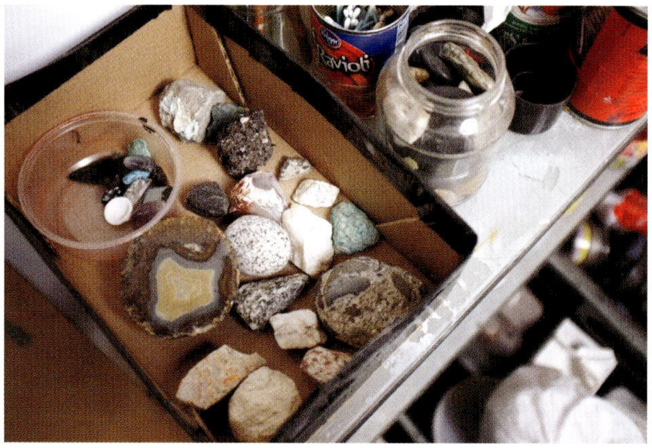

Studio image by Steve Kim

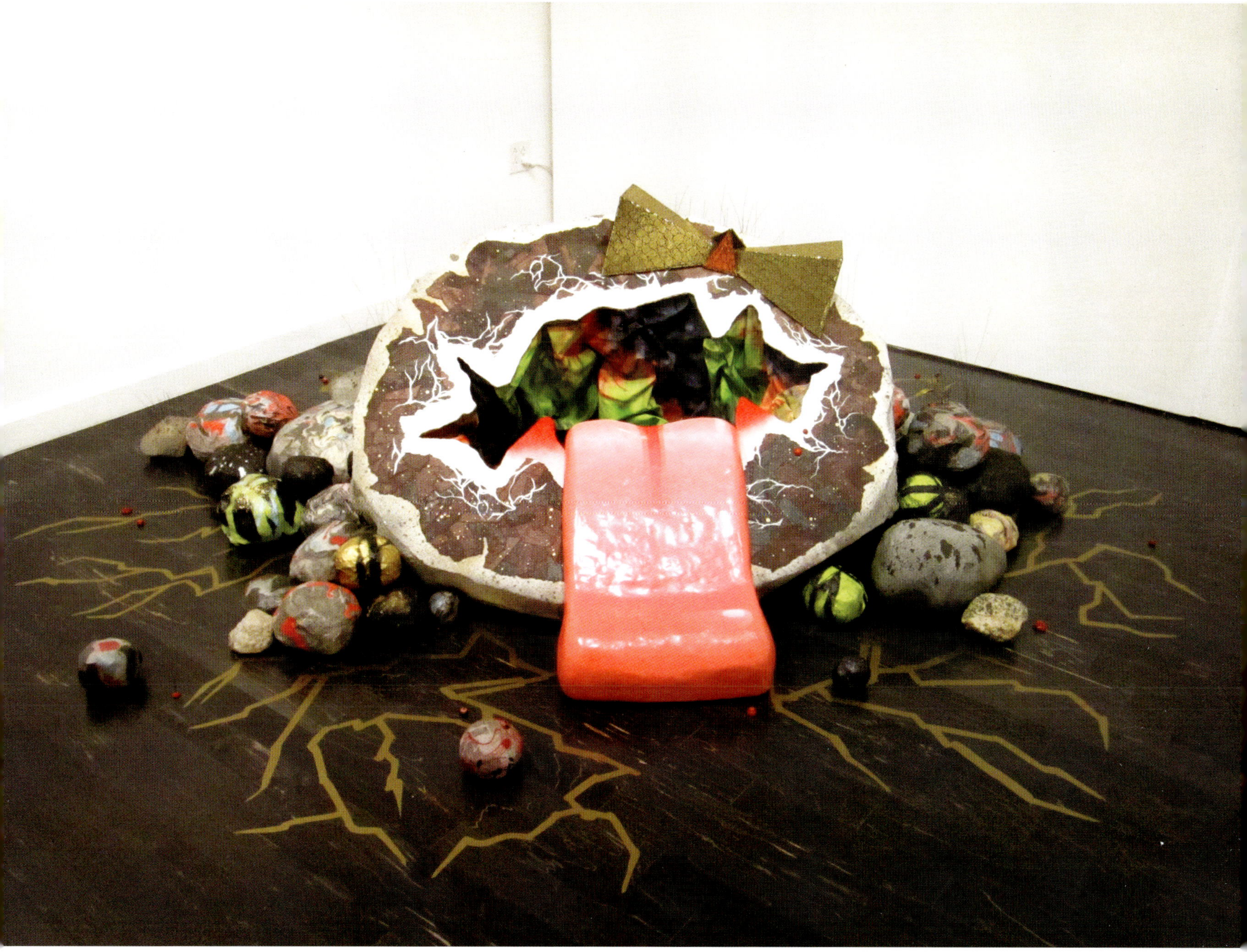

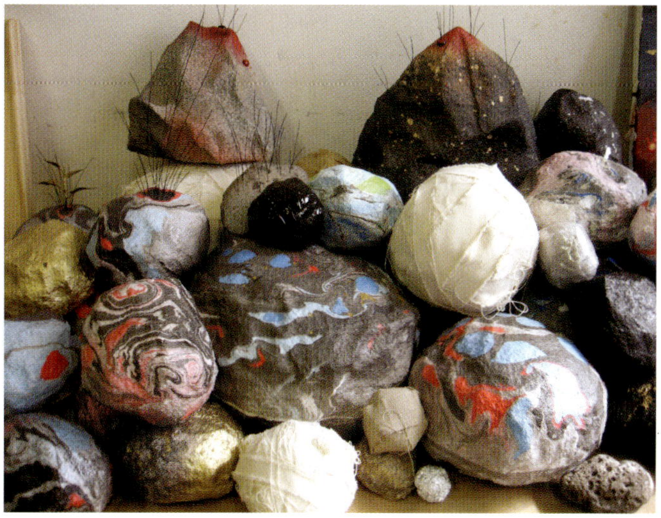

"Heave Ho" 2006-2012
Papier-mâché, fabric, wire mesh, paint, vinyl, and Fimo
Dimensions vary

"Rocks" 2006-2012
Rock sculptures in the studio
Dimensions vary

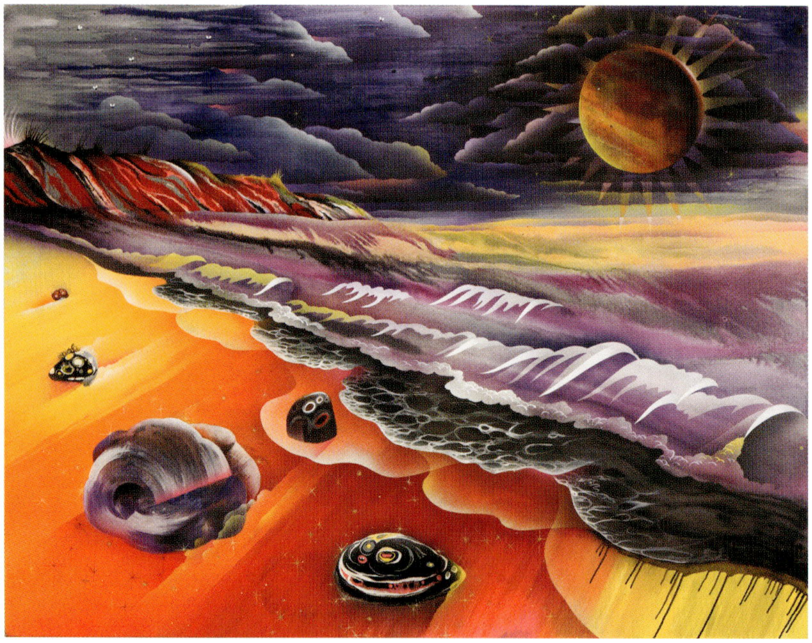

"Beach" 2010
Oil-based enamel on canvas
46 x 60 inches

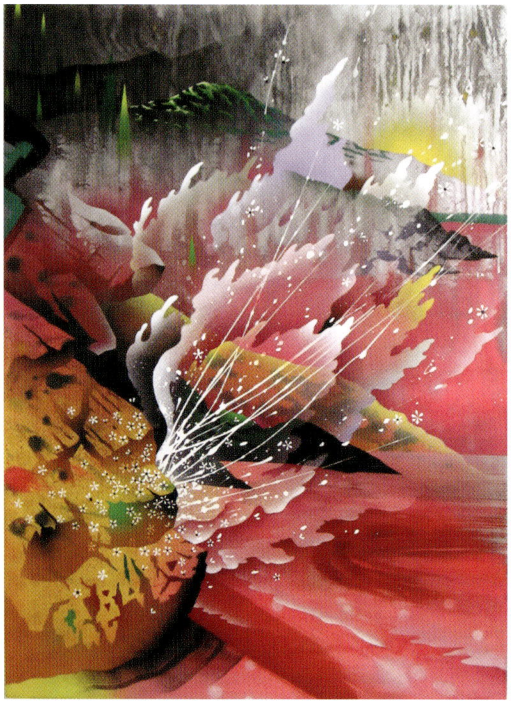

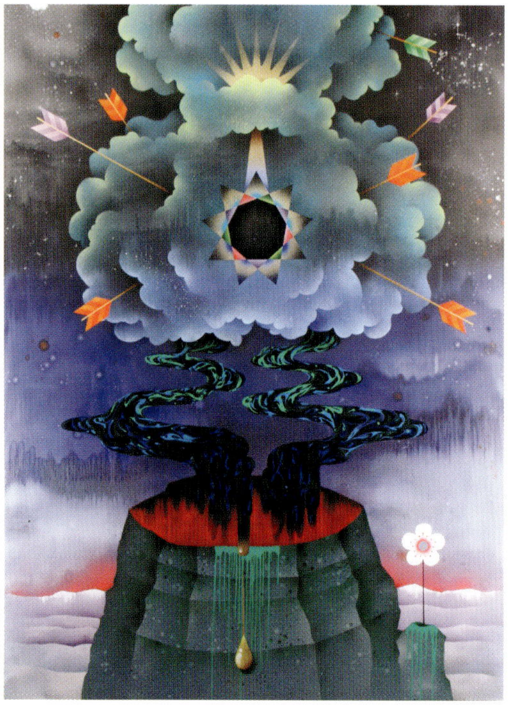

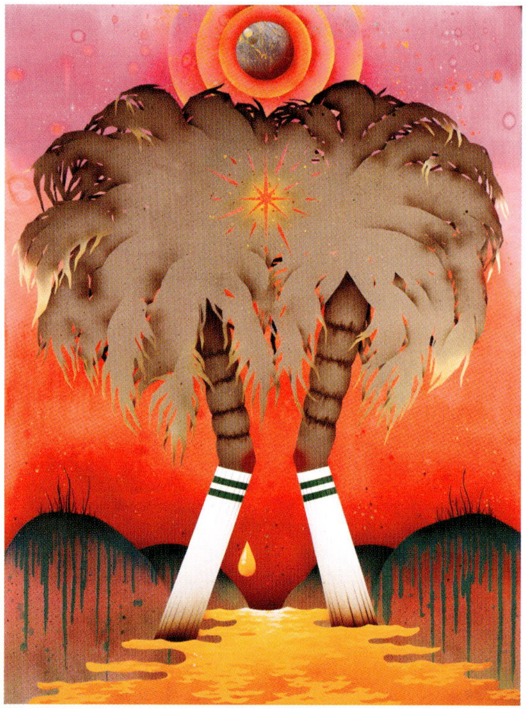

"Gush Buster" 2011
Oil-based enamel on canvas
40 x 30 inches

"Saint Perpetuumr" 2007
Oil-based enamel on canvas
96 x 72 inches

"Sightly Stunner" 2007
Oil-based enamel on canvas
96 x 72 inches

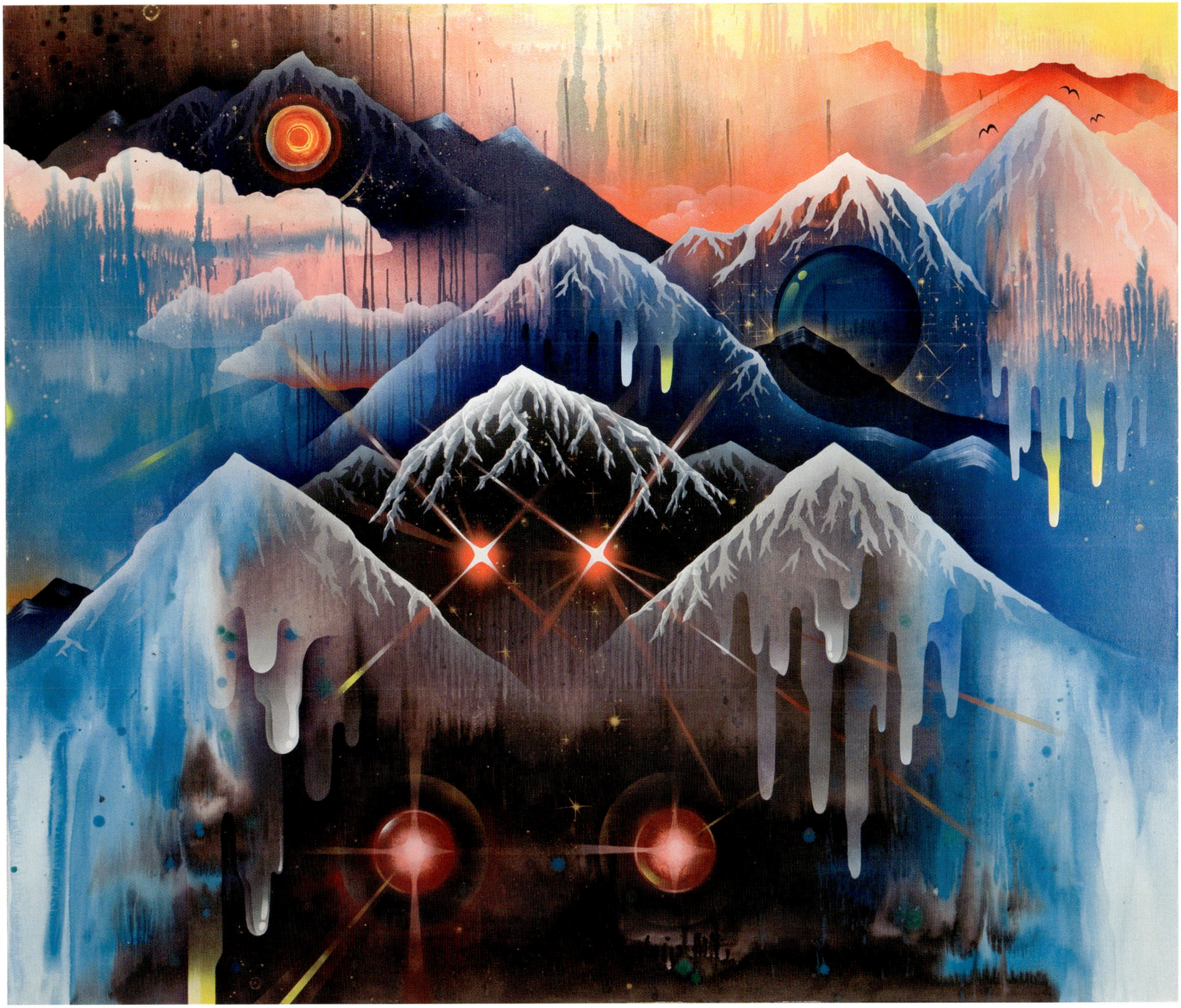

"Slow Creep" 2010
Oil-based enamel on canvas
96 x 72 inches

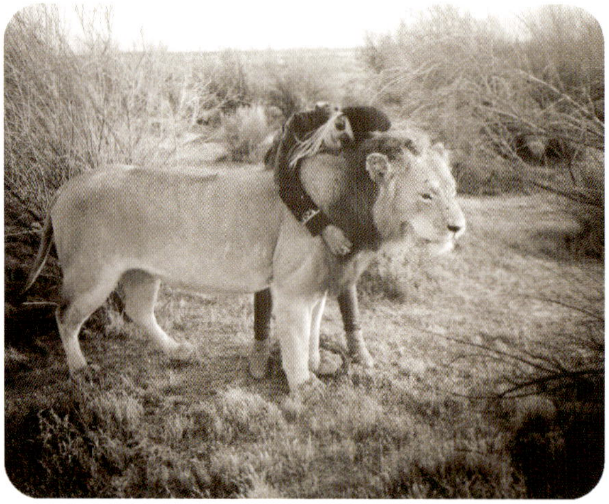

HARPER SMITH

Los Angeles, California
harpersmithphotography.com
iheartreps.com

Self Portrait, 2012

I moved to California from Iowa with my family when I was thirteen. This place was so intimidating to me when I first arrived: big, vast, loud. It scared the shit out of me; it was '94. Within that year I saw my first wildfire, riot, and high-speed chase (OJ of course). Then came the earthquake. ... It was insane. I finally found the beauty in all the chaos when I picked up my camera and started shooting. Now I realize I couldn't live anywhere else.

The influences of the Midwest have stuck with me, and because the landscape of California is so diverse I feel like I am still able to tap into those scenes on my shoots. You can really make California look like anywhere, which is why Hollywood was built. Not only landscape but the diversity of the people who live here and the free spirited feel of our population. Also, I never get tired of the desert—there is so much space—it's the perfect palate for a shoot. You really get a chance to focus on your subject without letting the surroundings take over.

I love insanity, imperfection, and turmoil. Even when my shoots feel softer and more feminine there is usually an opposing force with a little of those qualities. I have met some incredible people in California who continue to inspire me. Stylists, models, all with that LA attitude and mentality. When I shoot elsewhere, I feel like a little of that connection is lost; it is really important in my work.

When I work here, I am always driving past incredible locations that were built on love (Salvation Mountain), or insanity (hoarders' homes), or abandonment, and these places are priceless. They really help me build a true story about what and why I am shooting a particular concept.

This shoot was originally created after the stylist and I watched Lykke Li's "Get Some" video. We loved the mirroring images and the supernatural feel of the video. In general, I am inspired by music, cinema, and things that make us uncomfortable. Justin Blyth, our designer, has also greatly influenced my interest in these subjects and has helped me materialize a way to show these ideas within my photography.

Designed by Justin Blyth. Co-conceptualized and styled by Madley.

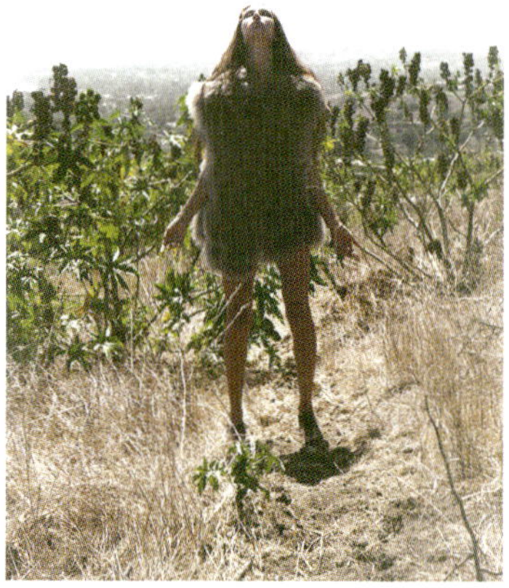

"Get Some" 2011
Digital photographs
Dimensions vary

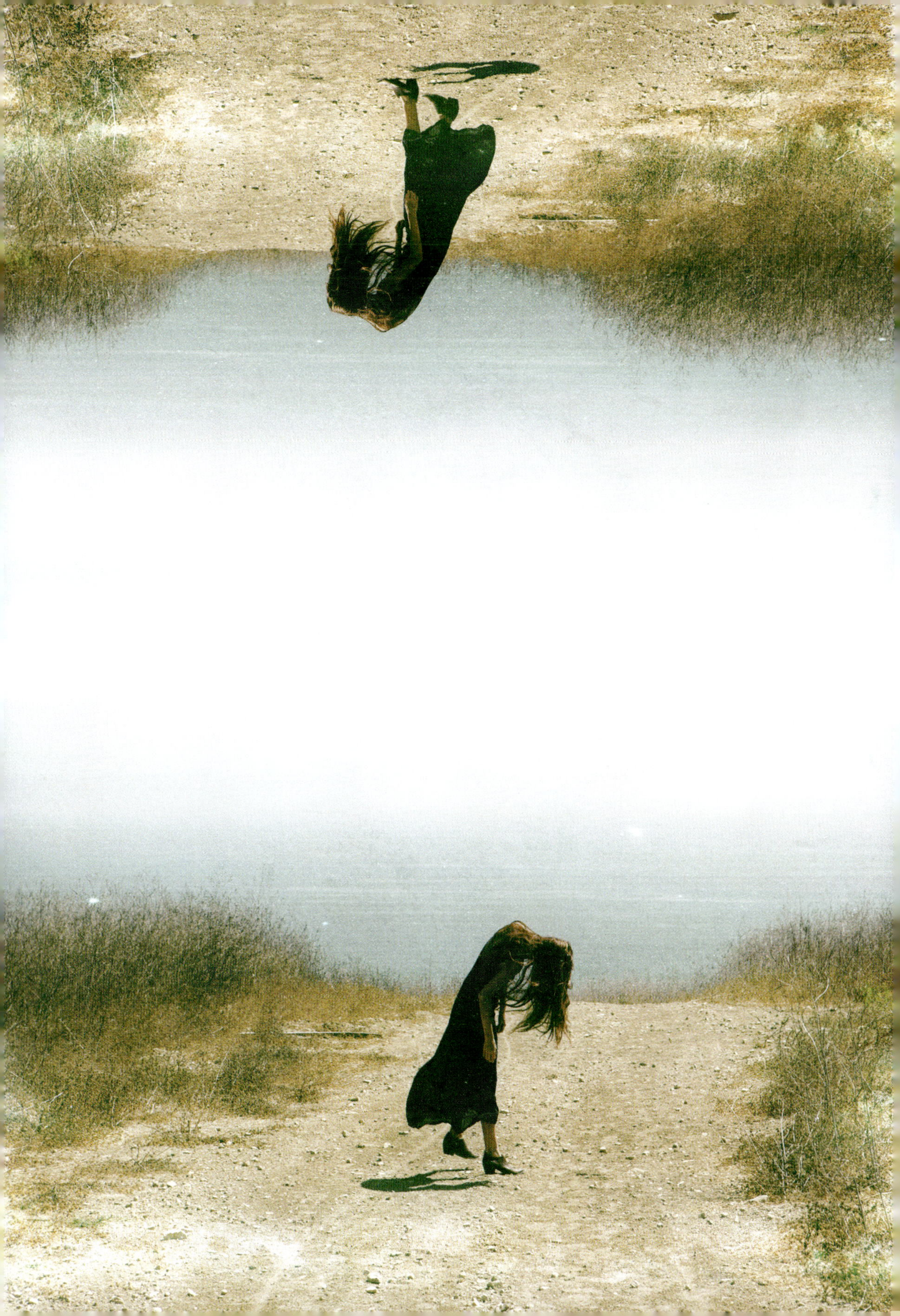

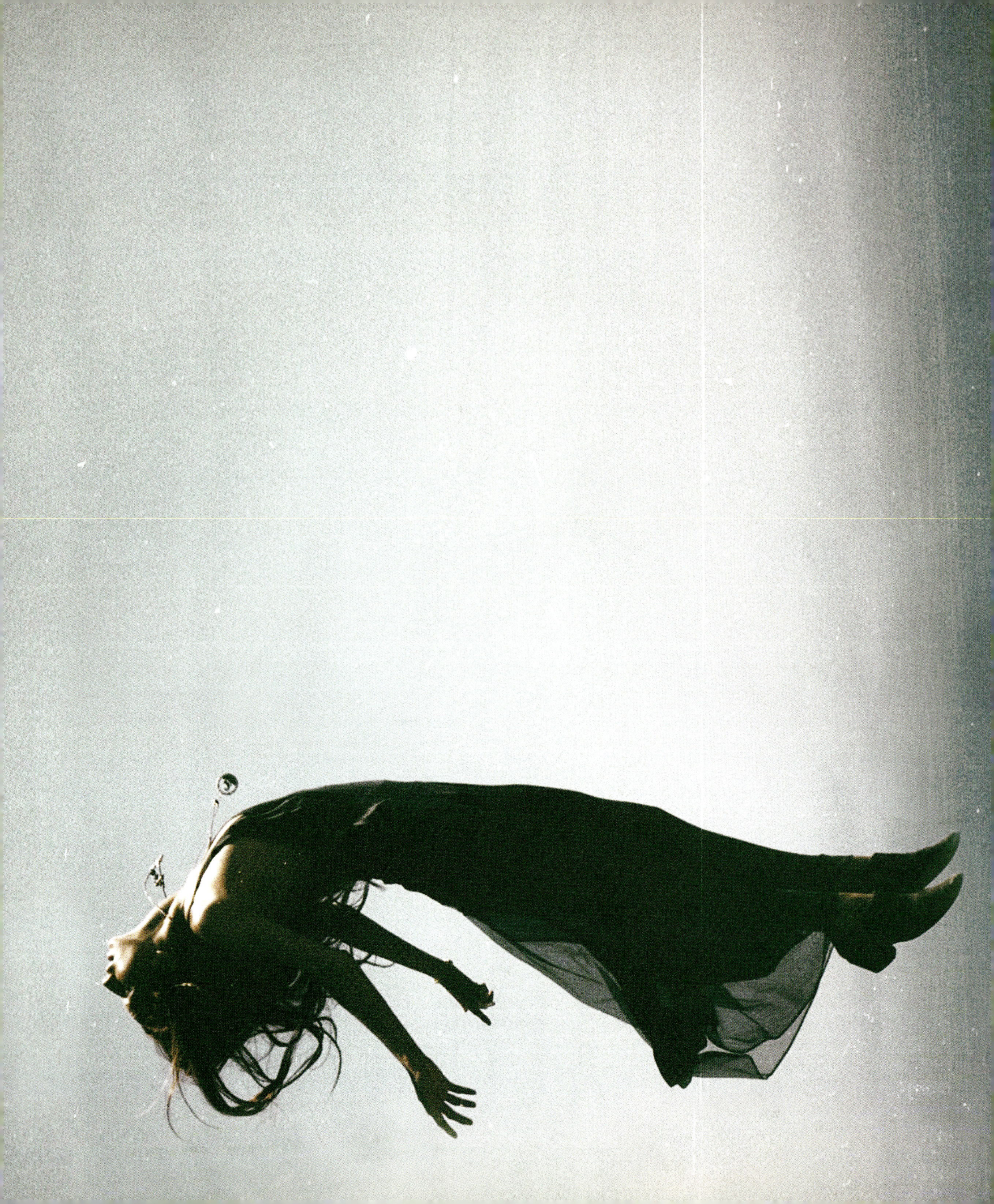

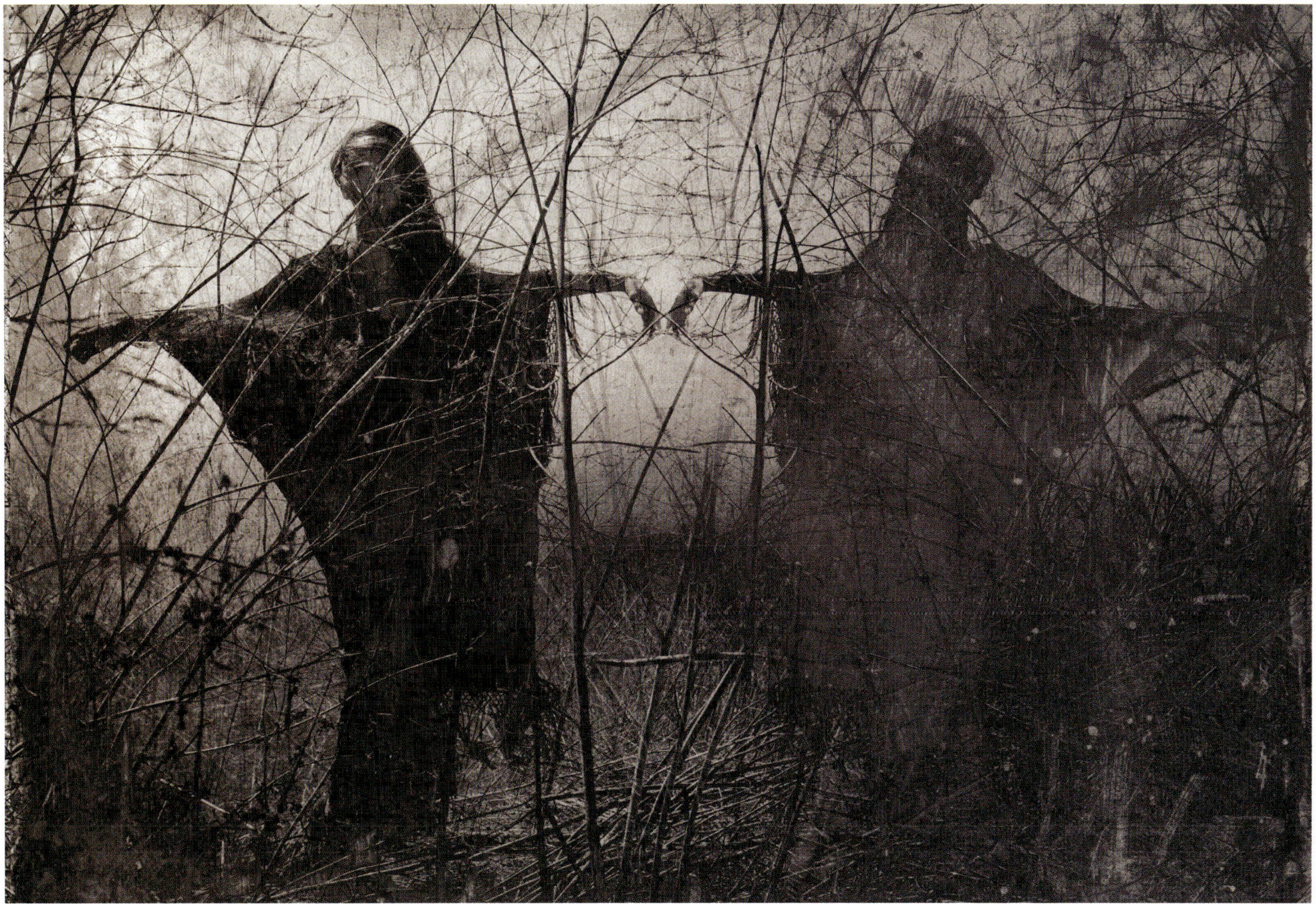

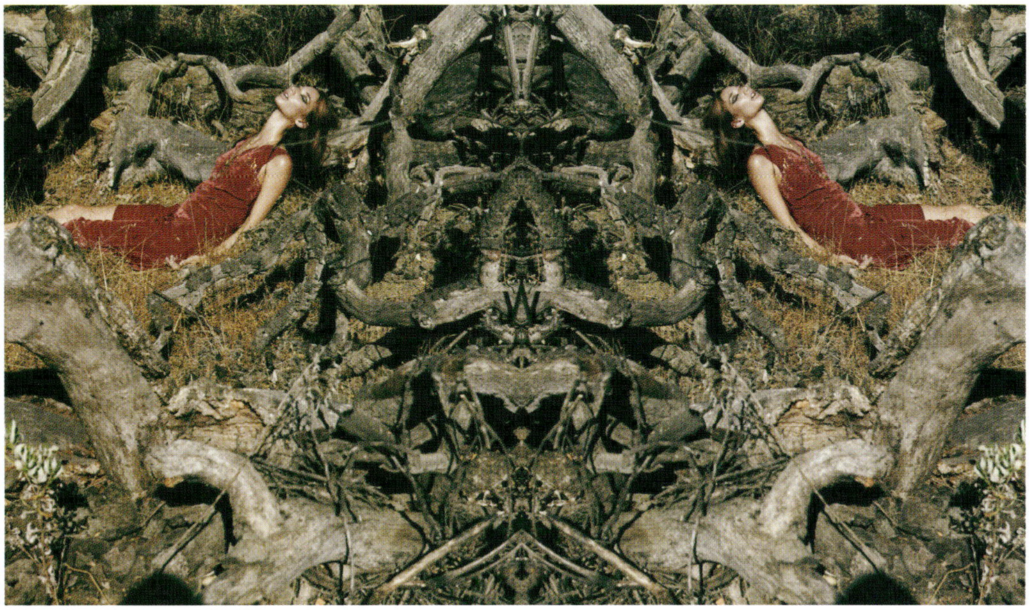

"Get Some" 2011
Digital photographs
Dimensions vary

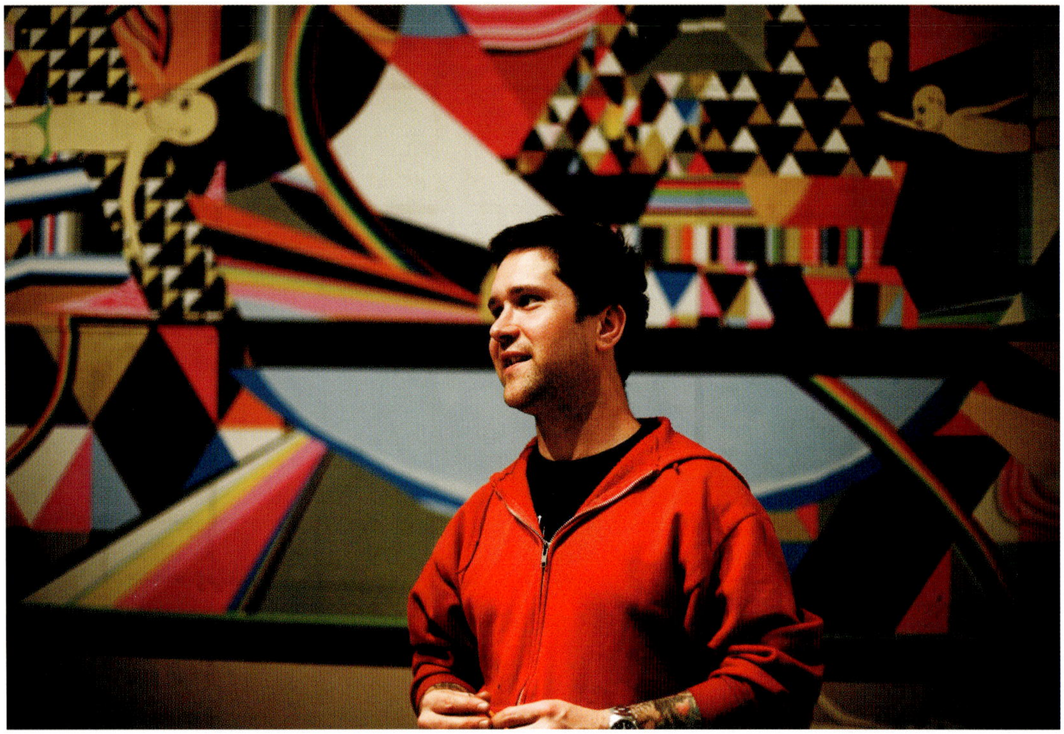

RICHARD COLMAN

San Francisco, California
richardcolmanart.com
V1 Gallery, Denmark

Self portrait, 2012

I'm not sure what really brought me out here. I was living in NY before I came west. I had been there for a while when the opportunity presented itself, and I just sort of figured why not? I was about twenty-six at the time and had done a bunch of moving around, just seeing new places, and I happened to land here. That was about 2004, I think, and I've been here ever since: first in Los Angeles and now in San Francisco. I've been here for about five years.

I like it here; I like the city, it's surrounding areas, and the people. It is a great place to be creative. There are a lot of interesting people doing a lot of interesting things, and I'm always meeting new people. The weather agrees with me, too.

There are always advantages and disadvantages no matter where you are, but I think part of being creative is being able to adapt to what ever situation you happen to be in. I think no matter where I would be I would still be making things, as for what that may be I can't say because I'm not there. I'm here. But again, I really enjoy the people here. It is a great creative environment, there are a lot of people making things, and it does seem that you get more for my money, space-wise out here. The studios I've had here I have space in and good light, whereas before, on the East Coast, they all seemed cramped and dark. One of the tough things for me about being in California, though, is that it is very far from my family and core group of friends, most of whom are still on the East Coast.

What I think influences me the most is the diversity of environments here and the people. As for process, it seems to be a lot easier for me to make the things I want to make here. It's pretty nice weather-wise here all the time, so I don't have to worry about that. I don't have to lug anything on the subway or anything, and I have a lot more space, so for me there is a lot more freedom working here. There are always hurdles to overcome, and nothing is perfect, but here I feel like I can come a lot closer to making the things I really want to make. There are less things in my way.

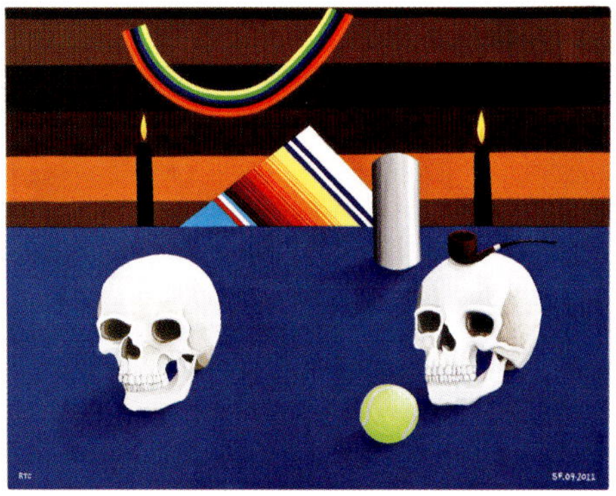

"Still Life on Canvas (Two Skulls)" 2011
Acrylic on canvas
14 x 14 inches

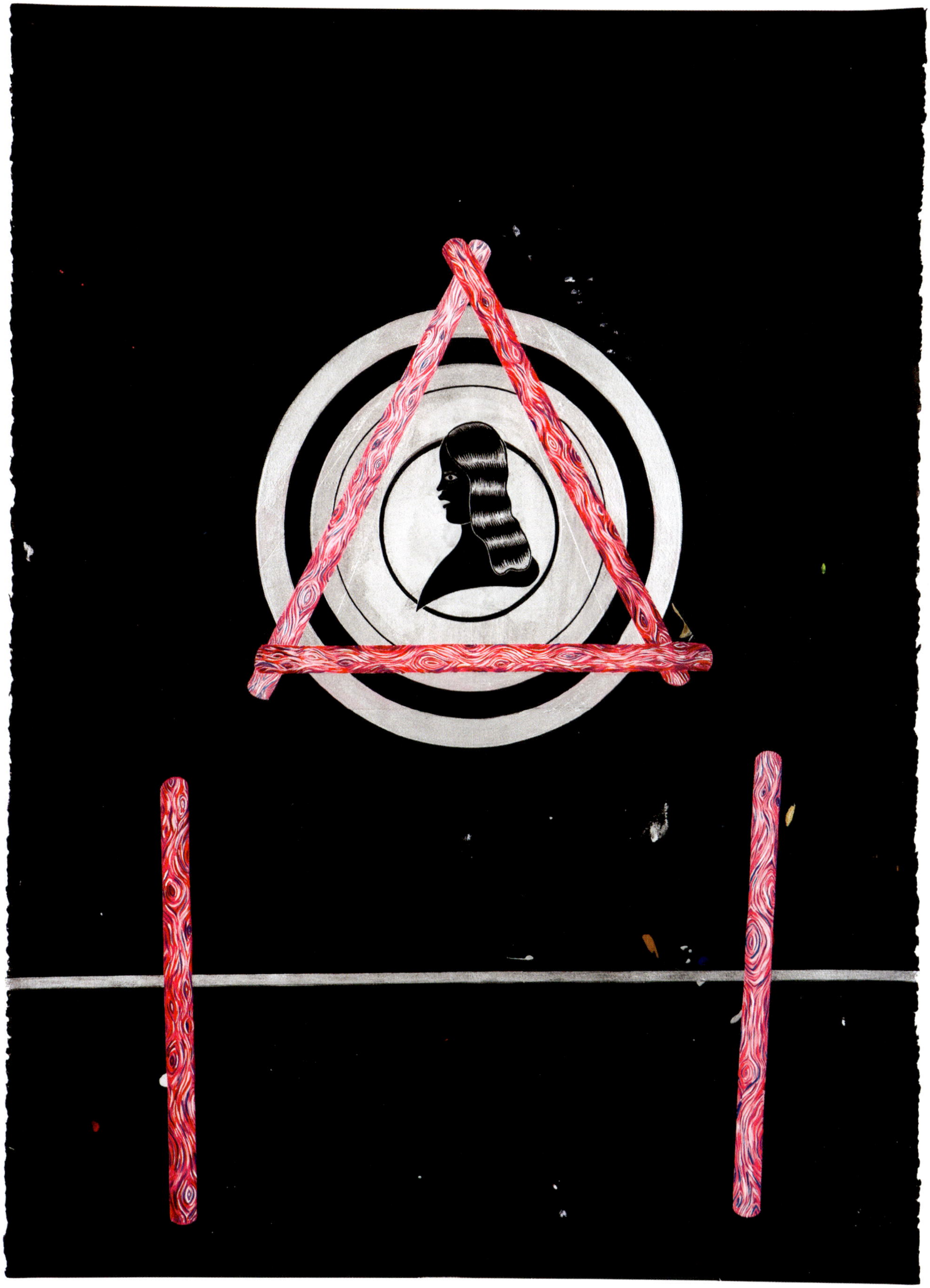

"Five Sticks with Silhouette" 2010
Acrylic and spray paint on paper
22 x 30 inches

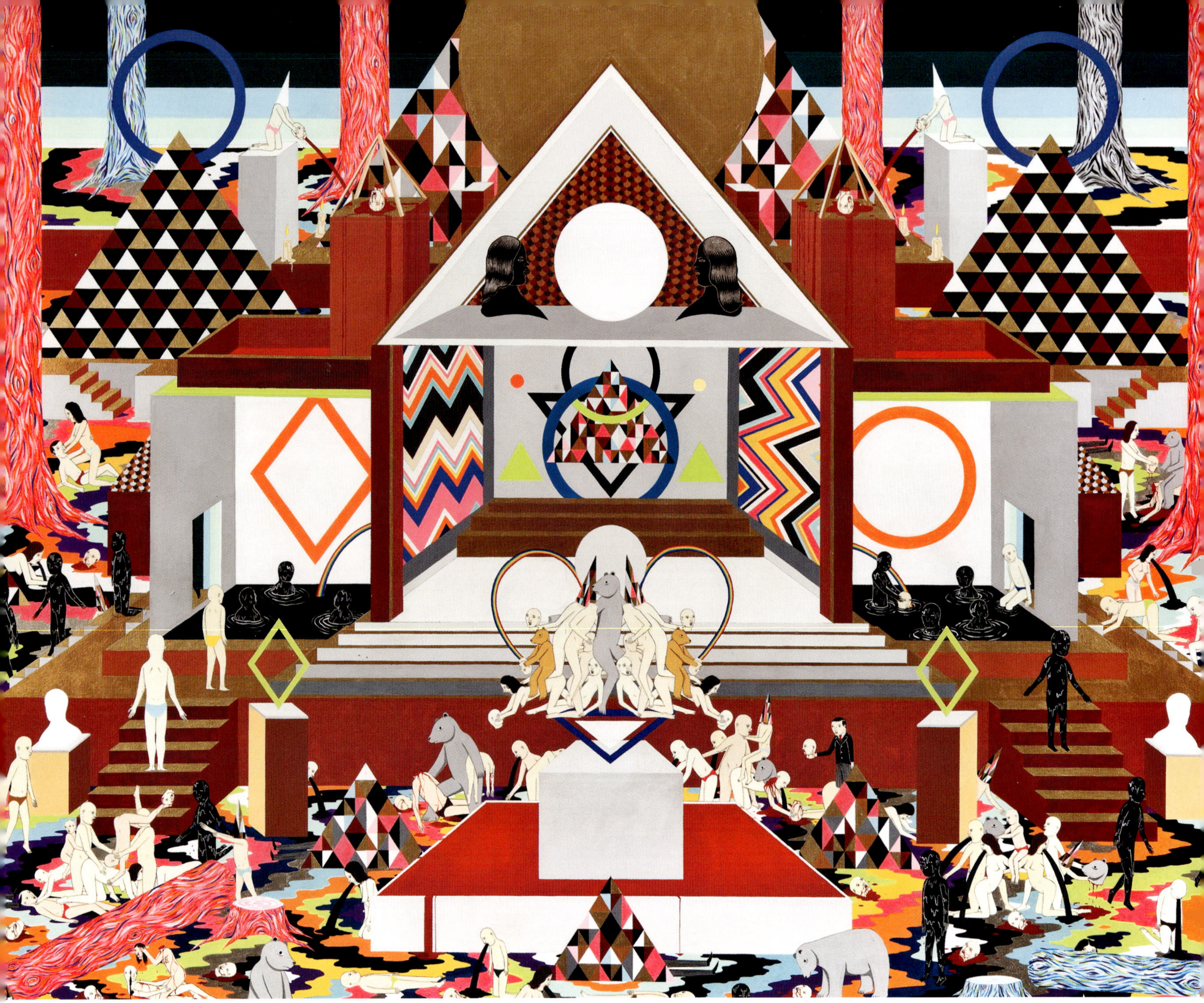

"Tuesday" 2010
Acrylic on wood panel
50 x 40 inches

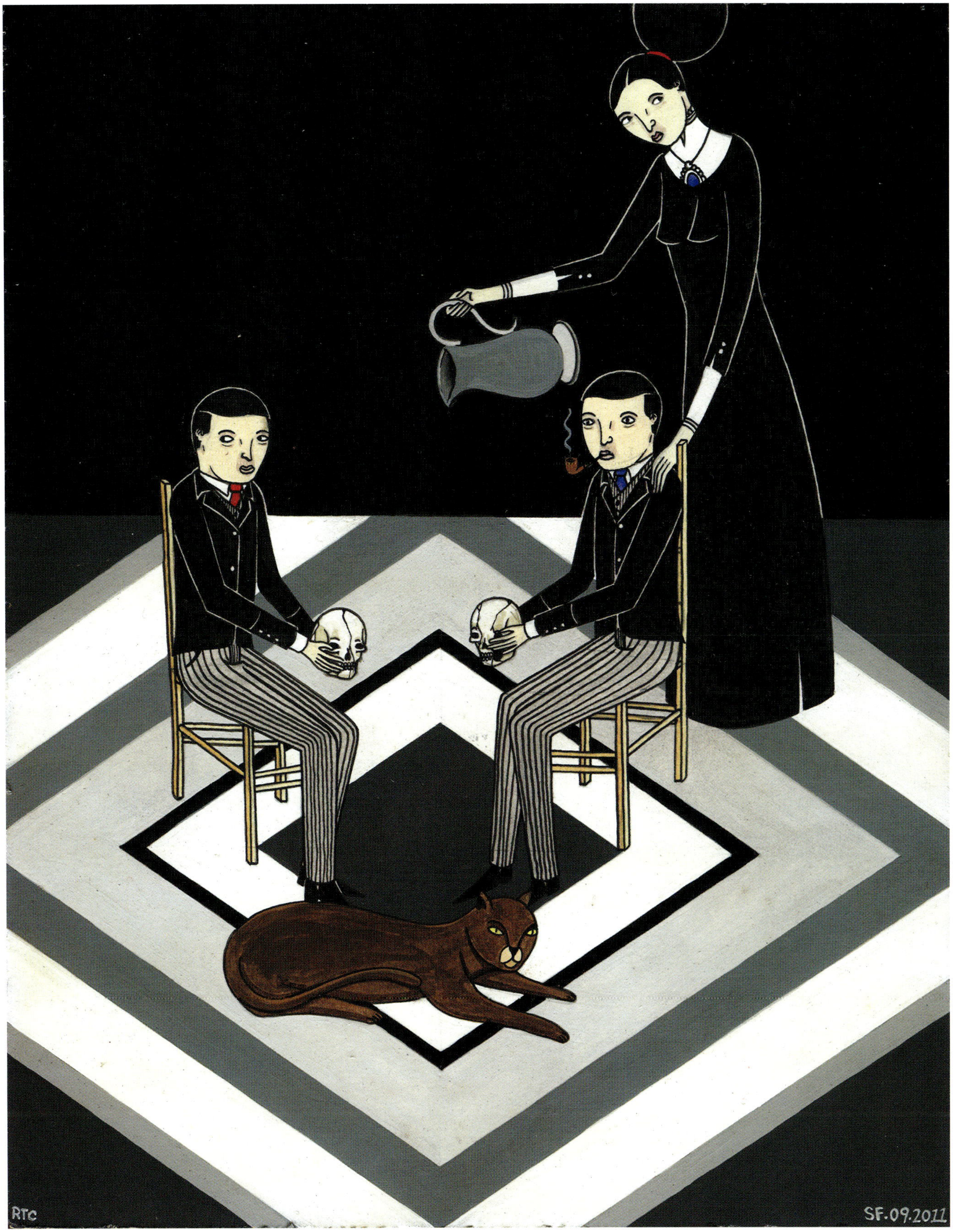

"Seated (With Two Skulls)" 2011
Acrylic on paper
9 x 12 inches

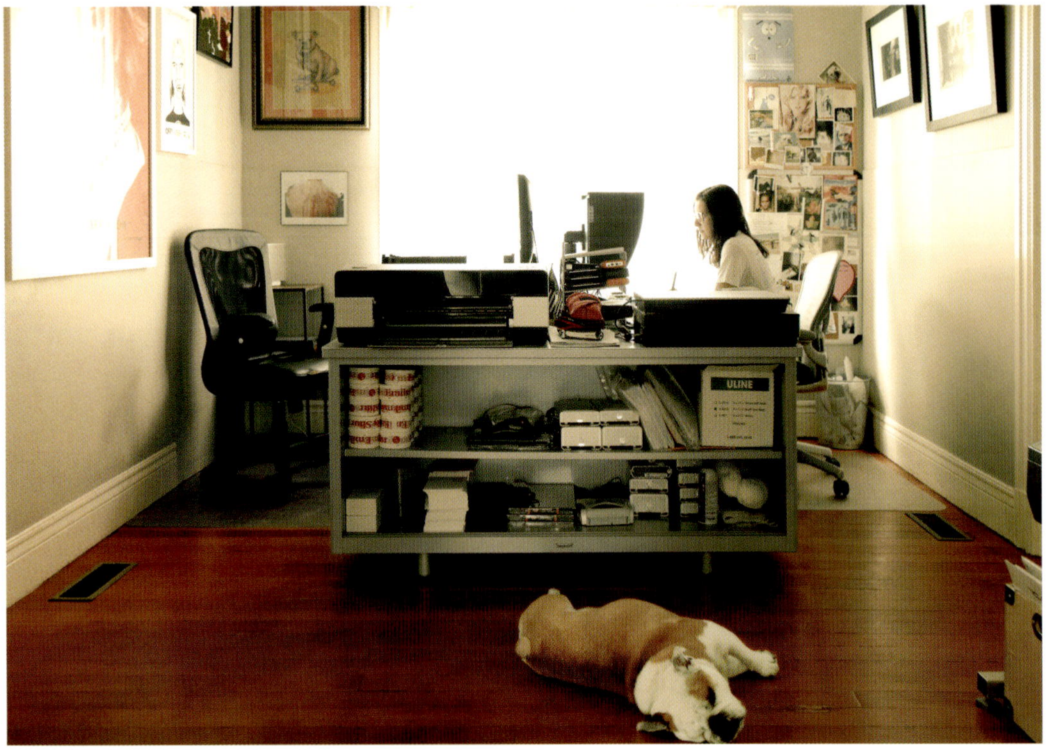

Self portrait—Echo Park office, 2012

EMILY SHUR

Los Angeles, California
emilyshur.com
giantartists.com

I moved here after almost twelve years in New York; I had had my fill of long winters and small apartments. I had been coming out to California periodically for work and always enjoyed my time here. The weather was so nice, and everyone seemed to have such a good quality of life. So, I decided to make a big change and moved to LA in 2005. I have never once regretted that decision. Soon after relocating, I met my husband. We bought a house that contains more than one room and windows that don't face brick walls. We have a lazy bulldog. Life is good.

The advantages of living here are being able to shoot outdoors all year round, the fact that I have an actual office in my house as opposed to a cramped desk area with stacks of prints in boxes up to the ceiling, and the geographic variety California offers cannot be beat. I can shoot at the beach, in the mountains, the desert, a mansion in the hills, on an urban downtown street, or in a canyon. It's all a short drive away. The only thing we don't have too much of are gloomy skies, so I suppose that could be considered a disadvantage to some.

How California influences my work and process is twofold for me. I make a living shooting celebrity portraiture, so California has a definite impact on that aspect of my work. Just being here allows me to do shoots that don't happen anywhere else.

In terms of my personal work, I am very inspired by the natural world and conventional landscape photography. In California, I never have a hard time finding a good landscape, beautiful light, or an amazing view. Whether I am working on a project here or somewhere far away, I have constant inspiration around me that keeps my eye working.

Also, and I never thought I'd find myself saying this, but I do enjoy having a car. There is freedom in throwing your camera in the backseat and taking off on a photo adventure.

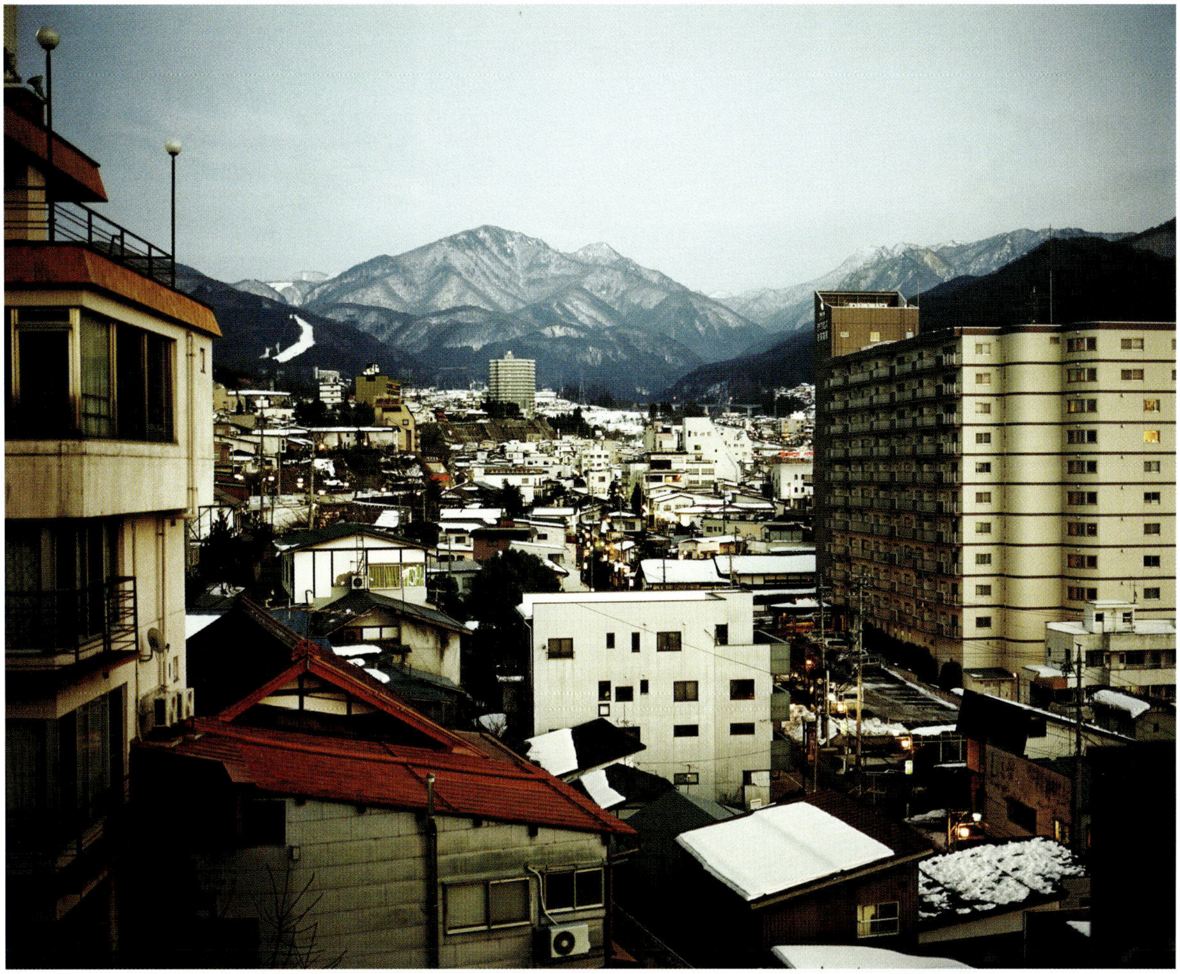

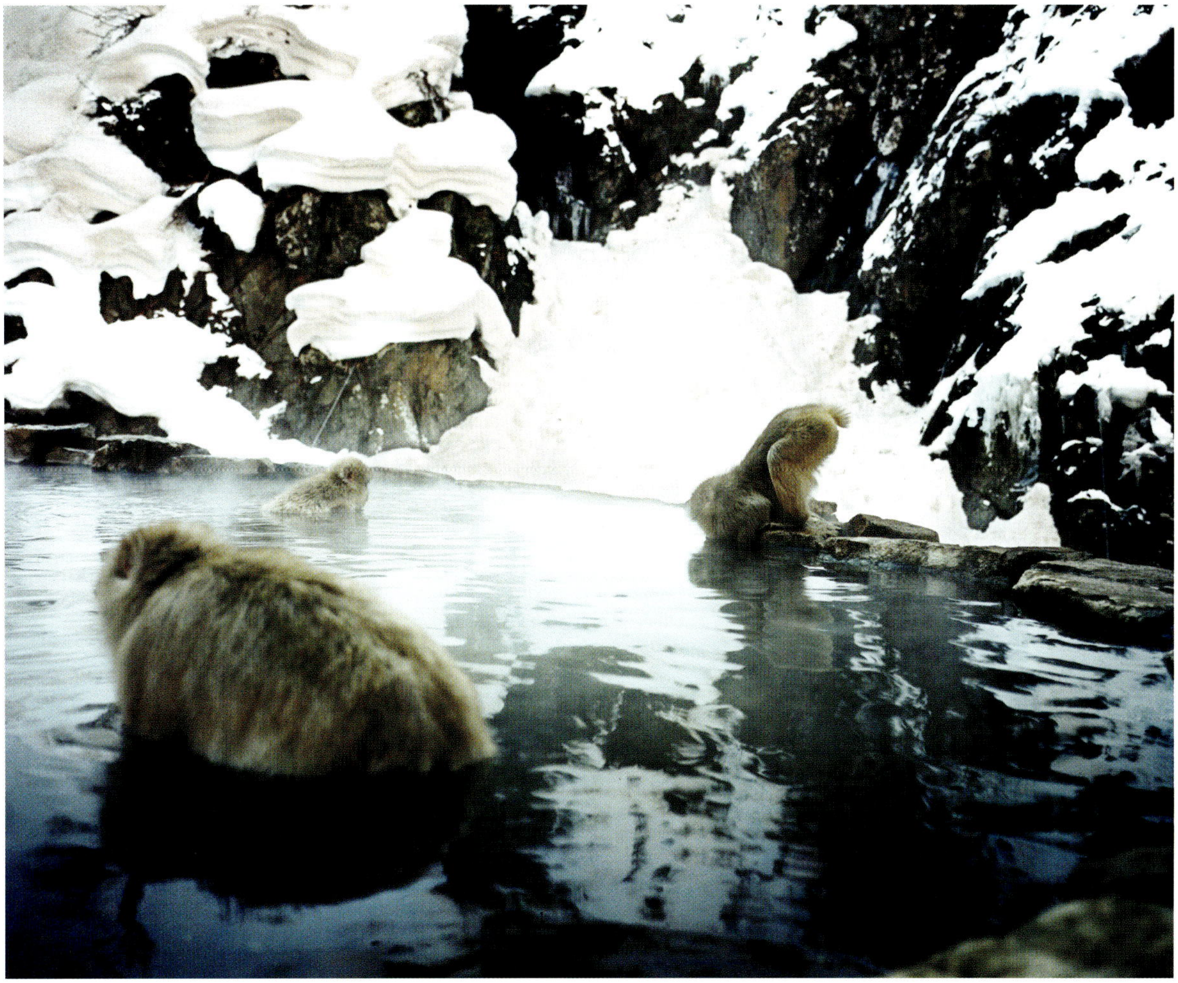

"Jigokudani Monkey Park, Yamanouchi" 2011
Photography (color negative film)
Archival pigment print
30 x 40 inches

"Sunset, Yudanaka" 2011
Photography (color negative film)
Archival pigment print
30 x 40 inches

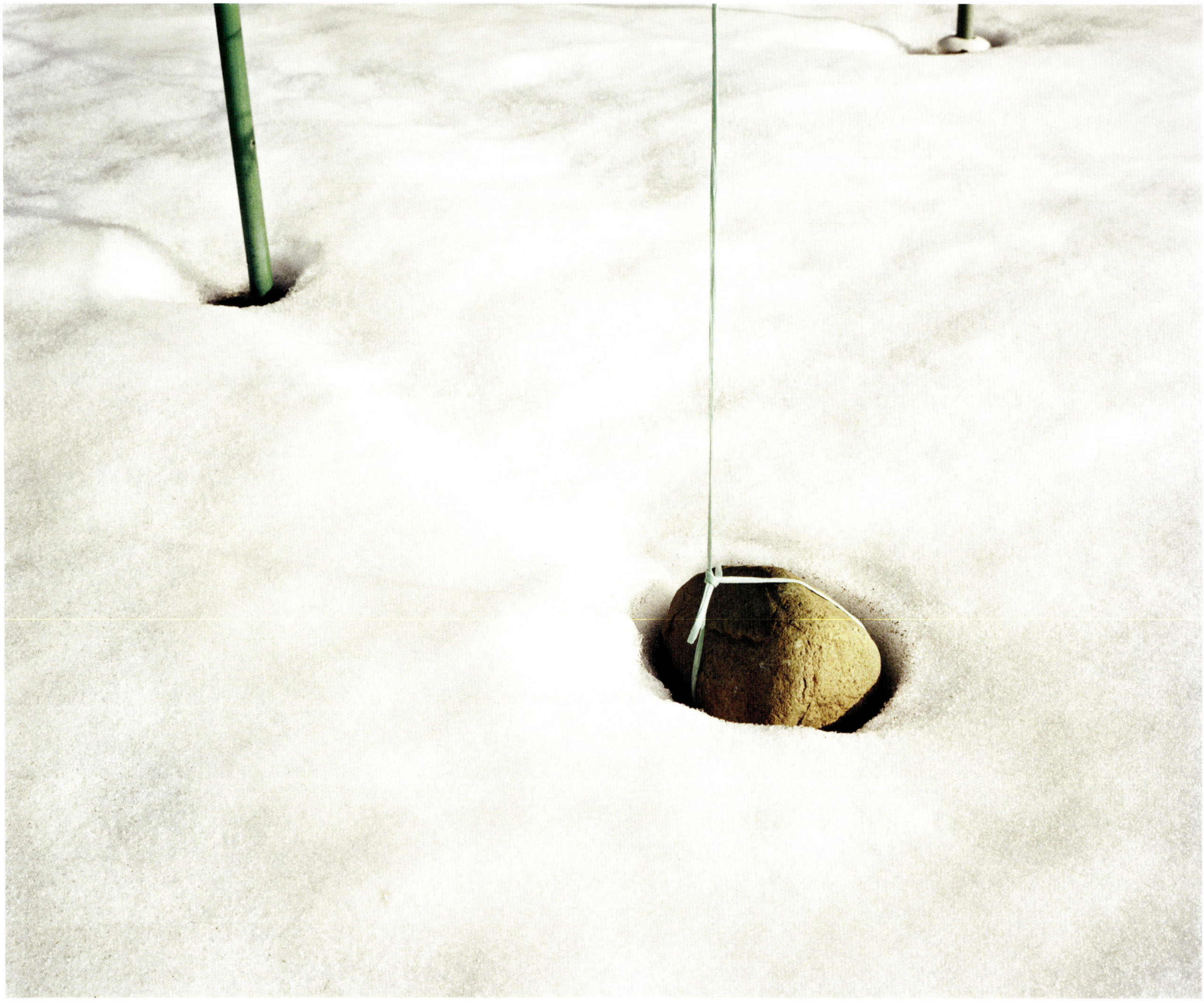

"One Swan, Mito" 2010
Photography (color negative film)
Archival pigment print
30 x 40 inches

"Sleeping Cat, Asakusa" 2011
Photography (color negative film)
Archival pigment print
30 x 40 inches

"My Bed, Yudanaka" 2011
Photography (color negative film)
Archival pigment print
30 x 40 inches

"Stone in the Snow, Yudanaka" 2011
Photography (color negative film)
Archival p.gment print
30 x 40 inches

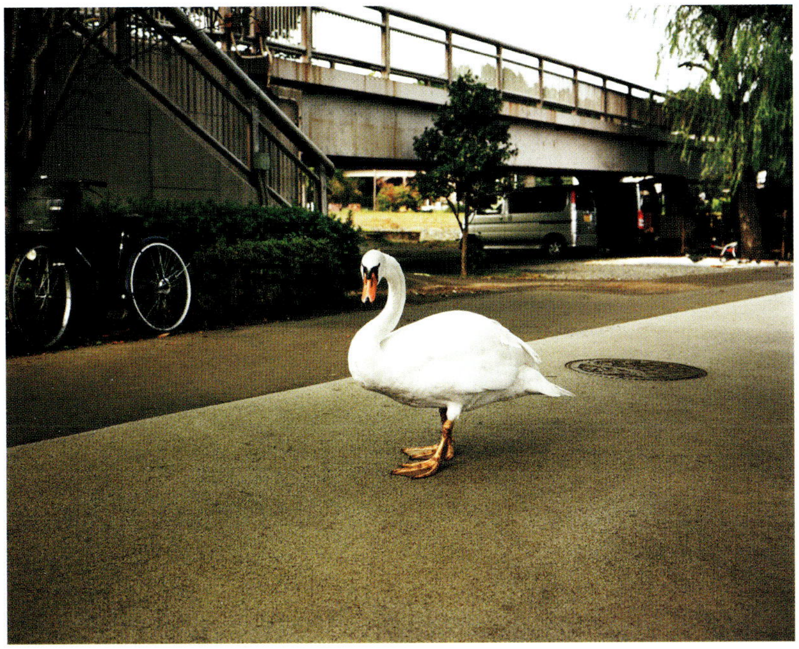

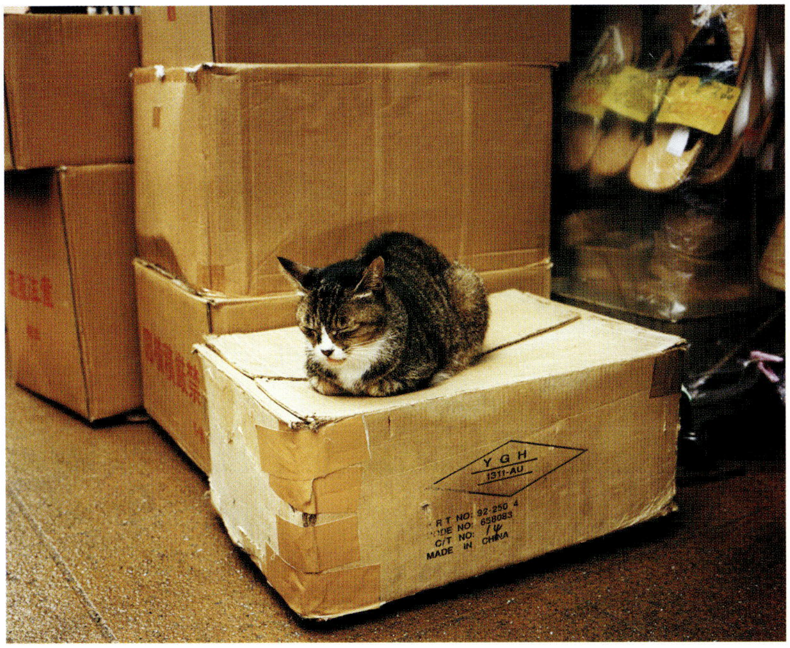
YGH
1511-AU
NO: 92-250 4
NO: 658083
C/T NO:
MADE IN CHINA

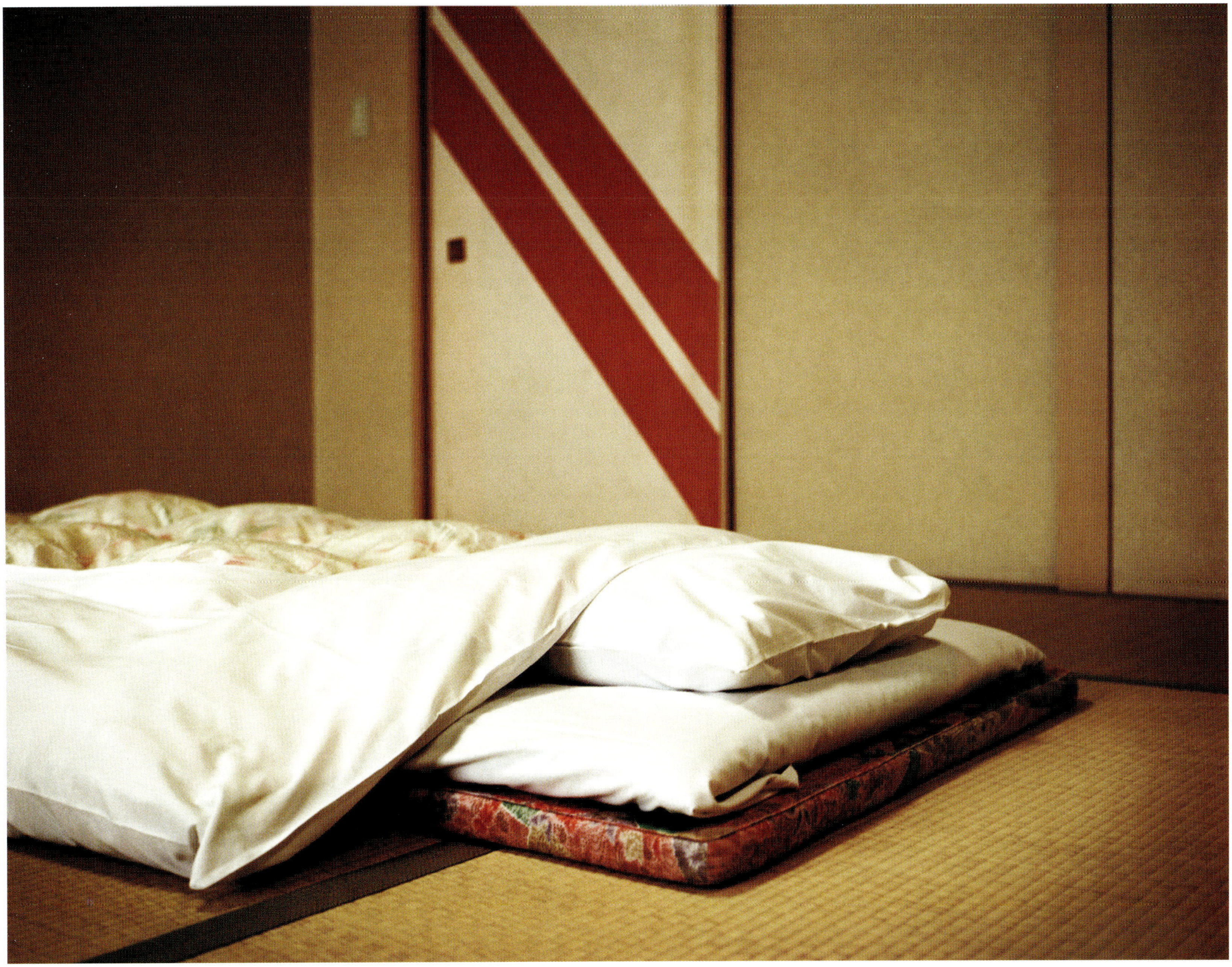

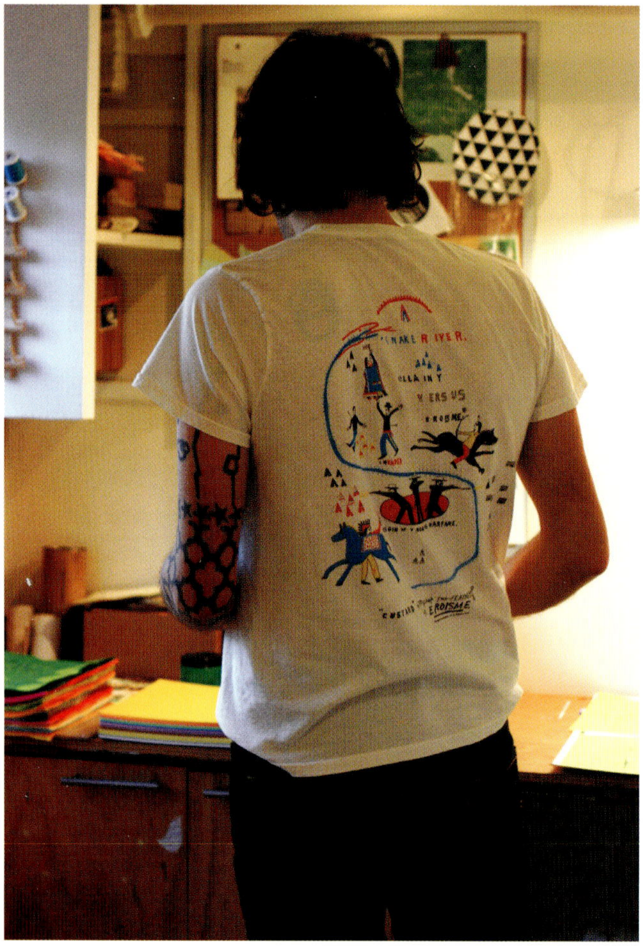

Self Portrait, 2012

CHRISTOPHER BETTIG

San Francisco, California
christopherbettig.com
mcdermottmanagement.com

I graduated from college and needed a change. California was 3,000 miles away from anyone I knew, and it offered a completely new world, different from the East Coast cities I had lived in previously. I've been here for twelve years now; it's my home. I can't imagine living anywhere else.

Some of the advantages of working in California are: space & opportunities. The amount of space available compared to NYC is unreal, and Los Angeles, specifically, is the center of so many creative industries that there are endless opportunities available that I had never thought possible.

The environment, the vastly changing landscapes in such a small area, having the beach, the mountains, the desert & forests all within two hours of each other, as well as the architecture of California, which also changes just as rapidly from house to house, are definite influences. It is so inspiring to see so much variety on a constant daily basis, which is completely the opposite of the environments and cities where I grew up.

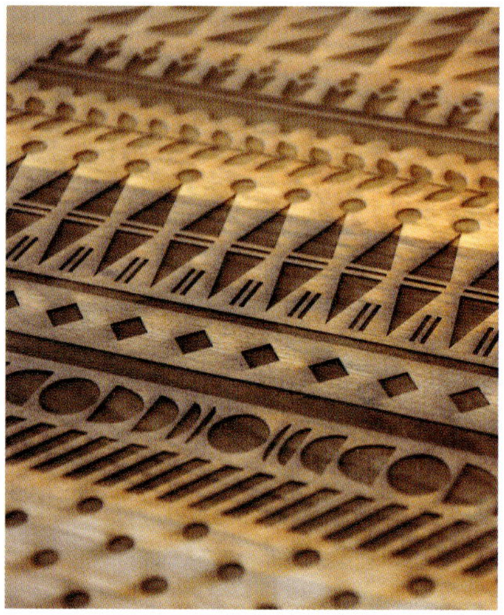

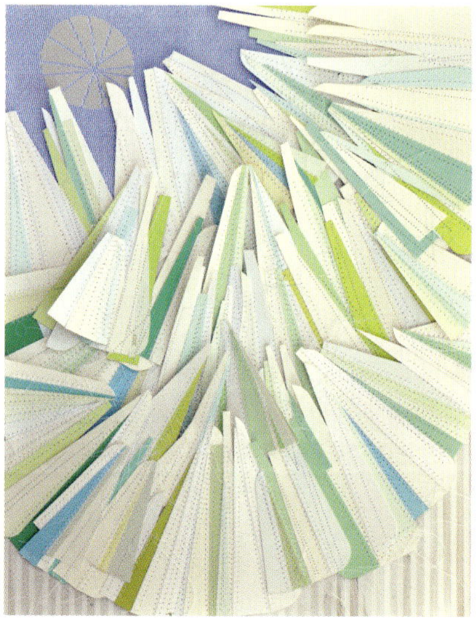

"Untitled" 2008
Laser-etched walnut (wood)
12 x 14 inches

"Untitled" 2010
Paper, acrylic, pen, paper, thread, screen print on wood
14 x 18 inches

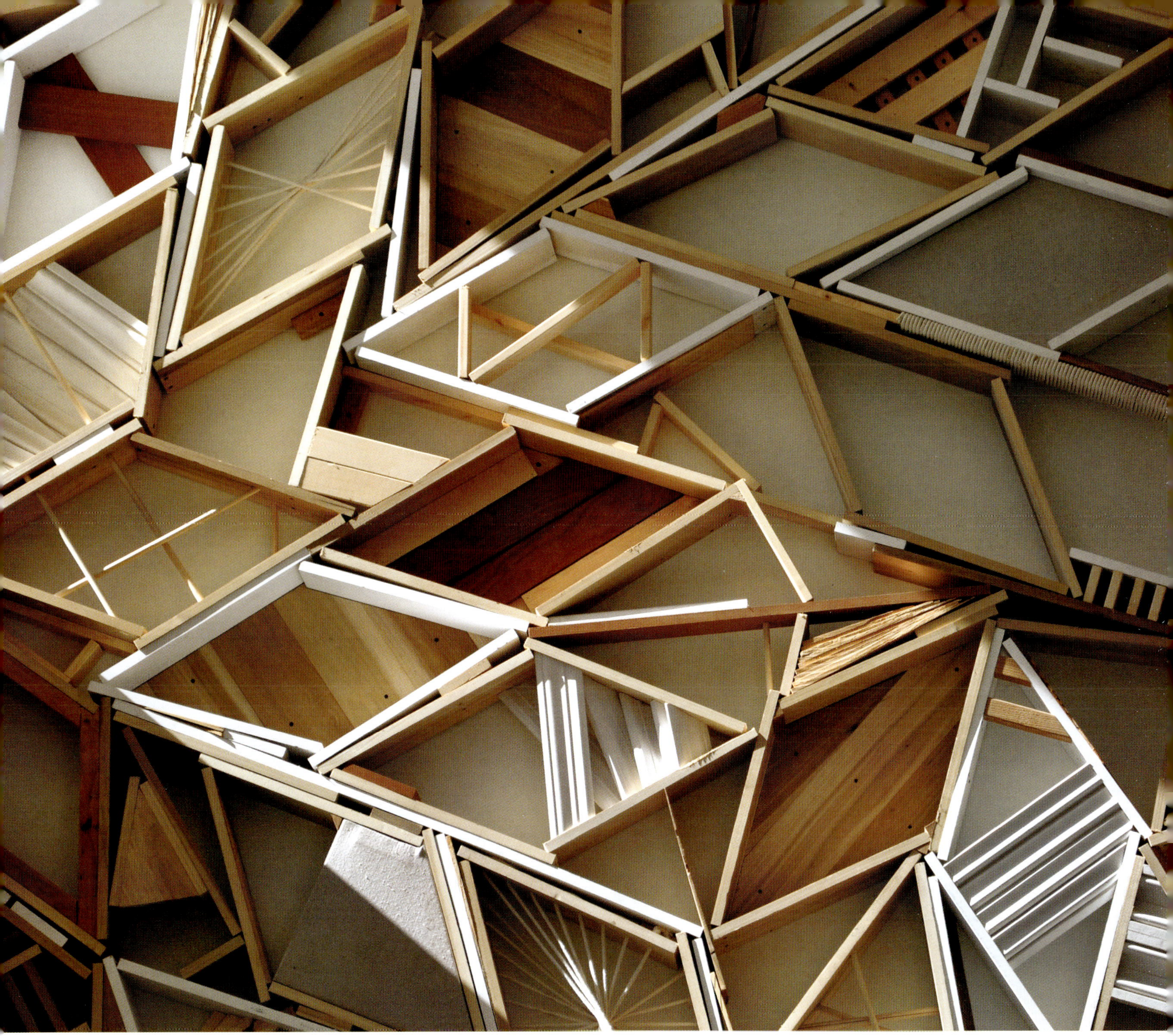

"J.Crew, New York City" 2012
Paper, acrylic, pen, paper, pine, cedar, oak,
mahogany, canvas, rope, molding
216 x 420 inches

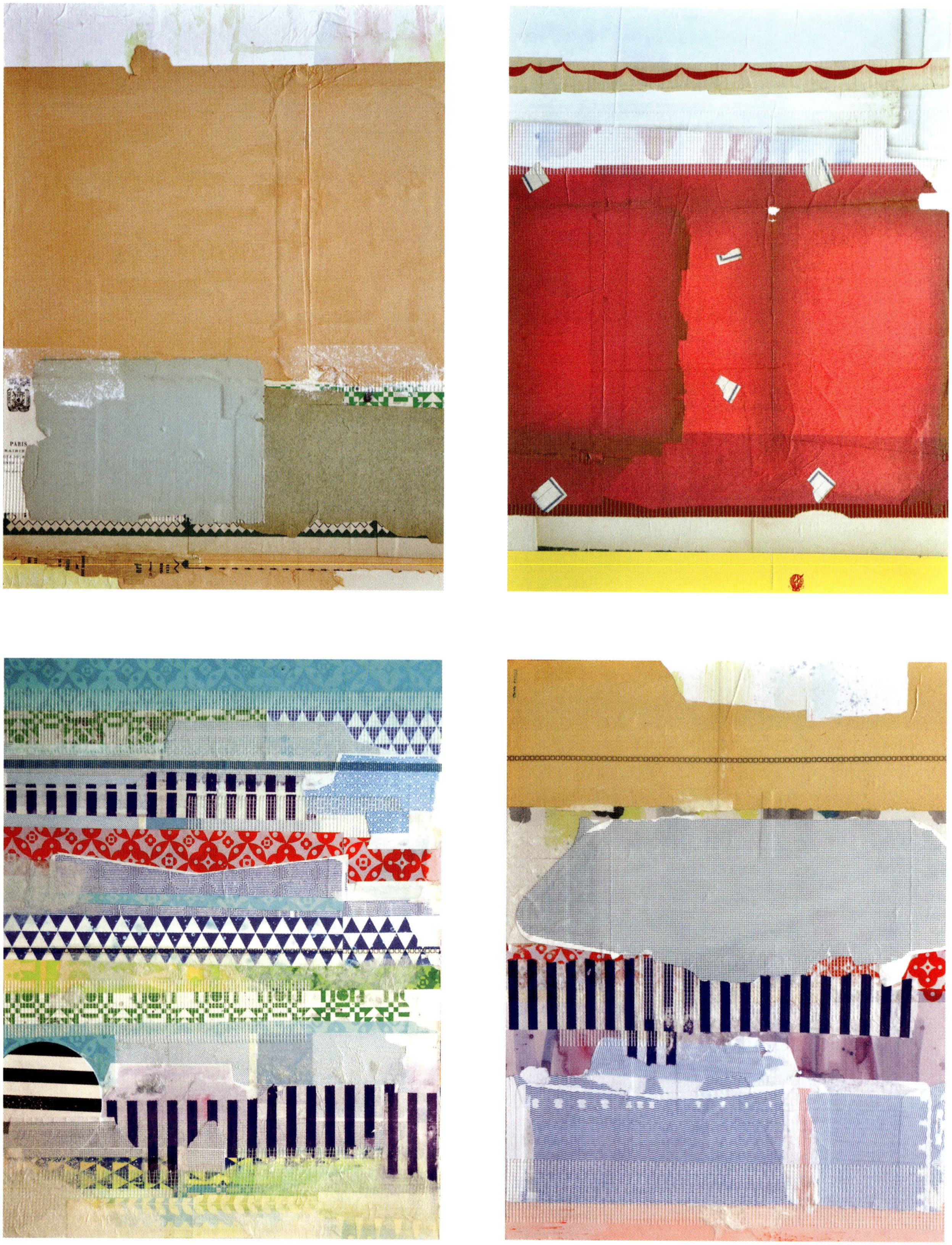

"Untitled (1-4)" 2012
Paper, screen print, water color on wood
14 x 18 inches

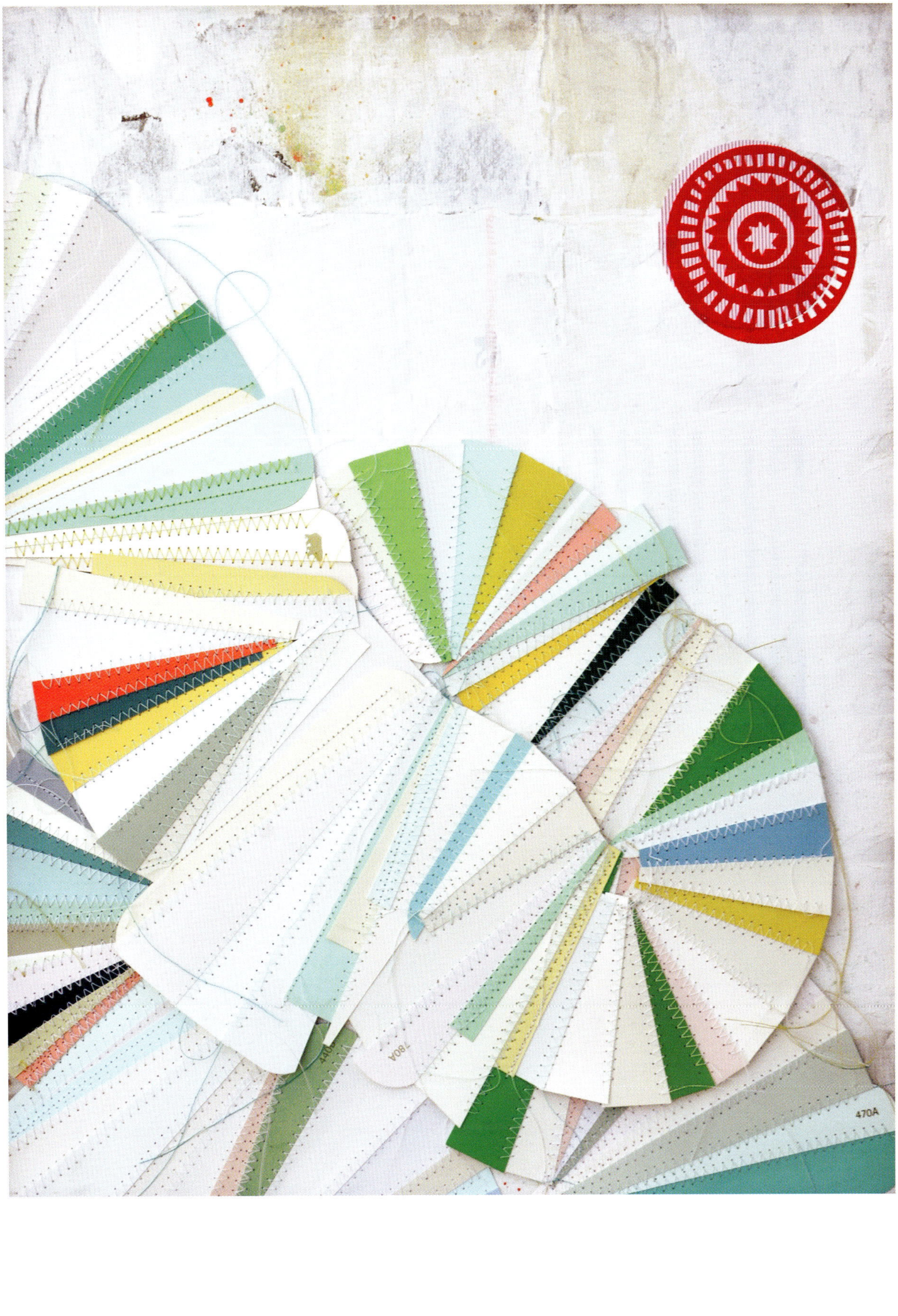

"Untitled" 2010
Paper, screen print, water
color on wood
14 x 18 inches

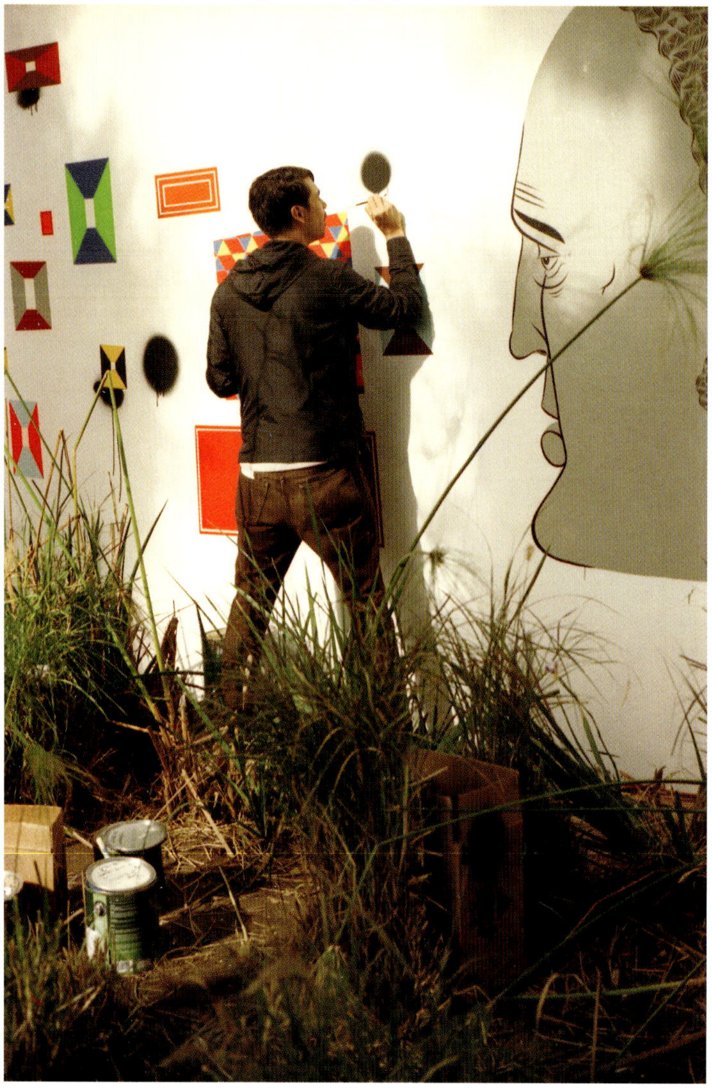

Photo by Casey Holland, 2010

BARRY MCGEE

San Francisco, California
Ratio 3, San Francisco

I was born in SF at a very young age, which was my first advantage. San Francisco and its colorful inhabitants inform my work and my mind-set. It's hard not to pay attention to the rich surroundings we have here in the Bay Area.

There are many great things about living and working in California. I like that it is the end of the line. ... It's as far west as you can go. The climate is fairly neutral: anytime you step outdoors it is usually warm, sunny, and inviting. I like working on pieces outdoors. There are no disadvantages other than everyone is crazy here.

Perhaps the lighting has become a part of my concepts and process. The landscape is naturally sun-drenched, combined with a morning and evening sea layer makes for fascinating filtered lighting. It's very rare to see a true black color in nature here.

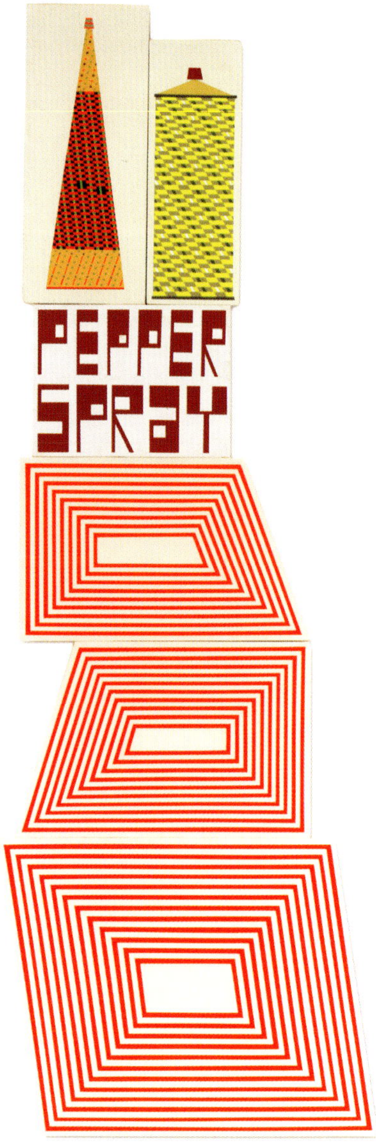

"Untitled" 2011
Paint on panel, 6 elements
90 x 39 inches

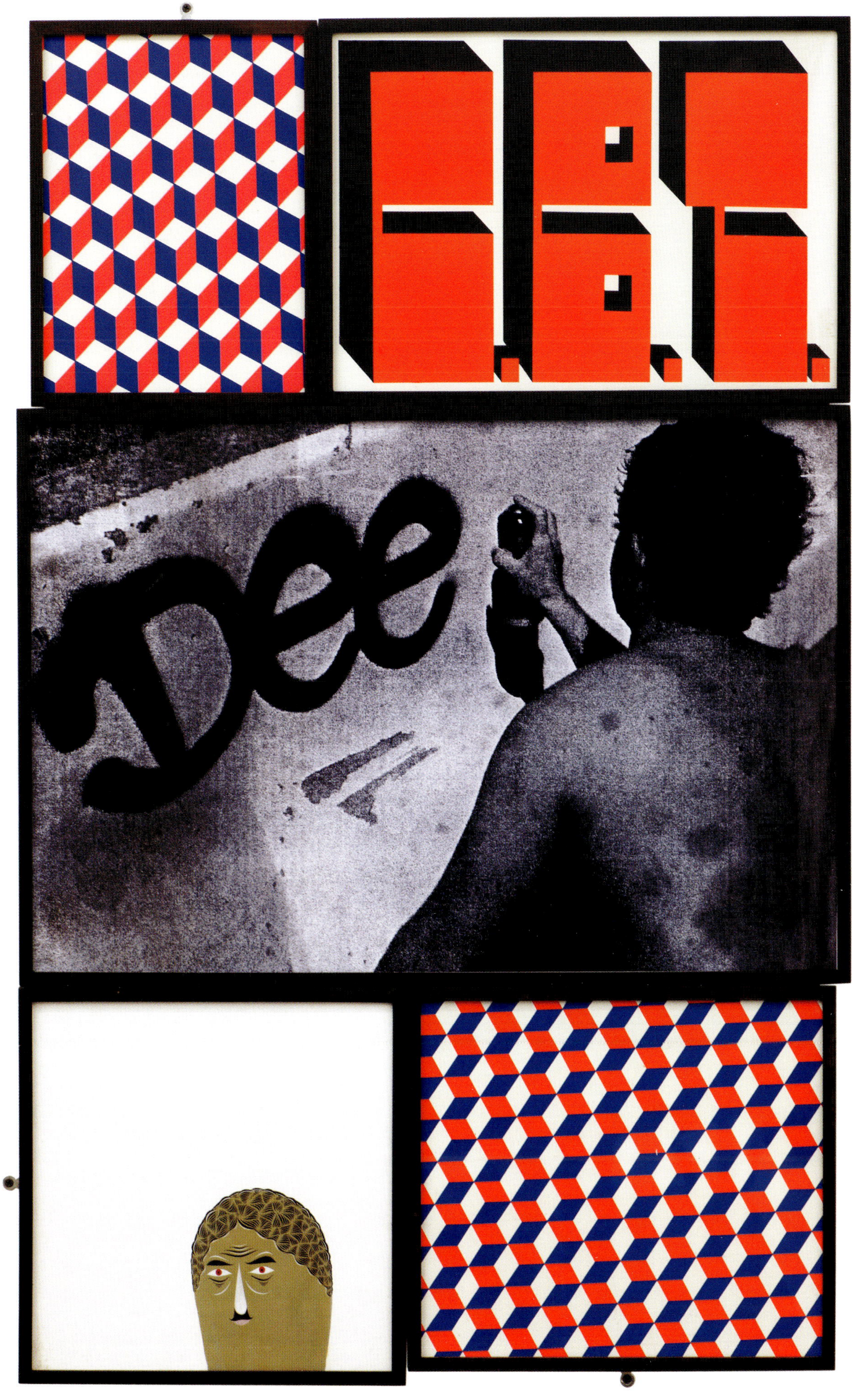

"Untitled" 2011
Mixed media, 5 elements
48 x 30.5 inches

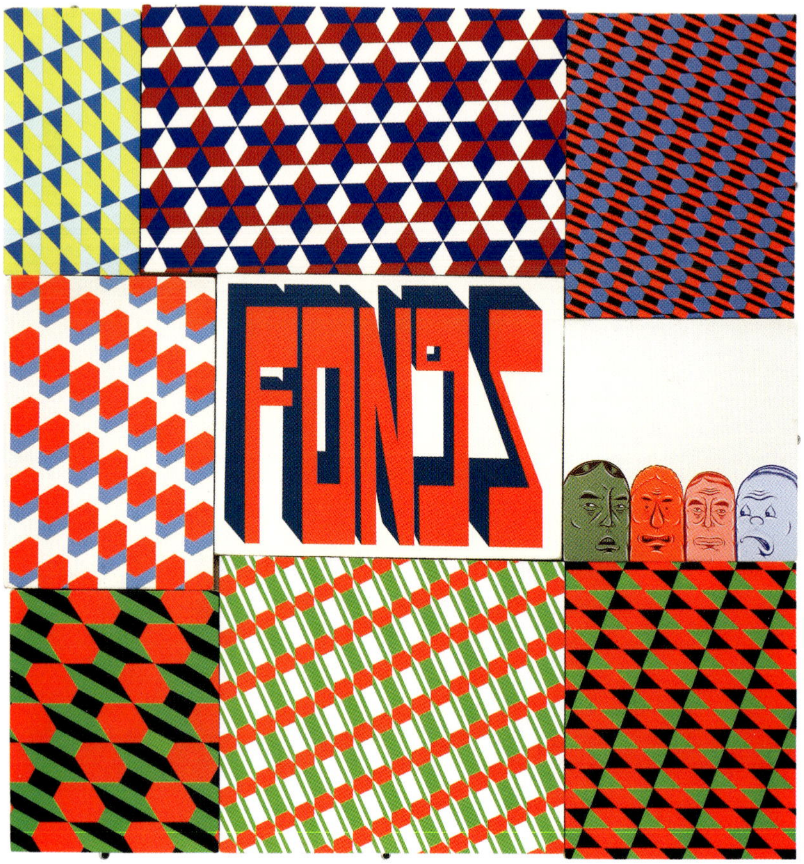

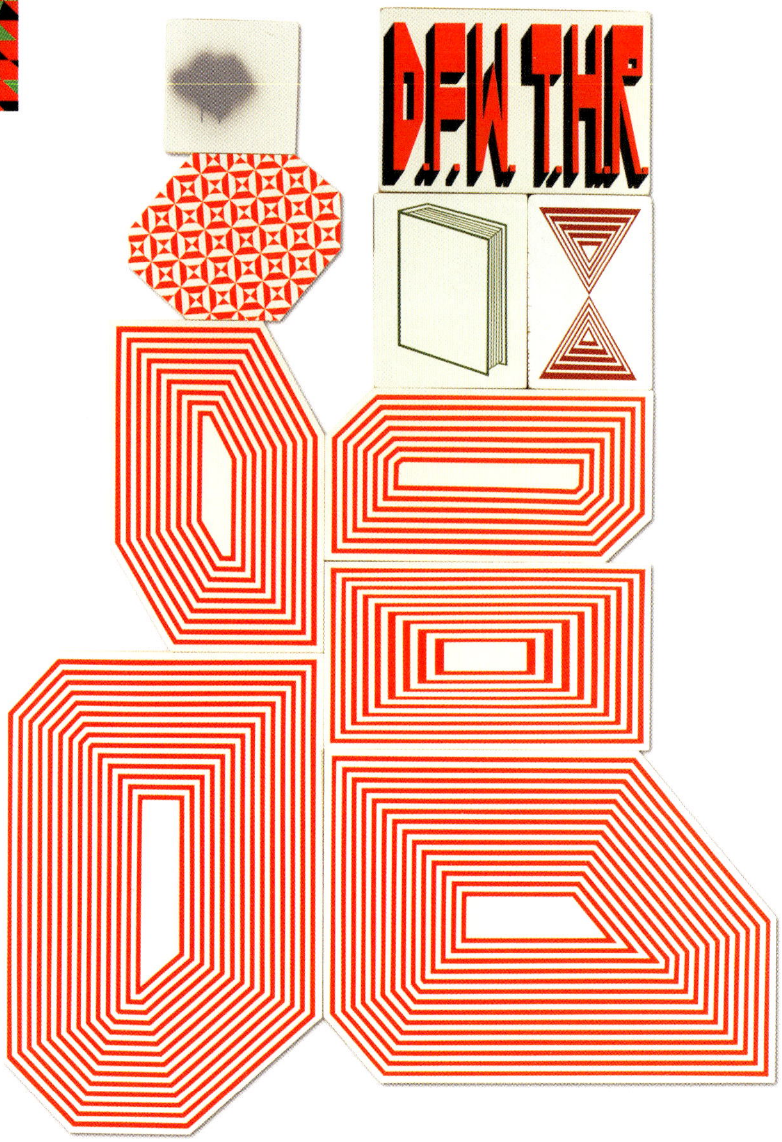

"Untitled" 2011
Acrylic on wood panel, 9 elements
41.5 x 40 inches

"Untitled" 2011
Paint on panel, 10 elements
77 x 57.5 inches

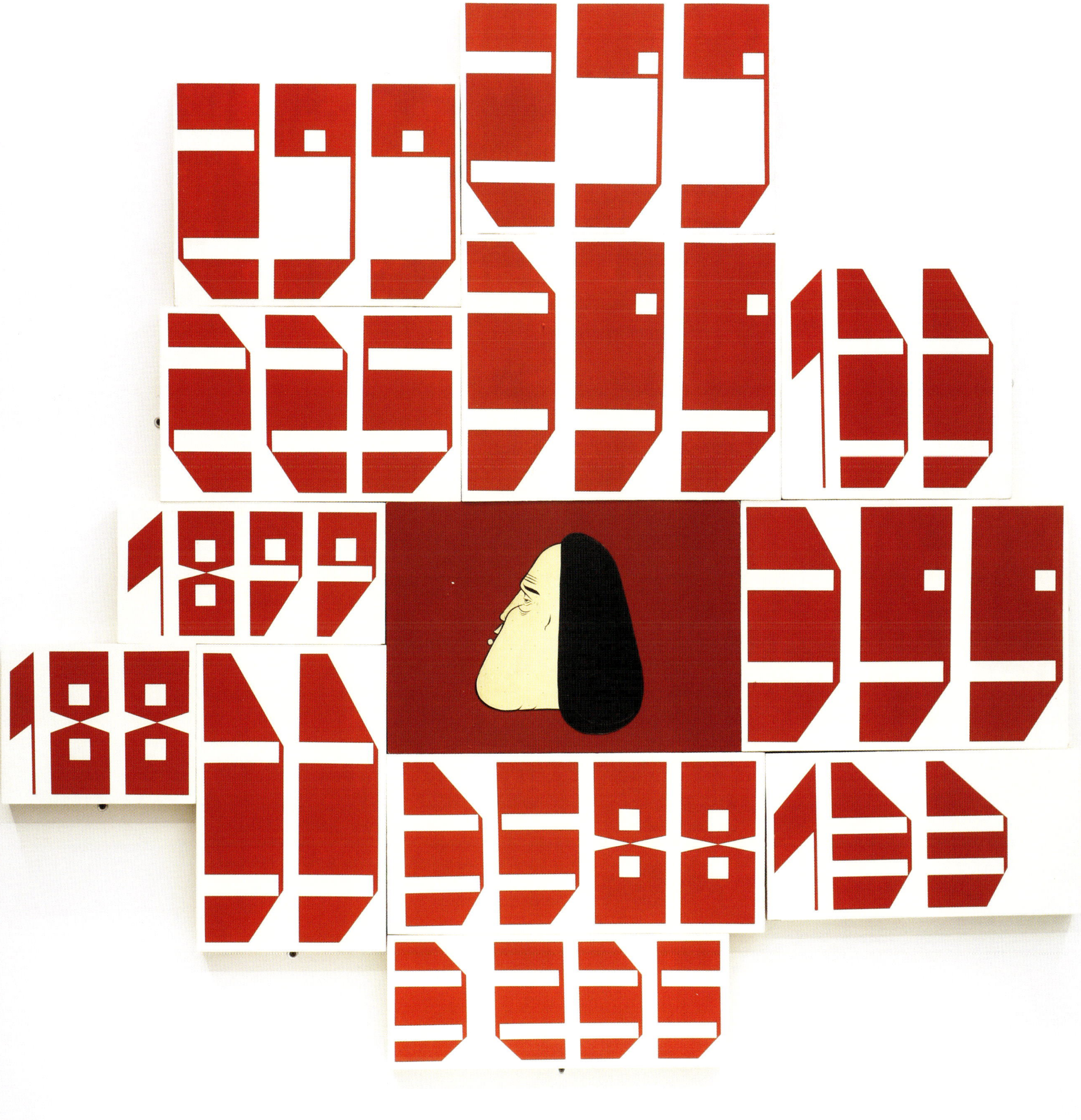

"Untitled" 2011
Paint on panel, 13 elements
51.5 x 53.5 inches

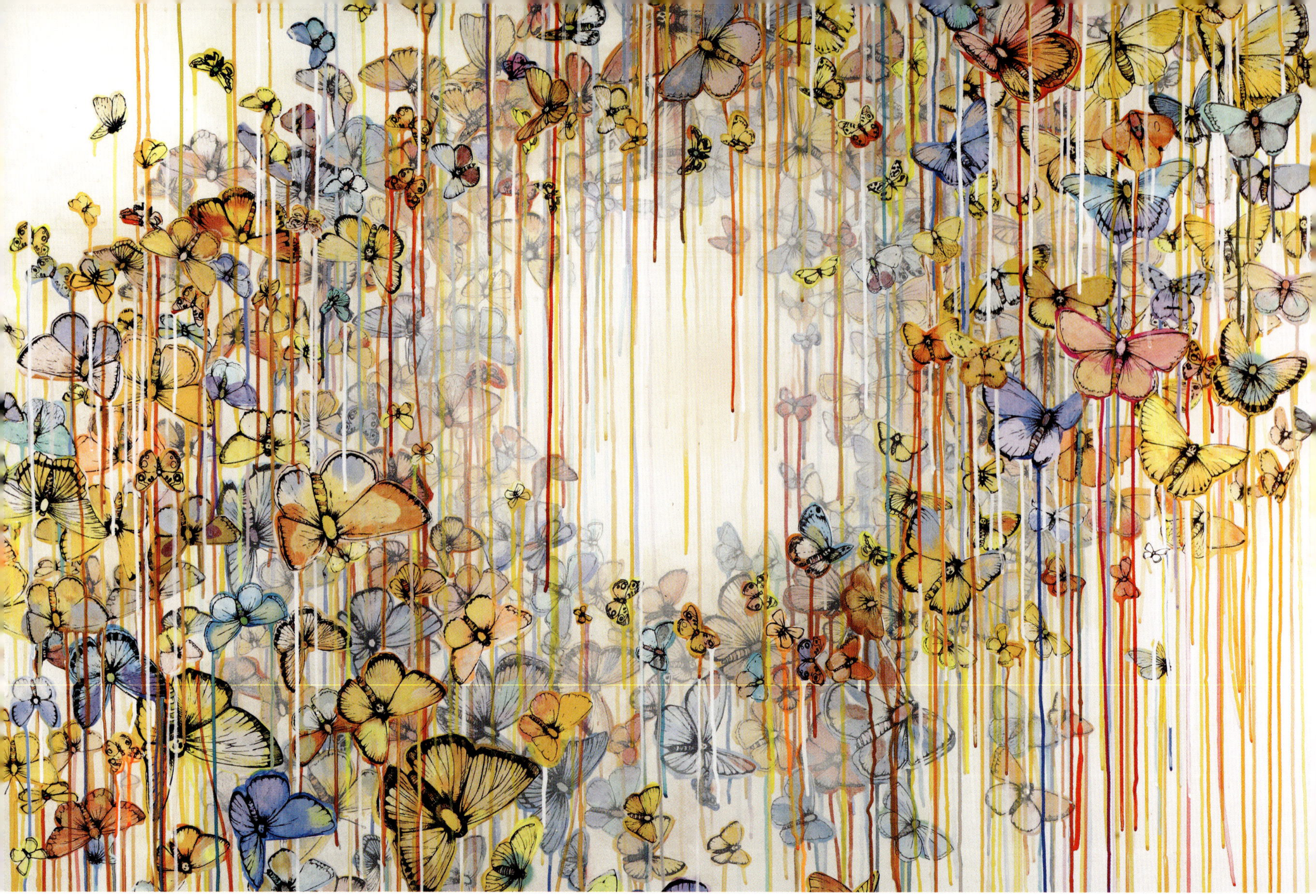

SHELLEY LEOPOLD

Los Angeles, California

Contemporary art in California, Los Angeles in particular, is a complicated mix of personalities and methods—old and new, aerosol and acrylic, performance versus the written word. LA's canvas is nontraditional and accepting of all mediums. Whether that freedom is defined by space, emotion, or influence is up to either the artist or the audience. Many artists find their way to California from somewhere else: the other side of the country, or the world, perhaps. However, the concepts and images created here become indelibly woven into the landscape.

It's usually a beautiful day in LA. The everyday saturation of the sun and the color of the sky have inspired generations of film directors, painters, even architects. It is no accident that our spectacular sky blue is the perfect backdrop for the crisp lines of Richard Neutra's buildings that are designed with glass walls to invite in the light. You'll notice the light in one of Dan Monick's photographs as he catches the first sun flare of the day reflecting off a surface of skin or metal. Or sparkling at dusk as it sets behind a viaduct marked by a faded Retna call out. This is the land where dreams are made, splashed across a Pantone sky, and punctuated by the sway of rustling palm trees.

Current contemporary Californian art may have been born from countercultures not experienced anywhere else

Sage Vaughn
"Ring Cycle (Rhinehold)" 2011
Oil, acrylic, ink, and vellum on canvas
60 x 60 inches

in the world. Form following function as a skateboard graphic, Mickey Dora surfboard, hot rod, a Chris Duncan fanzine or MFG show flyer. Maybe it's a mundane short film of a friend shooting a friend in the arm as a war protest piece (Shoot, Chris Burden 1971). Anyone can be an artist/ skater/surfer/protester/tagger. While doing it yourself and calling it art is not a uniquely Californian ideal, here it may create different opportunities.

Art in California lives in the present while it glances back to a not-so-distant past. A Robert Williams ZAP Comics panel is just as relevant today as it was in 1972, when he made it. The clean lines of an Eames chair are just as beautiful today as they were in 1945 when the DCW (Dining Chair Wood) was designed. Los Angeles is a young city, and it takes chances. It makes space for new ideas. It has a culture that will show up to an art opening simply because it's happening.

Contemporary art is undefined. Contemporary art is marketed. That's what we love about it. That's what we despise about it. Academics brand it post modernism. We might call it accessible.

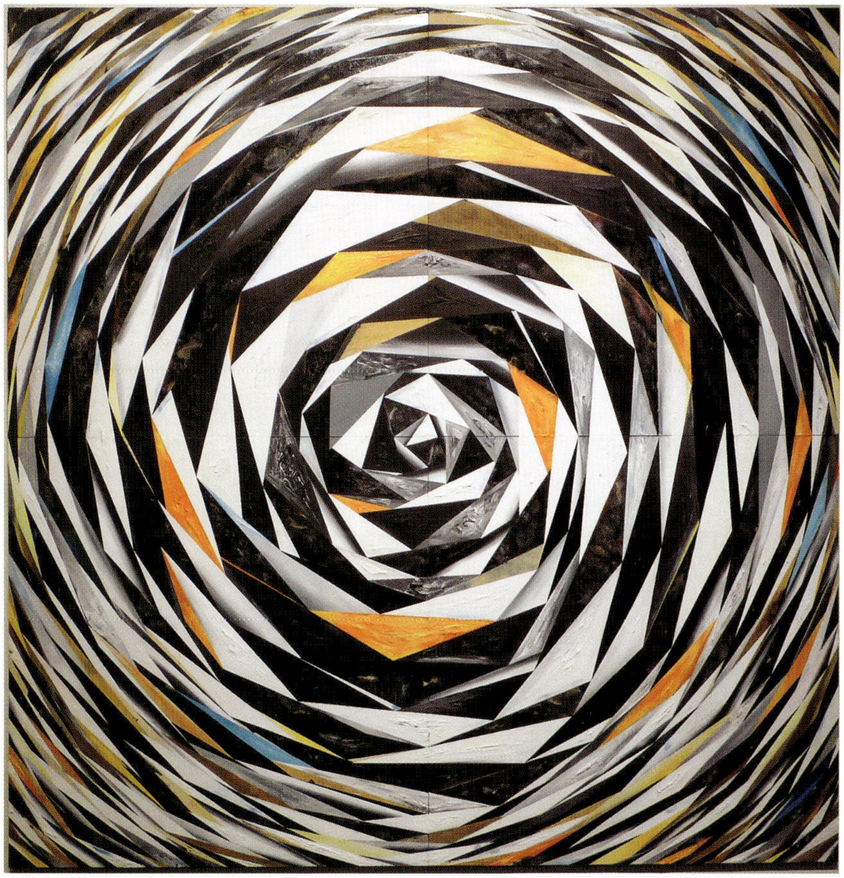

Chris Duncan
"Painting" 2012
Mixed media on wood panel
168 x 168 inches

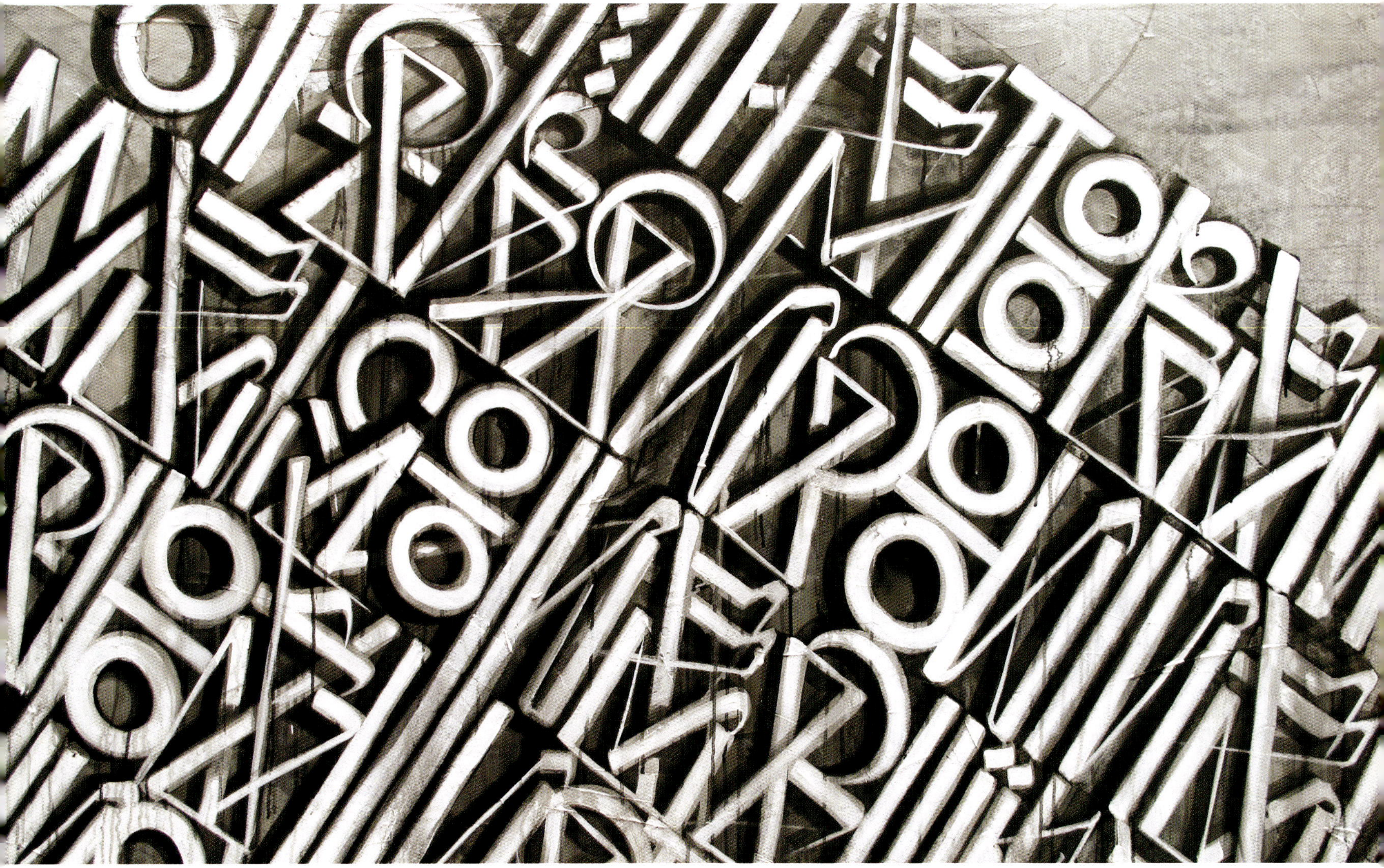

RETNA
"The Torment" 2010
Oil and acrylic canvas
72 x 48 inches

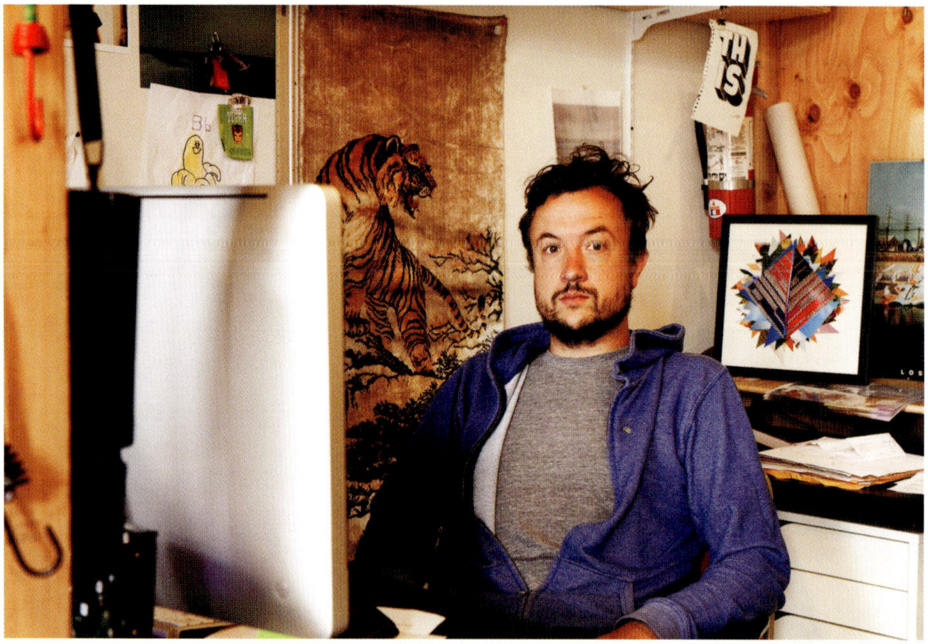

Self portrait, 2012

AARON FARLEY

Los Angeles, California
aaronfarley.com
mcdermonttmanagement.com
THIS los angeles

I came to LA the week before the tech bubble burst to work for a website (laughs). My friend Travis, who lived down here, told me, 'If you are going to be a photographer, you have to move to either LA or NY.' At that time I was in Portland, OR, during a long rainy spring and decided that LA sounded really nice, and seemed like the place I was supposed to be for awhile. That was in 2000.

Now I really can't imagine living anywhere else. The weather is beautiful, my wife, and kids, and I live in Eagle Rock—which is a little neighborhood where we can walk to everything—30 minutes from the beach, 30 minutes from the mountains, 45 minutes to the desert. It's great. And people here seem like they love to get out and do things. I think it's all the sunshine.

There is a lot going on in LA, and it seems like people like being busy, hustling, and coming up with new ideas and things to work on. People move here who are motivated to do something, so the city always seems to be changing, plus you can find anything you need here.

There is an openness to new ideas here. These works are not real photographs of real things. The original photographs are of water and clouds and these are photographs of those photographs, turned on their side, moved, reshot, reprinted, cut and folded, and reassembled to create a different scene, which still looks familiar.

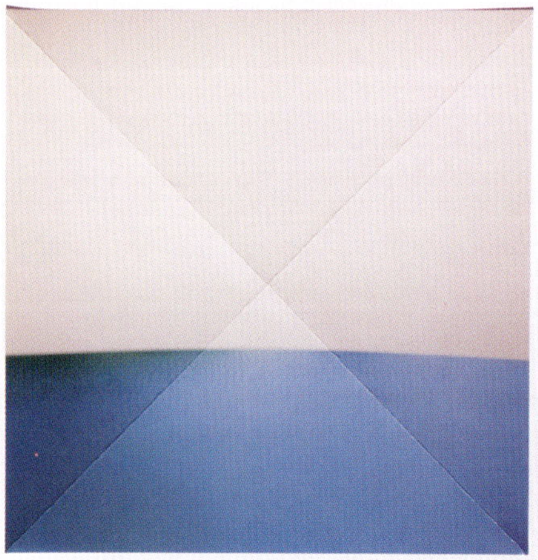

"Aqua cropped with X fold" 2012
8.5 x 8.5 archival inkjet folded two times in an *X* mou..ted on archival paper
11 x 14 inches

"Gold Clouds with 4 folds" 2012
Archival lightjet print
20 x 30 inches

"Blue cropped to square with vertical fold" 2012
8.5 x 8.5 archival inkjet folded vertically
Archival lightjet print
11 x 14 inches

"Blue clouds cropped and reassembled" 2012
4 archival inkjet prints reassembled and mounted on
archival paper
20 x 20 inches

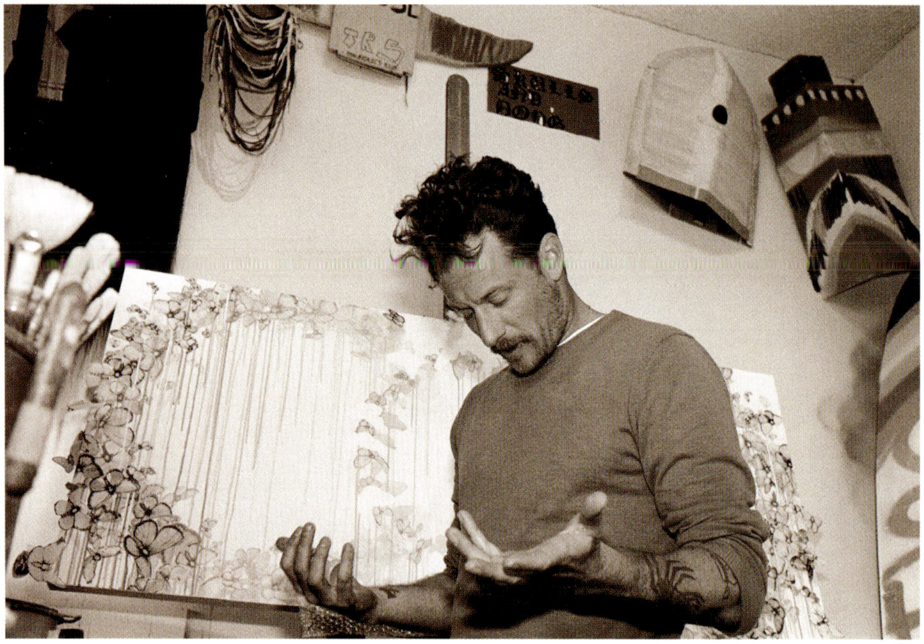

Photo by Amy Davis, 2011

SAGE VAUGHN

Los Angeles, California
sagevaughn.com
Lazarides, London
Galerie Bertrand and Gruner, Geneva
Fabien Fryns, Beijing

My folks moved to California from Oregon a few years after I was born. Living and working anywhere else: Life's hard; living in LA is easy.

The light in the sky and the sheer absurdity of the people here are a big inspiration. My work looks at the coastline between wilderness and society. I try to portray the overlapping edges of chaos and control within our environment and our lives. Like grass growing through a crack in the sidewalk, a bird landing on a telephone wire, or a coyote stealing your cat, the feral aspects of the outside are constantly encroaching upon our conceptions of the inside, putting into question the exact reach of our control.

With the Ring Cycle pieces, like the cover image, I used the opening musical arrangements of Wagner's "Ring Cycle" as a jumping off point. Quickly (and probably horribly) paraphrasing, the dwarf, Alberich, goes to the bottom of the River Rhine to steal the magic gold. He then forges a ring of power from the gold, thereby taking something from the natural world and creating something synthetic. In the piece, Ring Cycle "DawnLand", I've composed the swarm of butterflies into an unnatural and synthetic shape: taking what nature has provided and creating something more powerful.

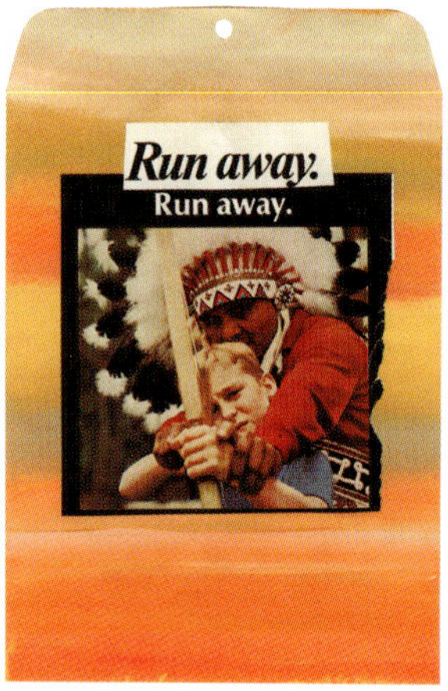

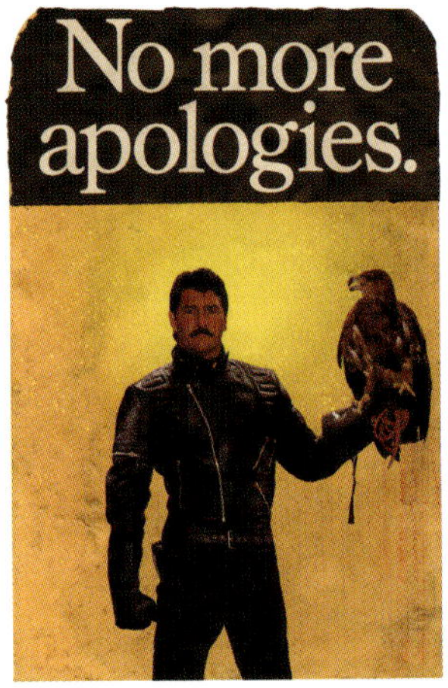

"Run Away" 2011
Mixed media
9 x 13 inches

"No More Apologies" 2011
Mixed media
9 x 12 inches

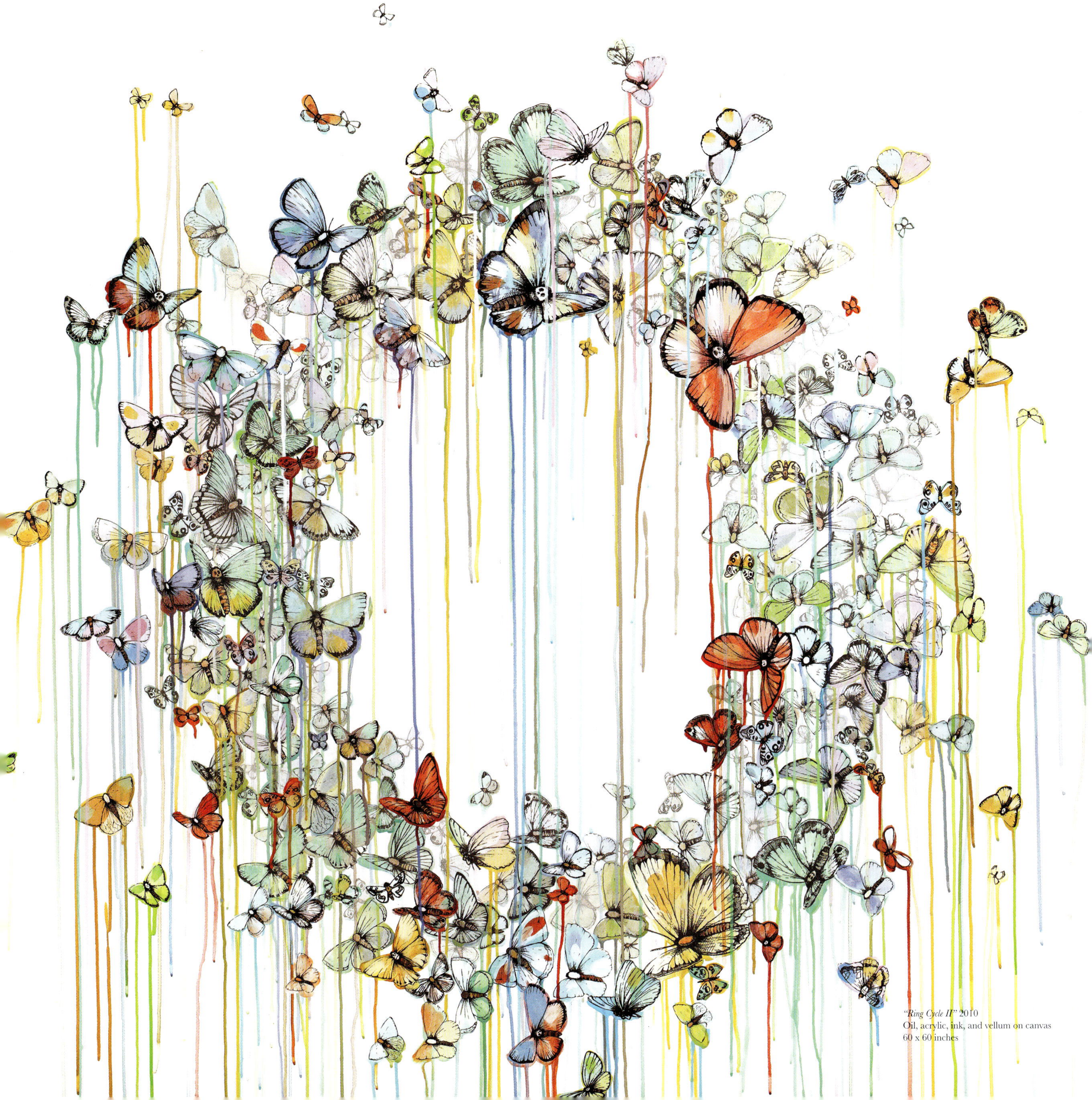

"Ring Cycle II" 2010
Oil, acrylic, ink, and vellum on canvas
60 x 60 inches

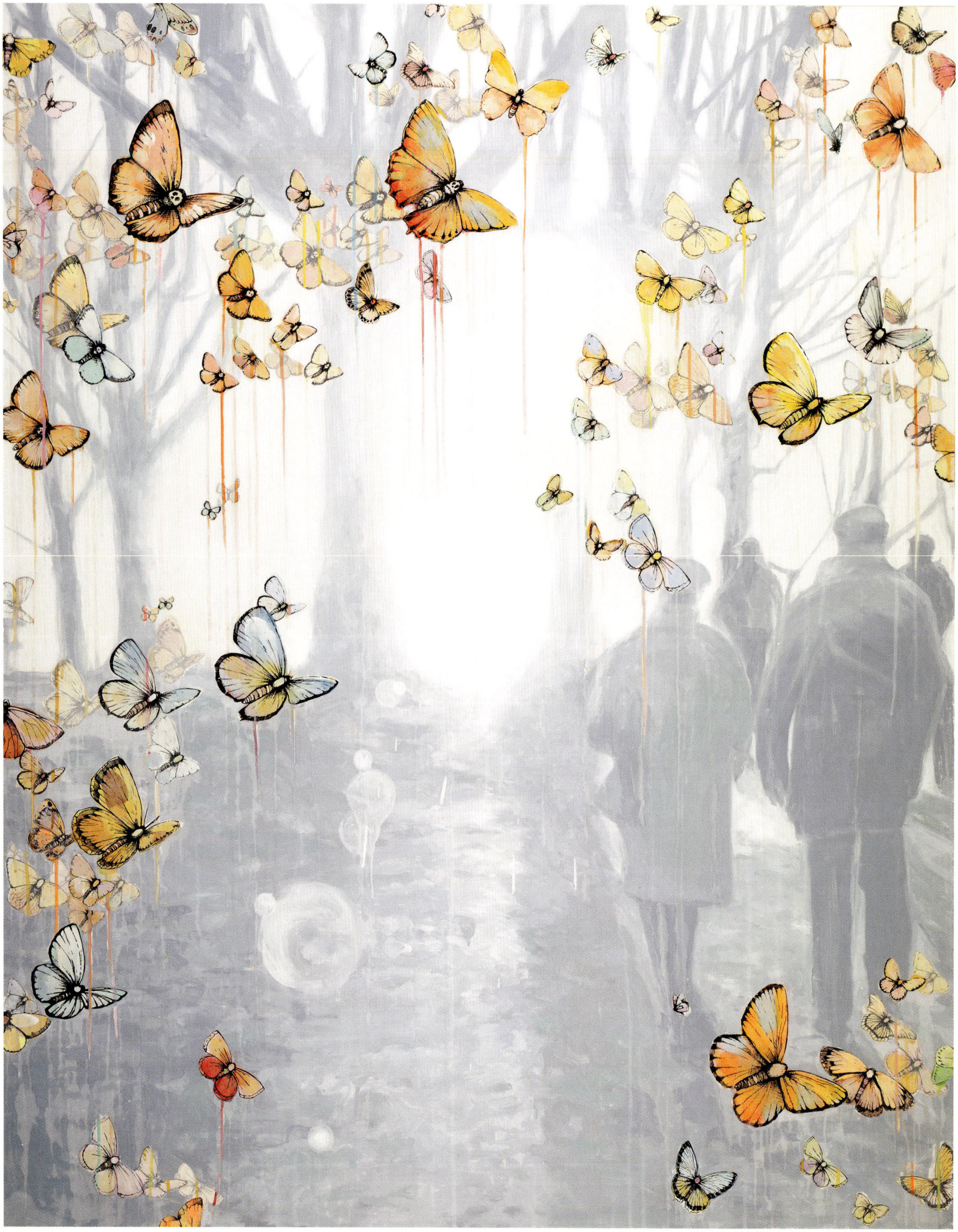

"You Will Miss Me When I'm Gone" 2010
Oil, acrylic, ink, and vellum on canvas
48 x 60 inches

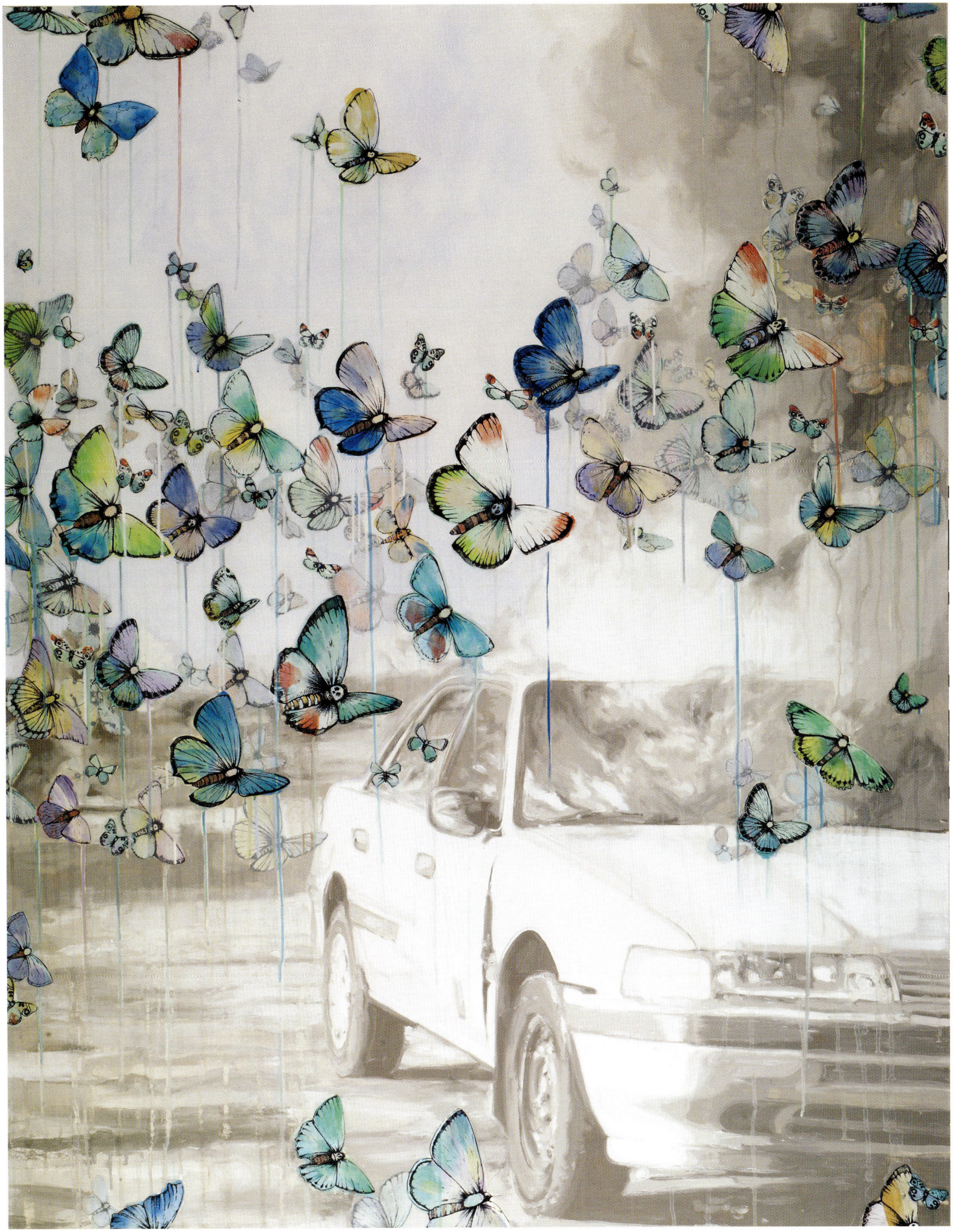

"You Can't Take It With You" 2011
Oil, acrylic, ink, and vellum on canvas
48 x 60 inches

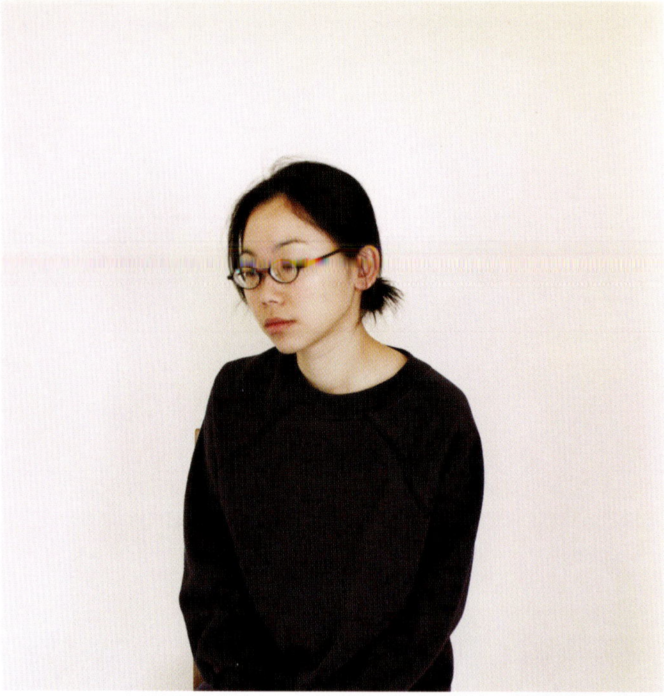

Self portrait, 2012

YE RIN MOK

Los Angeles, California
yerinmok.com

My family immigrated to California from South Korea when I was twelve years old.

The advantages of living in California are being near the ocean, the mountain, and the desert that's just a few hours drive away. The disadvantage for me would be not having four defined seasons.

I enjoy shooting outdoors in natural light, which California offers plenty of.

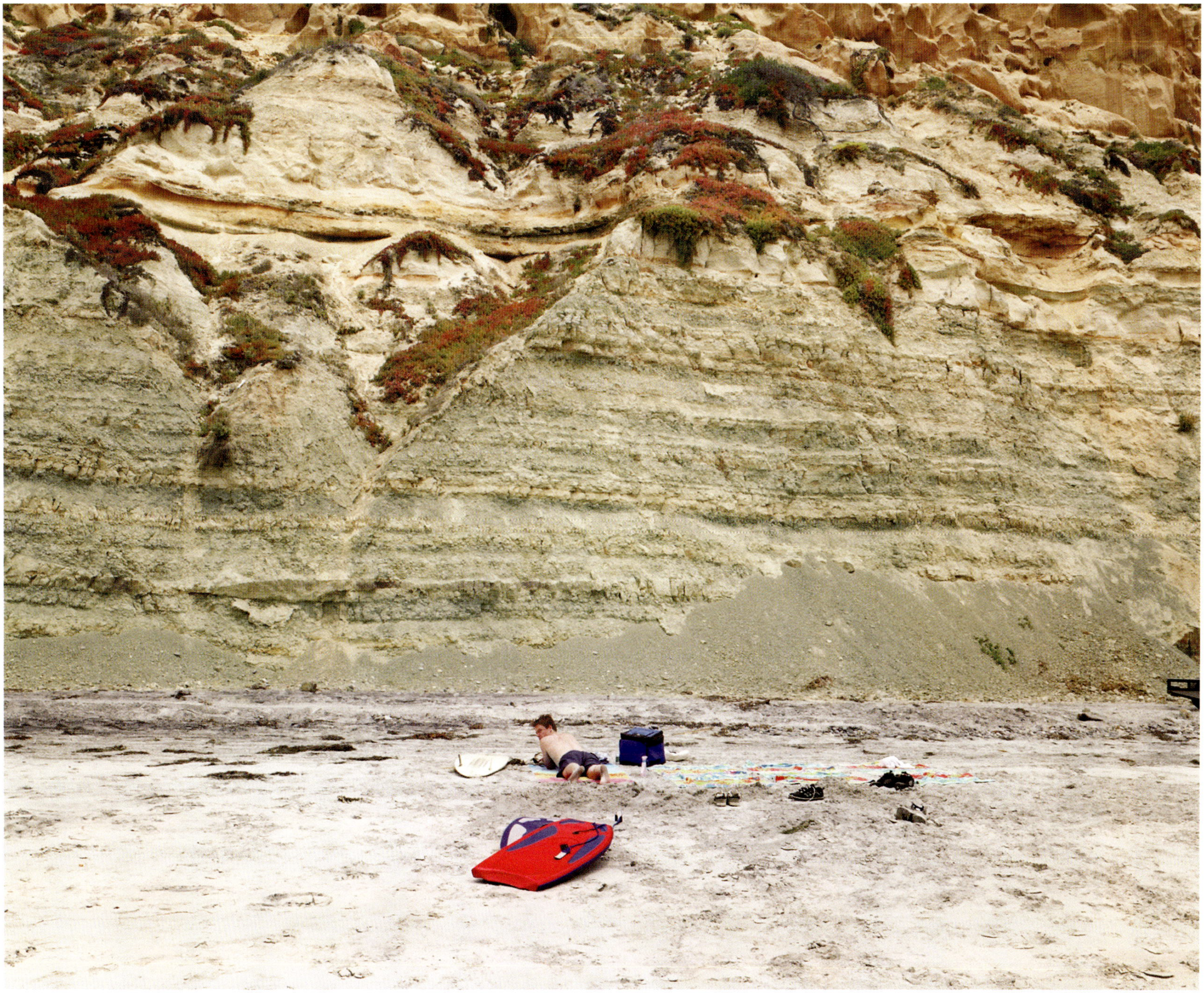

"Untitled 01" 2012
Digital photograph
Dimensions vary

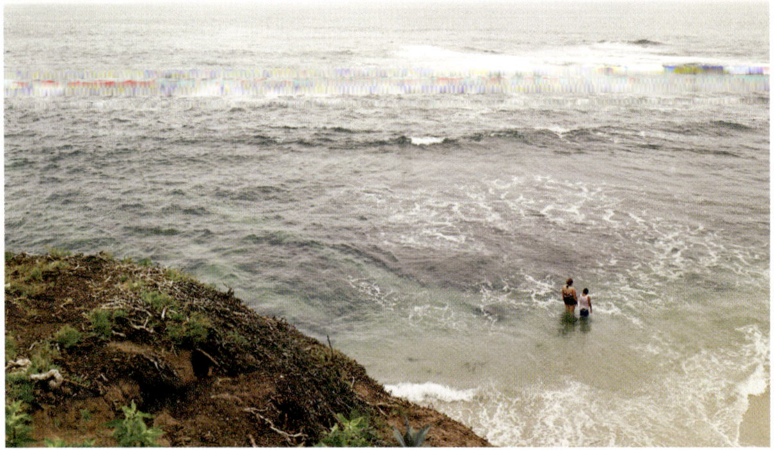

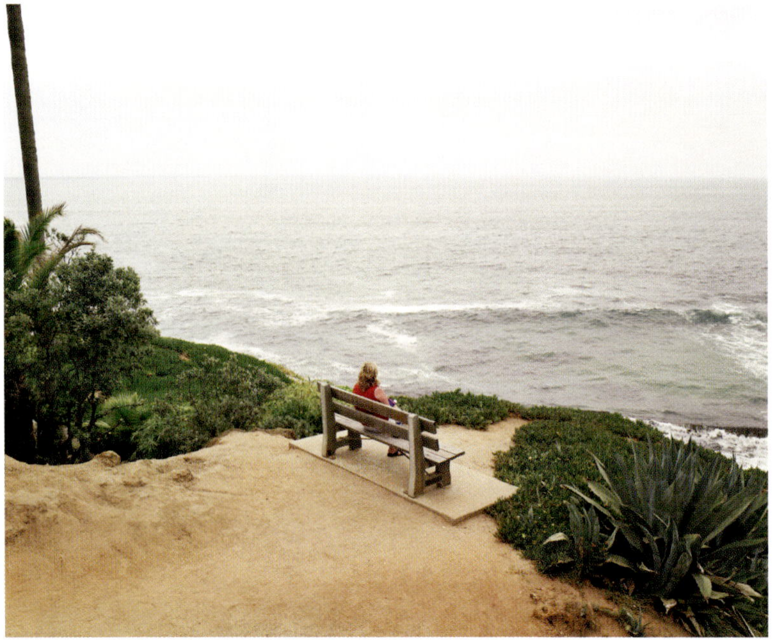

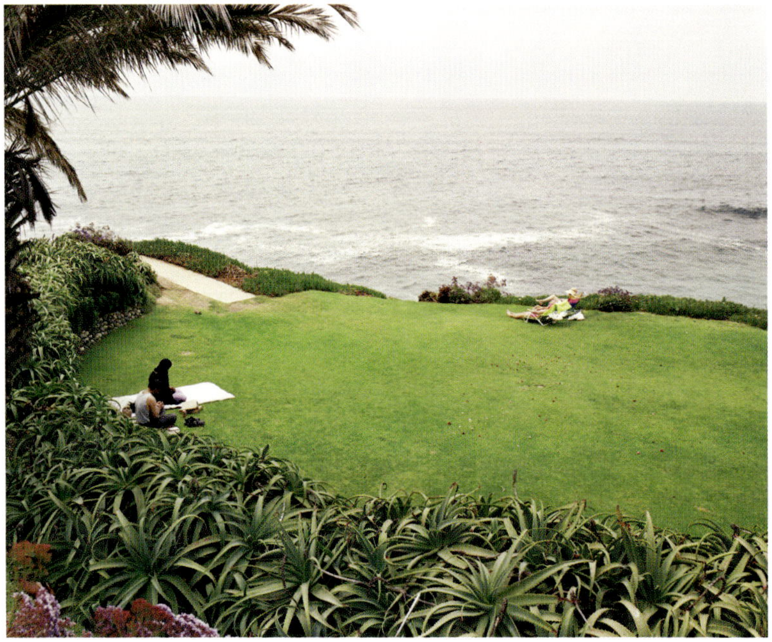

"Untitled 3,5,6" 2012
Digital photographs
Dimensions vary

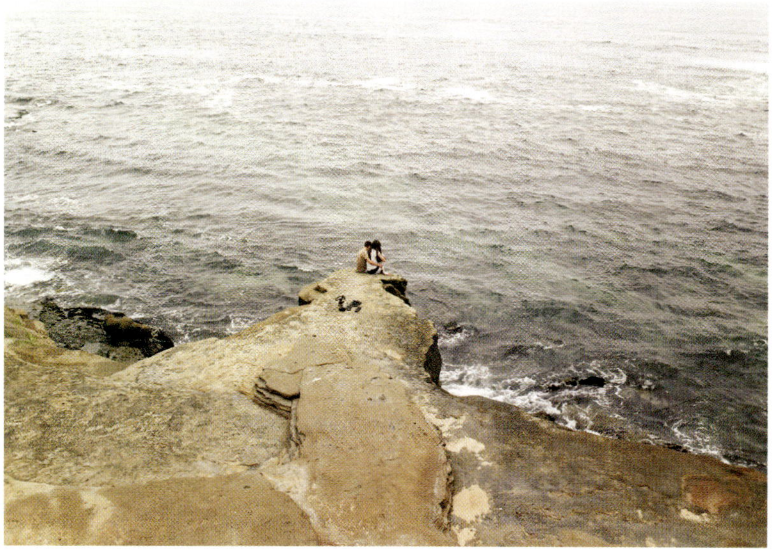

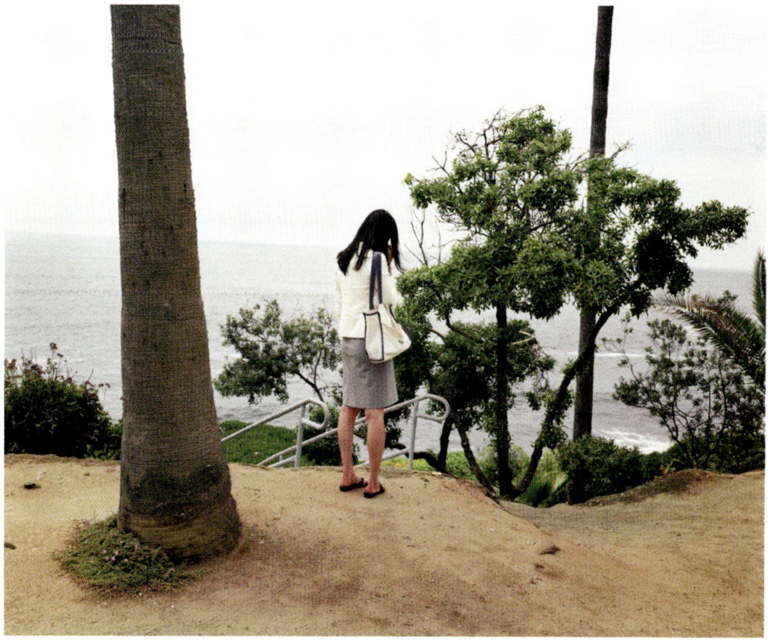

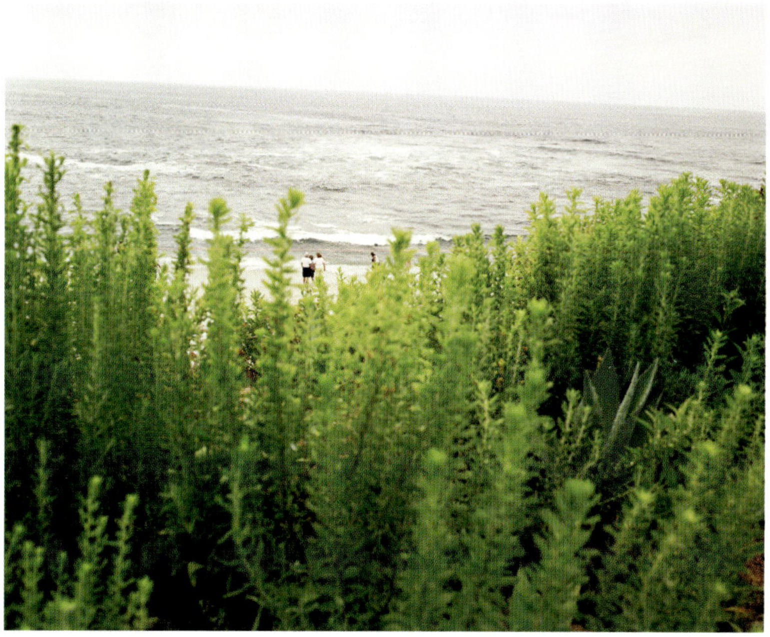

"Untitled 2,7,4" 2012
Digital photographs
Dimensions vary

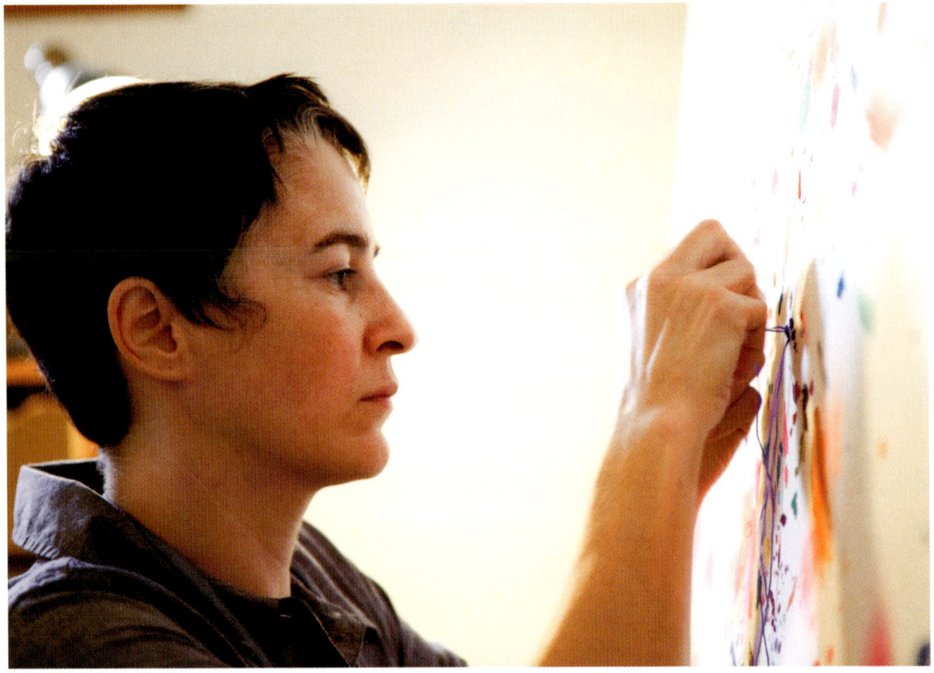

Photo by Aaron Farley, 2011

MEGAN WHITMARSH

Los Angeles, California
meganwhitmarsh.com

Both of my parents grew up in California. As a child I lived in California only briefly, but I visited it almost every year, and it felt like home. I moved 10 times during my childhood, and California felt familiar at least. After living in the Deep South, the Midwest, the East Coast, and the middle West, I guess it just felt right to move here. All my best memories from childhood seem to center on California: the smell of gardenias and jasmine on the night air in my grandmother's yard in Pasadena, shining sun and dusty roads in Grass Valley, picking blackberries and painting my other grandmother's horse fence white in Sacramento.

When I was a kid, California felt like Shangri-La and I was really jealous of my cousins who had grown up here. I thought it was like a fantasy to get to live here. It still is a kind of fantasy life for me, and I guess that is what keeps me here. I can see the drawbacks pretty clearly: smog, traffic, expense of living … and yet it still feels pretty Shangri-La to me. I get to smell gardenias, feel the sun, and pick blackberries.

I can only say what I see as advantages and disadvantages from my own experience as a working artist. I lived in New Orleans, Brooklyn, and Los Angeles as an adult. I guess the advantage it has in my mind over New York City is that you can have more studio time and space (requires less money to live, and space is cheaper). An added benefit for me was the quality of being left alone. New York felt too crowded for me both physically and psychologically, but for some artists this is a stimulant. I think it really depends on one's character.

I loved New Orleans, but it was difficult to make a living, and I sought a less predictable cultural context. New Orleans has an amazing cultural context but not as varied as New York or Los Angeles, which are in my mind the only two cities in the US that are too large and too diverse to be absorbed. A New Yorker once remarked that, although very different, Los Angeles had the same sense of mayhem that NY has, and I think this is exactly right. I think I like to be in a place I cannot define easily.

I am pretty happy here, and I think that influences my work. I take more risks and feel free to explore my creative impulses. I feel a sense of community here that is optimistic and generous, and this feels directly supportive of being an artist. I have a life that feels expansive and a process that feels open, and I think the weather, the diverse flora, and continual presence of nature all help to create that. California is a place of extremes and contrasts, and this oscillation between disparate things is very giving.

"Color Dance Bomb, and Color Dance Bomb(detail)" 2009
Embroidery thread, spray paint, and marker on fabric
36 x 36 inches

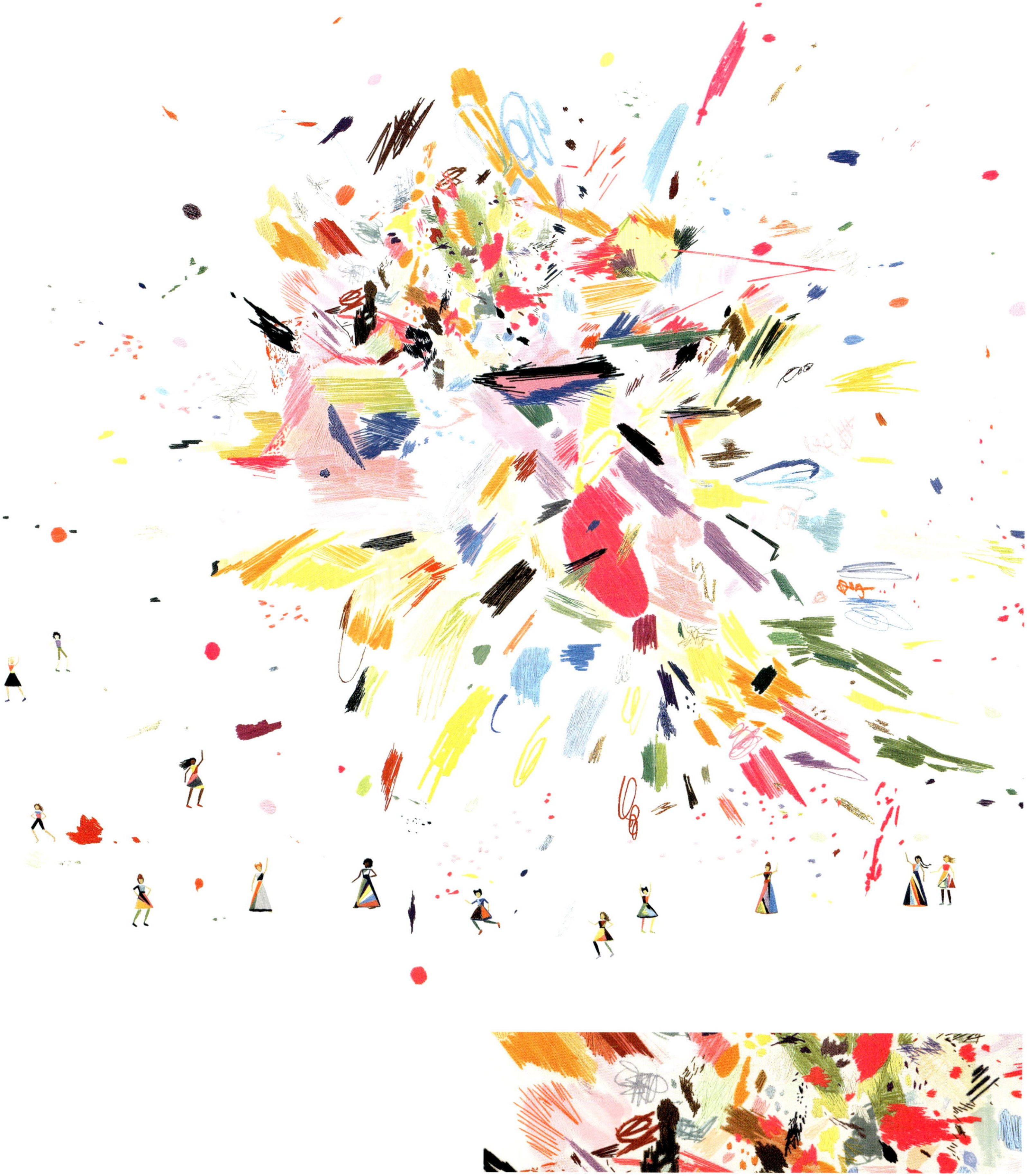

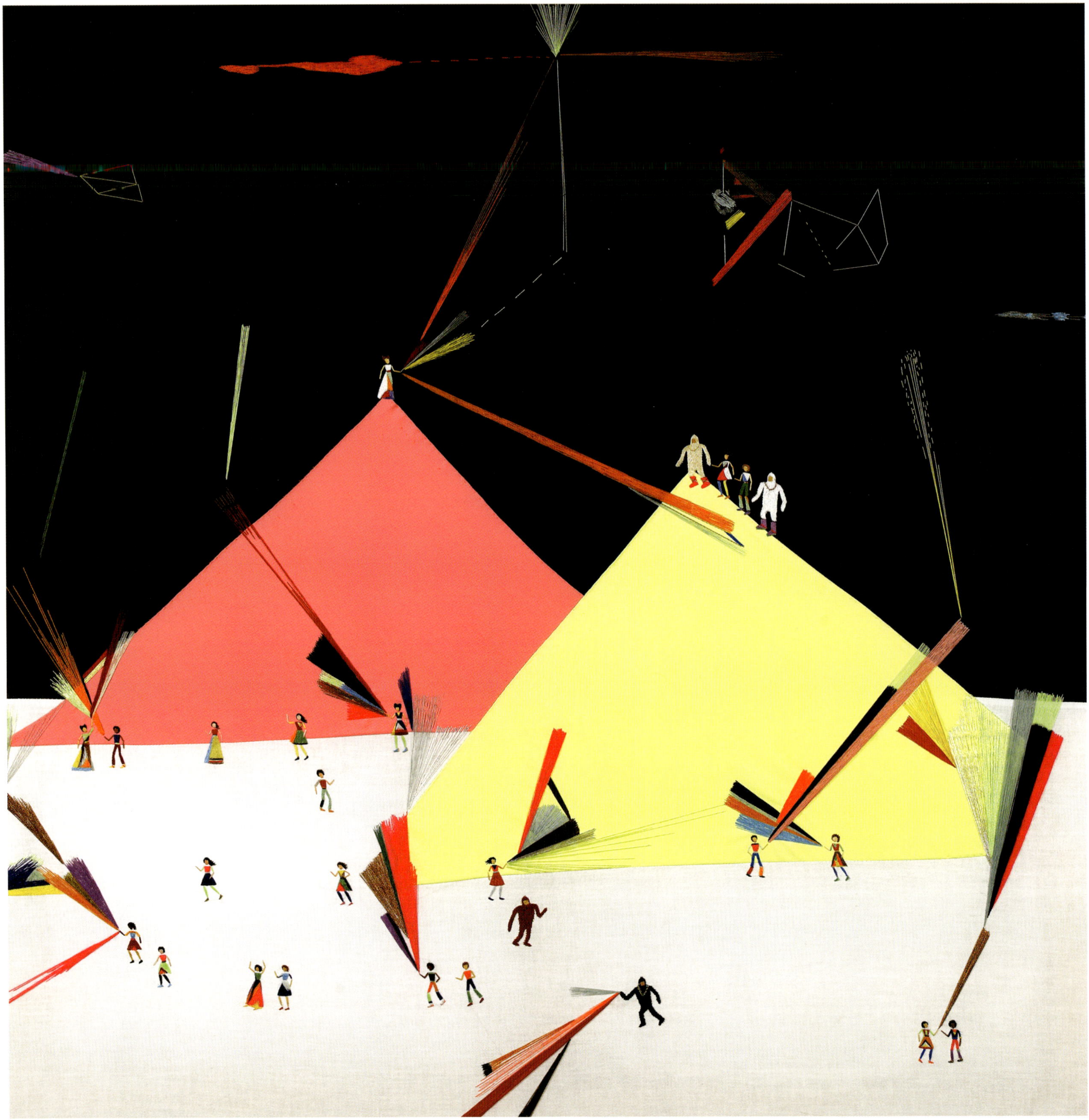

Opposite page:
"Shining Mountain" 2010
Embroidery thread, spray paint, and marker on fabric
70 x 55 inches

"Radiant Artifacts I (drawing)" 2010
Gouche, pencil, ink, and marker on paper
54 x 40 inches

"Laser Dance Wars" 2009
Embroidery thread on fabric
40 x 40 inches

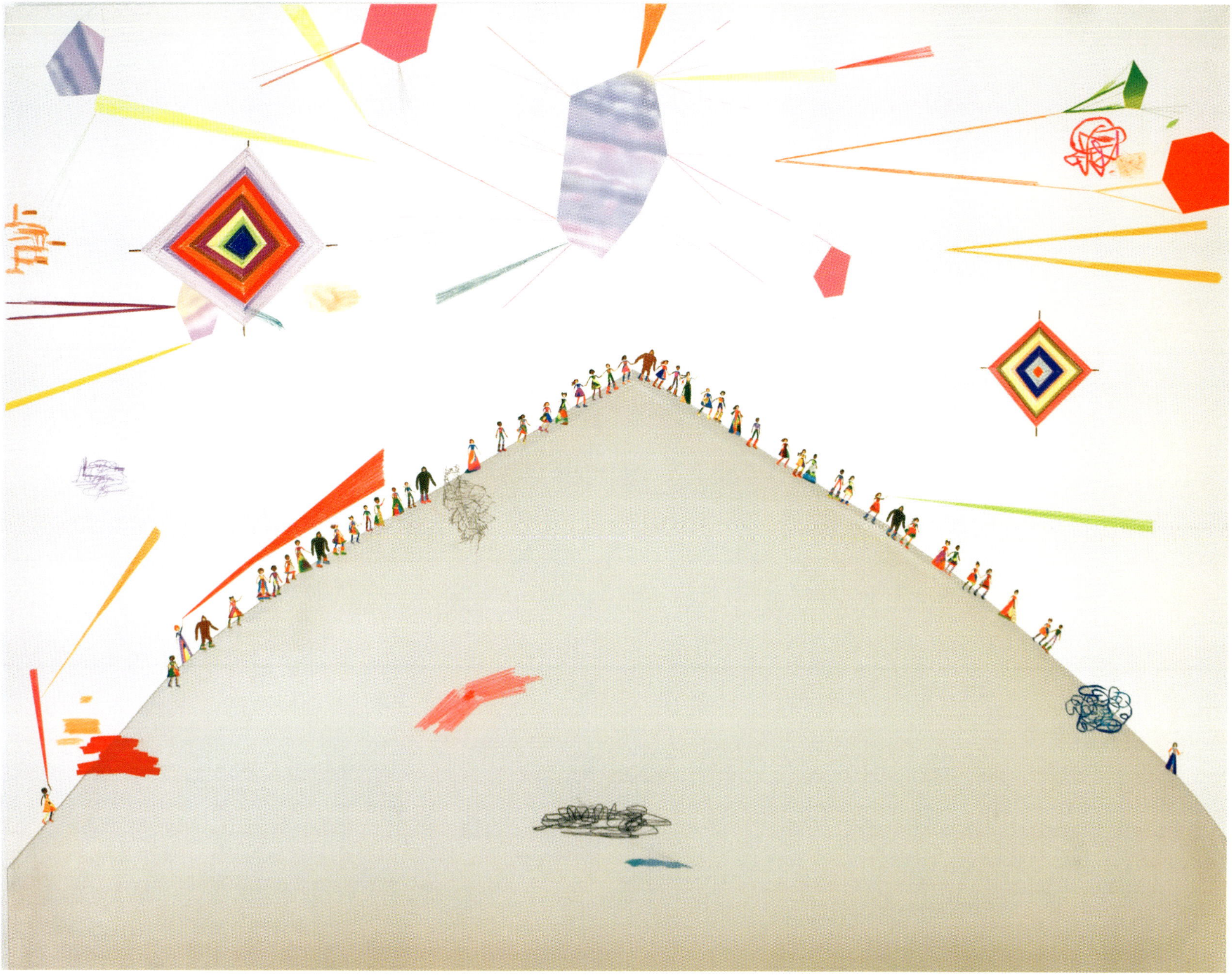

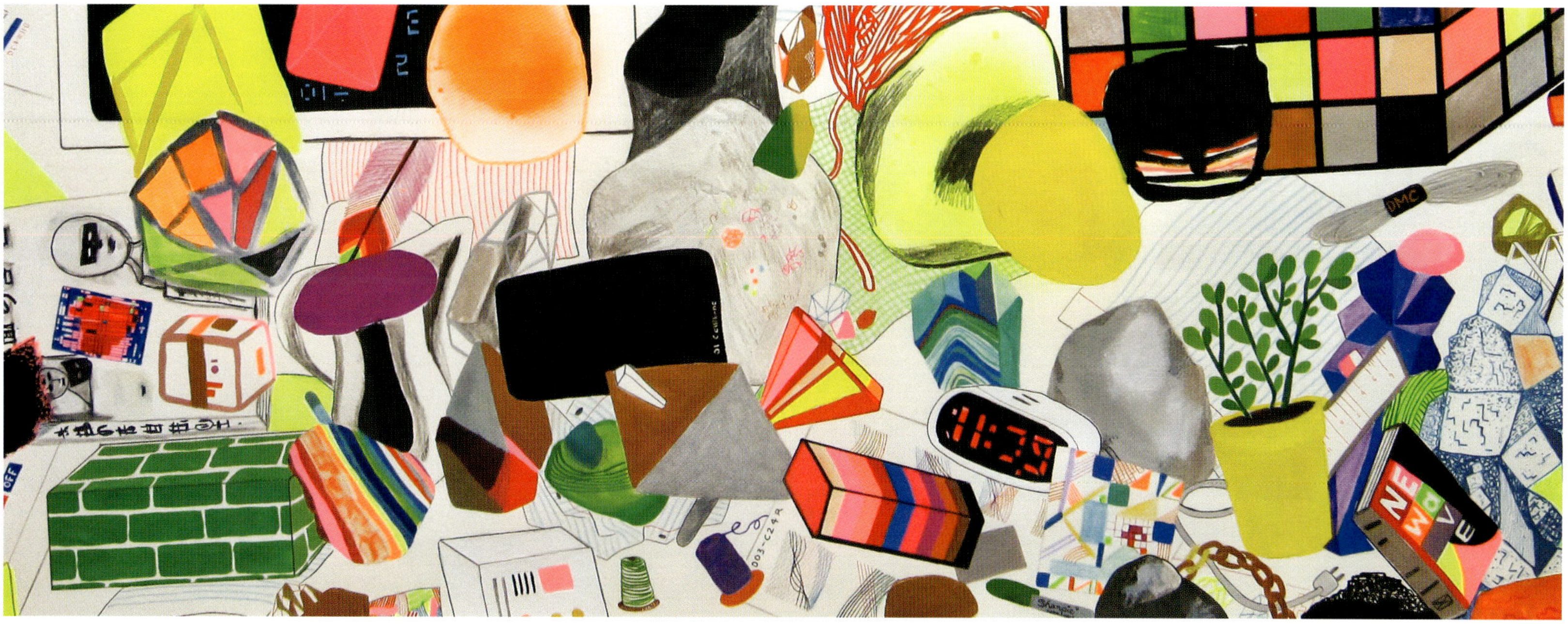

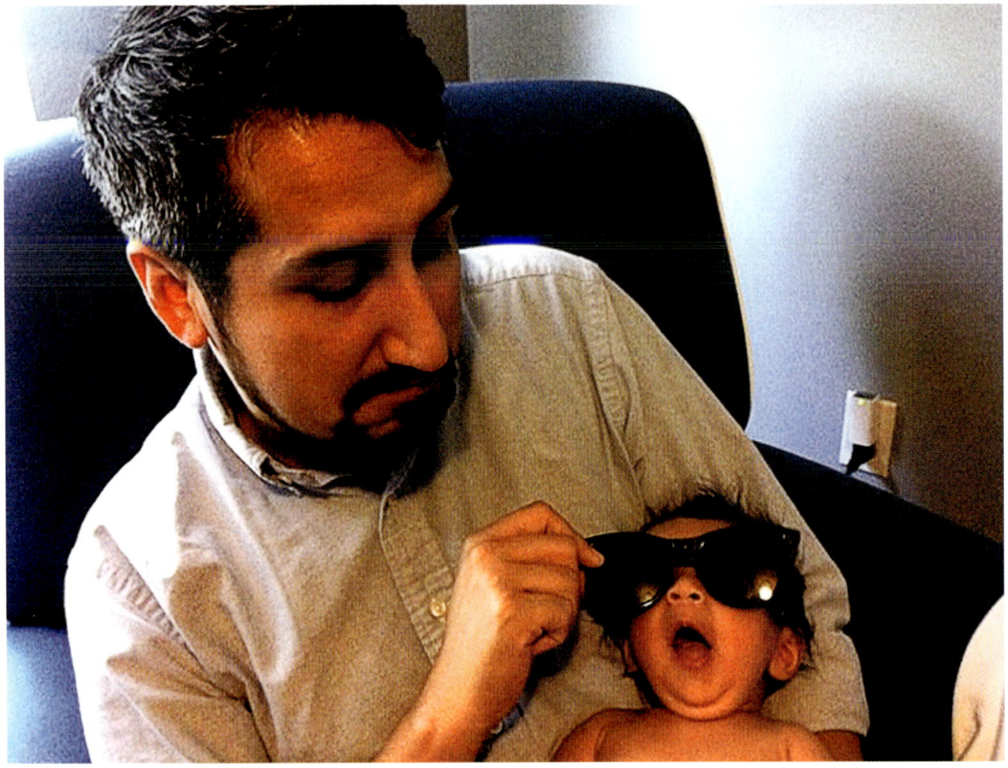

Photo by Stephanie Hutin, 2011

FLORENCIO ZAVALA

Los Angeles, California
bigskills.com
florenciozavala.com

My family has roots in Northern California, so Summer reunions brought me back year after year growing up. After school the migration was natural. Found a home in LA working for Shepard Fairey and Dave Kinsey and the rest is history.

LA is a dichotomy of many things. It's cozy but gets under your skin. I like that tension. And obviously you can't get any better weather. Anywhere. Sorry, but it's true. The access to nature is something you just can't take for granted. The land is such a resource. In LA foot traffic only gets you so far. Then you have to deal with the other traffic. :(

California influences my work and process through the lifestyle, the culture, the colors, the diversity, the individuality, the environment. I feel rich just living here.

It's a natural creative environment. Plain and simple. Not to mention we're in Hollywood. There's storytelling and fantasy woven into the fabric of the city. Being an author is instinctive. Formally my work is more a reflection of a city in constant transition. Kids scrawl graffiti on neighborhood walls only to be painted over the next day. Billboards rise and fall. Businesses come and go. The freeways push cars in all directions. You can only hope to capture a fraction of that in your work.

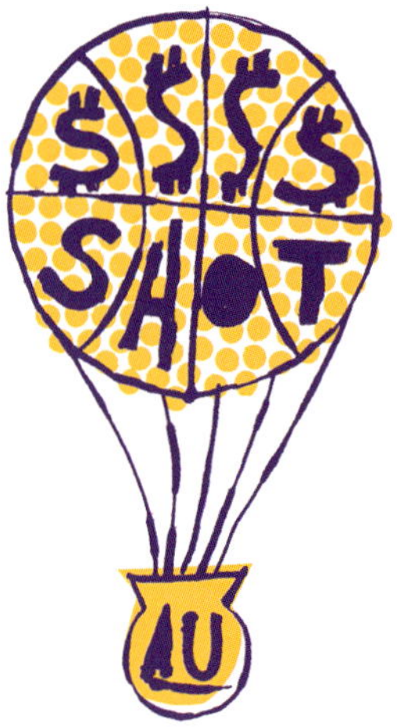

"Money Shot" 2005
Pen, ink, and cut paper
8 x 10 inches

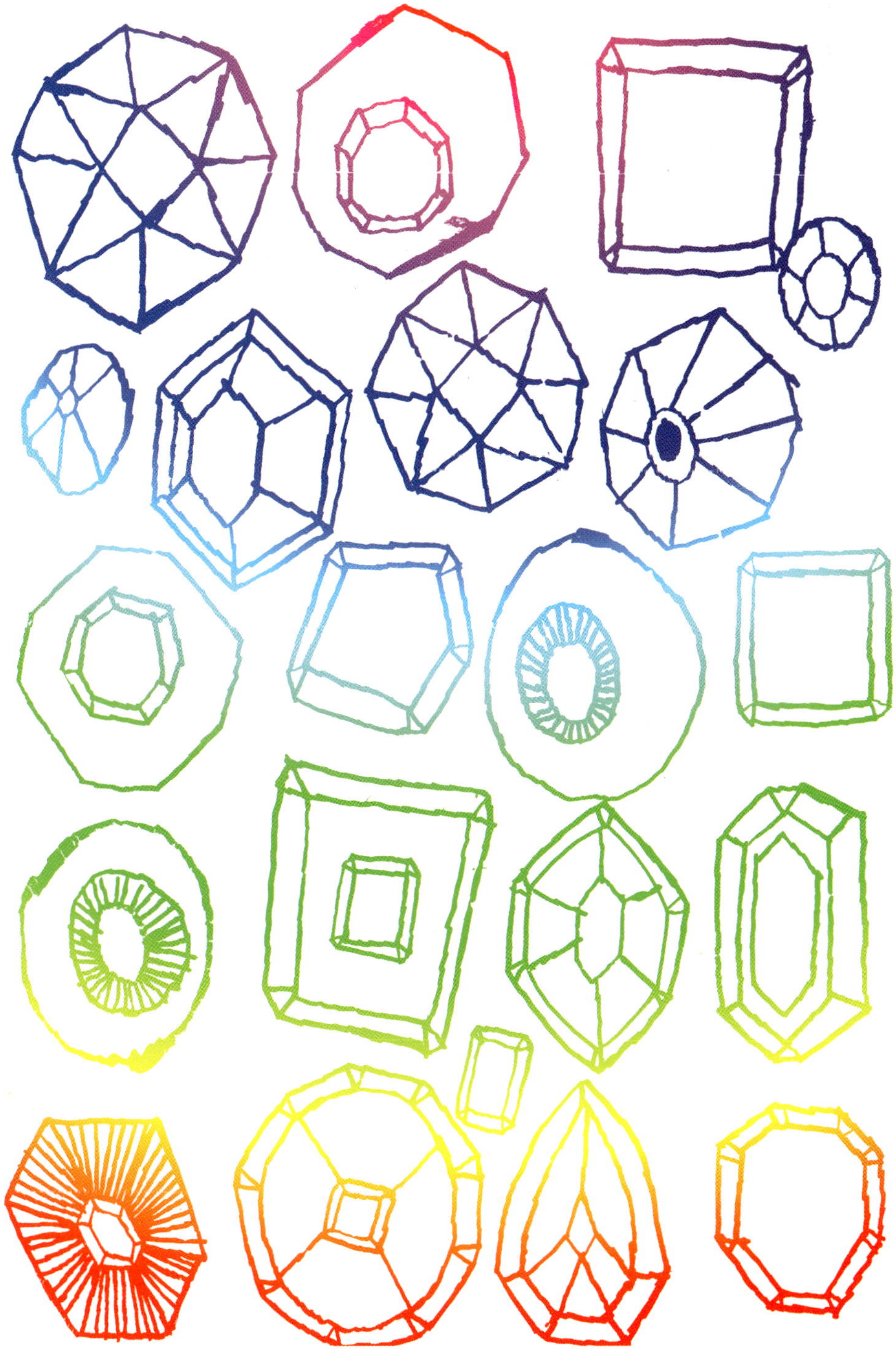

"Gems" 2006
Pen and ink
10 x 16 inches

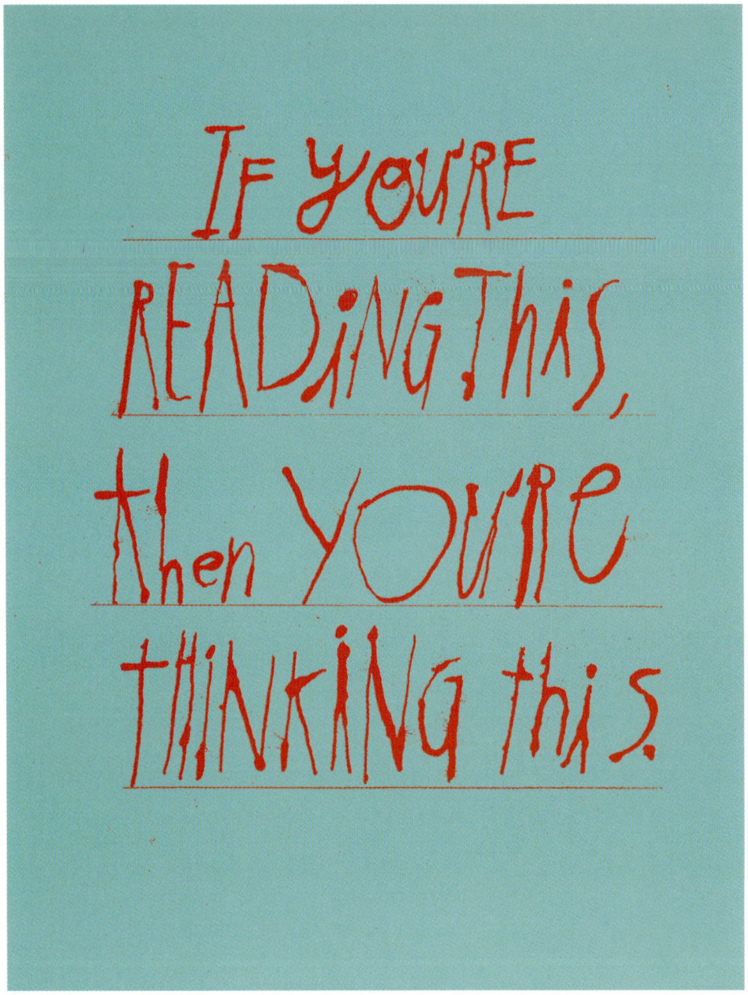

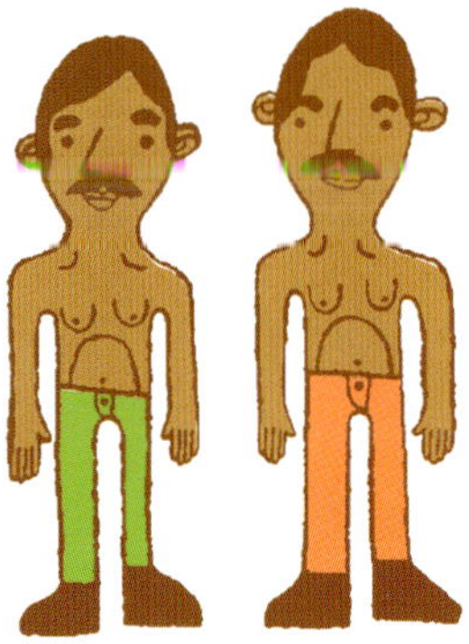

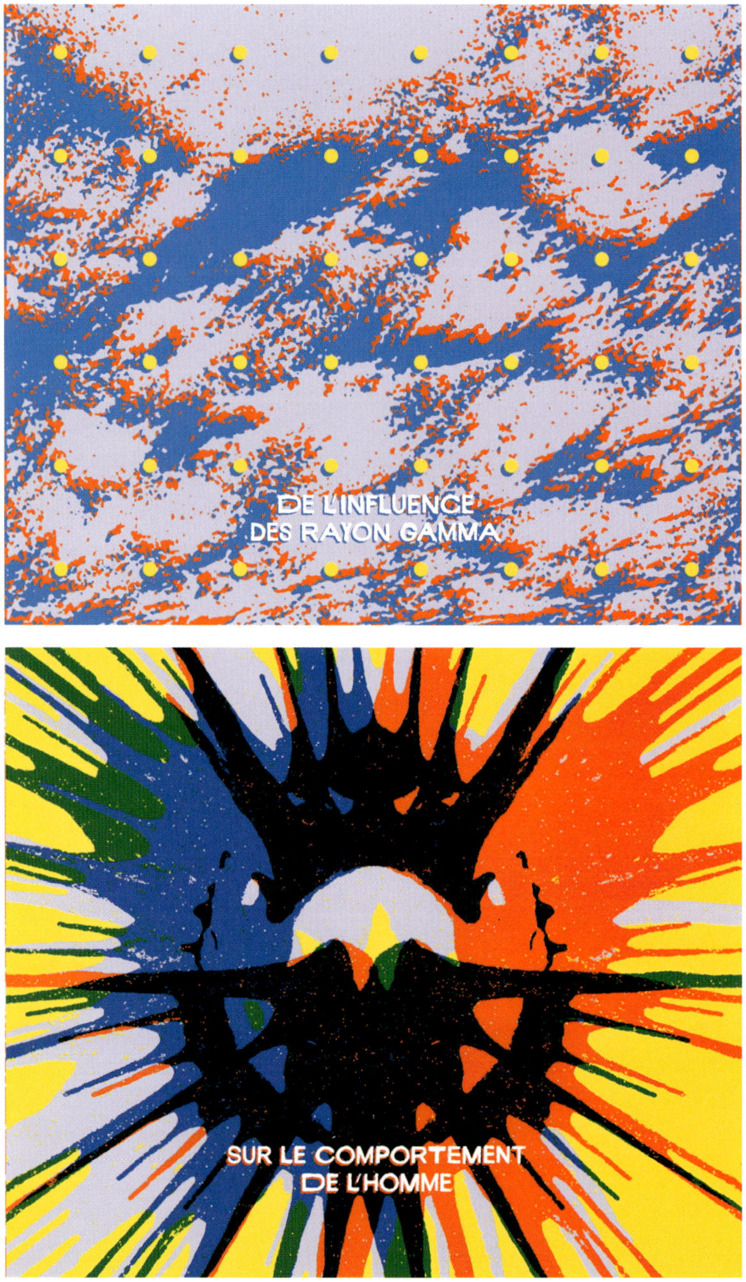

"Untitled" 2007
Pen and ink
8 x 10 inc..es

"Brothers" 2005
Pen and ink
10 x 16 inches

"De l'influence de rayon gamma (diptych)" 2010
Mixed media
22 x 18 inches individually

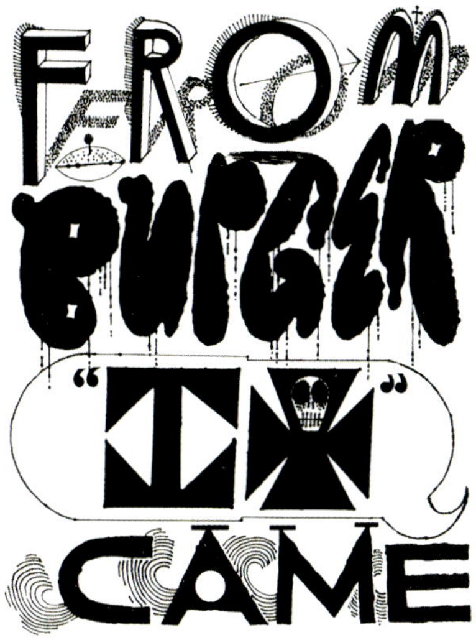

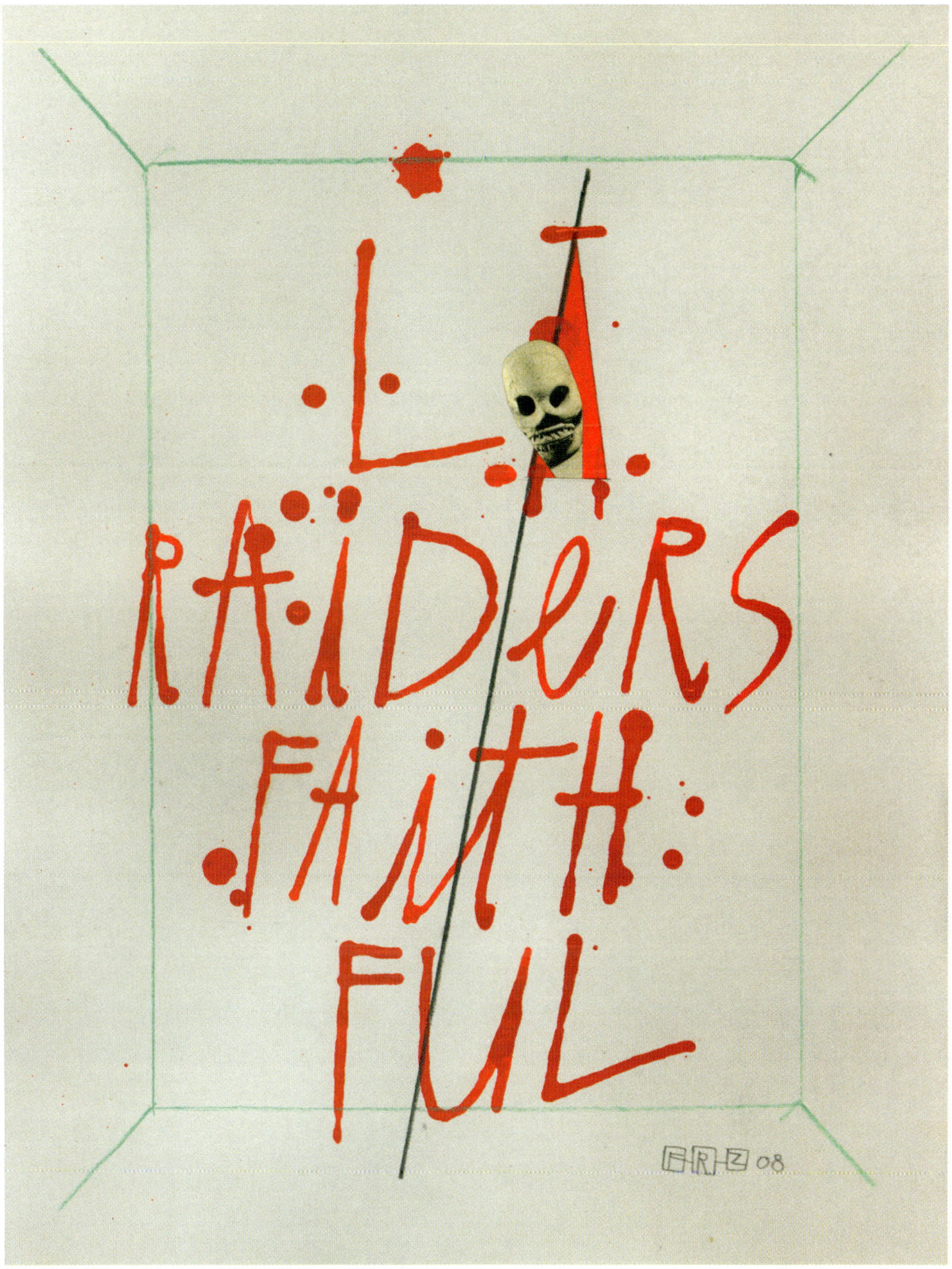

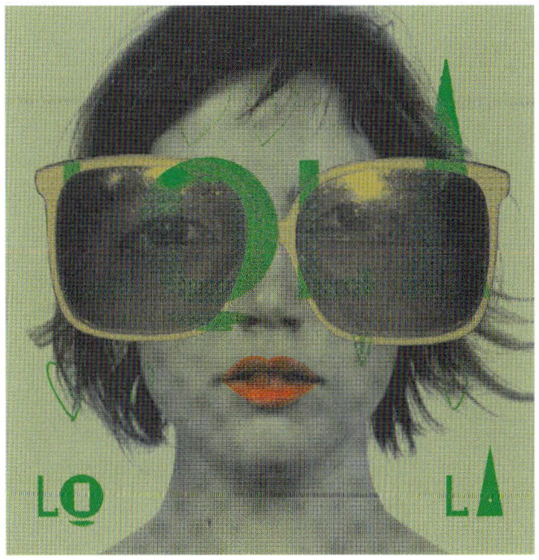

"LA Raiders Faithful" 2008
Pen, ink, and collage
8 x 10 inches

"From Burger It Came" 2008
Pen and ink
24 x 36 inches

"Lola" 2006
Screen print
27 x 27 inches

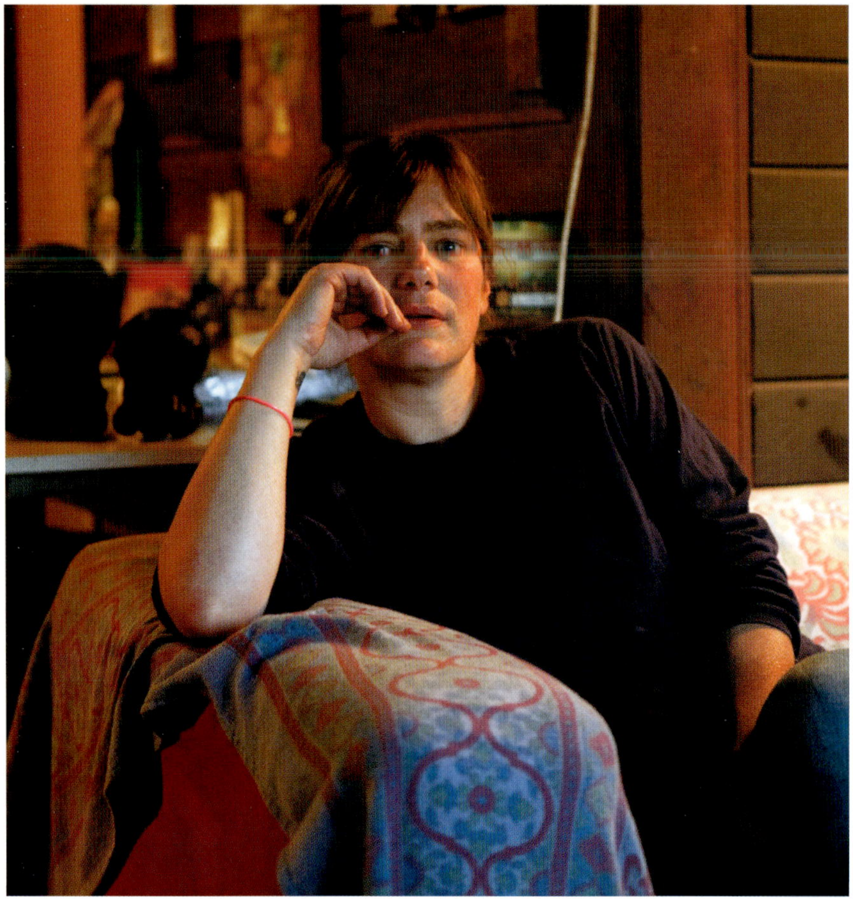

Photo by Aaron Farley, 2012

MEL KADEL

Los Angeles, California
melkadel.com

I'm still not sure what brought me to California, but there's a lot that keeps me here. Our place is surrounded by trees and animals (woodpeckers are in rare form right now), and it feels strangely remote for being two miles from Sunset Blvd. Whatever focus I have, I found here. And, when it's time to step away from the desk, there are endless ways to find adventure.

I see the advantages come with the people that flock here. It's a progressive place, full of creative risk takers. I'm constantly inspired.

The disadvantages can be how sprawling this city is, and how disconnected that feels.

I didn't draw as many sunbeams and rainbows until I moved to Los Angeles. As a whole, my work has become more positive, and I spend a lot more time on each piece. That must have something to do with my surroundings.

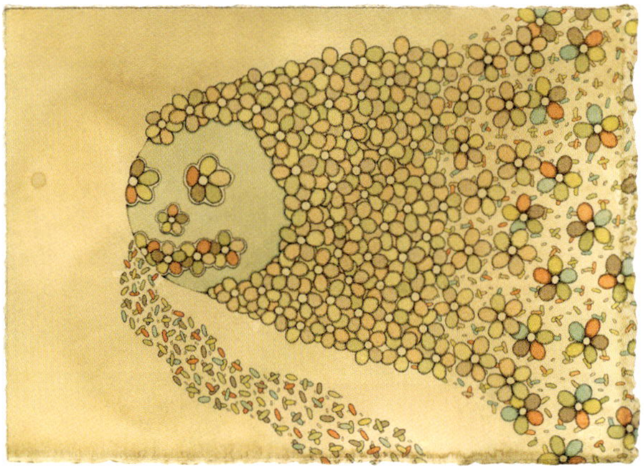

"Breath" 2011
Pen and ink on paper
12 x 16.75 inches

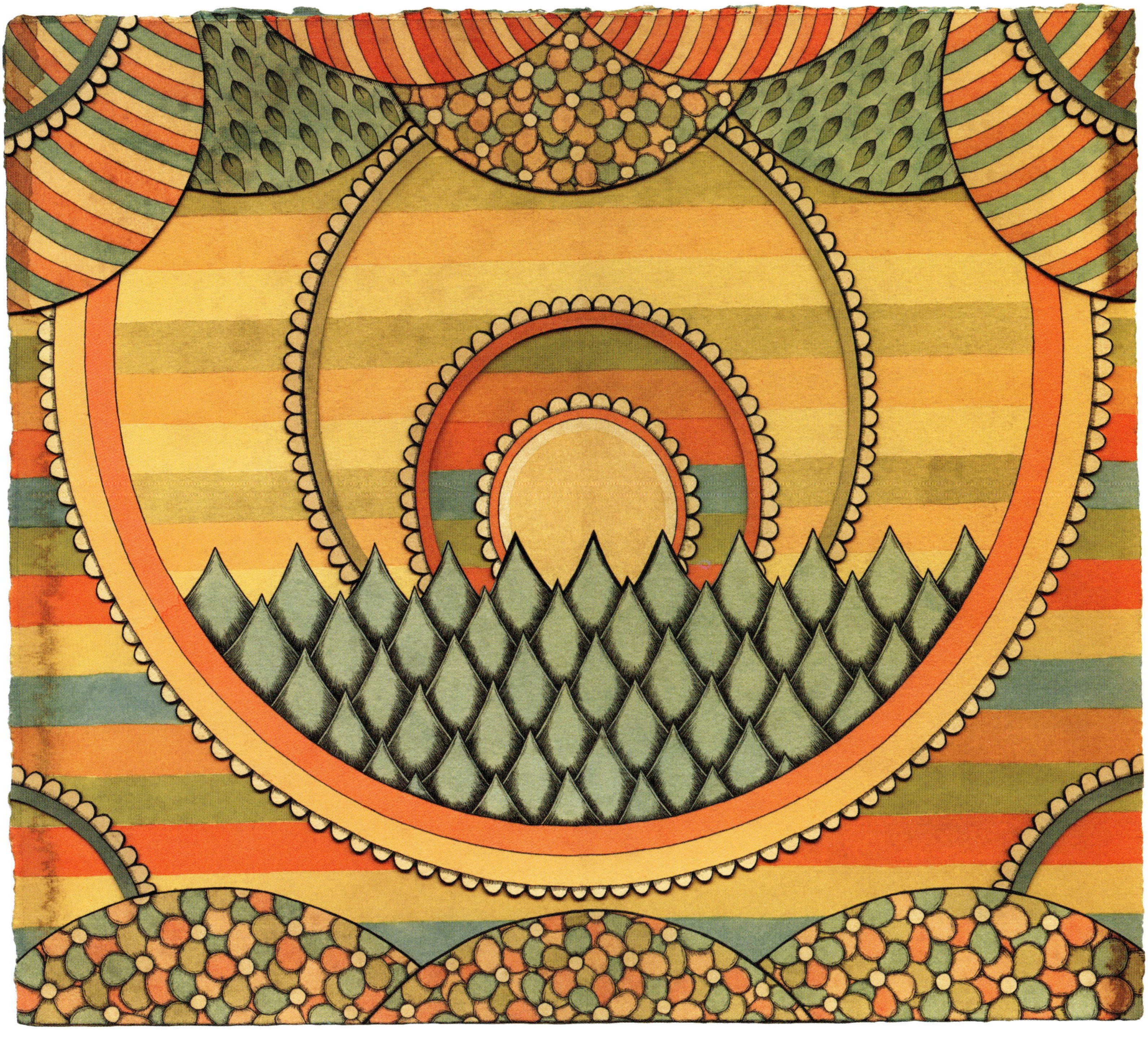

"Sunsets Today" 2012
Pen, ink, and collage on paper
11 x 14 inches

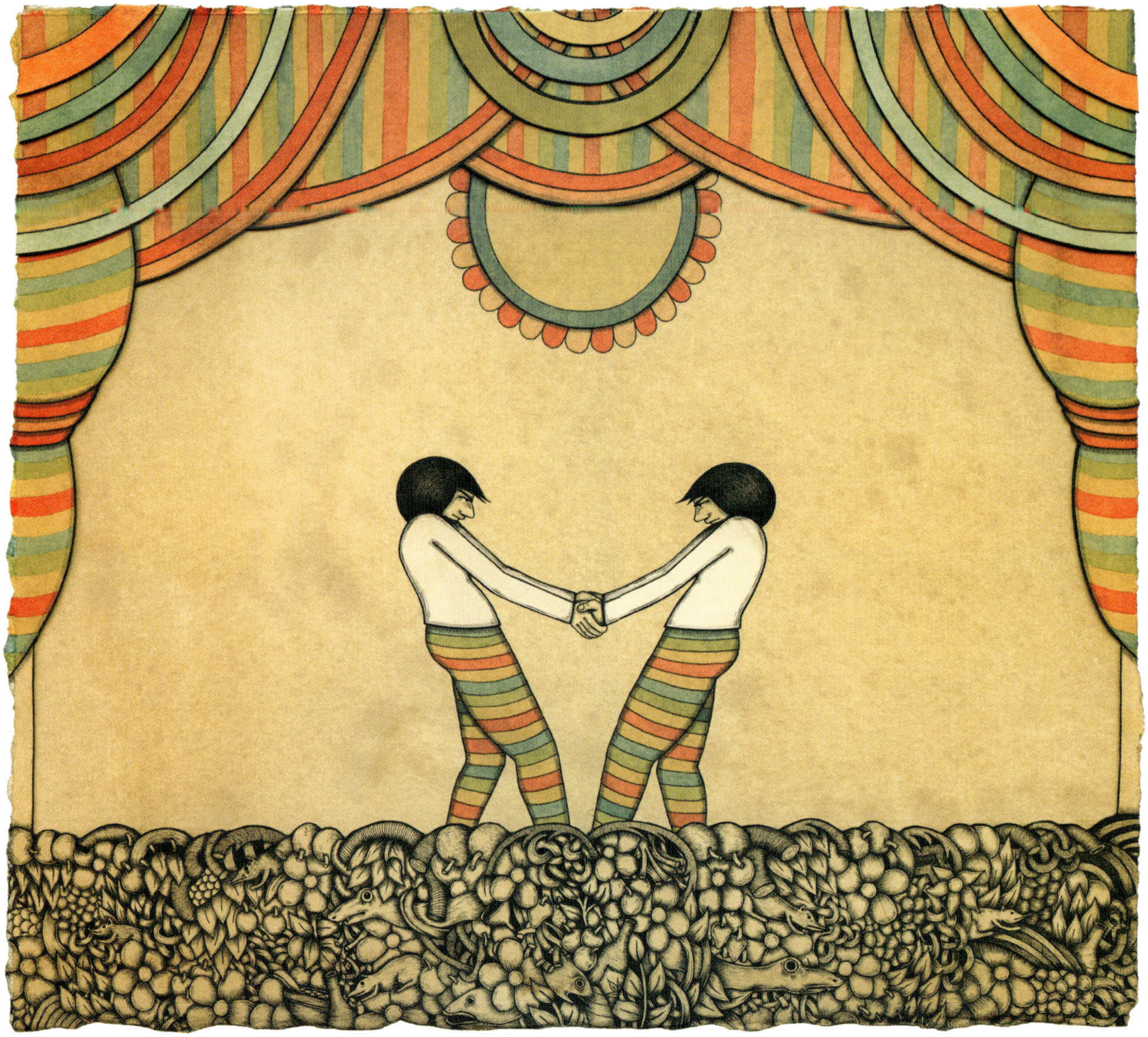

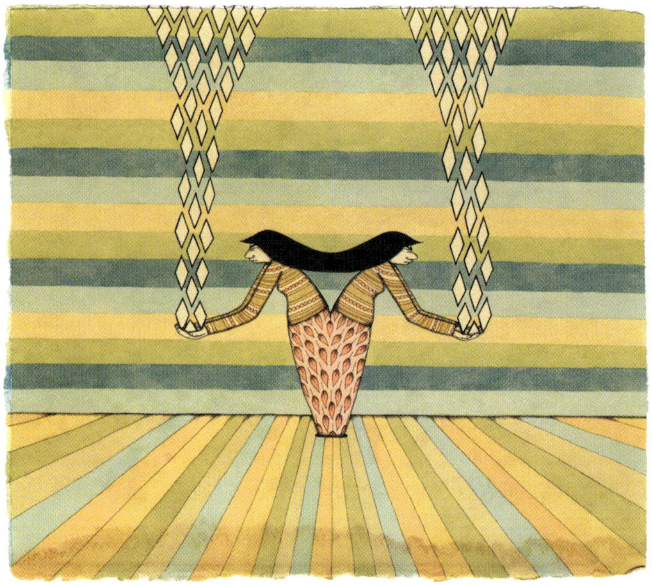

"Hold Hands" 2012
Pen, ink, and collage on paper
11 x 14 inches

"Diamonds" 2011
Pen, ink, and collage on paper
11 x 13 inches

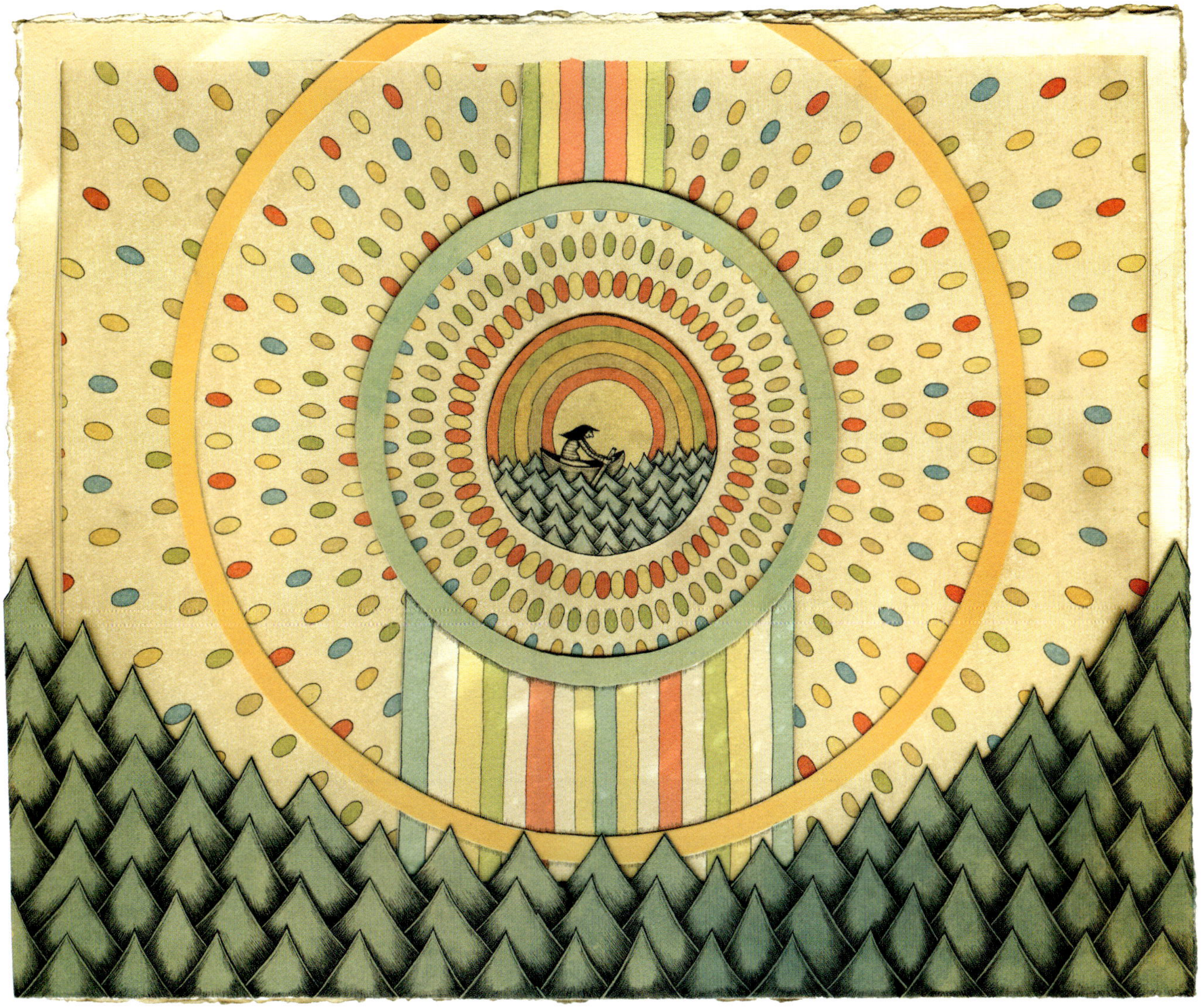

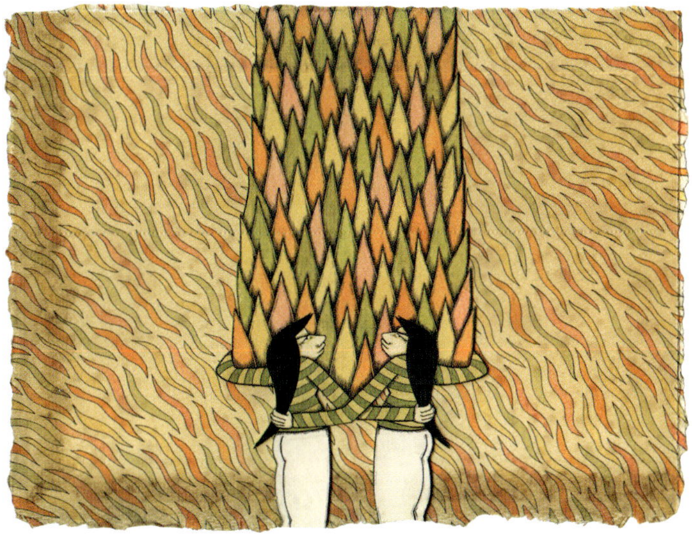

"Centered" 2011
Pen, ink, and collage on paper
11 x 14 inches

"Fueled" 2011
Pen, ink, and collage on paper
7.25 x 9.5 inches

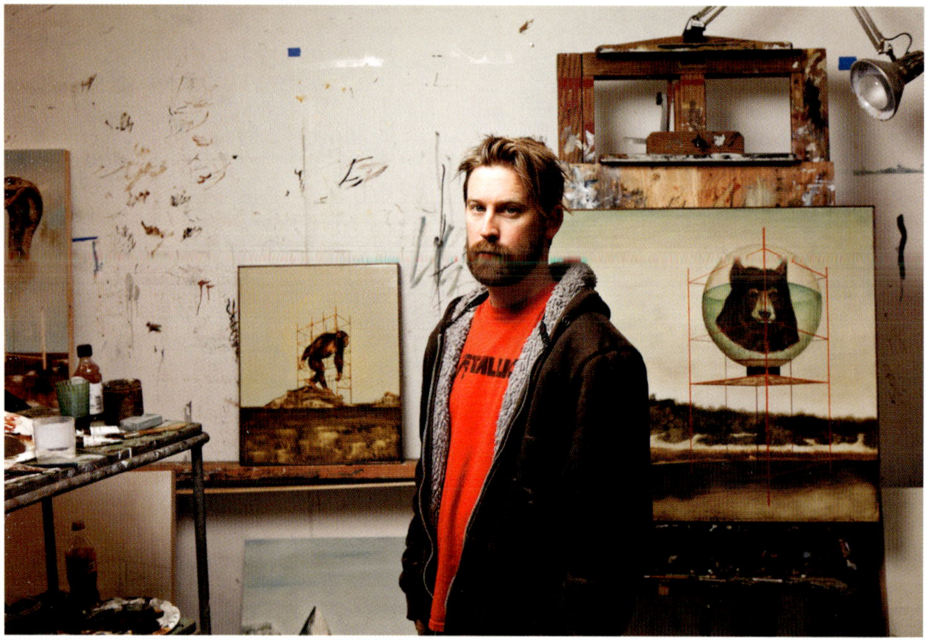

Photo by Winnie Wintermeyer, 2012

KEVIN TAYLOR

San Francisco, California
kevinearltaylor.com
Circle Culture, Berlin
Guerrero Gallery, San Francisco
Rebekah Jacob Gallery, Charleston, SC

[Before moving to California,] I felt myself getting comfortable in South Carolina, and I knew that couldn't be good. I came out for a show in Monterey in 2005 and stayed a week in SF. I felt a flow of energy that I'd been missing and didn't even realize it until it zapped me. I decided then and there to give myself a year to get out here, and I kept to that decision. I stick around because I can't think of anywhere else I want to put down solid roots at the moment. I'm actually getting a little bit restless to make a move, but not sure where. I do think this time, it'll be more off the radar and out of the rat race, however.

In addition to the obvious advantages—Mexican food, fresh vegetables, and lawlessness—I've been given opportunities and met so many great artists and colleagues that I would have never been in the mix with had I stayed in Charleston.

Some of the disadvantages are that I can no longer swim in the ocean without freezing my ass off, I miss black people, and I suffer from a serious thunderstorm deficiency.

California influences me to make work that is my own. I see quite a bit of style biting, and there's definitely a 'look' to a lot of art being crafted that isn't exactly difficult to achieve by imitation. That overflow keeps me pushing further.

I attempt to expose the animal within. Much of that which is assumed to be chaotic and incomprehensible within the human paradigm can be clarified through the observation that we, like all organisms, are bound first and foremost by natural law. Over time, civil responsibility has ordered a physical detachment from nature, however, a deeper mental architecture remains intact. It is this power play with which we struggle internally. I take interest in formulating a parody, amplifying an analysis, and offering visual depiction of this all at once grotesque, lovely, and hilarious production.

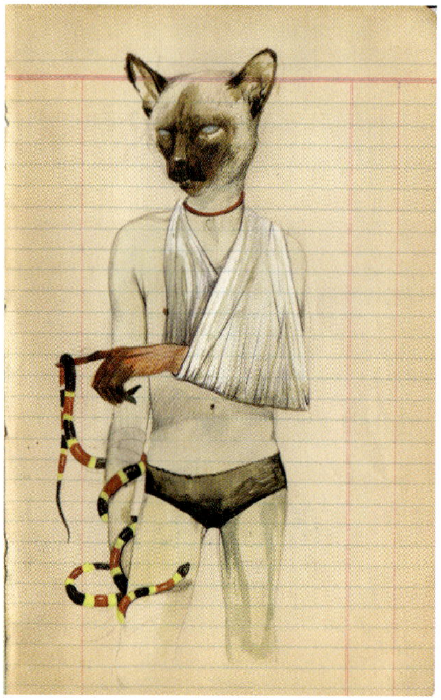

"Tourniquet" 2011
Gouache on paper
6 x 9 inches

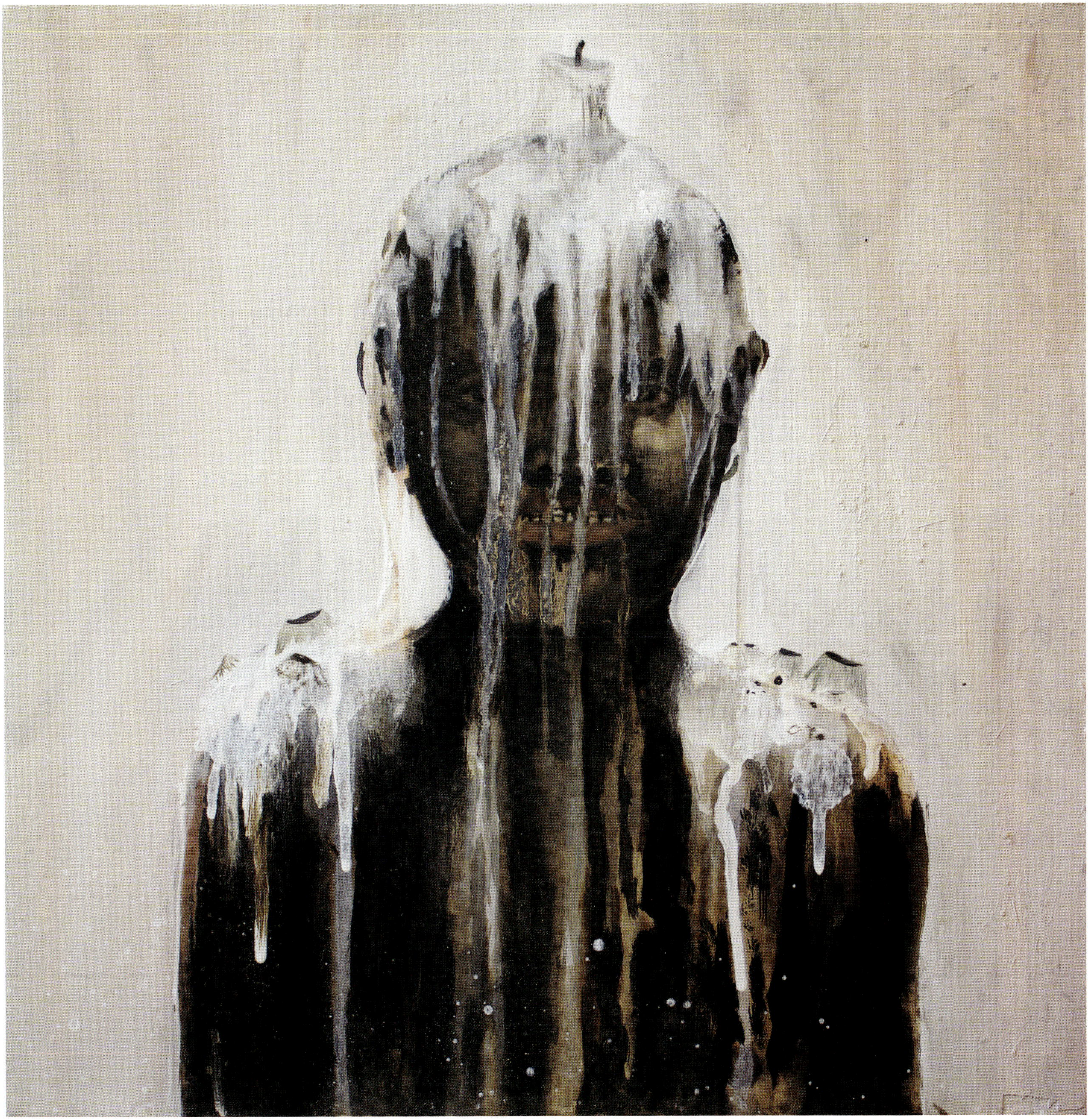

"Effigy" 2012
Oil on panel
12 x 12 inches

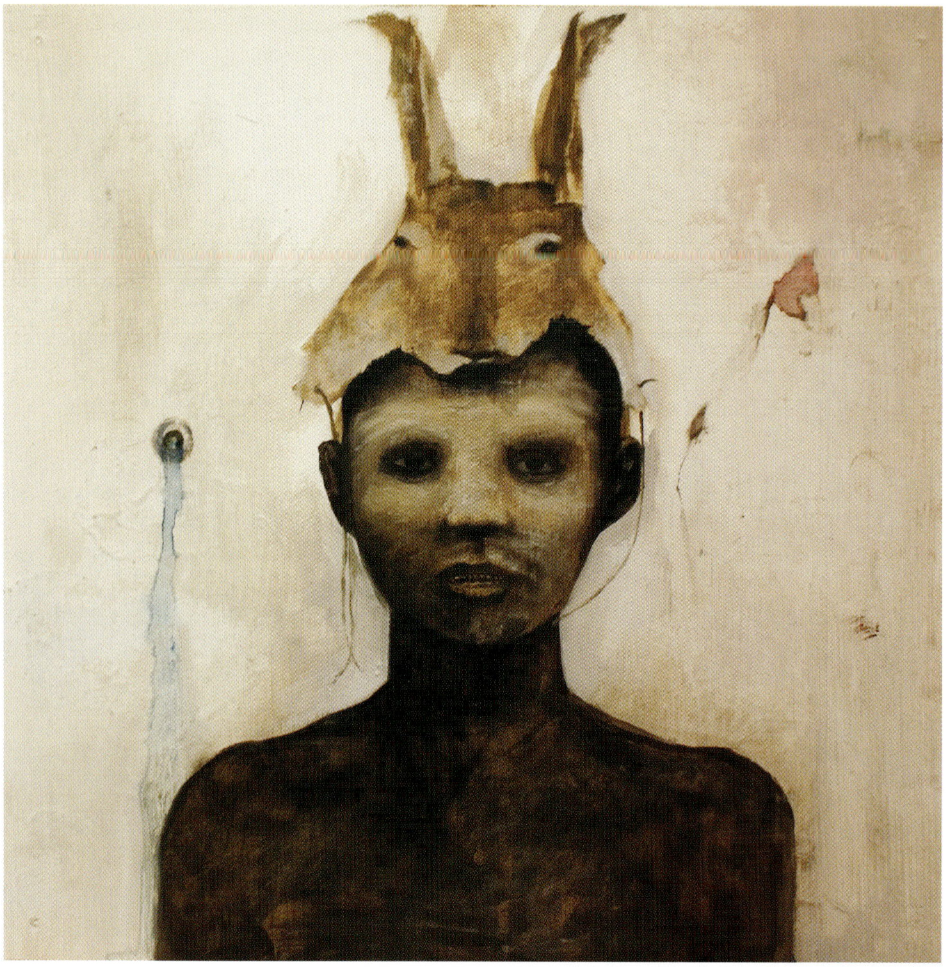

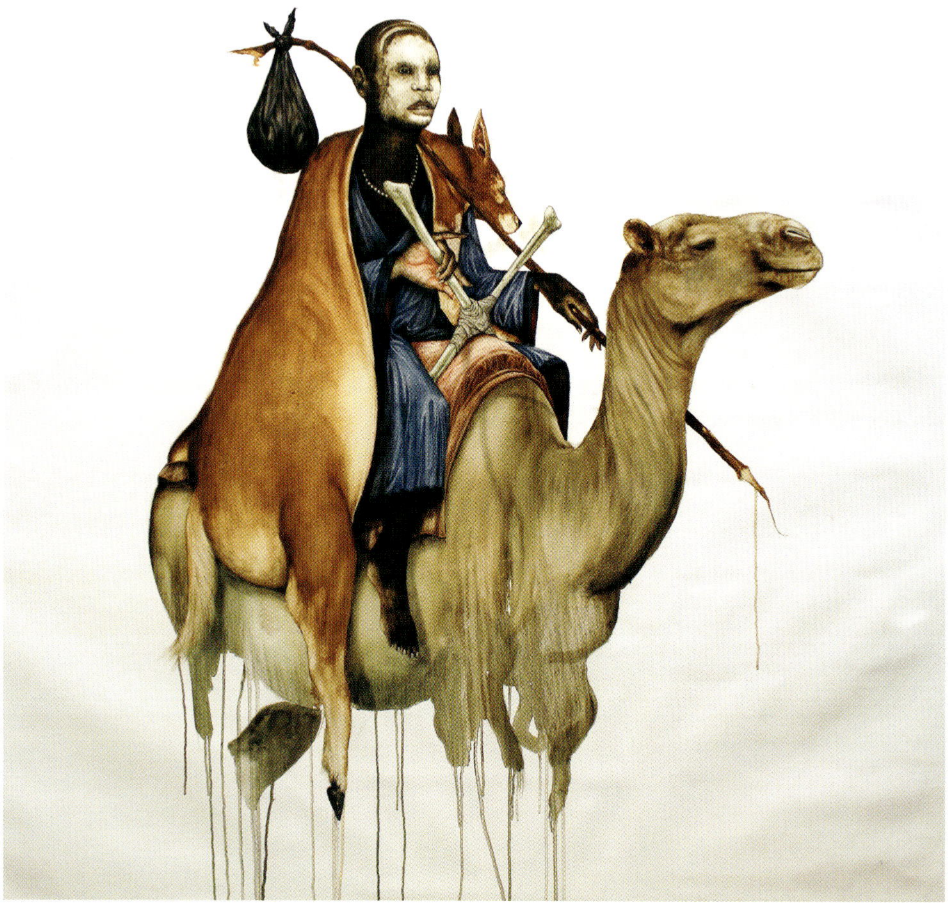

Top:
"A New Tribalism" 2010
Oil on panel
12 x 12 inches

"Pilgrimage" 2011
Oil on canvas
48 x 48 inches

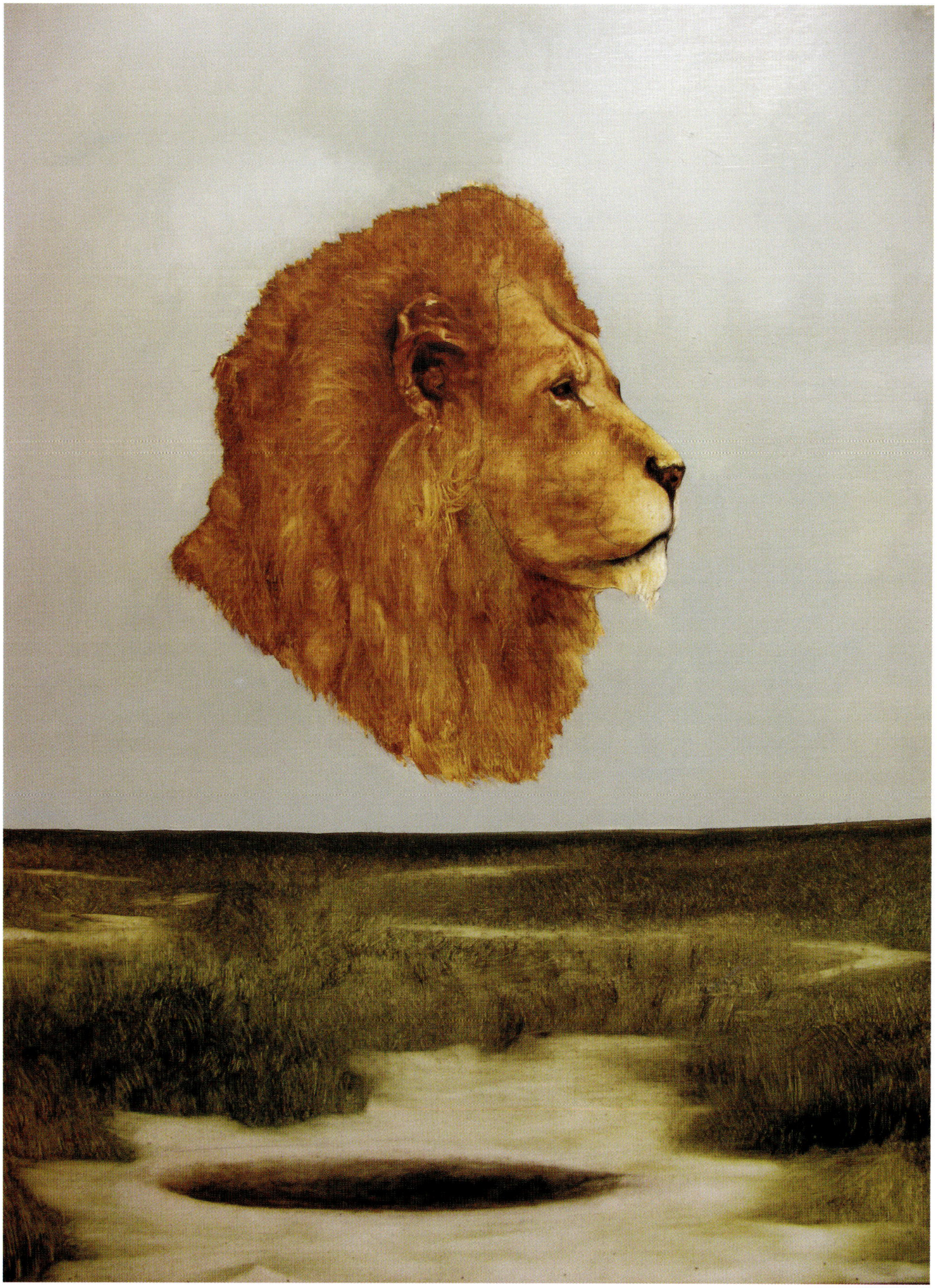

"Essence (detail)" 2012
Oil on panel
48 x 60 inches

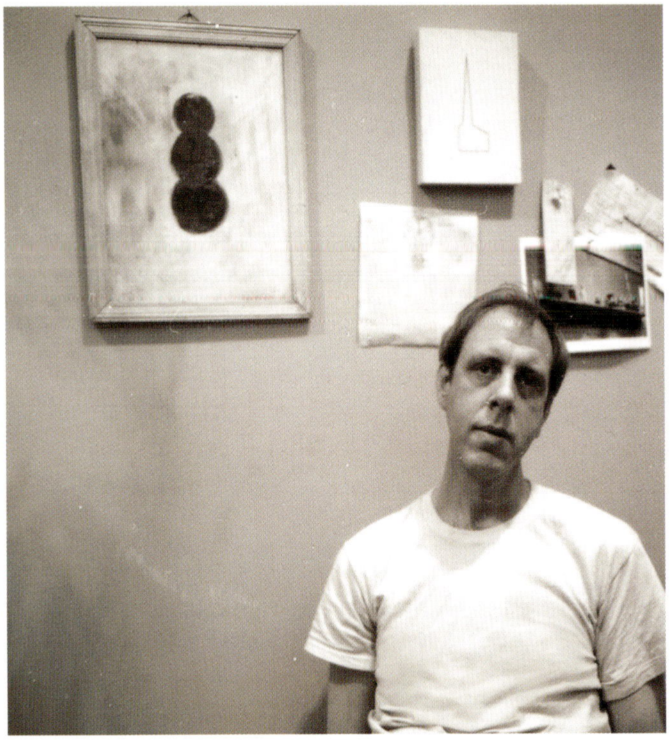

ROBERT THERRIEN

Los Angeles, California
Gagosian Gallery

Self portrait, 2012

I have lived in Southern California since 1971. Before that, I lived in Northern California, having spent my childhood in Chicago. Most of this Los Angeles time has been spent in a neighborhood on Pico Blvd. You know, the one between Crenshaw and Fairfax, storefronts, shops, beauty shops. Or, in the present studio, which is modeled after the Pico studio but more rooms and (ugh) facing south rather than north. Most of it seems like a matter of circumstance.

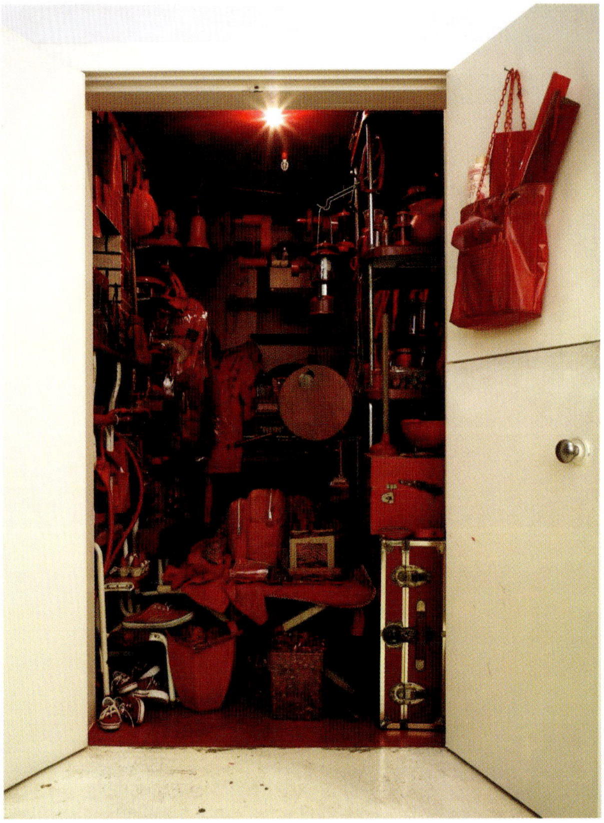

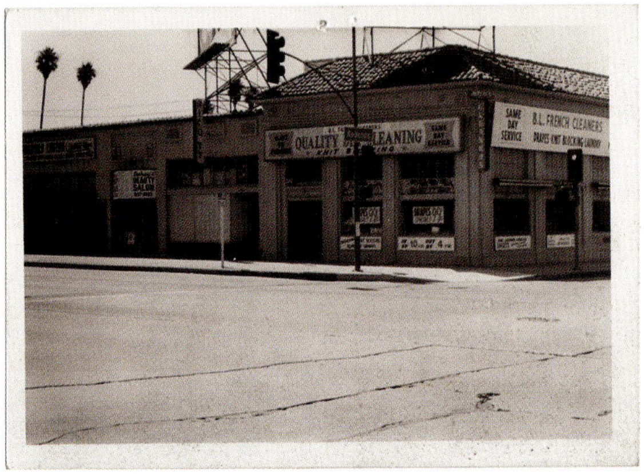

Pico Boulevard (TV)

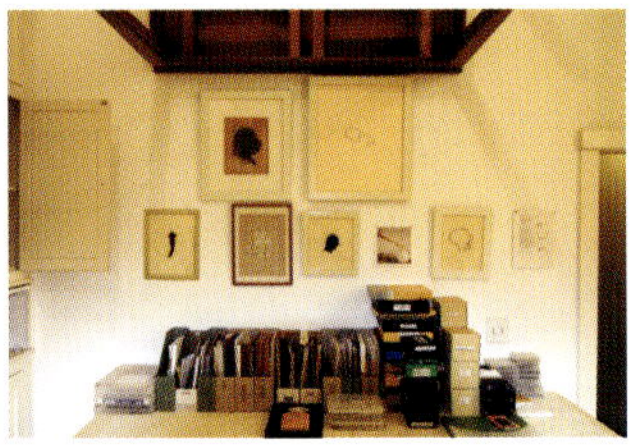

Studio Wall

"No title (Red room)" 2000-2007
Mixed media (approx. 888 red objects housed in a closet with no doors)
96 x 77 x 105 inches

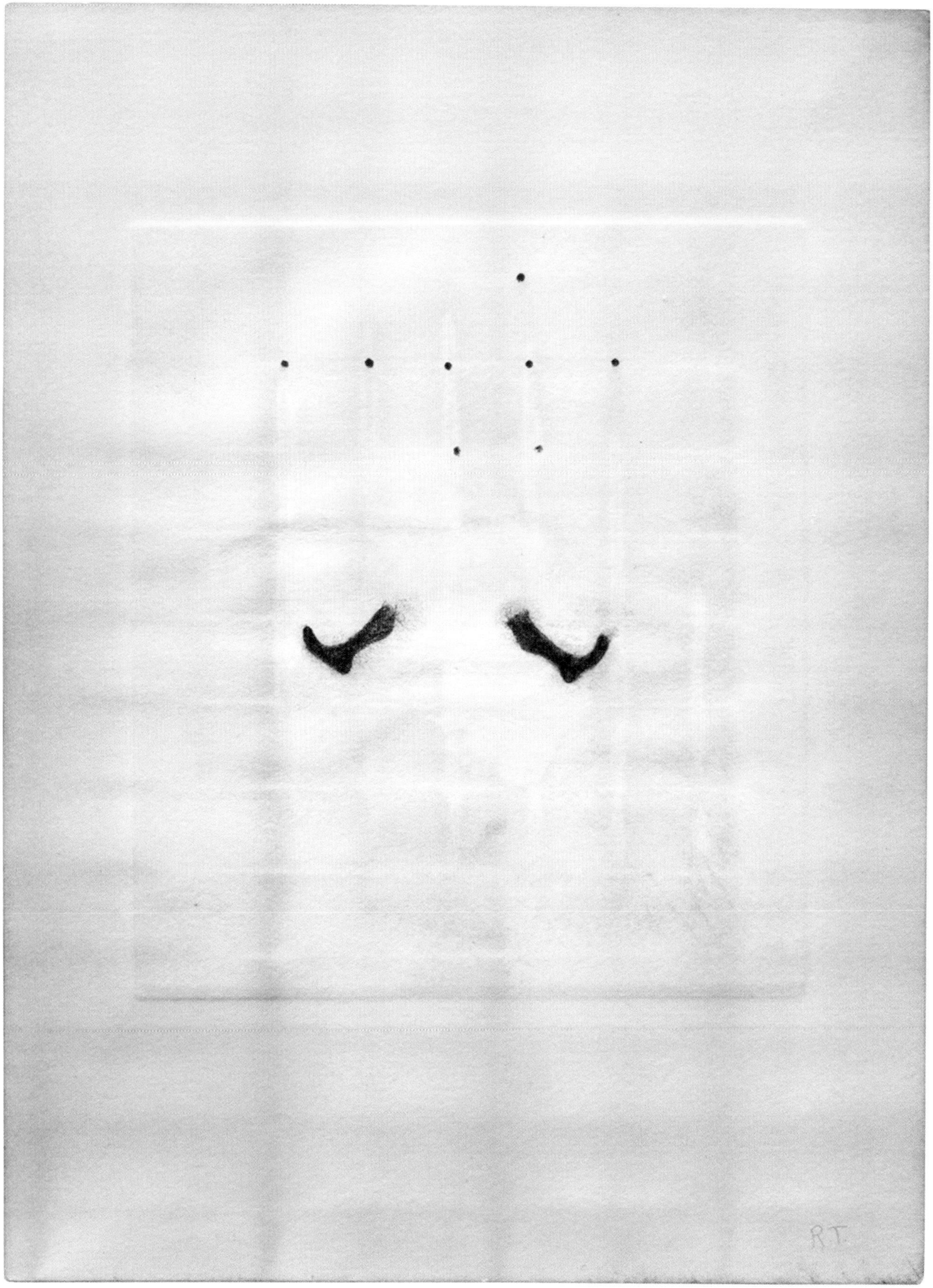

"*No title (Dots and legs)*" 2011
Pencil and bleach on paper
12½ x 10⅜ inches

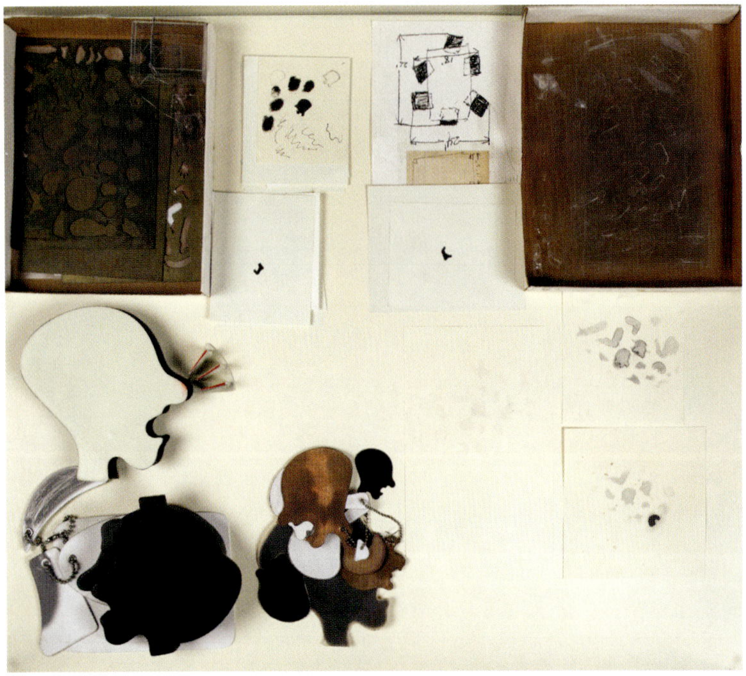

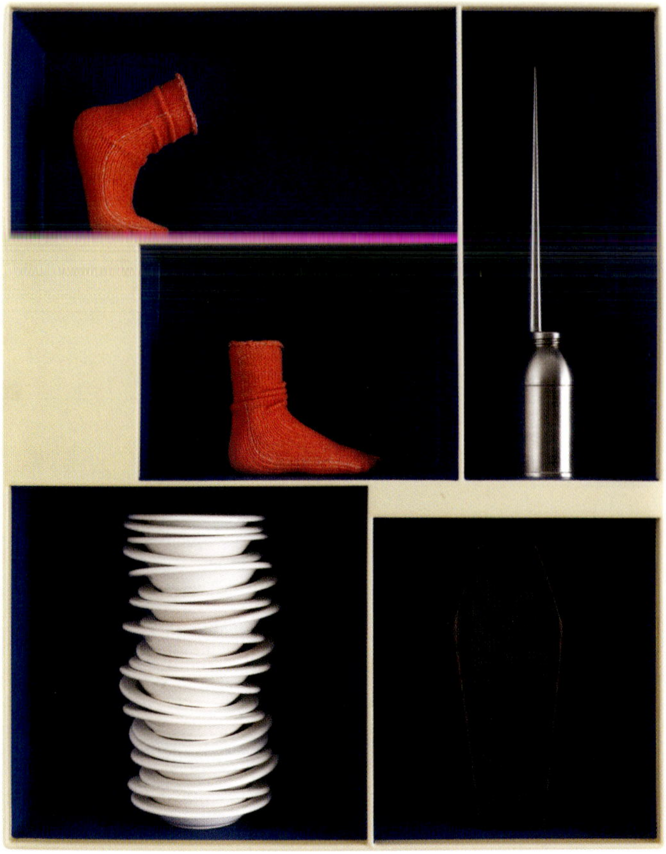

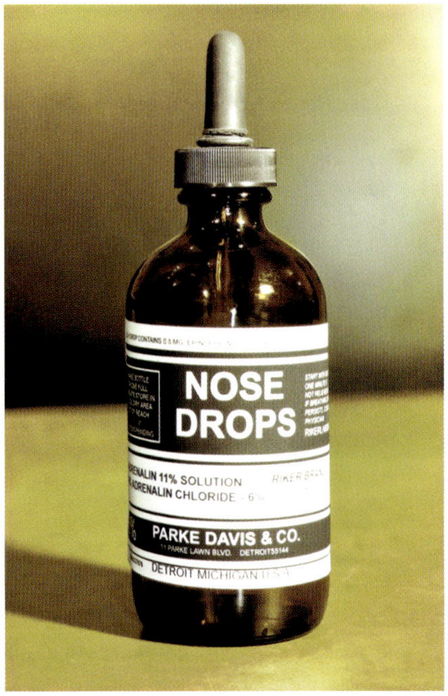

"*No title (Head and body parts vitrine)*" 2011
Mixed media
Vitrine: 7¼ x 31¾ x 37 inches

"*No title (Box edition)*" 2011
Mixed media
16⅜ x 13⅛ x 4½ inches
Edition of 15 blue/white with pink socks version

"*No title (Nose drops)*" 2011
Unique color photograph mounted on board
15½ x 23½ x 1¼ inches

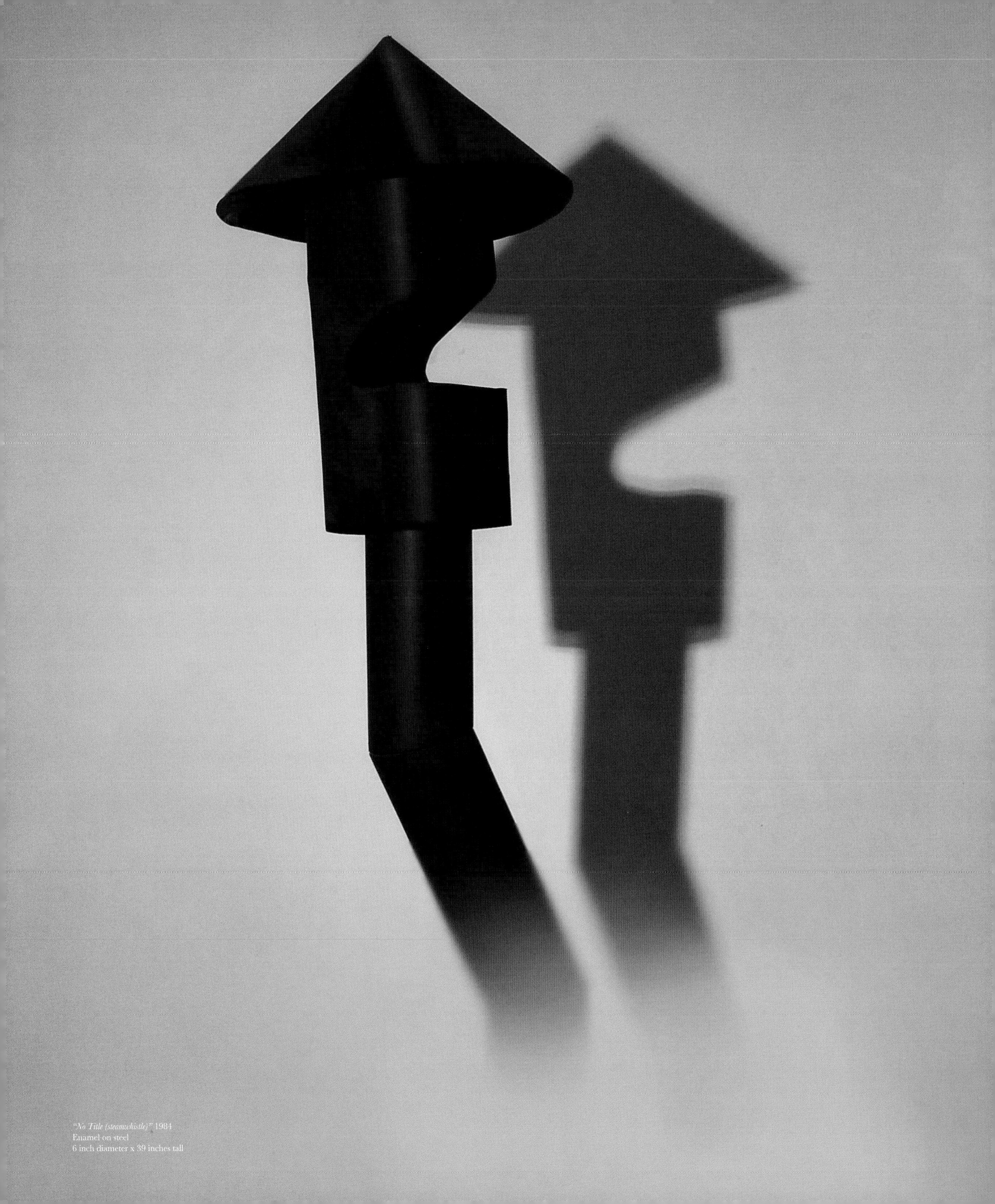

"No Title (steamwhistle)" 1984
Enamel on steel
6 inch diameter x 39 inches tall

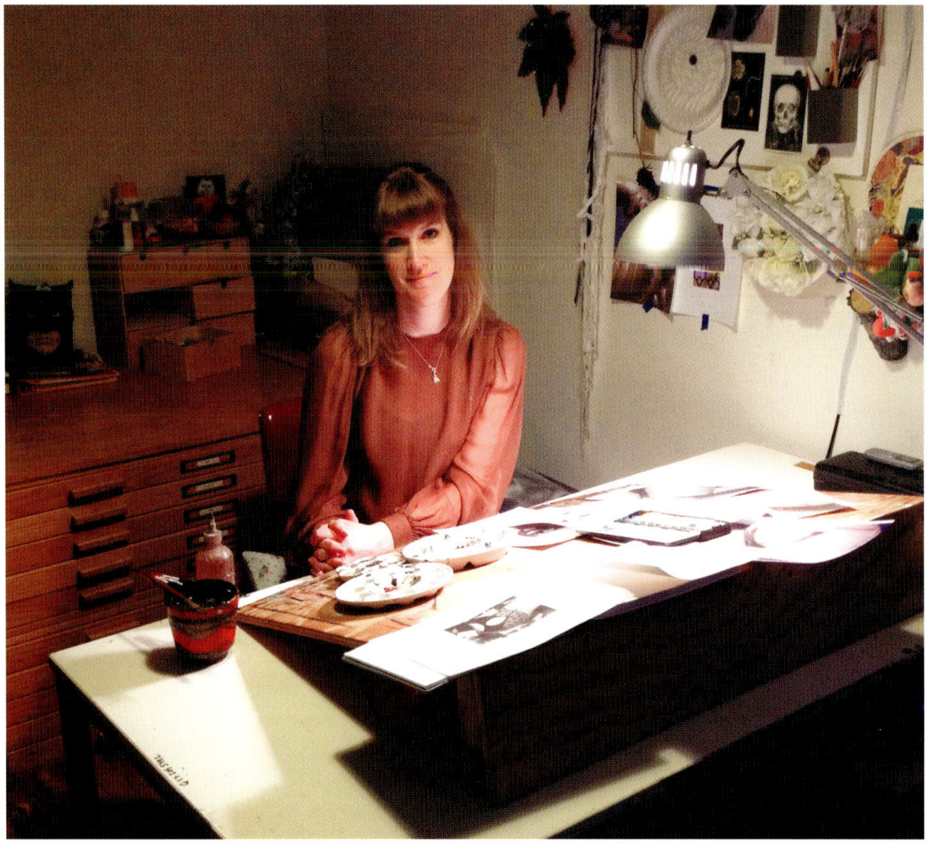

Self Portrait, 2012

ASHLEY SNOW MACOMBER

Los Angeles, CA
ashleymacomber.com

I came to California seeking an adventure and escape from the smells and memories I had grown up with on the East Coast. I stay here because it is my home. I have friends that are like family here, and California gives me a deep sense of peace and calm to focus on my work.

Space is the big advantage of working in California. Mental and physical space. This is the kind of place where you can become whoever you want to, and you can have the solitude and physical space to figure that out. I don't believe there are many disadvantages to working in California, however, living in Los Angeles can be difficult sometimes due to the dominance of the entertainment industry. It can be easy to fall prey to absurd aesthetic expectations.

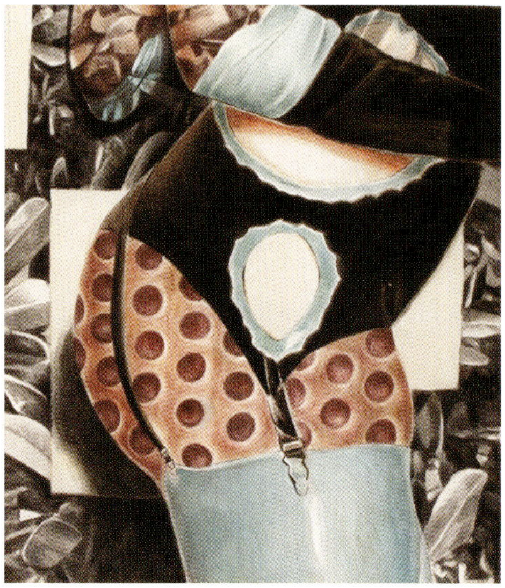

When I leave my house surrounded by fruit trees and succulents and I look into the sky on a sunny day, it makes me so happy. The flora and fauna are innately attached to the structure of the landscape. That is deeply inspiring to me. It has really enhanced my visual understanding of the natural world. I find reference for paintings constantly as I move through my day in the city.

"Asphyxia and Skin: Wailing Wallflower, Hustler Taboo pg.5, Dec. 2011" 2012
Watercolo. and gouache on paper
4 x 4.75 inches

"Bobbi no.2, A Stretch Behind Bars, Hustler Taboo pg.36, Dec.2011" 2012
Watercolor on paper
7.75 x 10 inches

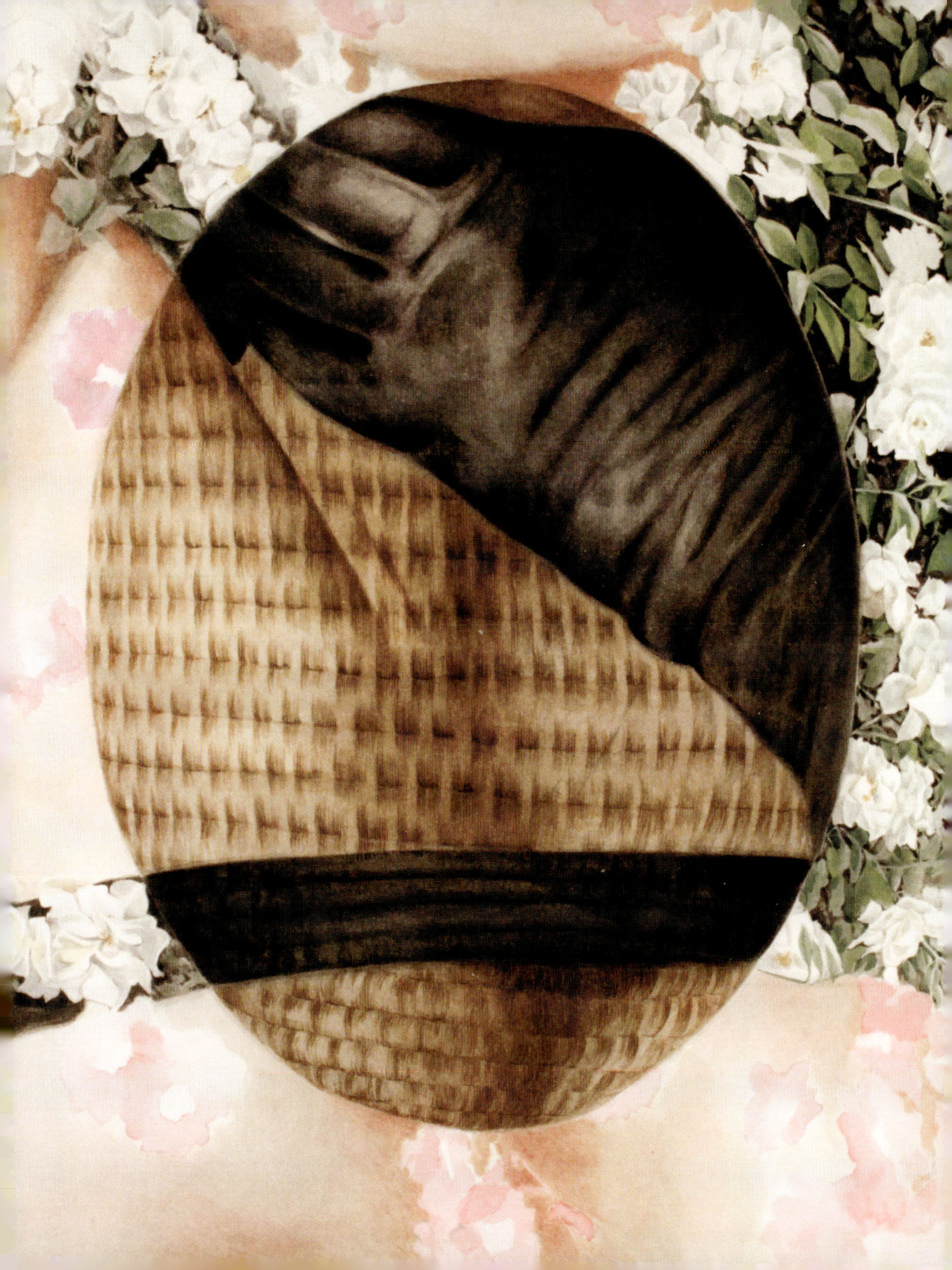

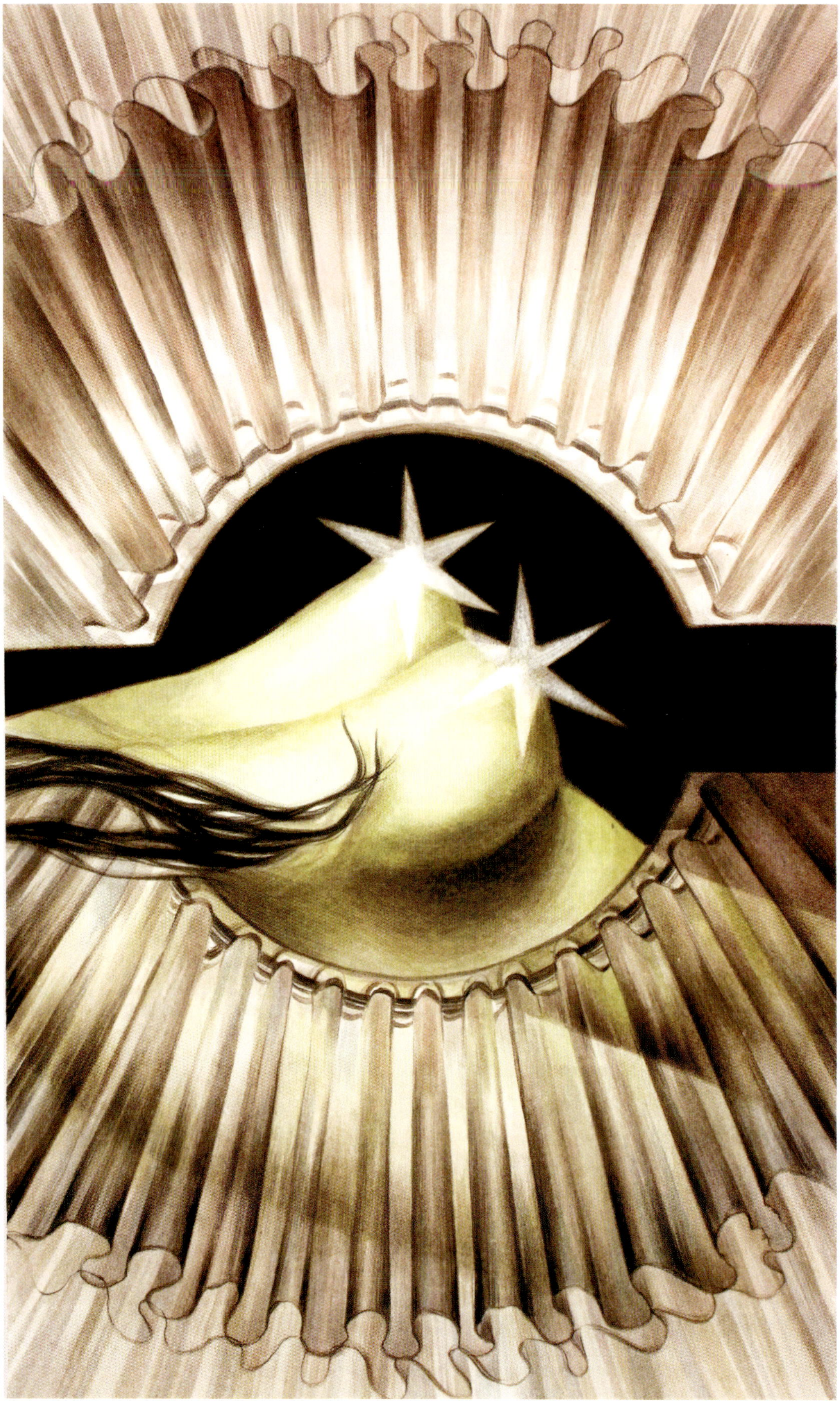

"Bella, $150, no hidden fees, Las Vegas, NV" 2012
Watercolor on paper
6.75 x 11 inches

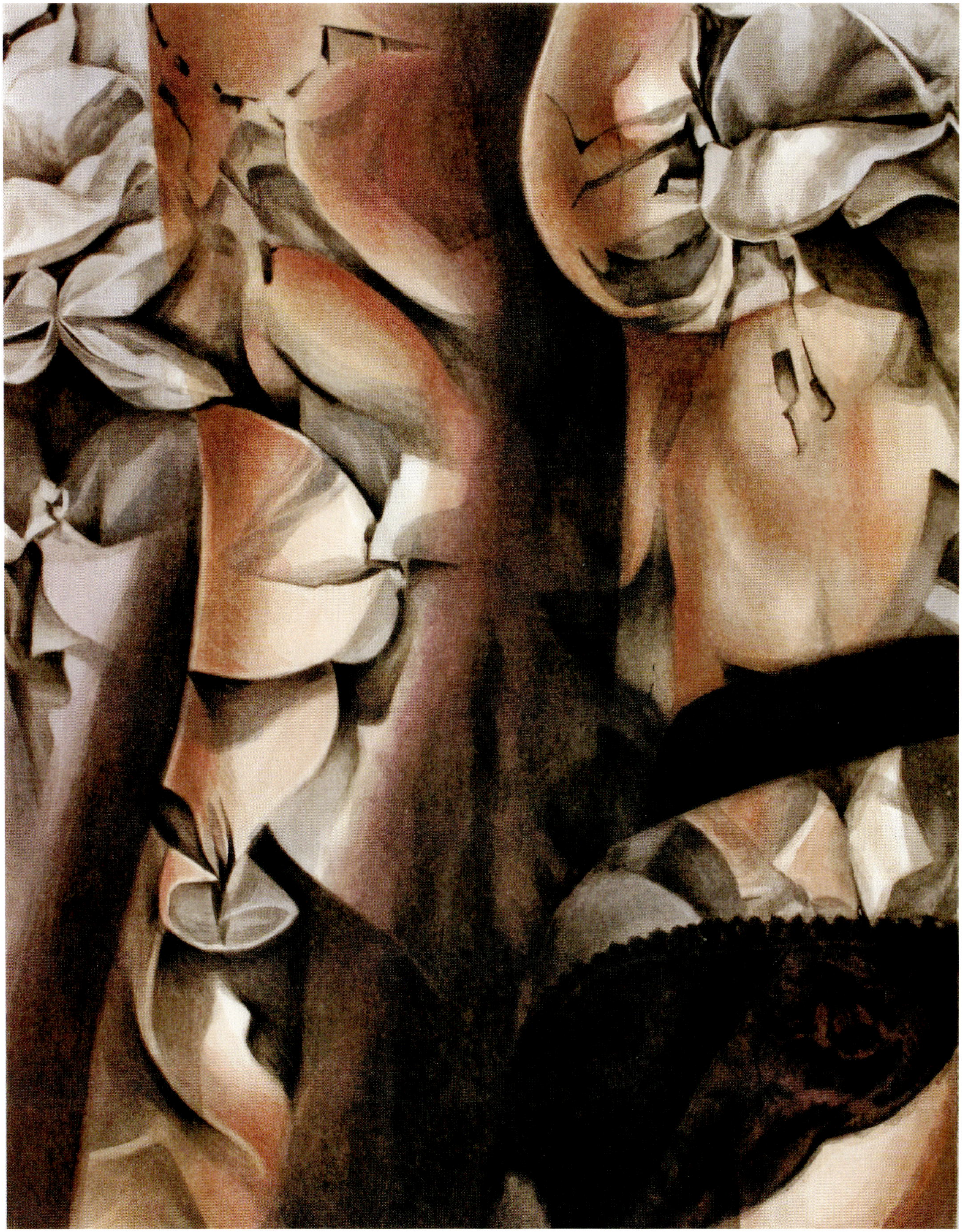

"Bobbi no.1, A Stretch Behind Bars, Hustler Taboo pg.36, Dec.2011" 2011
Watercolor on paper
8 x 10 inches

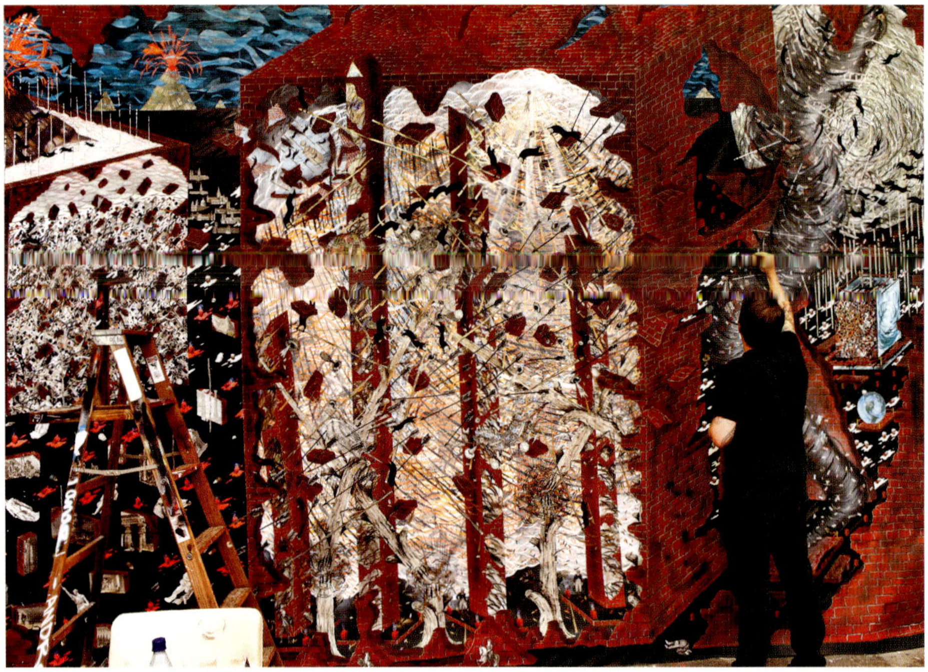

ANDREW SCHOULTZ

San Francisco, California
andrewschoultz.com
Mark Moore Gallery, Los Angeles
Marx & Zavattero, San Francisco
Morgan Lehman Gallery, New York
Jerome Zodo Contemporary, Milan
V1 gallery, Denmark
Ivory & Black, London

At work in the studio on the piece *Up in the Air* for The exhibition *Ultrasonic VI* Photo by Mark Moore Gallery, 2011

Skateboarding and Graffiti brought me to California. My great community of friends and peers that I have made over the past ten years keeps me here. I live in San Francisco and love it here, but I also love Los Angeles and somewhat consider that my community as well. It is very nice that I can be in LA in an hour on a plane or six hours in a car. It's very accessible and easy to be a participant in both cities. Leaving San Francisco and the West Coast would be hard because I would feel like I was leaving LA, too.

The advantages to California are many. I like the weather, and I like the easy access you have to so many different environments and climates. The general vibe to California feels a lot more warm and welcoming than the East Coast, which is something that I notice immediately as soon as I arrive in New York. California is a very culturally diverse state, and, in my opinion, feels very integrated, which I think adds to a richer life experience.

The politics and the diverse landscape and climate influence my work profoundly. The sunsets are amazing here. The more accepting and easygoing vibe that is prevalent in California has helped me develop my work in a more supportive environment. That has really enabled and inspired me to go in directions that push the limits of my work that I do not feel would be possible in any other place.

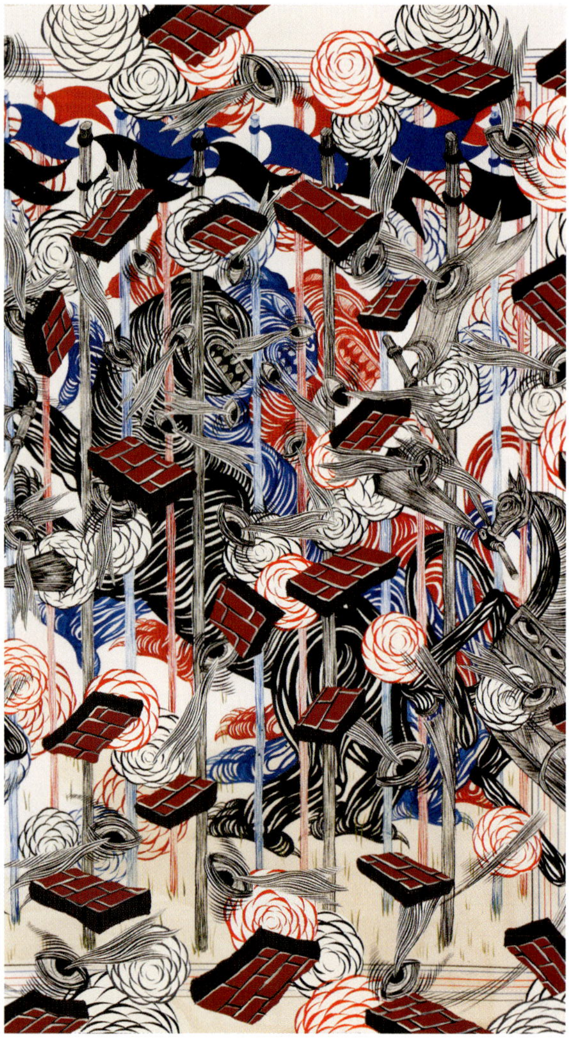

"Caged Beast Explosion (detail)" 2012
Acryic on paper
16 x 12 inches

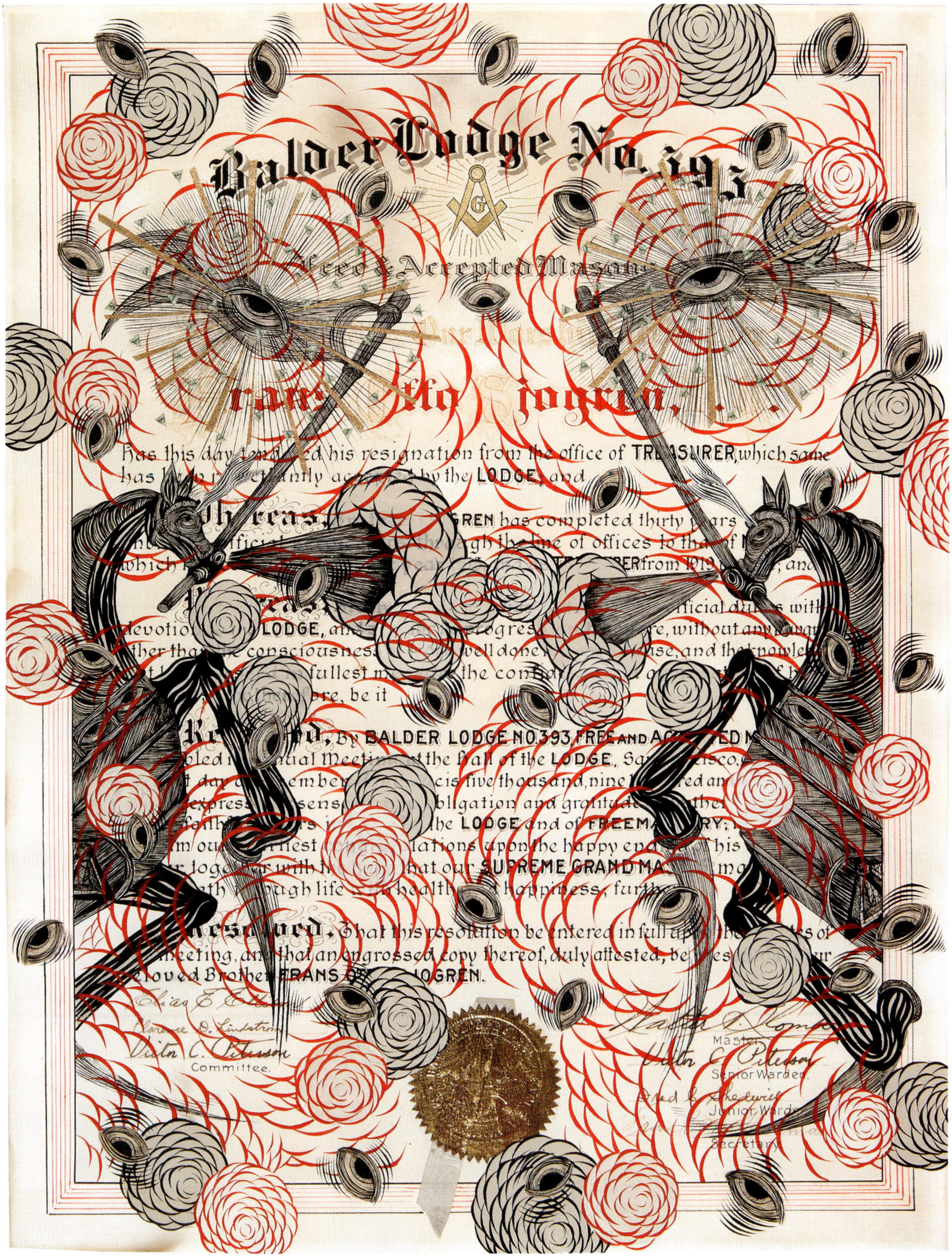

"Divine Resignation" 1947-2012
Acrylic, ink, and collage on found
Masonic treasurer resignation certificate
18 x 14 inches

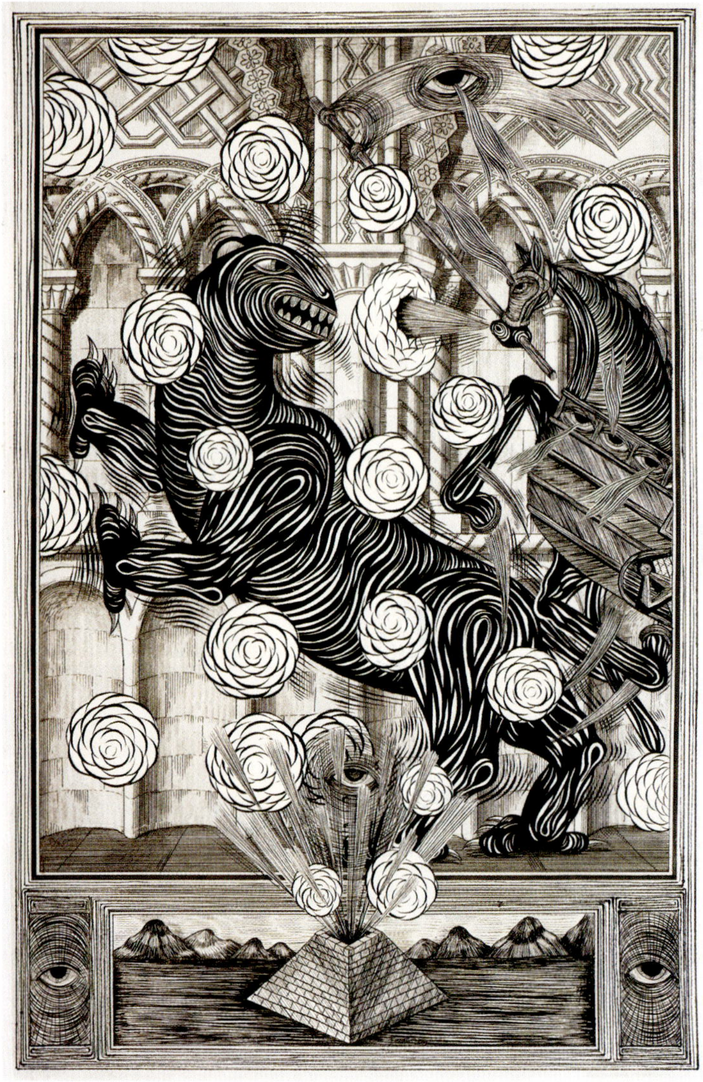

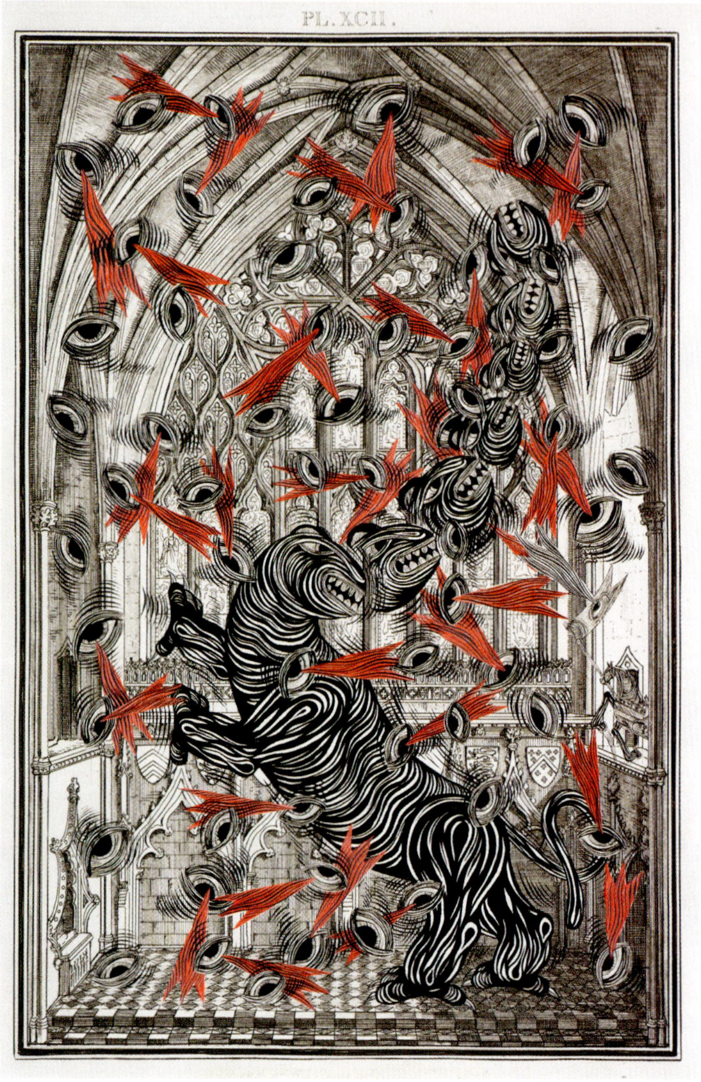

"The Horse on Our Back" 1798-2012
Acrylic on antique copper plate etching
16 x 12 inches

"Trapped Beast" 1798-2012
Acrylic on antique copper plate etching
16 x 12 inches

"Melting Lincoln" 2012
Acrylic, gouache, collage, and colored pencil on paper
16 x 12 inches

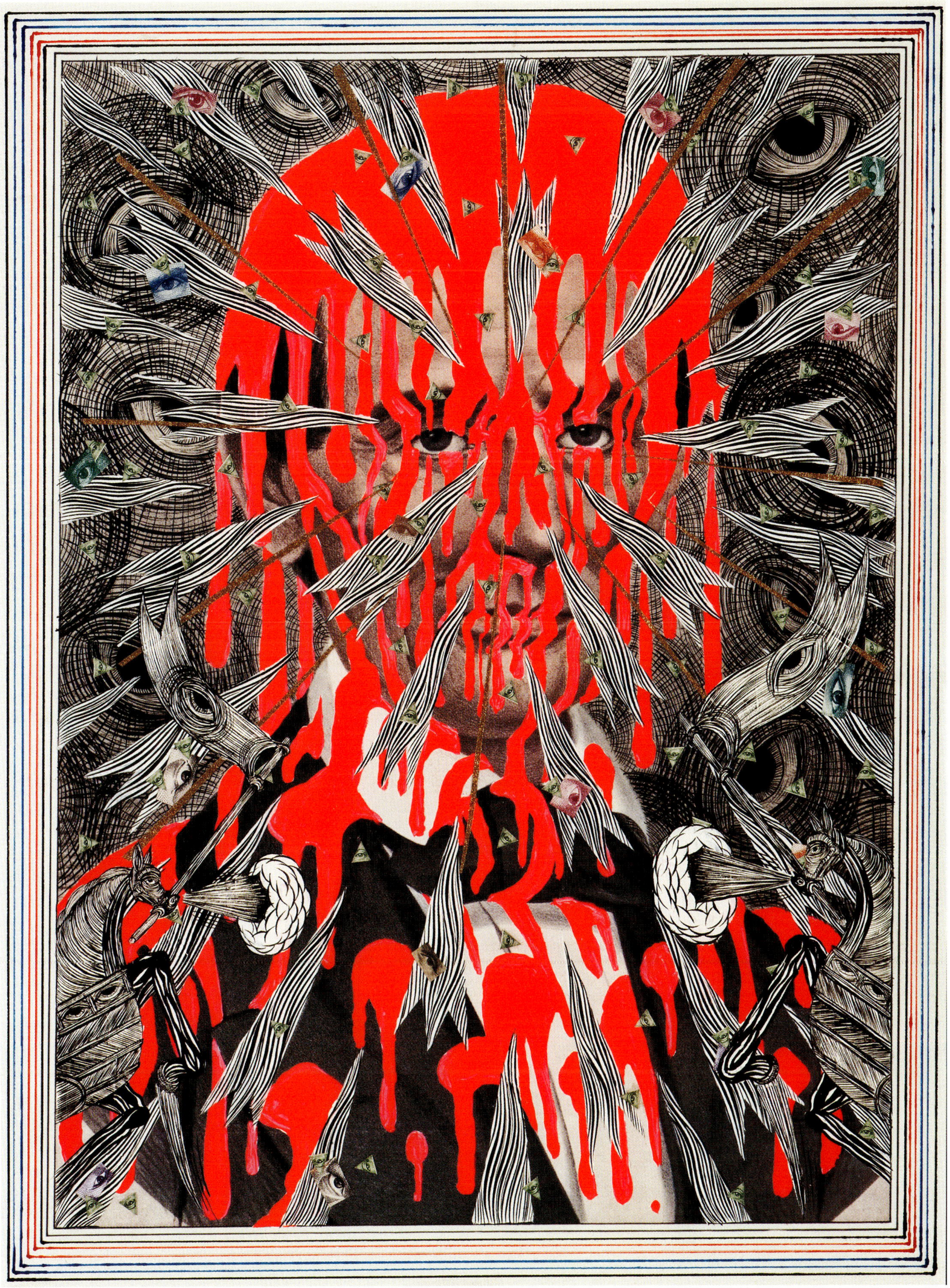

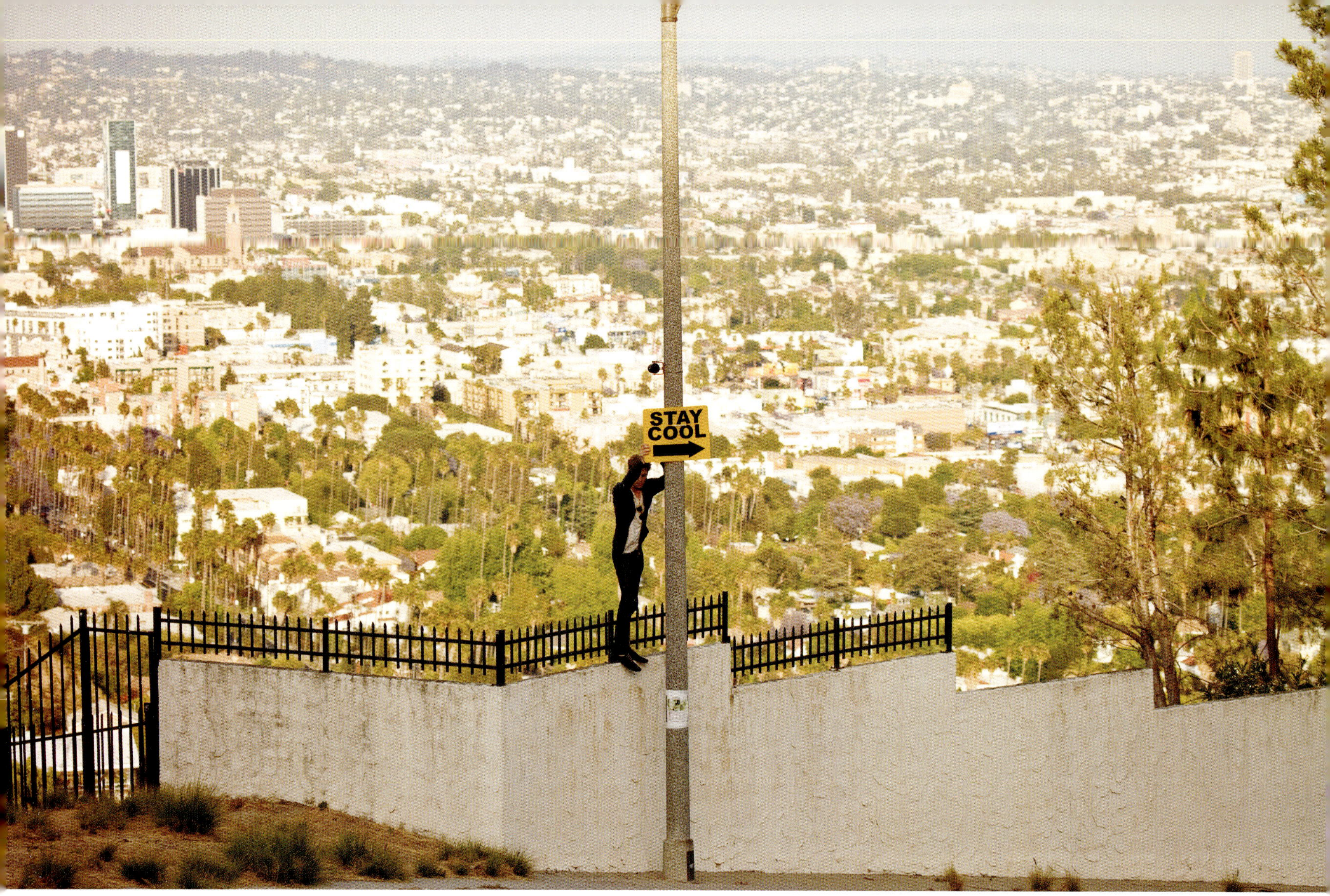

LUCY ROSE

Los Angeles, California
monsterchildren.com

When it was decided four years ago that the Australian publication I worked for was launching another version of the magazine in the United States, it wasn't even a discussion where we would set up our US offices. In hindsight, though, it does seem strange that Los Angeles was the natural choice with almost all of the magazine publishing industry being based in New York.

Los Angeles is such a beautiful city. It almost seems ironic to say, considering my feelings about the place on my first visit, which are certainly not isolated to myself. While I will refrain from quoting Roman Polanski, both because it's been done too frequently but also because I don't completely agree, Los Angeles isn't exactly world renowned for having a picturesque landscape. Los Angeles' beauty is in the details, the kind that you can drive past every day and only notice two years later. There is a form of inspiration on every corner if you're willing to look for it.

The sprawled city allows for so much freedom. The ocean, the desert, and the mountains are all so accessible. The space that is available and hugely obtainable, to work and live in, is unlike any other major city I know of. It allows the lifestyle you dream of without having to

RJ Shaughnessy
"Stay Cool #97" 2012
Digital photograph
Dimensions vary

compromise the luxuries of the city that we rely on. It is a city where art has always been extremely prevalent but has also always taken a back seat. When most people in this world think of California, and Los Angeles, I have no doubt that the majority of thoughts go instantly to Hollywood. While this is certainly not a representation of this place, I can't help but feeling that it removes a level of pressure. The art world in California has not had any form of definition in the past, and while great work has been coming out of here for decades, it still does not carry the reputation of a city such as New York.

What I have noticed about Los Angeles and California is that the air of support for new things and new people that are contributing to this culture is phenomenal. The cynicism, which is so common in the art scene, seems to be replaced by excitement. The attitude appears to me that there is always room for something or someone more. After two years in this city, I have no doubt we made the right decision: the energy in this city, the excitement when like-minded people only want to support what you're working on and to help you grow. The community really is just that. It seems as though everyone wants to grow this culture more—not to compete with bigger and 'more established' art cities but to gain recognition and awareness for the culture that is so prevalent here. Los Angeles and California is somewhat of an underdog in the historical sense of art internationally. While the work coming out of this place is far from second class, I can't help but think there is something to be said, something uniting, about having a common battle to fight.

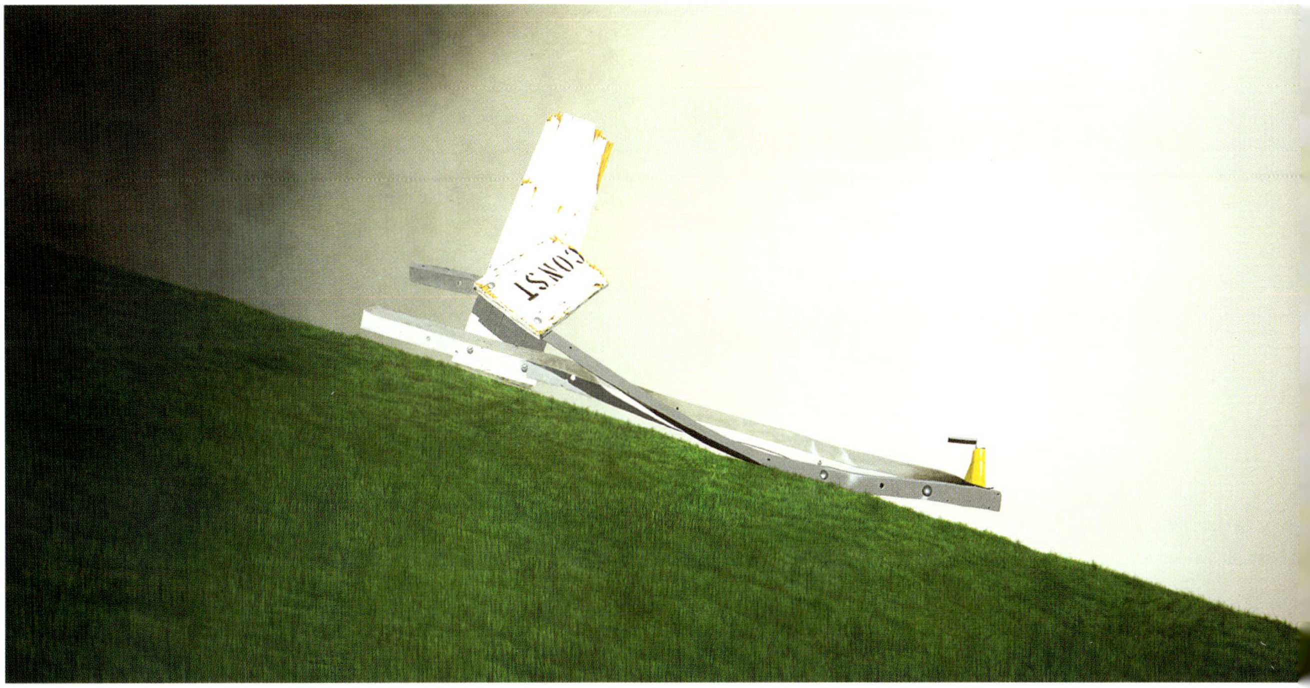

Ed Ruscha
"Psycho Spaghetti Western #3" 2010
Acrylic on canvas
60 x 112 inches

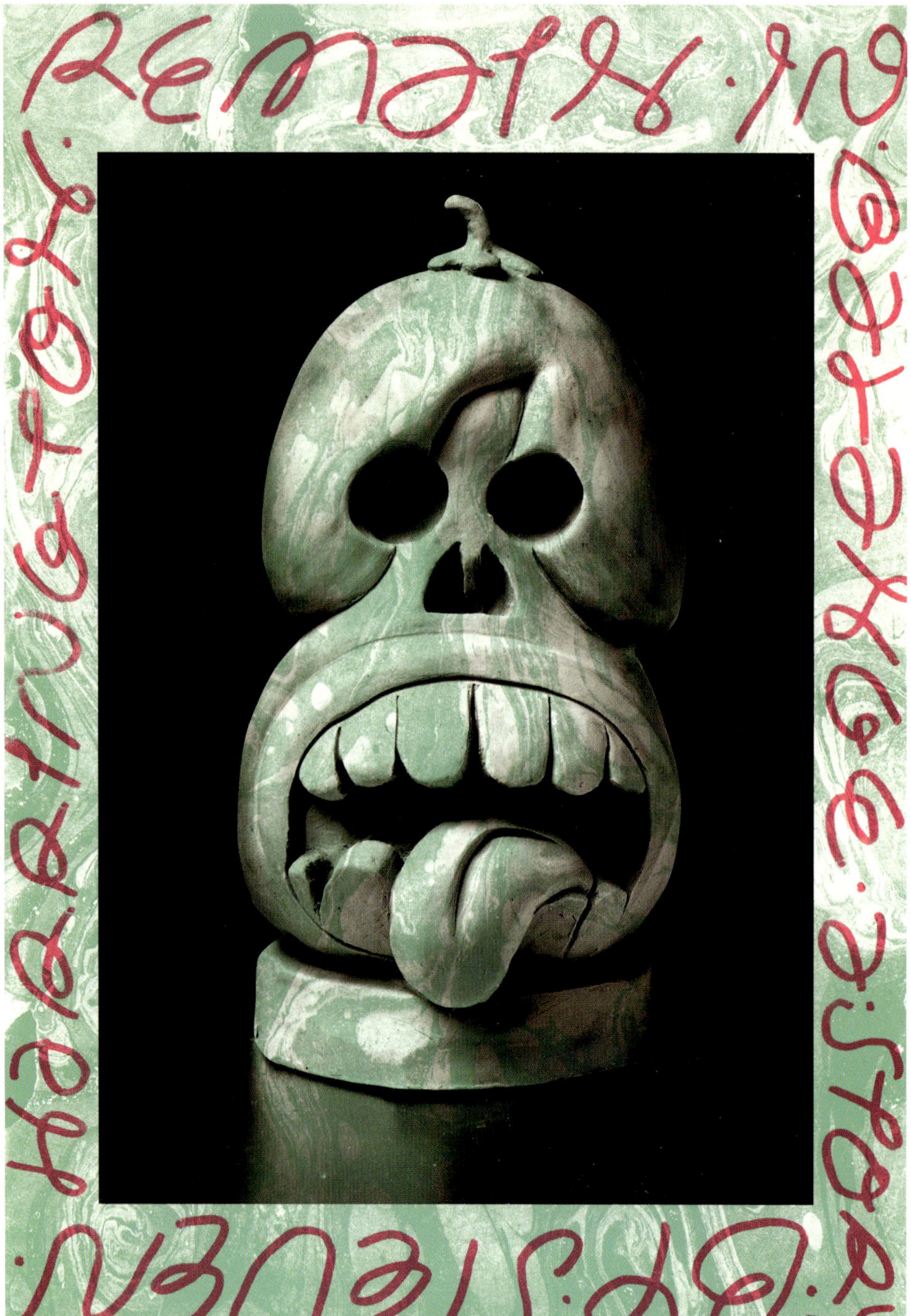

Steven Harrington
"Remain In Balance, A Story By Steven Harrington, Book Cover" 2012
Hand-shaped polymer clay
8 x 13 inches

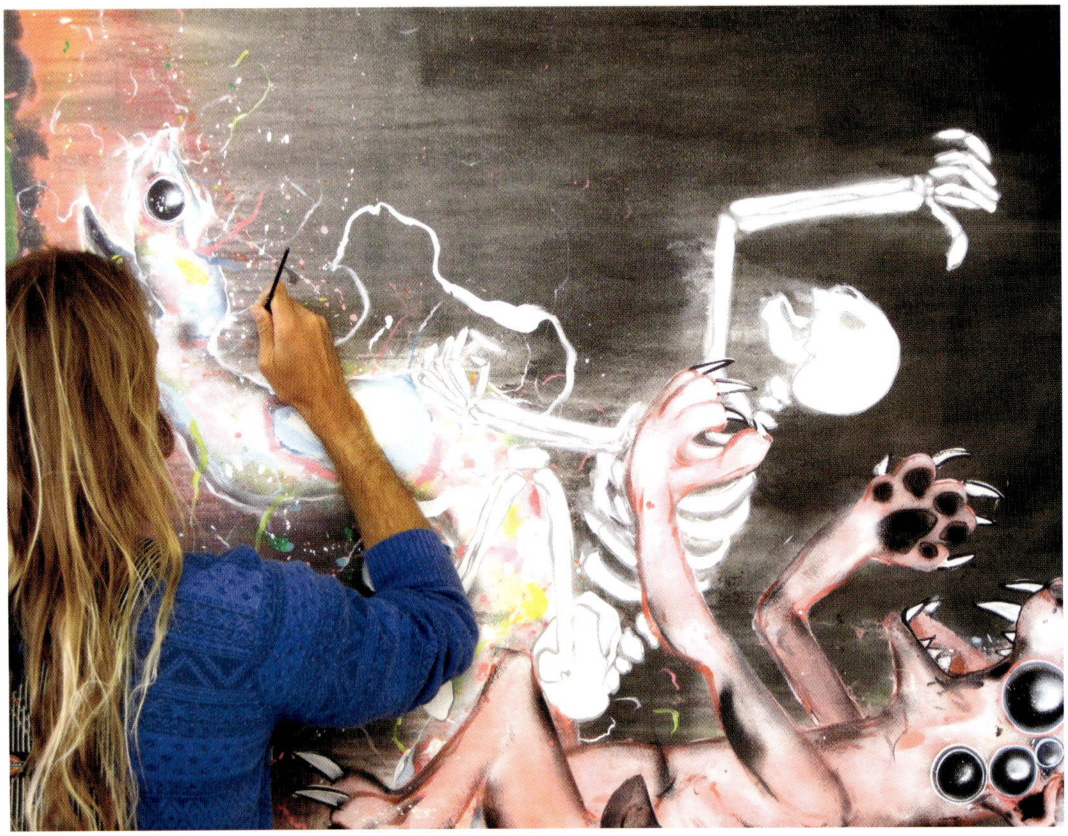

Self Portrait, 2012

KELSEY BROOKES

San Diego, California
kelseybrookes.com
Quint Contemporary Art, San Diego
Circle Culture Gallery, Berlin
Lazarides Gallery, London

Waves brought me here, and the people keep me here.

The waves, weather, and the people are both the advantages and disadvantages to living and working in California.

California has influenced my work and process by its ability to provide freedom and possibility.

My themes include expansion, intensity, enlightenment, purity, and, more recently, acceptance through a process of create, destroy, create, destroy, create, destroy, create, destroy, worry, then hang.

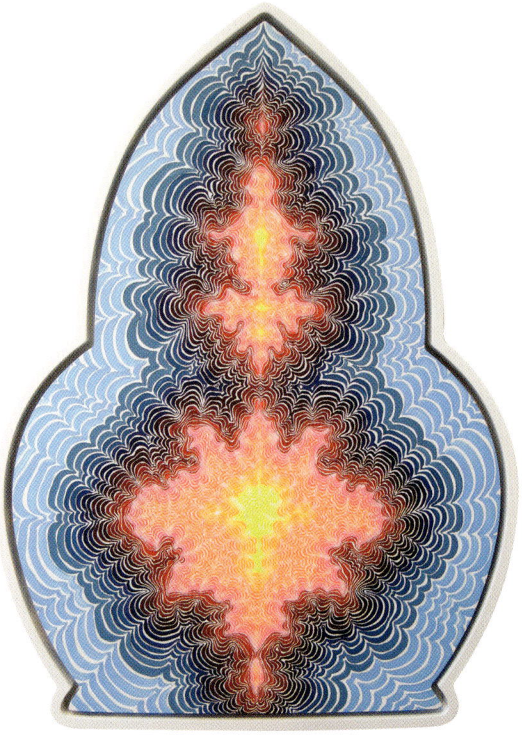

"*Window 1*" 2012
Mixed media on wood
18 x 24 inches

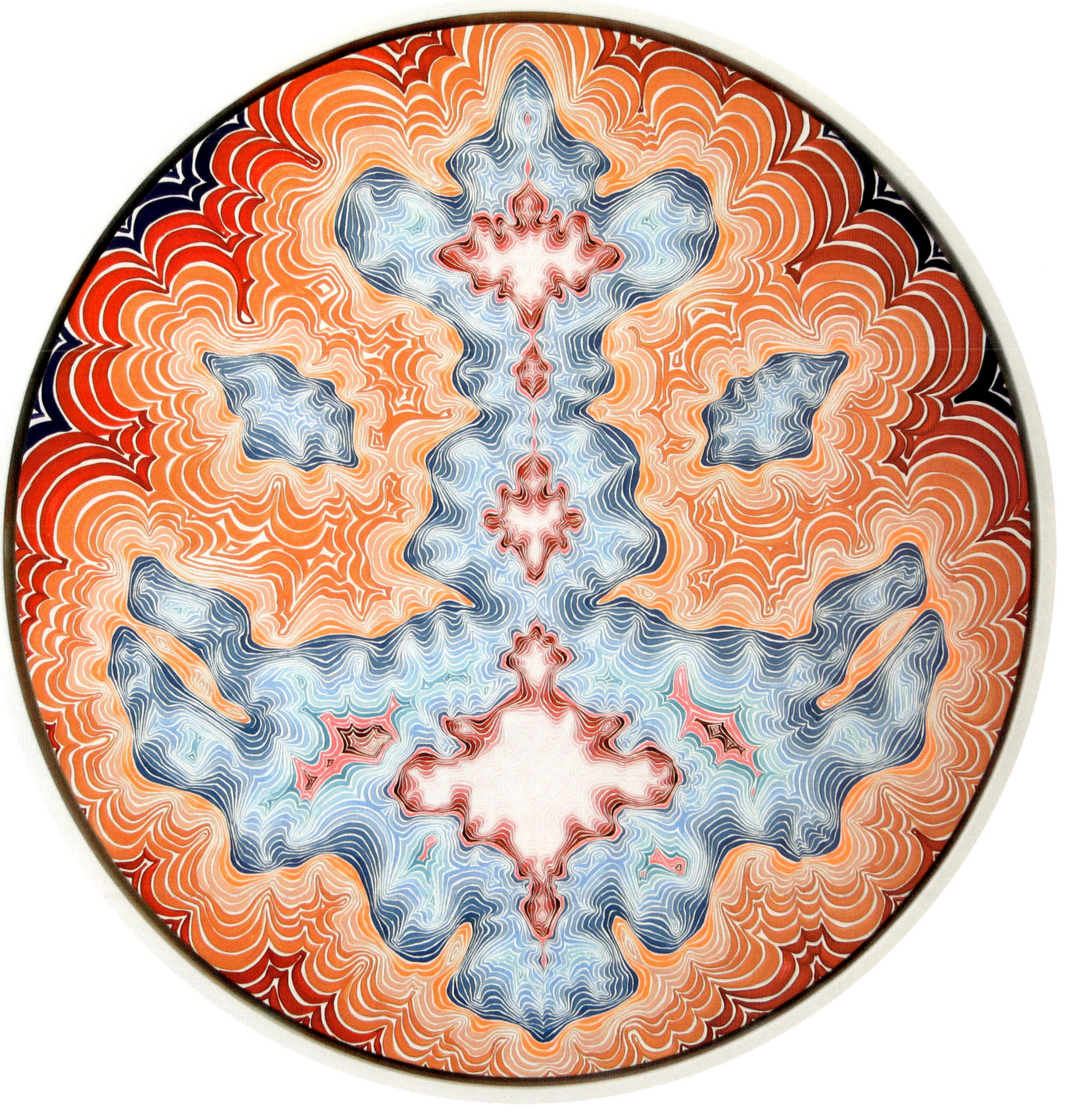

"Untitled 4" 2012
Mixed media on wood
24 x 24 inches

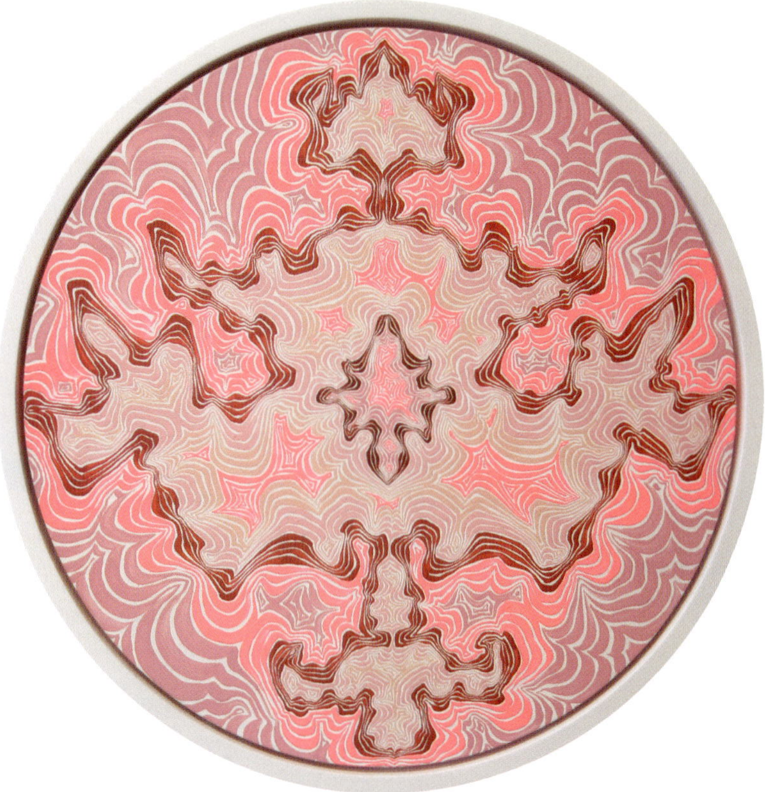

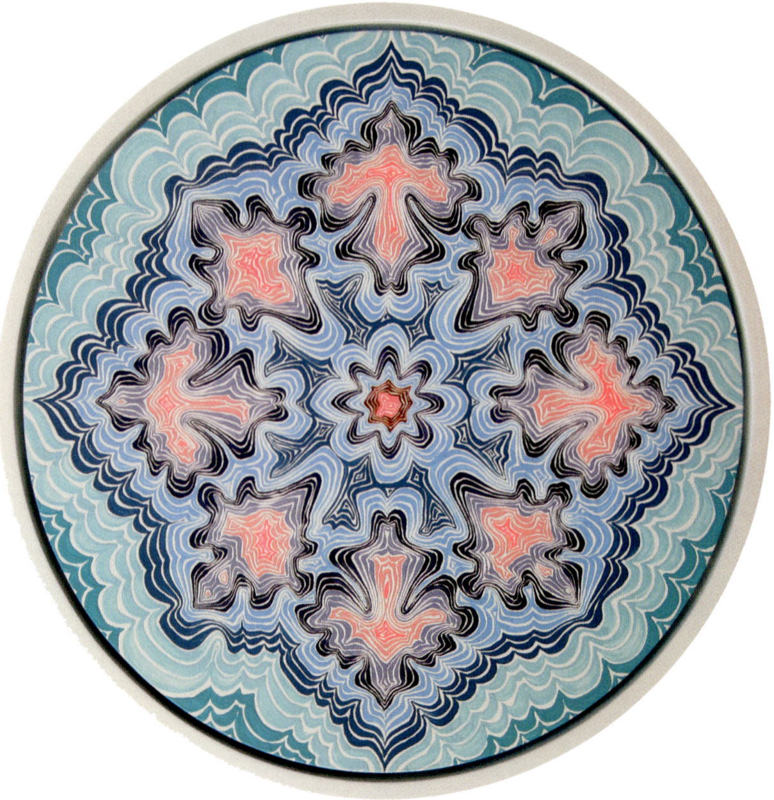

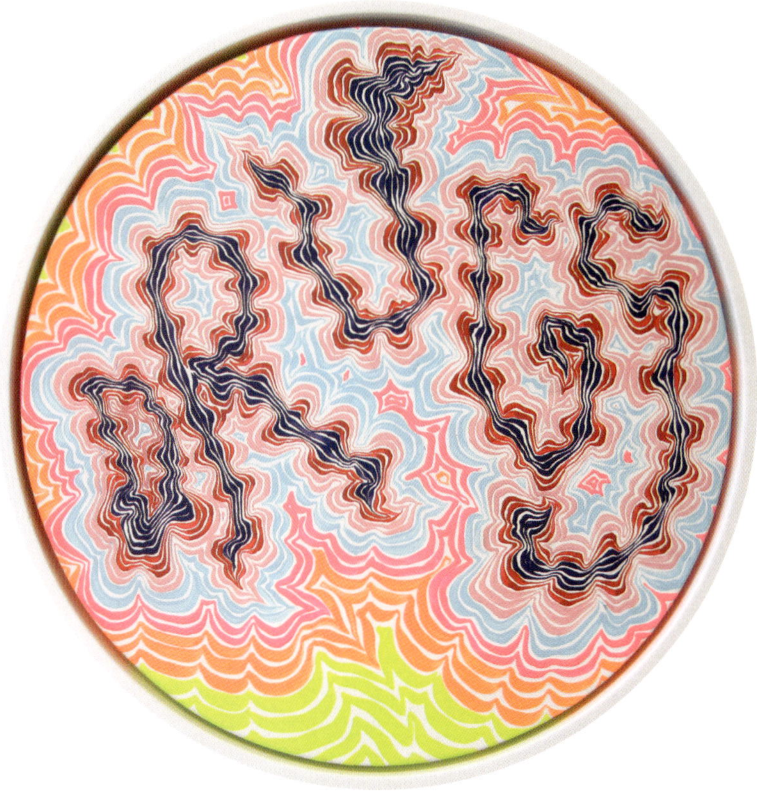

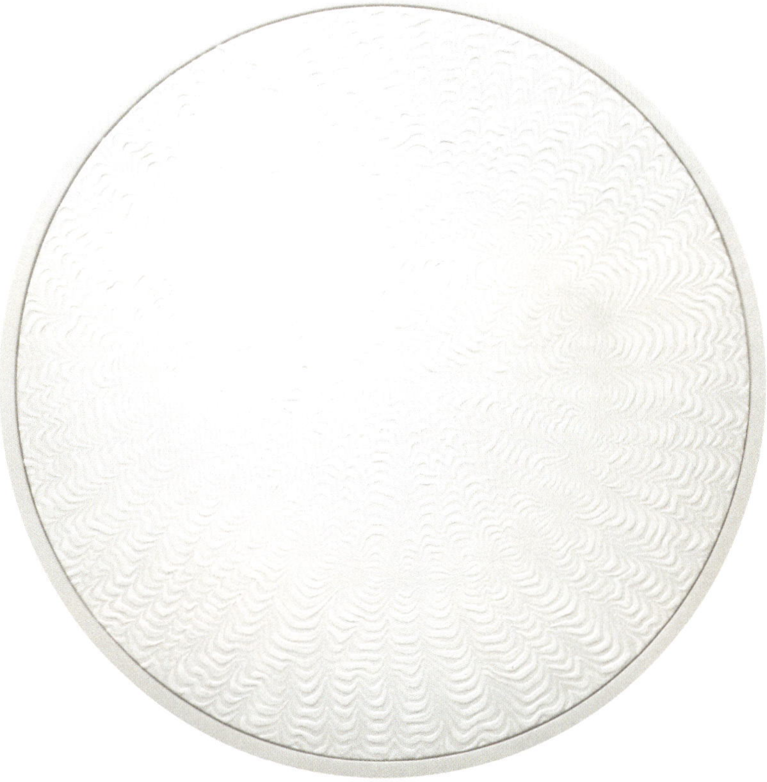

Top left:
"Untitled 7" 2012
Mixed media on wood
12 x 12 inches

Top right:
"Untitled 6" 2012
Mixed media on wood
12 x 12 inches

Bottom left:
"Drugs" 2012
Mixed media on wood
7 x 7 inches

Bottom right:
"White on White Smile" 2012
Mixed media on wood
12 x 12 inches

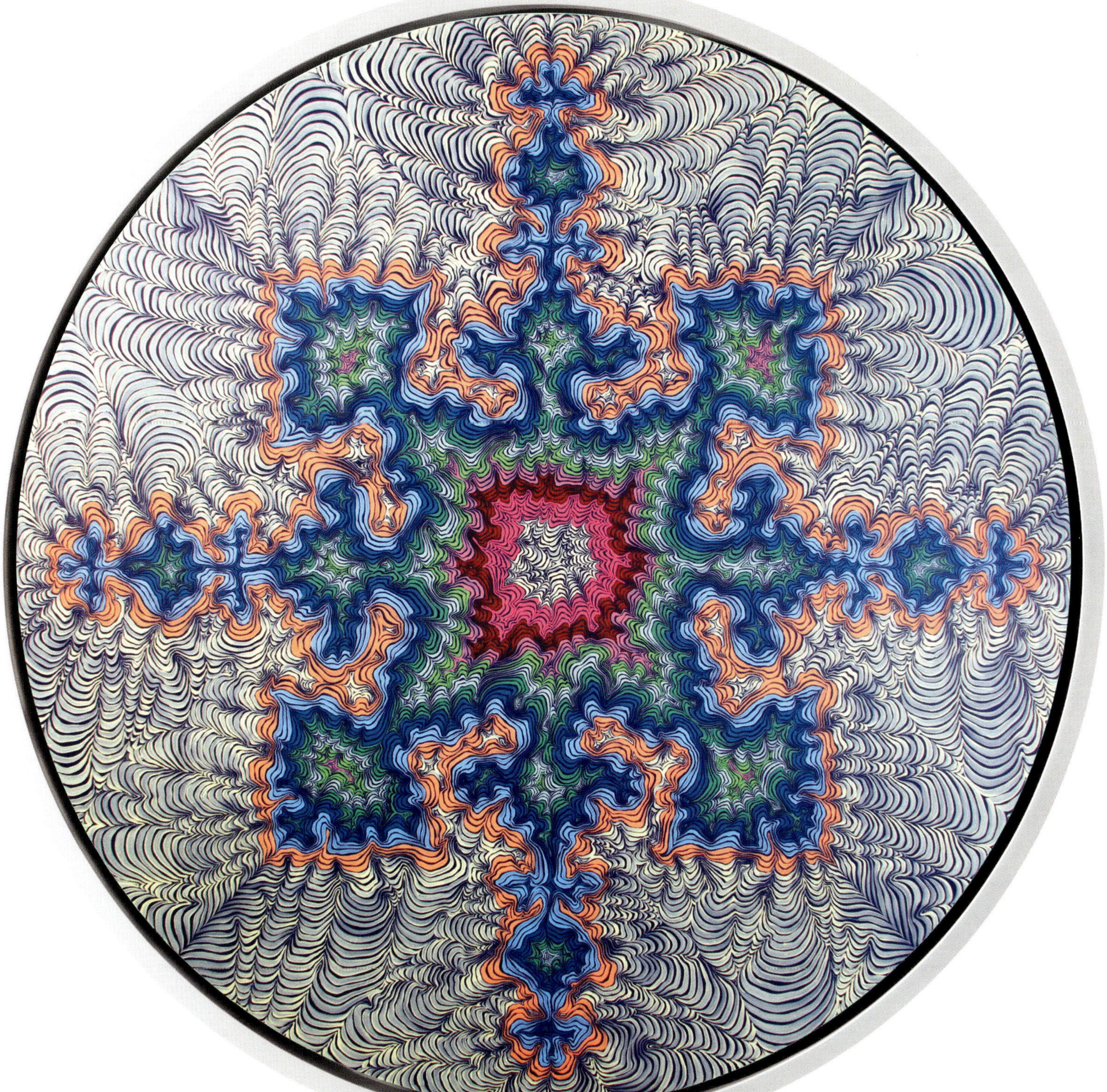

"Iris" 2012
Mixed media on wood
36 x 36 inches

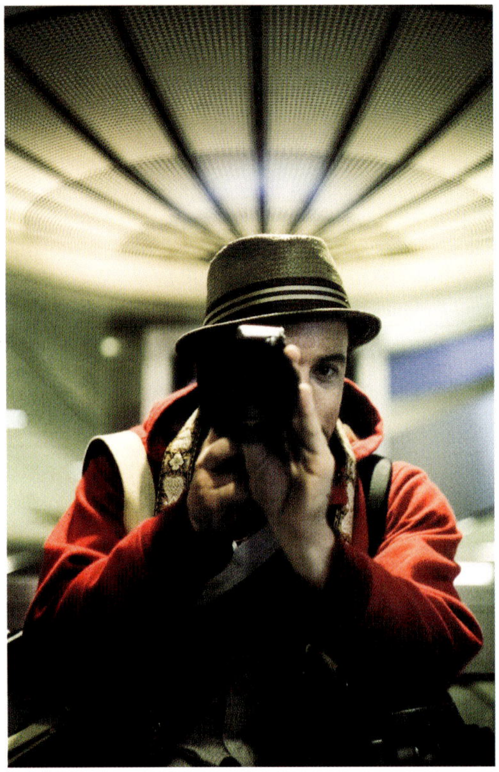

Self Portrait, 2012

G.LEWIS HESLET

Los Angeles, California
thecreativelives.com

My dad was a professor at UC Santa Cruz, and my mom was a student of his, and their love brought me to California, but what keeps me here are the people and the endless stories that California encourages and inspires. Painters, actors, writers, dancers, every dreamer of every variety throughout this sunny state, and you don't have to live in San Francisco or Los Angeles to feel that creative energy resonating and perpetuating itself in art shows, plays, and performances in small towns throughout the state. Finding those people and hearing those stories is what keeps me here. There really hasn't been a place like 21st century California since 16th century Italy. It's emerging to become a beacon to creative people worldwide.

The sun and weather are advantages, but I suppose everyone will say that. I'd say the support and encouraging nature of creative people is a huge advantage. Self-idolatry can be a big negative; too much support can spoil a talented mind. The arrogance of some Californians may be due to their constant praise for one another, but one must understand that it is this praise that fuels their dreams and leads them toward a greater end. Other positives include the food, the coastline, and the temperate rainforests, but again I assume everyone will say that.

The stories of creative people more then anything else [influence my work]. The same doubts, the same triumphs, the same awkward and incredible moments that occur every moment of every day across the great state. The creative spirit is visceral and yet indescribable; it's a feeling that hits you when you open yourself up to it. I have been fortunate enough to meet some of the most incredible people working in this state, and they have all been kind and encouraging of everyone around them, and that, I would say, is the true spirit of California. It's not just simply about making what you want to make; it's about encouraging others to create what they need to create.

All images from
"The Creative Lives" 2012
Assorted film stills

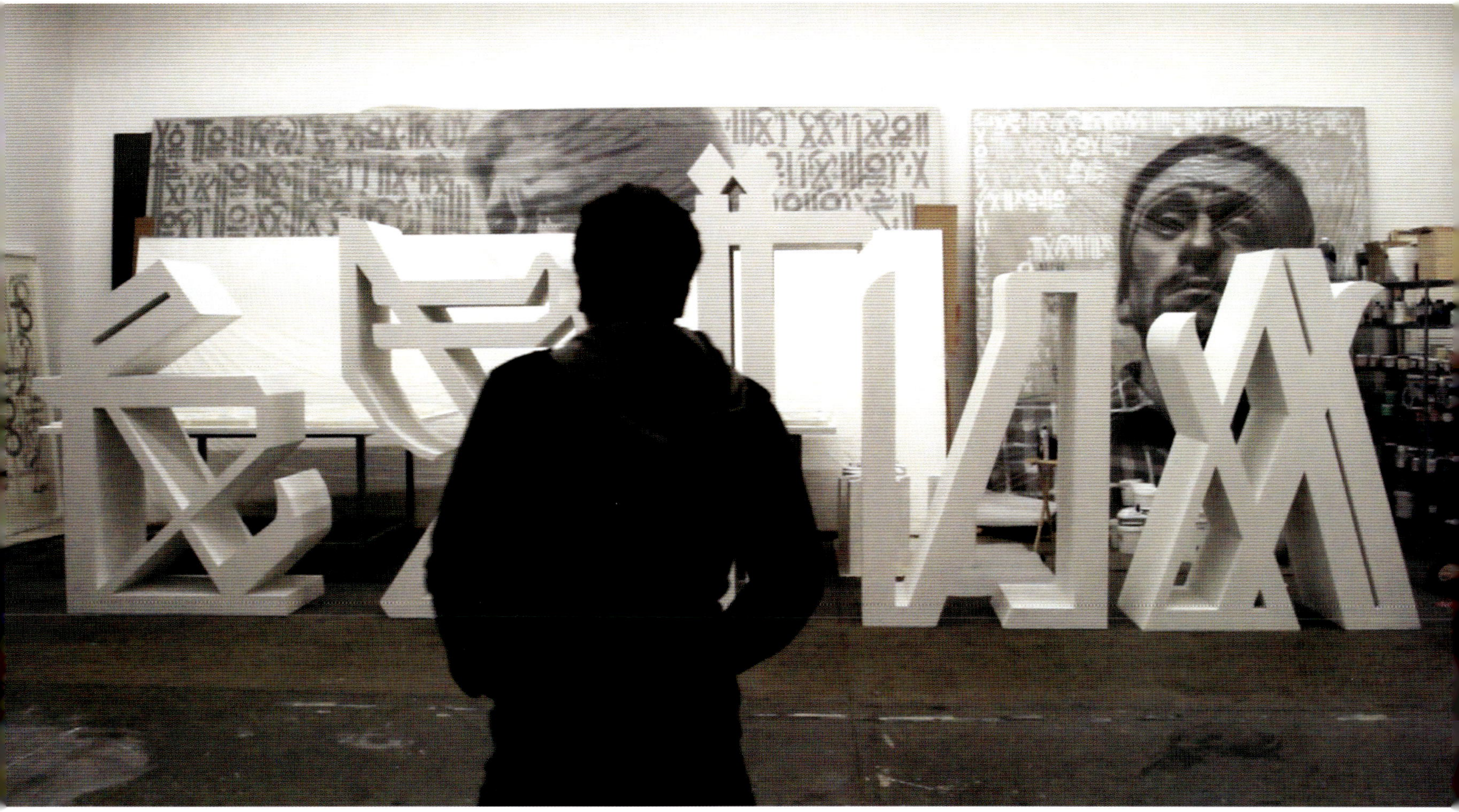

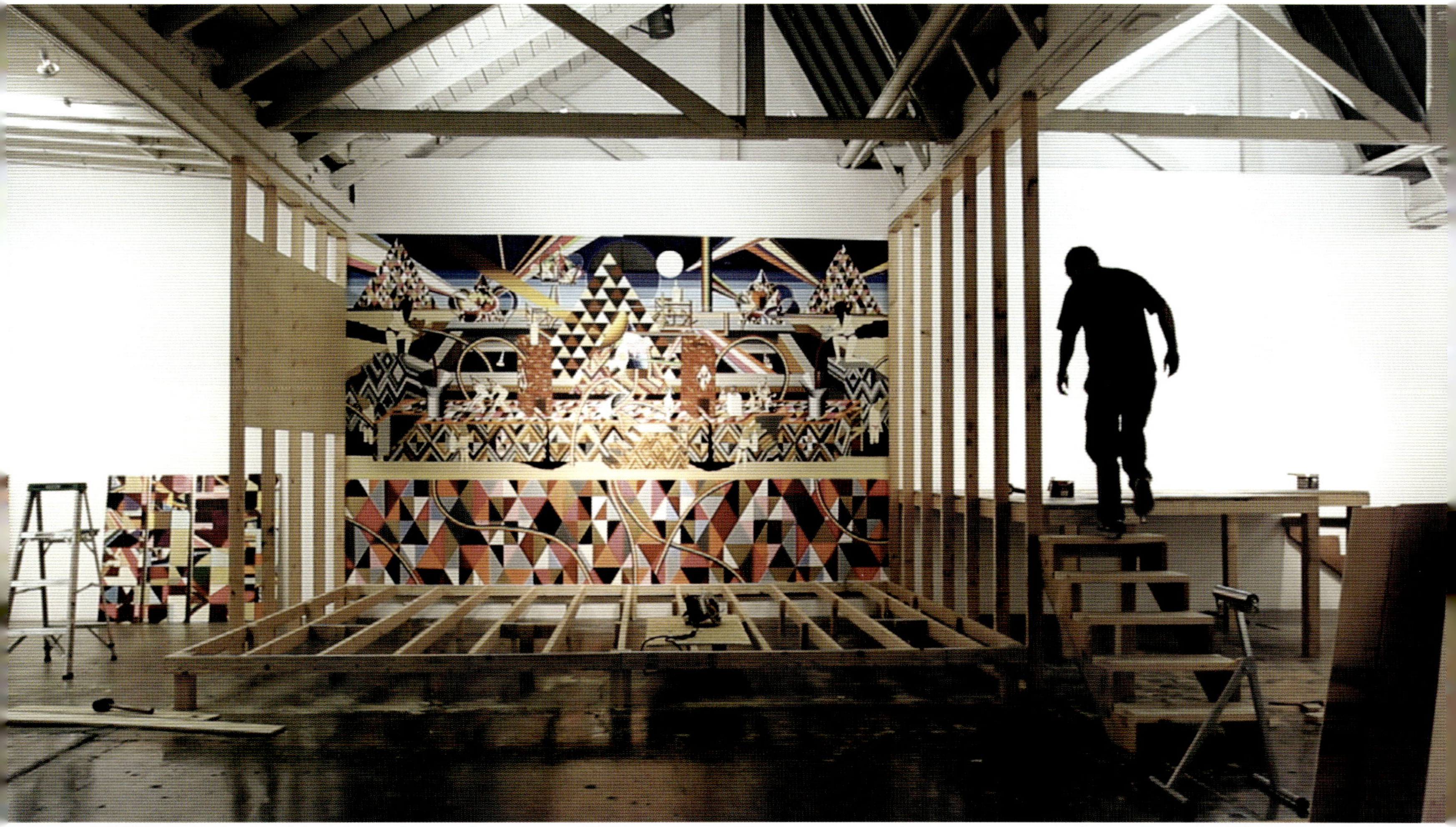

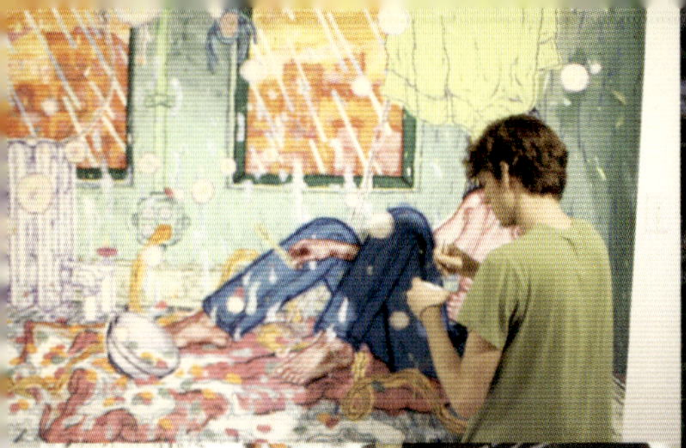
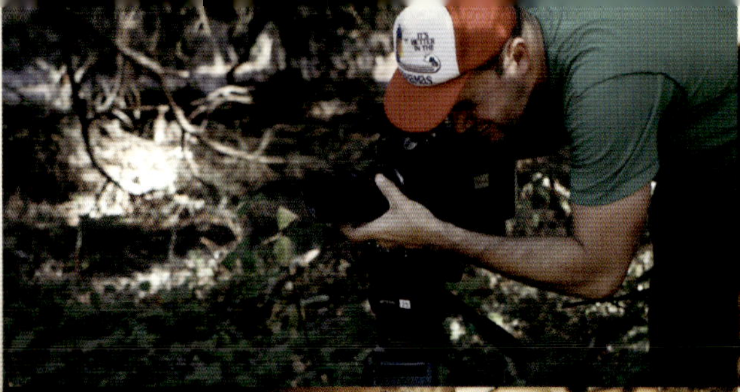
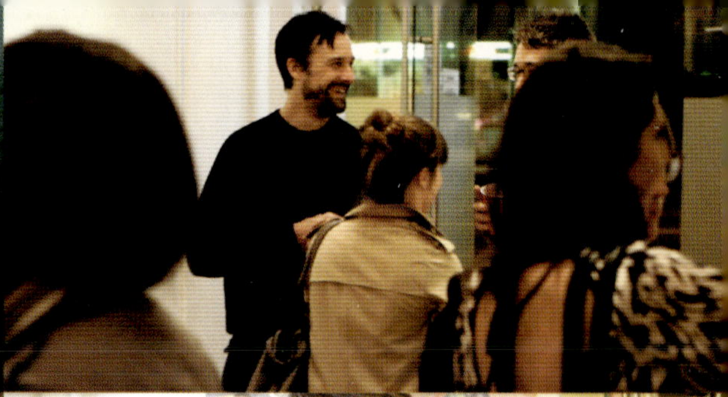
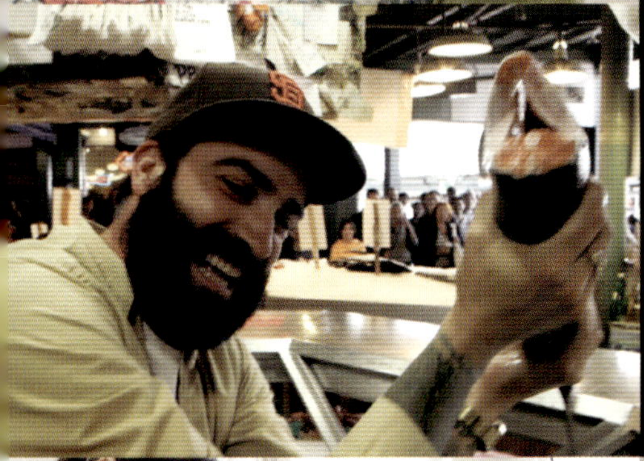
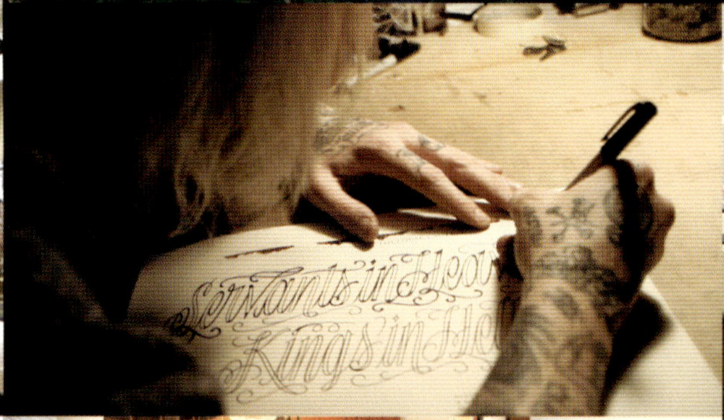
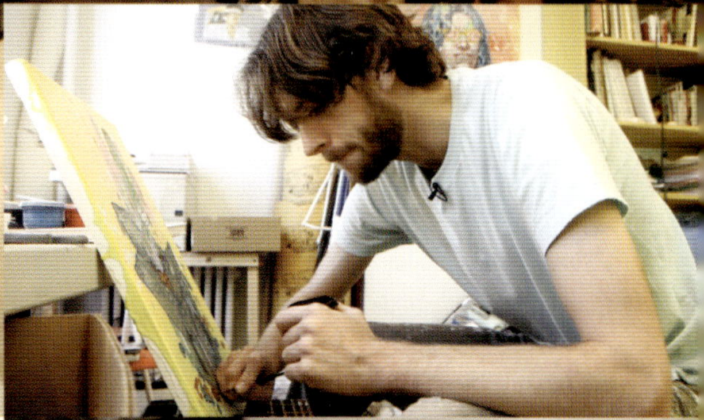
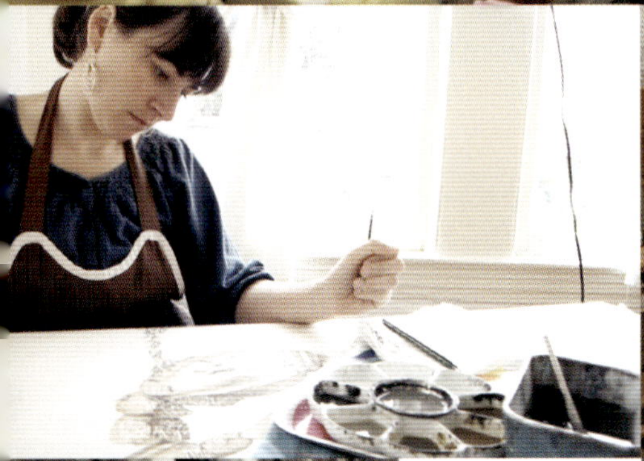
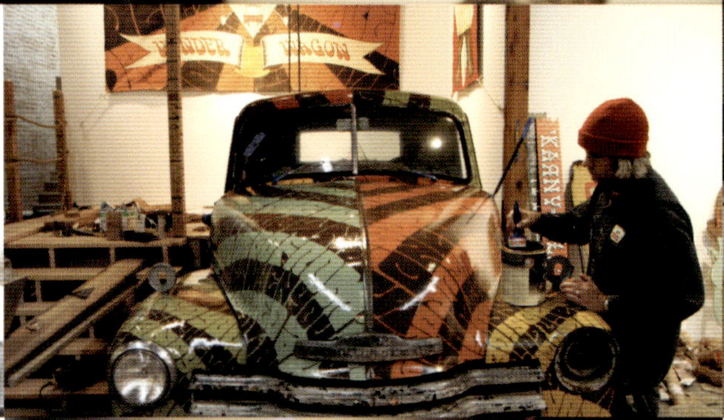
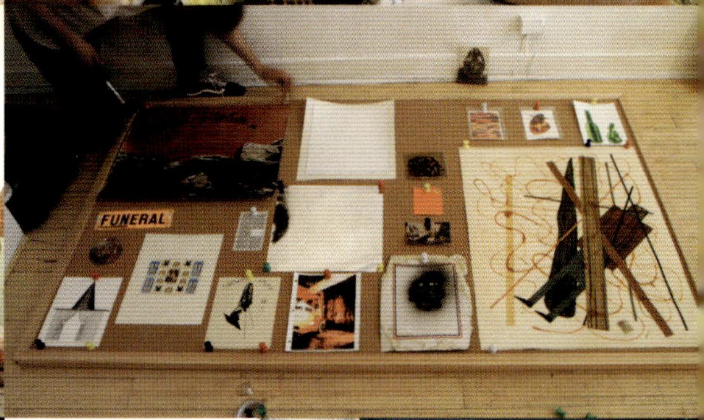
FUNERAL
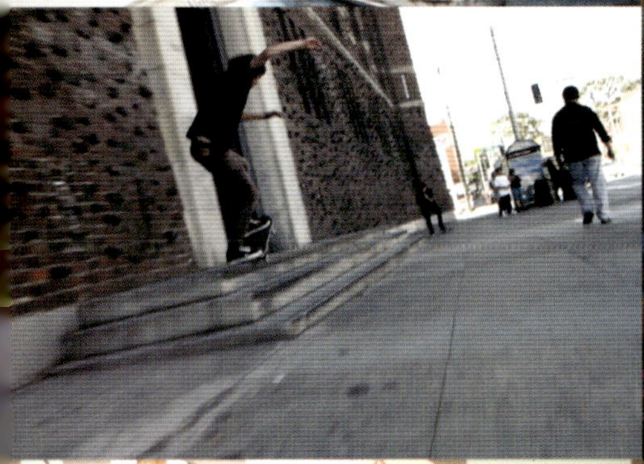
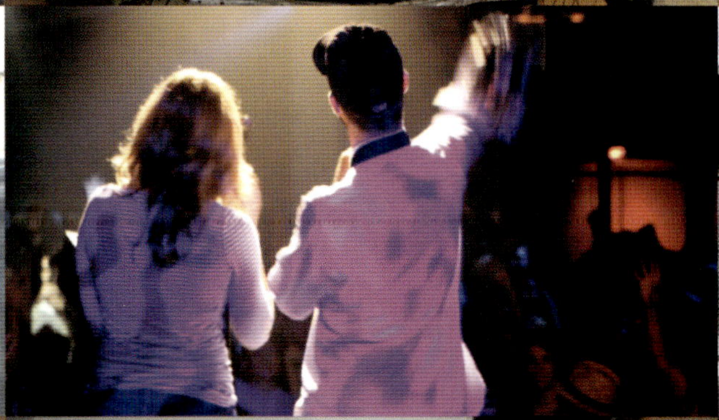
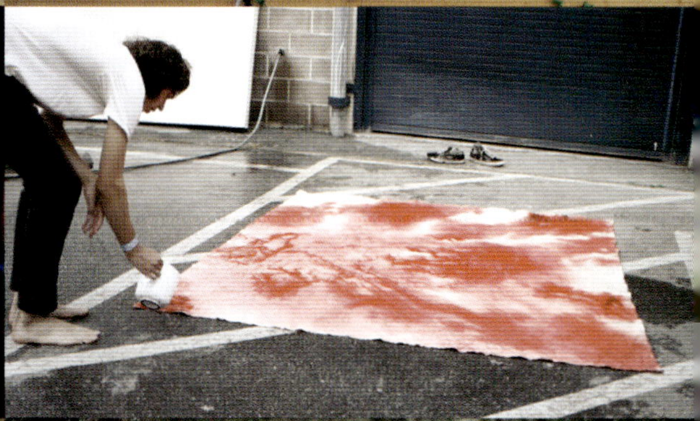
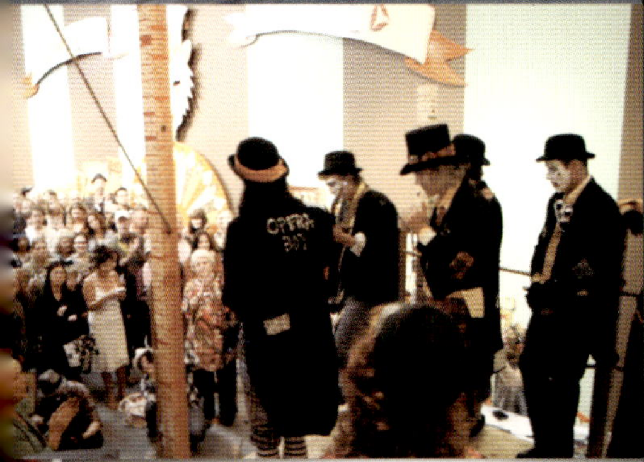
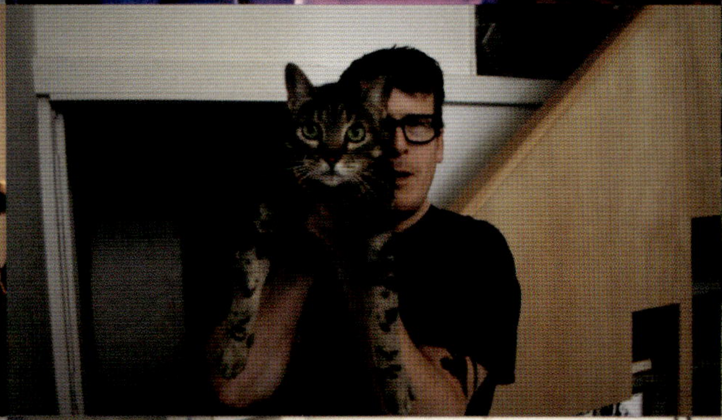
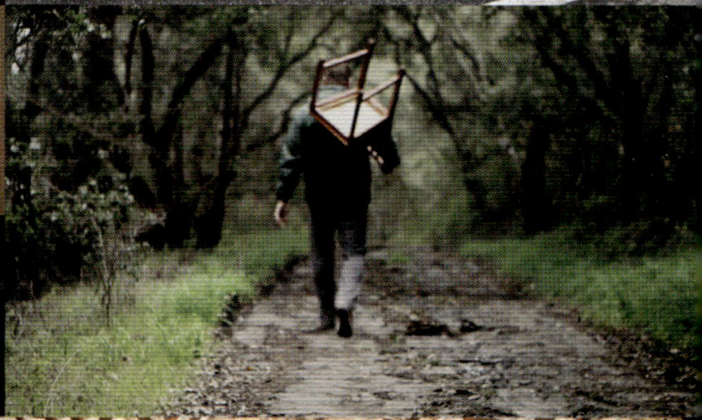
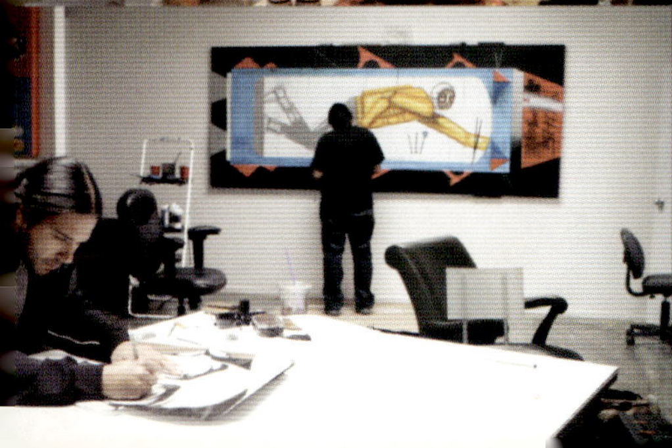
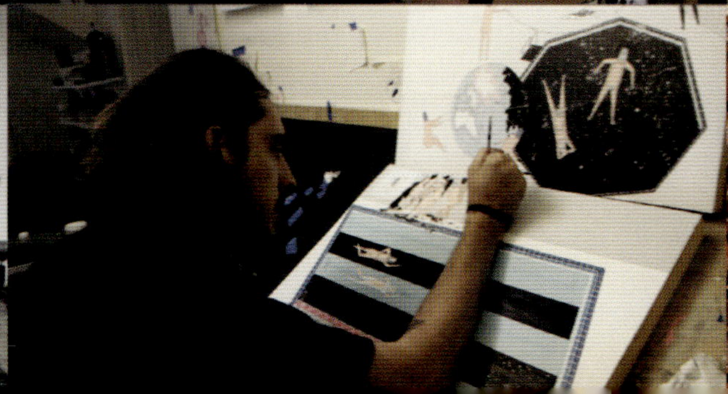
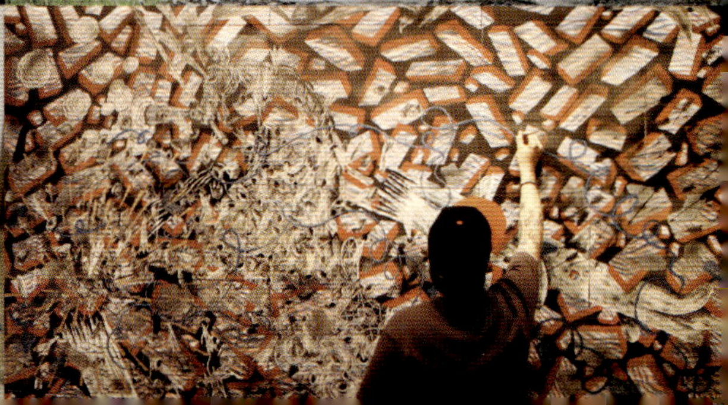

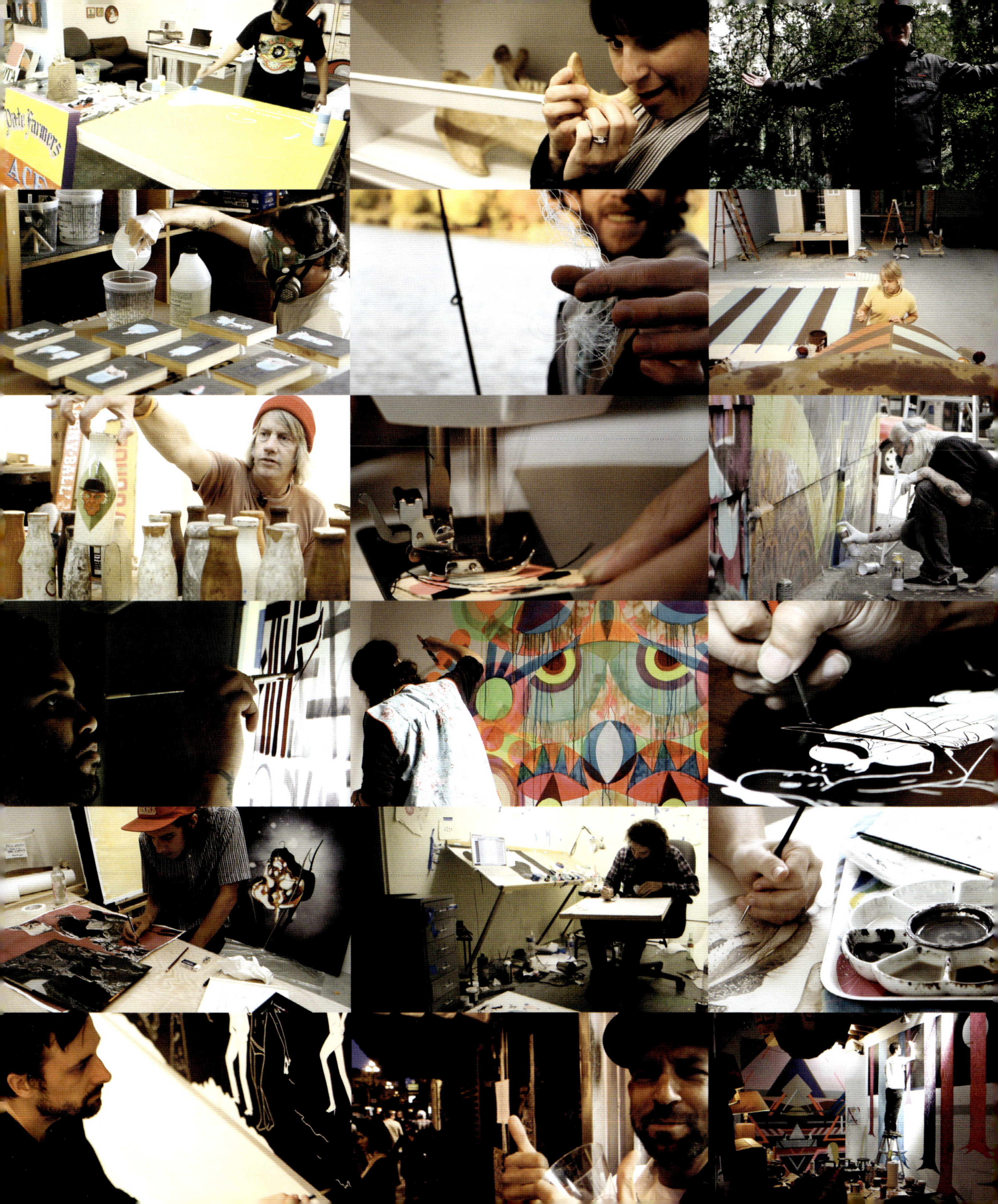
Dade Farmers

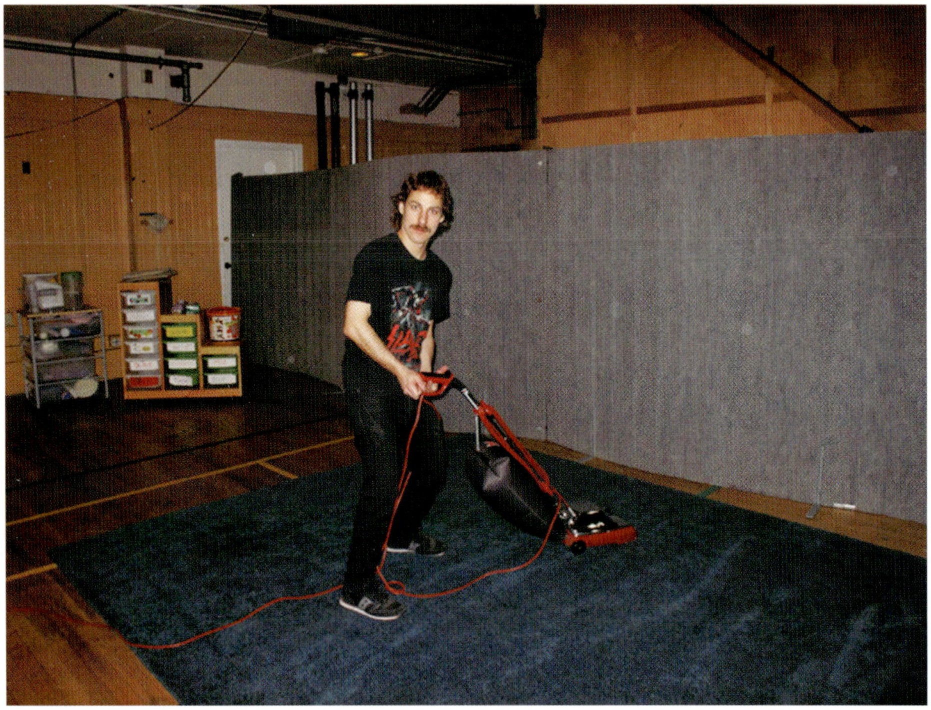

Self Portrait, 2012

BEN VENOM

San Francisco, California

benvenom.com

I moved to San Francisco, California, from Atlanta, Georgia, seven years ago to attend the Master of Fine Arts program at the San Francisco Art Institute. The people and the city are completely opposite from where I grew up, and I enjoyed the change. At this point I would find it very difficult to move back to the Dirty South ... you can't buy beer on Sunday!

A definite advantage to living in California is simultaneous access to the LA and SF art community. They are very different but share some similarities, and it's a short flight between the two cities. Being on the opposite side of the country from New York is a disadvantage. Especially when an artist is attempting to participate in the international gallery scene. I feel we as Californians are somewhat regulated to our own community.

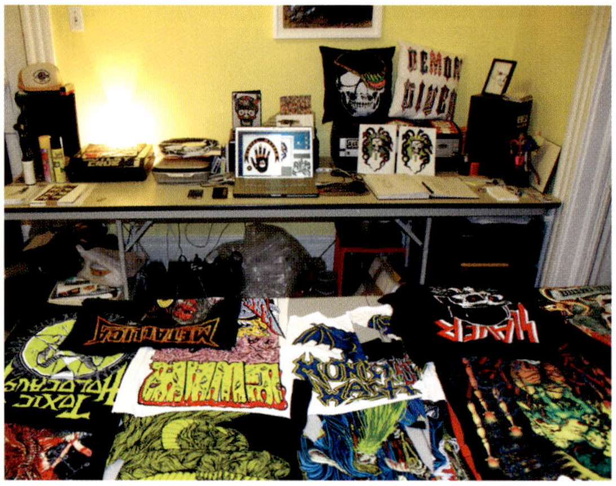

The progressive society and forward-thinking politics that are ever present in San Francisco, and California as a whole, influence my work. A large portion of the materials I use are recycled T-shirts donated by local musicians and friends. In California, recycling is taken more seriously, and a conscious effort is made to not use harmful or unnecessary products that would harm the environment. In San Francisco we have an artist-in-residency program at Recology SF that provides Bay Area artists with access to discarded materials, a stipend, and a large studio space. The idea being that artists can come and create works of art straight out of the trash can.

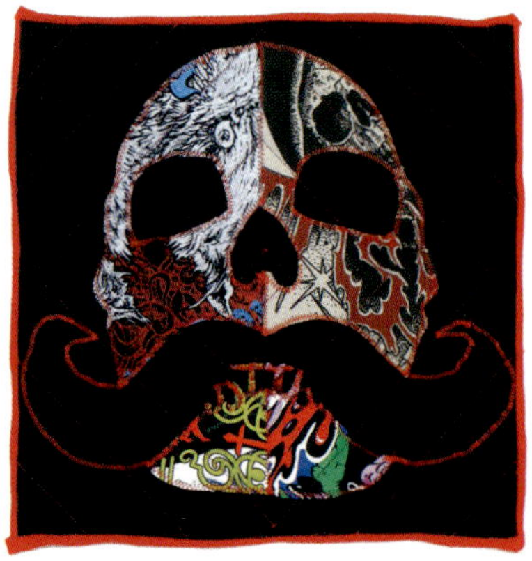

"Beneath the Remains" 2011
Handmade quilt, heavy metal t-shirts, fabric, batting, and thread
11 x 11 inches

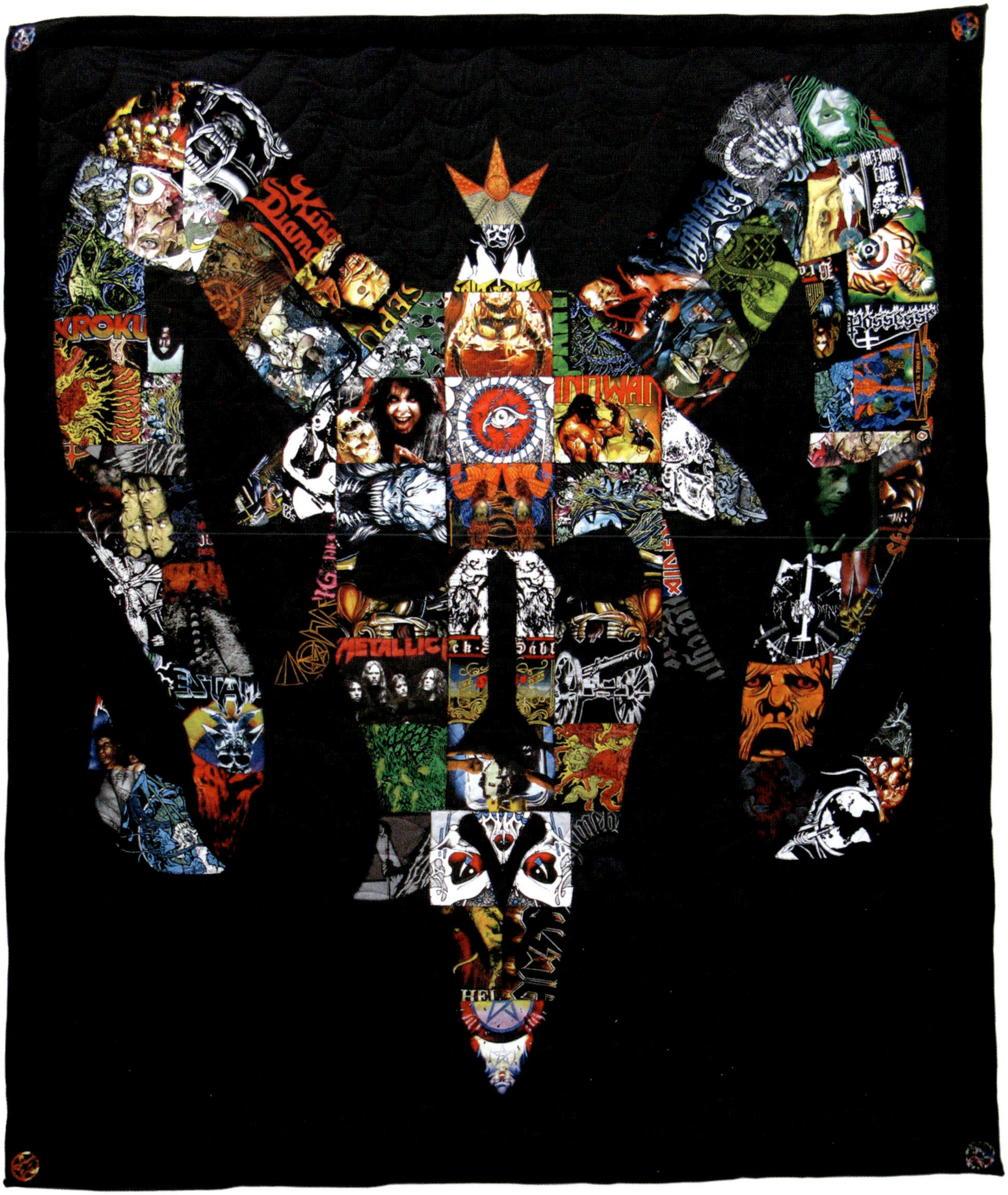

"Don't Wake Me Lucifer!" 2010
Handmade quilt, heavy metal t-shirts, fabric, batting, and thread
83 x 95 inches

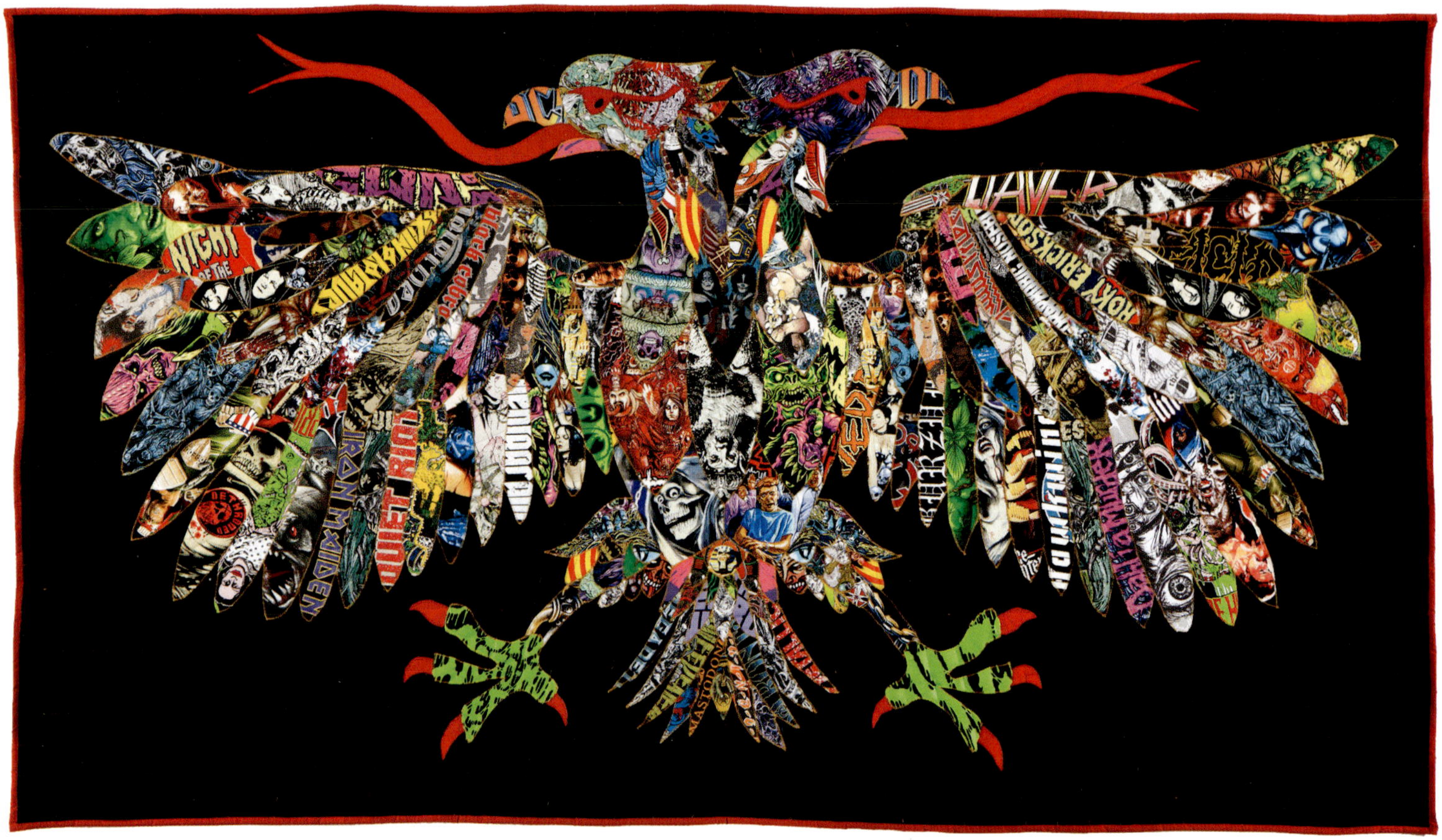

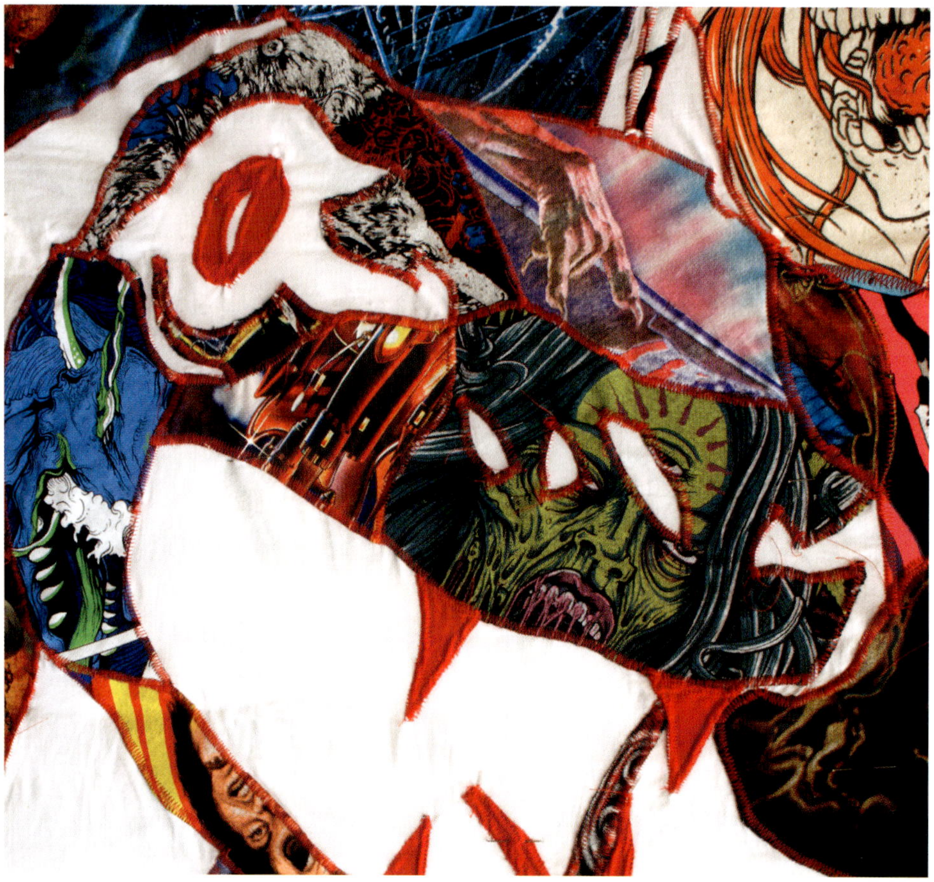

"I Go Where Eagles Dare" 2012
Handmade quilt, heavy metal t-shirts, fabric, batting, and thread
108 x 60 inches

"See You on the Other Side (detail)" 2011
Handmade quilt, heavy metal t-shirts, fabric, batting, and thread

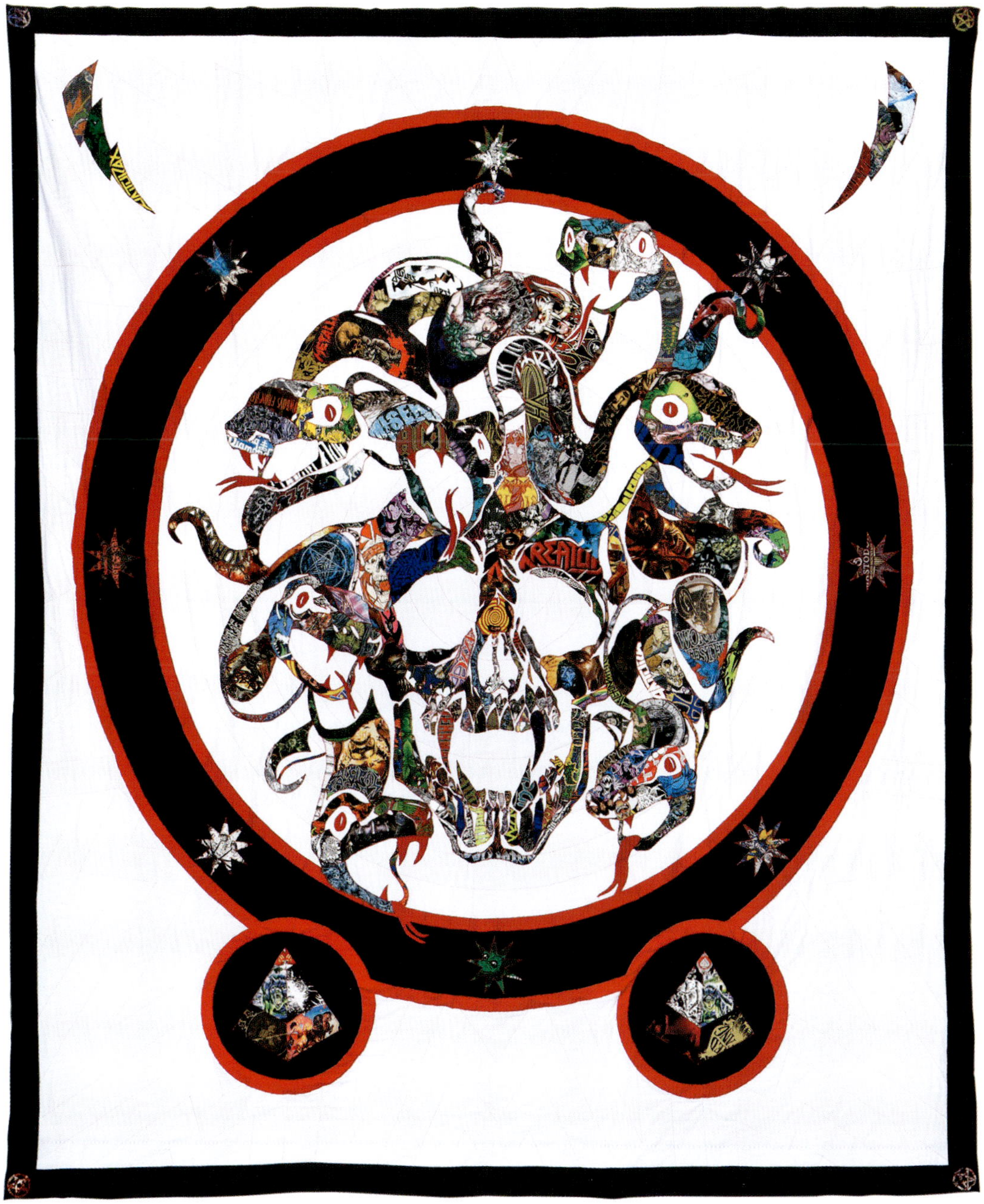

"See You on the Other Side" 2011
Handmade quilt, heavy metal t-shirts,
fabric, batting, and thread
155 x 175 inches

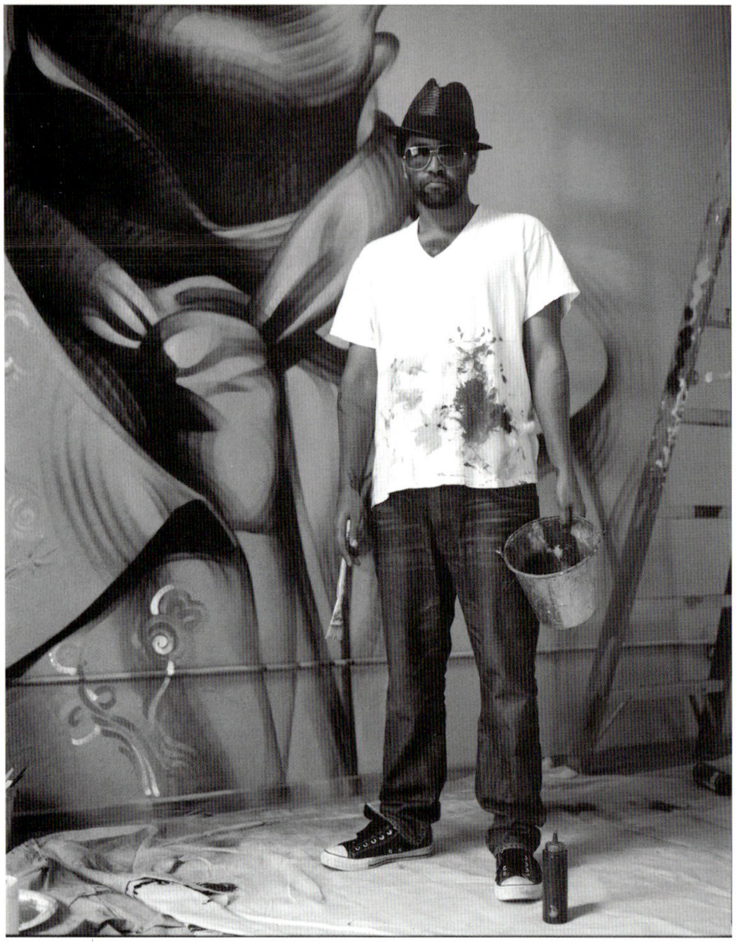

Photo by Greg Bojorquez, 2011

RETNA

Los Angeles, California
digitalretna.com
New Image Art, Los Angeles

Growing up in Los Angeles, the gang culture, graffiti culture, and the close proximity of so many different nationalities were the biggest factors in my upbringing. I have African American, Spanish, and Native American roots, so it was hard to know where I fit in at first. I spent countless hours working on my penmanship for the nuns in Catholic school. In a strange way, those hours spent practicing are a very big part of my work today.

There are some interesting advantages unique to Southern California, Los Angeles specifically, that played very big roles for me. Obviously the weather and space are great, but other factors like police helicopters made doing pieces and burners interesting. Also, the walls here get buffed so quickly that it forces your work to be really effective and memorable before they were covered up. Even though there are so many walls here, there are even more people trying to do pieces on them every day and every night.

I feel like the arrival of Jeffrey Deitch is another big advantage to California and the Los Angeles art scene. When he took over the role as the Director of MOCA, he spent, and continues to spend, a lot of time visiting studios, meeting with a lot of different artists. He is genuinely absorbing the scene here and I think that is really important. I feel that he has really made it a point to showcase some unknown and emerging artists in shows that have helped them to transition and gain credibility in the art world.

Today, my work now is still very heavily influenced by a variety of writing styles. Asian, Hebrew, and Muslim letterforms, Spanish and English gang letters are all mixing with graffiti into a form art that I feel is helping me to find my place as an artist.

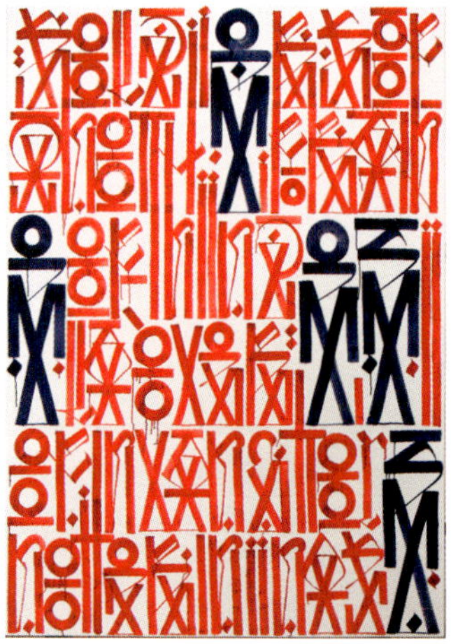

"Soldiers of Another Frame" 2011
Acrylic and enamel on canvas
60 x 84 inches

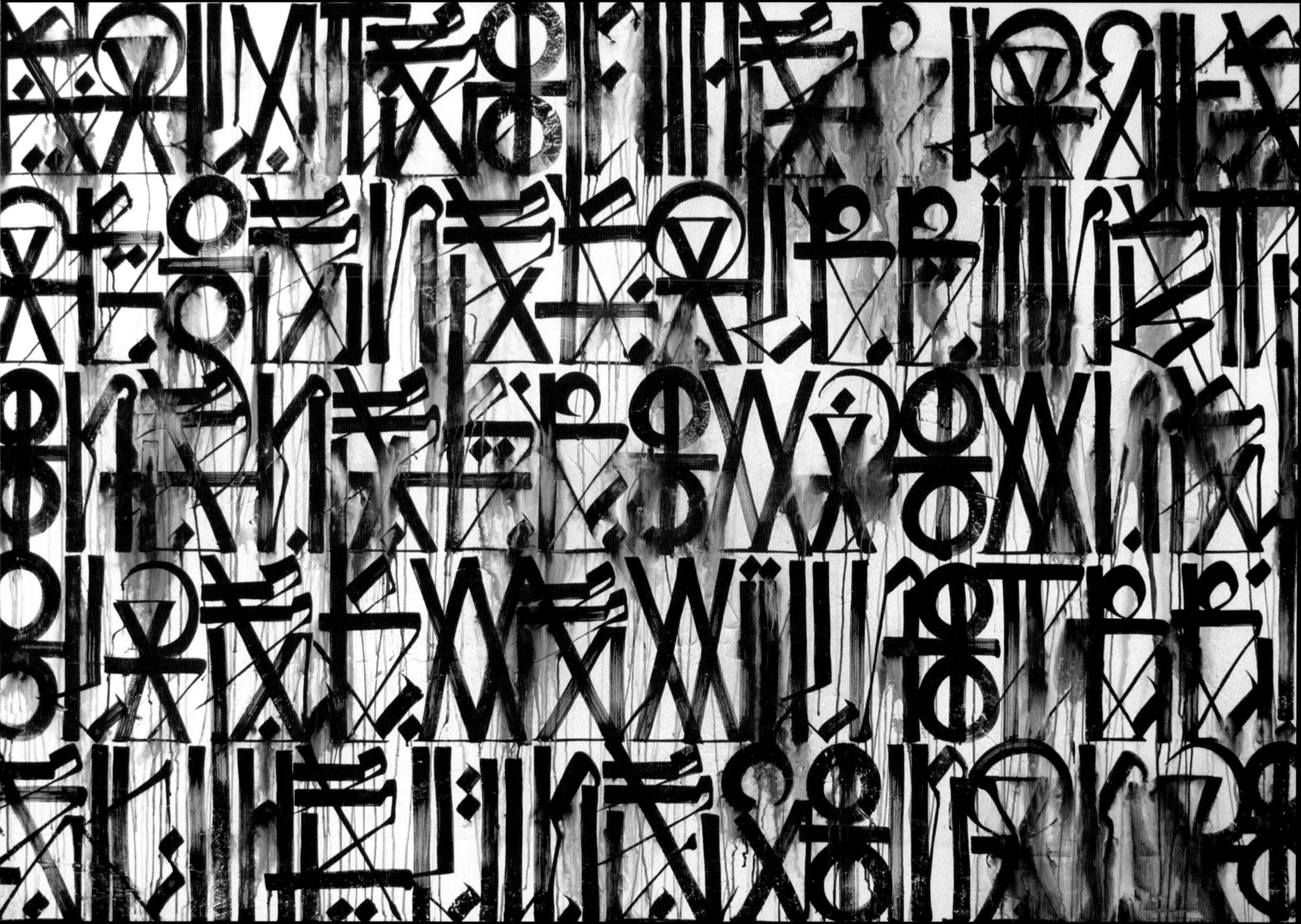

"Untitled (White on White dyptich)" 2011
Acrylic and enamel on canvas
144 x 72 inches

"Silent Night" 2011
Acrylic and enamel on canvas
107 x 97 inches

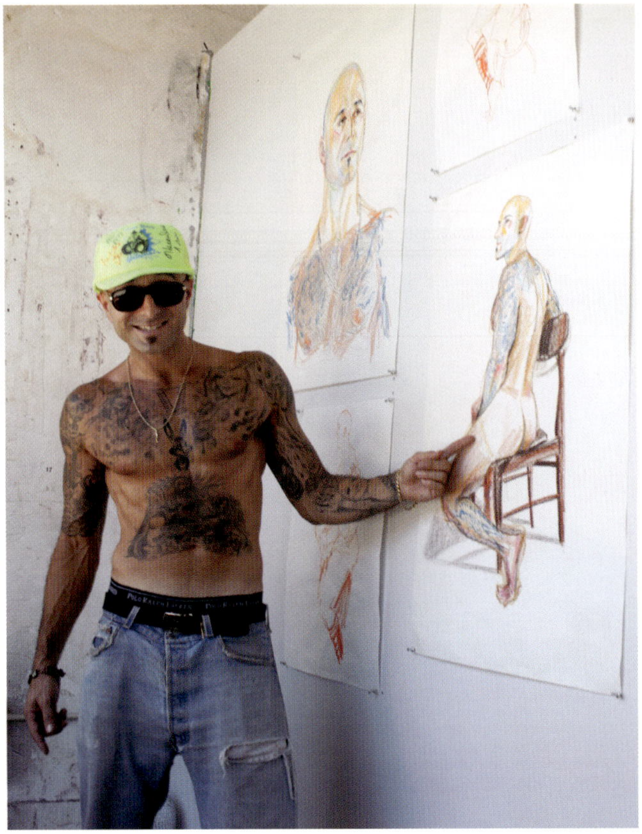

Self Portrait, 2012

GREG BOJORQUEZ

Los Angeles, California
gregorybojorquez.com

Way back in the '70s, my mother had an IUD and was on birth control, and my father wore a condom. Despite all of that, I was conceived with the IUD coil attached to my skull. I was born on an early summer morning at The White Memorial Hospital in Boyle Heights (the first suburb of LA) wearing a suit of armor. I stay in Los Angeles because I like hanging out at the El Super market on Lorena and Avenida De Cesar Chavez Avenue.

The obvious advantage to Los Angeles is that it is my home, and I am very familiar with it. Just about everything is readily available in Los Angeles. I do not really think there are disadvantages to being in Los Angeles. It could be competitive out here in LA, but that can make an inspired artist much better than hanging out where the level of things is much lower.

There are things in LA culturally that are not apparent outside of LA. I live in Boyle Heights now. The density of Latin Americans is the highest here in the entire nation. I sometimes feel like I am in another country. I can take a drive twenty minutes east and find myself in Beverly Hills. The contrast between the two neighborhoods is night and day, but I feel comfortable wherever I go. I can take bits and pieces from all the culture out here and come up with something very Los Angeles.

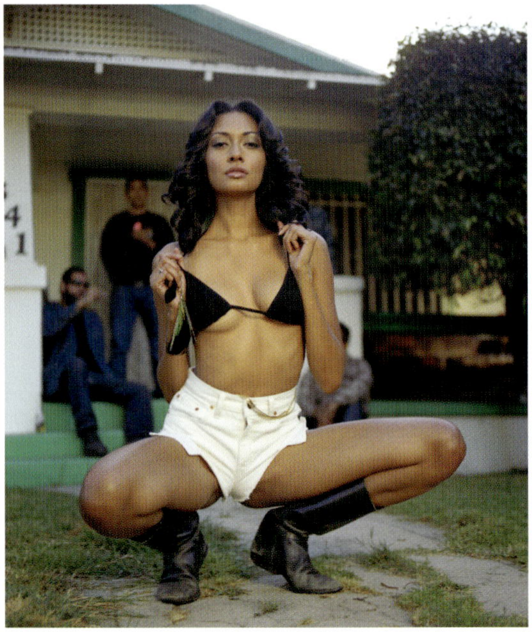

"*Alejandra In Boots*" 2011
Editions 20 x 24 inches, 30 x 40 inches

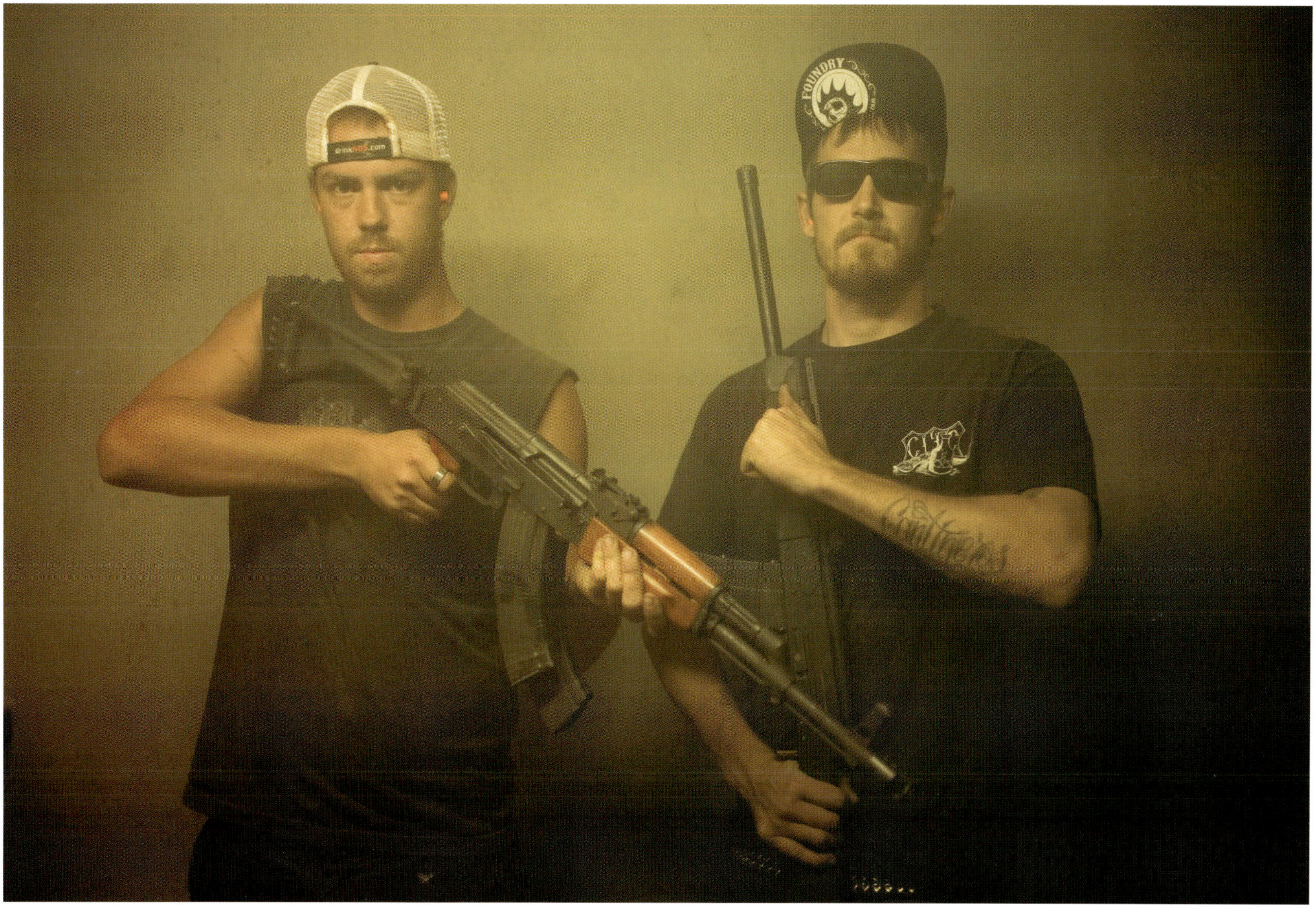

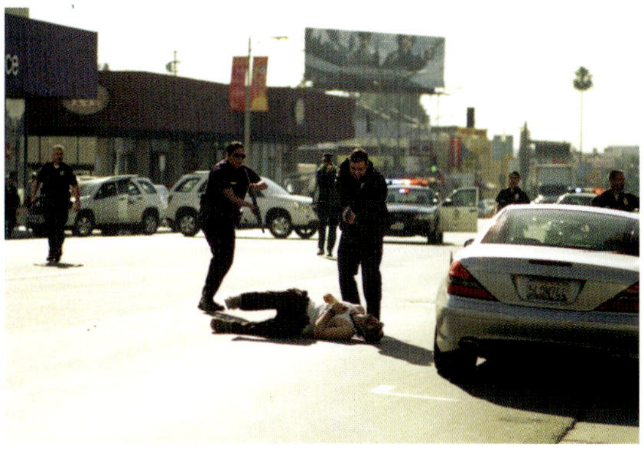

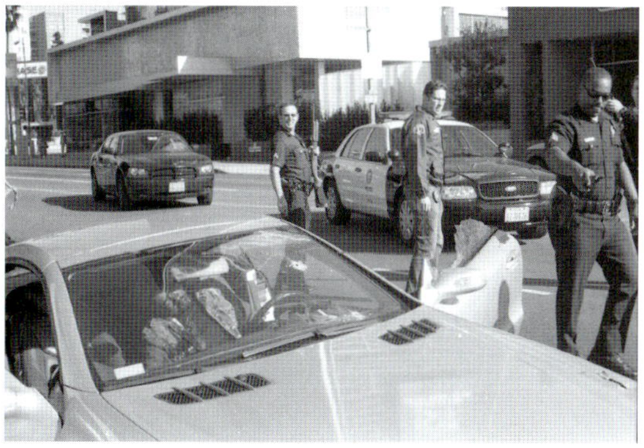

Top:
"Red and Pac Man" 2008
Edition 20 x 24 inches

Bottom Left:
"Shooter Down" 2011
Editions 16 x 20, 20 x 24,
and 30 x 40 inches

Bottom Right:
"Untitled" 2011

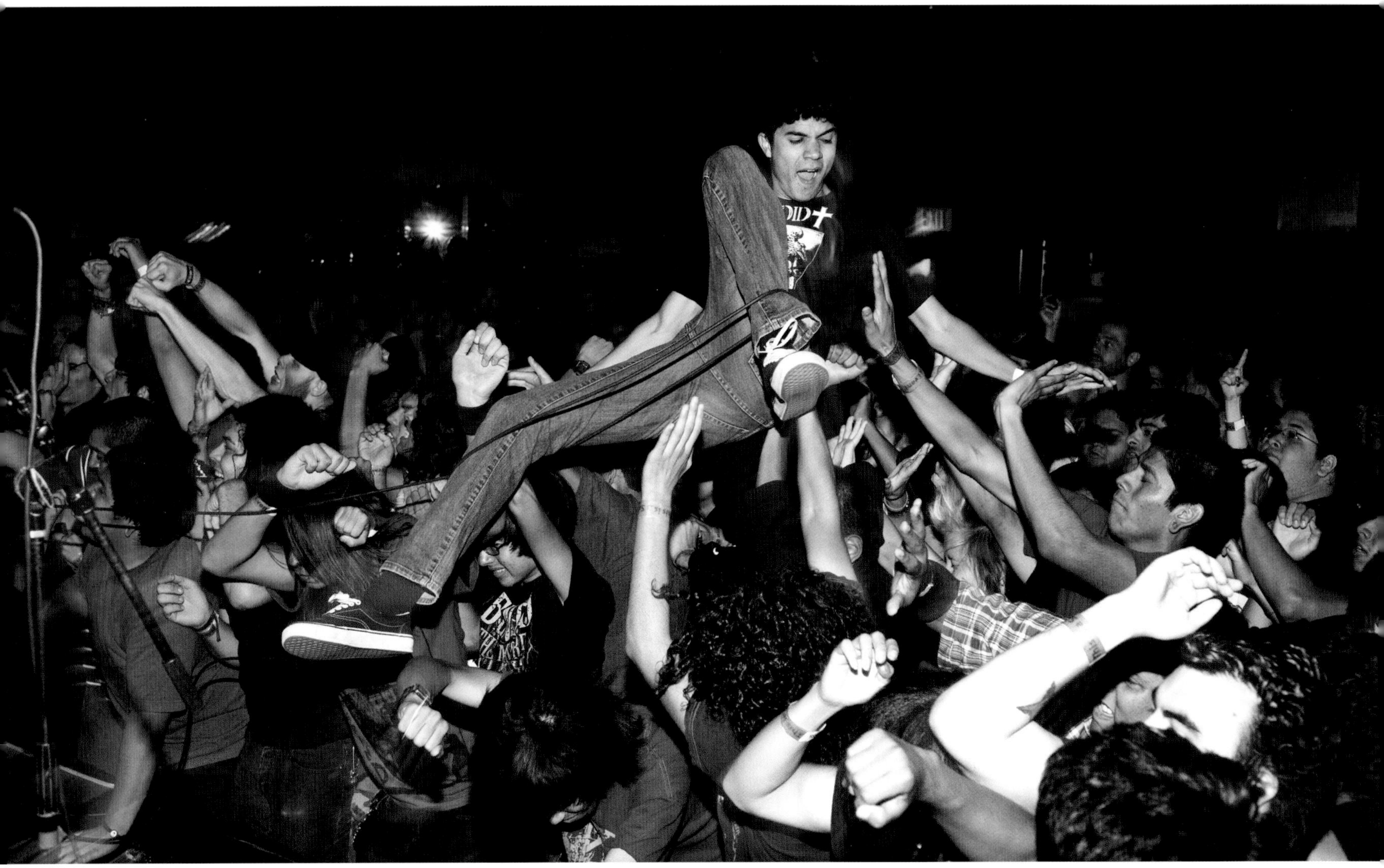

"Metal Matinee" 2011

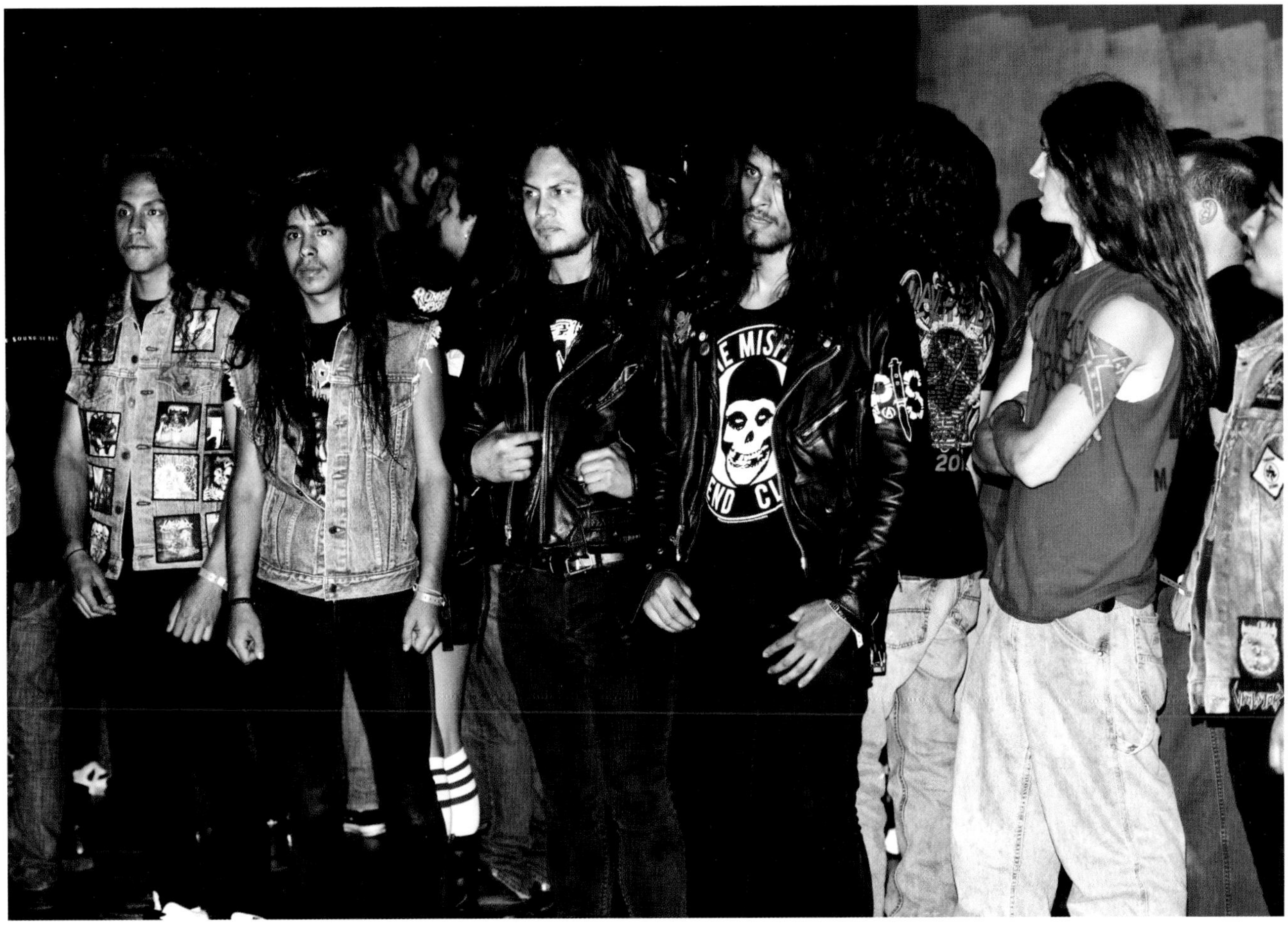

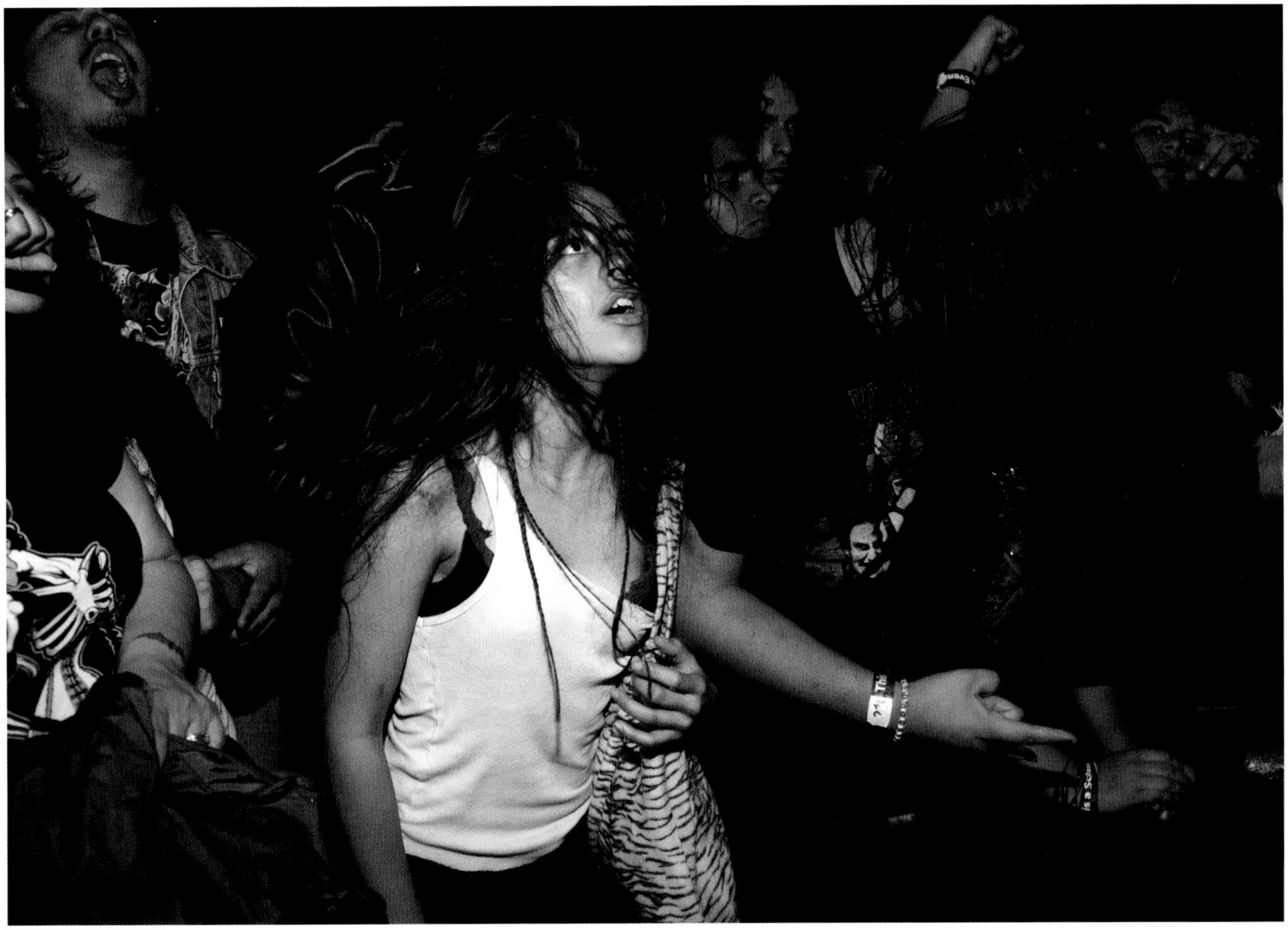

Top:
"Rockers" 2011
Edition 20 x 24 inches

"Girl in the Front Row" 2010
Edition 20 x 24 inches

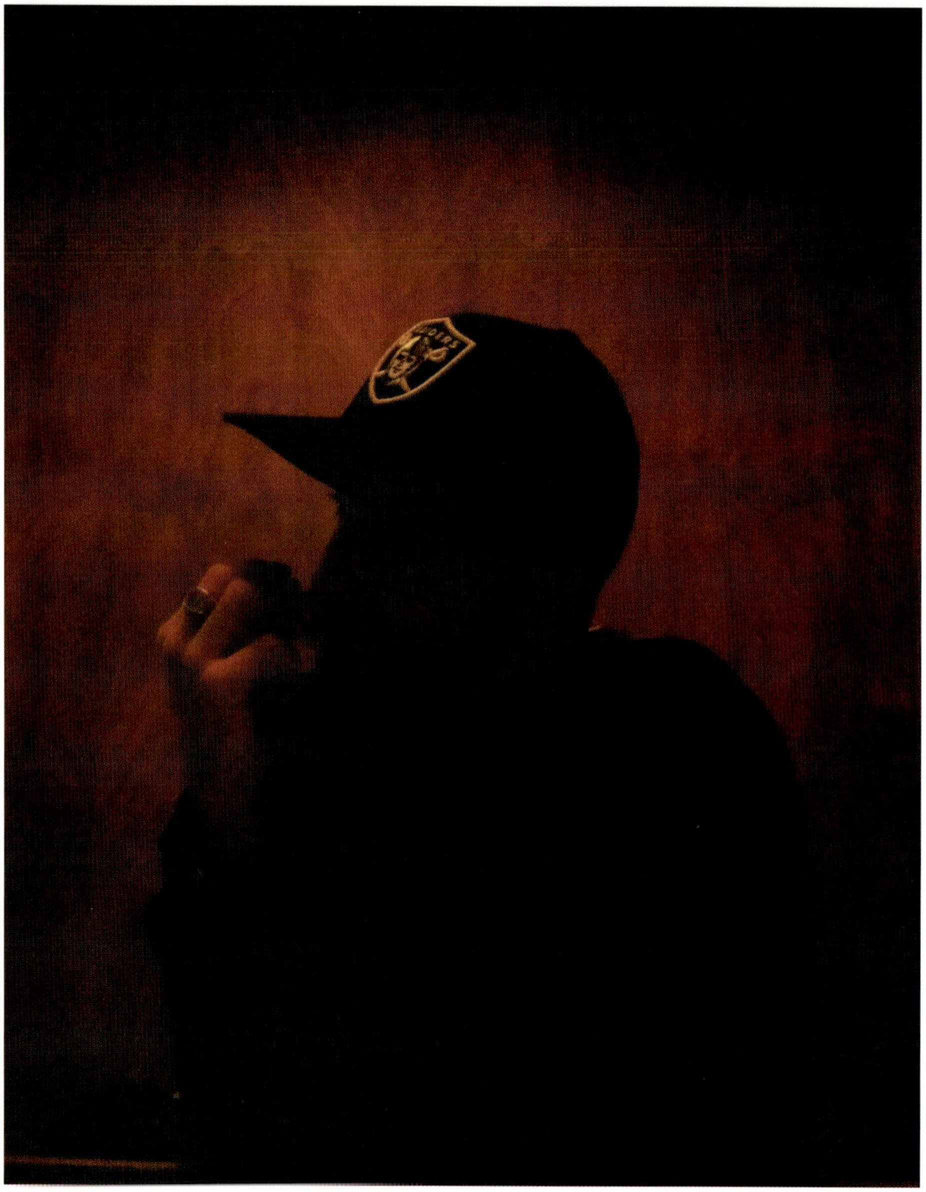

Self Portrait, 2012

PIERO GOLIA

Los Angeles, California
Gagosian Gallery

I came to LA in the summer of 2003, and I still remember driving up on La Cienega Boulevard towards Hollywood. I purchased a surfboard with the intention of learning how to surf, but things went differently. What keeps me here instead I don't really know, maybe my '69 El Camino or maybe just a sense of responsibility.

I take things as they are … I don't plan so much ahead, so I never really looked at advantages or disadvantages. ... If I don't like something, I just try to change it. I believe this is what I'm supposed to do.

I feel connected to the land and the people around me. But I aspire to build a universal model that has nothing to do with California. This is the big lesson I learned from Hollywood.

"Constellation Painting #12" 2011
Resin and debris
60 x 52 x 3 inches

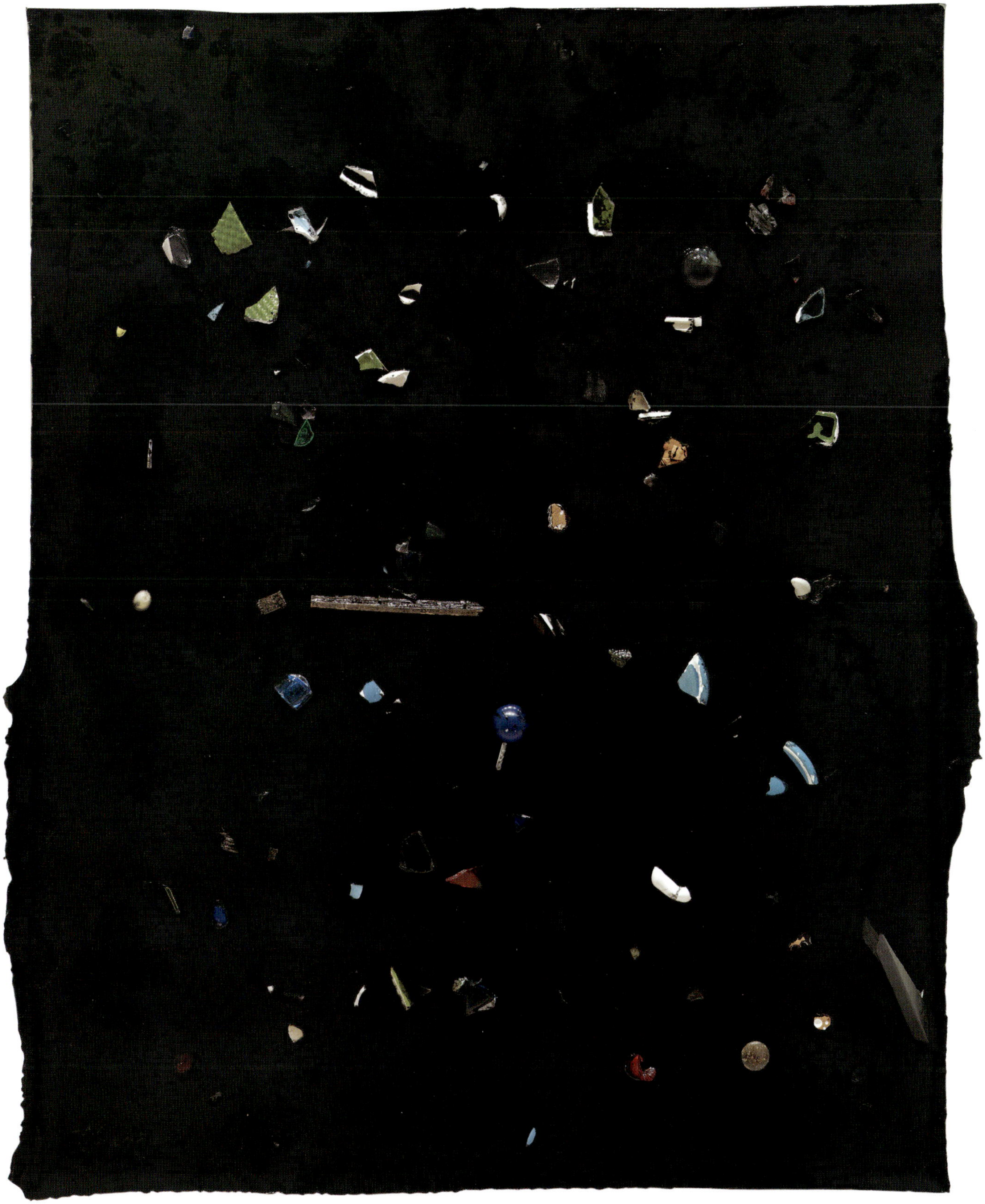

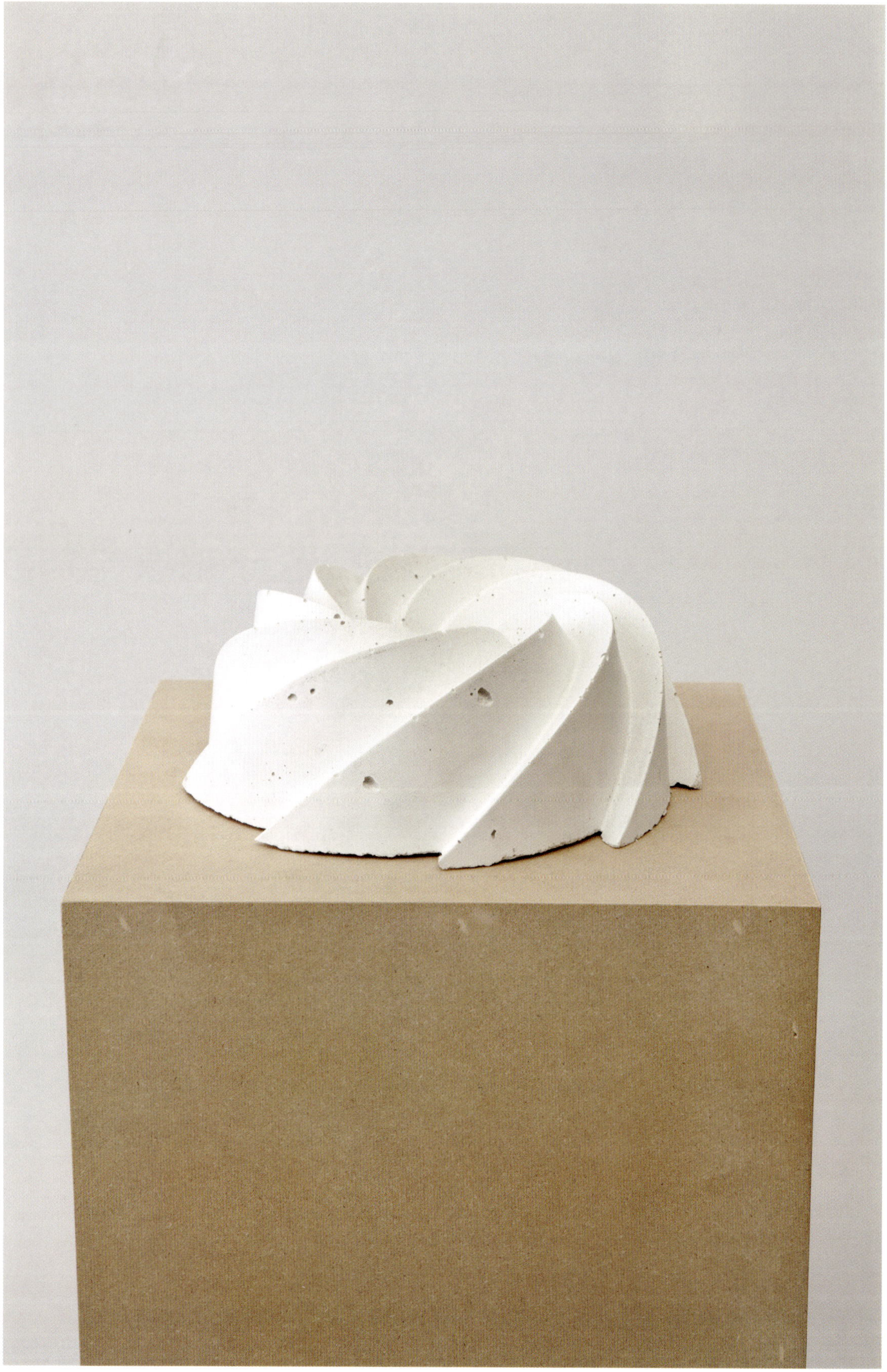

"Untitled #12" 2010-2011
Concrete
3½ x 6 x 6 inches

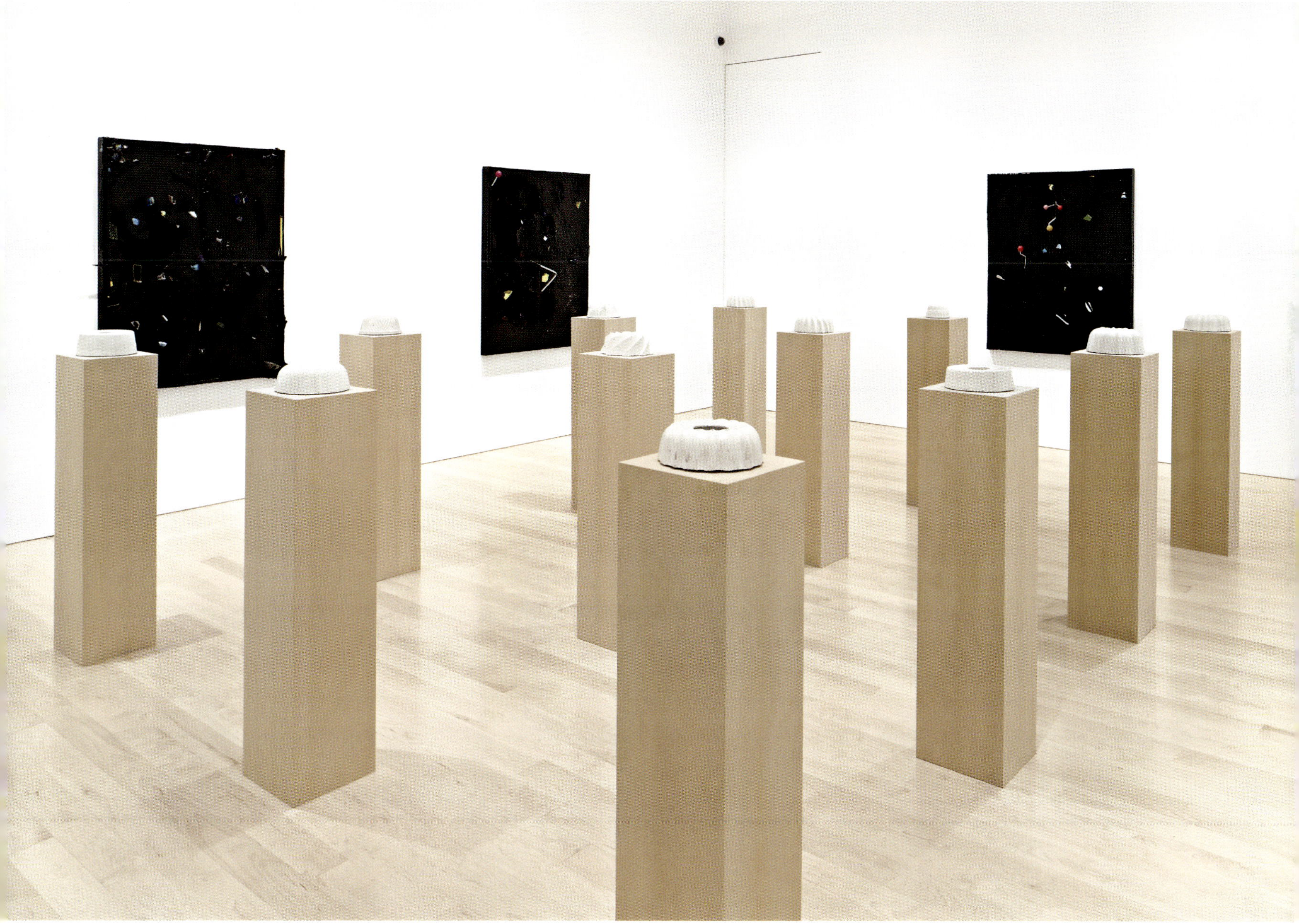

"Cakes and Constellations" June 23-August 5, 2011
Gagosian Gallery Beverly Hills

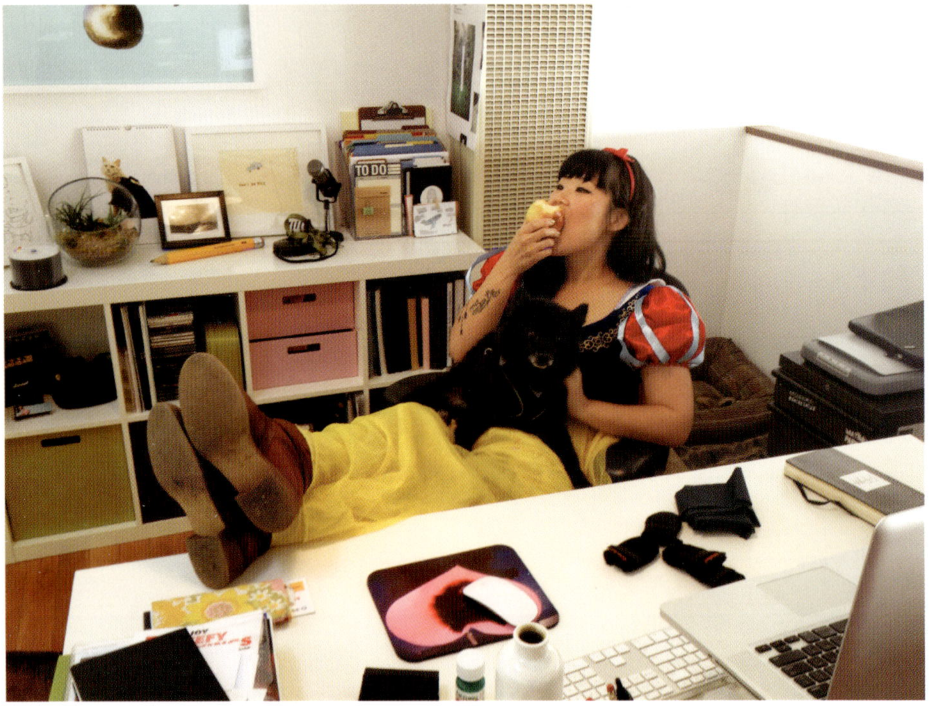

Self Portrait, 2012

LANA KIM

Los Angeles, California
hundreds-thousands.com

The film industry and a U-haul truck brought me to California. What keeps me here are my yards and my friends.

The advantages I have found are that California is filled with many people who make and do things better than you do. It's inspiring and helpful.

The disadvantages are that it's filled with many people who make and do things better than you do, and only so many opportunities.

The beauty of things that are real and also the beauty of things that are imagined, made up, and the boundless possibilities both can have are influences of California on my work and process.

"*Untitled (digital stills)*" 2011
Digital video

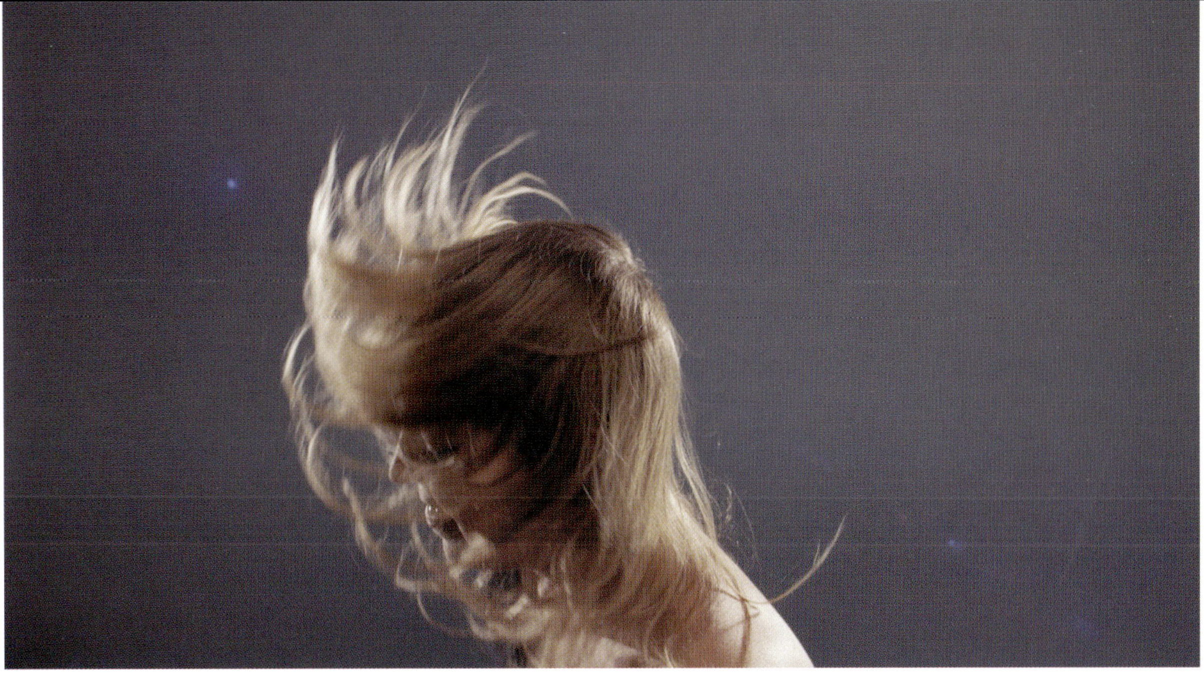

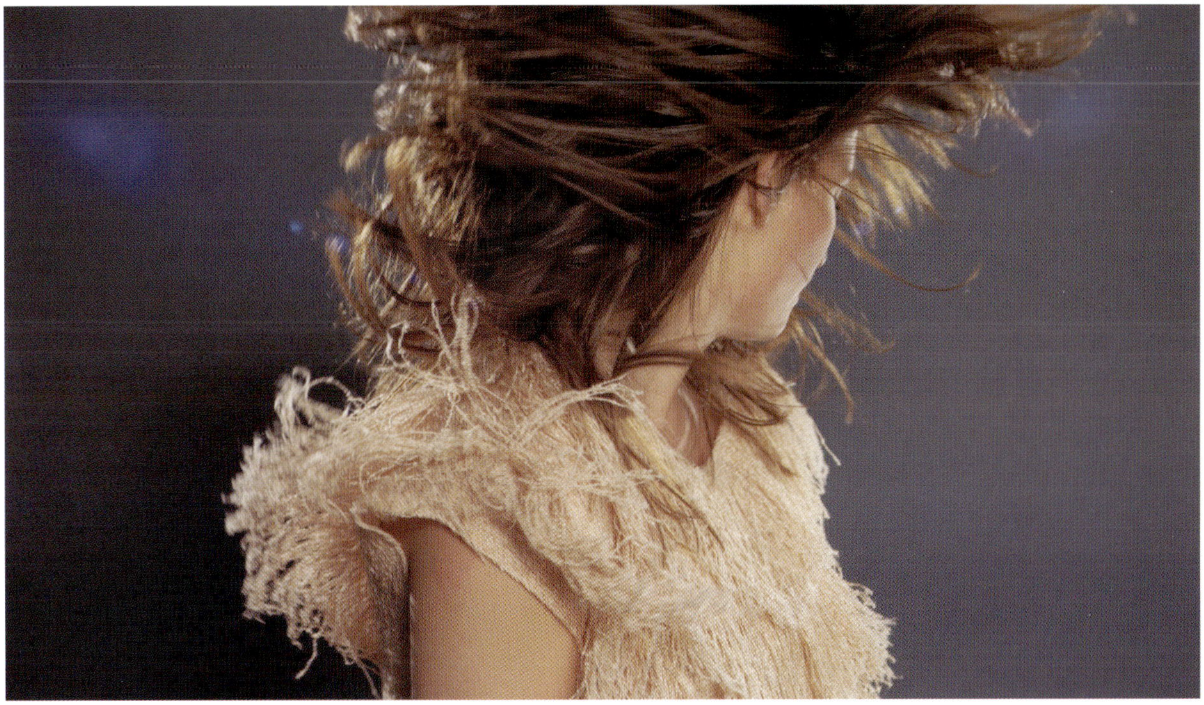

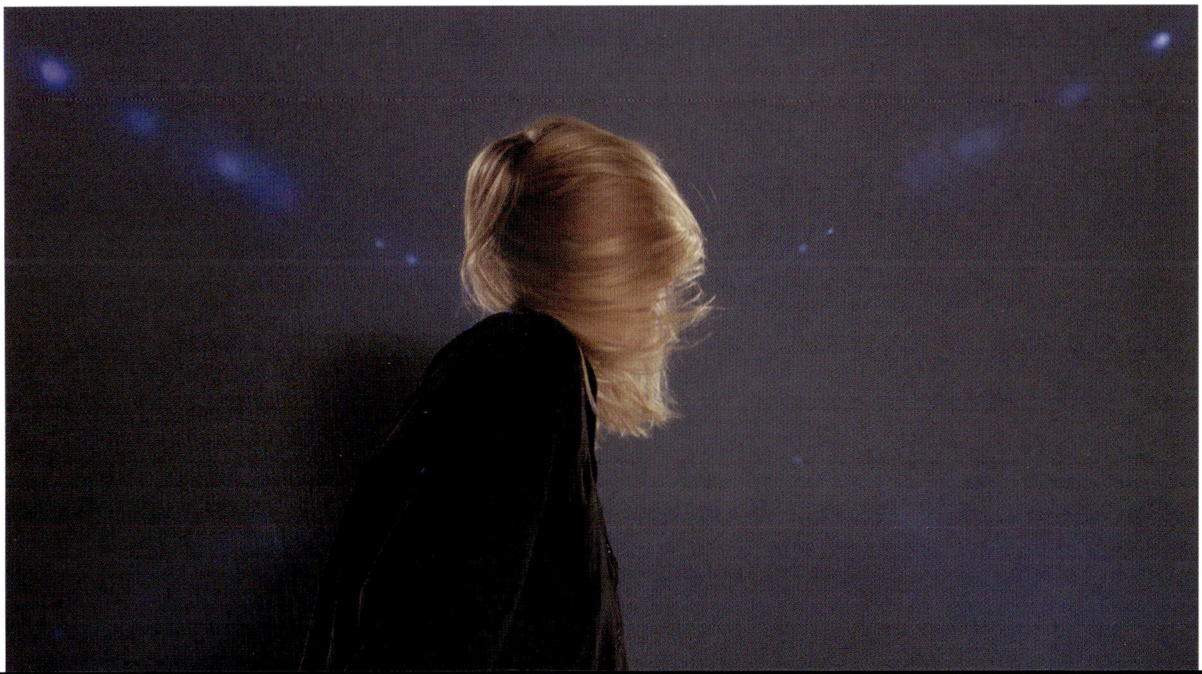

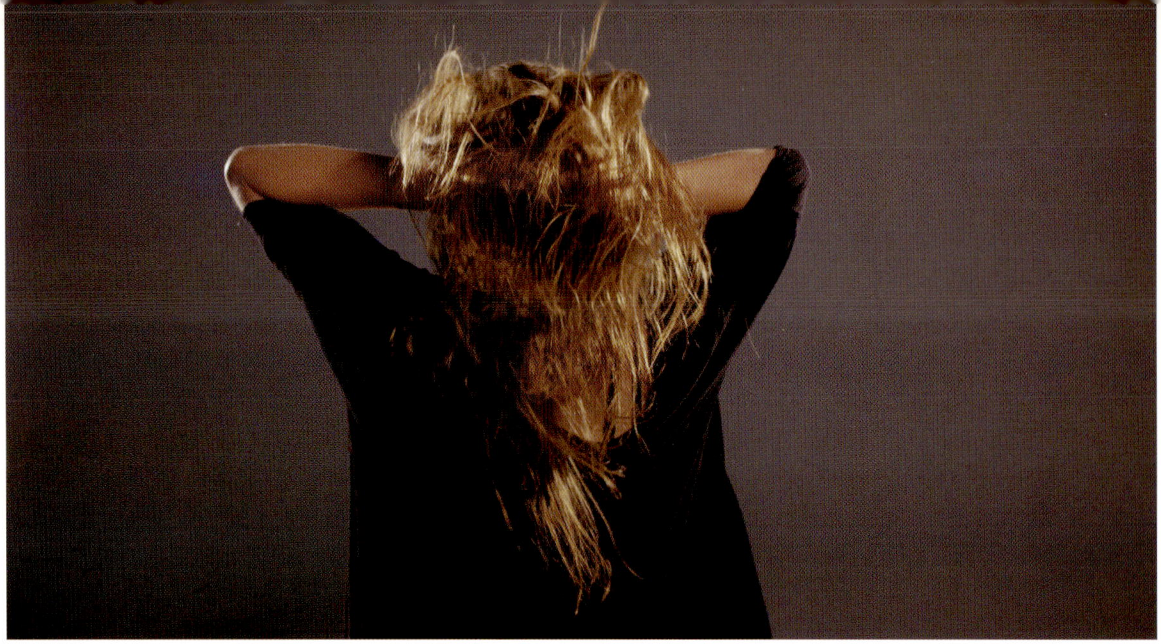

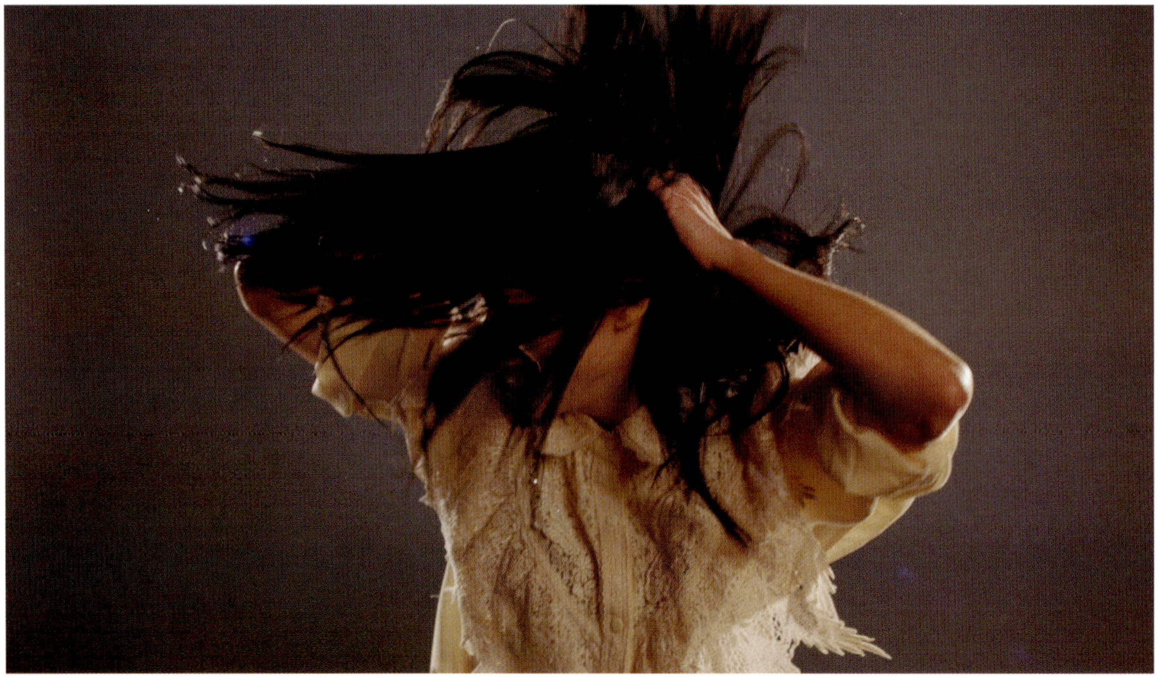

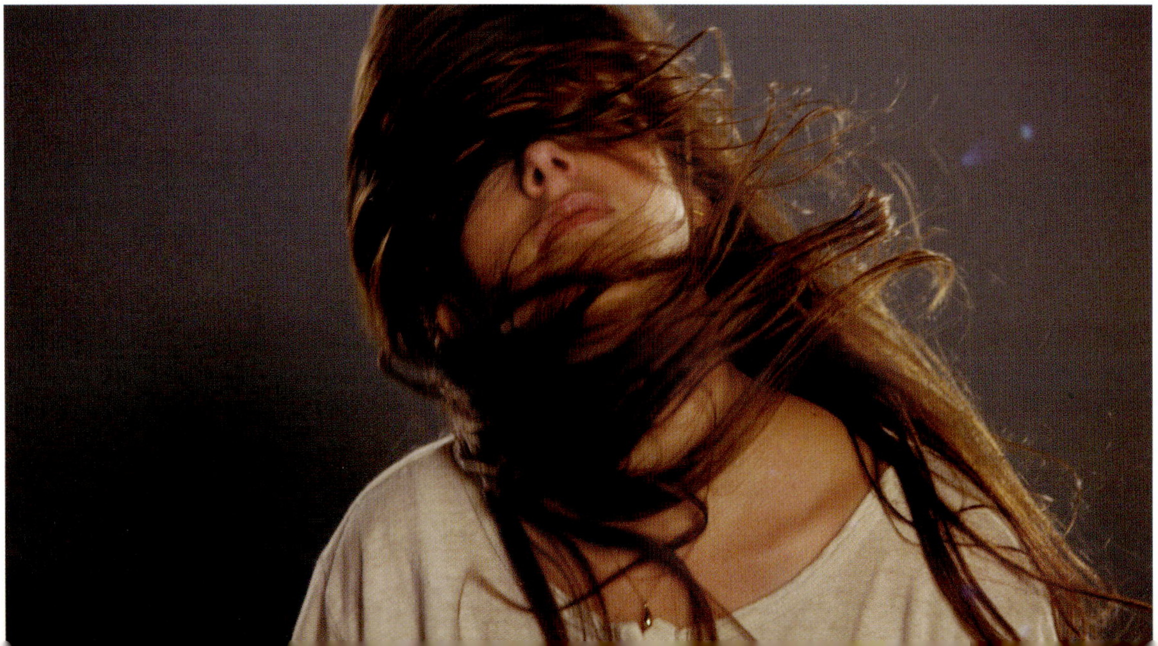

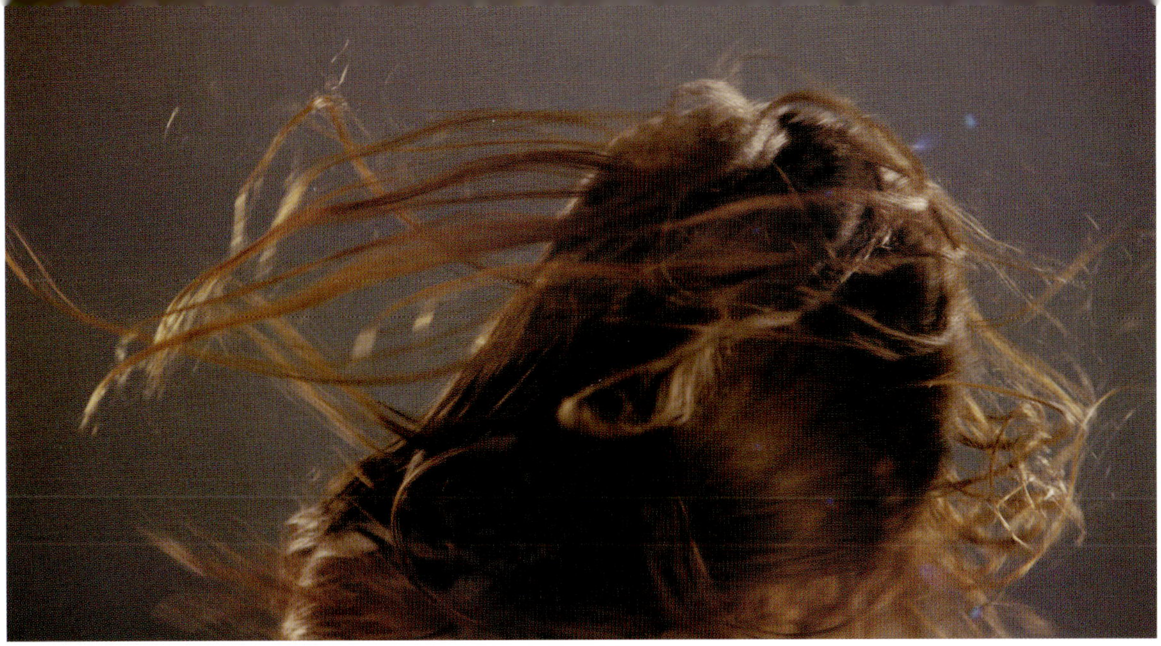

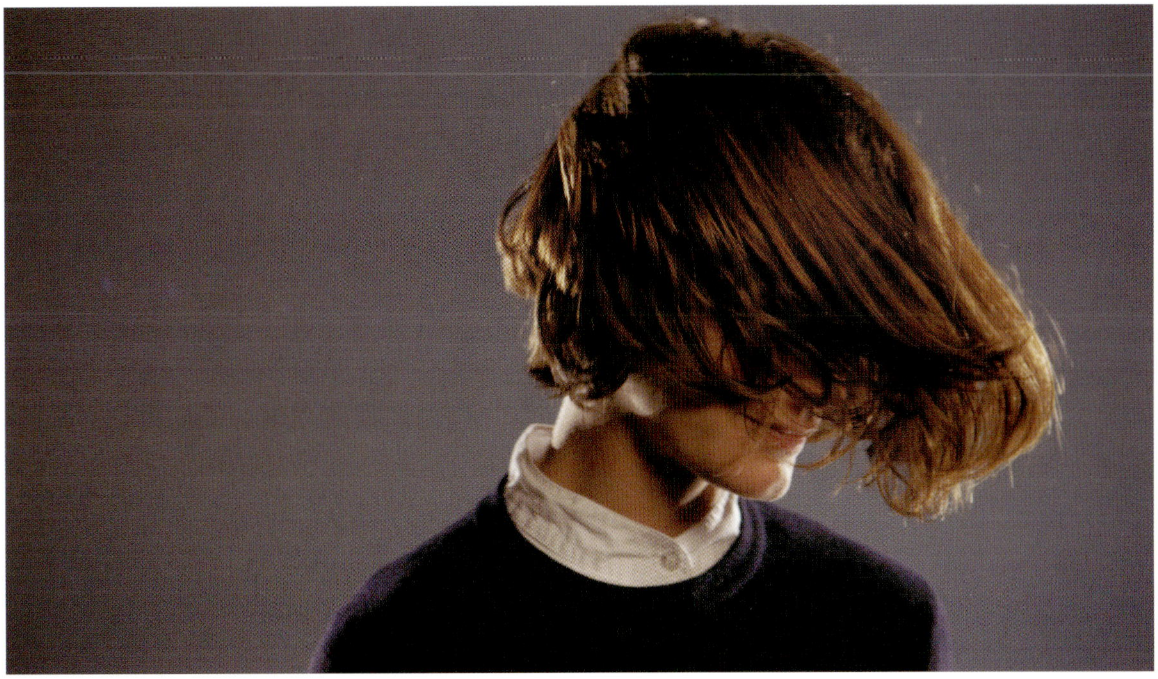

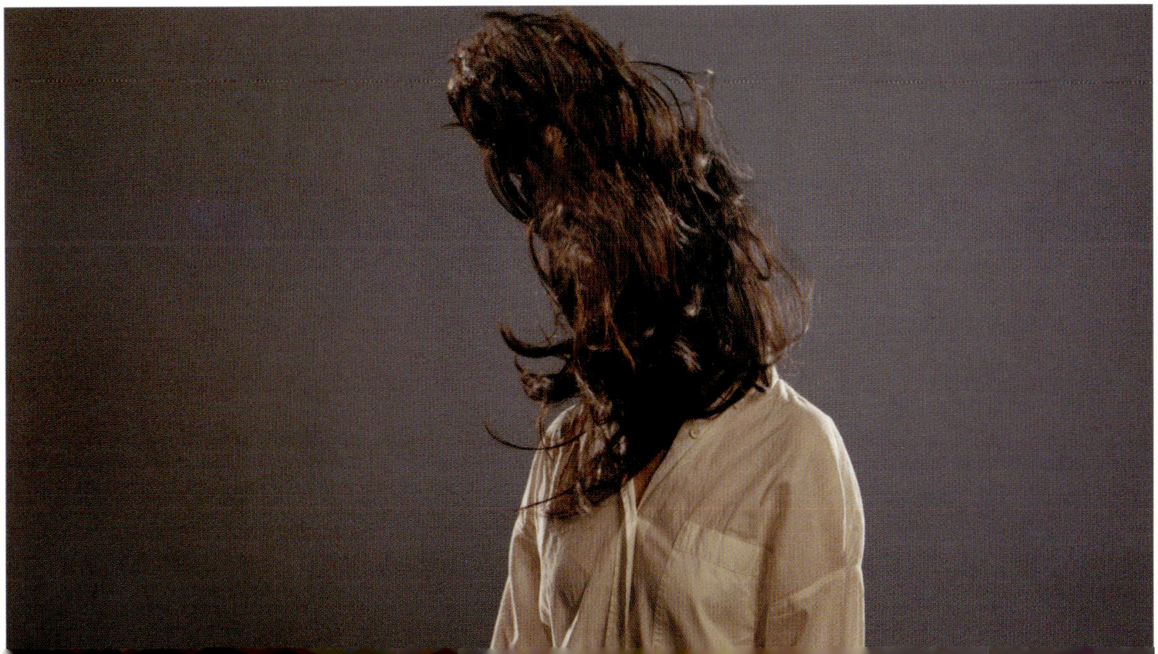

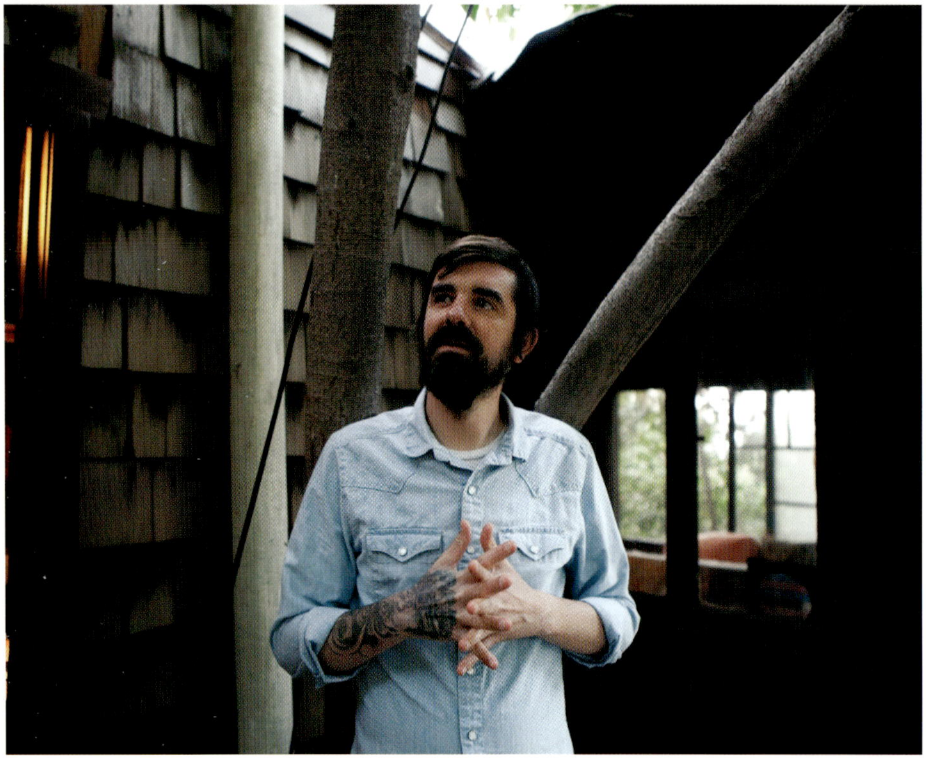

Photo by Aaron Farley, 2012

TRAVIS MILLARD

Los Angeles, California

fudgefactorycomics.com

I was living in a crappy Brooklyn apartment, trying to figure out how I was going to continue to make rent, and an old friend encouraged me to move to Los Angeles, where a much cheaper room awaited. So three days later, with no knowledge of the where I would be ending up, I packed a van and drove out in the dark of night. That was nine years ago, and the city is still fresh to me.

Maybe it's the absence of the J train running past my window every thirty minutes, or maybe it's the diversity of nature and fruit trees in the yard, but I found more peace and focus in LA. There's just more room to get lost in the woods here, both literally and figuratively.

I like that I can find so many different things to do on any given day, but also be just as happy wandering around the neighborhood or staying home and working at the desk. I guess the downside would be all the driving it takes to get anywhere. Some of my best friends live on the west side, which might as well be another city because it's such a commitment to make the journey.

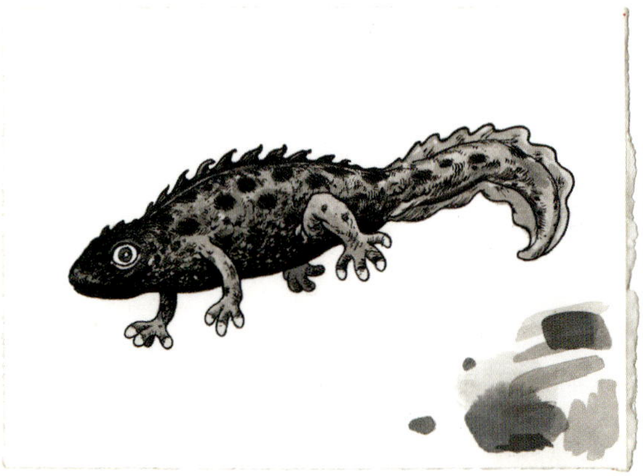

"Newt for That" 2011
Ink on paper
7 x 5 inches

"Splittin'" 2012
Ink on paper
10 x 12 inches

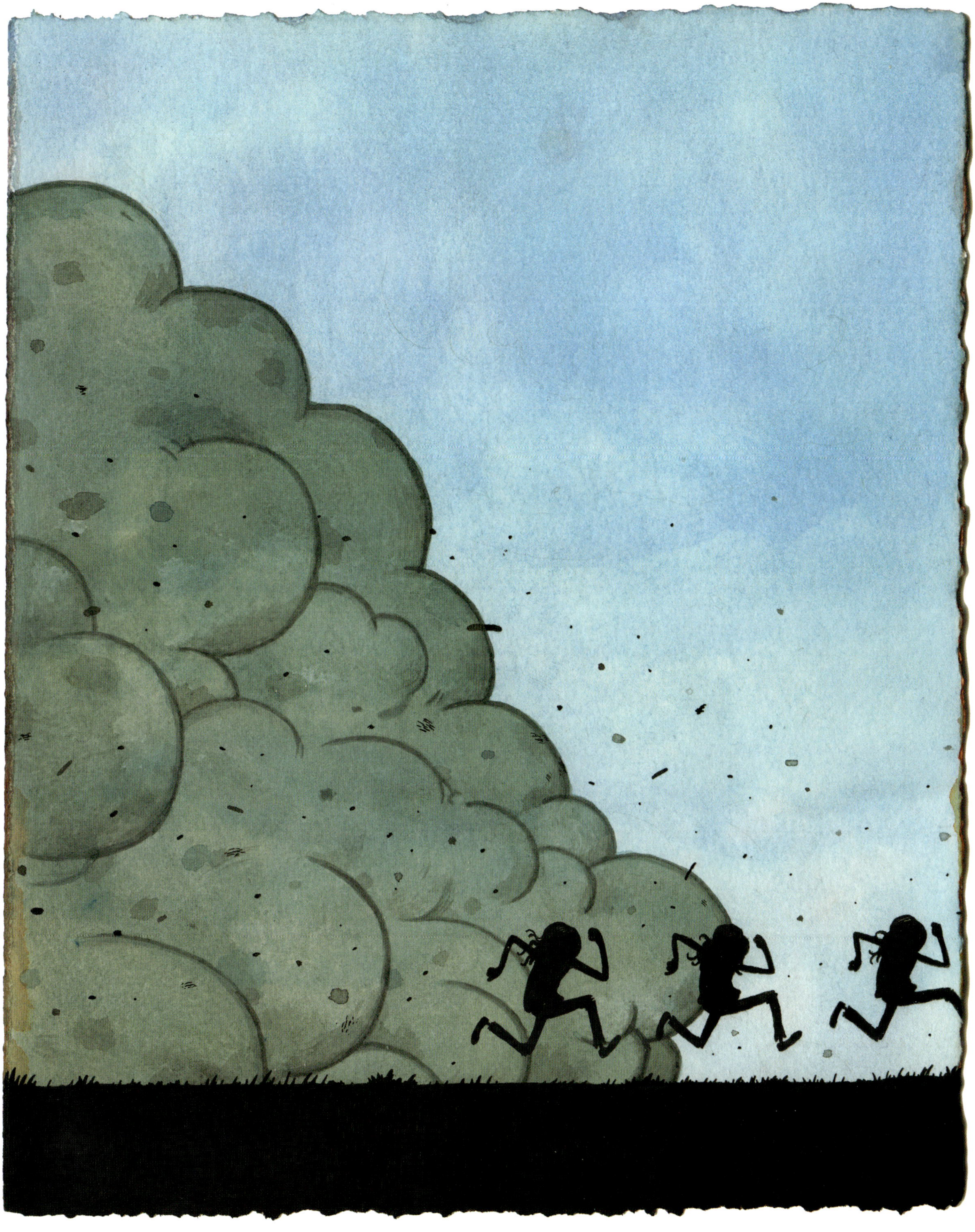

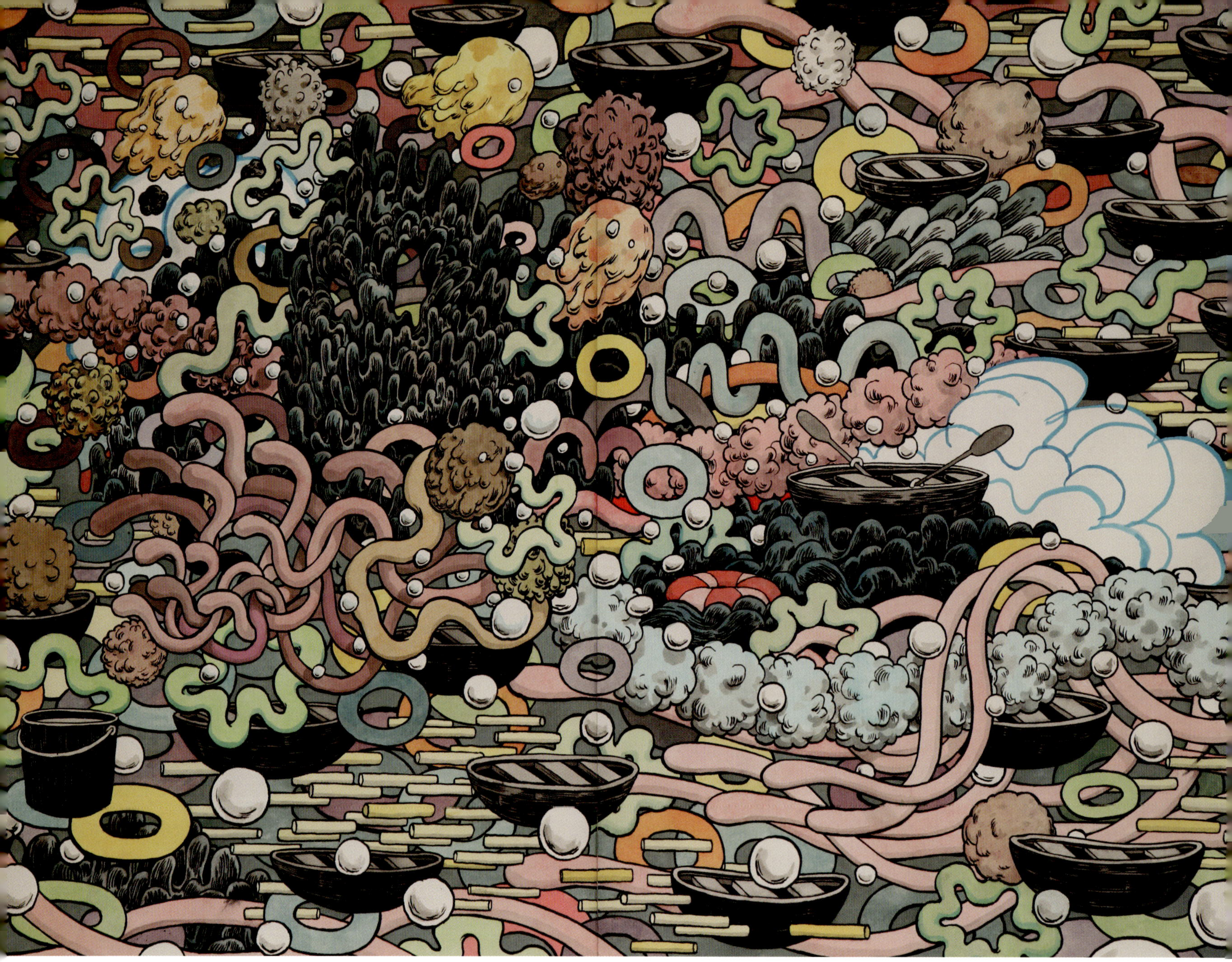

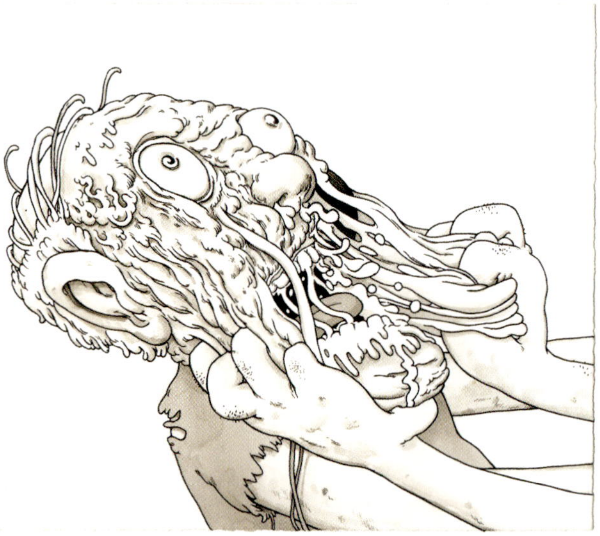

"Riverside" 2011
Ink on paper
39½ x 29½ inches

"Grab" 2011
Ink on paper
10 x 8 inches

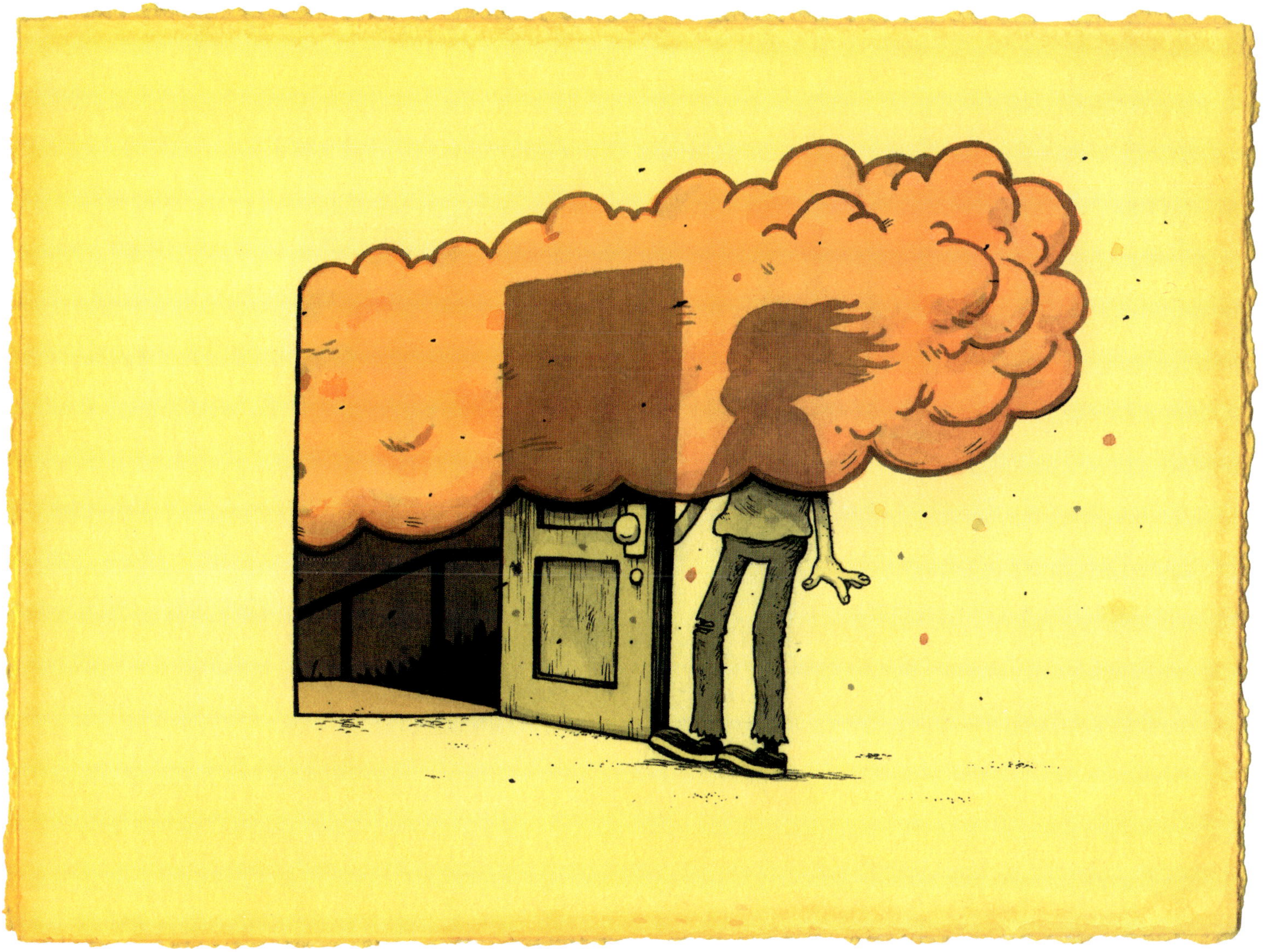

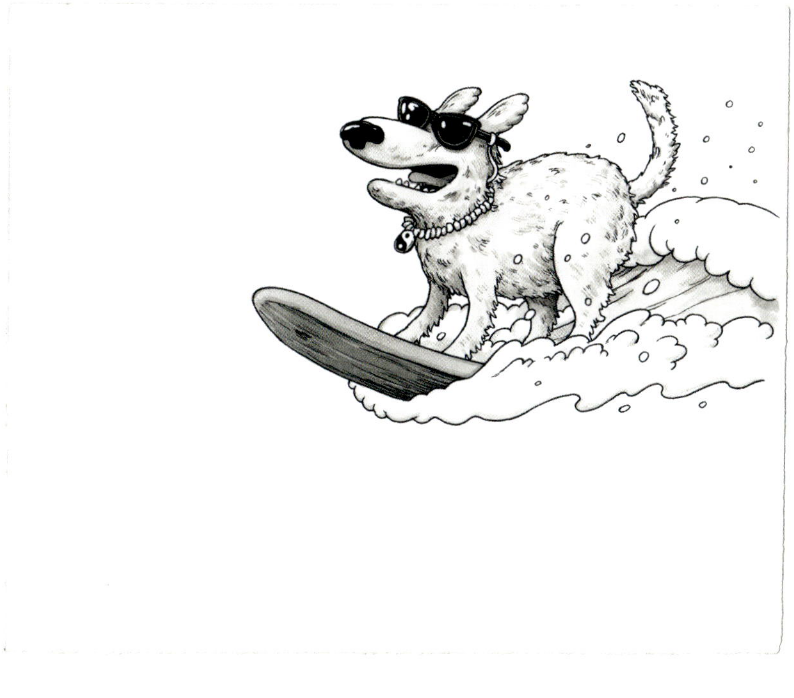

"Open the Door, Richard" 2012
Ink on paper
9 x 6½ inches

"Surfdog" 2012
Ink on paper
10 x 8 inches

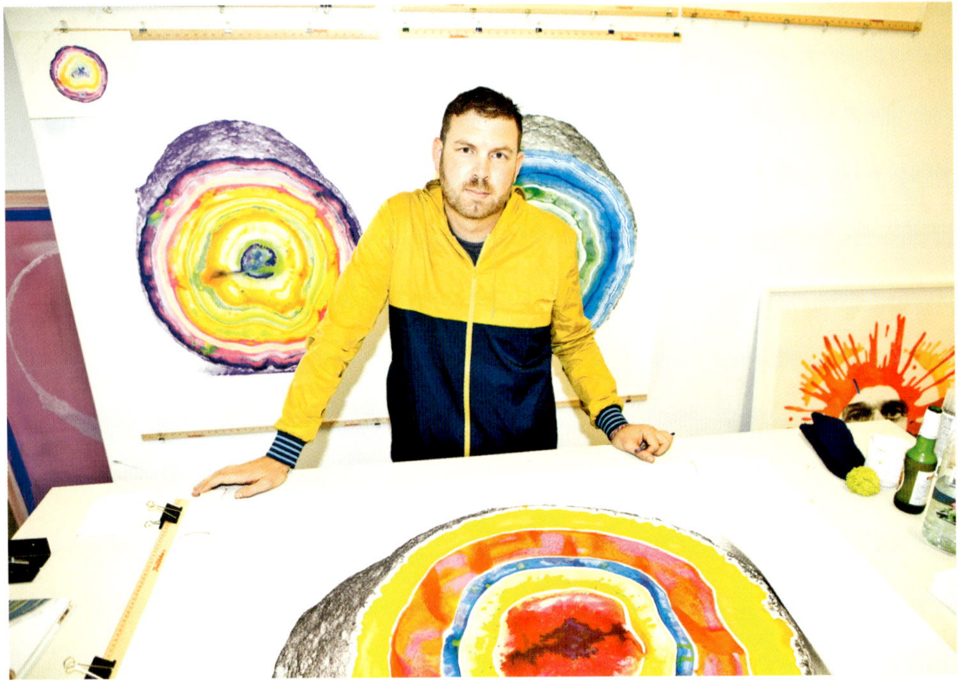

Photo by Meredith Jenks, 2012

JUSTIN KRIETEMEYER

Los Angeles, California
justinkrietemeyer.com
nationalforest.com

I was born and raised in California. I grew up surfing, well boogie boarding, in San Diego, moved to Santa Barbara, then San Francisco, and finally Los Angeles for college. California is in my blood. I have friends and family here in almost every city up and down the coast. I feel at home when I am in the ocean, the mountains, the desert, or the middle of the city.

I've only found advantages to working in California. The sun helps keep the optimism turned up to full blast. California, its cities, and subcultures have played a big part in informing my personality and perspective over the years. With that in mind, it makes sense that Cali continues to be a perfectly nurturing place to keep my creative mind moving.

The sun, the beach, the desert, the mountains, skateboarding, graffiti, Mexico, and the sense of optimism are all advantages to California. There are very literal influences here, like geodes found in the desert, or surf vans parked near the beach. I try to keep my work bright and positive and reflect a sense of optimism and mystery.

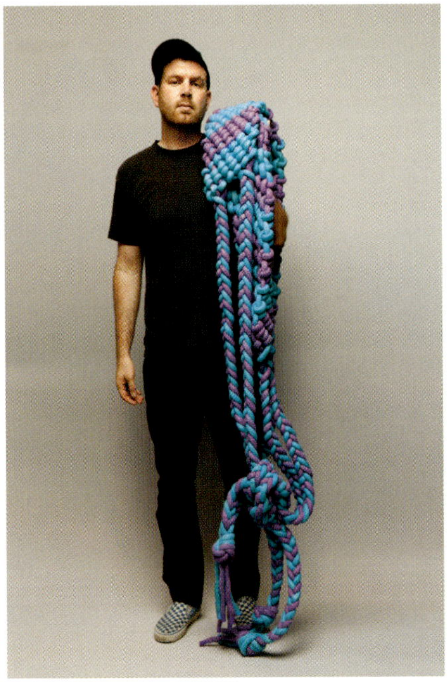

"Friendship Bracelet No. 1" 2011
Dyed cotton rope
18 x 30 inches
Collaboration with Meredith Jenks

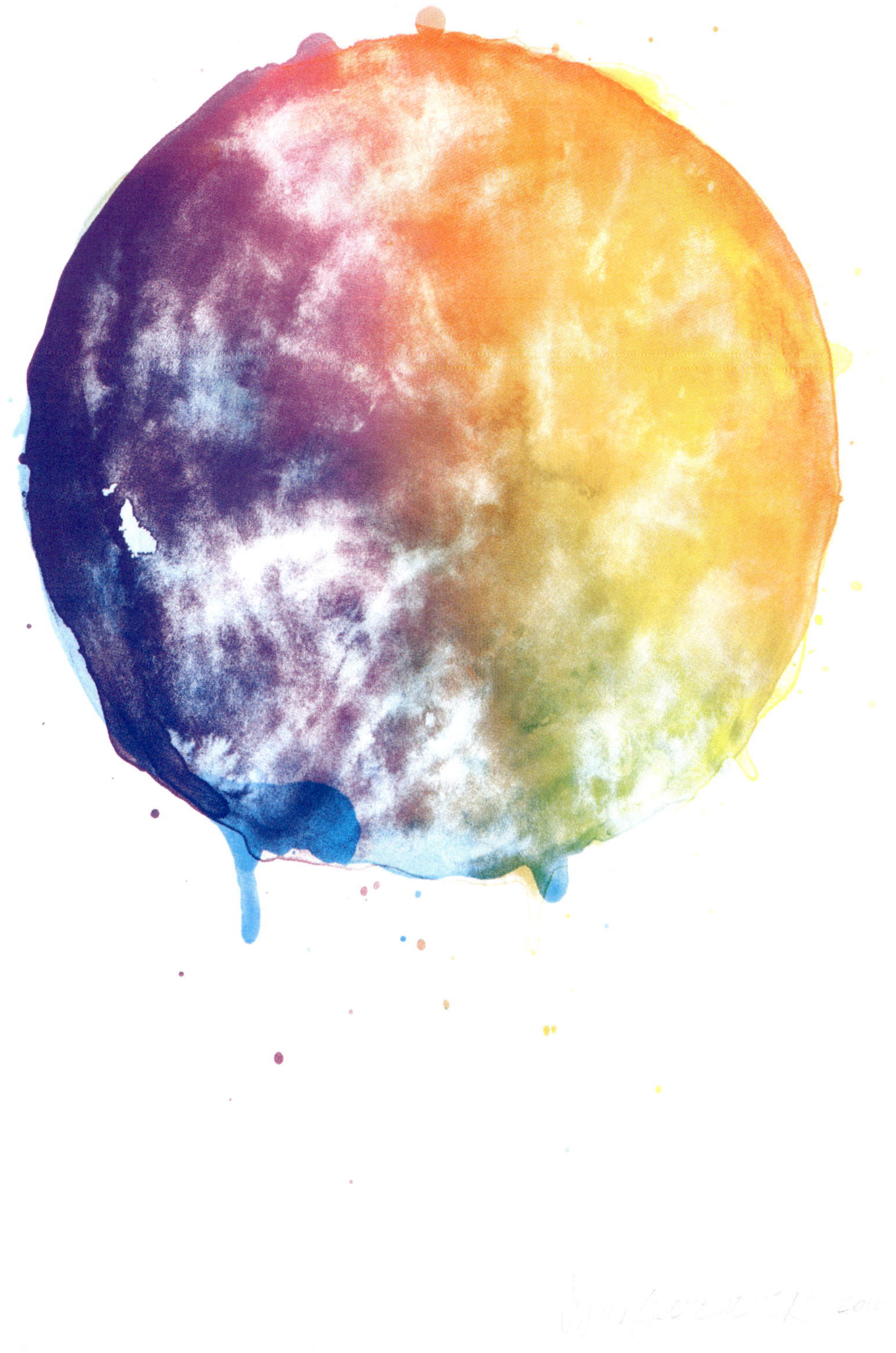

"Earth" 2010
Silkscreen
28 x 40 inches

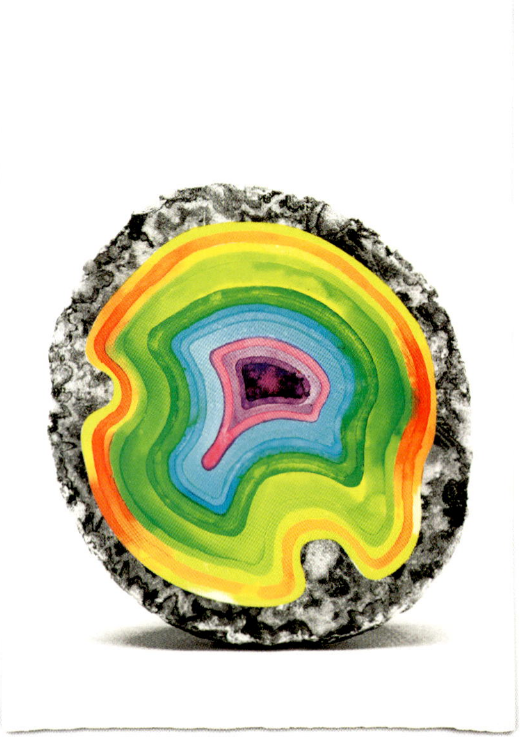

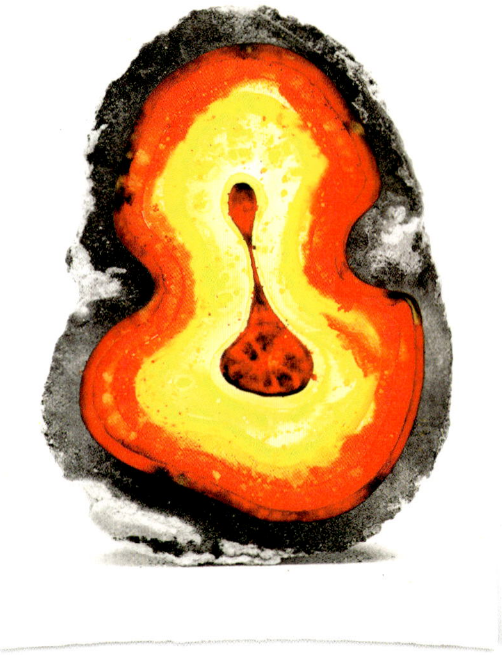

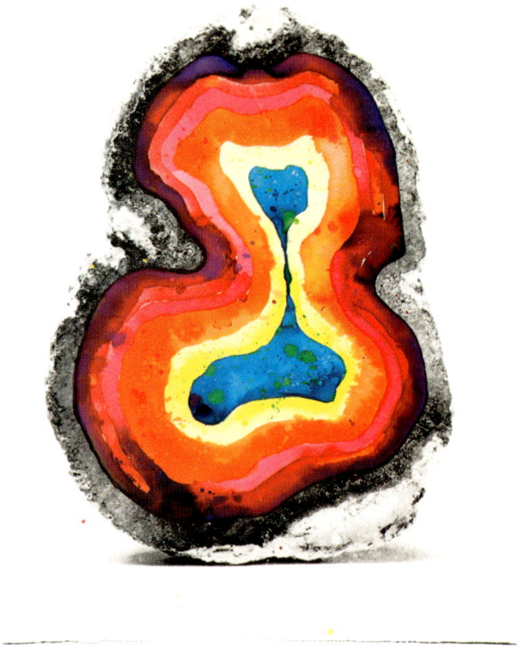

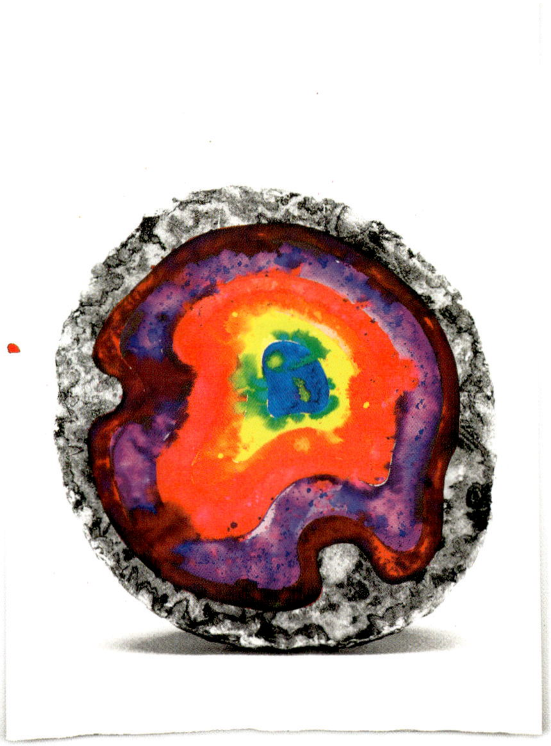

"Geode—No.13" 2011
Watercolor and silkscreen ink
22½ x 30 inches

"Geode—No.10" 2011
Watercolor and silkscreen ink
22½ x 30 inches

"Geode—No.8" 2011
Watercolor and silkscreen ink
22½ x 30 inches

"Geode—No.12" 2011
Watercolor and silkscreen ink
22½ x 30 inches

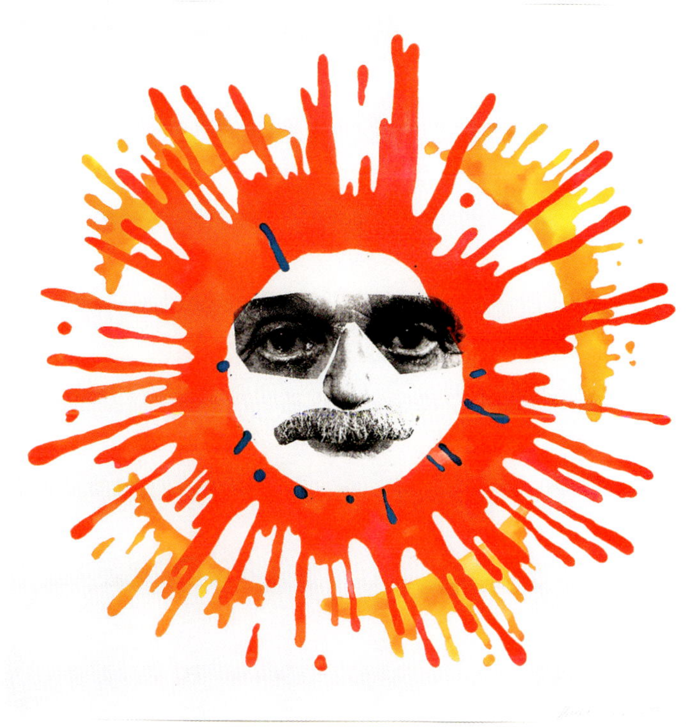

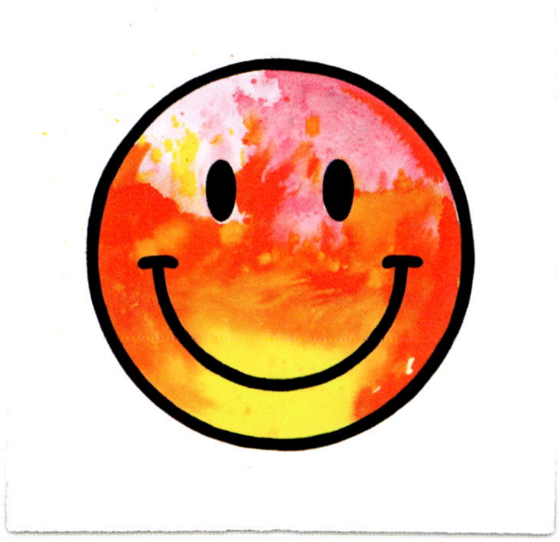

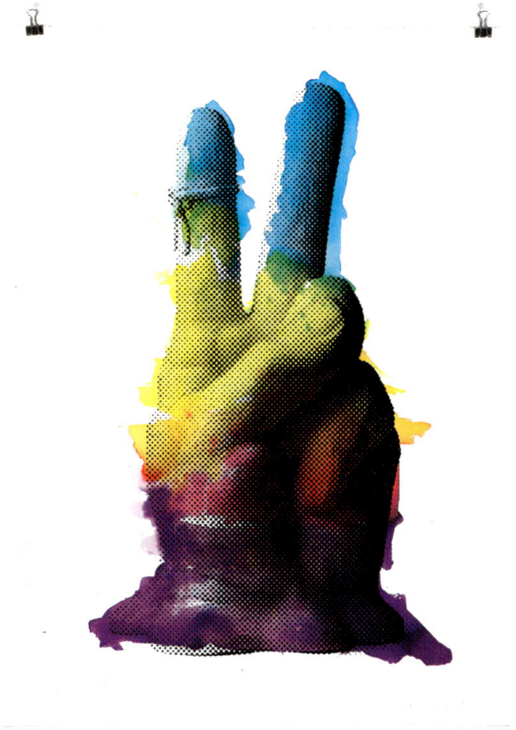

"Smiley" 2012
Watercolor and silkscreen ink
22½ x 22½ inches

"Sun" 2008
Watercolor and silkscreen ink
40 x 40 inches

"Peace Promise—Sun Prism" 2011
Handmade multiple/Edition 10
Watercolor and silkscreen ink
22½ x 30 inches

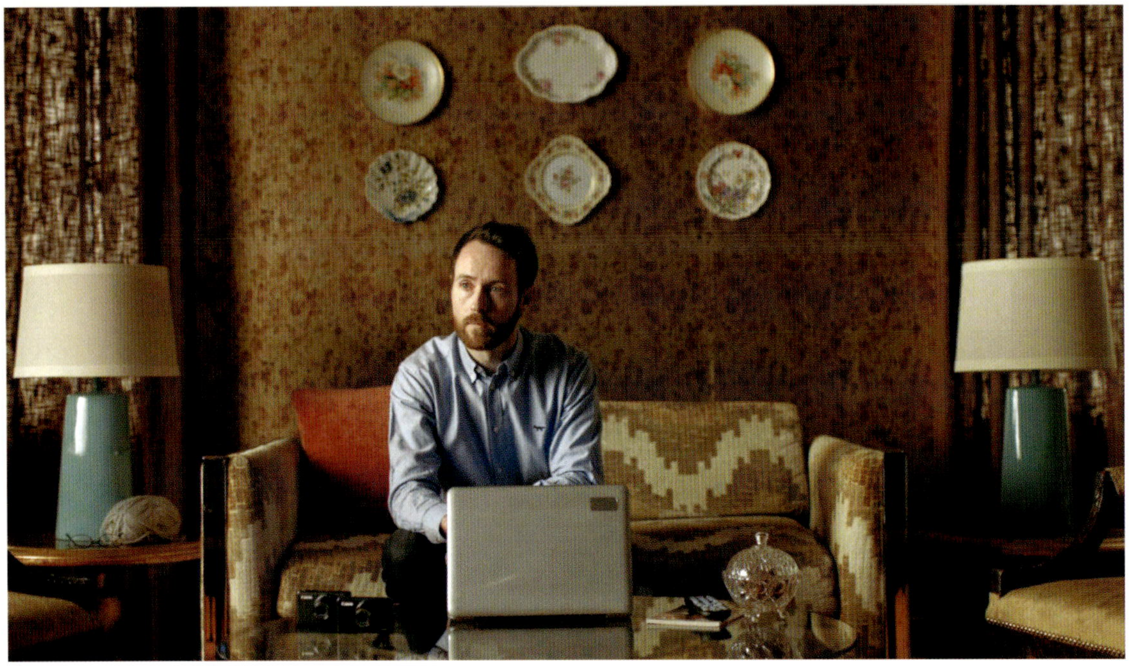

AARON RUELL

Pasadena, California

aruell.com

giantartists.com

Self portrait, 2012

I'm originally from CA, so I guess you could say birth is what brought me here. But I did move away for a little bit and made my way back here to make movies.

The absence of moderation becomes a looming influence. As an art maker, you can't be a stationary thinker in an isolation chamber. The necessity of mobility forces firsthand contact with a concentration of diverse craftsmen, industry, and culture.

This directly influences the evolution of your ideas and process while keeping your style and skills in check.

My entire working life has been spent in CA, so I don't have anything else to compare it to for advantages and disadvantages. But, as far as advantages go, you simply can't beat the landscapes that CA has to offer. It's a state that has such a diverse mix of geography so close together and that's what gives it a bit of an edge over other places in my opinion. One disadvantage that comes to mind is a lack of energy that is very present in NYC.

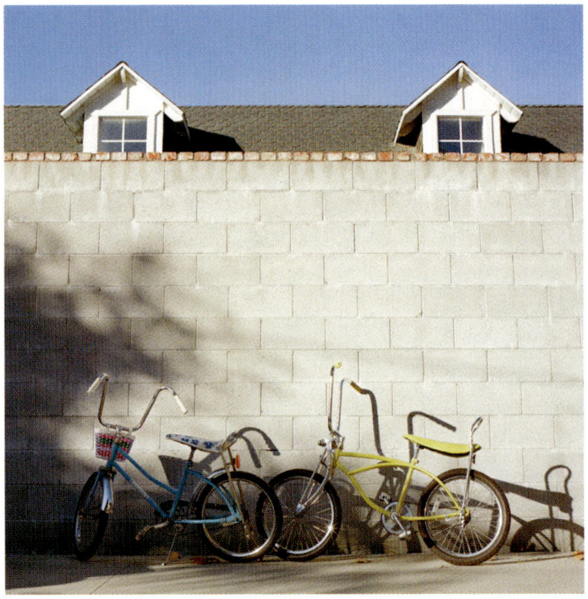

"Two Bikes" 2004

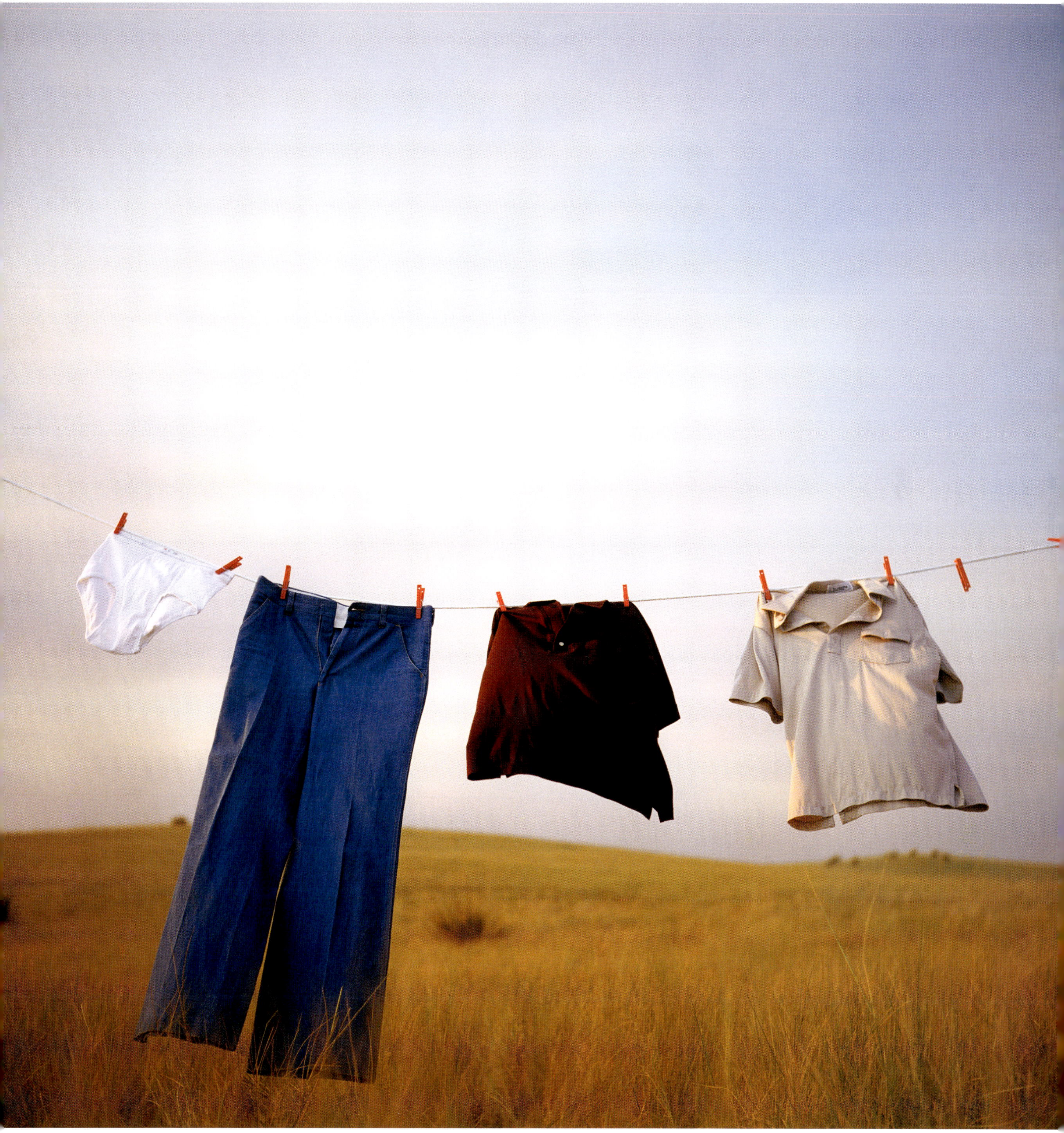

"Clothesline" 2004

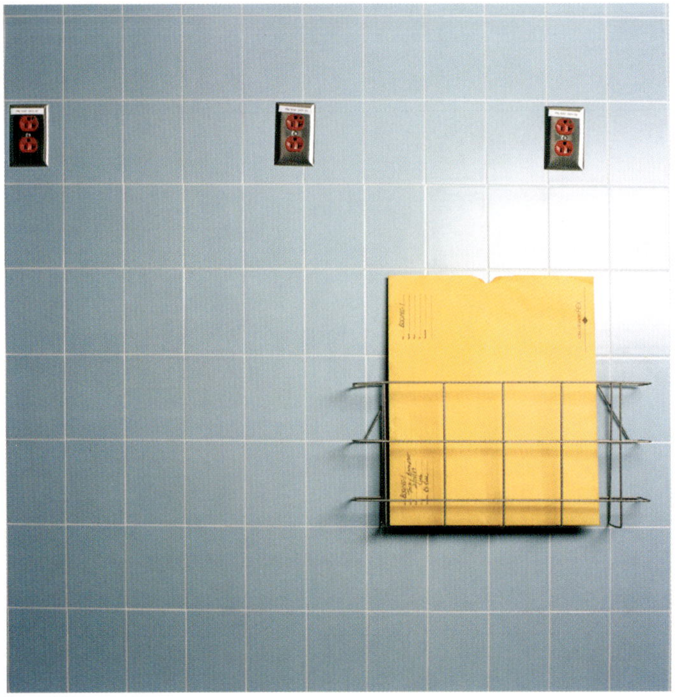

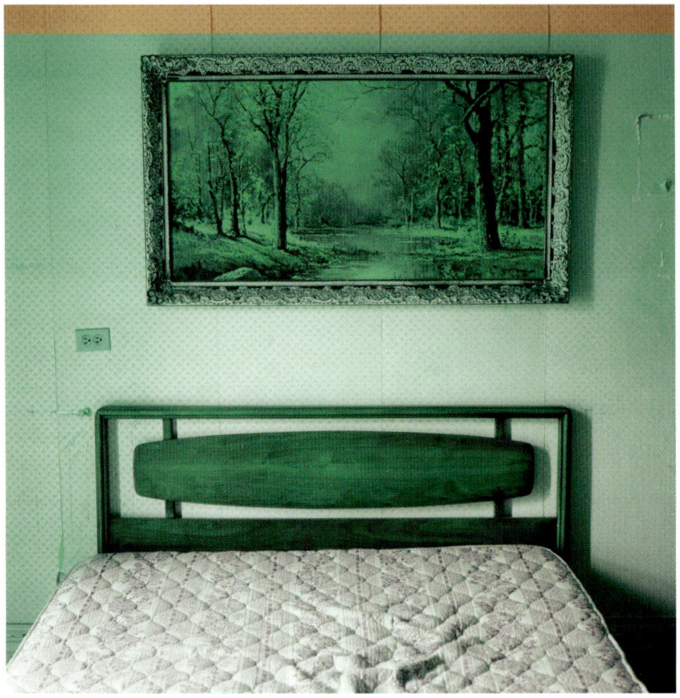

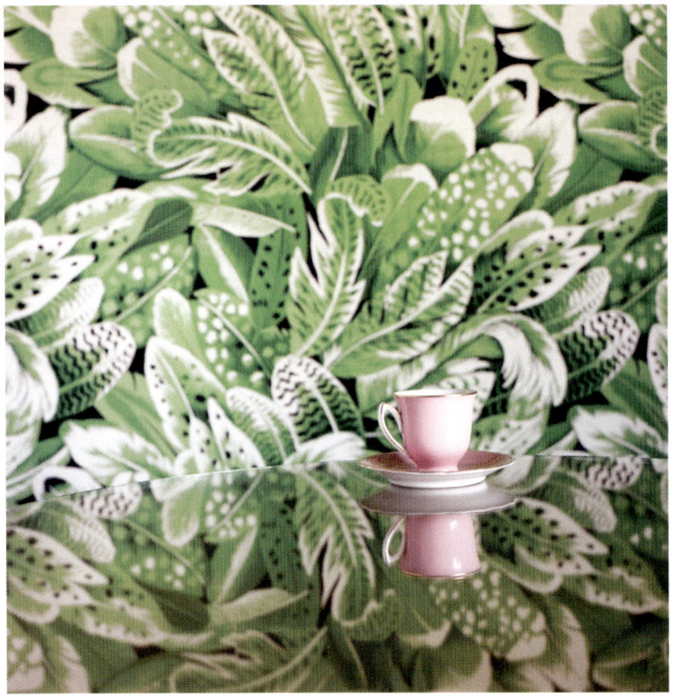

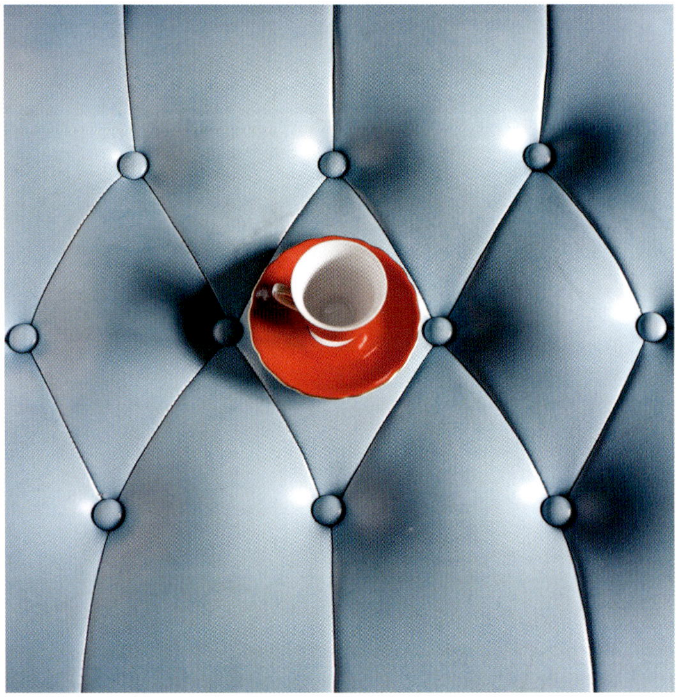

"Folder" 2006
Shot at an abandoned hospital outside of Los Angeles

"Roberts Bed & Painting" 2005
Part of a series shot in the historic Hotel Roberts shortly before it was demolished in the middle of the night, much to the surprise of the town

"Pink Tea" 2006
Part of an ongoing series of tea cups

"Red Tea" 2006
Part of an ongoing series of tea cups

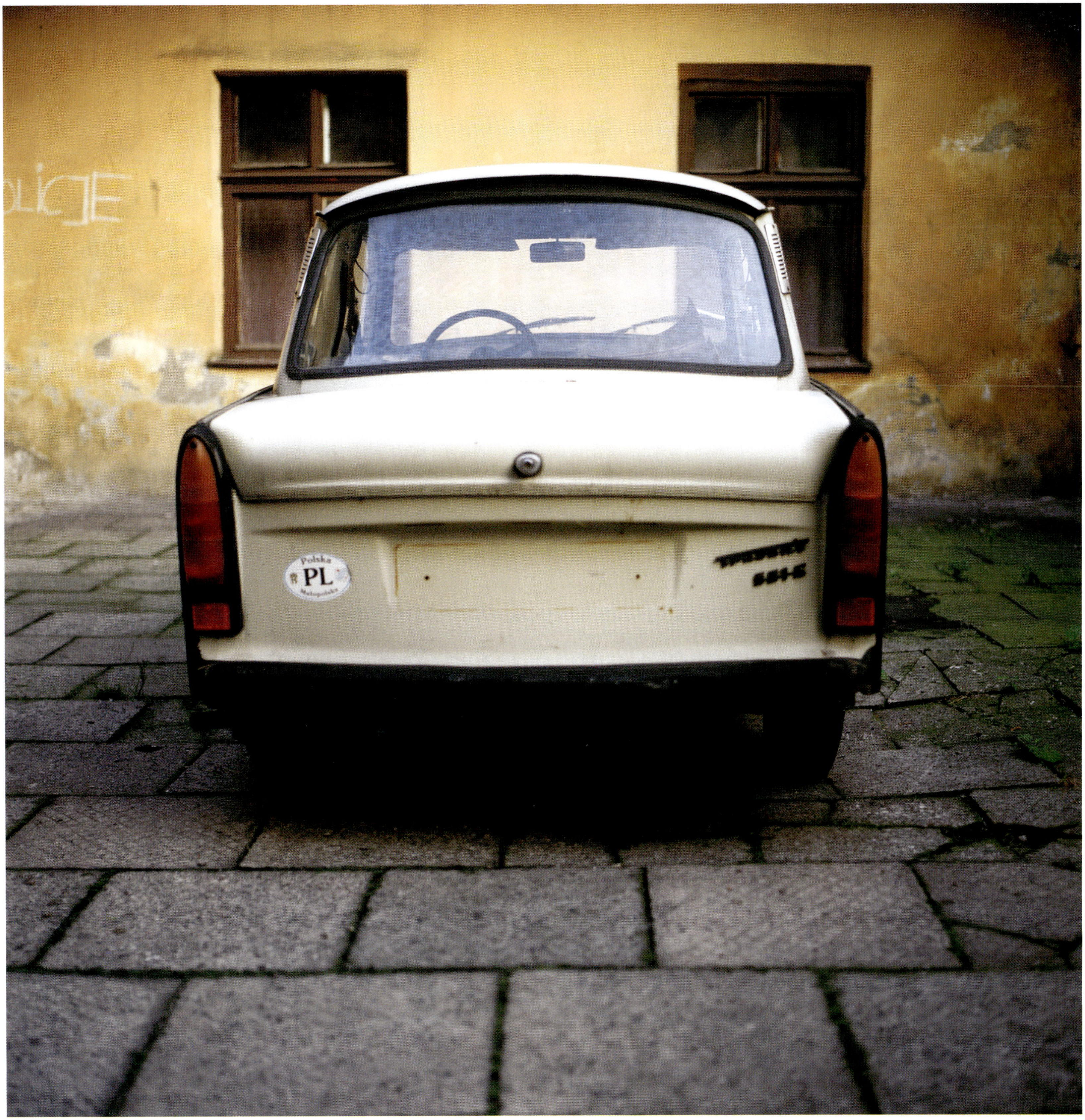

"Car" 2004
Shot during a trip to visit the Polish town of Sczynto where
Ruell's wife was born

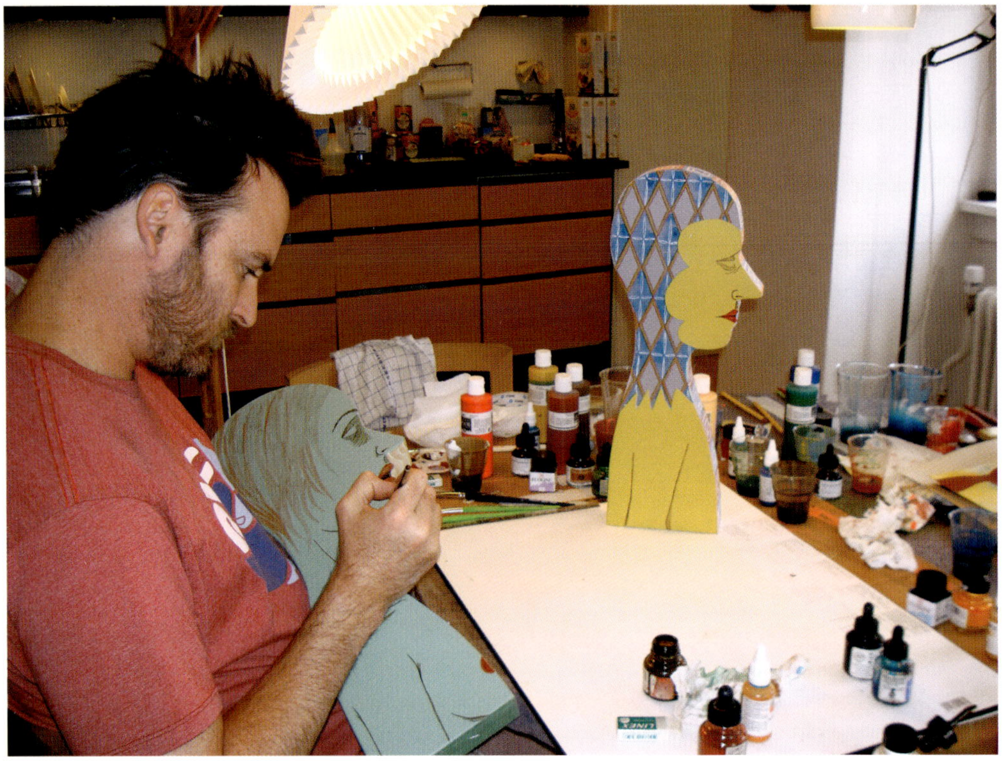

Photo by Deanna Templeton, 2011

ED TEMPLETON

Huntington Beach, California
toymachine.com/ed
Roberts & Tilton Gallery
Tim Van Laere Gallery
Nils Staerk Contemporary Art

I was born into this suburban mess south of Los Angeles; I cannot be held responsible. Skateboarding is what keeps me here. There is so much cement, and the industry resides here.

There is a growing advantage in that LA is rapidly rising as an art center. New York and London may be bigger, but LA is sunnier, and more spread out, so you can still be alone.

The suburbs and the particular fame-hungry population are a definite influence on my work and always fun to look at.

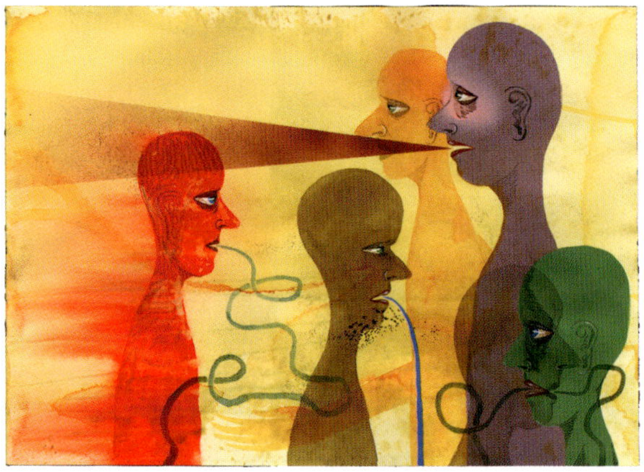

"Cacophony of Ideas" 2011
Acrylic and ink on paper
18 x 22 inches

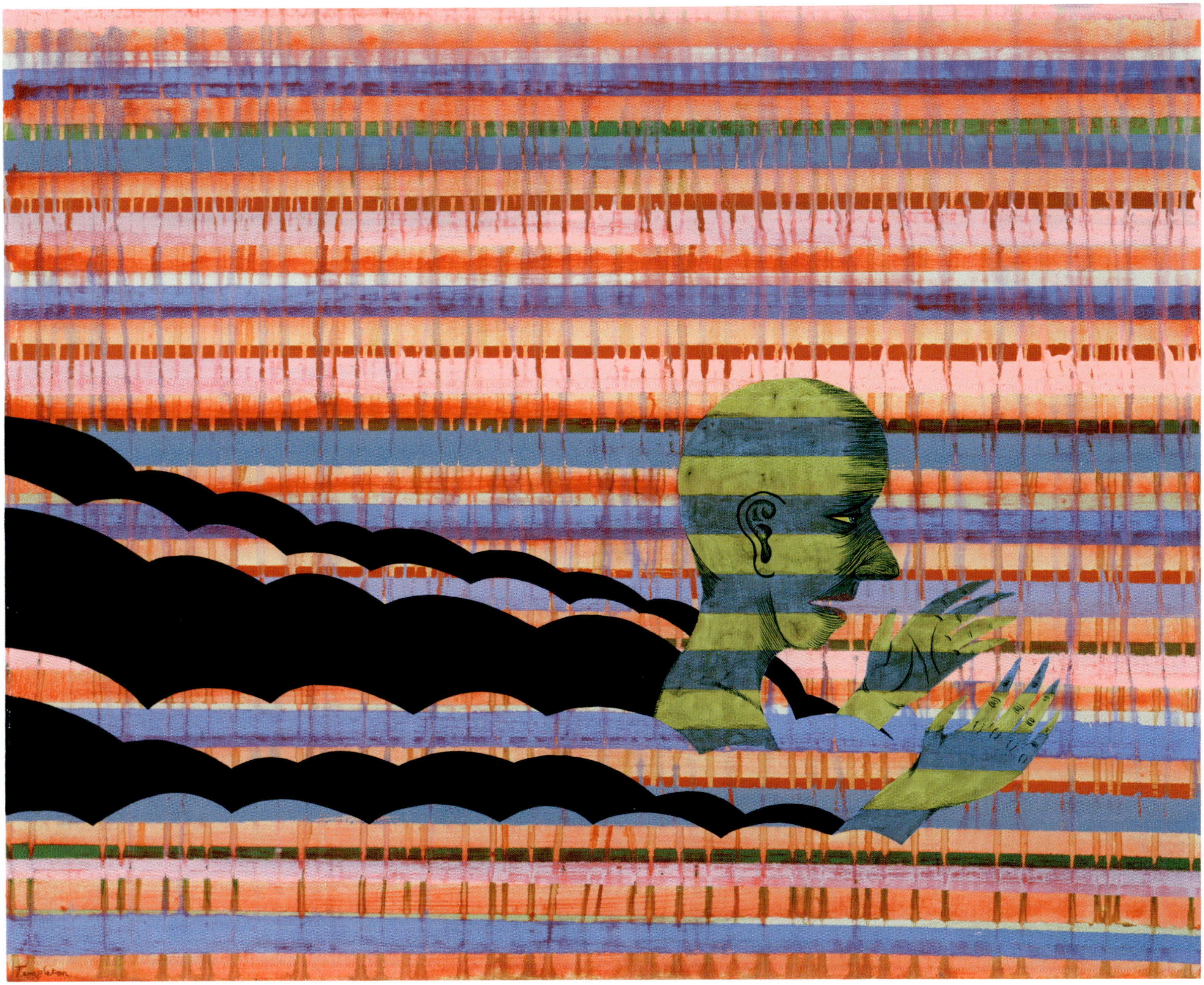

"Acid Dreams" 2006
Acrylic on panel
20 x 24 inches

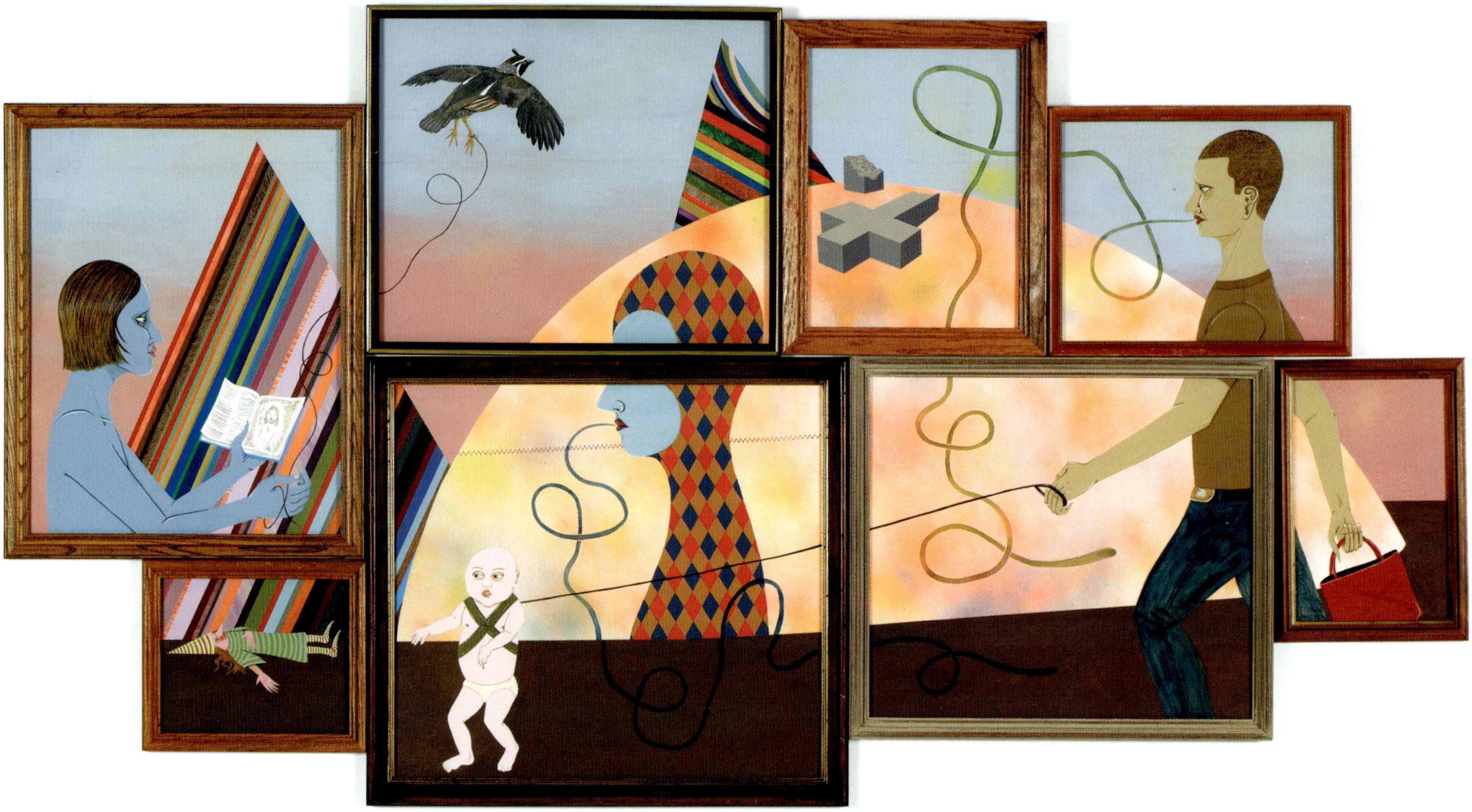

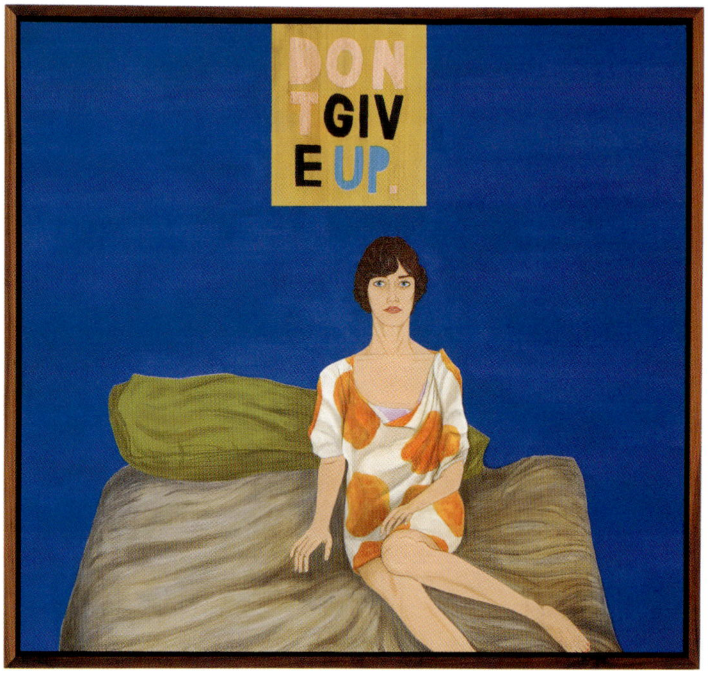

"Everyday Desires" 2011
Acrylic and ink on paper
38 x 73 inches

"Portrait of Miranda July" 2008
Acrylic on canvas
40 x 44 inches

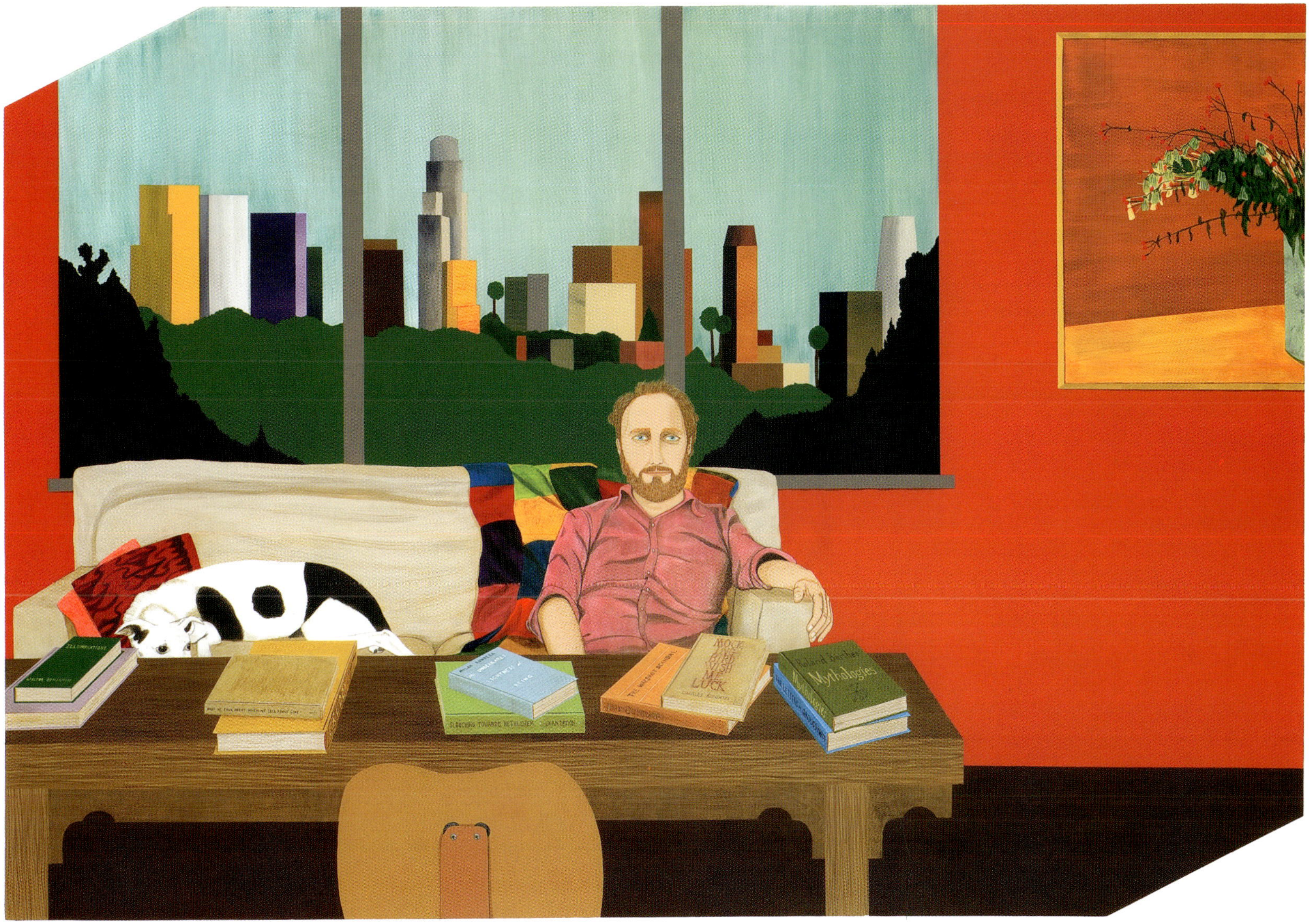

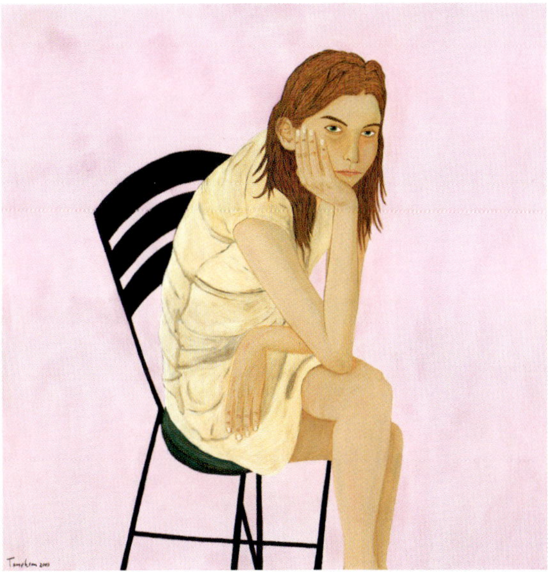

"Portrait of Mike Mills" 2008
Acrylic on panel
41 x 60 inches

"Portrait of Portrait of Ashley Thayer" 2005
Acrylic on panel
24 x 24 inches

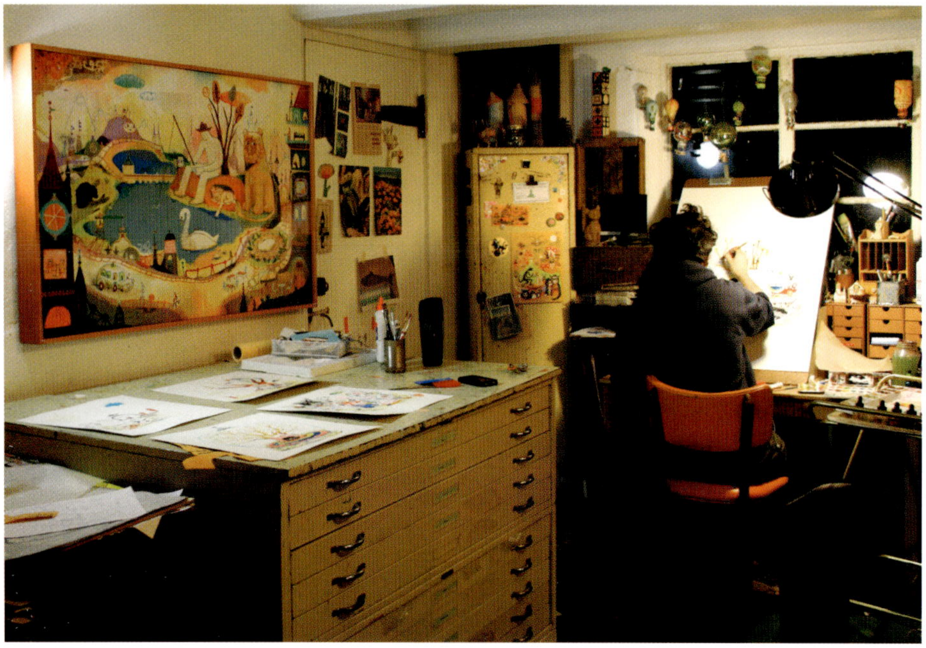

SOUTHER SALAZAR

Turlock, California
southersalazar.com
Jonathan Levine Gallery

Self Portrait, 2012

I was born and raised in California, so it's hard to imagine any other place feeling quite as much like home for me as California does. I've spent my whole life almost equally divided between the Bay, the Central Valley, and LA. I have this feeling like I should relocate for the sake of a new adventure, but it's hard because I really do love it here. The weather, my family and friends, my favorite spots ... my piles of junk ... I have all these little anchors.

It's a beautiful place, and this will probably sound cheesy, but I believe there is this sort of strange layer of positivity that floats around in the atmosphere a bit. It's like a sort of delusional, sunny spell that makes ridiculous ideas seem more plausible. People are willing to believe in something a little bit crazy. For me, that's an advantage because this environment has allowed me to make a career out of daydreaming. That behavior probably would've been less encouraged in many other parts of the world.

So many things about California influence my work and process—the geography, I think, makes it in. I've spent a lot of hours daydreaming on the 99 freeway. I think the rolling hills and oak trees sneak into those dreams. Some of my recent paintings were specifically inspired by time my wife and I spent living on the Tuolumne River in the Central Valley. Another thing is I'm always digging around here and there for little found items, stuff to add to my sculptures while wandering around the state. So there is a direct connection in that the actual bits of this place sometimes end up in my work.

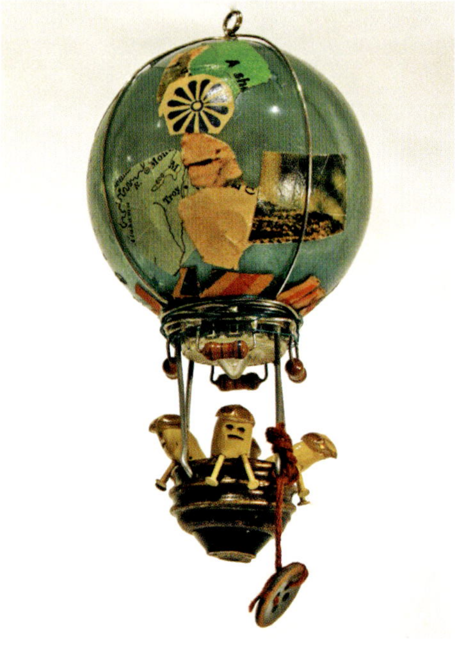

"The Exploratoriers" 2011
Acrylic, collage, polymer clay, and found materials
5 x 2¼ x 2¼ inches

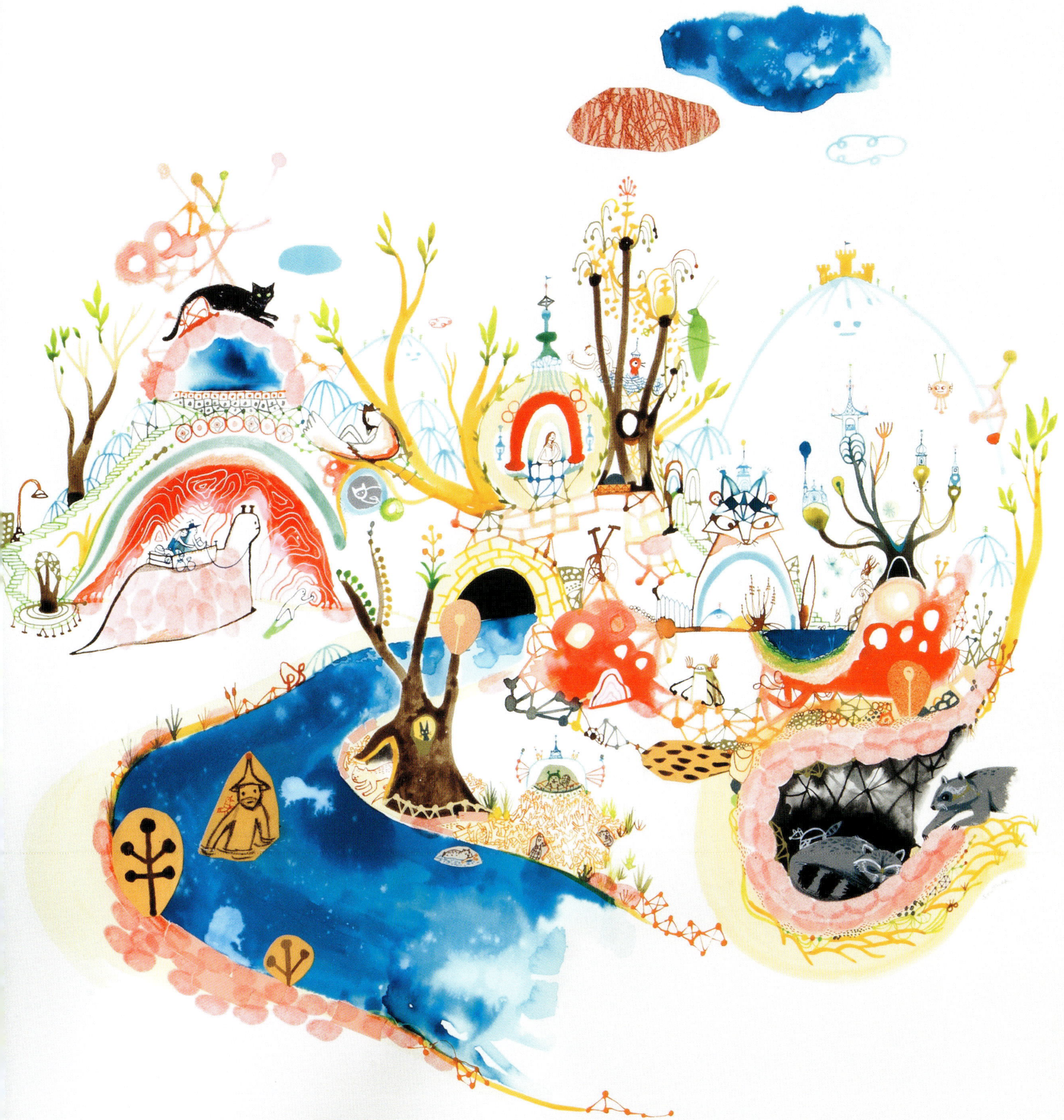

"The Way Home" 2011
Ink, watercolor, collage on paper
34 x 36 inches

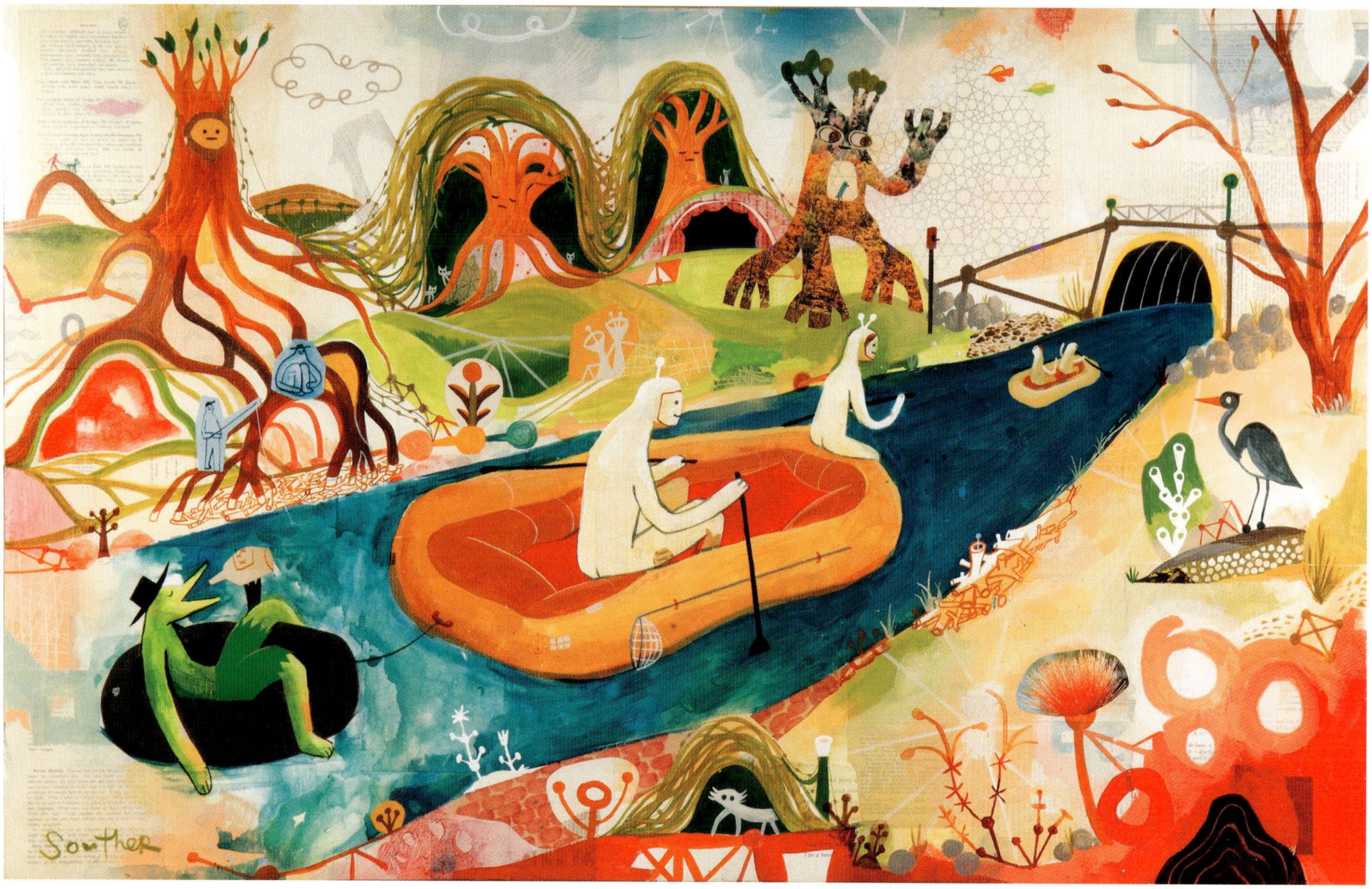

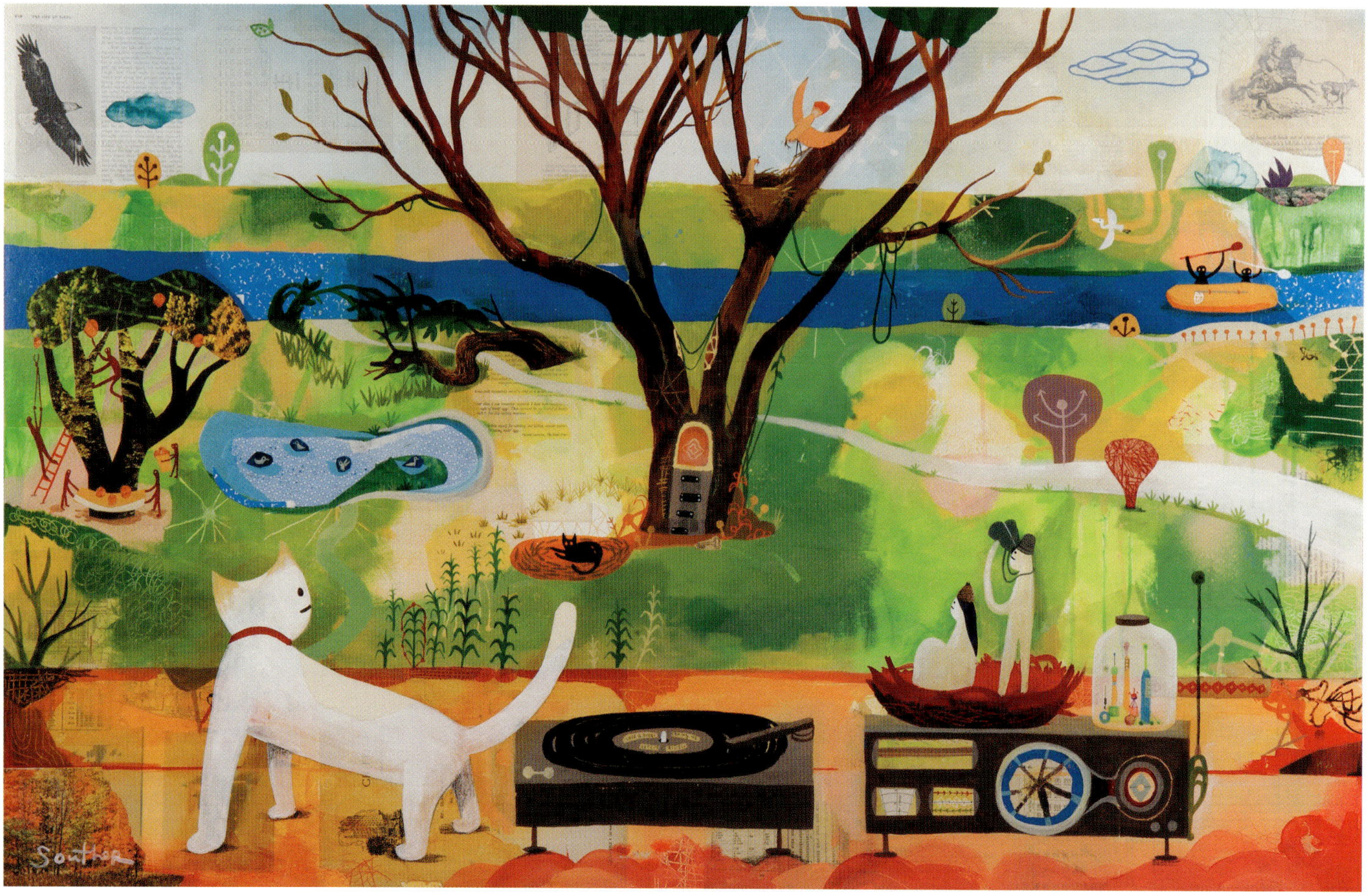

Top:
"We Don't Know Where This River Goes" 2011
Mixed media on wood panel
30 x 48 inches

Bottom:
"Throw Out the TV" 2011
Mixed media on wood panel
30 x 48 inches

Opposite:
"Home Base" 2011
Polymer clay, glass, resin, moss, and found materials
5 x 4 x 4 inches

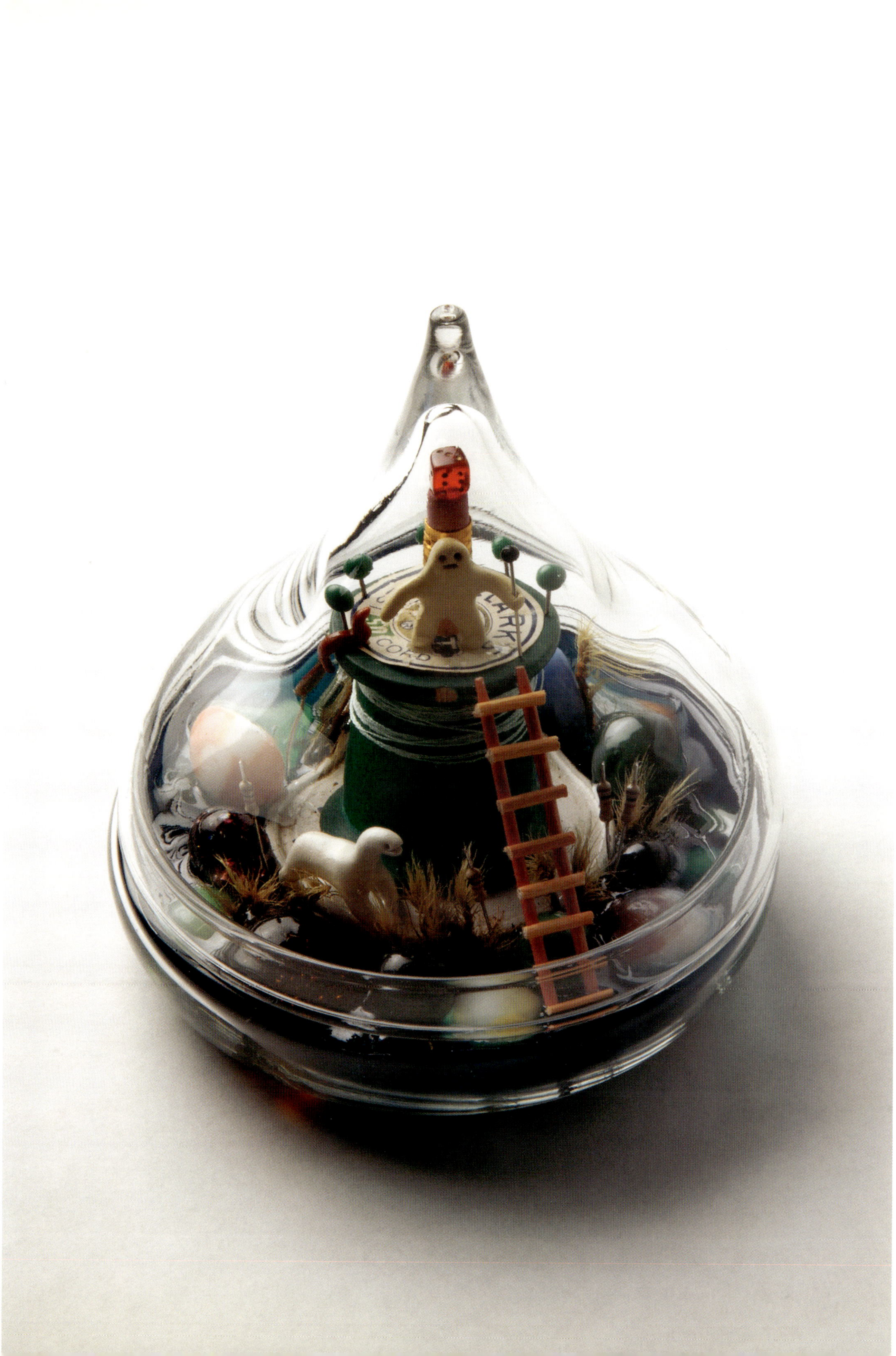
CORD

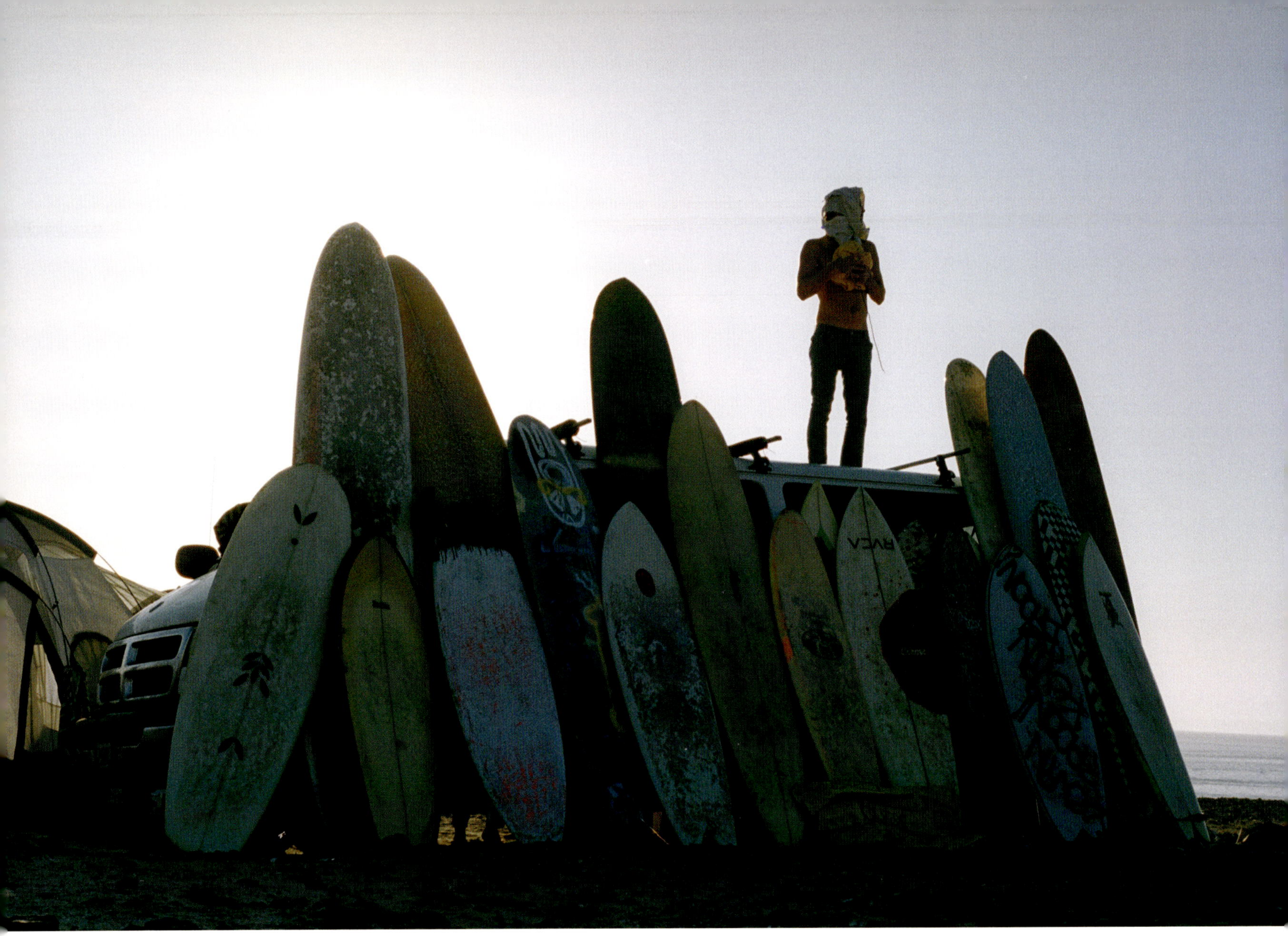

PM TENORE

RVCA Founder \/\ rvca.com
Costa Mesa, California

PM Tenore interviewed by Justin Van Hoy, May 2012

Pat Tenore (founder of RVCA) is an enigma. He is a charming and energetic person who is unique to the creative California landscape. To many, he is only the name printed on the tags of their RVCA garments (PM Tenore). But to a select few, he is the conduit in crafting a creative community involving many different groups of people all over California, as well as the world. Pat has spent his life in the Orange County sun surfing, skateboarding, and working on projects he is inspired to create and share. By living in the middle of the action sports mecca in Orange County, Pat was able to work and interact with industry professionals and start a clothing line at a young age. This proximity to the surf industry, coupled with his mind-set of doing what feels right rather than what makes sense on paper, has resulted in a unique home for artists in Southern California, as well as creative minds all over the world.

RVCA (pronounced roo-kah) is a men's and women's lifestyle clothing brand that was founded in the early 2000s in Pat's backyard garage, three miles away from the beach in Costa Mesa.

"Working with clothing lines as a freelance designer, I was able to observe, learn, and realize a new way of approaching the apparel industry. The natural next step was

Nolan Hall for RVCA
"Alex Kopps, Mexico" 2008

to create a brand that appeals to athletes, musicians, and general street culture, but create a platform for artists to interact and create at the same time. Right away I wanted to make RVCA unique by working with artists rather than having artists only do the work for the company. This decision to exhibit artists on an equal playing field, along with athletes and street culture personalities, was the only way to grow RVCA organically. Too many times the designer or artist remains anonymous when creating artwork for a brand. I didn't want that to be the case with RVCA. I wanted it to be a platform for artists to showcase their talents and take credit for the work.

"There have been so many legendary graphics and designs that artists have created, but few people know who actually did them. Like the Spitfire logo that Kevin Ancell created years ago. Everyone has seen that logo on shirts, stickers, and wheels thousands of times, but few people know he actually designed that logo."

The same day the RVCA brand was born, so was the Artist Network Program (ANP). It is a platform for an ever-growing number of artists, athletes, musicians, and galleries to come together and create. When an artist designs an ANP shirt, a portion of proceeds from that ANP shirt is donated to a charity of the artist's choice. By incorporating this type of mentality for a clothing line, Pat has helped create something far larger than just garments. This platform has given artists, athletes, and musicians the opportunity to all collectively share in the process of creating projects individually, and with each other, that many times would not be possible without support. RVCA has supported ANP artists in order to showcase their talents all over California and the United States, as well as in Asia, Australia, South America, and Europe. This allows for known artists to broaden their reach and unknown artists to reach audiences that might not have ever seen their work, given their geographic locations.

Over the years, the Artist Network Program has continued to grow and evolve, connecting artists and the RVCA community. When the audience is involved like this, it only creates a more rewarding experience and furthers our belief in working together. It creates a better product and collaborative experience; it creates a community, and that is the most important thing.

"Calling it a Network sounds like a cheesy marketing buzz word—that I don't like—but that is really what it is. By identifying with artists and groups that we believe in—rather than just who is popular at the moment—we are introduced to more and more people that share in our same sensibilities. A lot of great art world figures like Aaron Rose, Barry McGee, Ed Templeton, and Craig Stecyk have brought their shared histories and experiences, which have shaped the ANP over the years.

"Aaron Rose brings his insights and experiences from his *Alleged Gallery* in New York City and the *Beautiful Losers* school, which really helps grow the *ANP Quarterly*. Ed is a legend in the skate and art industry, and Craig has been a pillar in the creative athlete coming of age in Southern California."

Along with the RVCA ANP collaborations, Pat had a vision for *ANP Quarterly*, a free magazine that was started as a platform to showcase artists, musicians, and experiences of the art world in print.

"Current editor Aaron Rose and Art Director Casey Holland, along with past editors Ed Templeton and Brendan Fowler, put together a magazine that has created an enormous sense of anticipation when the new issue is set to come out. *ANP Quarterly* always brings together such a great selection of stories and insights that shed light on what is happening creatively all over the world."

Not having to rely on sponsors and advertisers allows *ANP Quarterly* to cover a broader group of stories and experiences that other magazines might overlook. Focusing on quality of content, versus just what is popular, has given *ANP Quarterly* a large community of followers worldwide.

RVCA also works with several fine art galleries. Los Angeles galleries KNOWN, New Image Art, and THIS los angeles, as well as The Luggage Store Gallery in San Francisco, and they have all created a niche in their cities that RVCA has grown to respect and support.

I trust what is happening in these galleries because they are a part of our artistic community. They are all coming from very different places, and that presents a unique view of what is happening in the art world. The art and artists they exhibit continue to grow our ANP network and continue to inspire myself, RVCA, and each other. They are all doing very different things, but they are all valuable pieces of our collective.

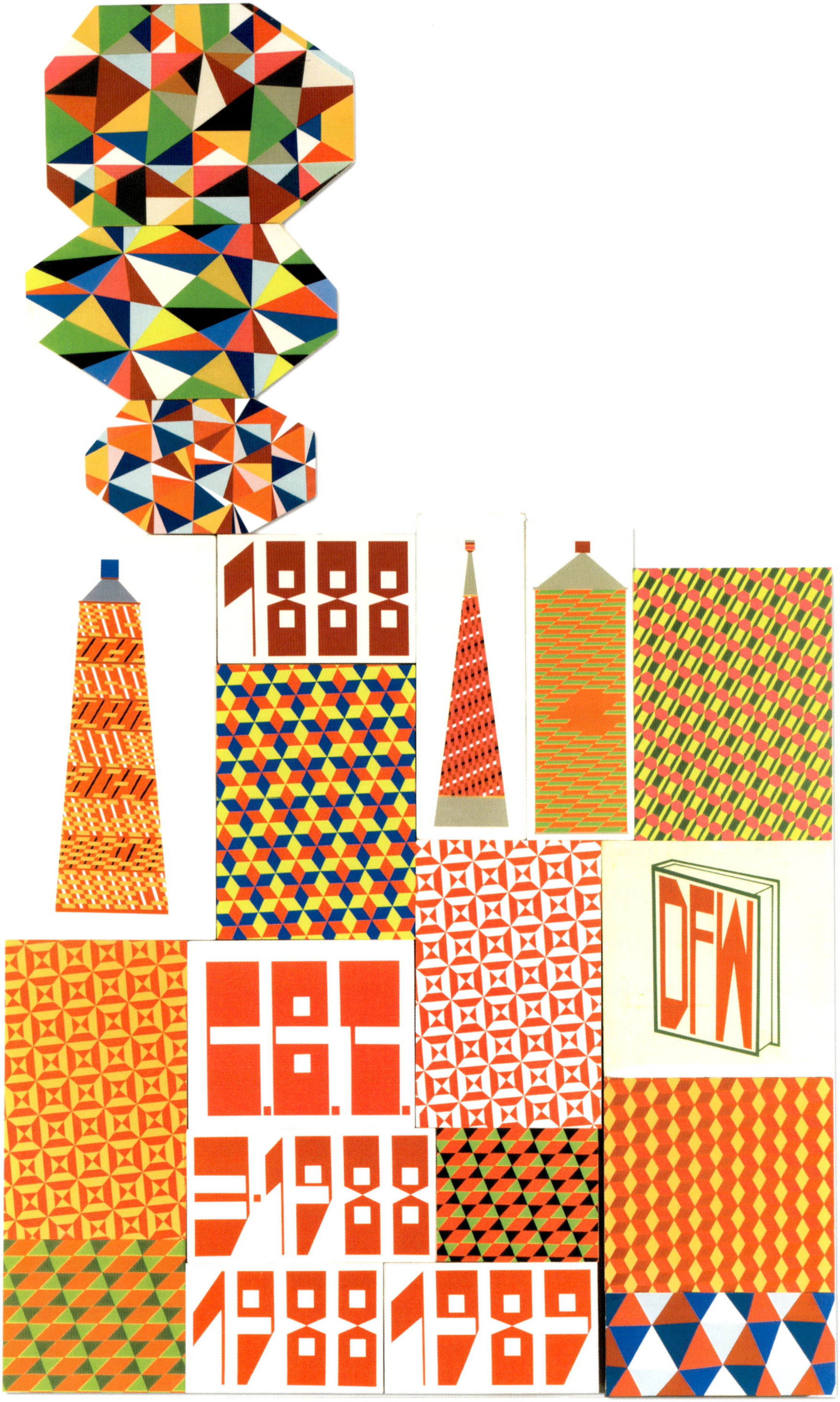

Barry McGee
"Untitled" 2011
Paint on panels
81 x 59 inches

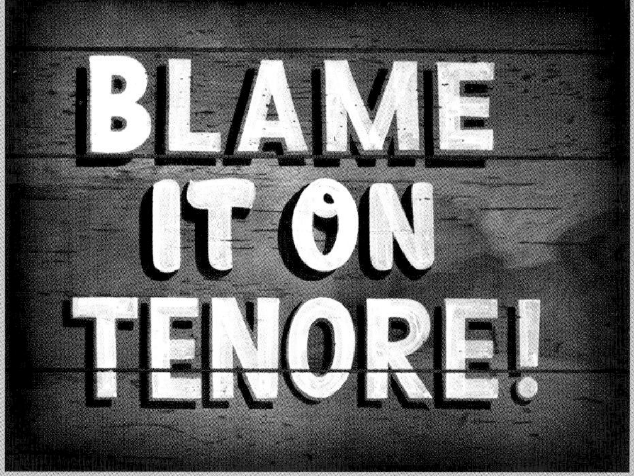

Alexis Ross
"Blame it on Tenore" 2011
Hand-painted sign
10 x 9 inches

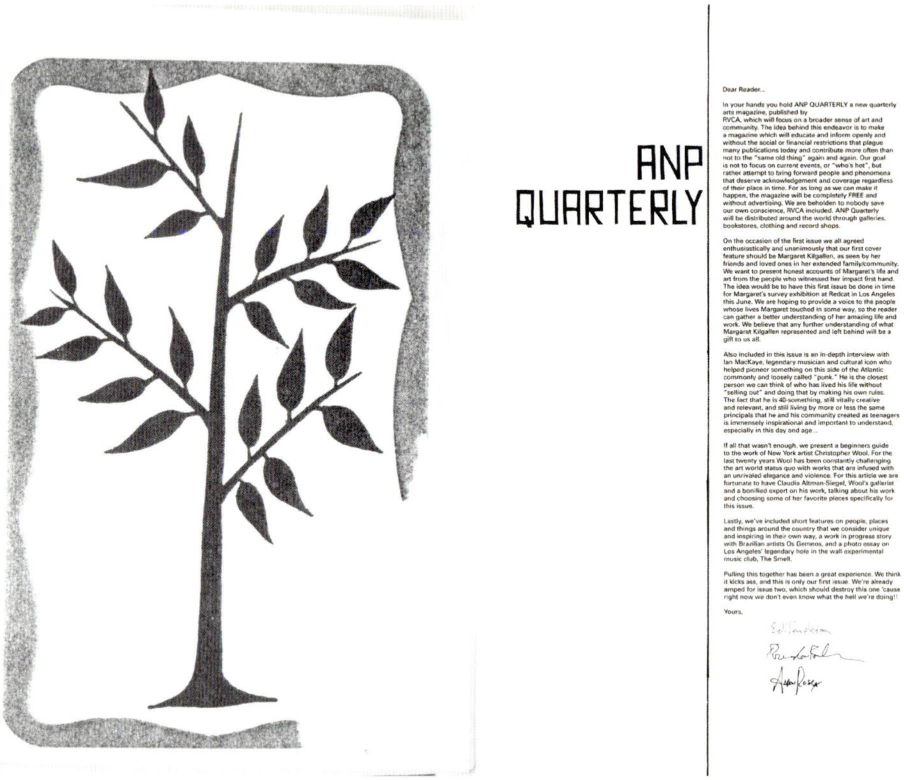
ANP QUARTERLY

Dear Reader...

In your hands you hold ANP QUARTERLY a new quarterly arts magazine, published by RVCA, which will focus on a broader sense of art and community. The idea behind this endeavor is to make a magazine which will educate and inform openly and without the social or financial restrictions that plague many publications today and contribute more often than not to the "same old thing" again and again. Our goal is not to focus on current events, or "who's hot", but rather attempt to bring forward people and phenomena that deserve acknowledgement and coverage regardless of their place in time. For as long as we can make it happen, the magazine will be completely FREE and without advertising. We are beholden to nobody save our own conscience, RVCA included. ANP Quarterly will be distributed around the world through galleries, bookstores, clothing and record shops.

On the occasion of the first issue we all agreed enthusiastically and unanimously that our first cover feature should be Margaret Kilgallen, as seen by her friends and loved ones in her extended family/community. We want to present honest accounts of Margaret's life and art from the people who witnessed her impact first hand. The idea would be to have this first issue be done in time for Margaret's survey exhibition at Redcat in Los Angeles this June. We are hoping to provide a voice to the people whose lives Margaret touched in some way, so the reader can gather a better understanding of her amazing life and work. We believe that any further understanding of what Margaret Kilgallen represented and left behind will be a gift to us all.

Also included in this issue is an in-depth interview with Ian MacKaye, legendary musician and cultural icon who helped pioneer something on this side of the Atlantic commonly and loosely called "punk." He is the closest person we can think of who has lived his life without "selling out" and doing that by making his own rules. The fact that he is 40-something, still vitally creative and relevant, and still living by more or less the same principals that he and his community created as teenagers is immensely inspirational and important to understand, especially in this day and age...

If all that wasn't enough, we present a beginners guide to the work of New York artist Christopher Wool. For the last twenty years Wool has been constantly challenging the art world status quo with works that are infused with an unrivaled elegance and violence. For this article we are fortunate to have Claudia Altman-Siegel, Wool's gallerist and a bonified expert on his work, talking about his work and choosing some of her favorite pieces specifically for this issue.

Lastly, we've included short features on people, places and things around the country that we consider unique and inspiring in their own way, a work in progress story with Brazilian artists Os Gemeos, and a photo essay on Los Angeles' legendary hole in the wall experimental music club, The Smell.

Pulling this together has been a great experience. We think it kicks ass, and this is only our first issue. We're already amped for issue two, which should destroy this one 'cause right now we don't even know what the hell we're doing!!

Yours,

ANP QUARTERLY

Costa Mesa, California

rvcaanpq.com

rvca.com

ANP Quarterly is an arts magazine published by RVCA that focuses on a broader sense of art and community. The idea behind this endeavor is to make a magazine that will educate and inform openly and without the social or financial restrictions that plague many publications today and contribute more often than not to the same old thing again and again. The magazine's editorial goal is not to focus on current events or who's hot but rather to bring forward people and phenomena that deserve acknowledgment and coverage regardless of their place in time.

Releasing 15,000 copies per issue, *ANP Quarterly* is available for free at leading galleries and museums, bookstores, record stores, and fashion boutiques around the world.

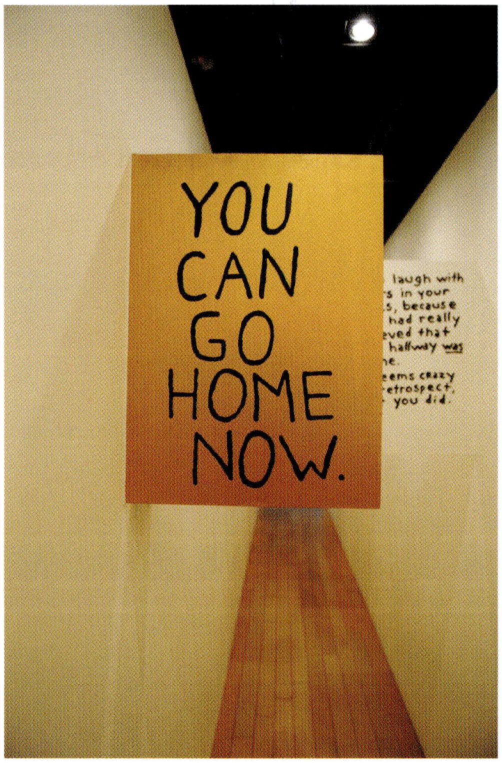

All images taken from RVCA *ANP Quarterly* Magazine

GARRY TRINH:
GIANT BONSAIS 2005–2007

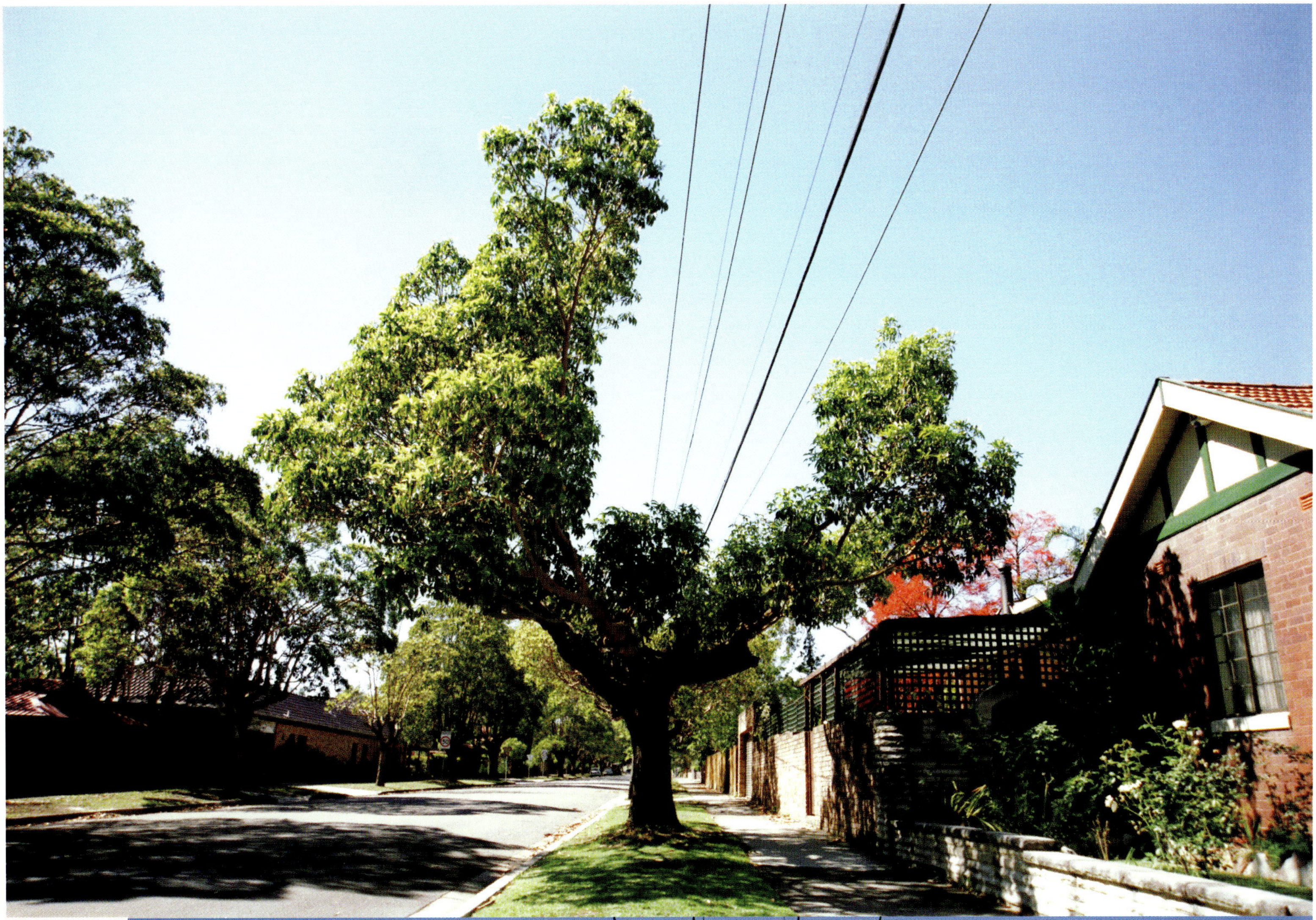

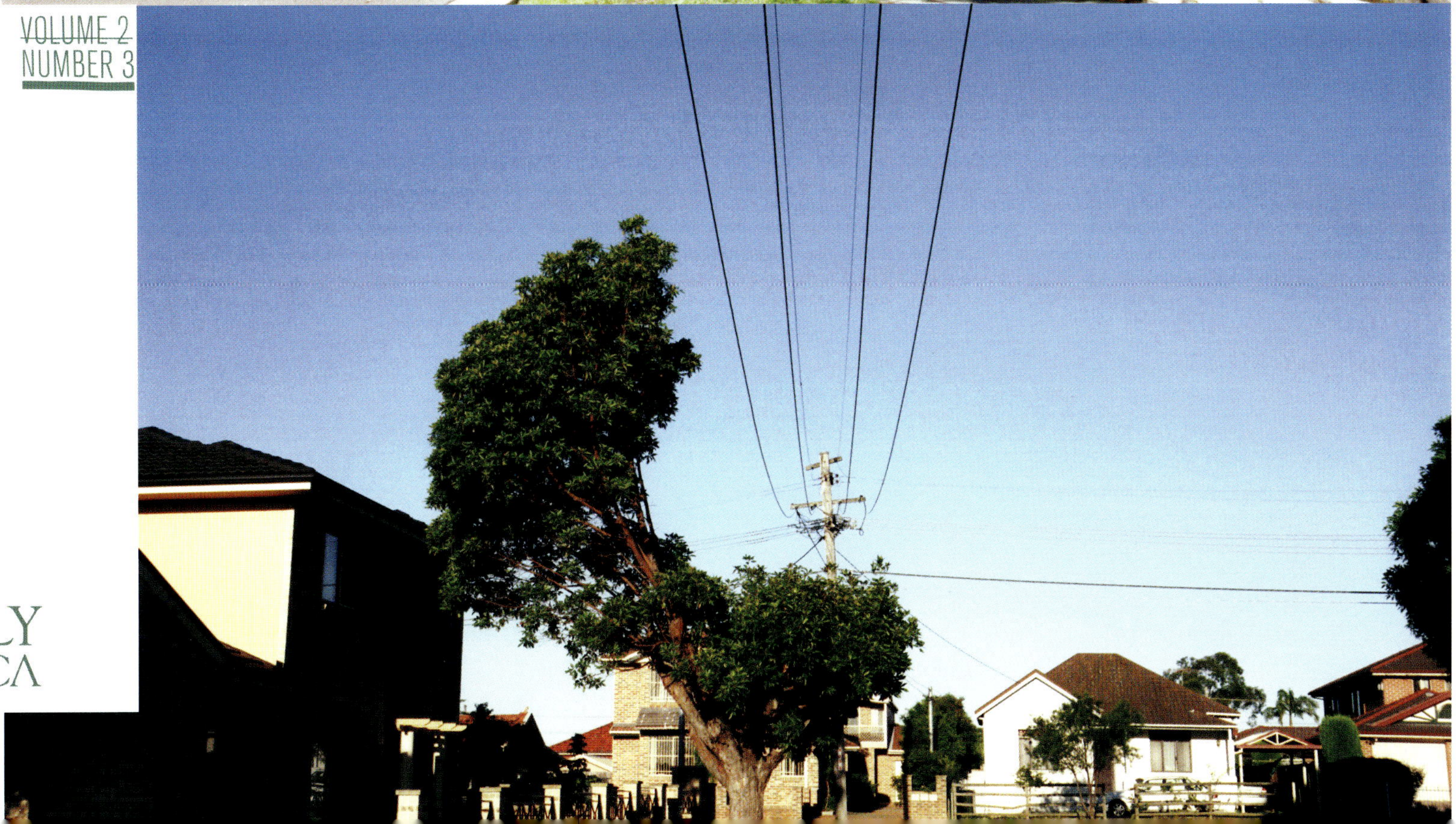

GEOFF MCFETRIDGE

Interview by Brendan Fowler
Installation photographs by Joshua White, all other courtesy the artist

Geoff McFetridge is a Los Angeles-based artist and graphic designer. For the last ten years he has slowly built a successful career working in virtually every medium imaginable. In the design world, he has created graphics and logotypes for companies such as ESPN, Nike, Girl Skateboards, Stussy, Patagonia, Pepsi and others, yet has always managed to avoid the usual trappings of being called a "sellout." This is possibly because, as this article illustrates, he has such a singular vision as a creator that even the work he does for hire maintains a very personal flair. In the gallery world, McFetridge has mounted exhibitions of his work in New York, Berlin, London, Paris and Tokyo and was included in the 2003 Cooper-Hewitt National Design Triennial in New York. In addition to paintings and prints, his installations have included everything from furniture, sculpture, film and video, fabrics and wallpaper. McFetridge's designs have also been featured on t-shirts, album covers, watches, rain jackets, surf trunks, bottles, toys, stickers, buttons, patches, and shoes. This interview was conducted on the occasion of Geoff's recent solo exhibition titled "The Line That Rhymes" at New Image Art in Los Angeles.

Brendan Fowler: Geoff, where did you grow up?
Geoff McFetridge: I grew up in Calgary, Alberta, Canada. I was born in 1971.
BF: When did you move to California?
GM: Not till around '93? '94? ...'93.
BF: Do you remember the first thing that you were really into as a kid, or as a teenager?
GM: As a teenager: skateboarding. It was like, from war, with full camo web gear and digging trenches, straight to skateboarding.
BF: Web gear?
GM: Yeah (laughing) you know, like G.I. Joe. I had all the army stuff (imitates torso covered in full army regalia). I had backpacks, and helmets. Camo.
BF: You would gear up and run around alone or with friends?
GM: Um, either/or.
BF: Did you spend a lot of time alone as a kid, solo?
GM: (laughing) Ah, yeah...kinda...fifty-fifty. But yeah, pretty much, I guess.
BF: I was alone a lot, too. I was just sort of picturing a lot of alone time.
GM: Yeah, I was alone a lot for sure. Lots of drawing by myself, and then lots of—because, where we lived was the crazy suburbs, so behind our house was, like, nothing, forever. If you looked on a map it would be, like, "There's behind our house, and there's British Columbia." It just goes. So I would put on full camo and just wander around. And sometimes I would meet friends out there, like, "Meet me in the woods," and you'd go out there, build lean-to's, it was pretty crazy.
BF: Did you have any urban experiences?
GM: When I got into skating. The suburbs were actually good for skating, because everything was concrete, but then we started going *downtown*. We would take the bus and go skating all day and all night. We knew every alley, every loading dock, every parking structure and it was like all abandoned at nighttime. And that's when you suddenly make friends with kids with tattoos and kids that were sleeping on the streets, cause you're there and they become your friends.
BF: You met kids that were way rawer.
GM: Way rawer. And I don't think that they necessarily thought, like, "This kid doesn't come from a broken home." And it didn't necessarily occur to me that we were so different, but then there was stuff like, "Wait, that *is* a real tattoo. He had a rad creature tattooed on his arm and he's 14." (laughs)
BF: And this is, in the early '80s?
GM: Yeah I got into skateboarding when I was in 7th grade and then went to my first punk show in 9th grade...it was D.O.A.

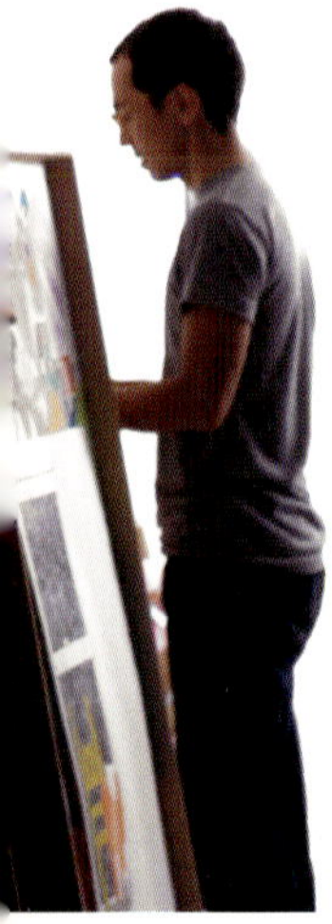

Geoff McFetridge, 2006, photo by Joshua White

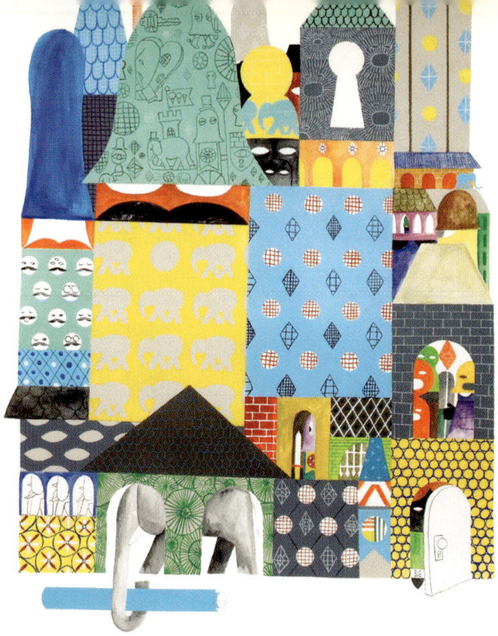

(Opposite)
"A City of Elephants" 2006
44.25" x 60"
paint, ink, pen, wax pencil on paper

TEENAGE TEARDROPS

Interview by Jessica Hopper / Photo by Betsy Adams

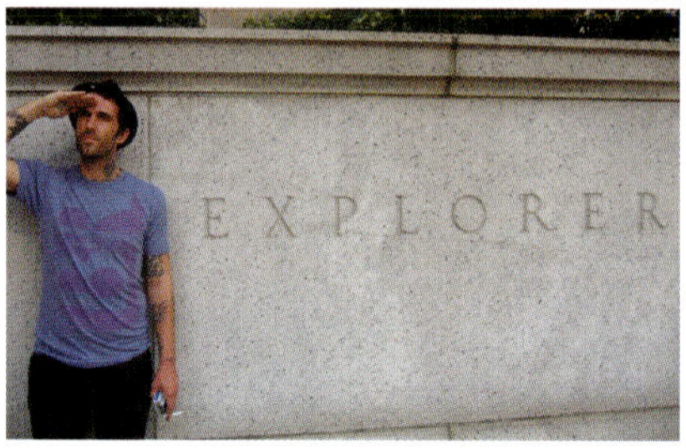

Cali DeWitt is my second oldest friend in the world; we've been down since teenhood. The mixtapes and drawings he made for me then, the books he sent me in the mail were crucial and influential in my development as a punk, an artist and a writer. This is not an uncommon story in regards to Cali, he has served as a beacon and influence to many; he's a grown up golden boy with a California head and a true-punx-heart. He has an easy way about him that makes life come into technicolor relief when you are around him, the way he enjoys things is infectious. After years on the medians of the music biz, he's downscaled to impresario of art label Teardrops, where he puts out tiny amounts of elaborately packaged vinyl records as well as books and art zines. He is also a late blooming artist himself, coming into great talent as a photographer and as a painter, though he will not cop to this.

I feel like Teardrops is much more than a record label; you specify it as an art label—which I think supposes an attitude and intent. Record labels just serve to sell things.

Well, why limit yourself? I love records and music so there will be plenty of that, but why can't I make a book? Why can't I make prints, dvds, skateboards? To me, art is something that gives me a physical and emotional response when I look at it. As an 'art label' I have the freedom to release anything that hits me, that feels honest, and that I can afford to manufacture.

Some of the fundamental aspects of early hardcore- "PMA" and inspiration, legacy, the young idea/ youthful spirit, the address of community—is constant in Teardrops. How did that happen?

I spent the late mid to late 80's listening to the Bad Brains and Urban Waste. It stuck. It is the foundation from where the tenacity comes I guess. As far as youth, I think I like to try and hold onto a certain kind of fearless naive idealism that is most often associated with the young. I am uninterested in becoming a jaded cynic who talks long shit about 'back in the day'.

What are you working on?

This spring will see the release of a 12" single by LA's NO AGE, a book of drawings by Mark McCoy of Das Oath/Youth Attack fame. A photo zine by Nate Harrington and myself called Post Teen Fury, Various silk screened ephemera, and a 'Teardrops Fest' on Bainbridge Island in Washington this summer, which, if I can pull it off, will be an all day group art show music fest in the woods.

How did you become an artist yourself?

I don't think of myself as an artist. I keep trying.

You've been a private artist for a long time--how did you come into making yr artwork public? Are you a late bloomer? Or was it just a matter of getting serious?

Again, I have been drawing and doing my best to make things for years. If I seem to be sharing some of those things more it's just because my heart has become more open of the years, and I am less afraid.

How much of yr teenage vision(s) about art and what you want to put into the world are informing what you do now? How have your ideas about art evolved?

Creativity and originality laid bare and with fearless honesty cannot be beat. The things I love took a risk on the part of who created them.

How much does love factor into what you are doing?

At this point in life love factors into everything I do. The love of my girlfriend, friends, and family inspire me on a daily. The love I feel for people who create the things that touch me inspires me to give total respect whatever it is Teardrops makes, and to do it justice.

What is the role of Los Angeles in what you create?

Los Angeles! The Los Angeles I live in is a small community. I often think that the city I love hasn't existed in many years. I live in Joan Didion's Los Angeles, Joan Didion's California. When I leave Echo Park every morning to go to work I spend the day fantasizing about leaving. I do, however, LOVE my little east side enclave and the piles of inspirational folks who inhabit the hills of the area.

With all you have done in your life and how long you have been around music, working with it professionally, you should be jaded. Instead, you present yourself as someone who has a continual capacity for inspiration–is that a matter of the heart, or is it principle or just dumb luck?

Without inspiration I feel I would be living a bleak life. It is a matter of the heart, and as long as there are people trying new things and moving forward and doing so independently, I will always have inspiration.

What inspires you?

Everything inspires me. Over the years it has changed, from darkness to light, from night to morning. I like to go slower and look at everything now. Lately my direct inspiration comes from my relationship, the bands on

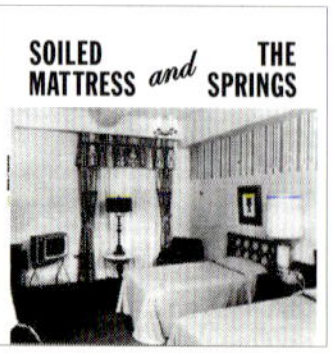

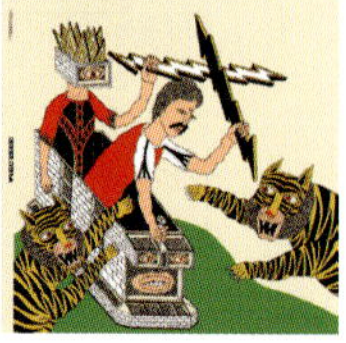

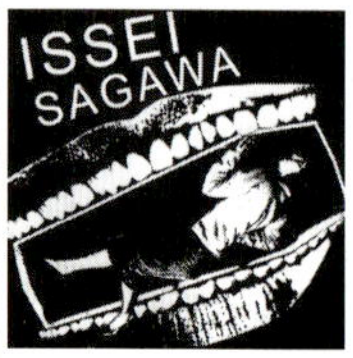

Teardrops who I am honored to be working with, Joan Didion's non-fiction, Bone Awl, and Giulietta Masinas performance in La Strada. I am also inspired by people living unconventional lives and love and honesty in the face of a very ugly, fast paced, extreme culture. People who take what they do seriously inspire me. Sobriety inspires me.

Much of the work you have put out so far is limited quanitites, with huge attention to details; it's very tangible, almost archaic way of making records; making a fine product. How much of what you do is a rebuke of technology?

Craft and care seems like it's dying. I hate the idea of nothing being made by hand anymore. I want to touch things and pick them up and wear them and use them. I want to make one thing at a time, I want to take each one of these things seriously, I want to make it as beautiful as I can.

http://teenageteardrops.abstractdynamics.org/
www.teenageteardrops.com

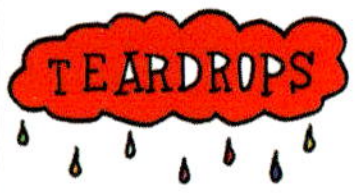

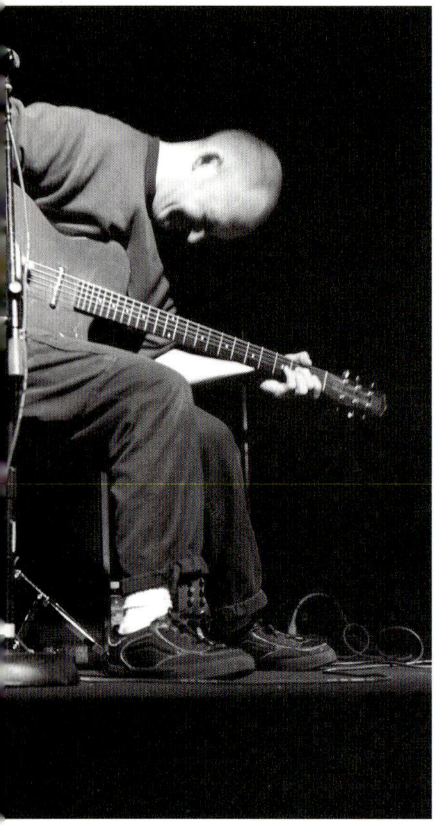

Whoa.
His daughter had talked to him about it.
Did he know you were there?
Yeah. He invited us. And we're sitting there and he said, basically, that we are fighting an incredible fight in a industry, which can be best described as bullshit, and at most, an ugly industry -I'm paraphrasing- then he goes, "it's nice to know that as links we share the chain." That makes me happy as hell to hear those words; and I feel the same about people. I feel like, the work that I am involved with is merely keeping that flame alive so that people can continue to come and ignite. I thought a lot about the way I perceive music, and for me, music is a gift. It was an incredible gift and when I get a gift I take care of it. And then I try to pass it along. Now other people have come across this gift and they looked at it and said, you know what? If I polish it I can sell it. But once you sell it it's no longer, it's not a gift! It's a commodity. So I think that I continue to give. That's my idea.
Well, going along those lines... In all of your bands- here, let's use Fugazi as the example-as a band, an independent creative unit, there are so many different venues and ways to make things and output stuff: there's shows and records and things like that; but then there's also "merch" stuff to sell: shirts and stickers and whatever things. And you always refrained from making that stuff, even in spite of the fact that it was getting made; clearly there was a demand for it. You know, people were making bootleg shirts and everything. Why, didn't you do it when A), it was being to underscore the existence of this parallel economy to music. It's one that's just filled with avarice. It's such a greedy, parallel economy. It's basically, like, if you create anything that people come to, somebody's gonna put a fucking hot dog stand next door. But why should we engage in it? But look, if I see a band on tour and there's six people at the show, I'll buy their T-shirt if *they* made the T-shirt.
Wait, you personally do?
Sure I would buy them.
(LAUGH)
I would never *wear* them, but I'll *buy* them. Because, why not? Like, help the damn band out, you know? If they sat there and silk screened them - that makes sense to me.
[Laughing]
What doesn't make sense is when you've got a couple a guys in a U-haul truck *following* the band around, they're like a merchandising company that's, like, made a deal; that's just not interesting to me. It's like the roar of merchandise drowns out the music. But I think that one issue that does come back to me a lot is the money. And I just kinda find it so fucking repugnant, man. It's disgusting. The money issues just drive me crazy. And I think in a way- you know, my mom died last year and we had some amazing conversations about sorta the psychology of our lives and we were talking one day and I was like, "you know, it's weird, I always felt like we were poor." And she said, "yeah, me too." But my father always thought we were rich. (LAUGH) You see, my father's parents had a little bit of dough. But

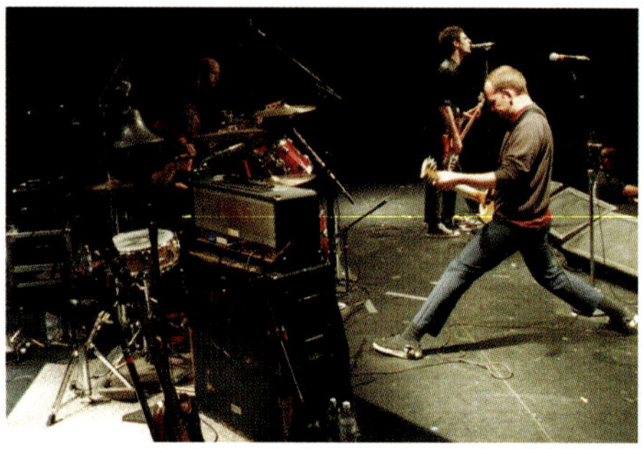

made already, without your consent, and B), you guys could have done it and been the ones receiving the benefits rather than exploitative third parties.
Well, we didn't want to do it. So can you think of a worse reason to do it? The fact that somebody else is doing it- I mean, in our mind, we were a band, we made music. The whole merchandising aspect of music was really, I mean, you knew you were in trouble when people were worrying more about their T-shirt designs than they are about their songs. And I'm not joking about that. I actually think that you can really see a decline in the music. You can really, really see the kind of songwriting and the decline of songwriting in music 'cause people were just not - the dialogue wasn't about the music anymore. [And] It went from merchandise straight to contracts. I remember the first time we we didn't have the dough. His parents had the dough and then, all that money just disappeared when my grandmother broke her hip and then was basically in homes and so forth, and so all the money just got used up. But my father, in his life he's always felt like he's well to do; but my mother's always felt really poor 'cause she grew up really poor- relatively poor. So I think that the money issue, like, that kind of pinch in between the two of them, probably really set me off, like, just to thinking: "...man, money's just fucked up!"
Yeah. It's really hectic.
It's just so screwed up. And what people will do for money is so discouraging.
Yeah.
And the justification for what they do for money is even more discouraging. And then you have all these other

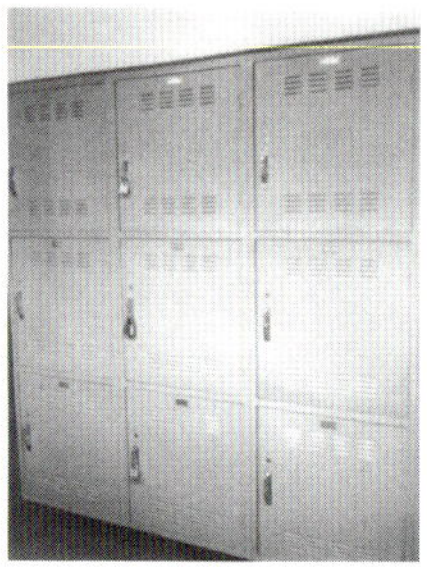

Five Day Locker Piece (1971)
University of California, Irvine, California
April 26-30, 1971

I was locked in locker number 5 for five consecutive days and did not leave the locker during this time. The locker measured two feet high, two feet wide and three feet deep. I stopped eating several days prior to entry. The locker directly above me contained five gallons of bottled water; the locker below me contained an empty five gallon bottle.

CB: Well unfortunately the school that I taught at was one of the leaders of that whole phenomenon. I remember having a conference with a student and I said, "Well I think this painting should be this or that or why don't you try this..." and the student says, "Well my art dealer says that these paintings are just fine and he wants me to paint more like that." So he and I are trying to have a critical dialog and it's like, "Well if you have an art gallery, maybe you shouldn't be here."

ANP: That's crazy!

CB: Well it's bad for the students even though it appears good because they never have time to percolate. You know, making mistakes and feeling unsure and trying to come to grips with yourself. Now you don't have any quiet time.

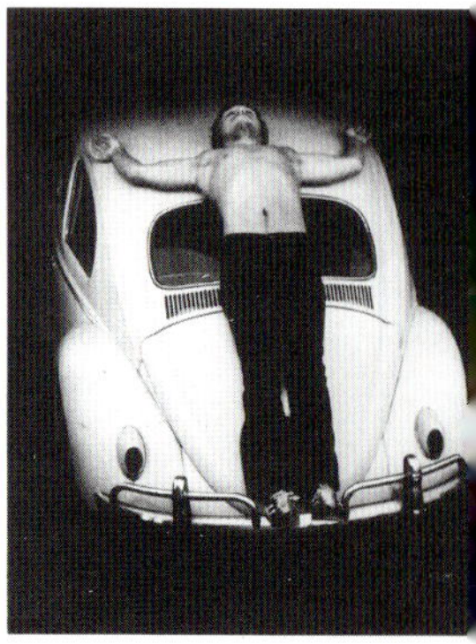

Trans-fixed
Venice, California: April 23, 1974

Inside a small garage on Speedway Avenue, I stood on the rear bumper of Volkswagon. I lay on my back over the rear section of the car, stretchi arms onto the roof of the car. The garage door was opened and the car w pushed half way out into the Speedway. Screaming for me, the engine was at full speed for two minutes. After two minutes, the engine was turned and the car pushed back into the garage. The door was closed.

did, it all sort of happened at once, right?
K: Yeah, it was a good timing. I met Nigo in 1997 and we had this relationship.

Kimpsons #1, 2004, acrylic on canvas, 8X9'
Kimpsons #2, 2004, acrylic on canvas, 80X80"
Kimpsons #3, 2004, acrylic on canvas, 80X80"
Kimpsons #4, 2004, acrylic on canvas, 40X40"
Kimpsons #5, 2004, acrylic on canvas, 40X40"

A Bathing Ape 2005 S/S catalog cover

KAWS designs for A Bathing Ape, 2005

(opposite)
Small KM-Landscape, 2001, acrylic on canvas, 48X48"

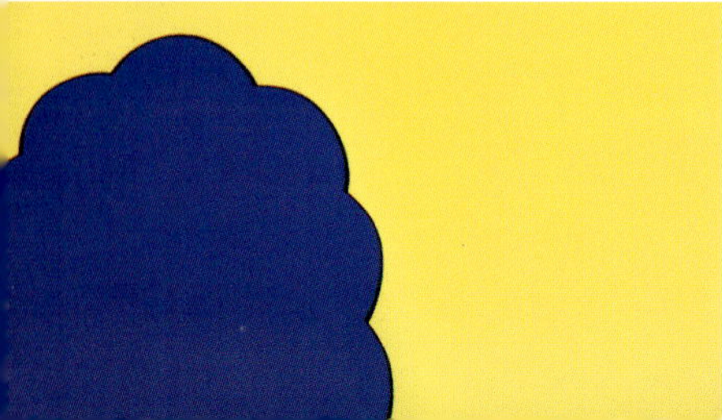

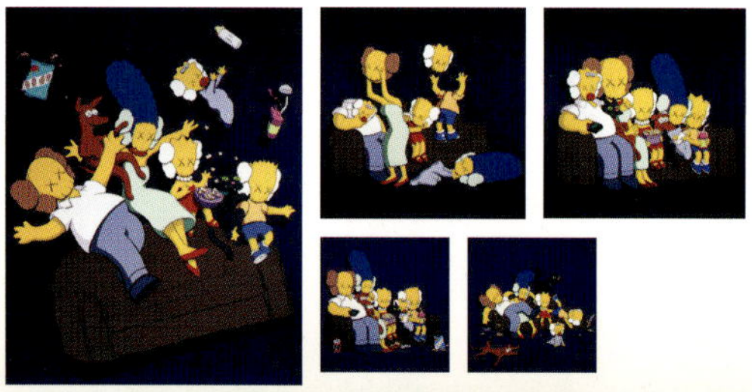

~~BLACK~~ DICE

BEEF PROFILE

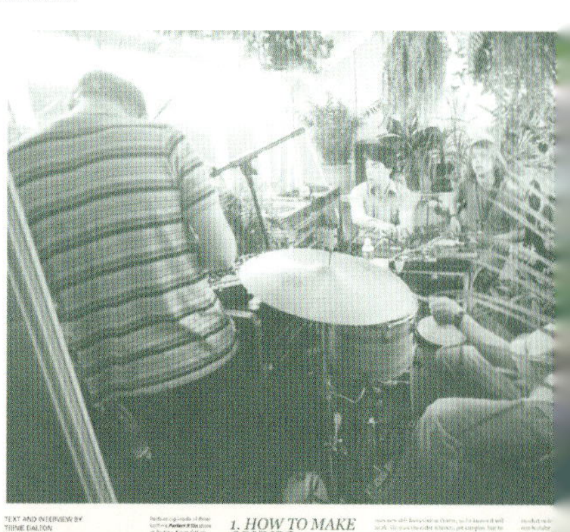

TEXT AND INTERVIEW BY
TRINIE DALTON
PHOTOS BY
JEFF WINTERBERG AND
JASON FRANK ROTHENBERG

1. HOW TO MAKE SOUNDS

Trinie: It's hard for me to wrap my mind around how your music is made.

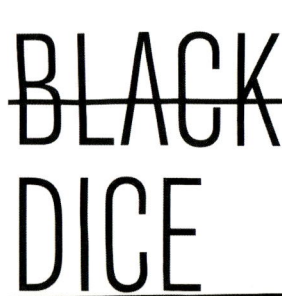

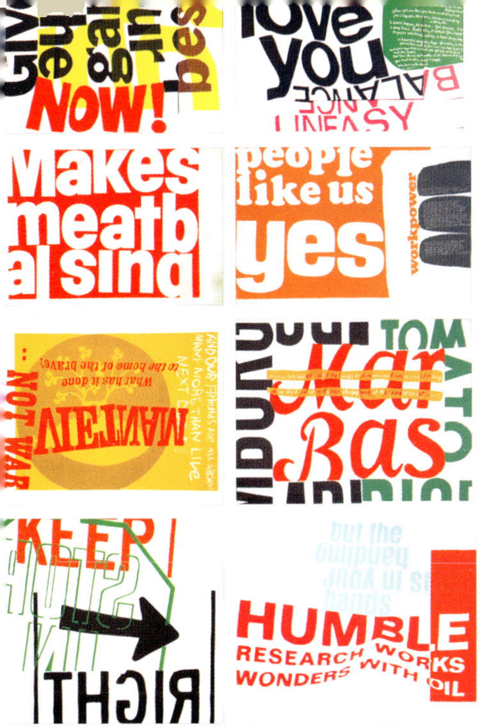

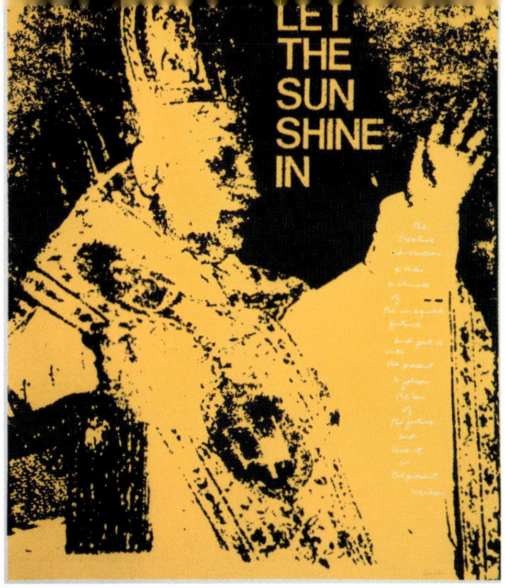

(Above)
Let the Sun Shine (1968)
Silkscreen on Paper
29 x 23 inches

(Opposite, clockwise from top left)
Give the Gang Our Best (1966)
Silkscreen on paper
30 x 36 inches

Feelin' Groovy (1967)
Silkscreen on paper
30 x 36 inches

People Like Us Yes (1966)
Silkscreen on paper
23 x 35 inches

Mary Does Laugh (1964)
Silkscreen on paper
29 ½ x 39 ½ inches

The Handling is in Your Hands (1966)
Silkscreen on paper
30 x 36 inches

Left (1967)
Silkscreen on paper
30 x 36 inches

Make Love Not War (1967)
Silkscreen on paper
30 x 36 inches

Song About The Greatness (1964)
Silkscreen on paper
29 ½ x 38 inches

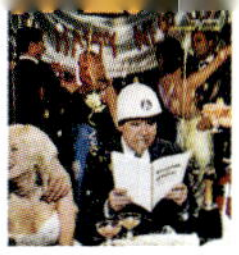

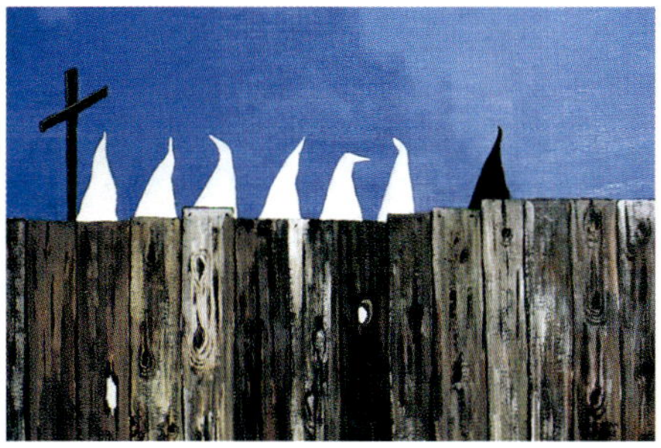

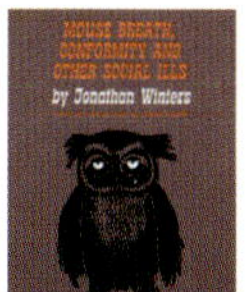

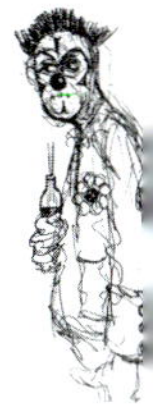

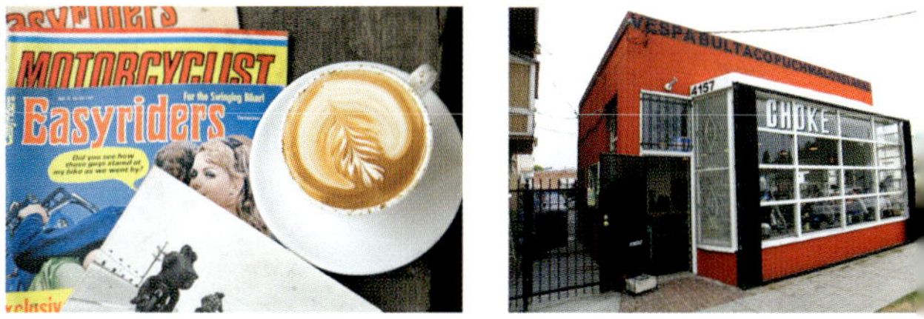

CHOKE

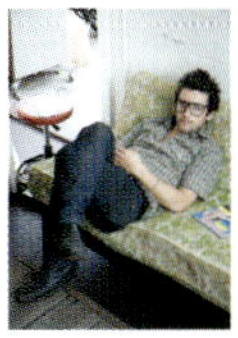

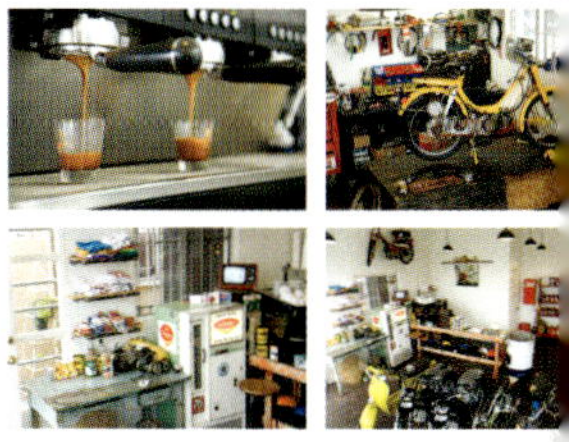

DAVID HORVITZ
XIU XIU POLAROID PROJECT 2

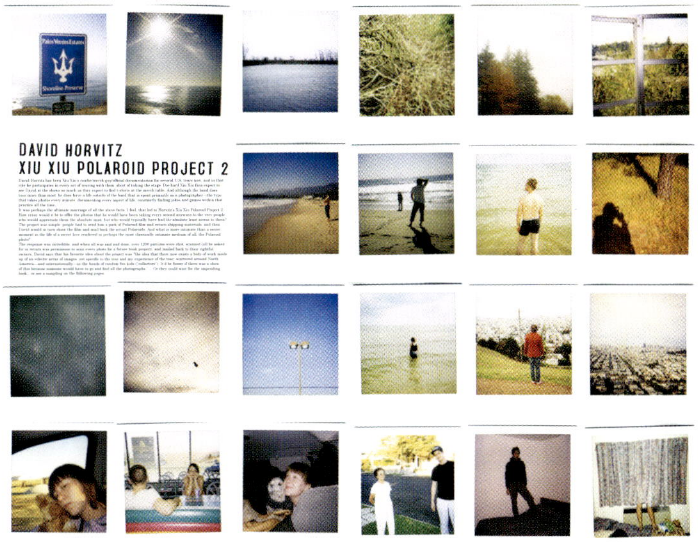

MONSTER CHILDREN GALLERY

Text by Wilfred Brandt / Photos courtesy of Monster Children Gallery

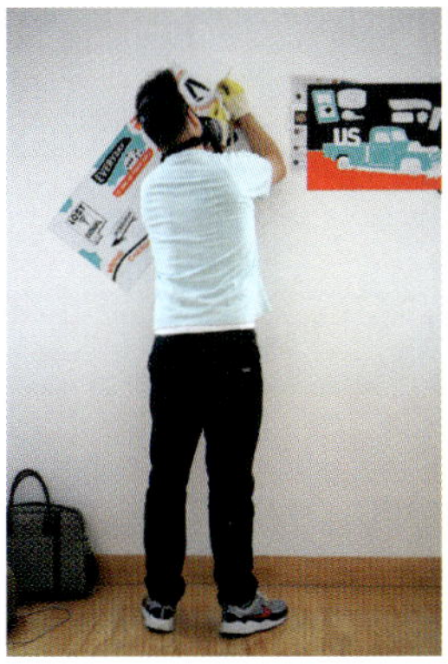

There's a corny old beer commercial that claims "Fosters" is "Australian for beer". The truth is its Australian for "crap". You'd be hard pressed to find Fosters in most Aussie bars. It's mainly brewed and bottled for exporting to the U.S., and it's a bland, watered-down version of Australian culture. Kinda like boomerangs, or Kylie Minogue.

For a real slice of home-baked Australiana, look no further than Monster Children magazine. It's sorta like Australian for "awesome". Sydneysiders Chris Searl and Campbell Milligan started this skate/surf/art and design mag five years ago with the goal of exposing Oz to an emerging international culture they were stoked on, and vice versa. And they've done well. Locals are hyped on the flippant Aussie attitude with which they cover the global scene, and their pages have brought worldwide exposure to homegrown heroes like The Presets, Josh Petherick, and Mike O'Meally.

But while Australian newsstands were eager to stock their uniquely formatted, beautifully designed publication, Aussie art dealers have been less-than-enthusiastic about hosting the unconventional artists the boys tried to pimp out.

"We'd have a gallery booked for a show, ready to go, and then a bunch of guys show up with tattoos carrying skateboards," Campbell recalls, "and all of a sudden we'd have to pay an additional deposit because they think we're going to trash the place."

So what to do? Rather than sit back and whinge about Australia's un-hip gallerists, Chris and Campbell threw their crisp, flat-brimmed caps into the ring. On May 26th 2005, Monster Children magazine give birth to a bouncing baby gallery. Chris and Campbell were proud pops at their first outing: Thomas Campbell and Alex Kopps.

"The show when we opened was amazing," Campbell beams. "Thomas and Alex painted non-stop for three days above the gallery while the thing was being built. There were big holes in the floor, walls not painted - it was a mess. And on the night, through some miracle it all came together. The doors opened, and the show was amazing, people were spilling out all over the road, and they sold pretty much everything."

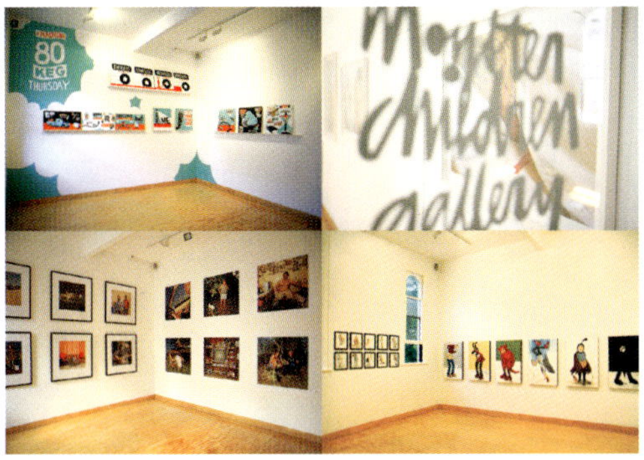

Those crowds spilling over into the streets have become a regular sight, as the gallery's opening night festivities often look more like a beachside barbee with bronzed Aussie blokes and Sheilas knocking back stubbies in thongs and singlets (that's Australian for "tan Australian dudes and chicks drinking beer in flip flops and tank tops").

"We love that our clientele are not always people who attend an art show," gallery manager Joseph Allen enthuses. "It is true that some see it as just a party. But if we can get them inadvertently looking at this great art while they down the Asahi, we still feel that we are achieving something. And when they return to have another look, we mark it down as a success. That being said, we do have T-shirts in production with the slogan 'It's an art gallery. Not a free bar'."

Joe's no stranger to the skate/art scene. A native Sydneysider, he worked as graphic designer for Kingpin Magazine in London, and was excited to take a job opening at the gallery when he moved back to Sydney a year ago. In that time he's seen the gallery go "from having no shows lined up to having almost a year of amazing shows by great local and international artists scheduled in". Past luminaries have included Neckface, Evan Hecox, and ESPO; future shows include Ed and Deanna Templeton, the Girl Art Dump, and DMOTE.

But getting artists down under ain't always easy. And as Campbell explains, it's not the 17-hour flight from the U.S. that's the big challenge...

"The main thing is money, getting artists here cost money. We have to hit up sponsors for the shows, and that can just be a right pain in the ass. Sometimes it's a breeze. But more often than not it's a nightmare making it all happen, and trying to fit in with schedules etc. And everyone from overseas wants to be here over summer. We could do 10 shows in three months, then winter comes and 'Nah, I'm good, how's November-December looking?"

It's not surprising international visitors would wanna visit Oz during the summer. Over 80% of Australians live on the coast, and for many of those, the beach is their way of life. Sydney has 37 beaches, most within a 30 minute bus ride of the city – an enticing alternative to three feet of snow at a December exhibit in Soho, for example.

"The rewarding thing is that when we do get these artists here, everyone is so psyched on it," Campbell says. "Usually it's the first time they have shown here solo, the artists have a great time in a new country, and people are always happy to see their favourite artists in the flesh, their work. And it gives them an opportunity to buy something that hasn't come from Ebay."

As far removed as Australia is from the western world, it's cool that our information age makes it possible for some kid to go from stencilling the bottom of his big brother's beat-up Variflex to a gallery wall just west of Woolloomooloo (pronounced "wool-uh-muh-loo" – I couldn't make this shit up). And while much of the globe is awash with chain stores and strip malls, it's great to see locals worldwide still do cool shit on their own terms. In the case of the MC gallery, the old phrase rings true: "necessity is the mother of invention". Or as the Australians might say, "she's a really Aussie battler, that one".

Fuck Fosters. When you come down to Oz, grab a Coopers, swing by the gallery and say g'day.

CREATIVE GROWTH

WORDS & PHOTOS BY CHERYL DUNN

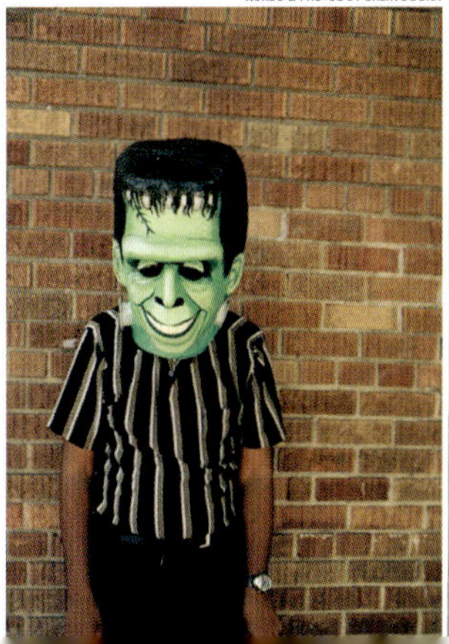

My mom's work is very fun. It is called Creative Growth and my favorite thing is the art! It's amazing! She works with people who have disabilities but they seem just like me. I have a dog named Fremont. He comes to work with us sometimes. But most importantly it's my favorite place! Sincerely, Lena O'Neal, 9 years old.

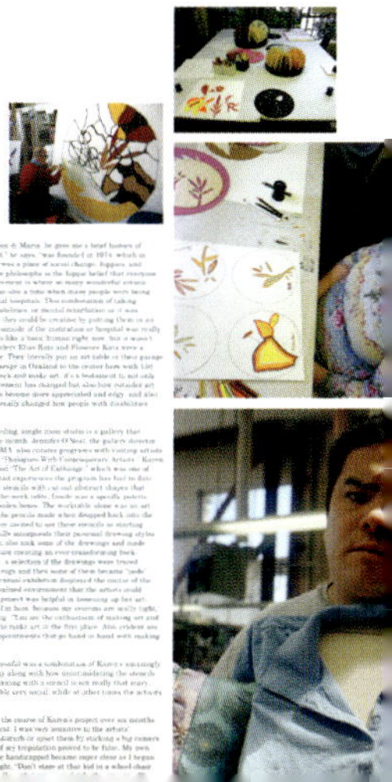

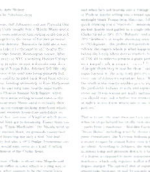

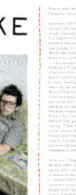

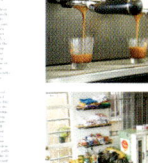

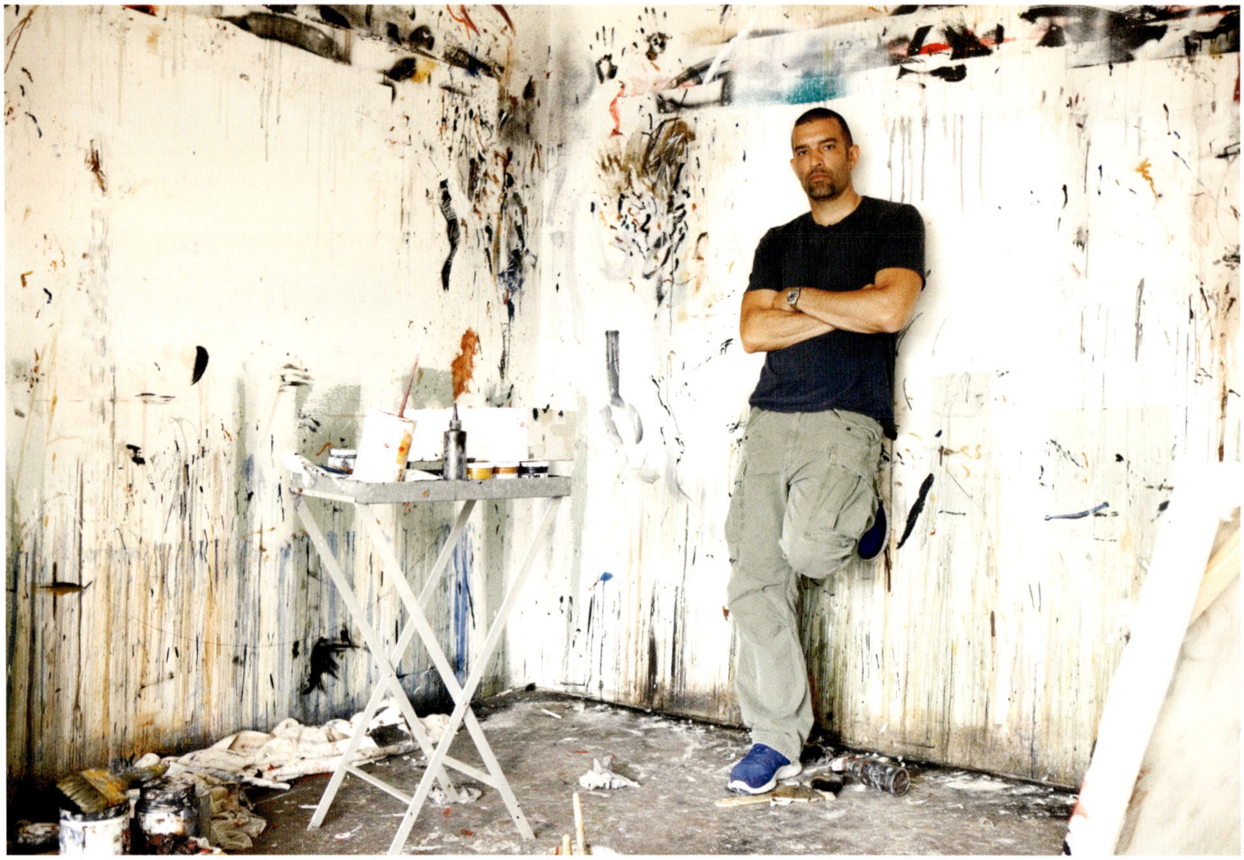

WEST ONE

Los Angeles, California
westonefc.com

Photo by Curtis Buchanan, 2012

Having been born and raised in New York City, there is an intensity, a grind, which becomes part of your daily rhythm. You are bombarded with sights and sounds, and people at all times, and there is no real sanctuary. The positive of that competitive environment is that is forces you to work, but the negative is that it's hard to hear the small voice inside that often guides your process.

In LA, I have lots of time in my own space, uninterrupted by anyone or anything. I hear that voice a lot more clearly here.

The main advantage for me working here is access to space. For years I was painting out of studios deep into Brooklyn or Queens, far from my apartment in Manhattan. In the winter I would have to trek to the studio in the cold, painting in boots, and sweaters, and hats. Here, my studio is next to my home, so I can simply walk into my studio at any time. For me, this is not so much a matter of convenience though. My paintings are layered and often develop over several weeks, and sometimes months. This allows me to act immediately; when I am in the process, sometimes I will jump in for ten minutes and add a few brush strokes to an existing painting and step away, and sometimes I will go in for ten to twelve hours at a time and come out, and just collapse in bed.

The main difference for me has been light and color. While in New York, my palette was predominantly dark. My paintings tended to be heavy, both aesthetically and emotionally. I am a bit color blind, so I struggle with color to begin with. Here, the natural light is constant, and the spaces are wide open. This has given me a certain freedom and looseness that has opened me up to a new relationship with color and lightness. One of my relatives told me when I got here that my paintings would change because of the environment, and they actually have. I've learned here that a painting can still be deep and layered, but also feel free and light.

"Freedom Suite (detail)" 2011
Acrylic paint and China marker
48 x 72 inches

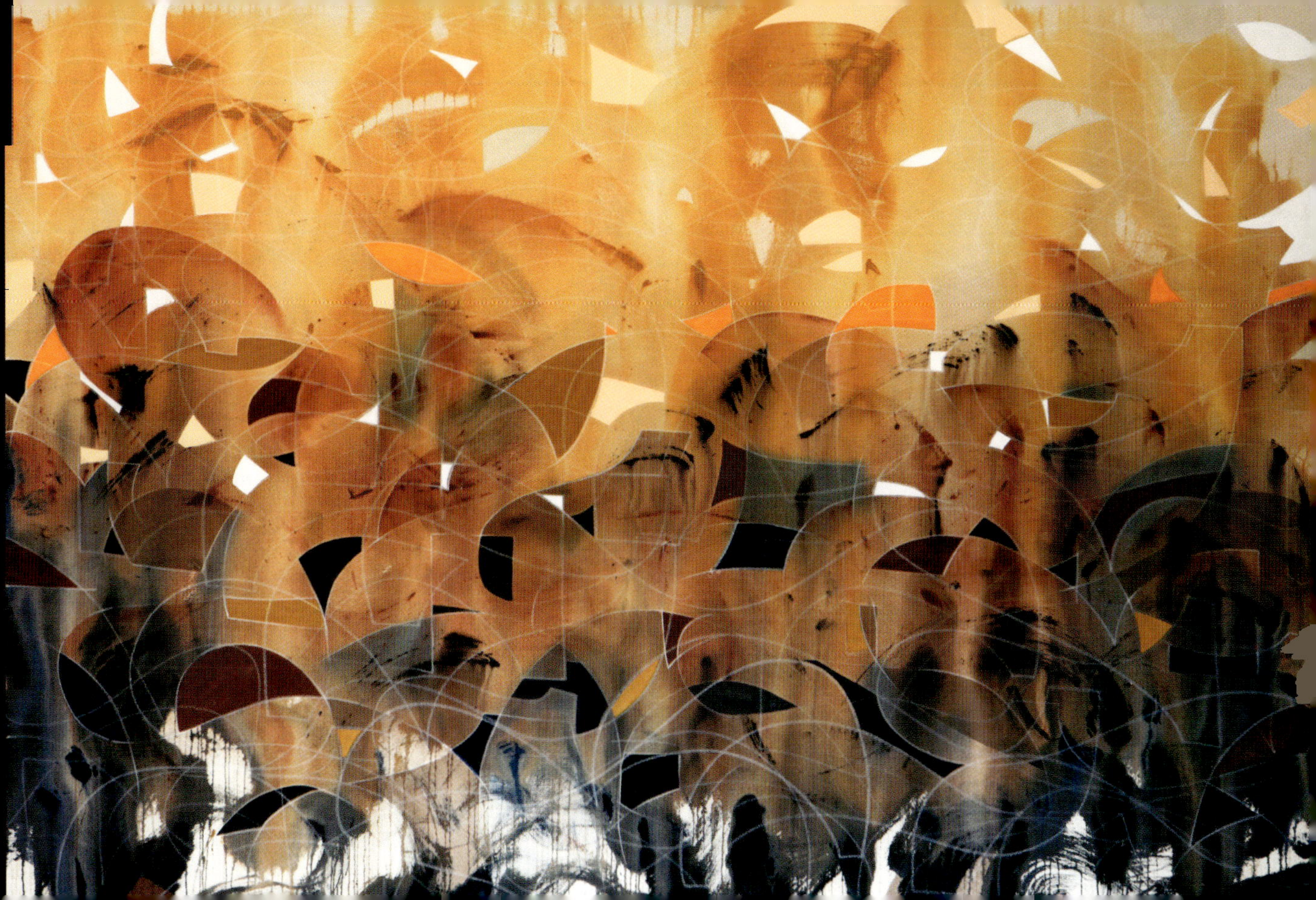

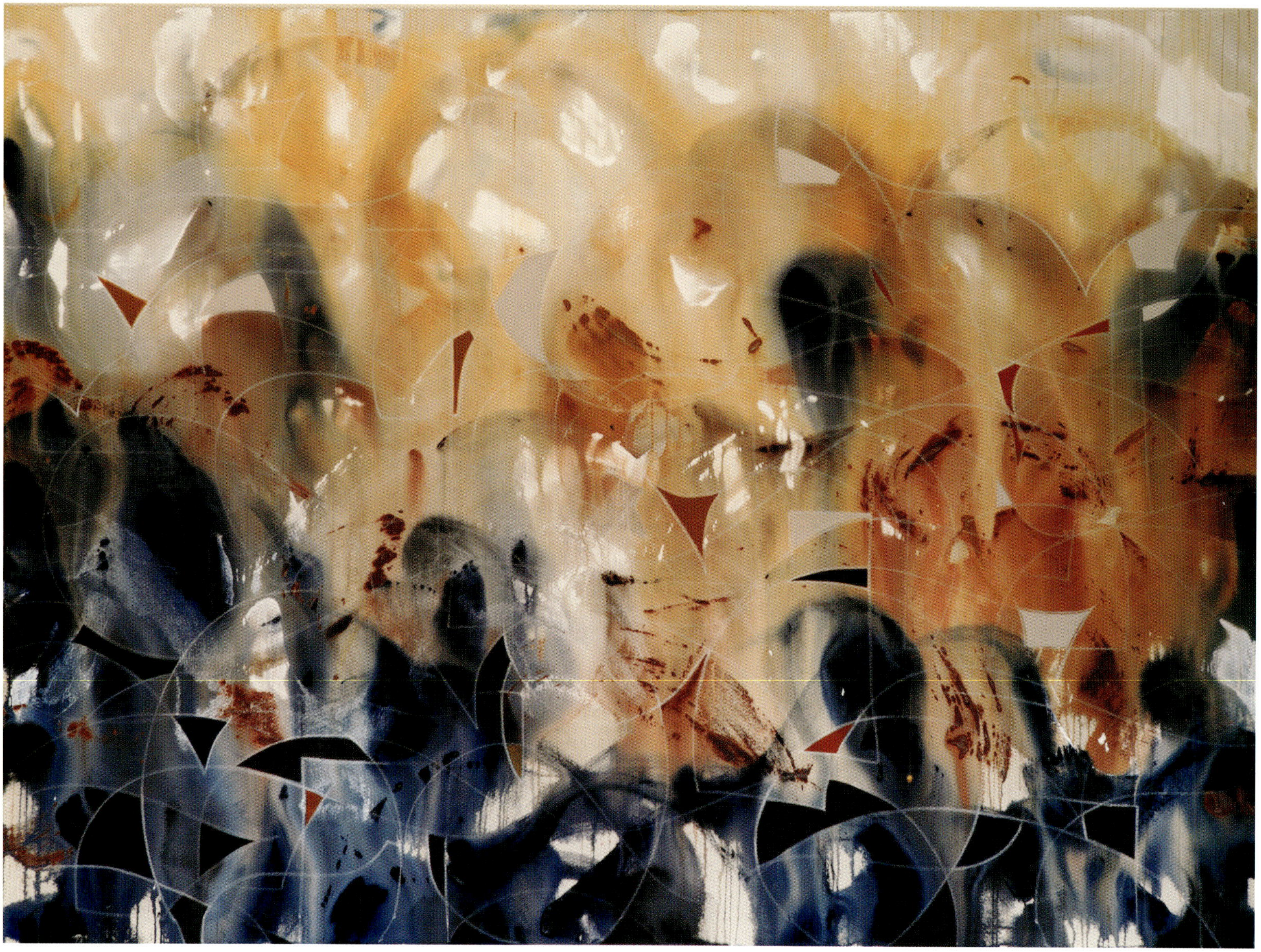

"Wood" 2011
Acrylic paint, gesso, and
China marker
42 x 58 inches

Opposite Top:
"The Immortal (KASE 2)" 2011
Acrylic paint, spray paint, gesso, and
China marker
48 x 72 inches

Opposite Bottom:
"Light" 2011
Acrylic paint, gesso, and China marker
42 x 58 inches

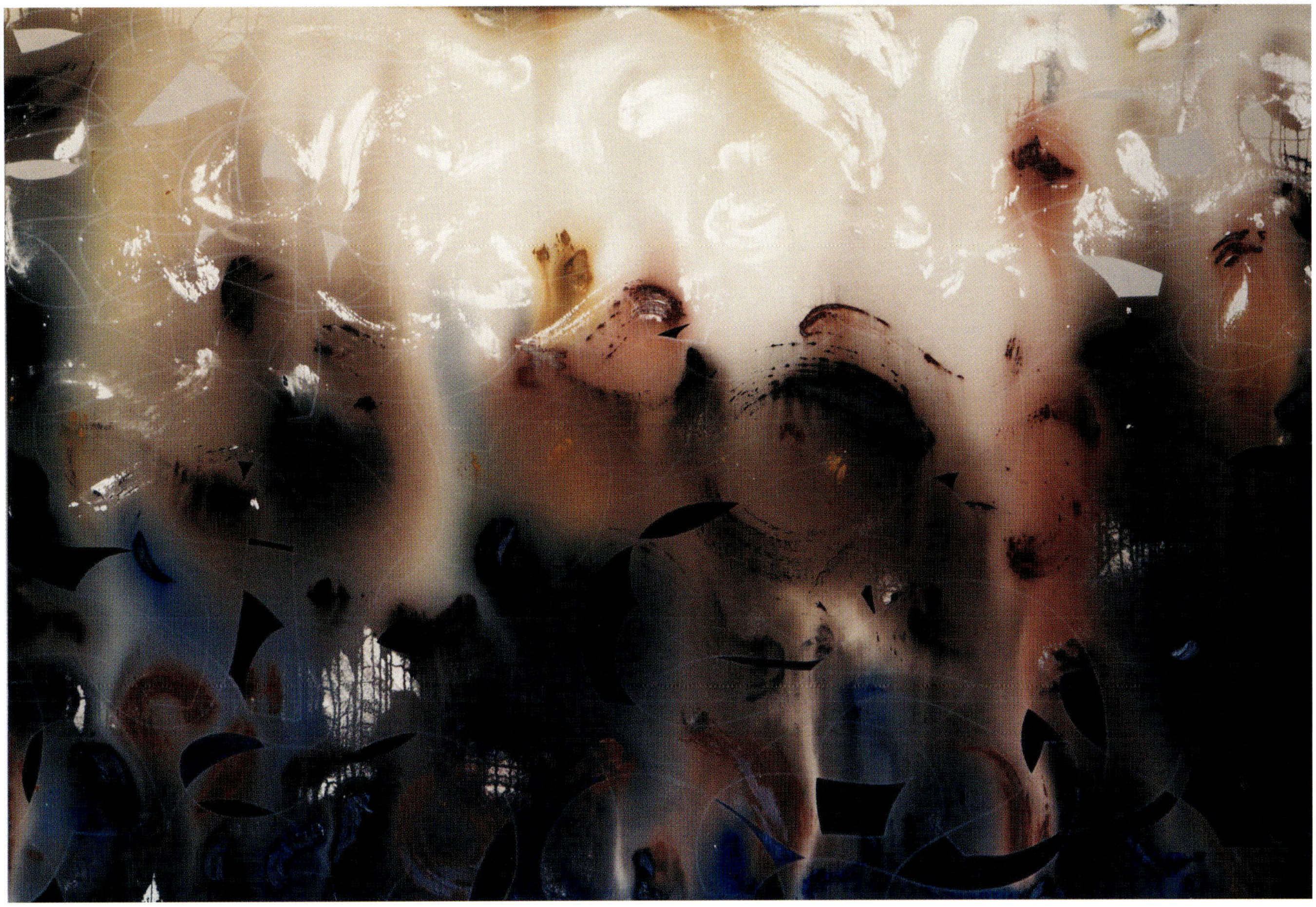
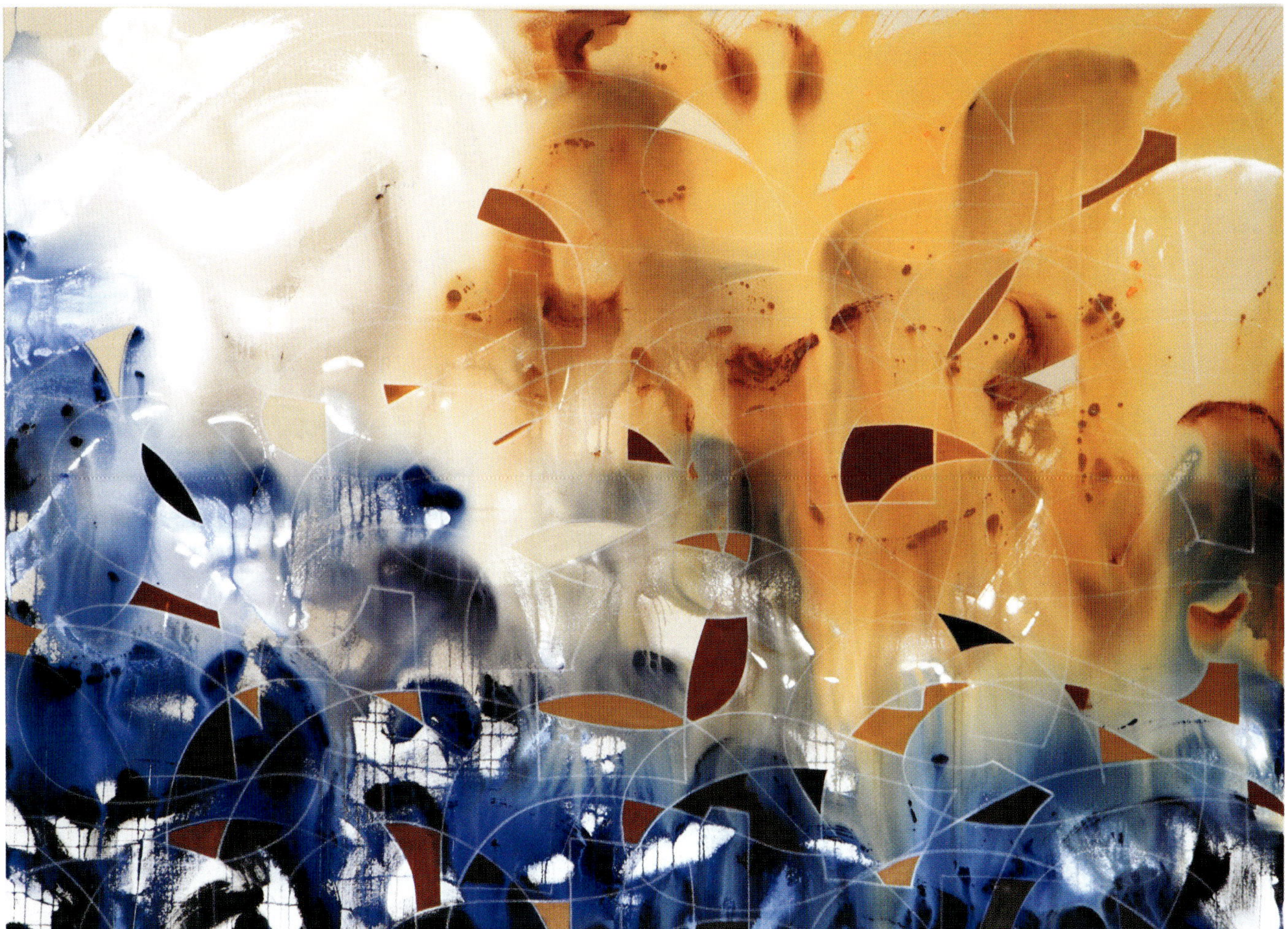

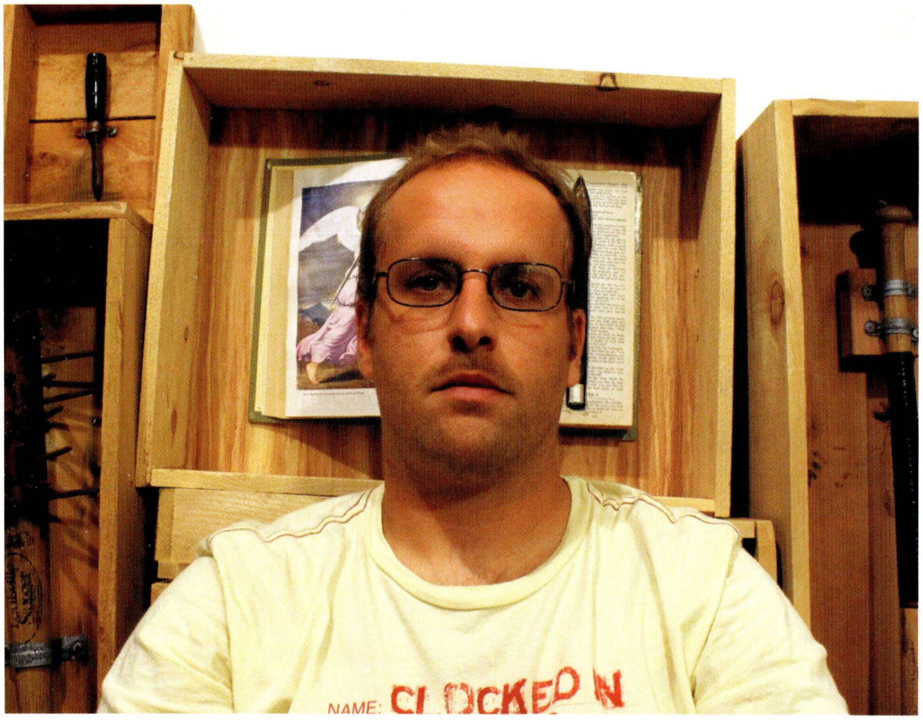

Self Portrait, 2012

BILL MCRIGHT

San Pedro, California
billmcright.tumblr.com

I initially came to California for two reasons: First, I had been excited about the culture and events I saw happening from a distance, and secondly, for work. More specifically, I got a job that would pay me more than I had been able to make anywhere else. The things that keep me here: work, the culture, and the weather. It seems like the perfect package to me.

The advantages for me about being in California are as follows: I get to see so much awesome stuff that keeps me inspired, the network of friends that I have here that are all doing amazing things, the ability to experience different climate within a few hours, the weather is almost always amazing (at least in Los Angeles), and the quality of life is pretty much top notch. On the downside, in LA everything is spread out, and it takes a lot of time to get used to. Having to drive a fair amount of the time can be a drag, but long commutes and a little confusion are a small price to pay for having a pretty rad life otherwise.

I'm still getting used to [living here] and feel like I'm just starting to hit my stride as a Californian. I would say there are a lot of things I have noticed about being out here that have started to inform my work: working with other artists, the constant sun, the huge differences between neighborhoods, gang graffiti, seeing low riders and classic cars every day, motorcycle culture, the varieties of plants and animals. I swear I see something new every day, it all has started to blur together, but it keeps me constantly stimulated.

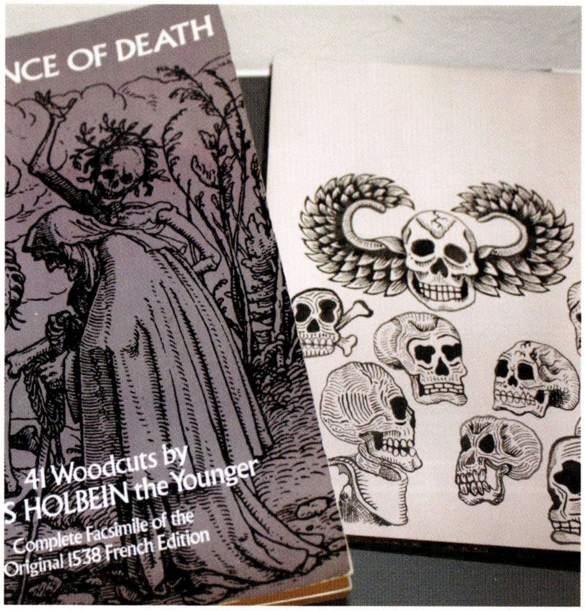

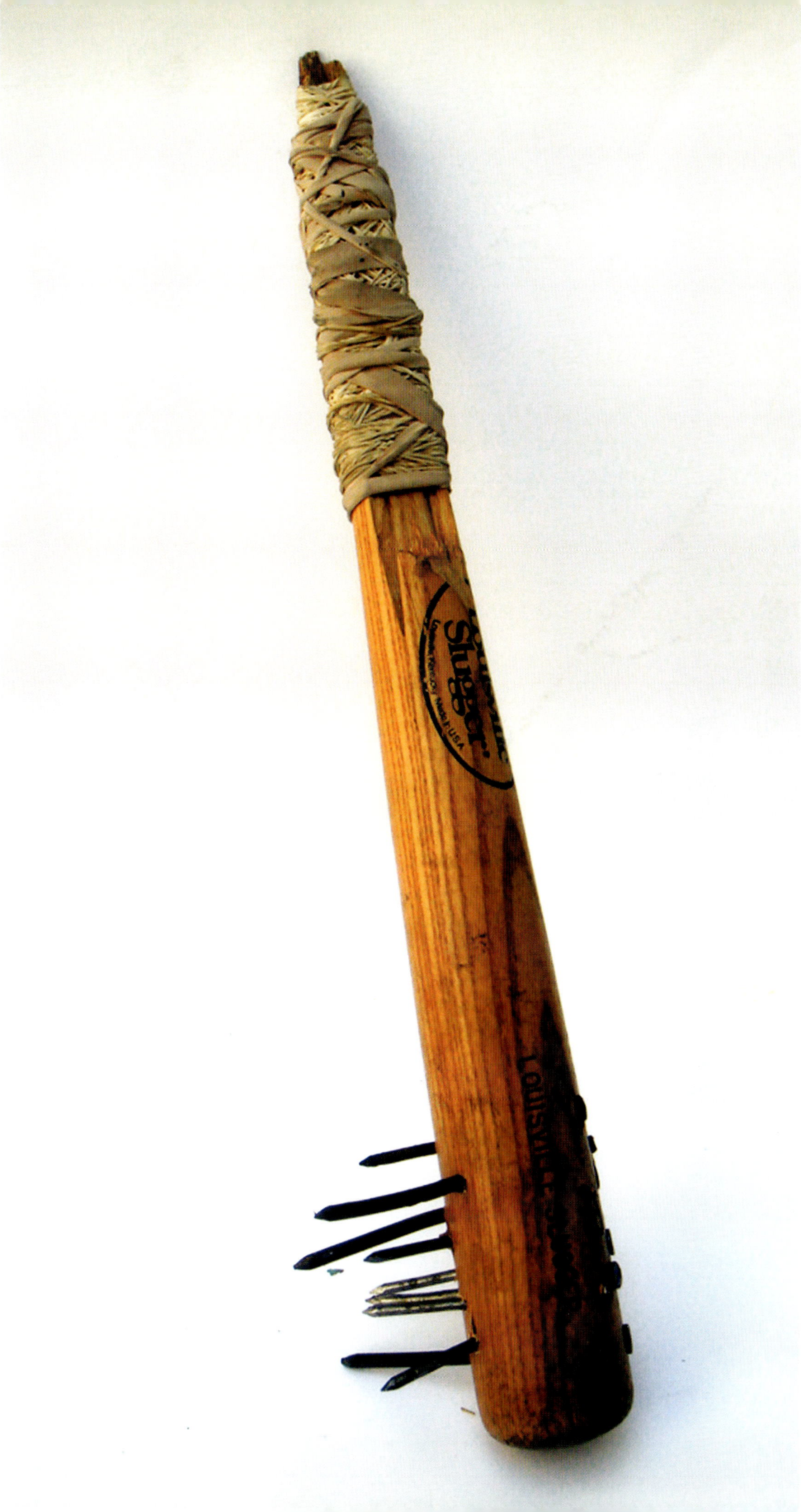

"Untitled (Bat)" 2011
Found object and reassembled
mixed media

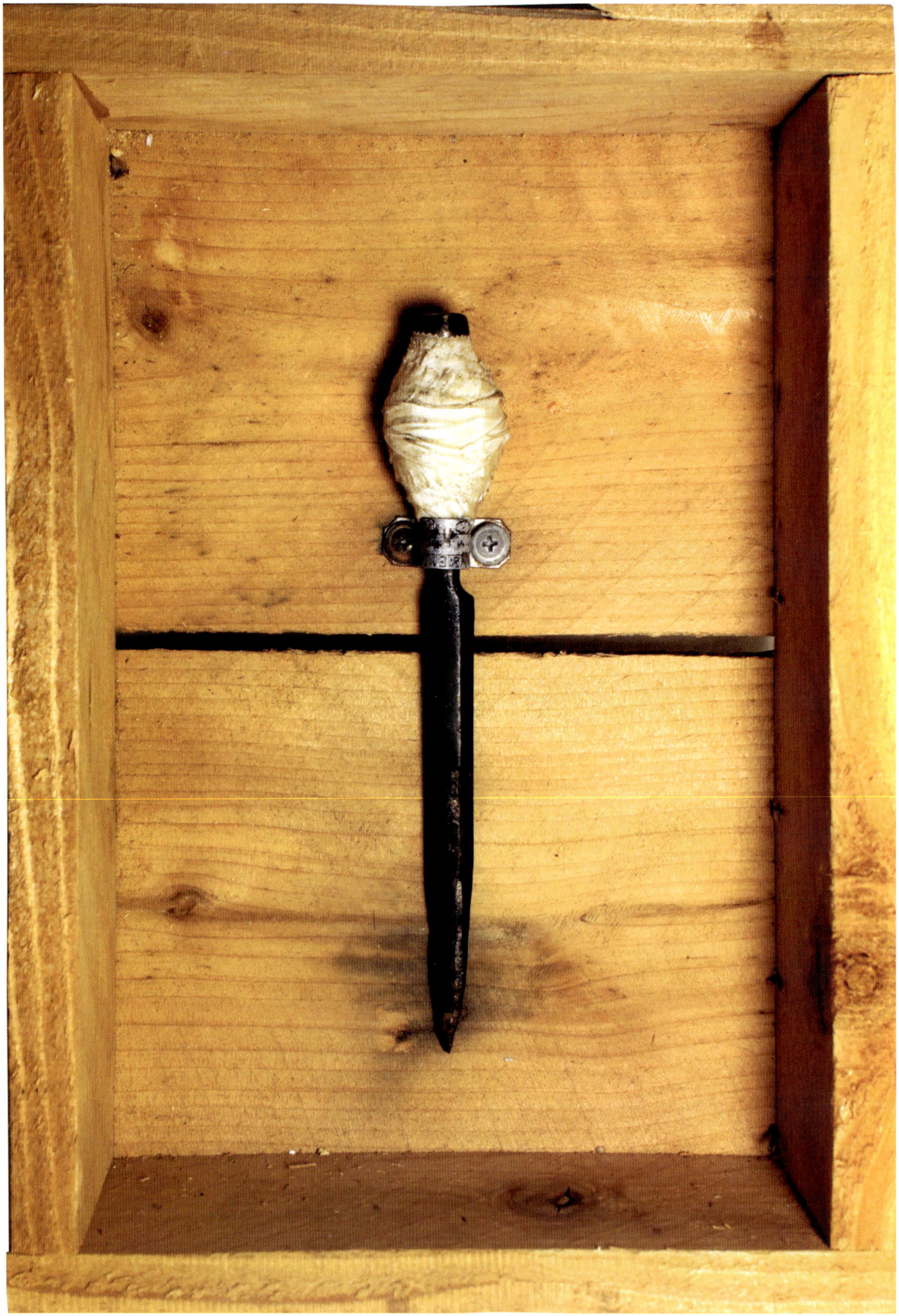

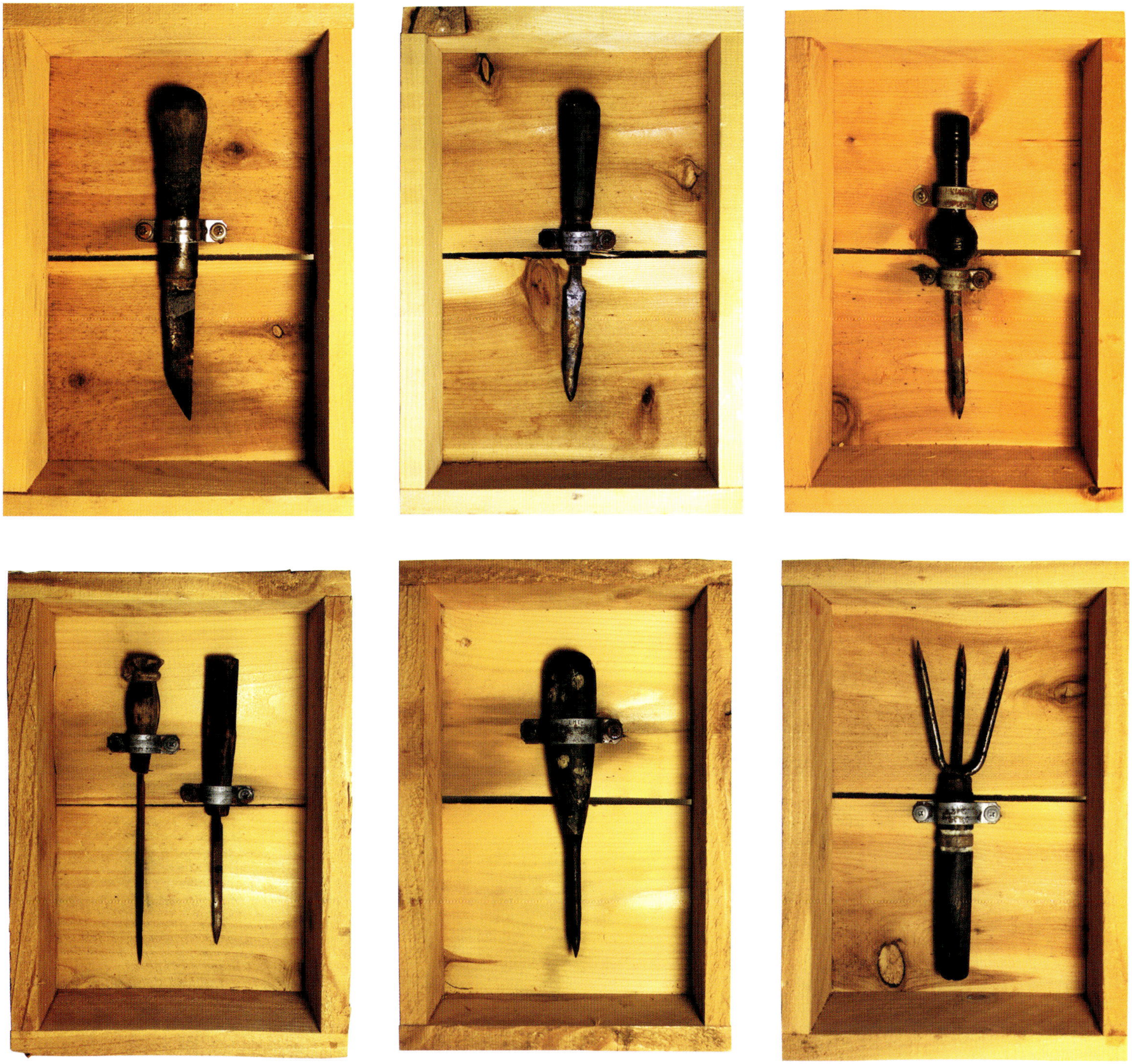

"Untitled (Shanks)" 2011
Found object and reassembled
mixed media

JOEL MORRISON

Los Angeles, California
Gagosian Gallery

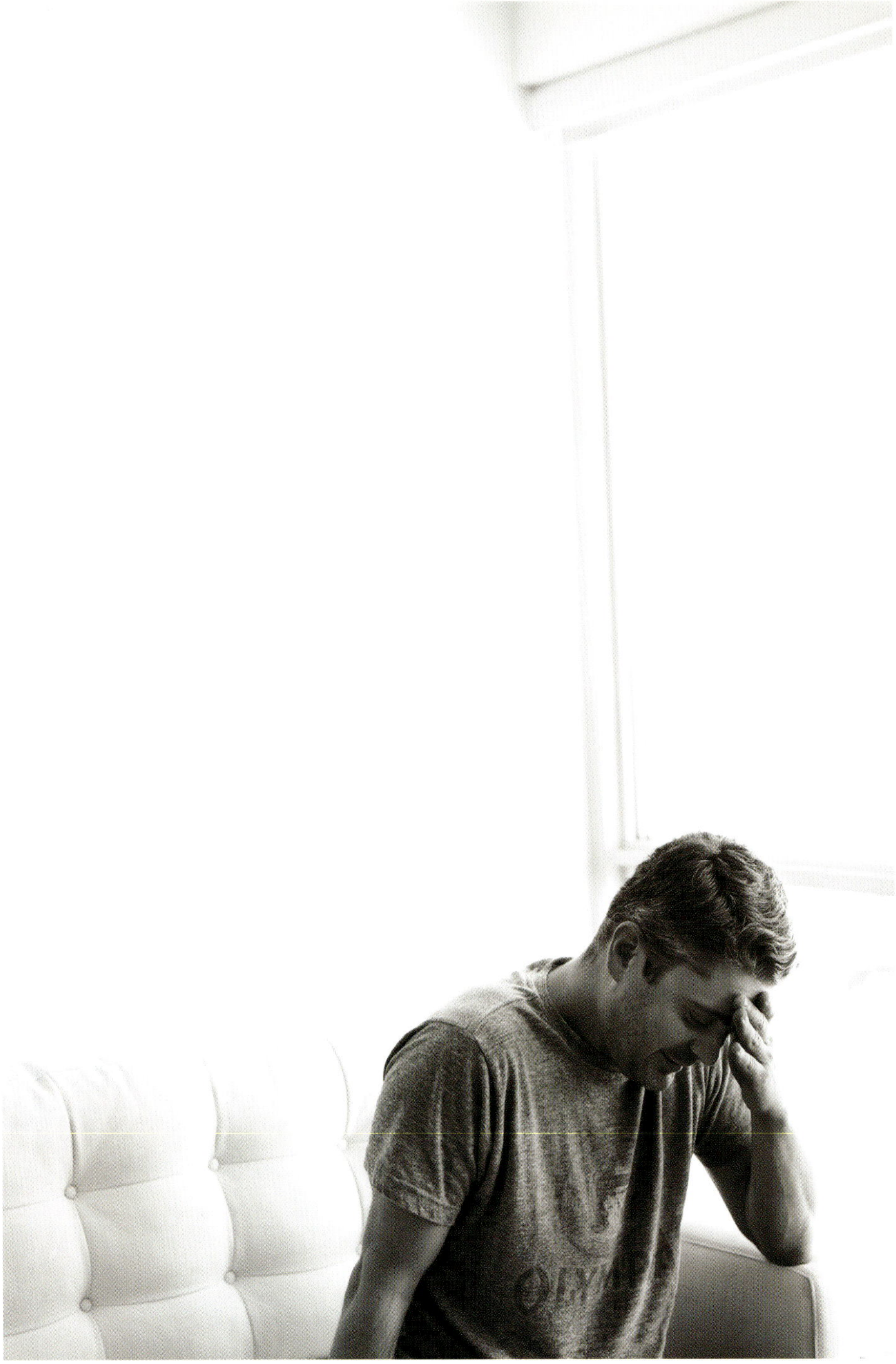

Photo by Dan Monick, 2012

The MFA mecca brought me to California and I'm acclimatized now.

The access to space and unlimited resources is an advantage. The disadvantage is sorting it all out and not losing your core. You eventually find what you are looking for. Through this hunt for a source you discover everything else.

The absence of moderation becomes a looming influence. As an art maker you can't be a stationary thinker in an isolation chamber. The necessity of mobility forces firsthand contact with a concentration of diverse craftsmen, industry, and culture. This directly influences the evolution of your ideas and process while keeping your style and skills in check.

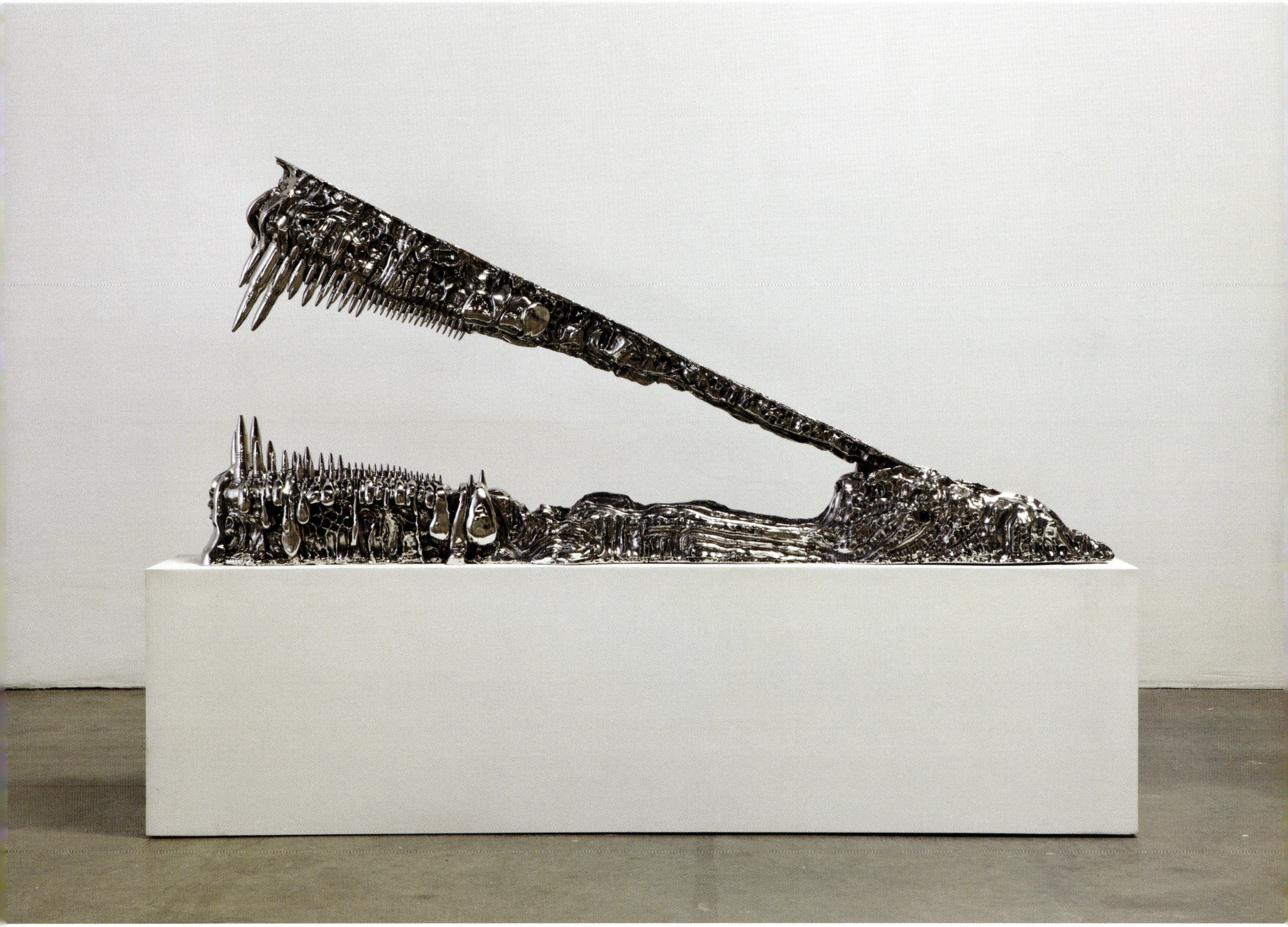

This page:
"Vic" 2011
Stainless steel
34 x 71 x 11½ inches
Edition of 2 + 1 AP

Following page:
"Tortilla Maker" 2012
Stainless steel
14 x 19 x 16 inches
Edition of 3

Following page:
"The Reaganomic Youth" 2011
Stainless steel
22 x 17 x 22 inches
Edition of 3 + 1 AP

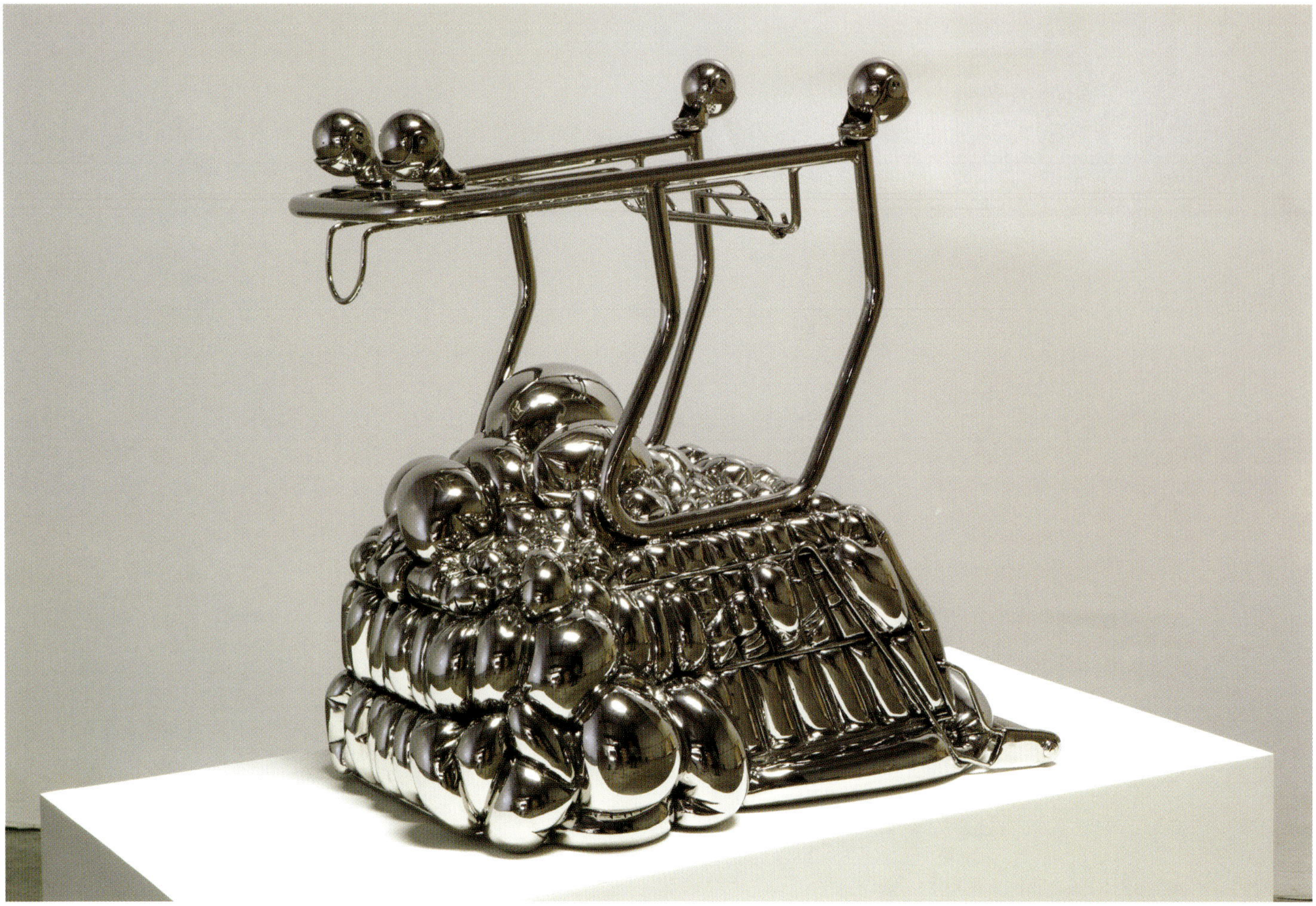

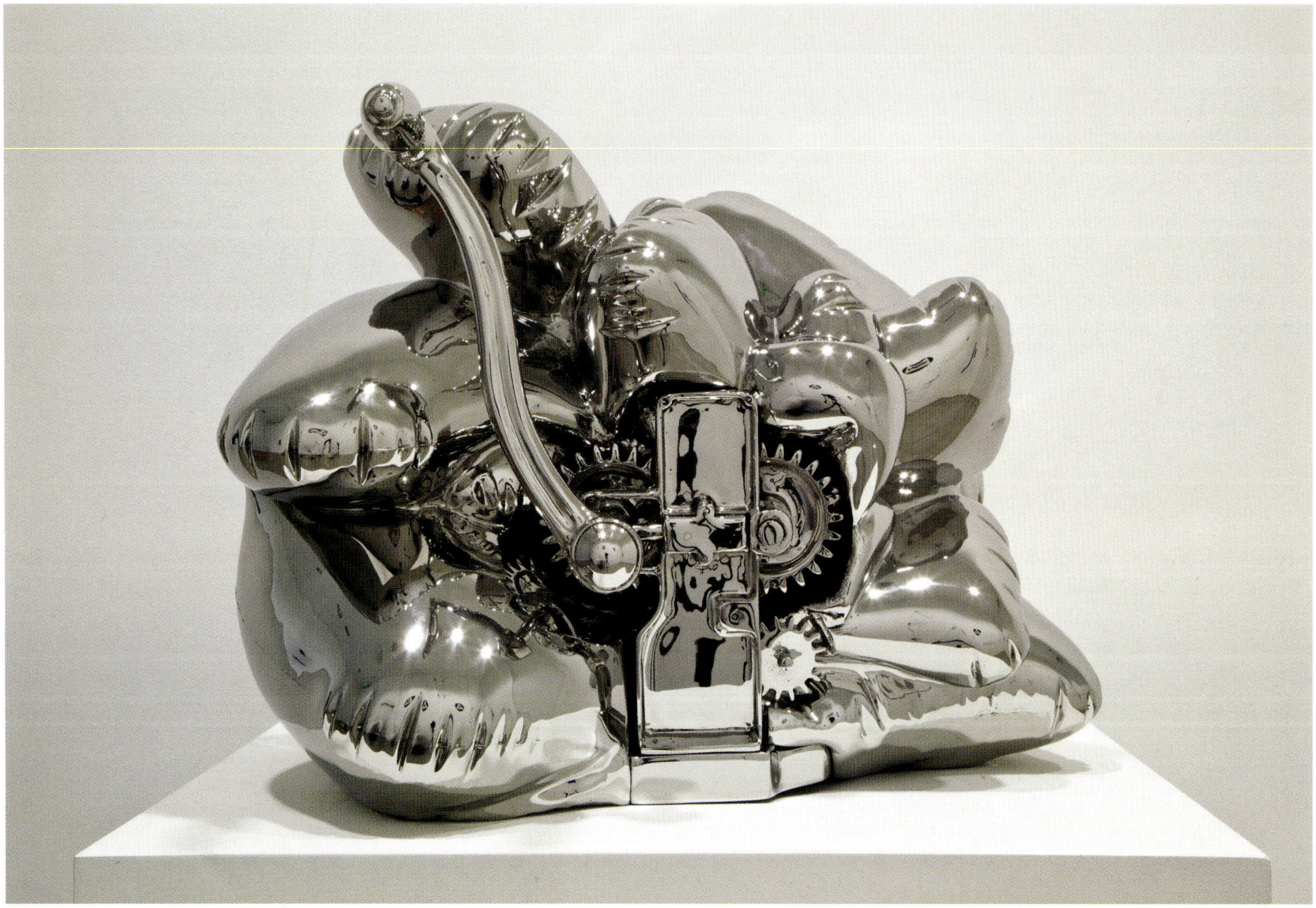

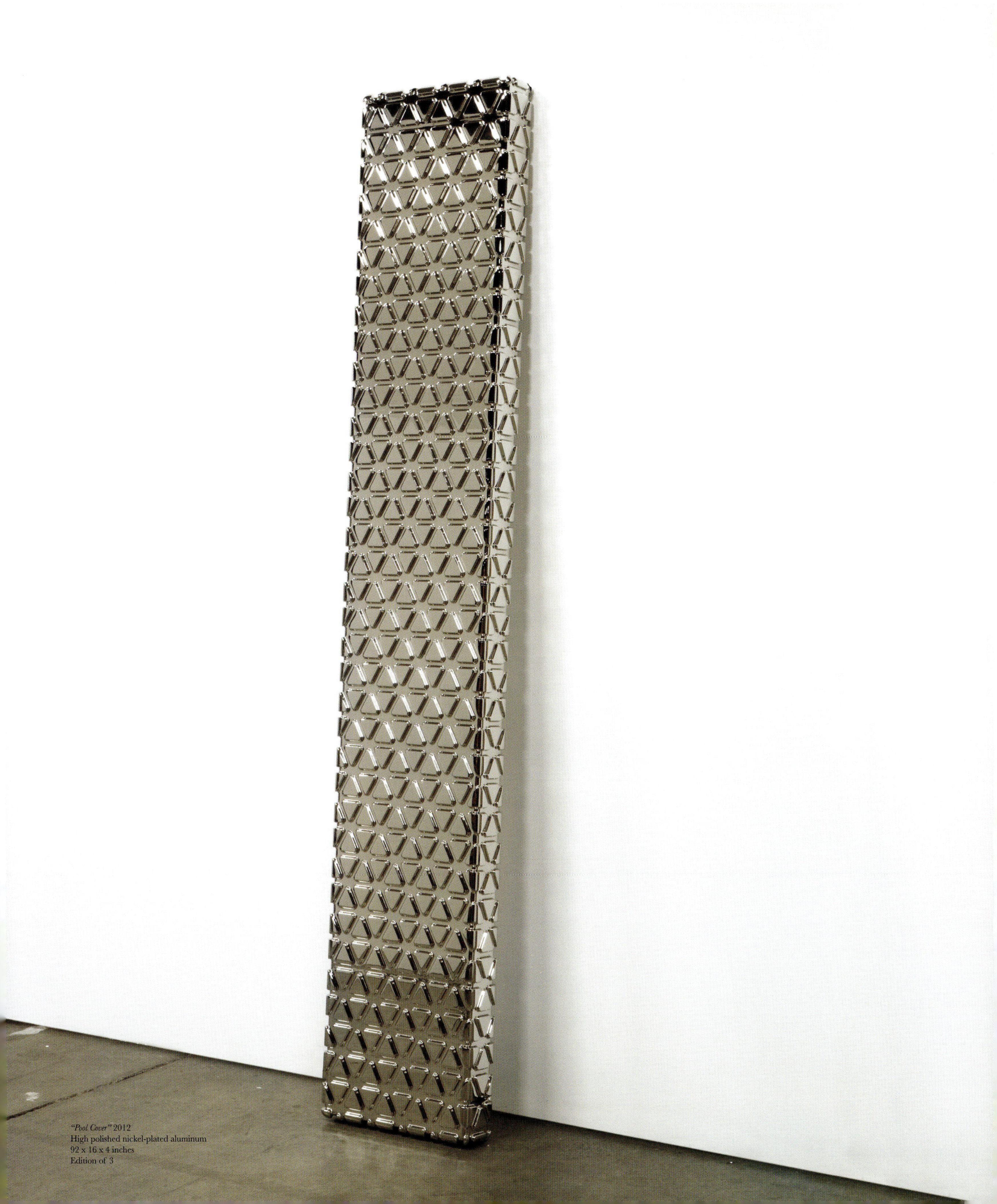

"Pool Cover" 2012
High polished nickel-plated aluminum
92 x 16 x 4 inches
Edition of 3

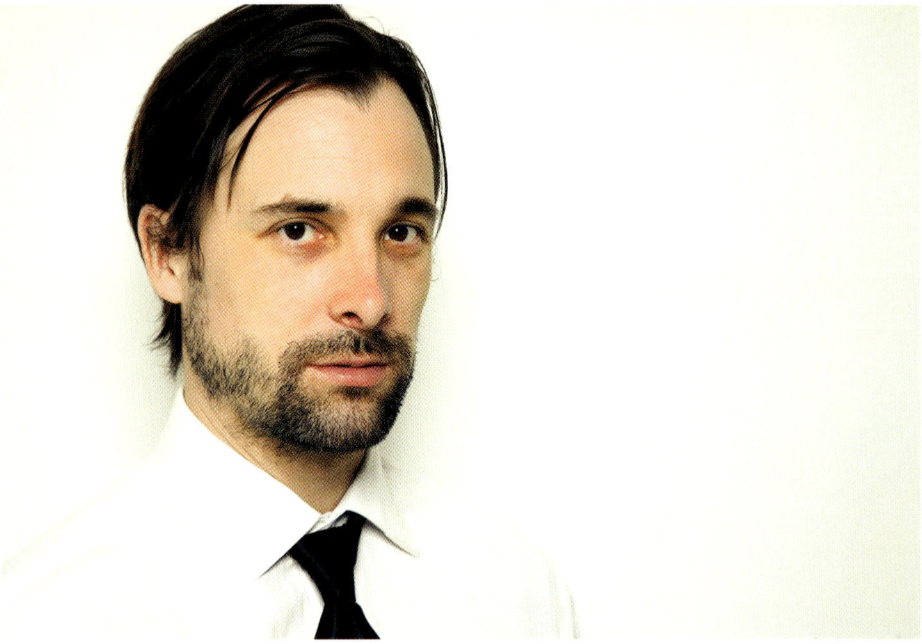

Photo by Aaron Farley, 2010

CLEON PETERSON

Los Angeles, California
cleonpeterson.com

New Image Art, Los Angeles
Cooper Cole Gallery, Canada
Guerrero Gallery, San Francisco
Alice Gallery, Brussels
Joshua Liner Gallery, New York
Ivory And Black, London
Prism, Los Angeles
THIS los angeles

The first time I ever drove down to California I was sixteen. I left from Seattle the first day I got my license. I remember seeing my first palm tree on the way down and thinking that I'd arrived in the promised land. I think that some people are made for the West Coast and that we have a completely different perspective on the world. Space is larger in the west, and to do what I want to do I need space, whether it be a living space or the outdoors.

I think that the California landscape is fertile because it encompasses so much variation. There's sun, rain, more sun, mountains, valleys, ocean, desert, and forests. There is also every imaginable culture and economic strata living around such diversity that gives us experiences we can draw from on a daily basis.

Making things is all I've ever known. Once, I tried getting a regular job. I walked around for days submitting applications and never got a response. Maybe not being hired is an act of providence for my type.

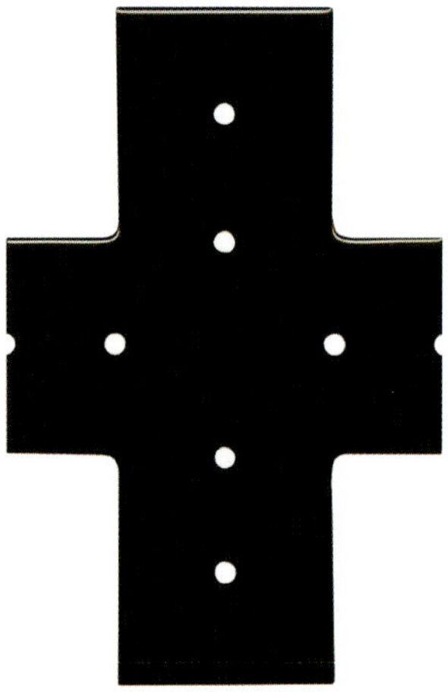

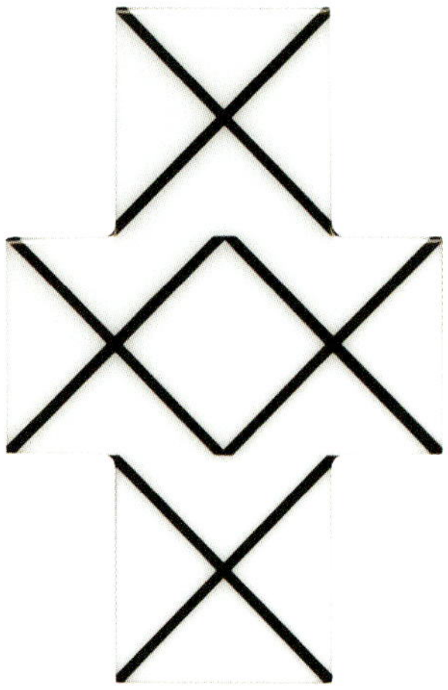

"Disambigulation 6" 2011
Acrylic, resin on wood
9 x 13 inches

"Disambigulation 5" 2011
Acrylic, resin on wood
9 x 13 inches

Opposite page:
"Struggle of Will (Power)" 2011
Acrylic on wood
66 x 88 inches

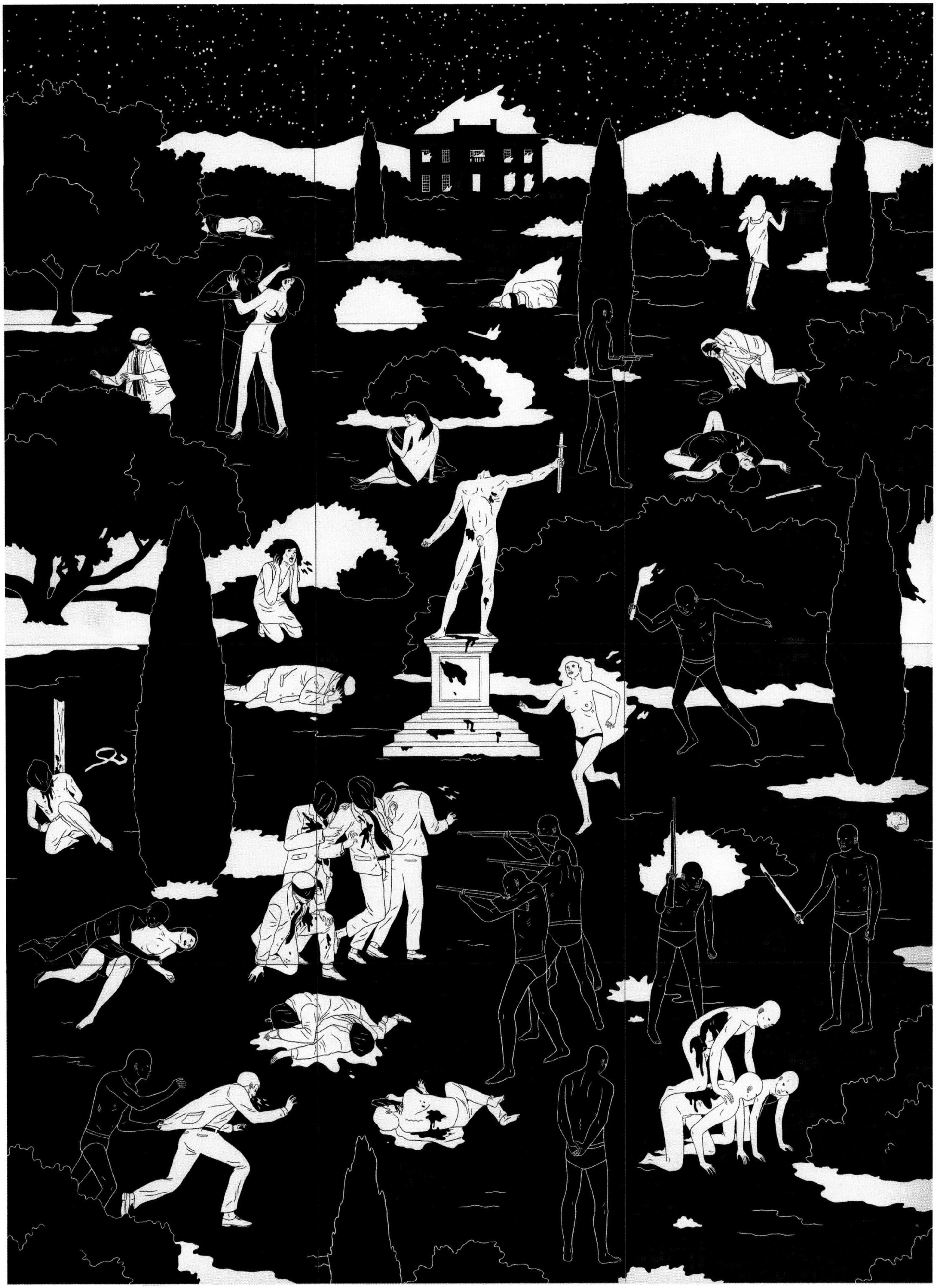

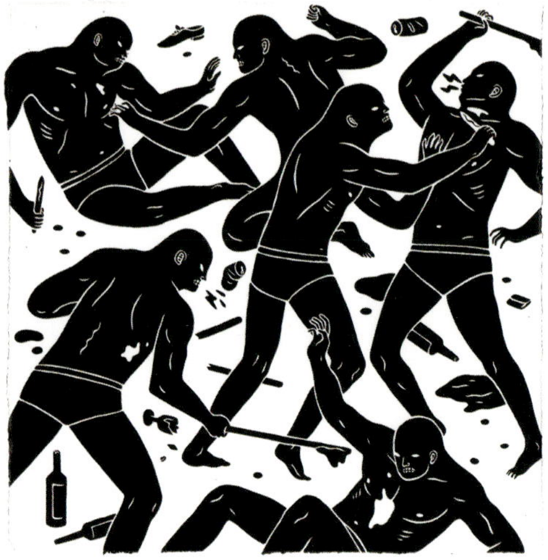

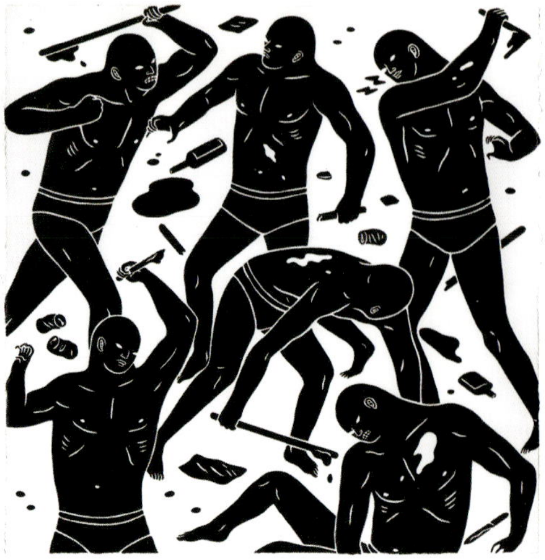

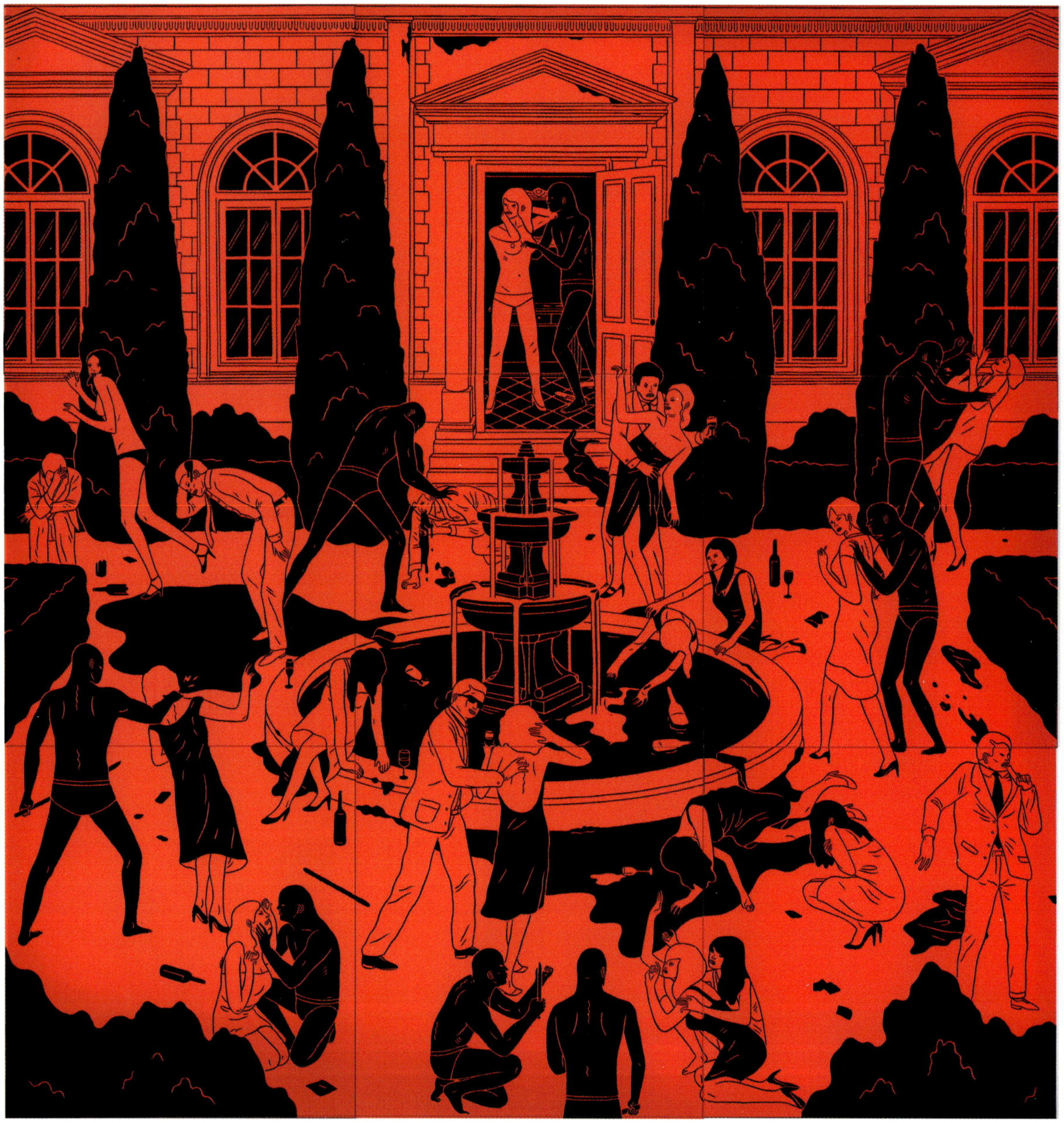

Top of Page:
"The Practice of Masters 4" 2011
Acrylic and gouache on paper
16 x 16 inches

"The Practice of Masters 6" 2011
Acrylic and gouache on paper
16 x 16 inches

Bottom:
"A Struggle of Will" 2011
Acrylic on wood
37½ x 39 inches

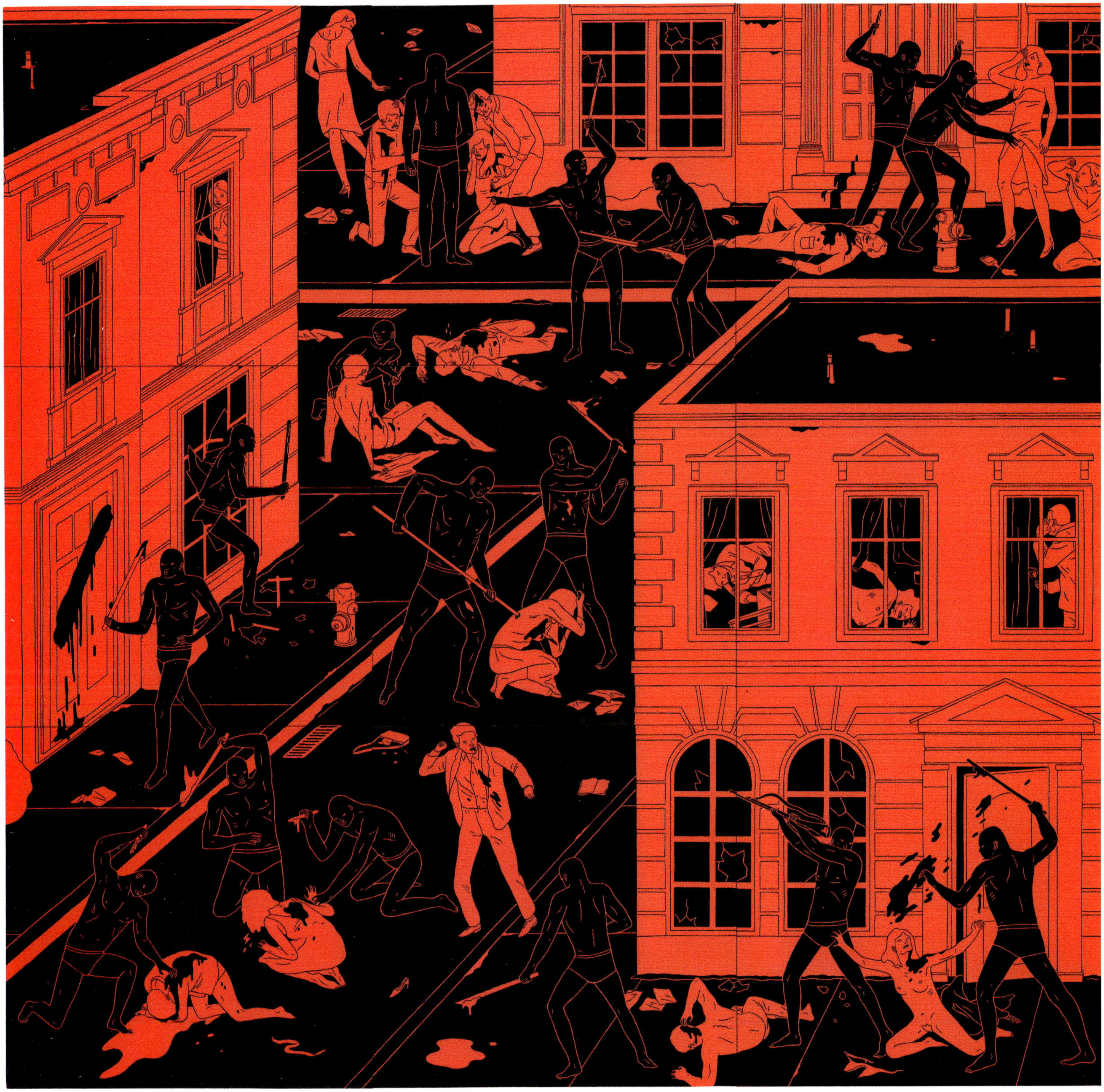

"Pink City 1" 2011
Acrylic, resin on wood
75 x 72 inches

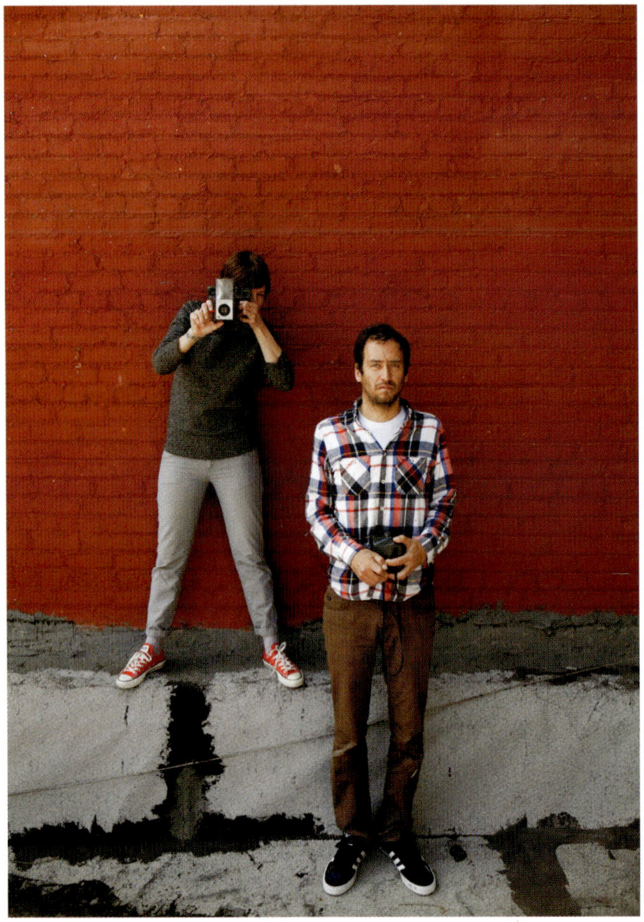

Photo by Aaron Farley, 2012

DAY19

Los Angeles, California
day19.com
giantartists.com
THIS los angeles

I originally moved to California in the mid '90s to snowboard all winter in Lake Tahoe. Once the snow melted, I accidentally moved to Orange County, which only lasted a couple months. After moving back to the East Coast for school, my wife Claire and I made our way west again, only this time together. We both honestly thought we would only live in LA a couple years and eventually move back east, but we slowly fell more and more in love with the place, and here we still are some twelve years later. California is one of the most magical places I've seen; you can head in any direction out of the city and be in totally different worlds.

I can only think of advantages of living and working here. A lot of our first photo work came mostly because we were in the right place at the right time, and this was the right place.

The sun, fun, mountains, ocean, woods, and concrete all influence our work and process.

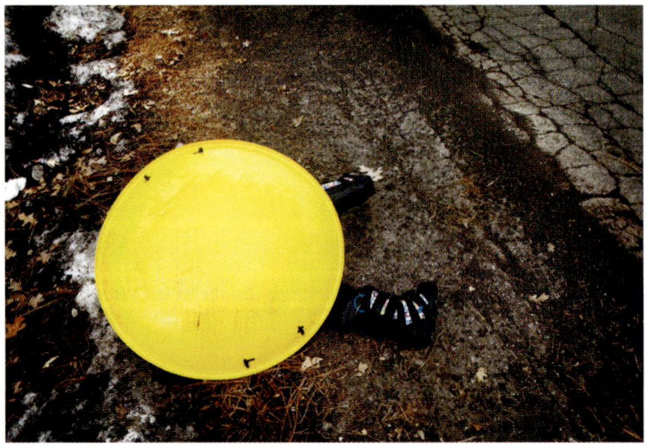

All images
"Untitled" 2011

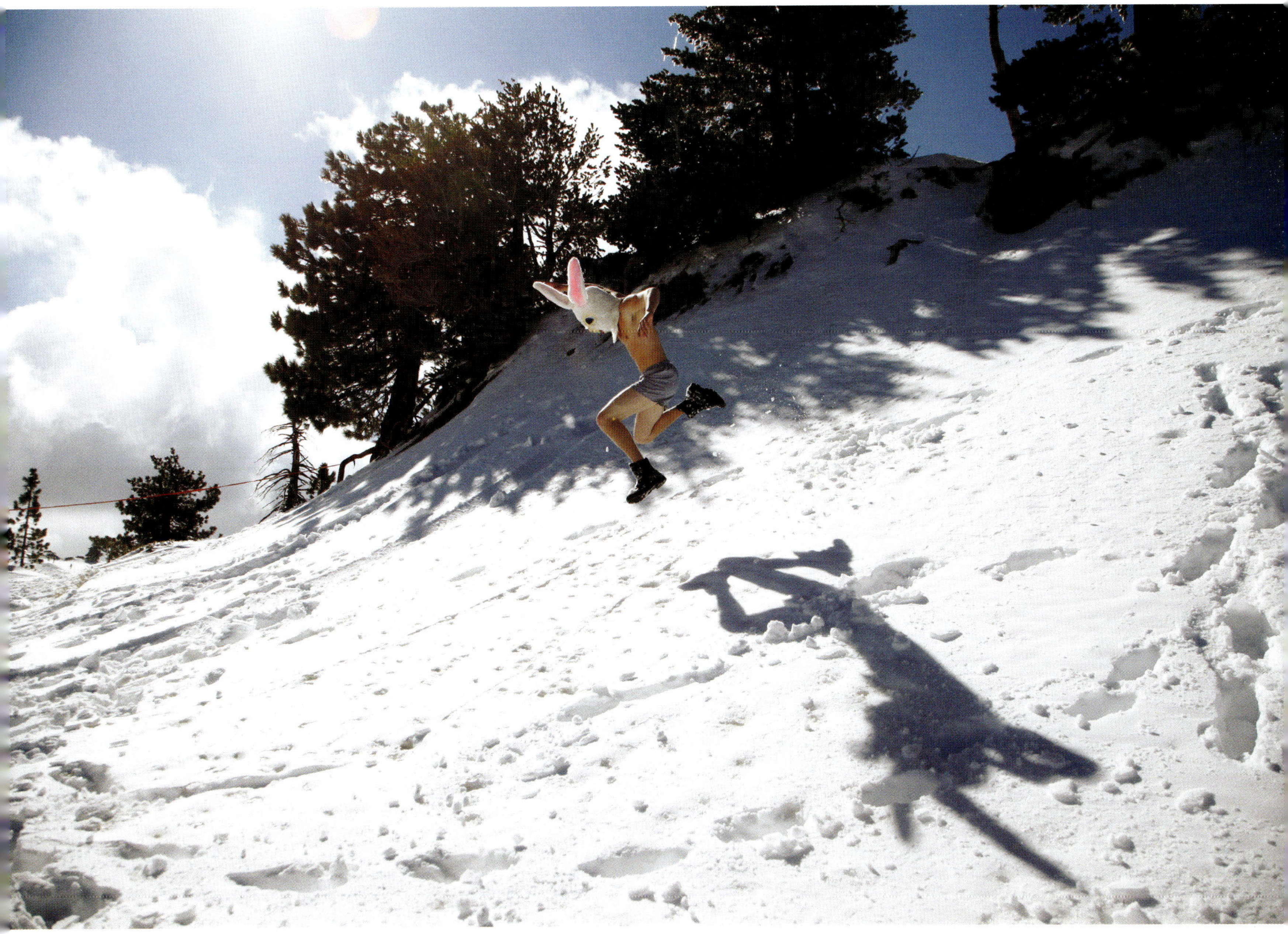

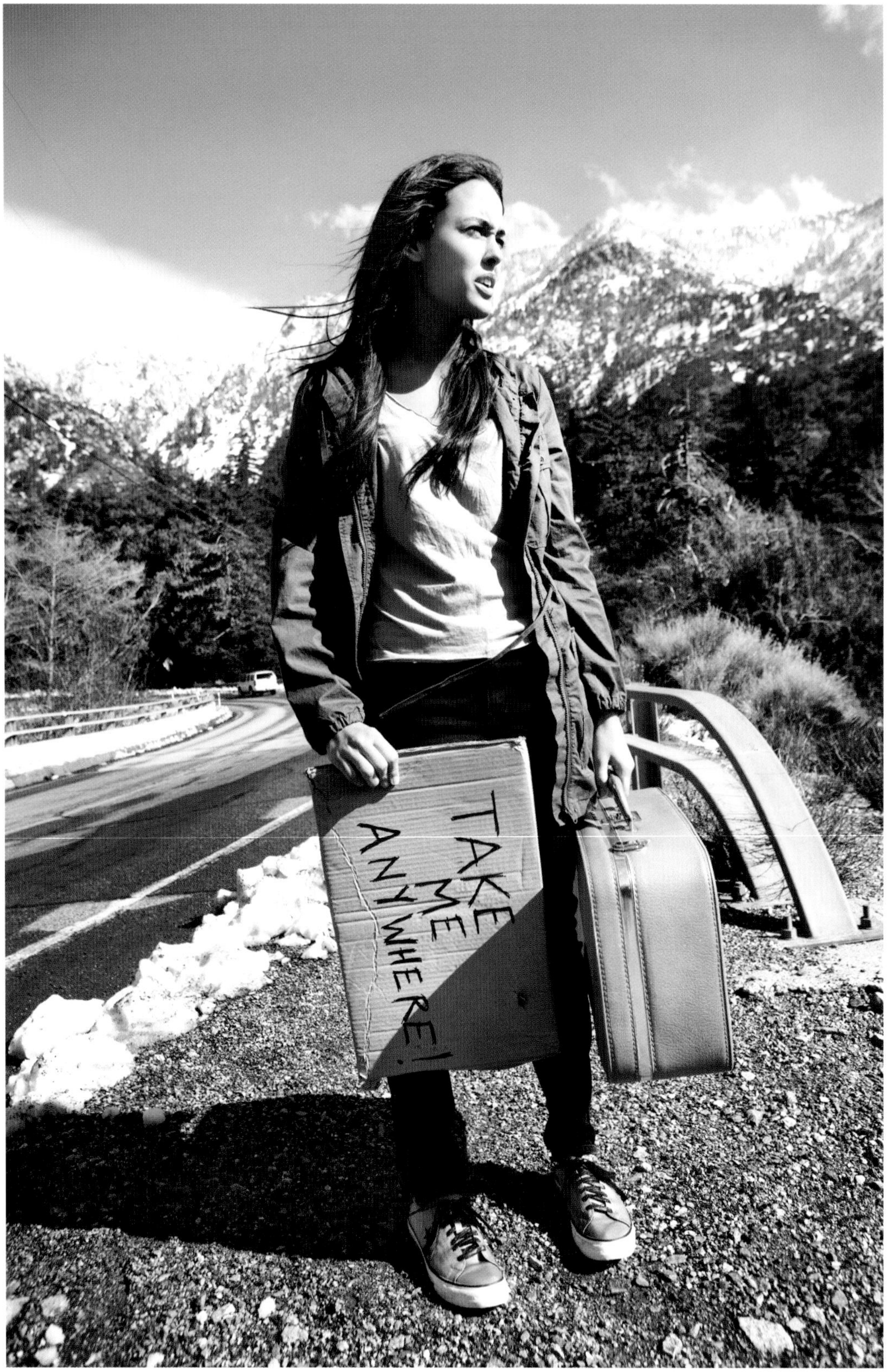
TAKE
ME
ANYWHERE!

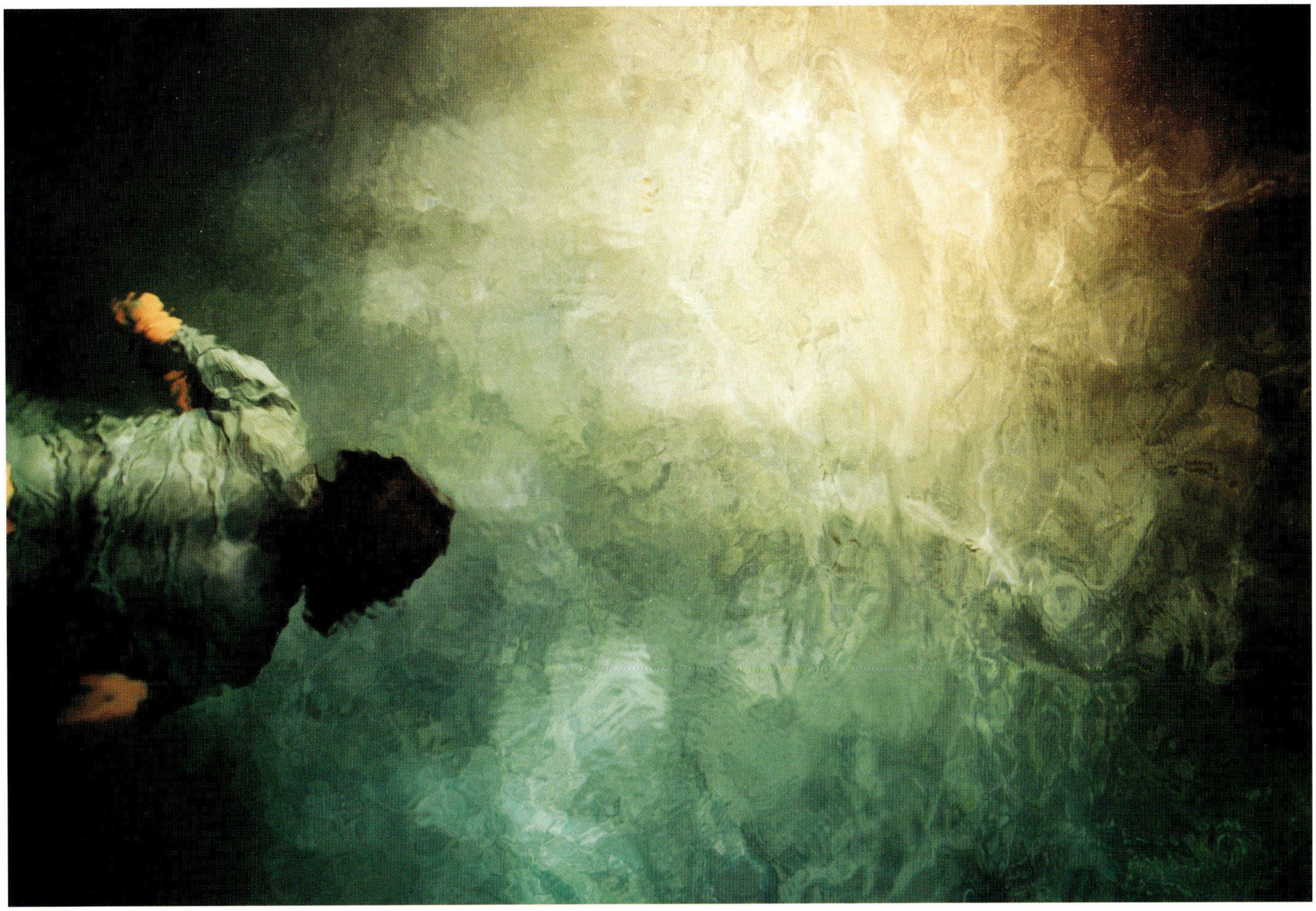

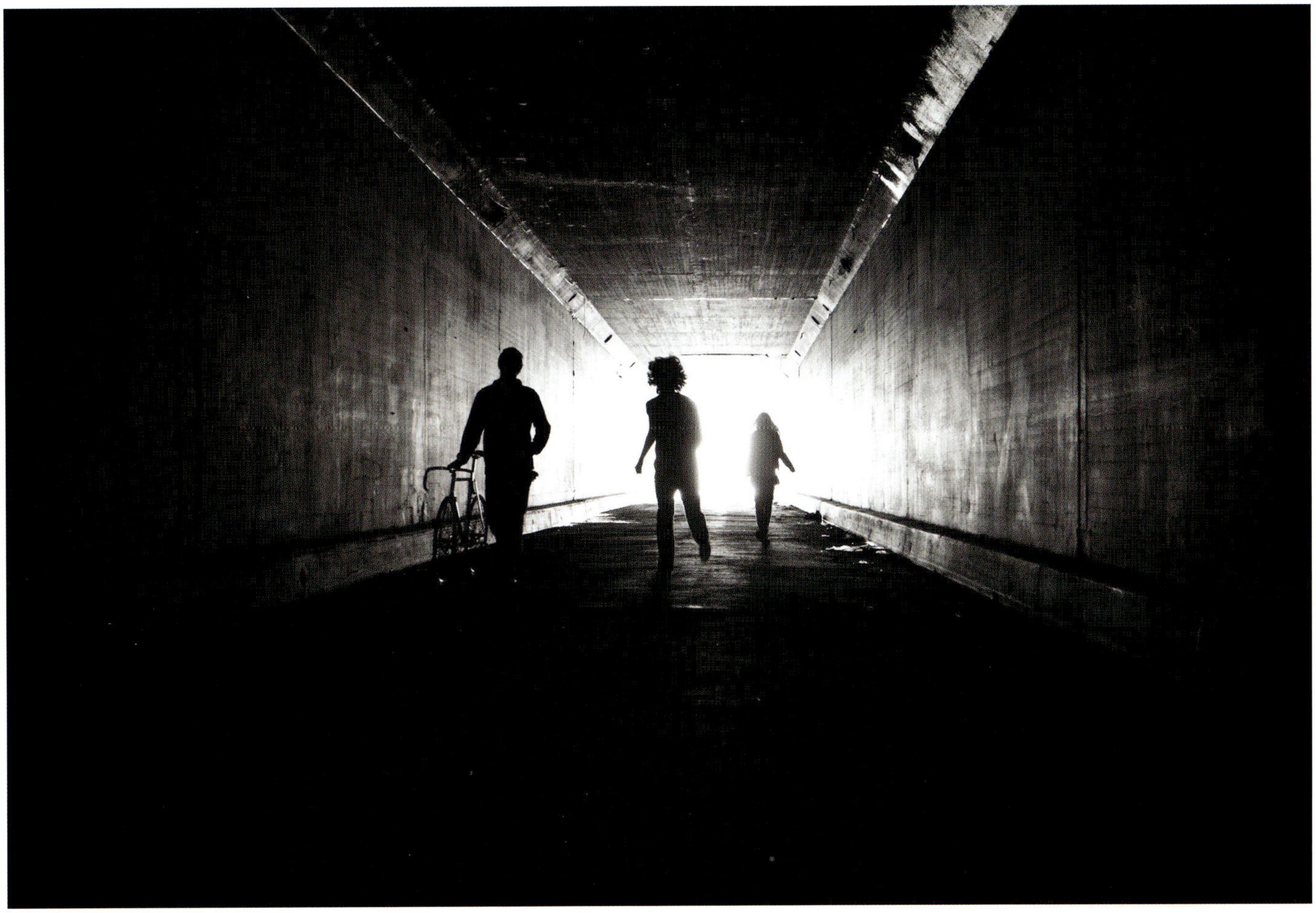

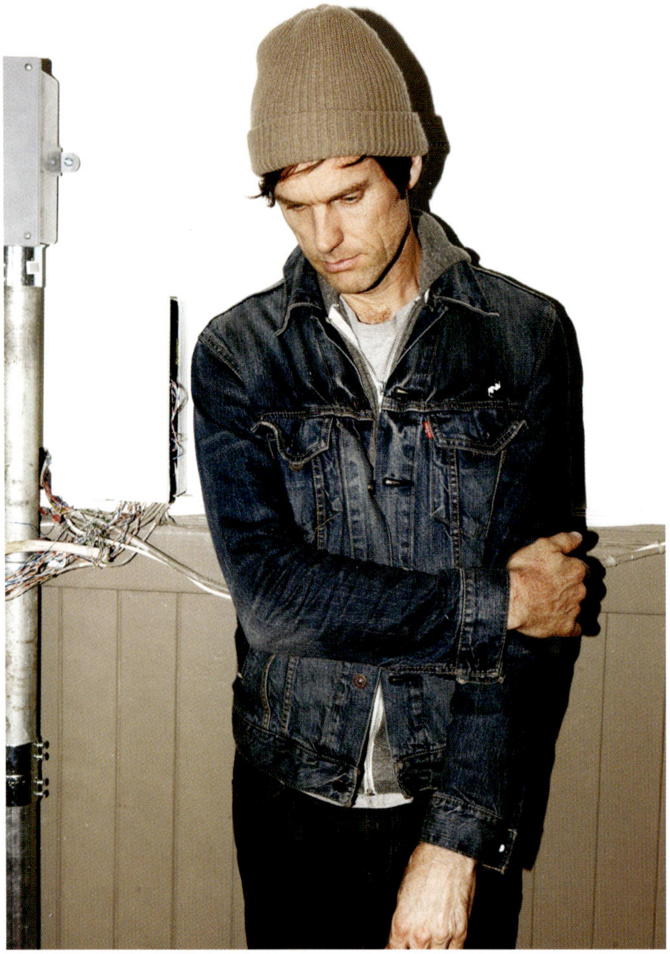

Self portrait, 2012

DAMON WAY

San Francisco, California
goincase.com

I lived in Southern California almost my entire life. ... I was born in Portland, Oregon, and by the time I was two and a half, my parents, who are natives of California, were following the hippie trailer back down the coastline from the Pacific Northwest.

I have always lived with water on one side of me, and the desert on the other. There is something magical about existing between these two distinct forces of nature, which I think permeates all who are receptive to its influence.

Adrift along the California coastline lurks a subculture of people who have found solace in clustered encampments of ragtag motor homes. This fragmented group of gypsies, vagabonds, derelicts, drop-outs, grifters, crazies, addicts and doomsday-ers, seem to be unknowingly leading the charge to a new paradigm of postmodern living … off the grid and out of sight. This selection of photos represents a clandestine look at the variety of mobile refuge put into action under this banner of blind freedom and dubious secrecy.

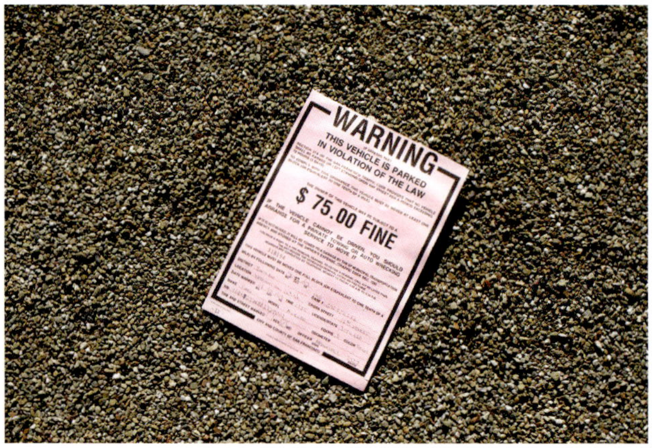

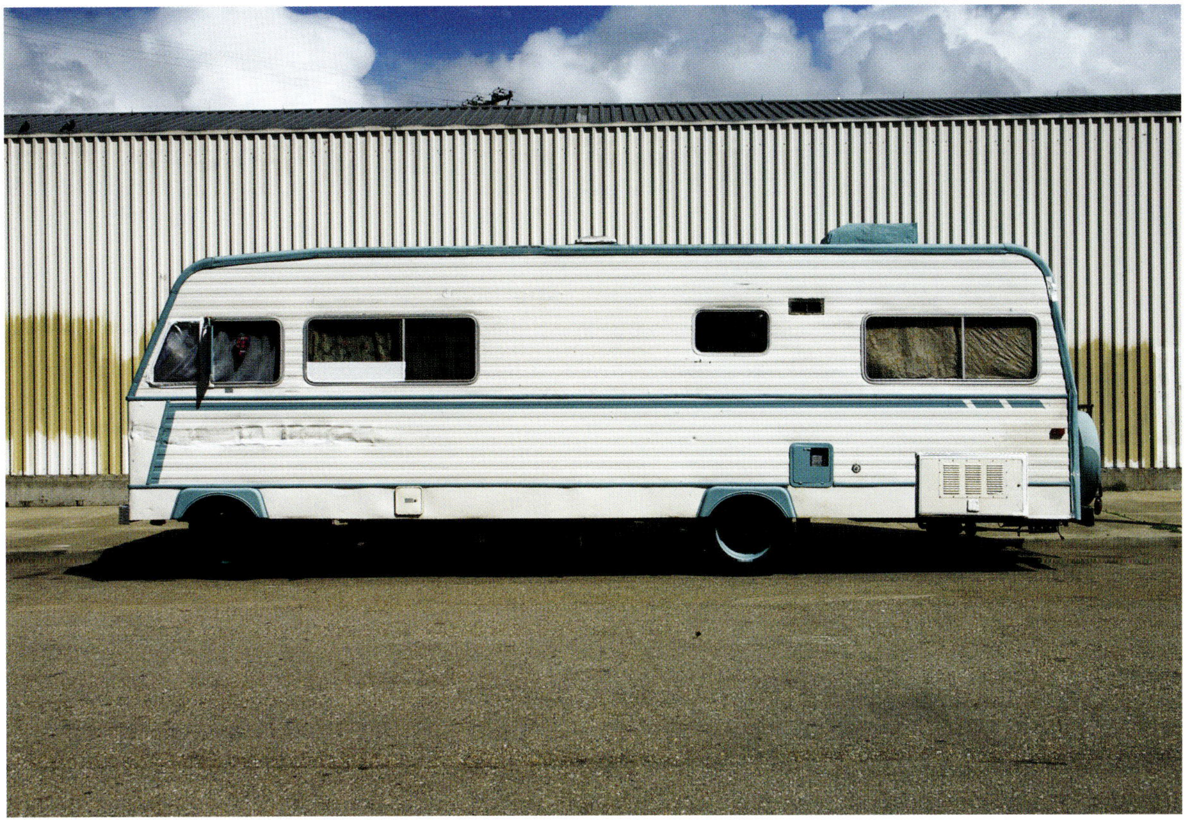

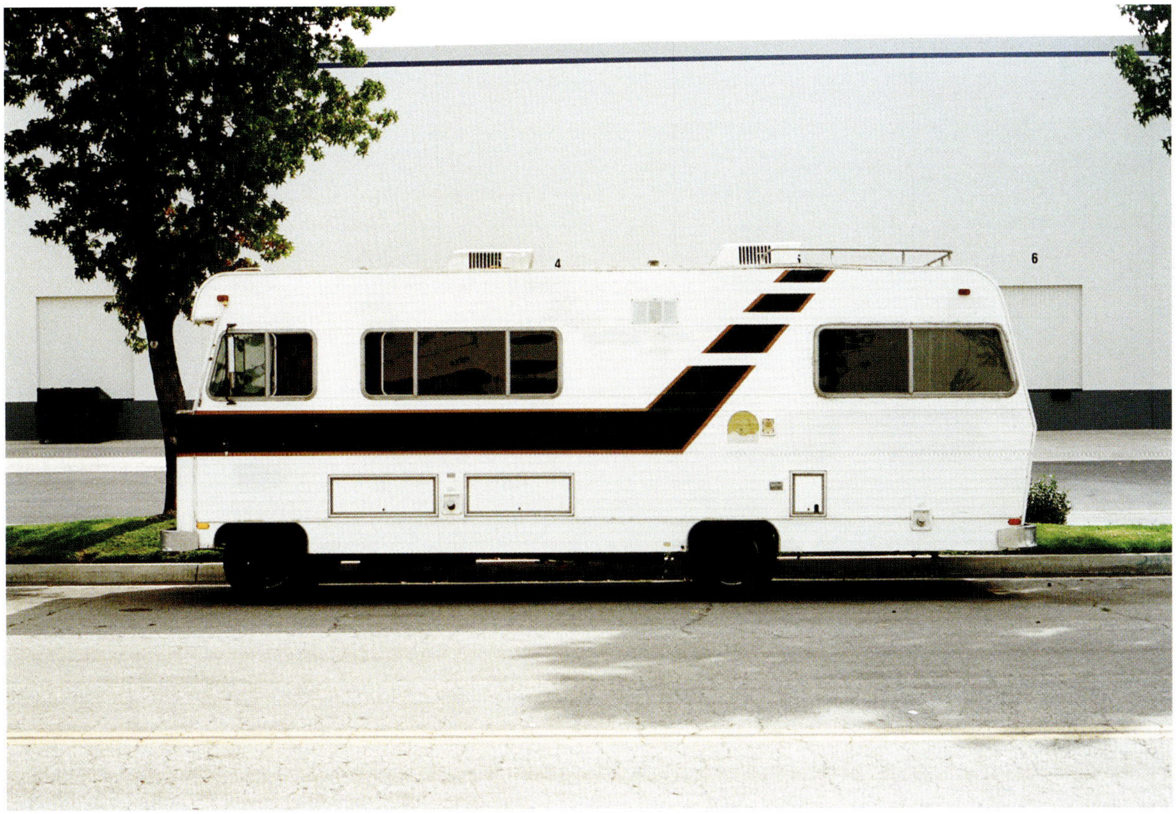

"Motorhome–San Francisco"

"Motorhome–Los Angeles"

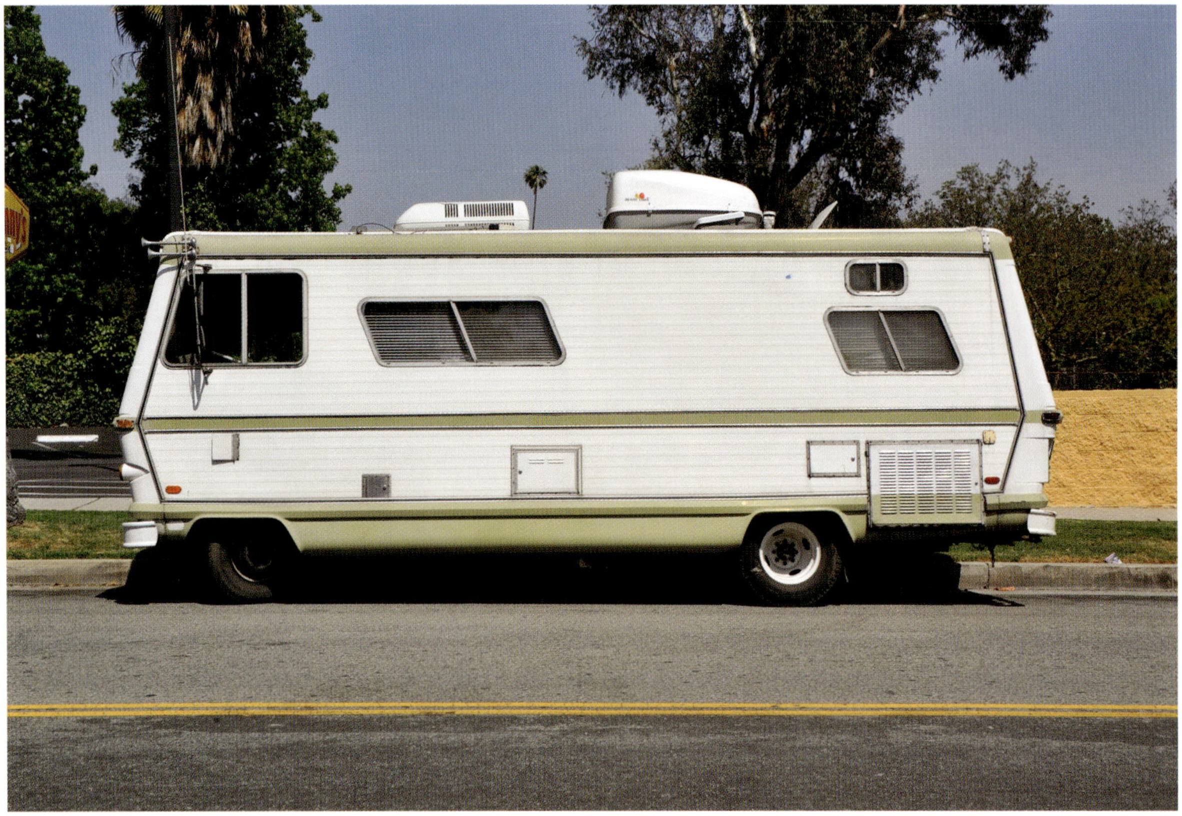

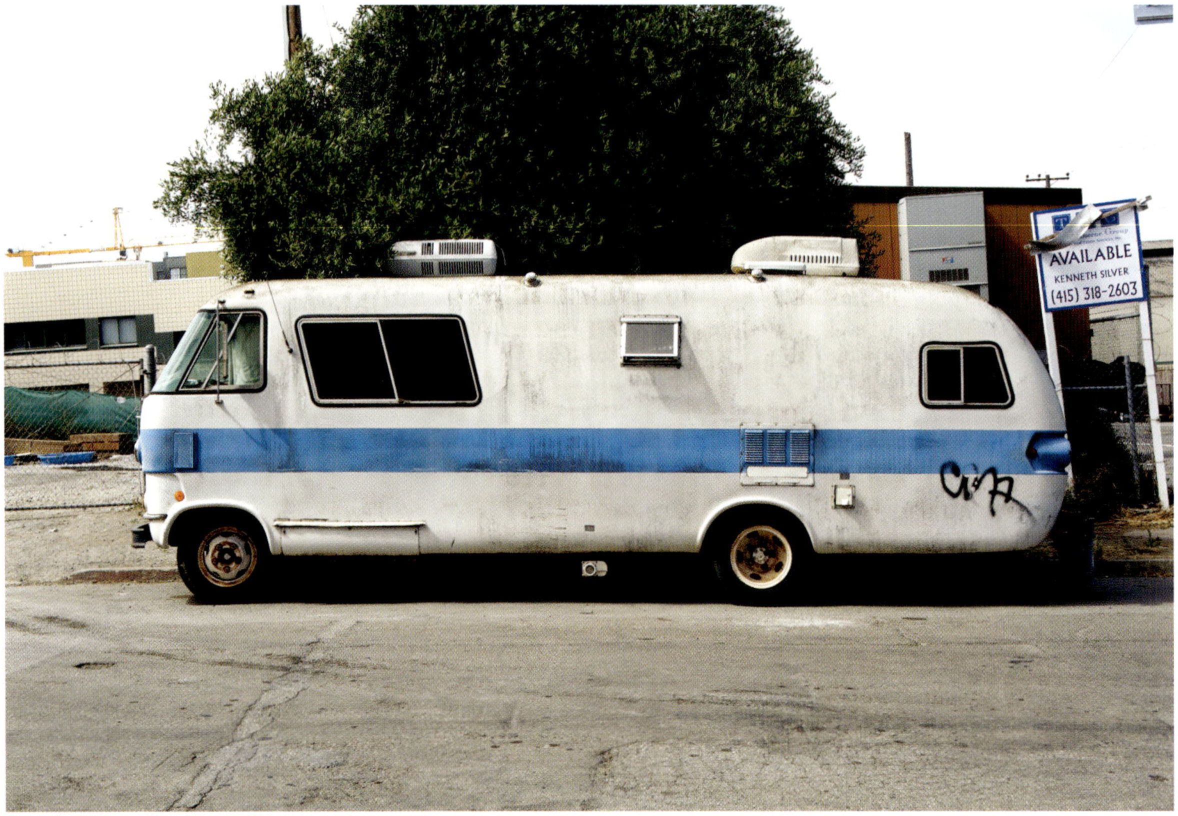

"Motorhome Los Angeles"

"Motorhome San Francisco"

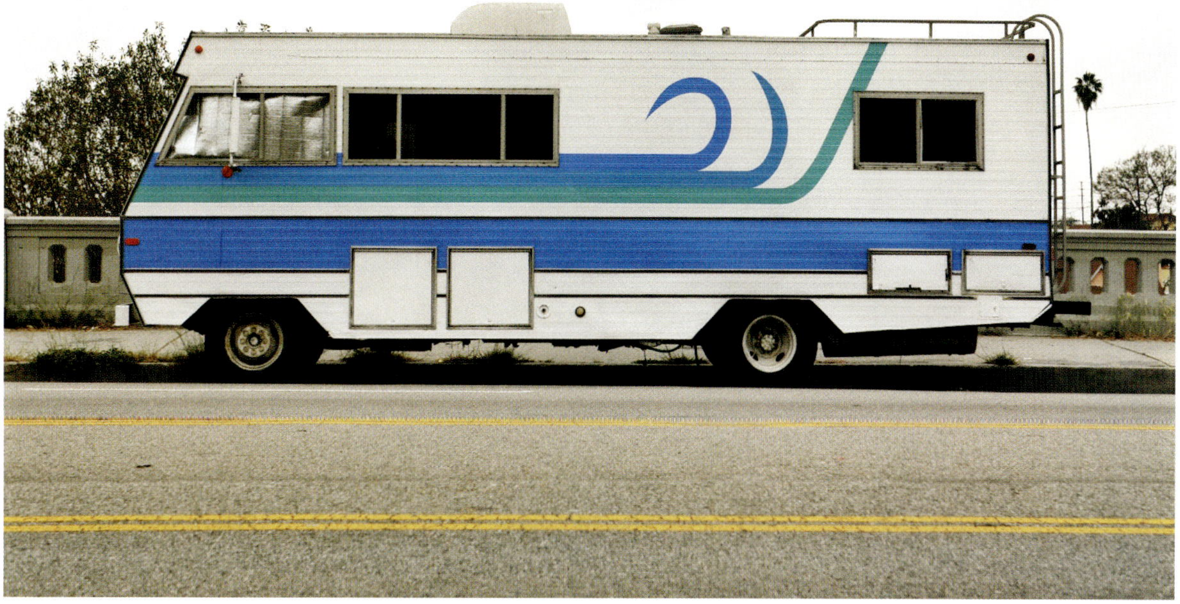

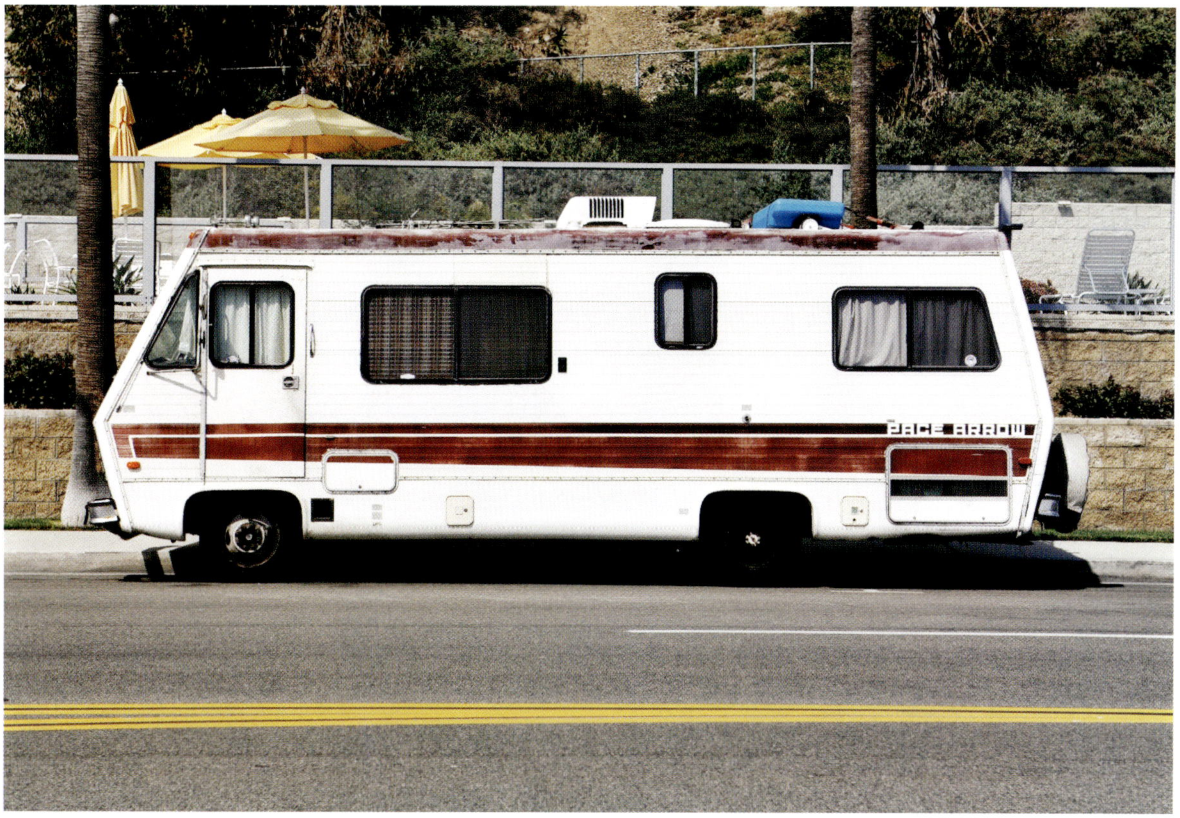

"Motorhome–Los Angeles"

"Motorhome–Los Angeles"

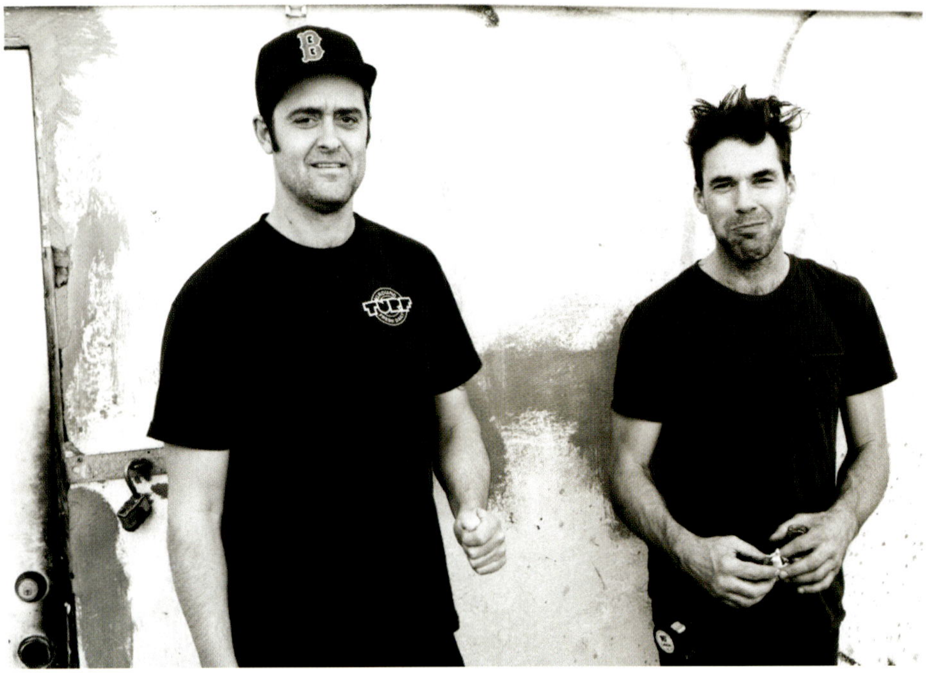

Photo by Chris Shonting, 2012

COAN BUDDY NICHOLS RICK CHARNOSKI SIX STAIR

Los Angeles, California
sixstair.com

Why did you first come to California, and what keeps you here to this day?

B: The weather and skateboarding brought me to California … I always wanted to be able to skate year-round and generally live a life without cold weather. I hate cold, and it makes my body hurt.

R: I spent my whole life in the Northeast. The same things that brought me here keeps me here: sunshine, surf, empty pools, and pinnacle levels of the good life. I'm not too deep.

What are the advantages and disadvantages of working in California vs. other parts of the world?

B: The advantages for me are the surroundings and the sun. I stay motivated to work because I get to do a lot of other things, and when it's time to work I can focus.

R: We basically make films about California and Californians. California is pretty much the backdrop to what we do. Sometimes it's better to have distance from your subject matter to get some perspective, but I travel enough to appreciate the Cali-vibe, and coming home is always a pleasure. Maybe the reason I like it here so much is because I'm not actually from here. I spent 35 years elsewhere, so I suppose I will always appreciate the ease of working and living here.

What about California influences your work and your process of making art?

B: I don't know. Like I said, the surroundings make me happy and in the mood to do stuff. I like having a great studio space and being around lots of people doing cool stuff all the time.

R: The good life. When the vibes are high, you're productive. California gets me stoked on life and making something of my time here on the big marble.

All Images taken from misc. film stills

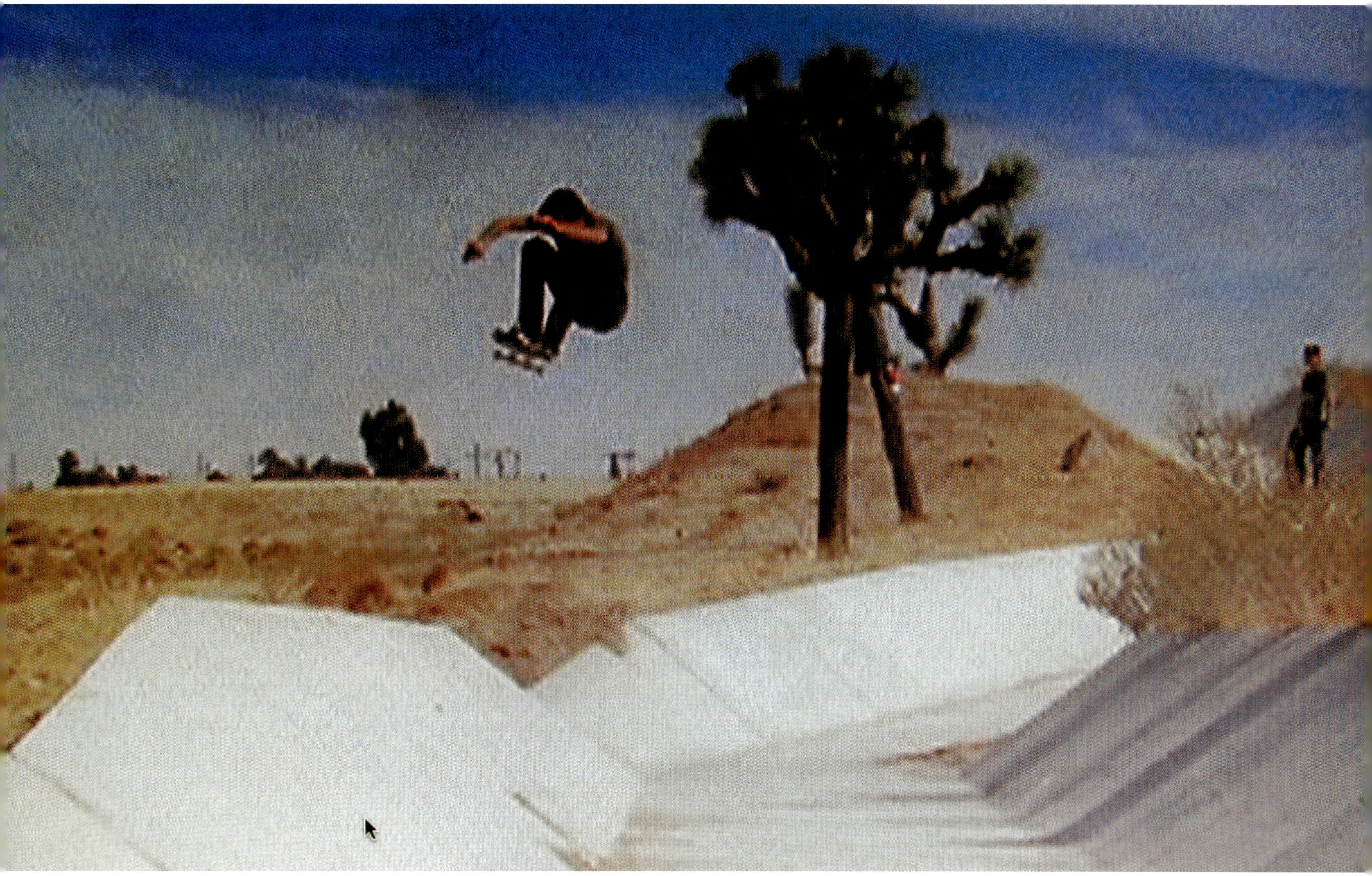

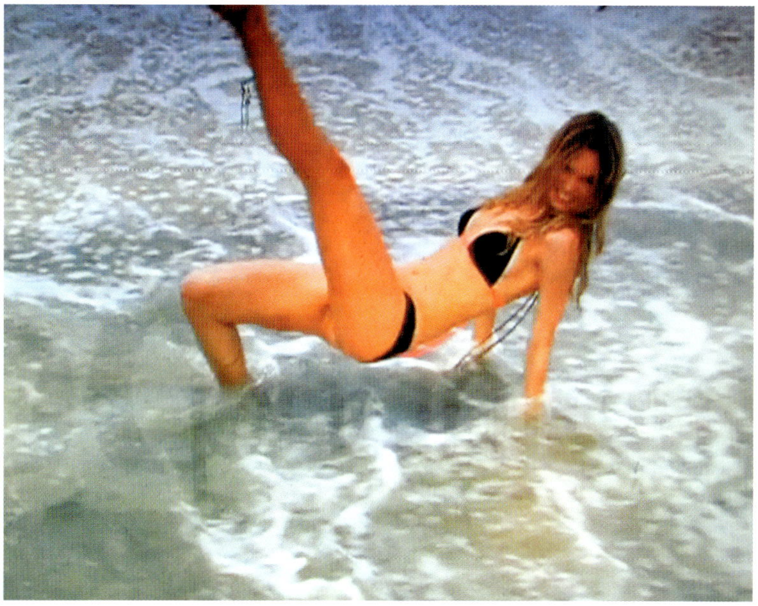

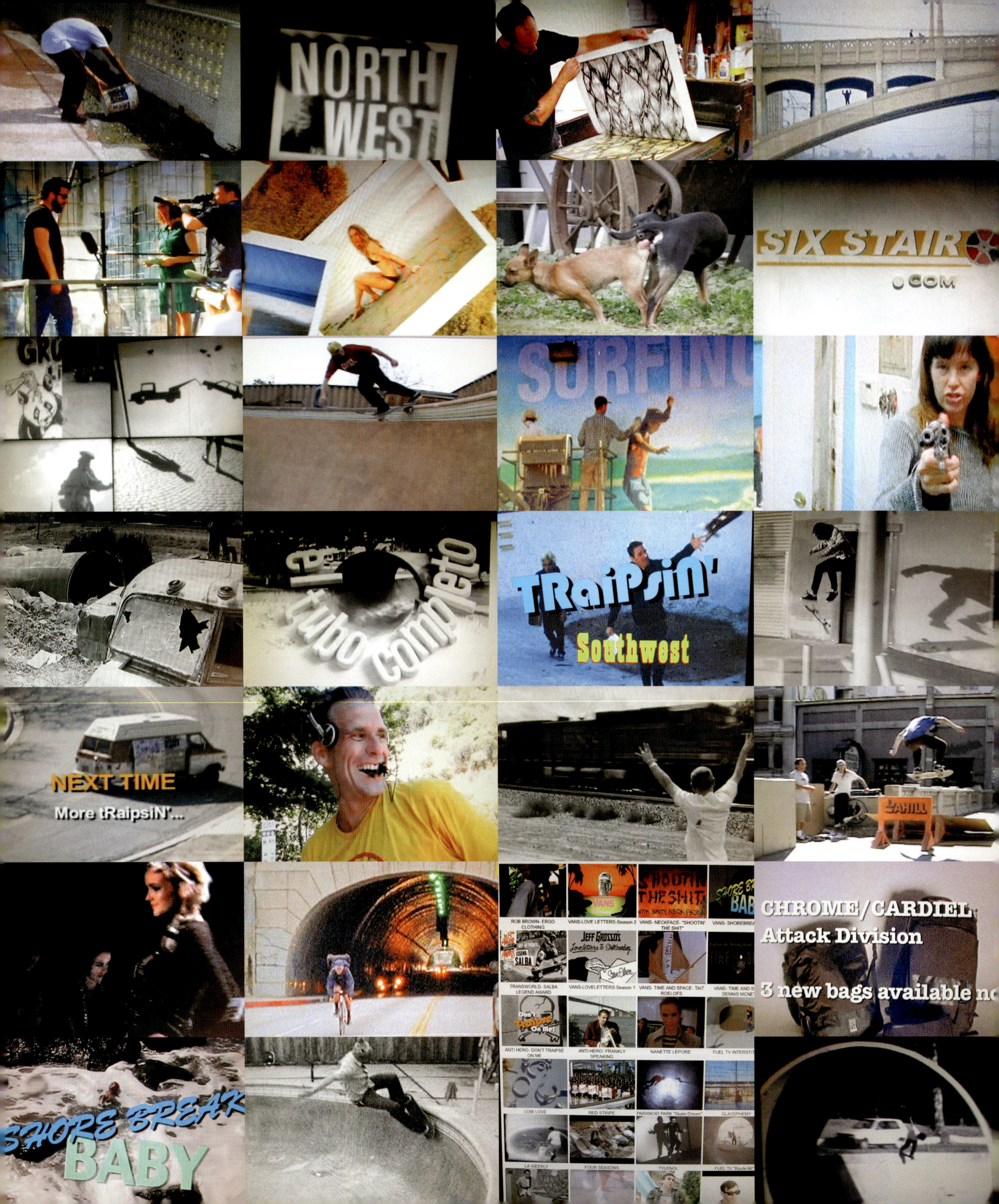
NORTH WEST
SIX STAIR
.COM
SURFIN
tubo completo
TRaiPsiN'
Southwest
NEXT TIME
More tRaipsiN'...
CAHILL
ROB BROWN- ERGO CLOTHING
VANS-LOVE LETTERS-Season 2
VANS- NECKFACE- "SHOOTIN' THE SHIT"
TRANSWORLD- SALBA LEGEND AWARD
VANS-LOVELETTERS-Season 1
VANS- TIME AND SPACE- TAIT ROELOFS
ANTI HERO- DON'T TRAIPSE ON ME
ANTI HERO- FRANKLY SPEAKING
NANETTE LEPORE
LOW LOVE
RED STRIPE
PARANOID PARK "Skate Dream"
GLASSPHEMY
LA WEEKLY
FOUR SEASONS
TYLENOL
CHROME/CARDIEL
Attack Division
SHORE BREAK
BABY

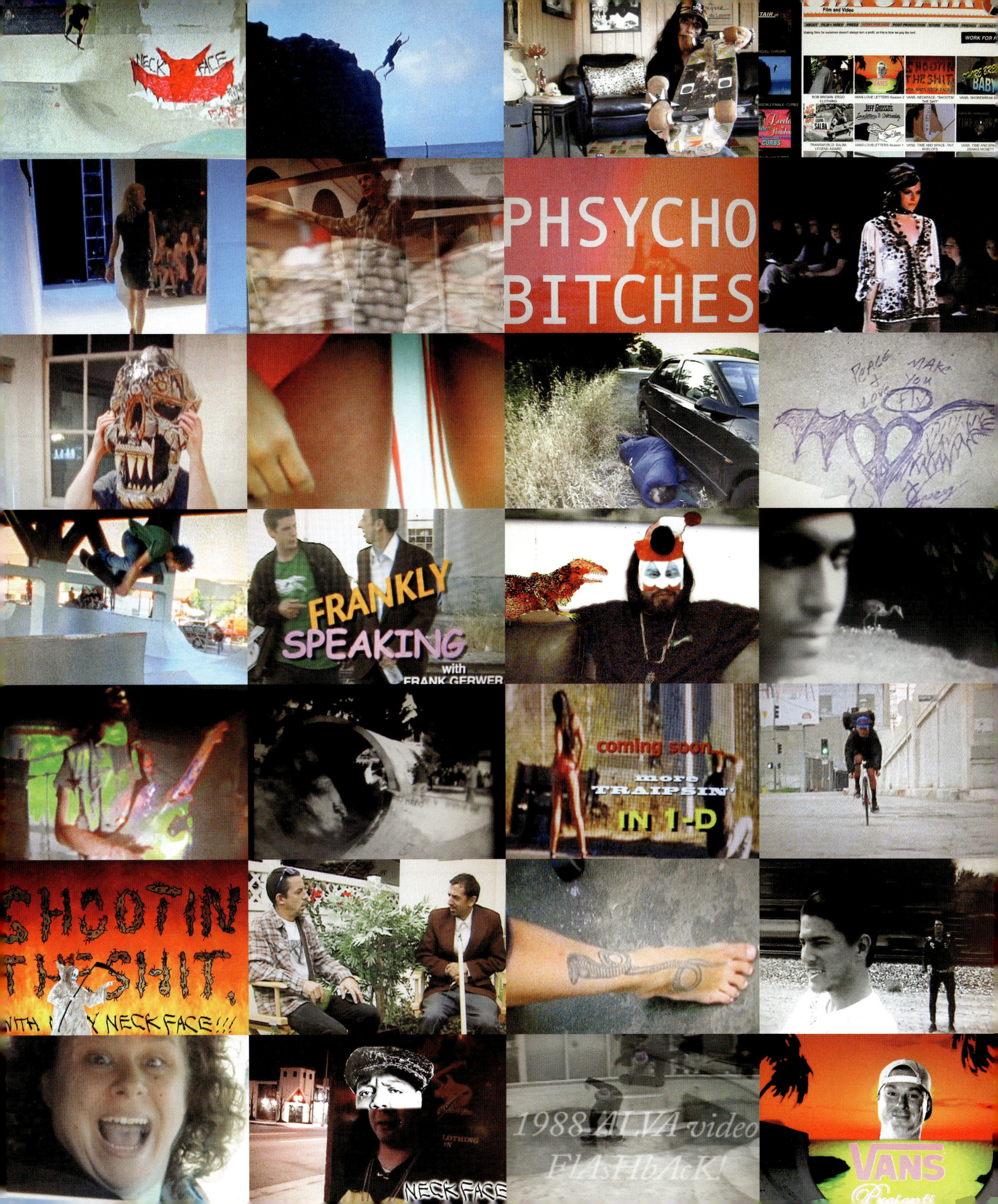
NECK FACE
PHSYCHO BITCHES
Peace & Love Make You Fly
FRANKLY SPEAKING
with FRANK GERWER
coming soon...
more TRAIPSIN'
IN 1-D
SHOOTIN THE SHIT.
NECKFACE!!!
NECK FACE
1988 ALVA video
FlAsHbAcK!
VANS

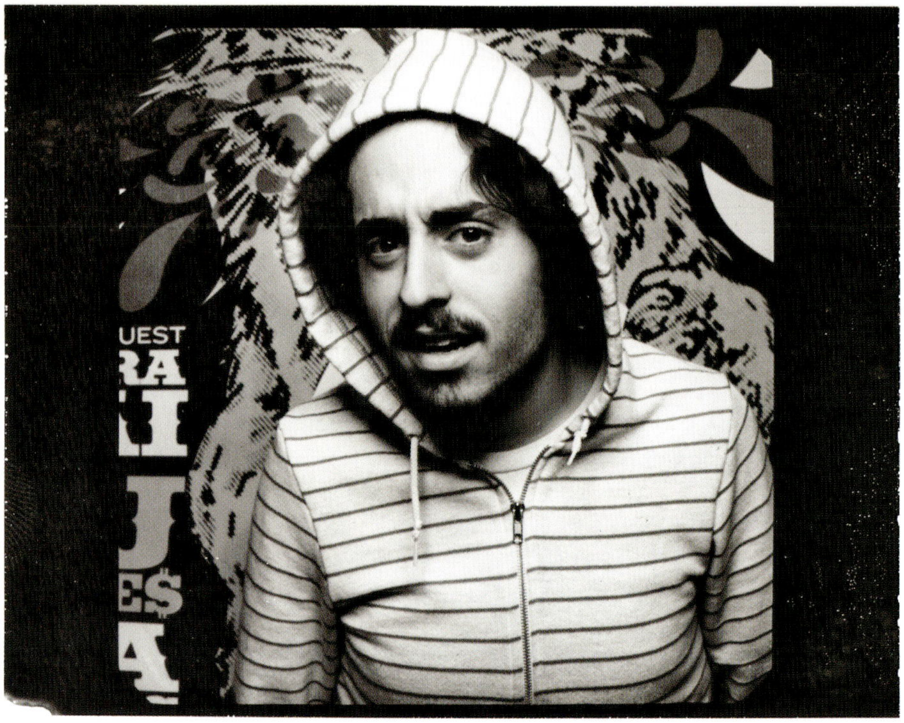

MFG

Los Angeles, California

mfgproductions.com

Photo by Rony Alwin, 2012

I was actually born here in Los Angeles. Each move felt like moving to a different city—even though it was just a consistent 15-20 minutes eastward—just because of the sheer size of LA and the sheer laziness of people to drive between suburbs to see each other. Going to UCLA and eventually working for Shepard Fairey both kept me in Los Angeles.

I love working in NY because I can get a head start on LA, and I can work later and still make LA deadlines. I think the advantage of working in Los Angeles is the diversity of the available work. I'd say that certain echelons of the design business are much more easily found in NY at bigger agencies, but for a few people, LA can also provide some great opportunities to work on awesome projects without having to suffer through the weather, people, and general anger in NY. That said, I absolutely love NY and constantly harbor a fantasy of being there.

I think that there's an openness to experimentation in design [in LA] that I think people who take it more seriously in other places don't have. I think the work overall suffers, but I like the happy accidents that come from not feeling like everything has to follow stringent design guidelines. I also like the Latin cultural influences and street culture that permeate Los Angeles. It also can make for a lot of not-amazing work, but the good stuff is amazing, and the fact that there is a non-American culture, with such a strong visual identity readily available is a great thing about working in LA.

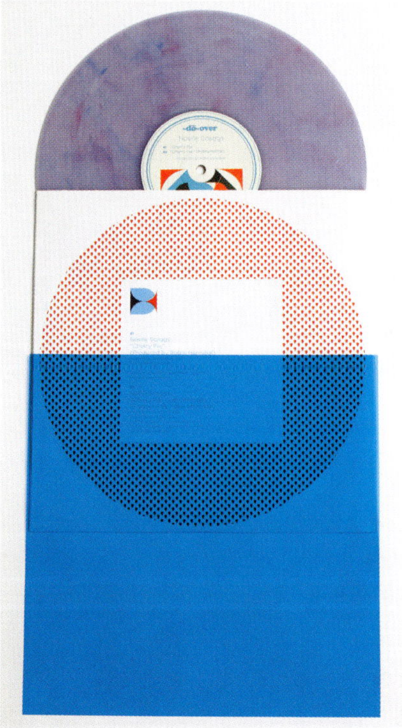

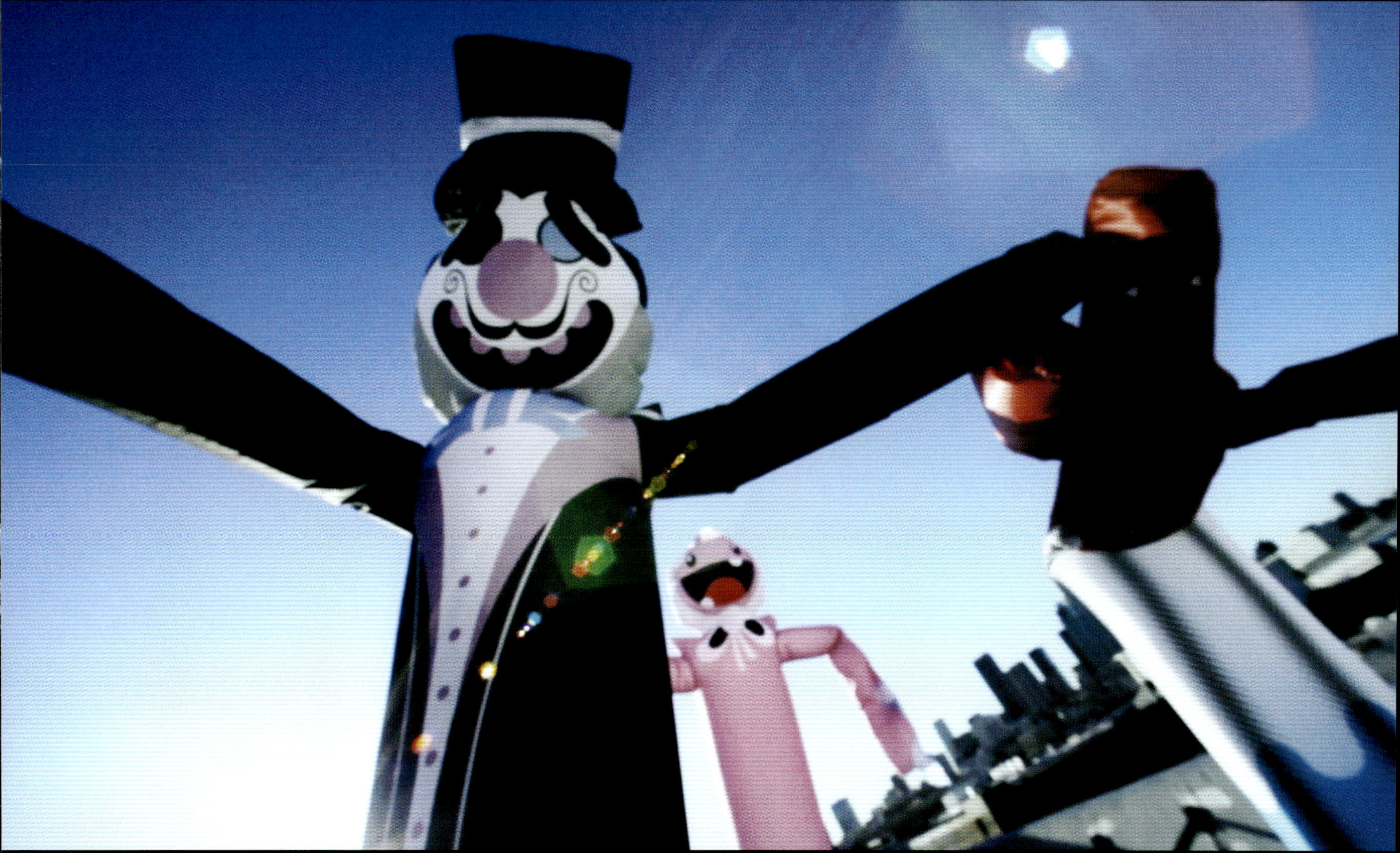

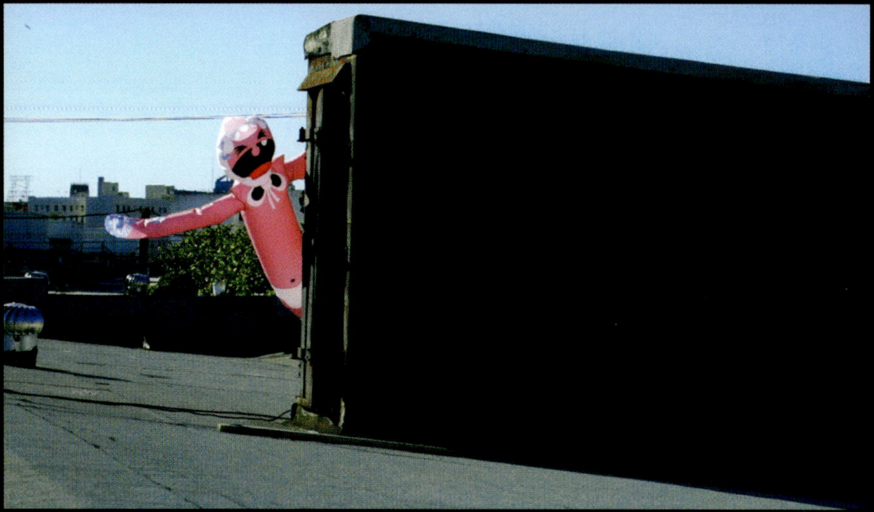

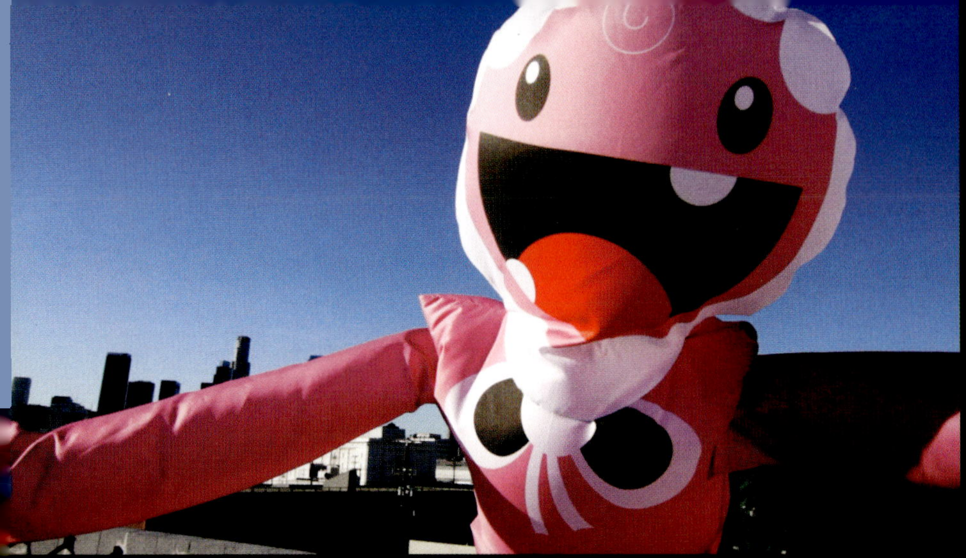

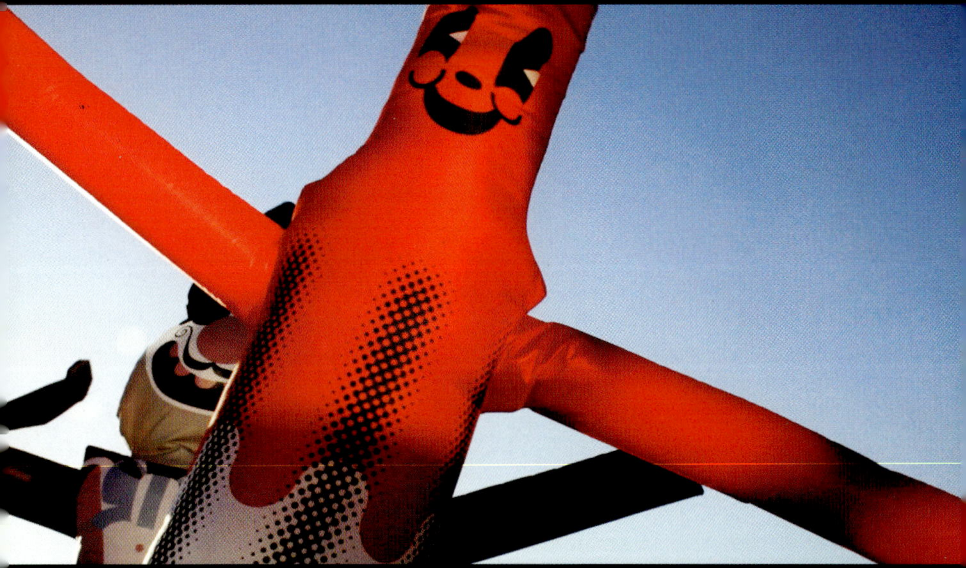

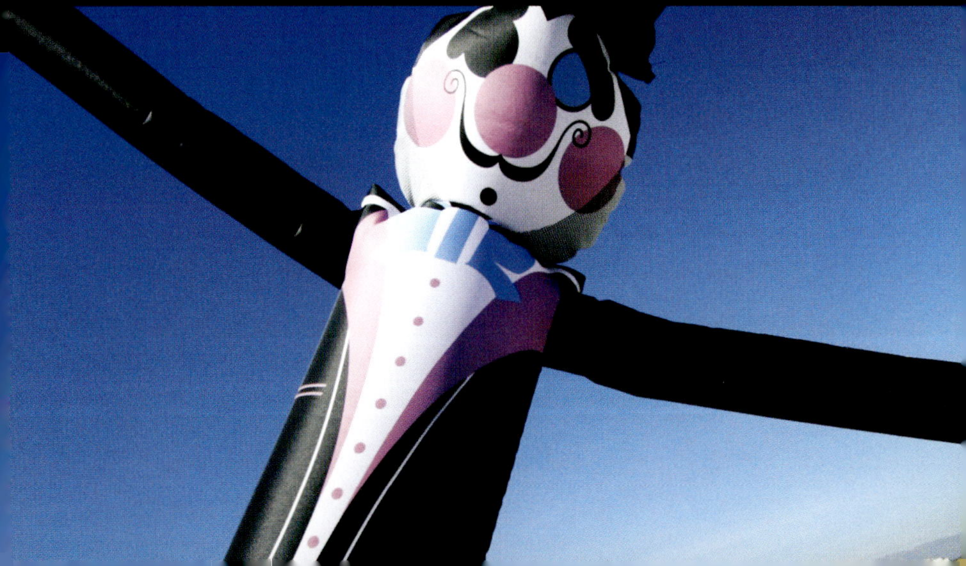

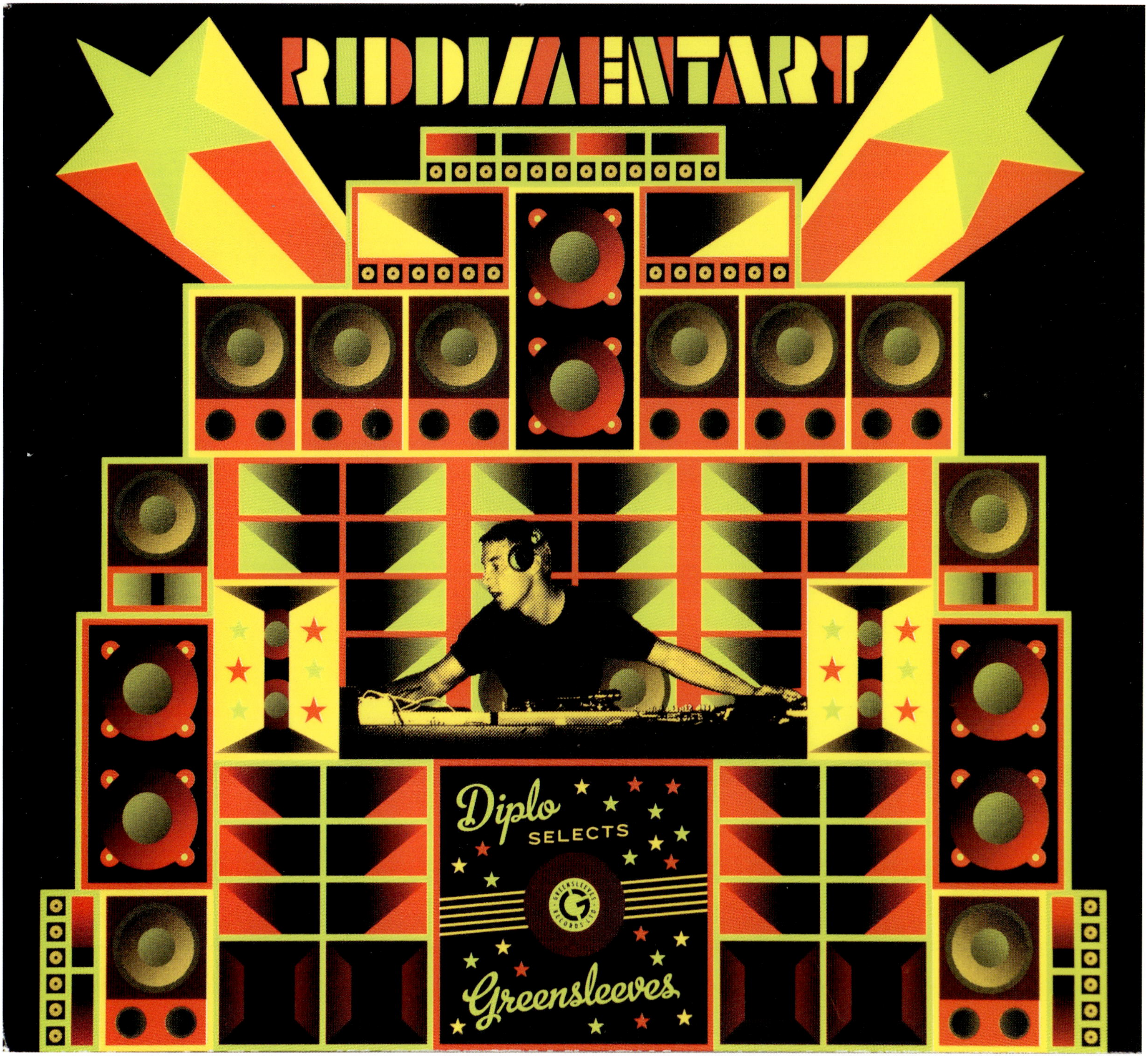
RIDDIMENTARY
Diplo SELECTS
GREENSLEEVES RECORDS LTD
Greensleeves
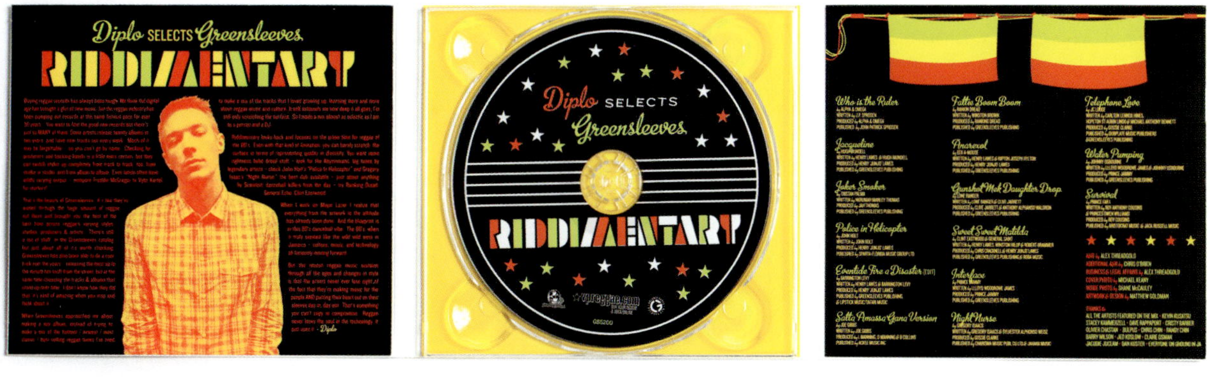
Diplo SELECTS Greensleeves
RIDDIMENTARY
Diplo SELECTS Greensleeves
RIDDIMENTARY

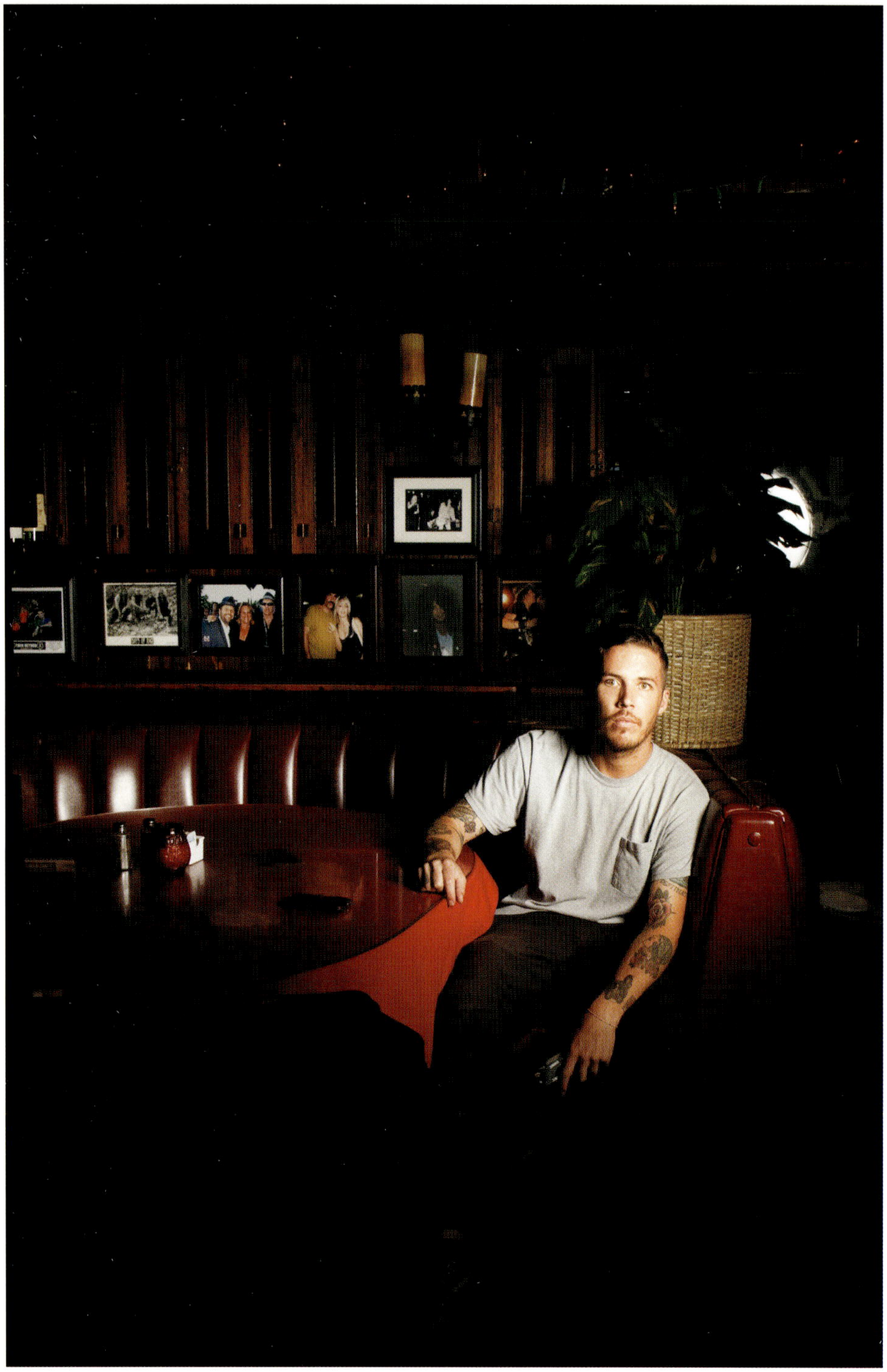

Self portrait, 2012

CURTIS BUCHANAN

Los Angeles, California
curtisbuchananphoto.com

Los Angeles is the best city in the world. It has the sense of pure nostalgia for me. It has the perfect amount of beauty and the perfect amount of ugliness.

There are only advantages to working here.

Everyone is creative and work is a reflection of their surroundings. Every pocket in Los Angeles has a completely different feel, and with that it gives me a different vision with every wave of inspiration that hits me.

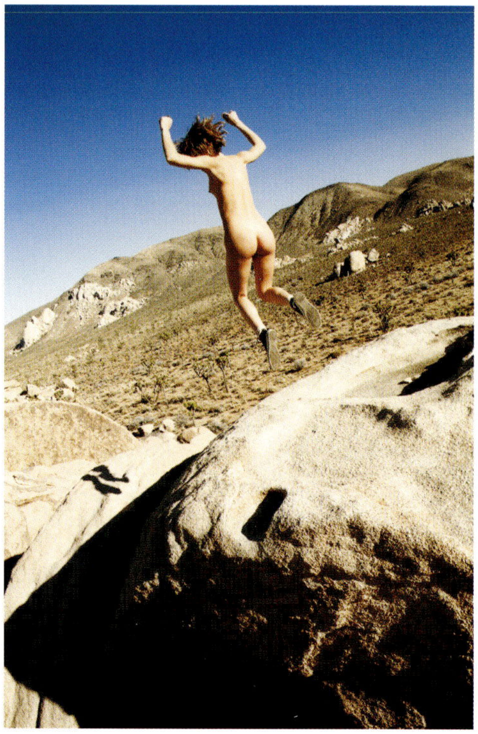

"Janell—Joshua Tree" 2012

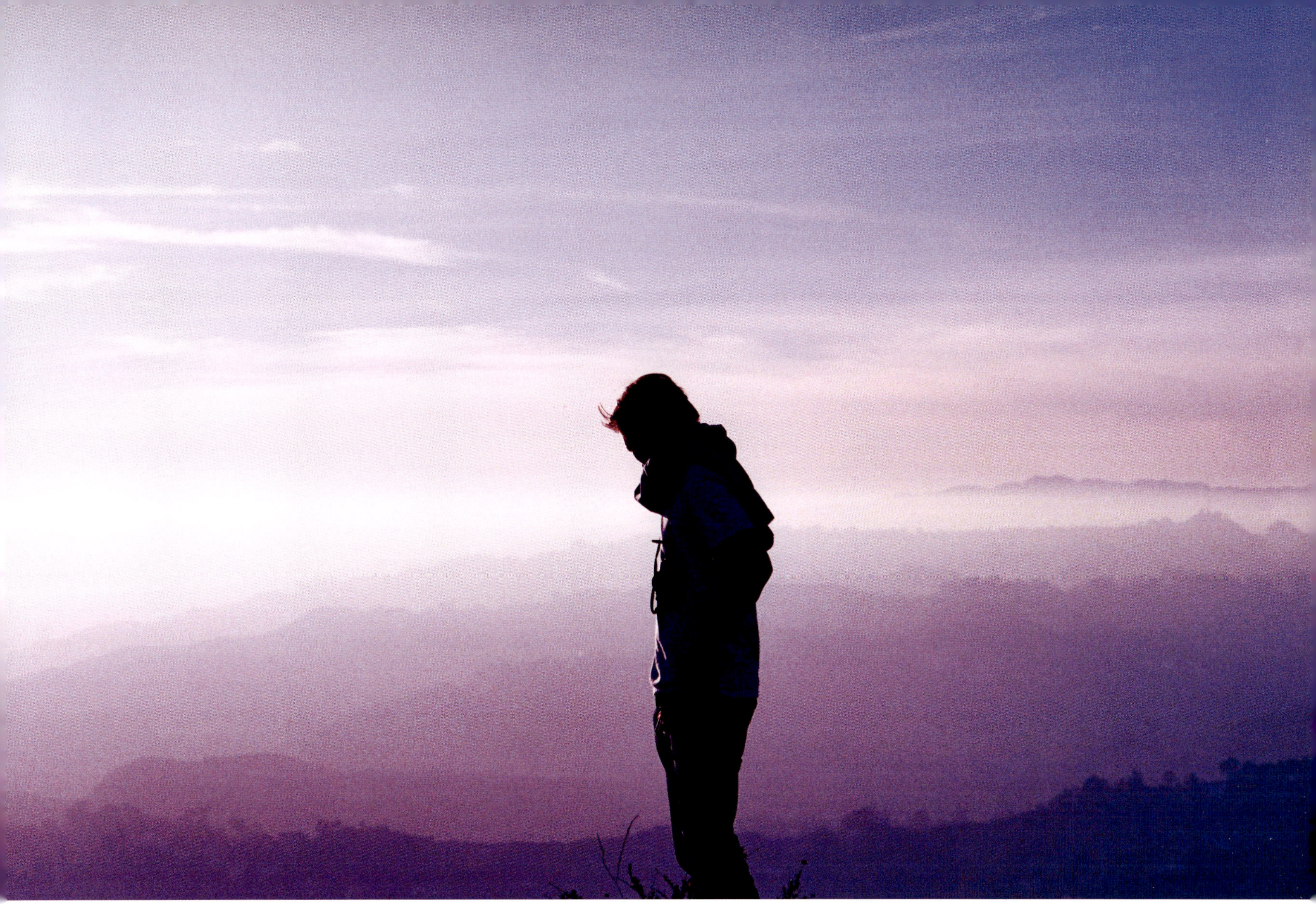

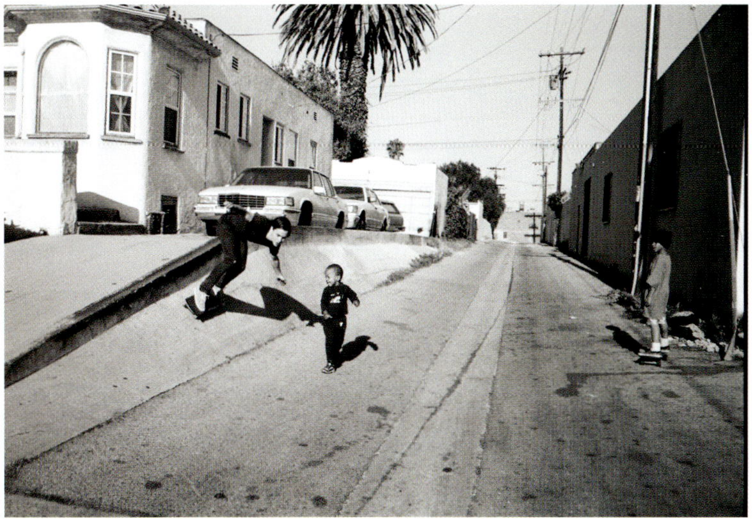

"Alex Olson" 2011

"Getting Tubed (Spanky)" 2008

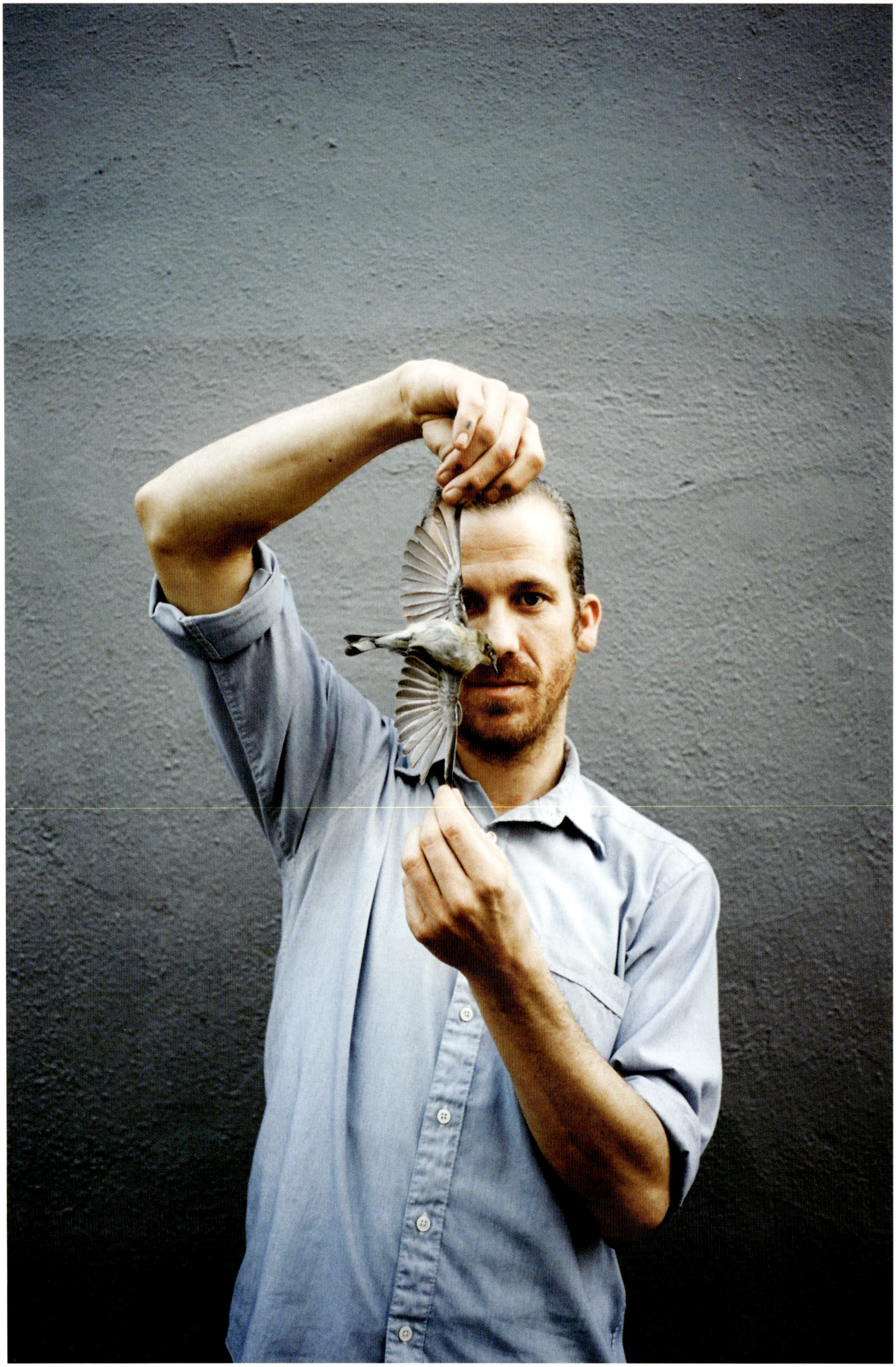

"No Dice" 2010

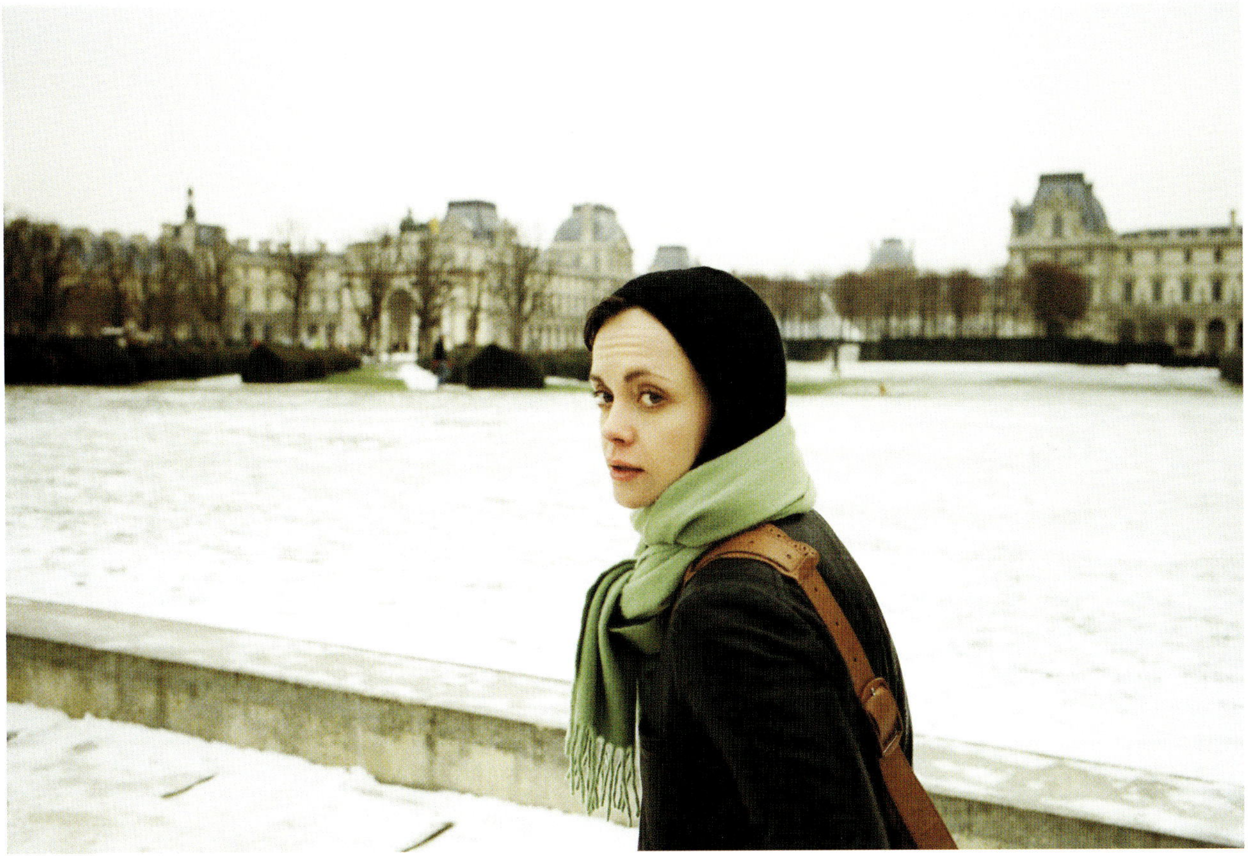

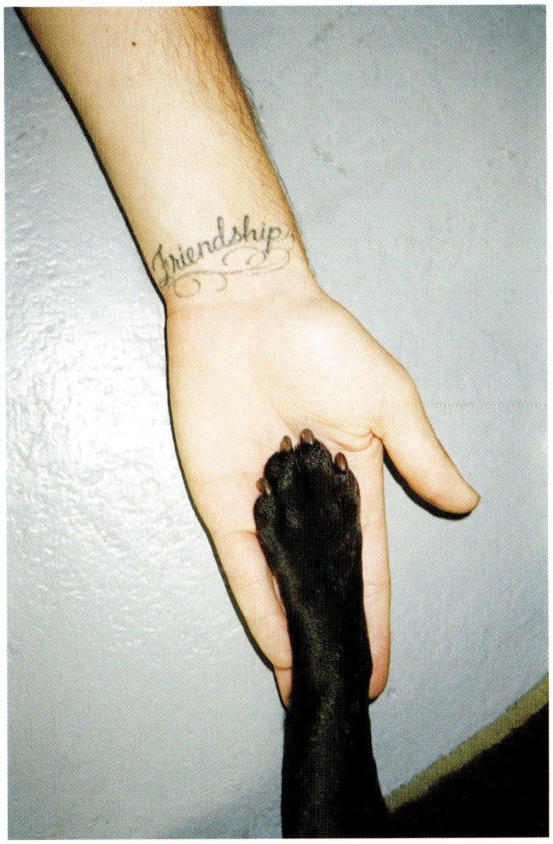

"Christina (Paris)" 2010 *"Friendship"* 2009

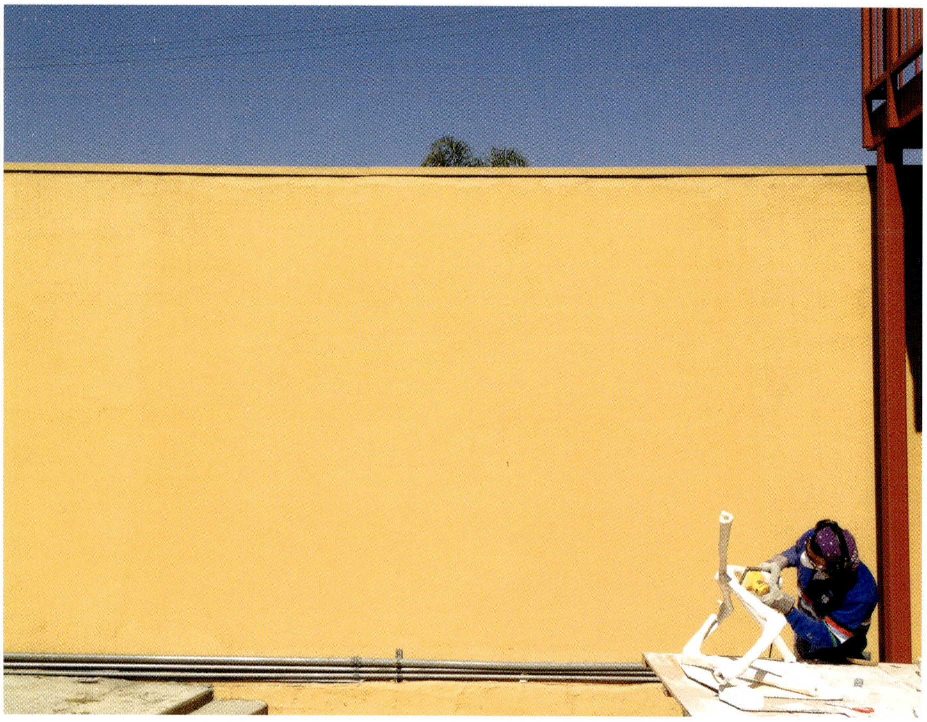

JON RAJKOVICH

Los Angeles, California
jonrajkovich.com

Photo by Justin Van Hoy, 2012

I came to California in 2005. I went to graduate school in South Carolina and lived in Atlanta for a couple of years, but I was always told by other artists that my work would fit in LA. I was driving a Ford F250 pickup and making brightly monochrome zoomorphic objects concerning the physical experience of sculpture—exploring how the body moves around the work and responds to color. Then my situation changed, and with the help of a couple of friends, I moved to Los Angeles.

The beach and the rich culture for art are great, but there are stretches in the summer when there is no place to hide from the blinding sun, helicopters, and heat pounding down every day. When I moved here, I felt totally exposed. I decided the work should be exposed too by leaving some surfaces unfinished.

Then I quit therapy and started online dating. This was a lot more fun. I got to know my city better and invented a new standard of reality. I traded my truck for a Ford ZX2.

My work changes when my environment changes. There may be a subject to the work, but through the making process my aim is for the art to balance the external circumstances with the personal and emotive, something which, in turn, can be a bit dark and perplexing. Sometimes I add a found object to balance things out: a cement lion paw I found in the LA River, for example. I'm most interested in these dark and mysterious currents. I have them. The city has them.

Many of the materials in my work have begun to impersonate other materials. Plastic looks like metal, wood looks like plastic. While this is a response to my dislike of informational placards in galleries and museums that give away all of the ingredients and date everything, it's also a response to the fact that much of this city is built on artifice. I like the way people portray someone else or their super-selves. Posture is important on the street and becomes so in the forms within my work. Romantic exaggerations and neurotic deceptions are commonplace, so a necessity in navigating this city and creating work is to locate verisimilitude.

I like LA. You think you know it; then you come across a neighborhood you never realized existed. You see and hear languages you know but don't understand. This is all I ever wanted from a city and what I want from art: a constantly changing, long-term relationship that never gives up all of its secrets, and a good place to be lost to be found.

"Profile" 2012
Plywood, steel, pigmented spackle, oil, and acrylic paint
42 x 39 x 17 inches

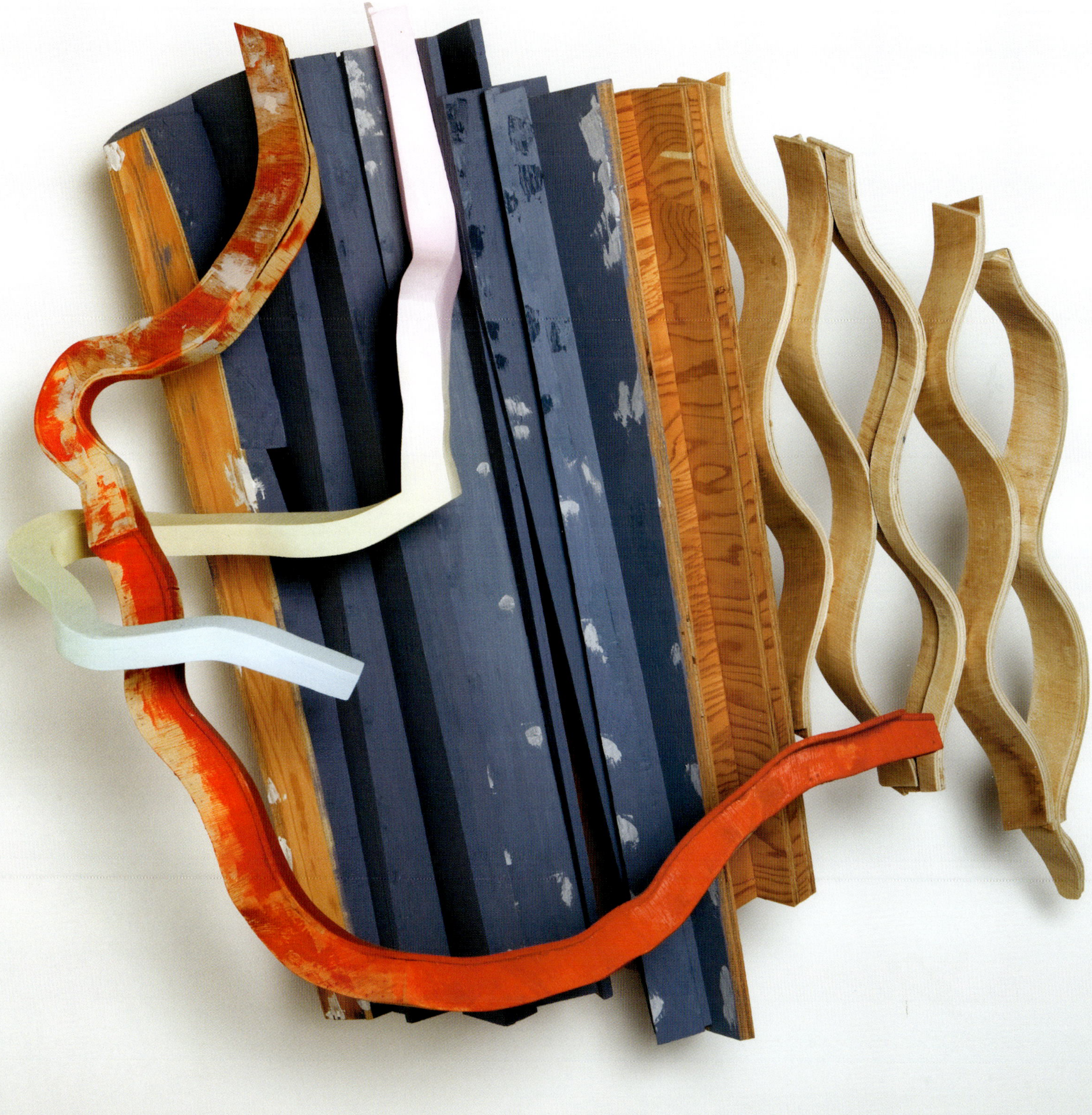

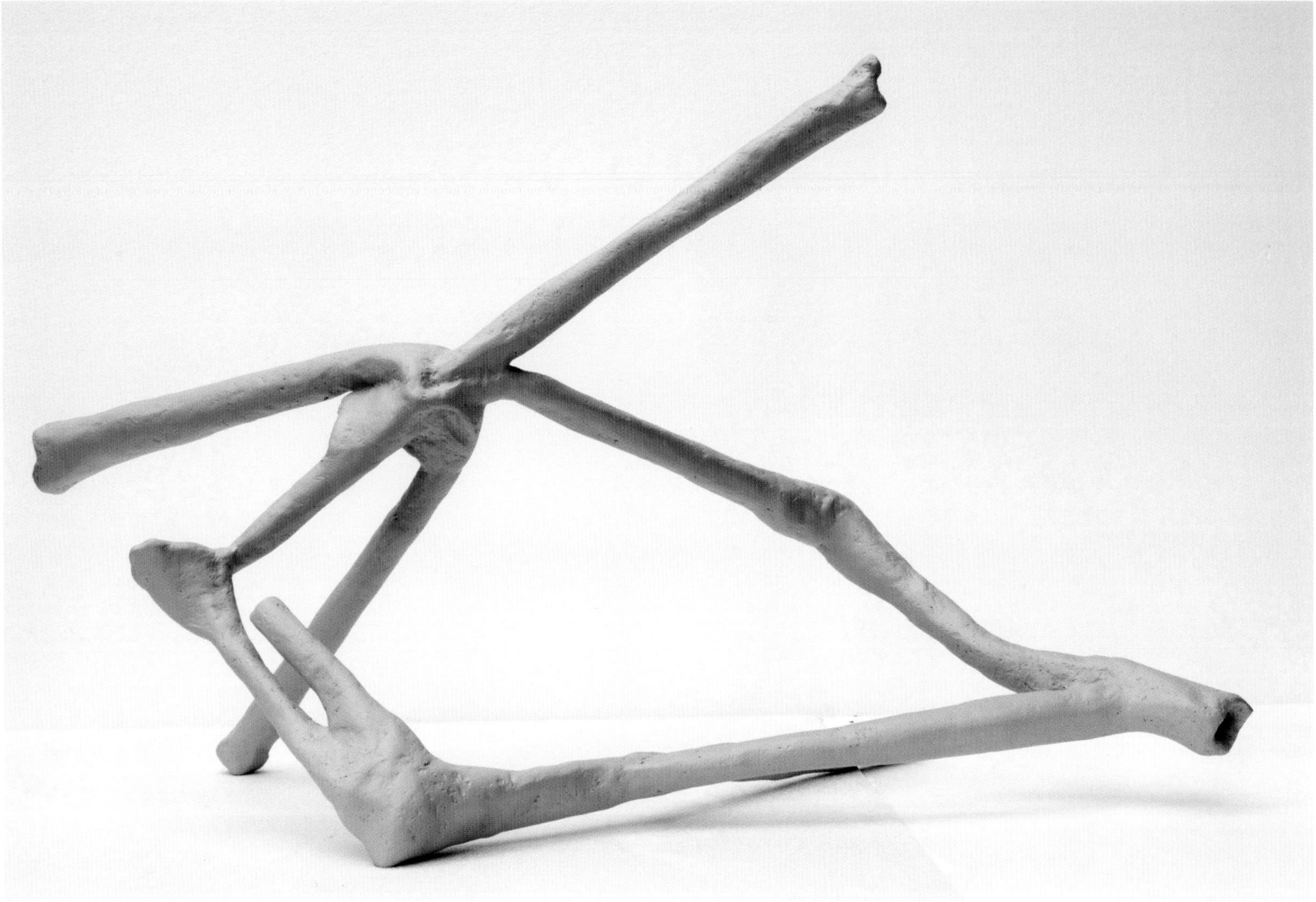

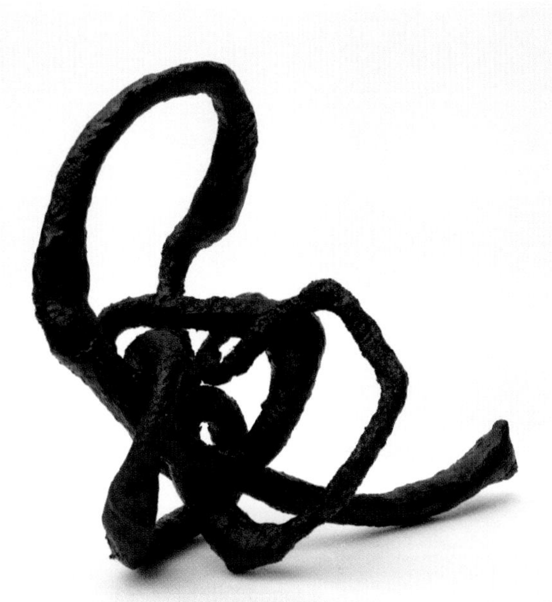

"Greyhound" 2012
Aluminum, aqua resin, oil, and acrylic paints
55 x 23 x 29 inches

"Untitled" 2012
Aluminum, aqua resin, oil, and acrylic paints
26 x 14 x 22 inches

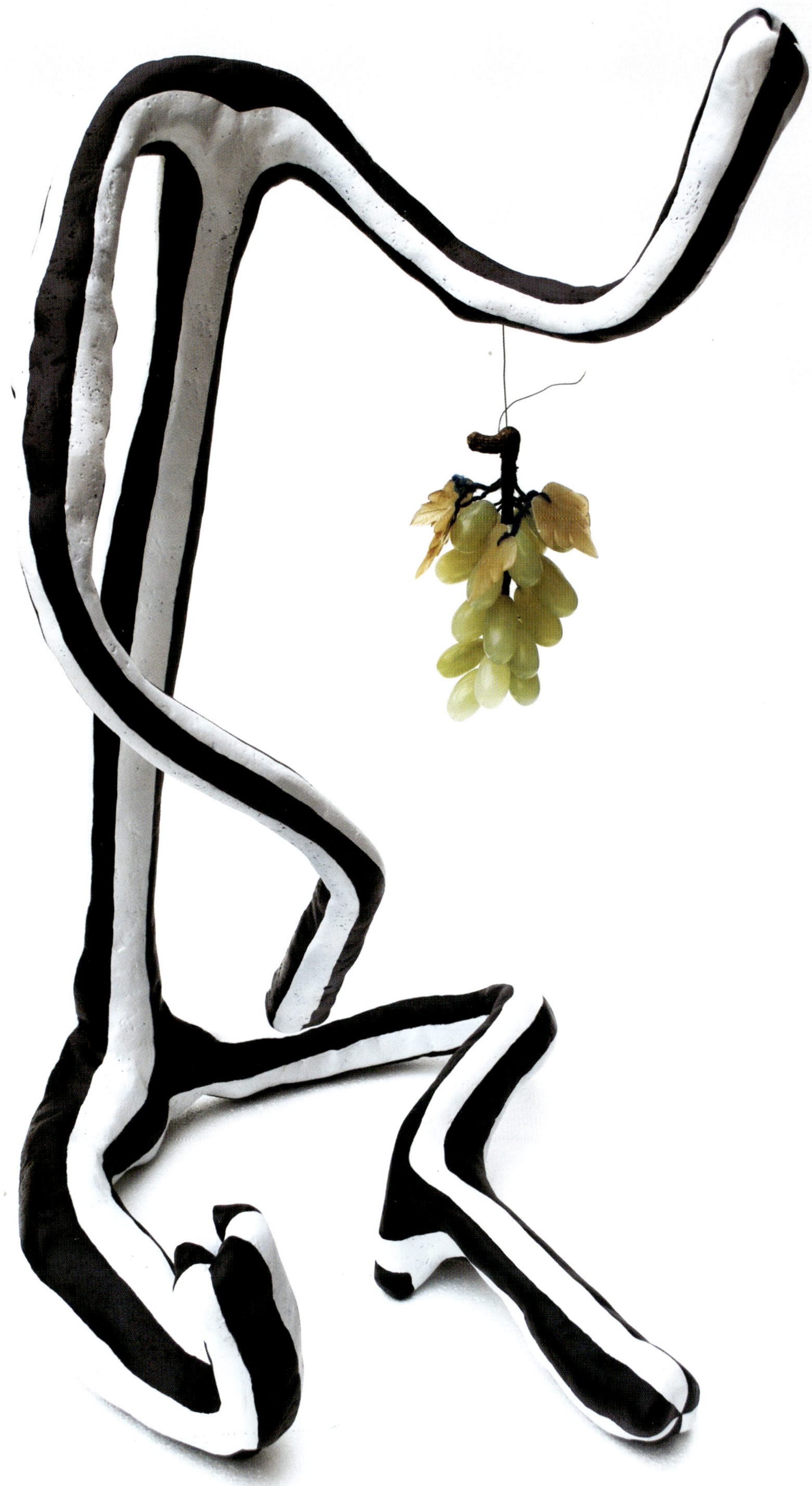

"Bacchus" 2012
Aluminum, aqua resin, found glass grapes, oil, and acrylic paints
33 x 23 x 18 inches

Kelsey Brooks
"Untitled 1" 2012
Mixed media on canvas
36 x 36 inches

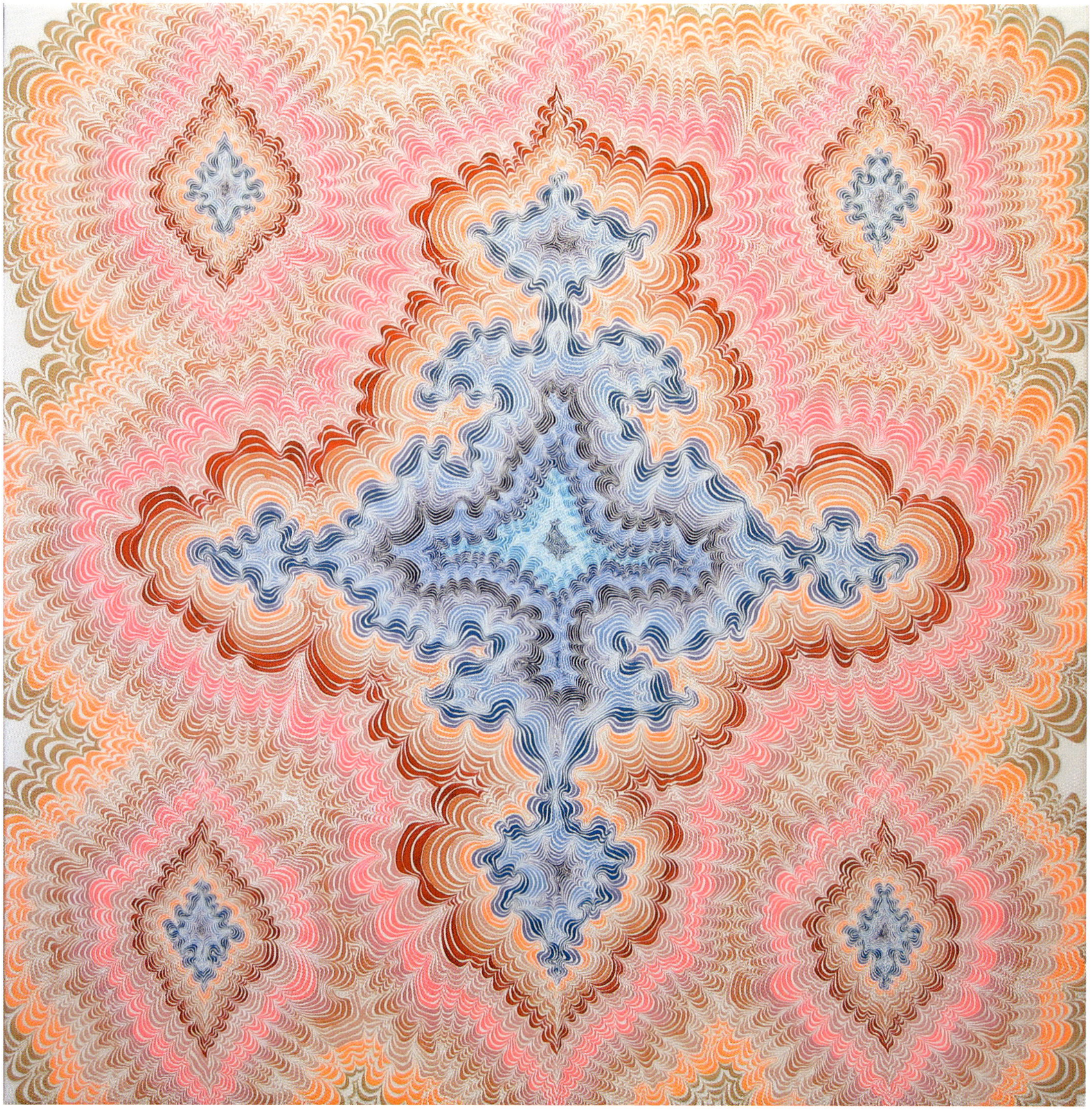

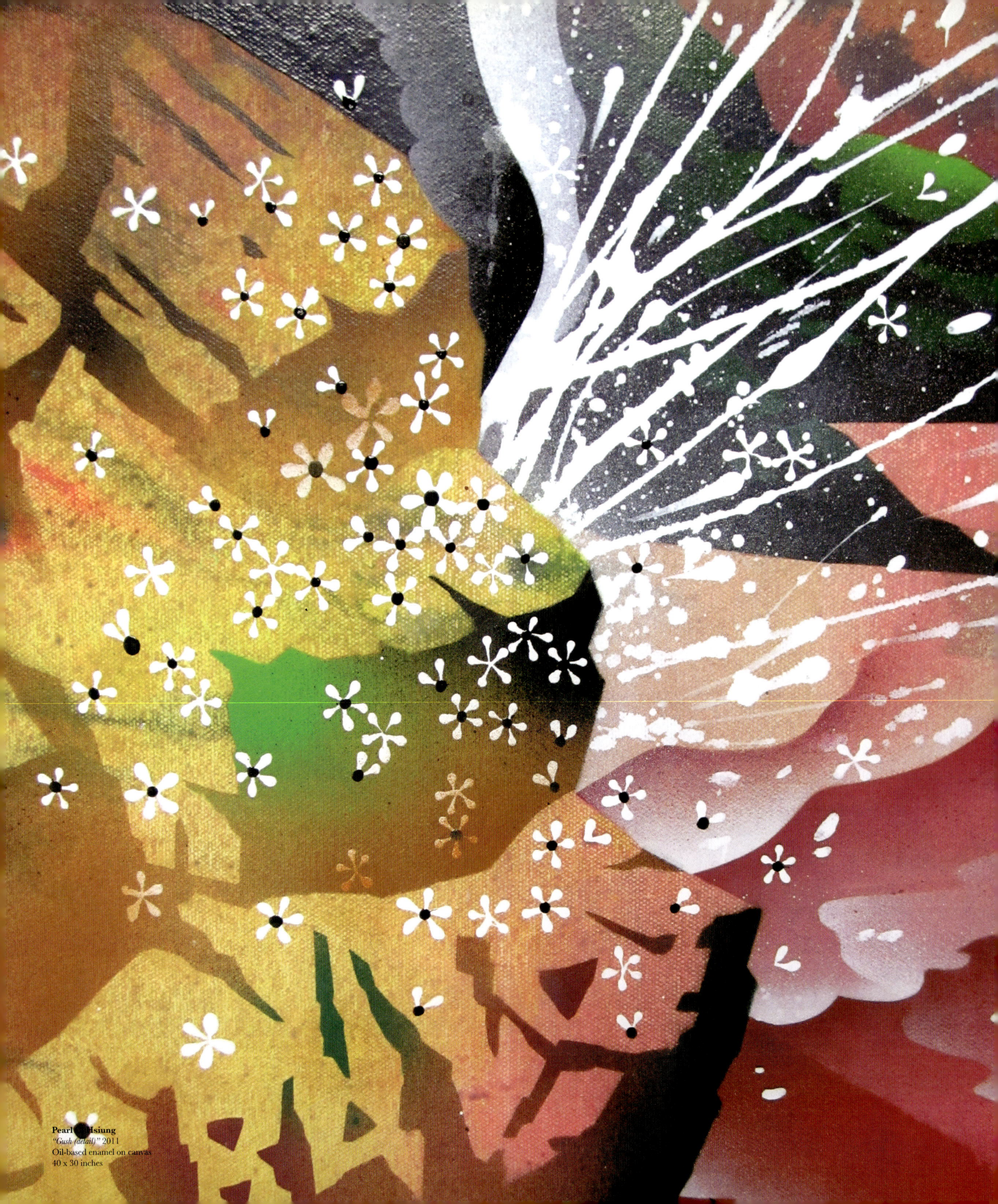

Pearl [illegible] Hsiung
"Gush (detail)" 2011
Oil-based enamel on canvas
40 x 30 inches

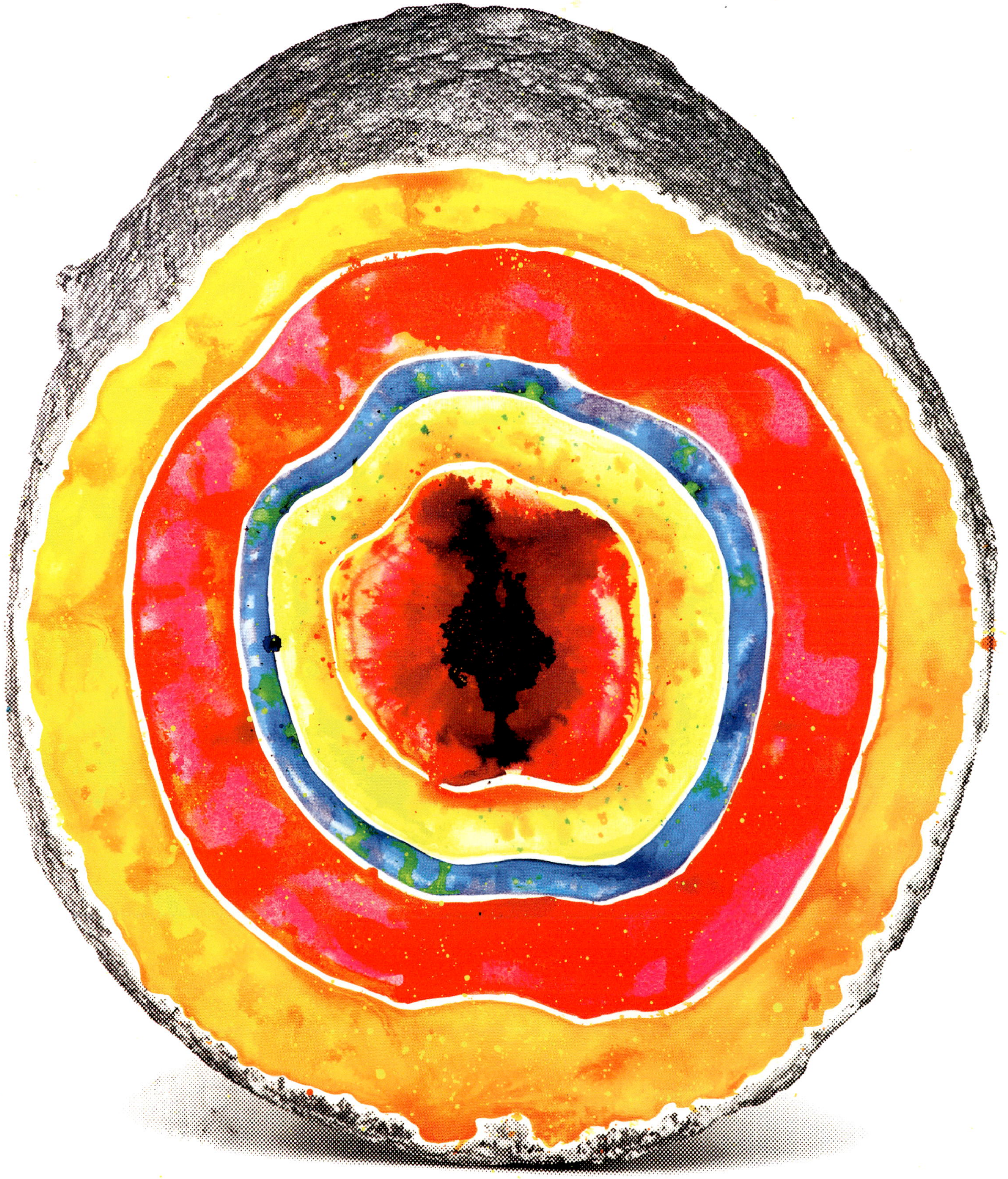

Justin Krietemeyer
"Geode—No.4" 2011
Watercolor and silkscreen
36 x 53 inches

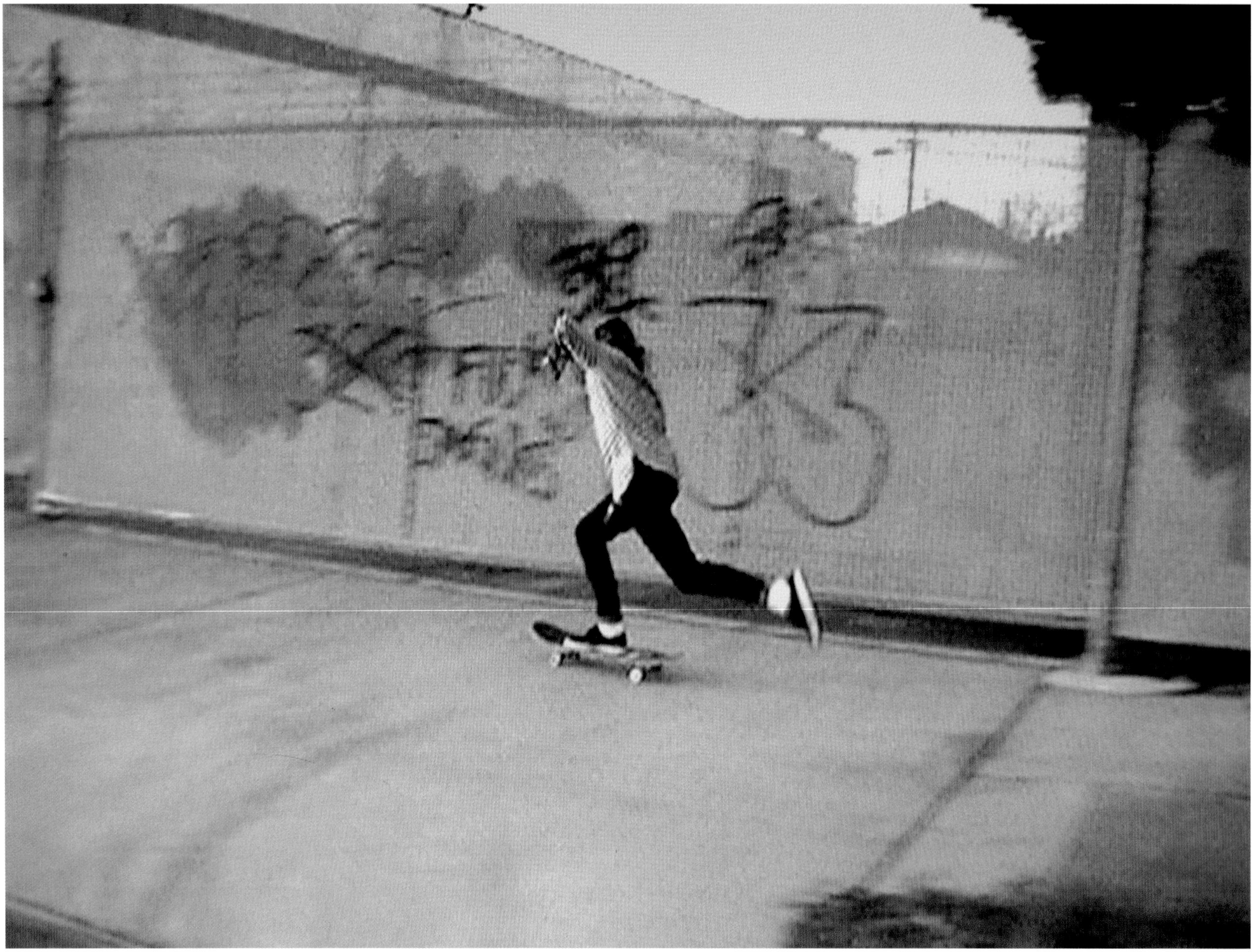

Six Stair
"Untitled" 2012
Film still

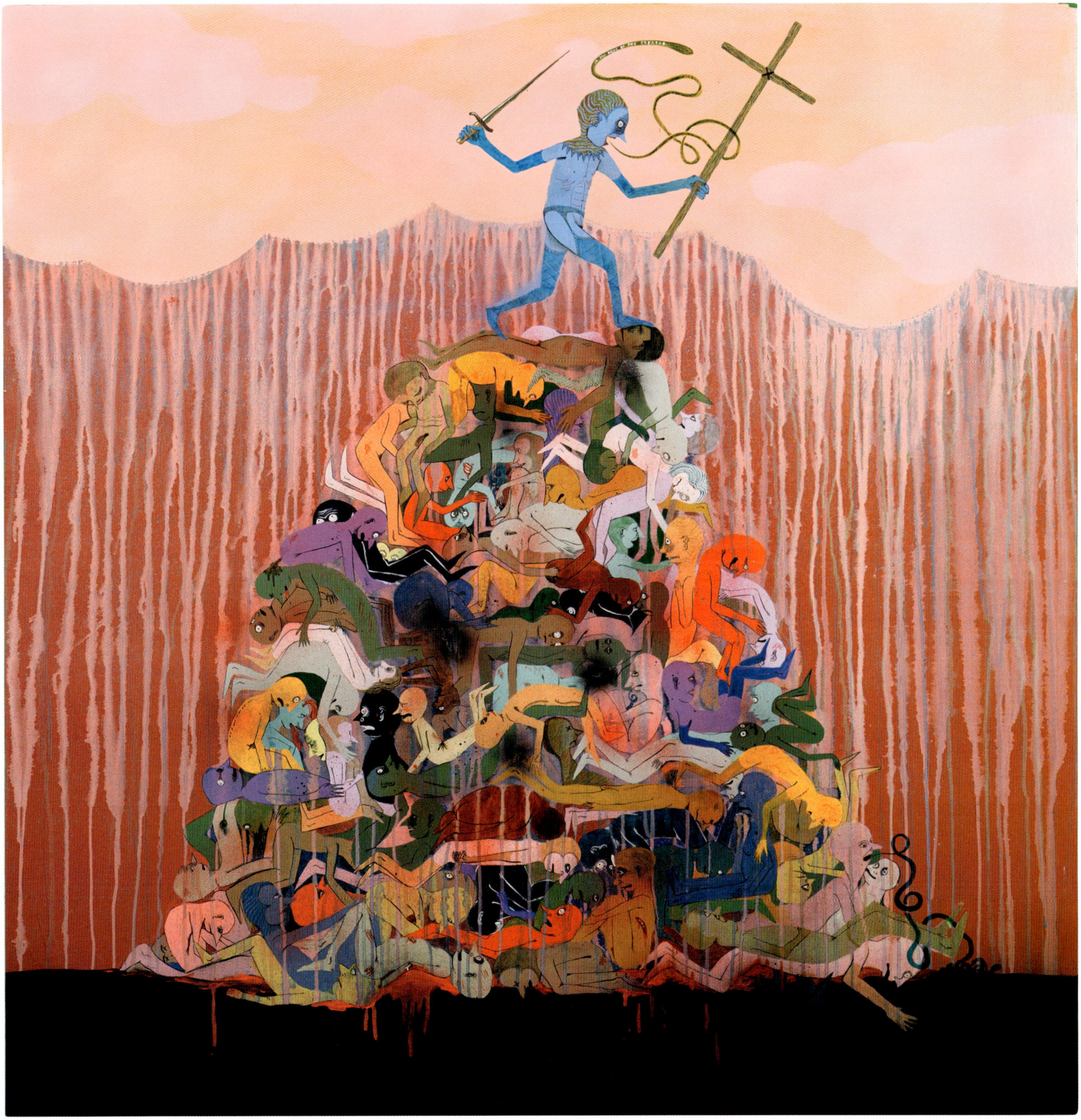

Ed Templeton
"In the Name of the Creator" 2006
Acrylic on panel
60 x 60 inches

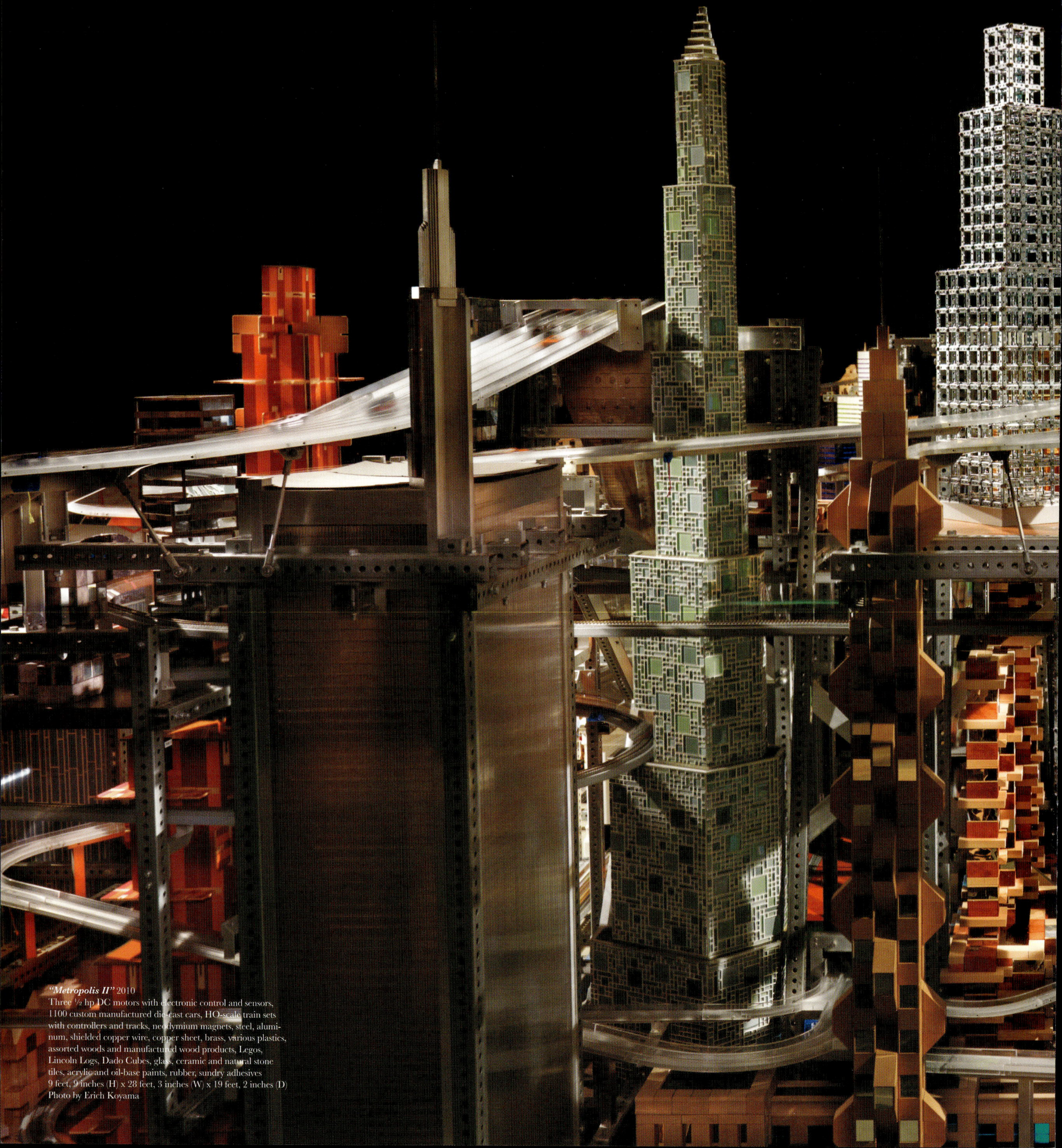

"Metropolis II" 2010
Three ½ hp DC motors with electronic control and sensors, 1100 custom manufactured die-cast cars, HO-scale train sets with controllers and tracks, neodymium magnets, steel, aluminum, shielded copper wire, copper sheet, brass, various plastics, assorted woods and manufactured wood products, Legos, Lincoln Logs, Dado Cubes, glass, ceramic and natural stone tiles, acrylic and oil-base paints, rubber, sundry adhesives
9 feet, 9 inches (H) x 28 feet, 3 inches (W) x 19 feet, 2 inches (D)
Photo by Erich Koyama

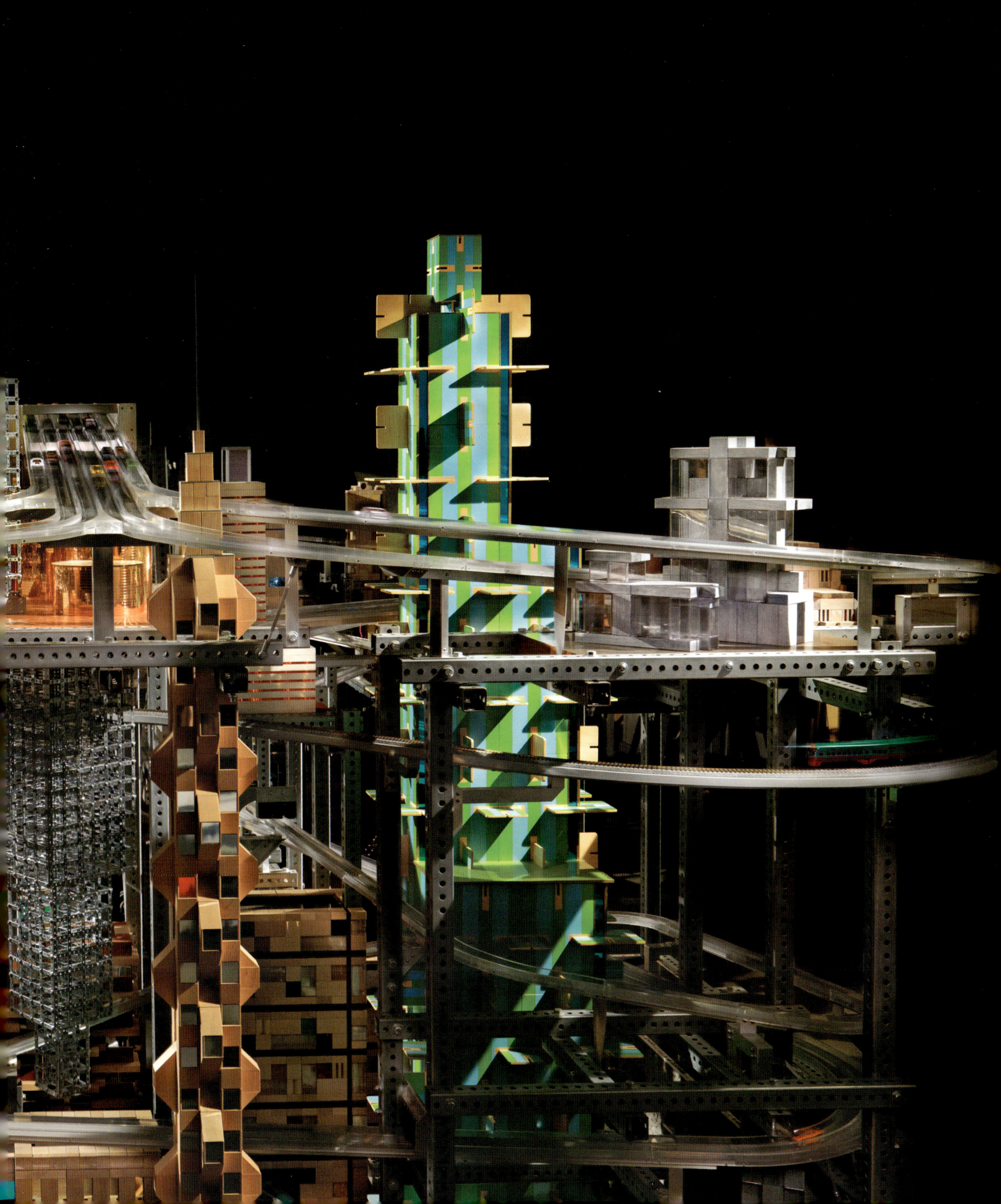

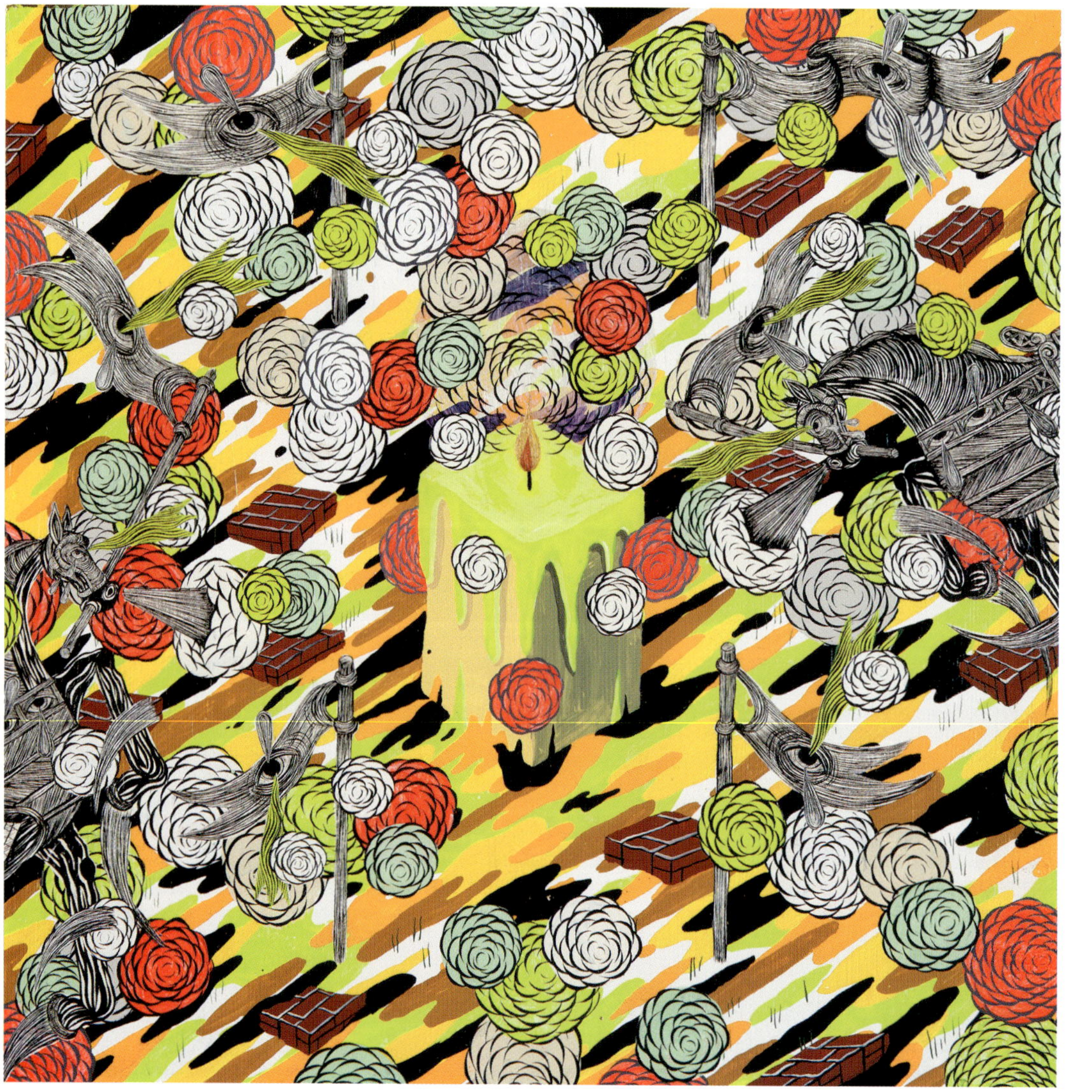

Andrew Schoultz
"Melting Candle (Yellow)" 2011
Acrylic on panel
14 x 14 inches

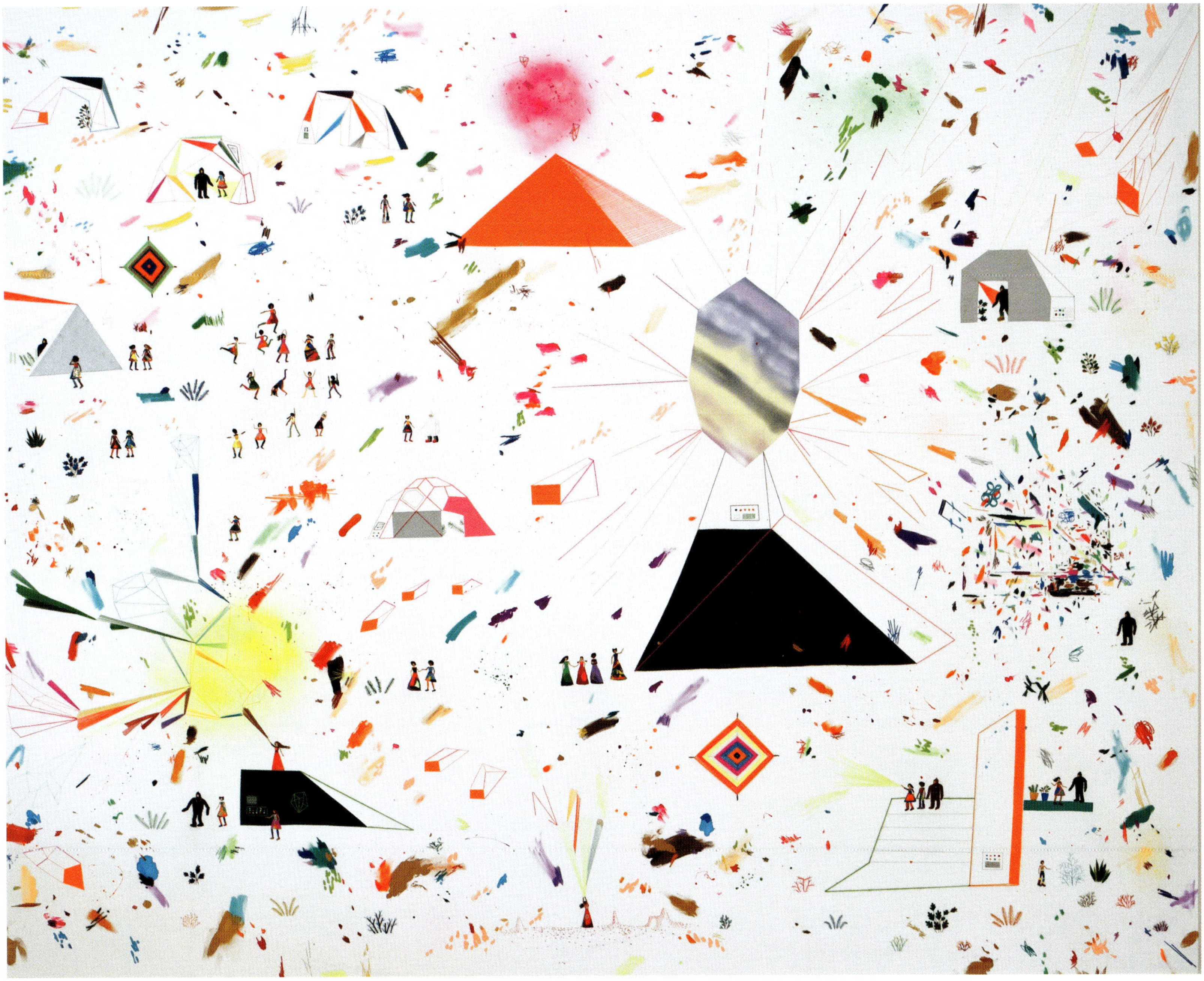

Megan Whitmarsh
"Radiant Future" 2010
Embroidery thread, spray paint, and
marker on fabric
70 x 55 inches

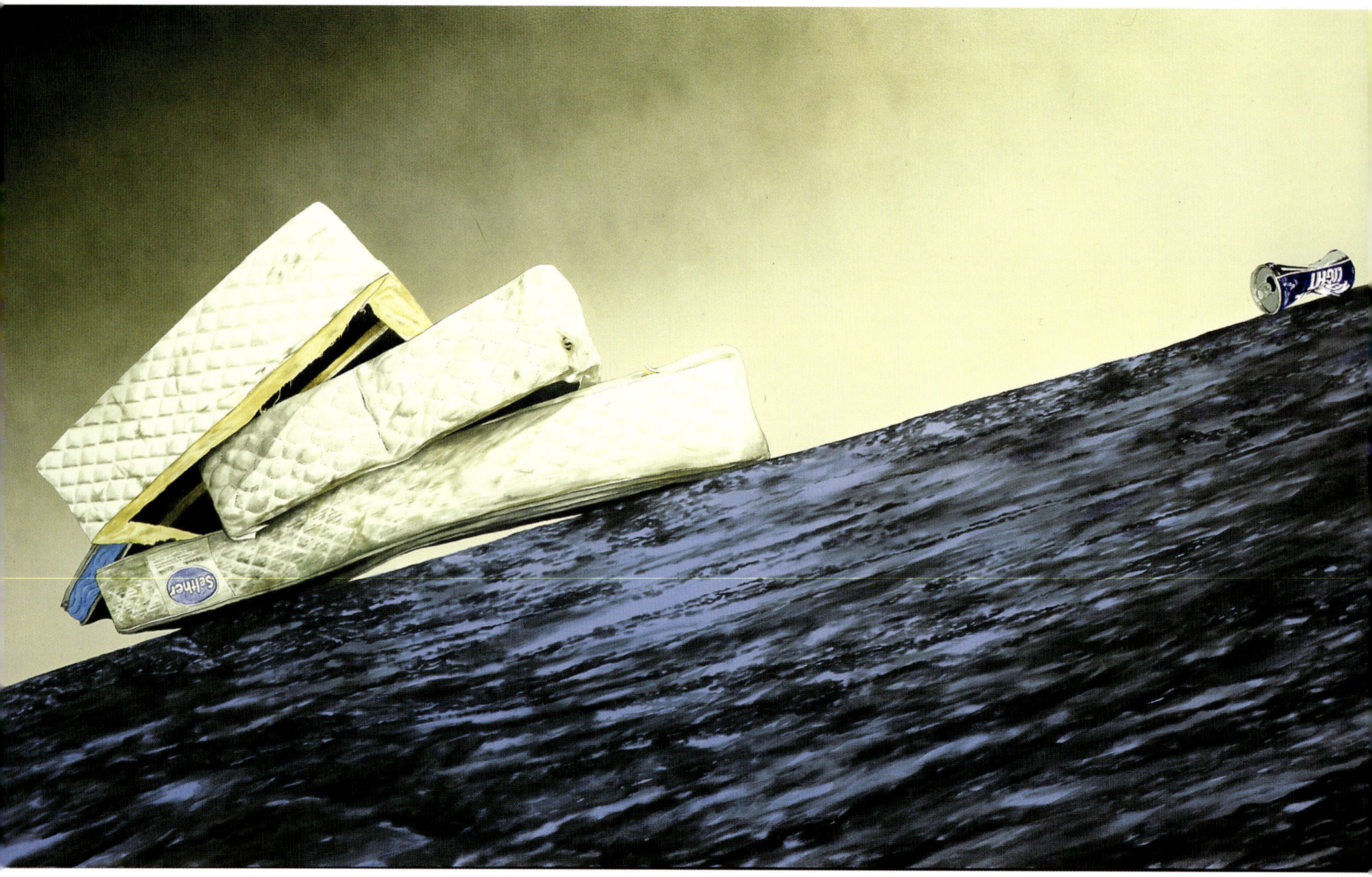

Ed Ruscha
"Psycho Spaghetti Western #2" 2010
Acrylic on canvas
42 x 72 inches

Aaron Farley
"Purple Clouds Cut and Reassembled" 2012
Archival inkjet cut vertically and reassembled
8½ x 11 inches

AMMO
AMERICAN MODERN **BOOKS**

MILK AND HONEY: Contemporary Art in California

by Justin Van Hoy

Published by AMMO Books, LLC

Design: Justin Van Hoy for The Dutch Press, LLC

Associate Editors: Steve Crist and Sara DeGonia

Photography: Aaron Farley, Curtis Buchanan, Greg Bojorquez, and Dan Monick

Acknowledgements: Steve Crist, Sara DeGonia, Casey Holland, Shelley Leopold, Lucy Rose, Jeremy Shockley, and PM Tenore.

Thank you to Holly, my wife and best friend. Mom, Dad, Ryan, Christin, and my supporting and loving family, The Snackers & The Buncle, Dr. Rodriguez, Dr. Sahebi, Dr. Spielberger, Roger Gastman, Jen Jenkins, Allyson Spellacy Smith, Larry Barnfield, Chad Dresbach, and all of the artists who trusted me with their work.

Front Cover Image: Sage Vaughn
Front endpapers: Joey Gallagher
Back endpapers: Richard Colman
Back Cover Image: RJ Shaughnessy

Printed and manufactured in China

ISBN: 9781934429099
Library of Congress Control Number: 2012933608

For more information on AMMO Books, please visit:
www.ammobooks.com

Dan Monick
"Every Pay Phone On Sunset Blvd (test)" 2012
35mm color negative film

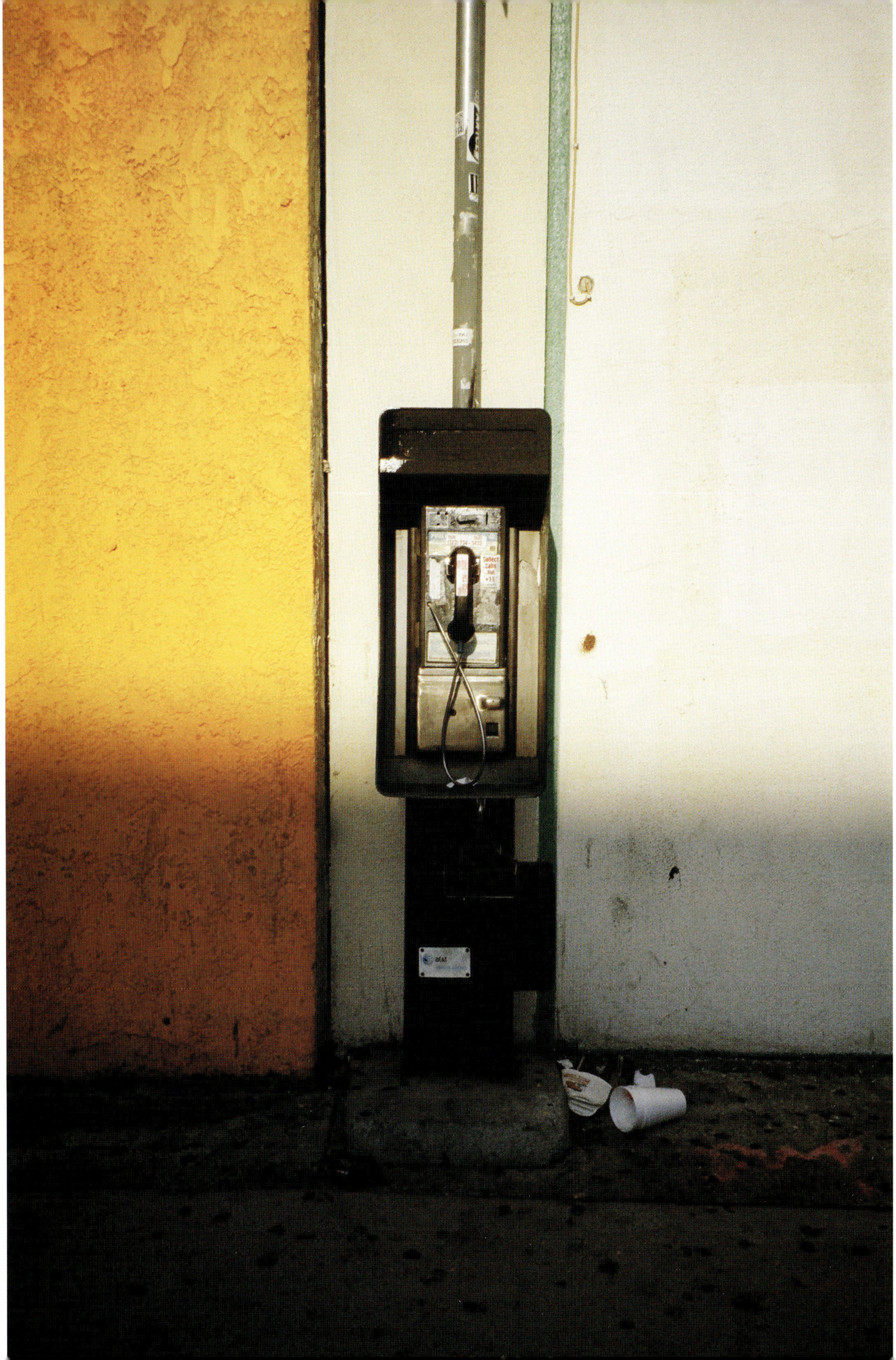

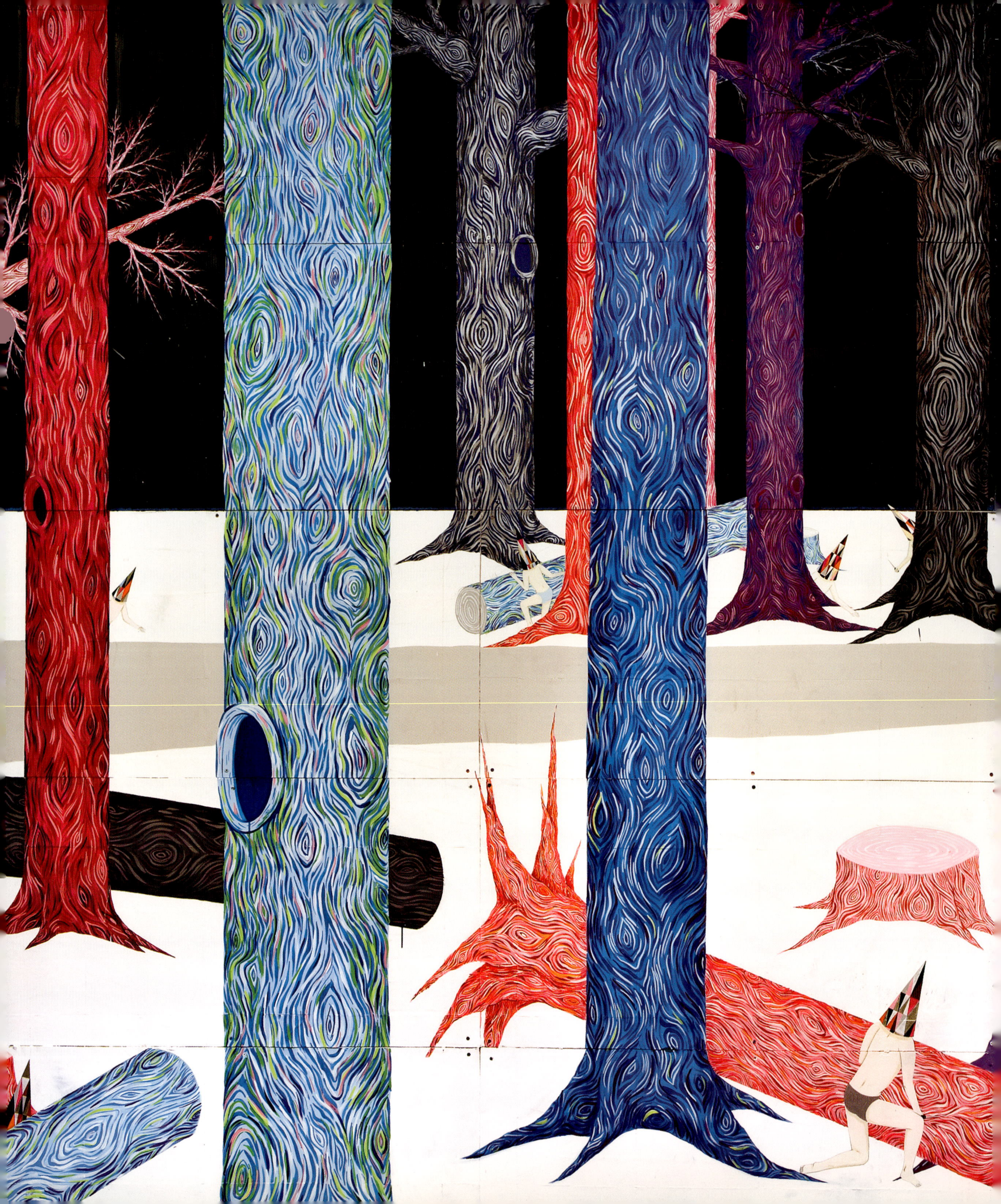